EUROPA INSTITUUT UNIVERSITY OF LEIDEN

JUDICIAL PROTECTION IN THE EUROPEAN COMMUNITIES

SECOND EDITION

HENRY G. SCHERMERS

PROFESSOR OF LAW UNIVERSITY OF LEIDEN

KLUWER – DEVENTER/THE NETHERLANDS
ANTWERP – BOSTON – LONDON – FRANKFORT

1979

The first edition of this book was published in the academic year prior to the retirement of Arnold J. P. Tammes, Member of the International Law Commission and Professor of International Law at the University of Amsterdam. It was dedicated to him.

The second edition describes Community law up to 1 April 1979, the date of the resignation of Judge André M. Donner from the Court of Justice, after more than twenty years of service.

To this esteemed scholar and co-developer of Community law this edition is dedicated.

ISBN 90 268 1096 2

Distribution in USA and Canada
Kluwer Law and Taxation
160 Old Derby Street
Hingham MA 02043   U.S.A.

Library of Congress Cataloging in Publication Data
Schermers, Henry G. — Europa Instituut, University of Leiden
   Judicial protection in the European communities.
   Includes bibliographical references and index.
   1. Judicial review — European Economic Community countries. 2. Court of Justice of the European Communities. I. Title.
LAW   341.5'5   79-16394

Printed in the Netherlands

TABLE OF CONTENTS

V

Chapter Three
OTHER TASKS OF THE COURT OF JUSTICE

Chapter Four
OTHER COURTS APPLYING COMMUNITY LAW

Chapter Five
STRUCTURE AND OPERATION OF THE COURT OF JUSTICE

TABLES

LIST OF ABBREVIATIONS

AA — Ars Aequi
AFDI — Annuaire Français de Droit International
AöR — Archiv des öffentlichen Rechts
AJCL — American Journal of Comparative Law
AJIL — American Journal of International Law
AWD — Aussenwirtschaftsdienst des Betriebs Beraters
BYIL — British Year Book of International Law
CCH — Common Market Reports (published by Commerce Clearing House, Inc. Chicago, Illinois)
CDE — Cahiers de Droit Européen
CMLR — Common Market Law Reports
CMLRev. — Common Market Law Review
ECSC — European Coal and Steel Community
ECR — European Court Reports
EEC — European Economic Community
ELD — European Law Digest
ELRev. — European Law Review
EuR. — Europarecht
Euratom — European Atomic Energy Community
GATT — General Agreement on Tariffs and Trade
GRUR — Gewerblicher Rechtsschutz und Urheberrecht
GYIL — German Yearbook of International Law
ICLQ — International and Comparative Law Quarterly
Jur. — Jurisprudentie van het Hof van Justitie van de Europese Gemeenschappen
JWTL — Journal of World Trade Law
LIEI — Legal Issues of European Integration
LQR — The Law Quarterly Review
NJ — Nederlandse Jurisprudentie
NJB — Nederlands Juristenblad
NJW — Neue Juristische Wochenschrift
NTIR — Nederlands Tijdschrift voor Internationaal Recht (Netherlands International Law Review)
OJ — Official Journal of the European Communities
RBDI — Revue Belge de Droit International
RCJB — Revue Critique de Jurisprudence Belge.
RdC — Recueil des Cours de l'Académie de Droit International de La Haye
Rec. — Recueil de la jurisprudence de la Cour de Justice des Communautés Européennes

Rec. D – Recueil Dalloz
RIDC – Revue internationale de droit comparé
RTDE – Revue trimestrielle de droit européen
RGDIP – Revue générale de droit international public
RMC – Revue du Marché Commun
RW – Rechtskundig Weekblad
SEW – Sociaal Economische Wetgeving
Stb – Staatsblad van het Koninkrijk der Nederlanden
Trb – Tractatenblad (Treaty Series of the Kingdom of the Netherlands)
UNTS – United Nations Treaty Series
WuW – Wirtschaft und Wettbewerb
YbWA – The Yearbook of World Affairs
ZaöRV – Zeitschrift für ausländisches öffentliches Recht und Völkerrecht

Introduction

I. Purpose of the book

§ 1. The Court of Justice plays a significant role in the development of the European Communities, to some extent comparable with the role of the Supreme Court in the early years of the United States of America. Both are constitutional courts charged with the preservation and the development of the law in a new society. The powers of both are in fact limited by the existing political situation.[1] Each court plays a vital role in the protection of the individual against a vast and increasingly influential administration.

In the present book the attempt is made to describe the nature of the judicial protection within the sphere of European Community law, that is available to individuals and undertakings as well as to the Member States. The study is heavily based on the case-law of the Court of Justice, which in principle is described rather than criticized, mainly for three reasons. (1) The author has great admiration for the Court of Justice and for the manner in which it operates. He considers that a detailed description of the Court's case-law portrays a fine legal system that is not susceptible to a great amount of fundamental criticism. (2) At their present stage of development the Communities are more in a position to benefit from a common effort to support and to utilise the structure laboriously built up by the Court of Justice than from any attempts to alter or demolish this structure. The Communities are of such recent origin and their legislative organs as yet function so badly that it is often more important that the gaps are filled by the case-law of the Court than it is to question whether this case-law is perfect in every detail. Lord MacKenzie Stuart's remark that 'Certainly the avidity with which reports of the decisions of the Court are devoured by certain writers would justify the legend "Here be dragons"[2] should therefore be seen as a positive sign which augurs well for the future. (3) Finally, a third reason for trying to describe the law as it is interpreted by the Court of Justice, is that practising lawyers have more need of a survey of the law as it stands, than of an opinion of how it should be.

---

1. See Robert G. McCloskey, *The American Supreme Court.* Seventh impression, University of Chicago Press, 1965. Many of his general conclusions are equally applicable to the Court of Justice of the European Communities. See also Werner J. Feld and Elliot E. Slotnick, *'Marshalling' the European Community Court: A comparative study in judicial integration*, 23 Emory Law Journal (1976), pp. 317-355.
2. Lord MacKenzie Stuart in 12 CMLRev. (1975) p. 512.

On the other hand a description of the system of judicial protection, within
the area of European Community law, on the basis of the case-law of the
Court of Justice leads to a certain imbalance. Community law is still in its
infancy. There is little more than twenty years of case-law. It is only natural
therefore, that in these initial years some branches of the law have received
more attention than others. The competence of the Community institutions
and coupled therewith, the review of the legality of their acts, received the
utmost attention right from the very first years, whilst other subjects, such as
suits for damages, received attention only much later. Furthermore, national
courts needed to go through a period of adaptation and learning before applying Community law. On this account the subjects which come primarily before these courts have had a noticeably shorter time to develop. The imbalance thus caused is reflected in the following chapters. Some are more
detailed than others, though not necessarily more important.

II. Schema

§ 2. The material of the present book has been divided into five chapters,
two on the legal order, and three on the courts. Chapter One contains a
description of the Community legal order: the rules which make up Community law. Chapter Two maps out the borderlines and extremities of this legal
order: the question of which acts still belong to it, the review of the validity
of acts taken by Community institutions. To a great extent, the completion of
the Community legal order is entrusted to the Member States. The validity of
the acts which the Member States perform in the field of Community law is
also concerned with the validity of Community acts and is therefore treated in
the same chapter. Although the case-law of the Court of Justice plays a
prominent role in the first two chapters, they do not basically deal with the
topic of the Court, but of the Community legal order. Even though it is
developed by the Court of Justice, the Community legal order is not a matter
for that Court alone. It is of equal relevance to national courts and to others
who are to apply Community law.

Chapters Three, Four and Five deal with the European and national courts
themselves and are therefore of a somewhat different nature from Chapters
One and Two. Chapter Three is concerned with the tasks of the Court of
Justice, other than that of judicial review. In carrying out these tasks the
Court has a more extensive role to play than when exercising its review
function as described in Chapter Two. As regards judicial review the Court
does not need to look beyond Community law: as long as Community law is
not violated there is no question of illegality. In relation to its other tasks the
Court must find a solution to a particular legal problem; this is not always to
be found in Community law; hence the Court may have to apply other legal
orders as well.

Just as the Court of Justice must sometimes apply the law of other legal
orders, other courts may have to apply Community law. The role played by
other courts is discussed in Chapter Four. In theory, these 'other courts'

include international courts, foreign courts and the national courts of the Member States. The first two categories are mentioned for the sake of completeness; in practice, the only one of significant importance is the application of Community law by the national courts of the Member States.

Chapter Five describes the structure and operation of the Court of Justice. Though rules of procedure may often be dull, they are of great importance to the law, as are the composition and functioning of courts.

§ 3. In *Judicial Remedies in the European Communities*[3] the attempt was made to clarify Community law by manner of excerpts taken from cases, with as little comment as possible. The present study represents a contrary approach: it presents a systematic arrangement of and commentary on Community law with many quotations of Court cases by way of illustration. It is hoped that both books can fulfil their own respective functions in the development and teaching of European law.

Some subchapters of the present book are revisions of the four articles published in 'Legal Issues of European Integration' under the title 'The Law as it stands on ...'[4] They have been updated and extended.

§ 3a. The schema of the *second edition* is almost the same as that of the first one. Very little of the first edition has been deleted. Some subjects have been added, others expanded in order to cover new developments. Only a few subjects have been rearranged (§ 178-192; § 275-283; § 377-379). For the sake of consistency the numbering of all other paragraphs is the same as in the first edition. Newly added paragraphs carry a letter (e.g. § 22a, § 25a).

Account has been taken of the cases of the Court of Justice decided up to 1 April 1979.

III. References

A. CASES

§ 4. Court cases are referred to by name rather than by number. In principle the name of the subject matter is preferred as it identifies the case most clearly. Both in Court cases (see the Court's page headings) and in literature the name of one of the parties is used more frequently, however, and in order to avoid the use of several names for the same case this practice has often been followed, particularly for cases of lesser importance. For the majority of cases the same names as in *Judicial Remedies* are used. Furthermore, cases decided by national courts bear names beginning with the nationality of the

3. L.J. Brinkhorst and H.G. Schermers, *Judicial Remedies in the European Communities* 2nd ed., Kluwer, Deventer 1977.
4. LIEI 1974/1 pp. 93-112 on preliminary rulings; LIEI 1974/2, pp. 111-139, on treaty violations by States; LIEI 1975/1, pp. 113-145, on the appeal for damages and LIEI 1975/2, pp. 95-142, on the appeal for annulment.

court: thus the *German Lütticke Case* refers to the case ruled upon by a German court, whilst the *Lütticke Case* was decided by the Court of Justice.

All quotations of cases are from the 'Reports of Cases before the Court' published by the Court of Justice of the European Communities. References to other publications have been added for the benefit of those who may not have access to these Reports.

In all cases references are made to the relevant page of the case. It was considered that this would be of more help to the reader than giving the page on which the case commences. For cases after 1 November 1978 no ECR publications were available. References are made to the considerations of the Court as numbered in the mimeographed texts. Unfortunately this numbering is not always the same as the one eventually used in the European Court Reports.

B. BOOKS AND ARTICLES

§ 5. A long bibliography of all books related to the subject has little practical value. It is better to consult a good library catalogue. I have tried to give further literature on each subject in footnotes to the paragraph concerned. Where a choice could be made preference has been given to recent literature and to literature in the English language. A list of authors at the end of the book should enable the reader to find the names of the books used.

In the same manner as with the references for the cases, references to books and articles will normally indicate the actual page on which the relevant passage appears. A reference, therefore, to an article, e.g. in Common Market Law Review, pp. 10-12, does not mean that the article contains only three pages; it may extend before p. 10 and after p. 12.

In general no references have been made to the relevant chapters of general books on Community law, such as the books by Cartou, Catalano, Ipsen, Kapteyn and VerLoren, Lasok and Bridge, Lipstein, Mathijsen or Parry and Hardy, it being assumed that the reader will find no difficulty in consulting these books.

Three books which were recently published cover almost the same field as the present one: G. Vandersanden and A. Barav, *Contentieux Communautaire*, Bruylant, 1977; L. Neville Brown and Francis G. Jacobs, *The Court of Justice of the European Communities*, Sweet & Maxwell 1977; and A.G. Toth, *Legal Protection of Individuals in the European Communities*, 2 Volumes, North Holland 1978. Only occasionally reference will be made to these books, when subjects are more extensively or differently treated than in the present work.

IV. Acknowledgements

§ 6. In the first edition acknowledgements were made to many people who assisted in its creation. For the second edition I want to repeat these acknowledgements. Most of the work of the first edition remained unchanged. In addition, I want to thank the authors who reviewed the first edition in legal periodicals.[5] I carefully studied their remarks. I am also grateful to Professor L. Neville Brown, Mr. H.J. Eversen and Mr. Alan Dashwood for their comments and to the European Communities, in particular to the staff of the Court of Justice, for their assistance. A special word of thanks is due to Miss Ester Davids of the Leiden Law School, who worked so carefully in completing all references and in finding cases and literature, and to my son Peter who again prepared the tables of cases. Mr. Neil C. Sargent linguistically revised the entire text, an effort for which I am very grateful.

I also want to express my gratitude to the publishers for the expert way in which they transformed a somewhat difficult manuscript into a book.

Leiden, April 1979.   H.G. S.

5. The following reviews came to my attention: Frances G. Jacobs, 14 CMLRev (1977), pp. 361, Valentine Korah, New Europe 1977, pp. 79, 80; 121 The Solicitor's Journal 11 Nov. 1977; Leon Goffin, 13 CDE (1977), pp. 681-683; T.C. Hartley, 2 ELRev. (1977), pp. 403, 404; Ignaz Seidl Hohenveldern, 13 EuR (1978), pp. 85-87; P. van Dijk, Themis 1978, pp. 40-42; Stuart S. Malawar, 71 AJIL (1978), pp. 191, 192; R.H. Lauwaars, 32 Internationale Spectator (1978), pp. 518-519; Daniel W. Martin, 71 Law Library Journal (1978), pp. 508, 509; Peter Hay, 26 AJCL (1978), pp. 367, 368; Hans G. Kausch, Jahrbuch für Internationales Recht, Kiel 1978, pp. 533, 534; Miren A. Letemendia, 1 Journal of European Integration (1978), pp. 411, 412; Torsten Stein, 39 ZaöRV (1979), pp. 165, 166.

CHAPTER ONE

The Community legal order

I. CONCEPT

§ 7. Each State has its own body of interlocking and complementary legal rules which taken together govern the legal relationships within the country. Within Community law these bodies of legal rules are normally called 'legal orders'.[1] Apart from these national legal orders international organizations have legal orders of their own.[2] In comparison with these the legal order of the European Communities is of particular significance not only because of the large number of rules it contains, and the preponderance and the frequent direct effect of these rules for a large group of people, but also due to its homogeneity.[3] Most international organizations embody their binding legal rules in treaties or conventions. These obtain force of law only after ratification by the States concerned. As in practice not all States ratify every convention, the binding force of conventions differs as regards territorial application. This precludes one convention being used for completing another. Because of the fact that not all legal rules bind the same States, they cannot form one legal order; each convention constitutes a legal order of its own. In the European Communities the three Treaties and all the rules of secondary Community law taken together form one legal order, equally binding within all Member States. The inherent unity of this legal order is of the greatest importance for its further development.[4]

§ 8. The Court of Justice has been careful to maintain this homogeneity of Community law. When, in the *Lead and Zinc Case*, Italy invoked some sort of reservation it had made at the adoption of the Acceleration Decision (which was taken under EEC Article 235 and therefore had to be unanimous) the Court replied:

1. This may not be a well known English expression, but it seems appropriate, see Lord MacKenzie Stuart. *The European Communities and the Rule of Law*, Hamlyn Lectures, Stevens 1977, pp. 2-4.
2. Henry G. Schermers, *International Institutional Law*, Vol. 2, Sijthoff 1972. Chapter Eight (pp. 458-536). See also Helmut Strebel, *Quellen des Völkerrechts als Rechtsordnung*, 36 ZaöRV (1976), pp. 301-346; Walter Ganshof van der Meersch, *L'ordre juridique des Communautés européennes et le droit international*, 148 RdC (1975V), pp. 1-433.
3. On the Community legal order see Riccardo Monaco, *The Limits of the European Community Order*, 1 ELRev. (1976), pp. 269-281.
4. On the question whether there are three Community legal orders or one, see Albert Bleckmann, *Die Einheit der Europäischen Gemeinschaftsrechtsordnung – Einheit oder Mehrheit der Europäischen Gemeinschaften*, 13 EuR (1978), pp. 95-104.

'In these circumstances (*i.e. those of Article 235*), a measure which is in the nature of a Community decision on the basis of its objective and of the institutional framework within which it has been drawn up cannot be described as an 'international agreement'.

The scope and effect of the Acceleration Decision must be assessed in the light of its terms and therefore cannot be restricted by reservations or statements which might have been made in the course of drawing up the measure concerned. Although formally addressed to the Member States alone this decision is intended to have repercussions on the Common Market as a whole and it conditions or prepares for the implementation of measures which are directly applicable within the Member States ...'[5]

§ 9. Being established by Treaty the Community legal order has its origin in international law, to which it is still closely linked. This link is exemplified by the provision that international agreements concluded by the Community are binding on the Community institutions and on the Member States without the need for any form of express transformation into Community law.[6] It is also demonstrated by the Court's decision that Community acts are illegal if they violate international law (see below § 292). On the other hand, it has been generally accepted that Community law is not just a branch of international law but forms a separate legal order.[7] This is important for those Member States where international law must be transformed into national rules before it can be applied (see below § 149-153). The recognition of Community law as a separate legal order enabled those Member States to make special provisions for the incorporation of Community law into their national legal orders (see below § 166-168).

The Community legal order is also closely linked to the national legal orders of the Member States. From those legal orders it derives many legal concepts (see below § 139-144); to those legal orders it introduces additional binding rules (see below § 145-192); and by way of those legal orders it must be enforced (see below § 713, 714).

II. SOURCES

A. TREATY PROVISIONS AND COMMUNITY ACTS

1. Texts

§ 10. The Community Treaties are the *primary sources* of Community law. They play the same role as is played by constitutions in the national legal orders. Their legality cannot be challenged and they take priority over all other rules of Community law.

5. *Lead and Zinc Case* (38/69), 18 Feb. 1970, [1970] ECR 56, 57; [1970] CMLR 90; CCH para 8100 (p 8448). See also below § 407.
6. EEC Art. 228 (2).
7. See quotations of the *Van Gend en Loos* and *Costa ENEL Cases* in § 160, 161 below.

8

This priority was demonstrated, for example, in the *Manghera Case*. According to EEC Article 37(1) State monopolies must be adjusted before 1 January 1970 so as to ensure that no discrimination exists between nationals of Member States. In practice this was not achieved and the Council adopted a resolution on 21 April 1970 by which the French and Italian governments were obliged to terminate all discrimination before 1 Januari 1976. Manghera disregarded the Italian tobacco monopoly after 1 Januari 1970 but before 1 January 1976 by importing tobacco from other Member States. The Italian court before which he was prosecuted asked the Court of Justice whether Article 37(1) had direct effect from 1 January 1970 and whether the Council resolution of 21 April 1970 could vary the effect of the article. The Court of Justice replied that upon the expiry of the transitional period Article 37(1) indeed had direct effect and, with respect to the Council resolution, continued:

'The said resolution which basically expresses the political will of the Council and the French and Italian Governments to put an end to a state of affairs contravening Article 37(1), cannot engender effects which can be used against individuals.

In particular the time-scale referred to in the resolution cannot prevail over that contained in the Treaty.[8]

§ 11.   The protocols annexed to the Treaties form an integral part thereof[9] and therefore share the same status as the Treaties.

Other primary sources have been added later by special treaties such as the Treaty establishing a single Council and a single Commission of the European Communities (the Merger Treaty), the Treaty and Act concerning the accession of Denmark, Ireland and the U.K. and the two budgetary treaties.[10]

§ 12.   The Treaties are composed of several parts and titles. The first title of each Treaty (for the EEC the first part) enumerates some general principles which are elaborated in the other parts and titles. These general provisions play an important role in the interpretation and application of the other provisions by the Court of Justice. In the *Continental Can Case* the Court of Justice rejected the applicant's argument that the introductory article, invoked in that case, merely concerns a general programme devoid of legal effect, because the article, (Article 3), considers the pursuit of the objectives which it lays down to be indispensable for the achievement of the Community's tasks. The Court then held that EEC Articles 2 and 3 set the limits to

8. *Manghera Case* (59/75), 3 Feb. 1976, considerations 16, 21, [1976] ECR 101, 102; [1976] CMLR 567, 568; CCH para 8342. See also Second Defrenne Case (43/75), 8 April 1976, considerations 4-40, [1976] ECR 471-476, [1976] 2 CMLR 122-125; CCH para 8346, on the direct effect of EEC article 119.
9. ECSC Art. 84; EEC Art. 239; Euratom Art. 207.
10. For a wider description of primary sources of Community Law see A.G. Toth, *Legal Protection of Individuals in the European Communities*, North Holland 1978, Vol. I, pp. 38-44.

the restraints on competition which the Treaty under certain conditions allows.[11]

§ 13. After the Treaties come the regulations, directives and decisions of the Community institutions, which are usually called '*secondary Community law*'. This law cannot restrict the application of the provisions of the Treaties. Whenever a rule of secondary Community law conflicts with a Treaty provision, the Court of Justice will refuse to give it legal effect.[12] Enforcement will be impossible. With respect to rules of law of other orders secondary Community law, being derived from the Community Treaties forms an inseparable part of the Community legal order. This means that it is impossible to treat secondary Community law differently from the Treaties themselves in the hierarchical relationship between legal orders.

§ 14. Sometimes it may be useful to dinstinguish as *tertiary Community law* those regulations, directives and decisions which obtain their legal force not directly from the Treaties but from rules of secondary Community law. The legal status of such tertiary rules may be disputed when the underlying rule of secondary law is annulled or withdrawn. Sometimes express provisions have been made, such as in Regulation 1035/72 of the Council which withdraws a number of prior regulations and then provides that all references to the withdrawn regulations should be read as references to the new regulation.[13] Thus the legal position of these references is safeguarded.

Only those rules should be considered as tertiary Community law whose legality directly depends on rules of secondary Community Law. This is not normally the case when a regulation empowers the Commission to enact further legislation. Such delegated legislation, made at the time when the Commission was authorized to do so, remains in force when the regulation granting the power is withdrawn.

The Court of Justice accepts that some regulations are subject to the provisions of others. In the *Bearings Cases* it held:

'The Council, having adopted a general regulation with a view to implementing one of the objectives laid down in Article 113 of the Treaty, cannot derogate from the rules thus laid down in applying those rules to specific cases without interfering with the legislative system of the Community and destroying the equality before the law of those to whom the law applies'.[14]

11. *Continental Can Case* (6/72), 21 Feb. 1973, considerations 23, 24, [1973] ECR 244; [1973] CMLR 223; CCH para 8171.
12. See e.g.. *First Rewe Case* (37/70). 11 Feb. 1971. consideration 4, [1971] ECR 34; [1971] CMLR 252; CCH para 8124; *Wine Duty Case (Commissionaires Réunis)* (80, 81/77), 20 April 1978, [1978] ECR 945-947. On the hierarchy of norms in Community law see also Jürgen Schwarze, *Die Befugnis zur Abstraktion im europäischen Gemeinschaftsrecht*, Nomos Verlag, Baden-Baden, 1976, pp. 45-53.
13. Regulation 1035/72, OJ 1972, Nr. L118. On this regulation see Th.C. Esselaar in *Tien jaren TMC Asser Instituut*, The Hague 1975, pp. 123-125.
14. *NTN Toyo Case* (113/77), 29 March 1979, consideration 21; *ISO Case* (118/77),

§ **14a.** Another category of rules which one could distinguish are rules of *pseudo-legislation*, which are applied by the Community authorities, though they have no formal legislative force, such as the opinion of the Committee on Common Tariff Nomenclature or the 'Notes Explicatives du Tarif Douanier Commun des Communautés Européennes' published by the Commission.[15] Their effect in Community law is of some importance.[16]

2. Interpretation by the Court of Justice[17]

§ **15.** The actual application of the Treaties and of Community acts depends to a large extent on the interpretation which is given to them. The only authentic interpretation is that by the Court of Justice. The Court has availed itself of four methods of interpretation.

a. LITERAL INTERPRETATION; CHOICE OF COMMUNITY LANGUAGE

§ **16.** When the text of a provision is clear and compelling, and apparently meant to cover cases such as the one in question, the Court of Justice will not depart from it. When in the *Sgarlata Case* the applicant submitted that a general principle of law existed which would entitle him to appeal against a regulation, the Court replied: *'These considerations, which will not be discussed here, cannot be allowed to override the clearly restrictive wording.'*[18] In the *Da Costa Case* the text of the Treaty provision was again clear, but there is seemed not to have been meant to cover cases such as the one before the Court. The question was whether a reference for a new preliminary ruling had to be made when the Court had already given the required interpretation in a previous case. Notwithstanding the clear wording of EEC Article 177(3) the Court held that no new preliminary ruling was required, considering:

'Although the third paragraph of Article 177 unreservedly requires courts or tribunals of a Member State against whose decisions there is no judicial remedy under national law — like the Tariefcommissie — to refer to the

---

29 March 1979, consideration 46; *Nippon Seiko Case* (119/77) 29 March 1979, consideration 24; *Koyo Seiko Case* (120/77), 29 March 1979, consideration 46; *Nachi Case* (121/77), 29 March 1979, consideration 22.
Nachi Case (121/77), 29 March 1979, consideration 22.
15. See, e.g. *Luma Case* (38/76), 16 Dec. 1976, consideration 5, [1976] ECR 2034, 2035.
16. See K.J.M. Mortelmans, *De rechtsbescherming bij pseudowetgeving in het Europees economisch recht*, 27 SEW (1979), pp. 16-30 and Schwarze (*op. cit.* note 12), pp. 60-72.
17. See also *Reports of the Judicial and Academic Conference*, Luxembourg, 27 and 28 Sept. 1976; L. Neville Brown and Francis G. Jacobs, *The Court of Justice of the European Communities*, Sweet & Maxwell 1977, pp. 193-214; Toth (*op. cit.*, note 10), Vol. II, pp. 226-234; Anna Bredimas, *Methods of Interpretation and Community Law*, North Holland 1978, pp. 33-148.
18. *Sgarlata Case* (40/64), 1 April 1965, [1965] ECR 227; 11 Jur. (1965) 284; 11 Rec. (1965) 296; [1966] CMLR 324; CCH para 8034.

Court every question of interpretation raised before them, the authority of an interpretation under Article 177 already given by the Court may deprive the obligation of its purpose and thus empty it of its substance'.[19]

§ 17.   The literal text of most rules of Community law is different in character from that of most national laws because of the authenticity of six (sometimes seven) languages.[20] This can entail greater precision: an expression which is vague in one language may be clearer in another.[21] It can also result in vaguer norms: the different languages may lead to varying meanings of the text. In the latter case the Court has more freedom to resort to one of the other methods of interpretation in order to reach the most appropriate rendering of the text. In the *Stauder Case* two of the authentic languages, four in number at that time, were more onerous to the individual concerned than were the other two. The Court of Justice then held:

'When a single decision is addressed to all the Member States the necessity for uniform application and accordingly for uniform interpretation makes it impossible to consider one version of the text in isolation but requires that it be interpreted on the basis of both the real intention of its author and the aim he seeks to achieve, in the light in particular of the versions in all four languages. In a case like the present one, the most liberal interpretation must prevail, provided that it is sufficient to achieve the objectives pursued by the decision in question. It cannot, moreover, be accepted that the authors of the decision intended to impose stricter obligations in some Member States than in others.'[22]

When the other languages demonstrate that the text in one language is wrong, the people who use that language may be in a difficult situation when in good faith they have relied on that text. Legal certainty is affected when one can no longer rely on each of the languages. Being aware of this problem the

19. *Da Costa Case* (28-30/62), 27 March 1963, [1963] ECR 38; 9 Jur. (1963) 77; 9 Rec. (1963) 75; [1963] CMLR 237; CCH para 8010. See also below, § 596.
20. The ECSC Treaty is authentic in French, the other Treaties are authentic in all seven languages, including Irish (Act of Accession, Art. 160) but secondary Community law is normally authentic in only six languages (Council Regulation No. 1 as amended, OJ L73/123 (1972)). On plurilinguism in general see Jean Hardy, *The interpretation of plurilingual treaties by international courts and tribunals*, 37BYIL (1961) pp. 72-155; on plurilinguism in the European Communities, see S.A. Dickschat, *Problèmes d'interprétation des traités européens résultant de leur plurilinguisme*, RBDI 1968, pp. 40-60; Lisbeth Stevens, *The principle of linguistic equality in judicial proceedings and in the interpretation of plurilingual legal instruments: the regime linguistique in the Court of Justice of the European Communities*, 62 Northwestern University Law Review (1967), pp. 701-734.
21. See e.g. *Matisa Case* (35/75), 23 Oct. 1975, consideration 6, [1975] ECR 1212; CCH para 8316; *Deboeck Case* (90/74), 16 Oct. 1975, consideration 35, [1975] ECR 1136; *Carstens Keramik Case* (98, 99/75), 18 Feb. 1976, consideration 12, [1976] ECR 252; CCH para. 8348; *Liègeois Case* (93/76), 16 March 1977, considerations 12, 13, [1977] ECR 549 [1977] 2 CMLR 764, 765; *Regina Case* (30/77), 27 Oct. 1977, consideration 14, 1977 ECR 2010 [1977] 2 CMLR 821; CCH para 8441; *Ganzini Case* (101/77), 13 April 1978, consideration 11, [1978] ECR 920.
22. *Stauder Case* (29/69), 12 Nov. 1969, [1969] ECR 424, 425 [1970] CMLR 118; CCH para 8077.

Court tries to avoid the conclusion that any texts in a particular language are not adequate. In the *Kerry Milk Case* it held:

'The elimination of linguistic discrepancies by way of interpretation may in certain circumstances run counter to the concern for legal certainty, inasmuch as one or more of the texts involved may have to be interpreted in a manner at variance with the natural and usual meaning of the words. Consequently, it is preferable to explore the possibilities of solving the points at issue without giving preference to any one of the texts involved.

...

It follows that any discrepancy between the versions in the different languages of Article 6 of Regulation No 1134/68 is irrelevant in the present context.'[23]

§ 18. In law, words such as 'public policy'[24] or *'force majeure'*, often express legal notions which have been evolved in the national legal systems. Even when the translation of such words causes no problem, their meaning may vary due to differences of development in their national legal systems. The expression *'détournement de pouvoir'* (misuse of powers) is interpreted with a different meaning even in Member States using the same language, such as Belgium and France. Literal interpretation of Community law is hampered by the fact that it may be unclear which legal notion the words refer to. Only gradually can the Court of Justice elucidate the Community law meaning of such words, although, sometimes it may be helped by the Community legislator which, for example, clarified the notion 'public policy' in certain directives.[25] When the Court had to apply the notion *'détournement de pouvoir'* in one of its early cases, the Advocate-General considered it necessary to make an extensive comparative study of that notion in the national legal systems of the Member States in order to come to a conclusion as to its meaning in the ECSC Treaty.[26]

§ 19. Whether a text is clear or not is a matter of interpretation. In order to arrive at the proper interpretation, the Court of Justice, like most Continental courts, considers itself less strictly bound by the letter of the law than most

23. *Kerry Milk Case* (80/76), 3 March 1977, considerations 11, 17, [1977] ECR 435, 436; [1977] 2 CMLR 781, 782; CCH para 8403.
24. Gérard Druesne, *La réserve d'ordre public de l'article 48 du traité de Rome*, 12 RTDE (1976), pp. 229-258.
25. See, e.g. EEC directives 64/221, 72/194 and 75/35. The Court restrictively interpreted this notion in the *Van Duyn Case* (41/74), 4 Dec. 1974, consideration 18, [1974] ECR 1350; [1975] 1 CMLR 17; CCH para 8283, and the *Regina Case* (30/77), 27 Oct. 1977, consideration 33. [1977] ECR 2013; [1977] 2 CMLR 824; CCH para 8441. On public policy see also H. Boonk, *De openbare orde als grens aan het vrij verkeer van goederen, personen en diensten in de EEG*, Thesis Groningen 1977.
26. Advocate-General Lagrange in the *First Assider Case* (3/54), 11 Feb. 1955, [1954-56] ECR 73-85; 1 Jur. (1954-55) 159-188; 1 Rec. (1954-55) 149-175. See also Christopher Dwyer, *Some Problems of EEC Legal Translations*, The Law Society's Gazette, 7 March 1979, pp. 244, 245.

British or Irish courts.[27] This may be illustrated by the *First Meroni Case*: the ECSC Treaty contains no general provision for the plea of illegality, it only mentions this plea in relation to individual decisions imposing pecuniary sanctions. In the *First Meroni Case* the High Authority had therefore submitted that in other cases the plea of illegality would not exist. However, the Court of Justice held that the express mentioning of the plea in one case only did not exclude it for other cases (for quotation, see below § 357).

§ 20. In general, one gets the impression that the Court was stricter as to the letter of the texts in its early days than it is at present. This may be a necessary development as the factual situation gradually evolves in such a manner that a text written in 1957 cannot be interpreted in exactly the same way in 1979. In this respect the Community Treaties differ fundamentally from national laws. When, within the national legal order, a literal interpretation of a law by a court leads to harmful effects, Parliament can change the law within a short space of time. But the Community Treaties have far more in common with a constitution. It is extremely difficult to amend them, and their development largely depends on the changing interpretation accorded to them by the judiciary.

b. HISTORICAL BACKGROUND[28]

§ 21. The *travaux préparatoires* of the Community Treaties are secret and cannot therefore be used by the Court. But following Continental judicial tradition the Court can make use of the preparatory documents of secondary Community legislation, such as debates in the European Parliament. It did so in the *Stauder Case* where it referred to the preparatory discussions in the Management Committee to establish that the meaning expressed by the Dutch and German texts had not been intended and that therefore the other texts should prevail.[29]

Another field in which the Court of Justice has resorted to the historical background of texts is that of *customs nomenclature*. In the *Bakels Case* the Court held: '*The Brussels Nomenclature, which was established by the Convention on Nomenclature for the Classification of Goods in Customs Tariffs of 15 December 1950, to which the Member States were parties, is undeniably the basis of the Common Customs Tariff*'. Hence the explanatory notes made under that convention '*cannot be ignored*' when the Community provisions come to be interpreted.[30]

---

27. On these differences see Lord Denning in the *English Champagne Case, Court of Appeal*, 22 May 1974, [1974] CMLR 118, 119.
28. See Bredimas (*op. cit.*, note 17), pp. 57-65.
29. *Stauder Case* (29/69), 12 Nov. 1969, consideration 5, [1969] ECR 425; [1970] CMLR 119; CCH para 8077. For another example in which the history of a regulation was taken into consideration, see *Pigs Marketing Case* (83/78), 29 Nov. 1978, consideration 54, [1979] 1 CMLR 203.
30. *Bakels Case* (14/70), 8 Dec. 1970, [1970] ECR 1009; [1971] CMLR 200; CCH para 8118. See also *Siemers Case* (30/71), 24 Nov. 1971, consideration 5, [1971] ECR 927,

c. SYSTEMATIC INTERPRETATION

§ 22. The Court makes use of the system of the Treaties.[31] The place of an article in a particular chapter of the Treaty is relevant for its interpretation. Also, the introductory articles setting out the purposes of the Communities play an important role in the interpretation of the other articles.

Thus, the Court considered in the *Manghera Case* that, as regards its interpretation, EEC Article 37(1), on State monopolies, *'must be considered in its context in relation to the other paragraphs of the same article and in its place in the general scheme of the Treaty'*[32] ; in the *Bresciani Case* the Court had to rule on the effect of EEC Article 13. It referred to Article 9 as well and then held:

'The position of these articles at the beginning of that part of the Treaty reserved for the "Foundations of the Community" is sufficient to indicate their crucial role in the construction of the common market.'[33]

§ 22a. A special form of systematic interpretation is interpretation by analogy.[34] In the absence of express provisions concerning a particular situation the Court then uses provisions applicable to similar situations elsewhere in Community law. When, for example, no clear time limit could be found in EEC Article 93(3) the Court applied the time limit contained in EEC Article 173.[35] When in one agricultural regulation no provision had been made on force majeure, the Court applied this principle by analogy with other regulations.[36] When no provisions had been made for the costs of proceedings brought by staff members of the European Investment Bank, the Court applied by analogy the rules provided for servants of the Communities.[37]

d. TELEOLOGICAL INTERPRETATION

§ 23. Although at first the Court was more strict, after gradually establishing its position it has increasingly used interpretations based on the purposes of

---

[1972] CMLR 142; CCH para 8151 and *König Case* (185/73), 29 May 1974, consideration 18, [1974] ECR 619; CCH para 8275.
31. See Bredimas (*op. cit.*, note 17), pp. 43-47.
32. *Manghera Case* (59/75), 3 Feb. 1976, considerations 6, 7, [1976] ECR 100; [1976] 1 CMLR 566; CCH para 8342.
33. *Bresciani Case* (87/75), 5 Feb. 1976, consideration 7, [1976] ECR 138; [1976] 2 CMLR 75, 76. CCH para 8347. See also *Gingerbread Case* (2,3/62), 14 Dec. 1962, [1962] ECR 431; [1963] CMLR 214-219; CCH para 8004.
34. See also John A. Usher, *Interpretation by analogy – contrasting cases*, 3 ELRev. (1978), pp. 387-390.
35. *Lorenz Case*, see below, § 76.
36. *Reich Case*, see below, § 105.
37. *Mills Case* (110/75), second judgement, 17 Nov. 1976, consideration 26, [1976] ECR 1626.

the Community Treaties.[38] It does not rely merely on the wording, the background or even the context of the provisions concerned, but chooses the interpretation which best serves the purpose for which the provision was made. For this type of interpretation the expressions *'effet utile'*, *'purposive'*[39], *'functional'* and *'teleological'* interpretation are used. It is employed either for the interpretation of the Community Treaties or for that of secondary Community law. In the former case the expression *'constitutional interpretation'* may be used in order to stress that the Treaties, the constitution of the Communities, are the basis for this interpretation. A legal order is developing out of the constitution, and in its constitutional interpretation the Court interprets that legal order as it has evolved and in such a way that it may fulfil its function most efficiently. The spirit and the purpose of the *constitution* form the core of this interpretation. As a similar kind of interpretation is used for secondary Community law, the expression *'teleological interpretation'* seems more appropriate as a general denomination.

The words *'effet utile'* and *'functional interpretation'* are avoided as they might suggest that the Court should interpret the law in the light of its own wishes as to how a future Community legal order should be. This is a manner of interpretation which the Court tries to avoid as much as is possible.

In principle, teleogical interpretation is of a subsidiary nature. The Court will apply it when the text and the history of the provision are insufficiently clear.[40]

Teleological interpretation is used for three purposes: (1) to promote the objective for which the rule of law was made, (2) to prevent unacceptable consequences to which a literal interpretation might lead, and (3) to fill gaps which would otherwise exist in the legal order. Each of these purposes may be illustrated by examples.

(i) Promotion of the objective

§ 24.   Because certain exchange markets within the Community had been disturbed, the Council had authorized the Member States to widen the margins of fluctuation for the exchange rates of their currencies. A perceptible

---

38. To some extent the Court used this method from its early days; see Scheingold, *The Rule of Law in European Integration*, London 1965, pp. 289-293. See also C.J. Mann, *The Function of Judicial Decision in European Economic Integration*, Nijhoff, the Hague 1972, pp. 378-383; Stuart S. Malawer, *International Law, European Community Law and the Rule of Reason*, 8 JWTL (1974), pp. 17-74; Robert Ormand, *La notion de l'effet-utile des traités communautaires dans la jurisprudence de la Cour de Justice des Communautés européennes*, thèse et d'après thèse, Paris I, 1975, 195 and 181 pages. Mustafa K. Yasseen, *L'interpretation des traités d'après la Convention de Vienne sur le Droit des Traités*, chapitre VII, *L'Effet Utile: Le principe Ut Res Magis Valeat quam Pereat*, 151 RdC (1976 III), pp. 71-77; Bredimas (*op. cit*, note 17) pp. 70-105; Robert Ormand, *L'utilisation particulière de la methode d'interpretation des traités selon leur 'effet utile' par la Cour de Justice des Communautés Européennes*, 12 RTDE (1976), pp. 624-634.
39. John Usher, *The Interpretation of Community Law by the European Court of Justice*, 11 The Law Teacher (1977), p. 165.
40. *Butter Sales Case* (11/76), 7 Feb. 1979, consideration 6; *Milk and Butter Sales Case* (18/76), 7 Feb. 1979, consideration 5.

margin of difference, within a Member State, between the current rate of exchange and the official parity could, however, give rise to difficulties for the agricultural market. The Council therefore issued Regulation 974/71, giving authority to Member States to apply compensatory amounts under specific circumstances.[41] The Regulation was amended several times and the Commission was charged to fix the amounts in certain cases. The question arose whether the compensatory amount on products imported from third countries could include the fixed component intended for the protection of the industry. The Court answered this question in the negative, considering:

'In fact, the sole objective of the introduction of compensatory amounts was to neutralize the effect of disturbances arising in agricultural trade provoked by the fluctuation of exchange rates for the currencies of certain Member States, as emphasized in the final recital of the preamble to Regulation No 974/71, according to which 'the compensatory amounts should be limited to the amounts strictly necessary to compensate the incidence of the monetary measures on the prices of basic products'.

...

In such a situation, it was contrary to the objective of Regulation No 974/71 to take account, by way of a 'charge on products imported', of the fixed component of the import levy on products derived from cereals, fixed by reference to considerations — the protection of the processing industry — which were totally extraneous to the objective of Regulation No 974/71.'[42]

§ 25. Under Community rules export refunds were paid on products subject to a single price system, but in the case of some countries, *inter alia* Morocco, the refunds were considerably higher than in the case of other countries. *Milch-, Fett- und Eier-Kontor* exported butter to Morocco, and unloaded it there. An affiliated company reloaded it again and subsequently sold it to a Czech company in Poland. Milch-, Fett- und Eier-Kontor claimed the refund applicable to Morocco. The German Customs authorities considered that the butter had not really been marketed in Morocco and only paid the refund applicable to Poland. The question was brought before a German court which requested a preliminary ruling on the regulations concerned. The Court of Justice held:

'Since these questions mainly raise the problem of the objective of the system of refunds, it is fitting to give a general answer to them.

...

The variation in the refund takes place by reason of the desire to take account of the peculiar characteristics of each import marked on which the Community wishes to play a part.

41. Council Regulation 974/71 of 12 May 1971, OJ 1971 Nr. L 106, p. 1.
42. *First Roquette Case* (34/74), 12 Nov. 1974, considerations 14, 19, [1974] ECR 1229, 1230; CCH para 8309.

If it sufficed for the goods simply to be unloaded to qualify for payment of the refund at a higher rate, the *raison d'être* of the system of varying the refund would be disregarded and abuse would be made possible to the detriment of Community interests.

It is therefore necessary for the goods to have been cleared through customs and put into free circulation at the destination.'[43]

§ 25a. One of the reasons why the Court of Justice held that Regulation 543/69, on the harmonization of certain social legislation relating to road transport, was applicable to independent traders as well as to employed drivers, was that *'the effect of an exemption would be to open a considerable breach in the effectiveness of the provisions of the regulation'.* [44]

(ii) Prevention of unacceptable results

§ 26. In the *Second Schlüter* and *Third Rewe Cases* the Court had to decide on the legality of Council Regulation 974/71 which provided for levies on agricultural trade between Member States to compensate for price differences caused by the revaluation of the Mark and the Guilder. The regulation was founded on EEC Article 103 and the Court first had to decide whether that article offered a sufficient legal basis. It found that Article 103 does not relate to the organization of agricultural markets and that Council Regulation 974/71 should therefore not have been based on that article, but on Articles 40 and 43, which require the advice of the European Parliament. The Court then went on:

'However, owing to the time needed to give effect to the procedures laid down in Articles 40 and 43, a certain amount of trade might then have passed free of the Regulations, and this could jeopardise the relevant common organizations of the market.

There being no adequate provision in the common agricultural policy for adoption of the urgent measures necessary to counteract the monetary situation described above, it is reasonable to suppose that the Council was justified in making interim use of the powers conferred on it by Article 103 of the Treaty'.[45]

The Court then had to decide whether the levies were compatible with EEC Articles 8, 9, 12 and 13, which prohibit all customs duties or charges having

---

43. *Second Milch- Fett- und Eier-Kontor Case* (125/75), 2 June 1976, considerations 3, 5-6, [1976], ECR 782, 783; CCH para 8366. For other examples in this category, see *Massonet Case* (50/75), 25 Nov. 1975, consideration 10, [1975] ECR 1481; *Schouten Case* (35/78), 14 Dec. 1978, considerations 30, 31, 35, 36, 39.
44. *Derycke Case* (65/76), 25 Jan. 1977, consideration 20, [1977] ECR 35; CCH para 8410.
45. *Second Schlüter Case* (9/73), 24 Oct. 1973, considerations 13-15, [1973] ECR 1152; CCH para 8233; *Third Rewe Case* (10/73), 24 Oct. 1973, considerations 13-15; [1973] ECR 1190; CCH para 8234.

equivalent effect on imports and exports in trade between Member States. The Court recognized that the levies constituted a partitioning of the market, but proceeded:

'Diversion of trade caused solely by the monetary situation can be considered more damaging to the common interest, bearing in mind the aims of the common agricultural policy, than the disadvantages of the measures in dispute'.

The Court concluded that the levies were conducive to the maintenance of the normal flow of trade, that they were intended to prevent the disruption of the intervention system, which is an essential element of the agricultural policy, that they were not introduced by Member States unilaterally but by the Community, and that therefore the Council, by adopting them, had not contravened the said articles.[46]

§ 27. In 1954 the High Authority had introduced an equalization system for scrap *purchased* during a particular period. In the beginning of that period the *Forges de Clabecq* had imported scrap which it had purchased at an earlier date. After the High Authority had imposed the levy due on this purchase, the forges lodged an action for annulment. The Court of Justice rejected the action, considering that the term 'purchase' could not be interpreted in its literal legal sense, since that would lead to a different regime for imported and for domestic scrap, a difference which had not been intended and would lead to the unacceptable consequence that the imported scrap would benefit from the equalization system (a subsidy on foreign scrap was paid when *imported*), while the scrap would not be counted for the levy all enterprises had to pay. Therefore the Court concluded that the date of delivery should be decisive. Usually the rejection of an action means that the party who initiated it bears all costs. As in this case the action had been caused by the defective formulation of the Decision by the High Authority, the Court decided that each party should bear its own costs.[47]

§ 27a. According to the Staff Regulations civil servants must avail themselves of an administrative procedure before they can appeal to the Court of Justice. The Court of Justice held that this requirement is 'devoid of purpose' in a situation where the competent authority would have no power to review the decision concerned. To take the requirement literally 'would merely result in a futile prolongation of the procedure' and was, therefore, not necessary.[48]

---

46. *Third Rewe Case* (10/73), 24 Oct. 1973, considerations 20, 21, [1973] ECR 1192; CCH para 8234. Consideration 33 of the *Second Schlüter Case* (see above note 45) reads the same; but there the national court had only asked whether the provisions of the Common Customs Tariff had been violated.
47. *Forges de Clabecq Case* (14/63), 16 Dec. 1963, [1963] ECR 371-373; 9 Jur. (1963) 780-783; 9 Rec. (1963) 748-752; [1964] CMLR 176, 177.
48. *Von Wüllerstorff Case* (7/77), 16 March 1978, considerations 7, 8, [1978] ECR 778, 779. For a case under the Convention of 27 September 1968 on Jurisdiction and Enforcement of Judgements in Civil and Commercial Matters, see *Somafer Case* (33/78), 22 Nov. 1978, consideration 7; [1979] 1 CMLR 502.

19

'*The necessity of the continuity of the service*' was accepted by the Court as a justification for not applying the rule that a jury for selection of personnel must be composed of three members.[49]

§ 27b. One of the reasons why the Court of Justice adjudicated in the *Nuclear Materials Ruling* that the Community must itself be a party to a convention relating to the physical protection of nuclear materials, was that otherwise '*it would not be possible for the Community to define a supply policy and to manage the nuclear common market properly.*'[50]

(iii) The filling of gaps

§ 28. Gaps occur in any legal system, but in a recently established one they will arise more frequently than in a system which has been developed over a long period of time. Normally the most important gaps should be filled by the legislator, but within the European Communities the legislator functions so imperfectly that it hardly fills any gaps in the law at all. The Court may fill such gaps by employing other sources of law, in particular general principles (see below § 33-118), but in addition teleological interpretation of existing rules can sometimes be used for the same purpose.

As the filling of gaps in a legal system comes close to enacting legislation, courts are not the most suitable organs for performing this function. They are not democratically elected nor controlled by an elected body. In cognizance of this the Court of Justice has always tried to avoid creating new law. As much as it possibly can it restricts itself to making declarations on the law as it was made or was meant to be made by the legislator. In a number of cases, however, the Court was compelled to fill gaps and therefore acted in an almost legislative capacity. Some examples may illustrate this position.[51]

§ 29. Unlike EEC Articles 12-17 (on the elimination of customs duties between Member States), Articles 18-29 (on the customs tariff) contain no provision on *charges having an effect equivalent to customs duties*, nor does Council Regulation 950/68 on the Common Customs Tariff. According to a Belgian law all persons importing uncut diamonds from outside the Communities into Belgium were obliged to pay 1/300 of the value into the Social Fund for Diamond Workers. Some Belgian importers contested this charge, and the Labour Court of Antwerp requested a preliminary ruling on the admissibility of this kind of charge under the Treaty and under Regulation 950/68. The Court of Justice held:

49. *Martin Case* (24/78), 13 Feb. 1979, consideration 20. At the time of writing no English translation of this case was available.
50. *Nuclear Materials Ruling* (1/78), 14 Nov. 1978, consideration 15.
51. For more examples see Henry G. Schermers, *The European Court of Justice: Promoter of European integration*, 22 AJCL (1974) pp. 459-464. See also: Gerhard Köpenik. *Die Ausweitung der Rechtssetzungsbefugnisse der Europäischen Gemeinschaften durch den Europäischen Gerichtshof*, Thesis München 1974, 225 pp.; Jean Boulouis, *A propos de la fonction normative de la jurisprudence. Remarques sur l'oeuvre jurisprudentielle de la Cour de Justice des Communautés européennes*, Mélanges Waline 1974, Vol. I, pp. 149-162; Schwarze (*op. cit.*, note 12), pp. 105-240.

'Although that Regulation does not expressly allow for the elimination or equalization of charges other than customs duties as such, it is nevertheless clear from its objective that under it Member States are prohibited from amending, by means of charges supplementing such duties, the level of protection as defined by the Common Customs Tariff.

Even if they are not protective in character the existence of such charges may be irreconcilable with the requirements of a common commercial policy.

According to Article 113(1) of the Treaty, the common commercial policy shall be based on uniform principles, particularly in regard to changes in tariff rates, the conclusion of tariff and trade agreements, the achievement of uniformity in measures of liberalization, export policy and measures to protect trade.

The definition of these uniform principles involves, as does the common tariff itself, the elimination of national disparities, whether in the field of taxation or of commerce, affecting trade with third countries.

...

It follows therefore that subsequent to the introduction of the Common Customs Tariff all Member States are prohibited from introducing, on a unilateral basis, any new charges or from raising the level of those already in force'.[52]

§ 30. In a regulation imposing a new levy on sugar as from 1 July 1968 no provision was made on the question whether an excess of sugar which comes to light on an official stocktaking after 1 July 1968 and which arose before this date, must be assigned, for the purpose of the calculation of the levy, to the period before 1 July 1968 or to the year after that date. The Court of Justice, which was asked for a preliminary ruling by a German court, considered:

'The regulations in force at the time were silent in this respect.

The rules of the common organization of the market in sugar must be regarded as forming a complete system in the sense that it does not leave the Member States the power to fill such a lacuna by resorting to their national law.

It is thus proper to seek a solution in the light of the aims and objectives of the common organization of the market, taking account of considerations of a practical and administrative nature'.

It then studied the system and the technical conditions for stocktaking, balanced the pros and cons of both possible solutions and concluded that the excess should be attributed to the marketing year in which it was ascertained.[53]

52. *Social Fund for Diamond Workers Case* (37 and 38/73), 13 Dec. 1973, considerations 13-16, 18, [1973] ECR 1623; [1976] 2 CMLR 233; CCH para 8258.
53. *Hannoversche Zucker Case* (159/73), 30 Jan. 1974, consideration 4, [1974] ECR 129; CCH para 8263.

§ 31. Illustrative also is the Court's reasoning in the *Cristini Case*. No specific provision existed on the entitlement of the widow and children of a migrant worker to a particular social benefit. The Court held:

> 'It would be contrary to the purpose and the spirit of the Community rules on freedom of movement for workers to deprive the survivors of such a benefit following the death of the worker whilst granting the same benefit to the survivors of a national'.[54]

§ 31a. Community law contains very few written rules in the field of industrial and commercial property. The EEC Treaty provides for one Common Market, but EEC Article 36 permits the Member States to restrict imports on the ground of the protection of industrial and commercial property. Initially it was not clear what restrictions are permitted under this heading. The Court of Justice interprets the exception of EEC Article 36 in a restrictive way. It has ruled that derogations form the free movement of goods are permitted only when they are justified for the purpose of safeguarding rights which constitute the *specific subject-matter* of industrial or commercial property rights.[55]

The import of goods may not be restricted for the reason that they bear a trade-mark which is identical to a national trade-mark, if both trade-marks have the same origin.[56] Nor may trade-marks be used for artificially dividing the Common Market.[57] In the application of these rules several specific problems have arisen. Here again the Court of Justice had to fill gaps. On the questions whether an importer or trader may repackage products imported under trade-mark, no rules were available. In principle the Court held that the proprietor of a trade-mark is entitled to prevent an importer from doing so; but it accepted the possibility of exceptions to this rule under the condition that the importer or trader gives prior notice of his intention to do so.[58] Such prior notice, however useful for the Market, could not be based on any existing rule of Community law.

§ 32. Although it may come close to legislation, teleological interpretation for the purpose of the filling of legal gaps is not legislation as the Court is not free to rule whatever it considers appropriate. It must interpret the law within the system of the existing rules and in the light of the purpose envisaged by the legislator when it first made the rules. This may lead to problems when

54. *Christini Case* (32/75), 30 Sept. 1975, consideration 16, [1975] ECR 1095; [1976] 1 CMLR 583; CCH para 8330. See also *Royer Case* (48/75), 8 April 1976, consideration 56, [1976] ECR 516; [1976] 2 CMLR 641; CCH para 8359.
55. See my contribution to the *Joint European-American Study on the Role of Judiciary in Economic Integration*. University of Michigan, to be published in 1980.
56. See *Sirena Case* (40/70), 18 Jan. 1971, [1971] ECR 69-91; [1971] CMLR 272; CCH para 8101; *Hag Case* (192/73), 3 July 1974, [1974] ECR 744; [1974] 2 CMLR 143-144; CCH para 8230.
57. *Grundig Case* (56, 58/64), 13 July 1966, [1966] ECR 344-346; 1966 CMLR 474-475.
58. *Second Hoffmann – La Roche Case* (102/77), 23 May 1978, consideration 12, [1978] ECR 1165; [1978] 3 CMLR 242; CCH para 8466.

the original legislator, normally the drafters of the Treaties, had in mind legal provisions which cannot now be supported by the practical developments of the law. Teleological interpretation may then lead to unacceptable results and may, therefore, be set aside by the Court. An example is offered by EEC Article 119 on equal pay for men and women. The drafters of the Treaty intended that this provision should be fully operative by 1 Januari 1962 for the old Member States and by 1 Januari 1973 for the new ones. In practice, however, this intention was not fulfilled. Though the Member States enacted the required legislation, it entered into effect in some of them only after a considerable delay. Miss *Defrenne* had invoked the Article before her national court and the court in question requested the Court of Justice to give an interpretation on the direct effect of the Article. If the Court had given the legally correct reply that the Article had such effect as from the dates mentioned above this would have caused a change in the national legal situation in some Member States of as great, if not greater, impact as important and sweeping legislation would have done. The Court of Justice considered that it should not engender such a change and ruled that '*it is appropriate to take exceptionally into account the fact that, over a prolonged period, the parties concerned have been led to continue with practices which were contrary to Article 119, although not yet prohibited under their national law,*'[59] and that therefore the principle of legal certainty should take priority (see below § 78). In doing so, the Court indicated that there are limits to the application of the law as considered by the drafters of the Treaties. The Court must have taken into account that it would run the risk that its decisions would not be followed, if it were to neglect the wishes and needs of contemporary society.

B. GENERAL PRINCIPLES OF LAW[60]

1. Various types of general principles of law

§ 33. No legal order can be composed solely of written rules. In all legal orders such rules are filled out by general principles of law accepted by the competent judiciary. On account of its lack of maturity and, as yet, great detail the Community legal order has need of even greater recourse to general principles for its completion than is the case with most national legal orders.

In the Community legal order one must distinghuish three groups of general principles:

---

59. *Second Defrenne Case* (43/75), 8 April 1976, consideration 72, [1976] ECR 460; [1976] 2 CMLR 128; CCH para 8346.
60. See also Albert Bleckmann, *Der Rechtsstaat in vergleichender Sicht. Zugleich ein Beitrag zur Rechtsquellenlehre des Europäischen Gemeinschaftsrechts*, 20 GYIL (1977), pp. 406-432; Neville Brown and Jacobs (*op. cit.*, note 17), pp. 215-228; Toth (*op. cit.*, note 10), pp. 85-94; Anna Bredimas, *Comparative Law in the Court of Justice of the European Communities*, 32 YbWA (1978), pp. 320-333.

§ 34. *a. Compelling legal principles*, stemming from the common legal heritage of Western Europe, and setting out binding legal rules.[61] These are a form of natural law which should be obeyed irrespective of whether they form part of the written legal order or not. The question of which rules belong to this category depends on the society concerned. Each society subjectively decides what legal principles it considers to be compelling and each society changes this notion slowly but continuously. A definition of these principles is therefore very hard to give.[62]

§ 35. *b. Regulatory rules common to the laws of the Member States.* These are all other rules, which for whatever reason happen to be common to the legal orders of all Member States. Unlike the compelling legal principles these rules do not necessarily contain an element of justice, fairness or equity. Additional to those rules which contain such elements the laws of the Member States have in common rules of a purely regulatory nature. It was, for instance, a regulatory rule common to the laws of the Member States that cars should drive on the right-hand side of the road. After British and Irish entry this is no longer a common rule. In the *Alma Case* the Court of Justice accepted as a general rule common to the laws of the Member States the rule *'that a written declaration of intent becomes effective as soon as it arrives in due course within the control of the addressee'.*[63] Perhaps, this can be seen as a rule of a regulatory nature.

Due to their common background in Roman law and a comparable level of cultural and economic development the Western European States have many legal rules in common.

§ 36. *c. General rules, native to the Community legal order.* The Community legal order is extended by means of legislative action and by the Court's cases. Within this legal order general principles of law will develop, independent of the national legal orders. If, within the Communities, a particular approach is adopted for many legal questions, that approach may become a general rule which is subsequently followed in other cases. Legal constructions repeatedly employed by the legislator, legal reasonings repeatedly followed by the Court will be gradually embodied into the general rules of the legal order. All Community institutions take part in this process. New legal principles may evolve not only from the case-law of the Court of Justice but also from the decisions and resolutions of the European Parliament or of other institutions. It is therefore to be expected that the Community legal order will gradually

---

61. For the meaning of the word 'principle' see below § 188. To make a distinction, the words *'rules* of law' are used below for those principles of law which are not of such fundamental nature.
62. Hans-Josef Rüber cites in his dissertion *Der Gerichtshof der Europäischen Gemeinschaften und die Konkretisierung allgemeiner Rechtsgrundsätze*, Köln 1970, pp. 25-33, some 20 authors who give some 20 different definitions. For the content of the compelling legal principles accepted in Western Europe, see also Ernst-Werner Fuss, *Die Europäischen Gemeinschaften und der Rechtsstaatsgedanke*, UGA Verlag 1967, p. 17.
63. *Alma Case* (8/56), 10 Dec. 1957, [1957-58] ECR 98; 3 Jur. (1957)201; 3 Rec. (1957) 190.

encompass more general rules of law within its own tradition and that the need to refer to the national legal orders will diminish accordingly.

The Court of Justice referred to indigenous rules of Community law when in the *Reliable Importers Case* it rejected the use of 'reliability of the importer' as a criterion for the suspension of an import levy, because this did *'not conform to the system of guarantees and proof introduced by the Community rules'.* [64]

In theory, the indigenous principles could be compelling legal principles as well as regulatory rules of law. In practice, however, the former will not develop separately from either the written texts or the compelling principles mentioned sub a), so that only rules of a more regulatory nature are relevant in this respect. The most important legal principle of the Communities themselves, such as the free movement of goods and persons [65] , have their basis in the Treaties and therefore form part of another source of Community law.

§ 37. The distinction between the different groups of general principles of law is important as the principles of the first group take priority over other elements of Community law, with the exception of the express provisions of the Treaties. However, other general rules of national laws or of Community law itself are used only when no other sources of Community law are available.

It is not too difficult to distinguish compelling legal principles from regulatory general rules. But it is hard to draw a clear-cut division between the two groups. Most compelling legal principles are at the same time regulatory rules common to the laws of the Member States, and such rules when continuously applied may gradually be seen as rules which ought to be applied.

However, some compelling principles are too vague to be general rules common to the laws of the Member States. For example, all the legal systems of the Member States provide for limitation periods, but they do it differently so that no general rule common to the laws of the Member States exists. On several occasions the applicability of a limitation period was invoked before the Court of Justice as a compelling legal principle, and the existence of such a principle was accepted by the Court, but it could not be applied because of the absence of a common rule with regard to its content (see below § 73).

2. Foundation of general principles in the Treaties

a. EXPRESS REFERENCES

§ 38. By the EEC and Euratom Treaties the establishment of non-contractual liability of the Communities has been attributed to the jurisdiction of the

---

64. *Reliable Importers Case* (39/70), 11 Feb. 1971, consideration 5, [1971] ECR 58; [1971] CMLR 293; CCH para 8132.
65. The Court of Justice mentions this principle as one of *'fundamental nature'* in the *Sotgiu Case* (152/73), 12 Feb. 1974, consideration 4, [1974] ECR 162; CCH para 8257 and as *'basic'* and *'fundamental'* rules in the *Marine Labour Code Case* (167/73), 4 April 1974, considerations 21-25, [1974] ECR 369, 370; [1974] 2 CMLR 228; CCH para 8270.

Court of Justice (see below § 448). But there was no Community law on non-contractual liability which could be applied. The Treaties therefore refer to the *general principles common to the laws of the Member States*. [66] As the laws of the Member States are far more complete than Community law, these common general principles were able to offer a rich source for filling gaps which otherwise would have existed in the Community legal order.

The reference to general principles is wide and therefore includes the compelling legal principles which must be applied as well as regulatory rules which may be applied at the discretion of the Court.

§ 39. In its review of the legality of Community acts the Court of Justice uses as one of the grounds which could lead to establishing illegality *'infringement of any rule of law relating to the application of the Treaty'* (EEC Article 173 see below § 292). The Court accepted that a violation of general principles of law would be covered by this ground and would therefore lead to the illegality of the provision concerned. Thus, this provision has become another Treaty reference to general principles of law.

b. APPLICATION WITHOUT REFERENCE

§ 40. Legal principles of a compelling nature will be applied even if they cannot be based on an express Treaty provision. According to Van Gerven the Court would prefer to apply legal principles in cases where it has a choice to apply either such principles or an express Treaty provision. [67] He refers to the *Köster Case* in which the Court discussed the submission that a general principle had been violated[68] instead of referring to EEC Article 40 on which the case could have been decided and which the Advocate-General actually had proposed as the legal basis for the decision. [69] Van Gerven's view may be correct for cases where the Treaty provisions and the legal principles do not conflict. In case of divergence the Court will probably apply the Treaties as it did in the *Sgarlata Case*, quoted above (§ 16). In the *CFDT Case* as well the applicant tried to establish a right to bring his case before the Court of Justice on the ground of general principles of law. The Court then held:

'Whilst the principles upon which the applicant relies call for a wide interpretation of the provisions concerning the institution of proceedings before the Court with a view to ensuring individuals' legal protection they do not permit the Court on its own authority to amend the actual terms of its jurisdiction.'[70]

66. EEC Art. 215; Euratom Art. 188.
67. Walter van Gerven, *De grenzen van de rechterlijke functie, en het gevaar van overschrijding, in het Europese Recht*, Rechtsgeleerd Magazijn Themis 1974, p. 645.
68. *Köster Case* (25/70), 17 Dec. 1970, considerations 20-22; [1970] ECR 1173, 1174; [1972] CMLR 292; CCH para 8127.
69. *Idem*, Opinion of Advocate-General Dutheillet de Lamothe, [1970] ECR 1146, 1147; [1972] CMLR 270, 271; CCH para 8127.
70. *CFDT Case* (66/76), 17 Feb. 1977, consideration 8, [1977] ECR 310; [1977] 1 CMLR 594, 596.

The Court demonstrated sympathy with the position of CFDT by not ordering it to bear all costs of the proceedings.[71]

§ 41. For legal principles of a compelling nature it may be clear that they should be applied in cases where the Treaties are silent; for regulatory rules common to the laws of the Member States this might be questioned.

The express reference to general principles common to the laws of Member States in the two cases quoted above (§ 38, 39) could mean that these principles should not be applied in other cases where they are not thus mentioned. This would make it impossible to fill up gaps in other fields of the Community legal order such as the judicial review of acts of Member States, pecuniary sanctions, civil servant cases or cases brought to the Court pursuant to an arbitration clause. This would not necessarily lead to a denial of justice as another legal order might offer an alternative. In the cases of judicial review of acts of Member States and arbitration between Member States this could be the international legal order; in the other cases mentioned it could be the most appropriate national legal order.

As has been seen above (§ 19) the Court of Justice is reluctant to apply a reasoning *a contrario*. For that reason it was unlikely that the Court would derive from the express mentioning of legal principles common to the laws of Member States in EEC Article 215 that these principles should not be used in other cases. In the *Algera Case* the Court, furthermore, applied these general principles as part of the Community legal order in a situation where no express rule of Community law existed. In that case the Court held:

'Unless the Court is to deny justice it is therefore obliged to solve the problem by reference to the rules acknowledged by the legislation, the learned writing and the case-law of the member countries.'[72]

Though acts of Community institutions were involved, the Court did not refer to the general rules of law relating to the application of the Treaty. The formula used would be applicable in all cases. It may therefore be safely concluded that the reference to general rules common to the laws of the Member States in EEC Article 215 and the implied reference in EEC Article 173 are just examples of a method generally applicable for filling gaps in the Community legal order, rather than exhaustive provisions.[73]

§ 42. So far the question whether gaps in the Community legal order must be filled by general principles of Community law, or by the rules of another legal order, has not been of great practical importance. The development of Community law — however rapidly it may proceed — will need a long time

---

71. *Idem*, considerations 18 and 19.
72. *Algera Case*, (7/56 and 3-7/57), 3 July 1957; [1957-58] ECR 55; 3 Jur. (1957) 120; 3 Rec. (1957) 115.
73. See also Fuss (*op. cit*, note 62), p. 13. For a reference to general principles of law in a case concerning the Convention on Jurisdiction and the Enforcement of Judgements, see *Gourdain Case* (133/78), 22 Feb. 1979, consideration 9.

before it can noticeably differ from international law in the field of treaty violations by States; cases of arbitration and pecuniary sanctions are rare; civil servant cases usually concern the validity of Community acts, which means that general principles can be applied on the ground of the implied reference to them in EEC Article 173 (the rules of law relating to the application of the Treaty).

§ 43. As the Community legal order develops as a homogeneous body of law, thanks in particular to there being a single Community Court, it may be expected that those general rules which have entered the Community legal order through the express openings of EEC Articles 215 and 173 will be applied throughout the legal order, that is also in cases in which no reference to general rules has been made.

3. Generality

a. COMPELLING LEGAL PRINCIPLES

§ 44. Compelling legal principles should be *generally* accepted in the national legal orders of the Member States in order to be general principles of Community law. 'Generally accepted' does not mean that they must be expressly enumerated in each of the legal systems. It would be sufficient if its content were accepted — possibly in a different form — in all the national legal orders.

Here one meets a wide range of possible roles which a legal principle may play within the national legal order of a State. Ranging from the one extreme to the other they may be roughly divided into the following categories:

a) The legal principle is guaranteed by its incorporation in the national constitution. Many basic human rights fall under this category.

b) The principle, though not regulated by the constitution, is accepted in the national legal order either by statute or by the case-law of the courts.

c) The national legal order is completely silent on the matter. This may be due to the underlying legal problem being solved in a totally different way. In order to find out whether the national legal order is also *indifferent* one may have to conduct further research.

d) The national legal order rejects the principle involved. General principles accepted in some legal orders, such as the right to strike, the freedom of opinion or the right to own private property, may be rejected by others.

e) The national legal order contains a constitutional prohibition of the legal principle. One could imagine such a constitutional denial of legal principles such as the right to strike or the right to own private property.

§ 45. It is manifest that a common legal order cannot be formed from national legal orders which contain diametrically opposite legal provisions in their national constitutions. The Community legal order could be created because of the degree of similarity in the national legal orders of the Member States. Even though the formulations may differ the legal notions are basically comparable. A principle classified under (a) in one Member State will never be classified under (e) or even (d) in another. Taking this as a starting-point it is not too difficult to accept as a primary rule that a principle classified under (a) in any of the Member States should be accepted as a general principle of Community law. [74] In practice this means that if any Member State considers a principle to be of such importance that it has incorporated it in its constitution, it should be accepted as a principle of Community law unless it can be demonstrated that the rule is contrary to the legal order of any of the other Members.

§ 46. In its early cases the Court of Justice seemed to reject this view. In the *Second Ruhrkohlen Case*, in which the applicant invoked the right to own property, guaranteed in Article 14 of the German Constitution, the Court held:

'It is not for the Court, whose function is to judge the legality of decisions adopted by the High Authority (...) to ensure that rules of internal law, even constitutional rules, enforced in one or other of the Member States are respected.

Therefore the Court may neither interpret nor apply Article 14 of the German Basic Law in examining the legality of a decision of the High Authority'. [75]

Also in the *Stork Case* the Court held that it could not *'examine a ground of complaint which maintains that, when the High Authority adopted its decision, it infringed principles of German constitutional law.'* [76]

In these cases, however, it was contended that the *German Constitution* should be applied by the Court of Justice. The situation may be different, however, when legal principles are invoked, in particular after the *Stauder Case* (see below § 53) in which the Court accepted that it must ensure the observance of general principles of Community law, and after the *Handelsgesellschaft Case* (see below § 53) in which the Court accepted the possibility that Community law contains guarantees analogous to those of the German Constitution.

§ 47. In the *Second Nold Case* quoted below (§ 54) the Court of Justice held that it *'cannot uphold measures which are incompatible with fundamental rights recognized and protected by the Constitutions of the Member States'.* [77] It is impossible to construe this statement to mean that every

74. See also Jozeau-Marigne Report, European Parliament document 297/72, 28 Feb. 1973, para 19.
75. *Second Ruhrkohlen Case* (36-38 and 40/59), 15 July 1960, [1960] ECR 438; 6 Jur. (1960) 920; 6 Rec. (1960) 890. On this issue see also Advocate-General Dutheillet de Lamothe in the *Handelsgesellschaft Case* (11/70), 17 Dec. 1970, [1970] ECR 1146; [1972] CMLR 271; CCH para 8126.
76. *Stork Case* (1/58), 4 Feb. 1959, [1959] ECR 26; 5 Jur. (1958-59) 66; 5 Rec. (1958-59) 63.
77. *Second Nold Case* (4/73), 14 May 1974, consideration 13, [1974] ECR 507; [1974] 2 CMLR 354.

fundamental right must be recognized by the constitutions of *all* Member States, for several Member States do not have constitutions guaranteeing fundamental rights. One is therefore, inclined to think that all fundamental rights which are guaranteed anywhere in any of the separate constitutions are meant. Hence the case-law of the Court of Justice is in conformity with the view expressed above (§ 45).[78]

§ 48. It is harder to establish whether general principles which are not mentioned in any constitution but are otherwise accepted in the national legal orders of Member States (above § 44(b)) form part of the Community legal order. This will be the case if all Member States have accepted them, either in laws, or in proposals for new laws or in their legal doctrine. But even if some of the Member States have not expressly accepted a legal principle, it may belong to the Community legal order as long as it does not conflict with the legal order of those Member States. From the case law of the Court of Justice quoted below (§ 53-118) it will be seen that some legal principles have indeed been accepted in the Community legal order without belonging to the legal orders of all the Member States.

b. REGULATORY RULES

§ 49. The purpose of employing general principles common to the laws of the Member States is to provide a solution in the event of a lacuna. To this end, it should not be a prerequisite that the principle exists in each of the Member States.[79] When there is no rule of law governing a certain situation and a regulatory rule must be found in order to prevent a denial of justice, it may be sufficient if such a rule is available only in some of the legal orders of the Member States, whilst the others remain silent. A legal solution of the problem is thus available within the legal orders of the Member States, and there is no reason to militate against using it. The provision may be lacking in the other national legal orders just because they did not need to solve that particular question. If *'common to the laws of the Member States'* means that the national legal systems must be unanimous, then one could analogously apply EEC Article 148(3) which provides: 'Abstentions ... shall not prevent the adoption by the Council of acts which require unanimity'.

---

78. *Kapteyn* comes to the same conclusion in 25 AA (1976), p. 115. See also Advocate-General Warner's opinion in the *IRCA Case* (7/76) of 7 July 1976, [1976] ECR 1237; CCH para 8348.
79. See Advocate-General Roemer in e.g. the *Plaumann Case* (25/62), 15 July 1963, [1963] ECR 116, 117; 9 Jur. (1963) 252-253; 9 Rec. (1963) 241, 242; [1964] CMLR 37, 38; CCH para 8013, or the *Schöppenstedt Case* (5/71), 2 Dec. 1971, [1971] ECR 990; CCH para 8153. See also Ernst-Werner Fuß, *Die Allgemeinen Rechtsgrundsätze über die ausservertragliche Haftung der europäischen Gemeinschaften, zur Methode ihrer Auffindung,* Festschrift Hermann Raschhofer 1977, pp. 43-57; Bruno du Ban, *Les principes généraux communs et la responsabilité non contractuelle de la Communauté,* 13 CDE (1977), pp. 397-402.

§ 50. The situation is different when the national legal orders offer divergent solutions for the same problem. One legal order may offer a solution which another has refused to apply, or two legal orders may present solutions which cannot be reconciled. In such cases there are no general rules common to the laws of the Member States. These situations are rare, however. Though the precise textual solutions may differ, the underlying general rules are usually the same in all Member States. Again — as is the case with compelling legal principles — the common legal, cultural and economic background usually leads to a similar outlook on legal problems.

4. General principles applied by the Court of Justice[80]

§ 51. There are many customary rules considered to be so self-evident, though of insufficient importance for codification in the Rules of Procedure, that they are applied by the Court more or less as a matter of course. The behaviour of the judges is to a great extent founded on the general rules common to the courts of the Member States. It is their similar background which enables the individual judges to work together as one court. The importance of the rules common to the national legal systems as a basis for the Court of Justice cannot be easily quantified, but it is clear that the Court would be unable to function if the judges had basically different ideas about right and wrong.

As regards the Court itself there is no need to express or to evaluate the importance of the Member States' common legal heritage; this factor should, however, be taken into account when the Court of Justice is used as a model for the establishment of other courts whether they be of a regional or a universal nature.

§ 52. Apart from such unobtrusive application, the Court has expressly referred to a number of general principles of law in its cases. The generally accepted principle of *implied powers* will be discussed in Chapter Two (§ 264-267); other general principles are discussed below. Sometimes several legal principles can be applied simultaneously. It will be seen below (e.g. § 69) that the Court of Justice may then accord priority to some principles in preference to others.

a. FUNDAMENTAL HUMAN RIGHTS[81]

§ 53. The Treaties contain no general provisions for the protection of human rights. This has led to a substantial amount of literature on the question as to what extent the Communities are bound to observe general principle of hu-

---

80. See also John A. Usher in 1 ELRev. (1976) pp. 362-368.
81. See also Meinhard Hilf, *Der Gerichtshof der Europäischen Gemeinschaften als Integrationsfaktor, dargestellt anhand der Rechtsprechung zu den Grundrechten*, in *Die Grundrechte in der Europäischen Gemeinschaft*, pp. 23-34.

man rights.[82] The absence of express provisions has caused some problems, particularly in Germany which has strict constitutional rules on human rights. For this reason German lawyers have found it difficult to accept that powers which Germany transferred to the European Communities would be removed from all control with regard to the protection of human rights. Accordingly both before the Court of Justice and before their national courts they have repeatedly pleaded that certain Community acts were void on account of their violating basic provisions of the German Constitution.[83] This plea sometimes succeeded before lower German courts[84] and finally reached the Federal Constitutional Court, the *'Bundesverfassungsgericht'*. In its decision of 29 May 1974 this court accepted the possibility that the execution in Germany of certain provisions of Community law would be held unconstitutional if they infringed basic human rights (see below § 714).[85] For the protection of individuals as well as for securing the full confidence of national courts it was of great importance that the Court of Justice recognised basic human rights as part of Community Law in the *Stauder Case*. In that case it was submitted that some EEC rules jeopardized basic human rights. The Court denied this on the facts, but said in an *obiter dictum* that *'the fundamental human rights are enshrined in the general principles of Community law and protected by the Court'*.[86]

In a later case where the plaintiff had submitted that an EEC decision was void for infringing a basic guarantee of the German Constitution, the Court denied that it could apply such a guarantee but continued:

82. See e.g. Pierre Pescatore in 4 CDE (1968), pp. 629-673, in CMLRev 1972, pp. 73-79 and in his report for FIDE 1975 (Brussels); E.A. Alkema, *West-Europa en de rechten van de Mens*, Civis Mundi 1974, in particular pp. 115-118; Ernst-Werner Fuss, *Der Grundrechtsschutz in den Europäischen Gemeinschaften aus deutscher Sicht*, UGA Verlag 1975, pp. 67-89; A.G. Toth, *The Individual and European Law*, 24 ICLQ (1975), in particular pp. 664-668; W.R. Edison and F. Wooldridge, *European Community Law and Fundamental Human Rights: some recent decisions of the European Court and of national courts*, LIEI 1976/1, pp. 1-54; Ch. Philip, *La Cour de Justice des Communautés et la protection des droits fondamentaux dans l'ordre juridique communautaire*, 21 AFDI (1975), pp. 383-407; M. Hilf, *The Protection of Fundamental Rights in the Community* in F.G. Jacobs (ed.) *European Law and the Individual*, North Holland 1976, pp. 145-160; Pierre Pescatore, *Bestand und Bedeutung der Grundrechte im Recht der Europäischen Gemeinschaften*, 14 EuR (1979), pp. 1-12.
83. See e.g. Court of Justice in *Stork Case* (1/58), 4 Feb. 1959, [1959] ECR 26; 5 Jur. (1959) 66; 5 Rec. (1959) 63; *Second Ruhrkohlen Case* (36-38 and 40/59), 15 July 1960 [1960] ECR 438; 6 Jur. (1960) 920; 6 Rec. (1960) 890, see quotation above, § 46; *Bundesverfassungsgericht*, 5 July 1967, 18 Oct. 1967, 9 June 1971 and 29 May 1974 all summarized in L.J. Brinkhorst and H.G. Schermers, *Judicial Remedies in the European Communities*, 2nd ed. Kluwer Deventer 1977, pp. 181-191. See also Peter Hay, *Supremacy of Community Law in National Courts, A Progress Report on Referrals Under the EEC Treaty*, 16 AJCL (1969) p. 524; Bodo Börner, *Deutsche Grundrechte und Gemeinschaftsrecht*, NJW 1976, pp. 2041-2-48.
84. *Finanzgericht* Rheinland-Pfalz, 14 Nov. 1963; *Verwaltungsgericht* Frankfurt, 24 Nov. 1971, Brinkhorst and Schermers (*op. cit.*, note 51) 1st edition 1969, pp. 144, 145 and Supplement 1972, pp. 74-77; *Hessischer Verwaltungsgerichtshof*, 1 March 1971, [1972] CMLR 841.
85. *German Handelsgesellschaft Case*, *Bundesverfassungsgericht*, 29 May 1974, see below § 171, 172.
86. *Stauder Case* (29/69), 12 Nov. 1969, [1969] ECR 425; [1970] CMLR 119; CCH para 8077.

'However, an examination should be made as to whether or not any analogous guarantee inherent in Community law has been disregarded. In fact, respect for fundamental rights forms an integral part of the general principles of law protected by the Court of Justice. The protection of such rights, whilst inspired by the constitutional traditions common to the Member States, must be ensured within the framework of the structure and objectives of the Community. It must therefore be ascertained, in the light of the doubts expressed by the Verwaltungsgericht, whether the system of deposits has infringed rights of a fundamental nature, respect for which must be ensured in the Community legal system'.[87]

Since then the Court has considered on several occasions whether rules of Community law were in conformity with basic principles of human rights.

§ 54. The best source for the human rights which are generally recognised in Western Europe is the *European Convention for the Protection of Human Rights and Fundamental Freedoms.* Since 3 May 1974 all the Member States of the European Communities have been parties to this convention and one may safely assume that the Communities are bound by its provisions (see below § 134). Before 3 May 1974 the convention itself could not be applied in the Community legal order as France had not ratified it. As France had, however, accepted most of the human rights enumerated in the Convention in its national law, the human rights themselves could be considered as general principles common to the laws of the Member States even then. As yet the Court has not expressly referred to the Convention. The furthest it has gone was in the *Second Nold Case* when it considered:

'As the Court has already stated, fundamental rights form an integral part of the general principles of law, the observance of which it ensures.
    In safeguarding these rights, the Court is bound to draw inspiration from constitutional traditions common to the Member States, and it cannot therefore uphold measures which are incompatible with fundamental rights recognized and protected by the Constitutions of those States.
    Similarly, international treaties for the protection of human rights on which the Member States have collaborated or of which they are signatories, can supply guidelines which should be followed within the framework of Community law'.[88]

The case is of interest both because of its express reference to the constitutions of the Member States and because of its reference to international treaties. Both will be taken into account by the Court of Justice.

---

87. *Handelsgesellschaft Case* (11/70), 17 Dec. 1970, [1970] ECR 1134; [1972] CMLR 283; CCH para 8126 (p. 7424). On this case see Fuss (*op. cit.*, note 82), pp. 79-89.
88. *Second Nold Case* (4/73), 14 May 1974, consideration 13, [1974] ECR 507; [1974] 2 CMLR 354.

§ 54a. In rejecting a plea of discrimination based on sex in the *Third Defrenne Case*, the Court of Justice referred to the *European Social Charter* as well as to Convention III of the International Labour Organisation.[89] Apparently these texts are considered relevant with regard to the establishment of basic human rights.

§ 55. On several occasions it has been proposed to codify the human rights to which the European Communities are bound and thus to give them a stronger basis than 'general principles of law'. The German Constitutional Court, the *Bundesverfassungsgericht*, made this suggestion in the *German Handelsgesellschaft Case* for the purpose of ensuring greater legal certainty when it held that legal certainty is not guaranteed merely by the decisions of the Court of Justice (see quotation below § 171). Codification of human rights could be achieved either by an express reference to the European Convention on Human Rights or by a separate enumeration of those human rights which are binding upon the Communities.[90] Against the former solution is advanced the plea that the European Convention is more than 25 years old and is not entirely representative of contemporary European standards, particularly as economic and social rights are lacking. Against the latter solution practical objections can be made: it would be difficult to draw up a list of rights which are relevant to the Communities and acceptable to all of its Member States. The suggestion for a separate enumeration of human rights was made by the Commission in its report on European Union in order to include more human rights than those of the European Convention, in particular economic and social rights.[91] In practice, the acceptance of human rights as general principles of law may be as good a solution as any, leaving it to the Court of Justice to develop the fundamental rights of the European Communities. In a joint declaration the European Parliament, the Council and the Commission have underlined the importance they attach to the protection of fundamental rights, as derived in particular from the constitutions of the Member States and the European Convention on Human Rights.[92]

§ 56. As long as there is no codification of Community human rights, it will be hard to establish which principles belong to this category, There is no sharp division drawn between basic human rights and other legal principles. Several of the legal principles recognized by the Court of Justice and mentioned below can at the same time be held to be basic human rights. One right of the European Convention on Human Rights which the Court of Justice has accepted in principle is the freedom to practise one's religion.[93] When duly informed, the

---

89. *Third Defrenne Case*, (149/77), 15 June 1978, consideration 28, [1978] ECR 1378.
90. Jozeau-Marigne Report, European Parliament document 297/72, 28 Feb. 1973, para 23. See also Henry G. Schermers, *The Communities under the European Convention on Human Rights*, LIEI 1978/1, pp. 1-8.
91. *Report on European Union*, Bulletin of the European Communities, Supplement 5/75 para 83.
92. Joint Declaration of 5 April 1977, O.J 27 April 1977, No C 103/1. See also John Forman, *The Joint Declaration on Fundamental Rights*, 2 ELRev (1977), pp. 210-215.
93. European Convention on Human Rights, Art. 9.

Community should not fix dates for written tests on religious holidays for any of the candidates for such tests.[94]

b. THE RIGHT TO BE HEARD[95]

§ 57. The right to be heard has often been discussed in cases concerning the *staff* of the Communities. Sometimes staff members of the Communities have been dismissed or demoted without having obtained an opportunity to defend themselves. In such cases the Court of Justice annuls the measure concerned because of the violation of a general principle of law. In the *Alvis Case* the Court held:

> 'According to a generally accepted principle of administrative law in force in the Member States of the European Economic Community, the administrations of these States must allow their servants the opportunity of replying to allegations before any disciplinary decision is taken concerning them.
> This rule, which meets the requirements of sound justice and good administration, must be followed by Community institutions.'[96]

By 1977 this 'principle in force in the Member States' had clearly developed into a general principle of Community law. The Court of Justice then spoke of: '*the general principle that when any administrative body adopts a measure which is liable gravely to prejudice the interests of an individual it is bound to put him in a position to express his point of view.*'[97]

§ 58. In the *First van Eick Case* the Court considered that the Disciplinary Board, even though it has only advisory powers, is obliged to respect basic principles of the law of procedure and that therefore it may not refuse to hear witnesses on specific questions when this has been requested for clearly defined reasons.[98]

§ 59. According to Article 50 of the Staff Regulations the Commission has very wide discretionary powers to dismiss staff members of the ranks A1 and A2 in the interest of the service. The Court considered in the *Almini Case* that when such power is exercised, the civil servant involved '*should first have an*

---

94. *Prais Case* (130/75), 27 Oct. 1976, considerations 10, 16, 19, [1976] ECR 1598, 1599; [1976] 2 CMLR 722, 723, 724. See also Trevor Hartley, *Religious freedom and equality of opportunity*, 2 ELRev (1977), pp. 45-47.
95. See Opinion of Advocate-General Warner in the *Transocean Marine Paint Case* (17/74), 23 Oct. 1974, [1974] ECR 1088-1090; [1974] 2 CMLR 469-471; CCH para 8241.
96. *Alvis Case* (32/62), 4 July 1963, [1963] ECR 55; 9 Jur. (1963) 118, 119; 9 Rec. (1963) 114; [1963] CMLR 404. See also *Pistoi Case* (26/63), 1 July 1964, [1964] ECR 354; 10 Jur. (1964) 730; 10 Rec. (1964) 698; *First De Greef Case* (80/63), 1 July 1964, [1964] ECR 407; 10 Jur. (1964) 834; 10 Rec. (1964) 796.
97. *Moli Case* (121/76), 27 Oct. 1977, consideration 20, [1977] ECR 1979.
98. *First van Eick Case* (35/67), 11 July 1968, [1968] ECR 342; 14 Jur. (1968) 480; 14 Rec. (1968) 501.

opportunity of effectively defending his interests'. As the Commission had granted him only four days to do so and as, furthermore, the reasons which had been given to him were not the same as those discussed by the Commission, the Court found that *'the elementary safeguards'* of the official had not been respected and annulled the decision by which Almini had been dismissed.[99]

§ 60. Also in *other* cases apart from staff cases the right to be heard is occasionally at issue. Regulation 99/63 of the Commission obliges the Commission to inform an undertaking of the objections raised against it, before the Commission may take action under EEC Article 85 to enforce the competition rules. In the *Transocean Marine Paint Case* the Court of Justice held that this regulation:

> 'applies the general rule that a person whose interests are perceptibly affected by a decision taken by a public authority must be given the opportunity to make his point of view known. This rule requires that an undertaking be clearly informed, in good time, of the essence of conditions to which the Commission intends to subject an exemption and it must have the opportunity to submit its observations to the Commission. This is especially so in the case of conditions which, as in this case, impose considerable obligations having far-reaching effects'.[100]

§ 61. In the above-mentioned case the Court clearly stated that the right to obtain information is an essential part of the right to be heard. In anti-trust cases the Court may, however, meet practical difficulties when it wishes to inform an undertaking. A large quantity of data is usually obtained from competitors and it may be inimical to their interests if such data are passed on to others.

In the *Grundig Case* the applicants pleaded that their right to be heard had been violated because they had not been fully informed about all the documents which had prompted the Commission to decide that their mutual agreement violated EEC Article 85. The Court of Justice then held:

> 'The proceedings before the Commission concerning the application of Article 85 of the Treaty are administrative proceedings, which implies that the parties concerned should be put in a position before the decision is issued to present their observations on the complaints which the Commission considers must be upheld against them. For that purpose, they must be informed of the facts upon which these complaints are based. It is not necessary however that the entire content of the file should be communicated to them. In the present case it appears that the statement of the Commission of 20 December 1963 includes all the facts the knowledge of

99. *Almini Case* (19/70), 30 June 1971, considerations 11, 15, 17, [1971] ECR 630, 631.
100. *Transocean Marine Paint Case* (17/74), 23 Oct. 1974, consideration 15, [1974] ECR 1080; [1974] 2 CMLR 477; CCH para 8241.

which is necessary to ascertain which complaints were taken into consideration. The applicants duly received a copy of that statement and were able to present their written and oral observations. The contested decision is not based on complaints other than those which were the subject of those proceedings.[101]

§ 62. As other parties' interests are often involved, it seems acceptable that the rights of the defence do not include a right to inspect all the documents in the possession of the Communities. Such interests of other parties should not, however, be exaggerated. In the *Chemiefarma, Buchler* and *First Boehringer Cases* the applicants had requested the Commission to inform them about the results of the investigations made by the Commission's officials on the concerted practices of these companies. The Commission refused to entertain the request referring to the need to protect the business secrets of other enterprises. The Court then held that the Commission *'could have requested the opinion of the other undertakings concerned with regard to the applicant's request for the communication of the documents relating to them'.*[102]

c. NON BIS IN IDEM[103]

§ 63. Another general principle of law which at the same time may be regarded as a basic human right and which has been accepted, albeit only to a certain extent, by the Court of Justice is the right not to be proceeded against more than once for the same act (*non bis in idem*). In the *Guttmann Case* the Court of Justice held:

'The applicant alleges that the rule *non bis in idem* was violated by the decision of 20 and 21 January 1965.

This rule prohibits not only the imposition of two disciplinary measures for a single offence, but also the holding of disciplinary proceedings more than once with regard to a single set of facts.'[104]

Later, after having obtained further information, the Court annulled the decision considering:

'In the light of the facts of this case, the possibility cannot be excluded that two disciplinary proceedings have been initiated on the basis of the same

101. *Grundig Case* (56 and 58/64), 13 July 1966; [1966] ECR 338; 12 Jur. (1966) 511; 12 Rec. (1966) 491; [1966] CMLR 469; CCH para 8046.
102. *Quinine Cartel Cases: AFC Chemiefarma* (41/69), 15 July 1970, considerations 35-40, [1970] ECR 685; CCH para 8083, (p. 8194); *Buchler* (44/69), 15 July 1970, considerations 13, 14, [1970] ECR 752; CCH para 8084 (p. 8216); *First Boehringer* (45/69), 15 July 1970, considerations 13, 14, [1970] ECR 797; CCH para 8085 (p. 8243).
103. See the Opinion of Advocate-General Mayras in the *Second Boehringer Case* (7/72), 14 Dec. 1972, [1972] ECR 1295-1303, [1973] CMLR 868-882; CCH para 8191.
104. *Gutmann Case* (18 and 35/65) 1st judgement, 5 May 1966, [1966] ECR 119; 12 Jur. (1966) 174; 12 Rec. (1966) 172.

set of facts known to the Commission at the opening of the earlier proceedings, and founded on the same complaint.'[105]

§ 64.   In the case quoted above the rule *'non bis in idem'* was invoked against two proceedings bearing on the same act or piece of behaviour and both initiated by Community institutions. The situation is different when an act or a particular piece of behaviour is proceeded against by Community authorities as well as by national authorities. In such a case the Court of Justice considered:

'The possibility of concurrent sanctions need not mean that the possibility of two parallel proceedings pursuing different ends is unacceptable. (...), the acceptability of a dual procedure of this kind follows in fact from the special system of the sharing of jurisdiction between the Community and the Member States with regard to cartels. If, however, the possibility of two procedures being conducted separately were to lead to the imposition of consecutive sanctions, a general requirement of natural justice, such as that expressed at the end of the second paragraph of Article 90 of the ECSC Treaty, demands that any previous punitive decision must be taken into account in determining any sanction which is to be imposed. In any case, so long as no regulation has been issued under Article 87(2)(e), no means of avoiding such a possibility is to be found in the general principles of Community law.'[106]

§ 65.   The situation is again different when an undertaking is prosecuted by an institution of the Community as well as by a non-Member State. This happened in the *First Boehringer Case*. Boehringer was fined by the Commission for the violation of the EEC rules on competition. For the same restrictive trade agreement it was also fined by a US court. It pleaded *'non bis in idem*, but the Court of Justice considered that the sanctions imposed in the US were in respect of restrictions on competition which took place outside the Community. Therefore they did not pertain to the same activity on behalf of the applicant and they could not be taken into consideration.[107] This position was confirmed in the *Second Boehringer Case* in which the Court held:

'In fixing the amount of a fine the Commission must take account of penalties which have already been borne by the same undertaking for the same action, where penalties have been imposed for infringements of the cartel law of a Member State and, consequently, have been committed on Community territory. It is only necessary to decide the question whether

---

105. *Idem*, 2nd judgement, 15 March 1967, [1967] ECR 66; 13 Jur. (1967) 81, 82; 13 Rec. (1967) 83.
106. *Walt Wilhelm Case* (14/68), 13 Feb. 1969, consideration 11, [1969] ECR 15; [1969] CMLR 120 (there it is consideration 9); CCH para 8056 (p. 7867).
107. *First Boehringer Case* (45/69); 15 July 1970, considerations 60, 61, [1970] ECR 807; CCH para 8085 (p. 8248).

the Commission may also be under a duty to set a penalty imposed by the authorities of a third State against another penalty if in the case in question the actions of the applicant complained of by the Commission, on the one hand, and by the American authorities, on the other, are identical.

Although the actions on which the two convictions in question are based arise out of the same set of agreements they nevertheless differ essentially as regards both their object and their geographical emphasis.

The Community conviction was directed above all towards the gentlemen's agreement for the division of the common market and Great Britiain ...

... the applicant has put forward nothing capable of confirming the argument that the conviction in the United States was directed against the application or effects of the cartel other than those occurring in that country.'[108]

d. FREEDOM OF TRADE UNION ACTIVITY

§ 66. In the *Union Syndicale* and *Syndicat Général Cases* the Court of Justice held:

'Under the general principles of labour law, the freedom of trade union activity recognized under Article 24(a) of the Staff Regulations means not only that officials and servants have the right without hindrance to form associations of their own choosing, but also that these associations are free to do anything lawful to protect the interests of their members as employees.'[109]

These cases demonstrate that the Court of Justice accepts the fundamental principles essential to the right to form trade unions. In the cases concerned the Court also stressed, however, that this right does not alter the fact that the procedure for complaints and appeals established by EEC Article 179 and Articles 90 en 91 of the Staff Regulations is designed to deal exclusively with individual disputes, so that a staff association cannot institute proceedings for the annulment of acts addressed to individual civil servants (see below § 325-328).

e. LEGAL CERTAINTY

(i) Concept

§ 67. In Community law an important role is played by the principle of legal certainty (*sécurité juridique*), a principle underpinning any legal system, ac-

---

108. *Second Boehringer Case* (7/72), 14 Dec. 1972, considerations 3-6, [1972] ECR 1289, 1290; [1973] CMLR 887, 888; CCH para 8191.
109. *First Civil Servants Unions Cases* (175/73), 8 Oct. 1974, consideration 14, [1974] ECR 925; [1975] 1 CMLR 140 and (18/74), 8 Oct. 1974, consideration 10, [1974] ECR 944; [1975] 1 CMLR 140.

cording to which the application of the law to a specific situation must be predictable. Often legal certainty can come into conflict with lawfulness. With sole regard to lawfulness, for example, there should be no time limits set on the action for annulment so that unlawful acts might be annulled at any juncture. Legal certainty requires, on the other hand, that acts which have been relied on as legal will not turn out to be invalid. The rule that the legality can be questioned only for a limited period of time is a compromise between the two requirements (see below § 661).

§ 68.   The following examples from the case-law of the Court of Justice may help to illustrate the concept of 'legal certainty'.

(1)   In the *Bosch Case* the validity of an agreement between Bosch and Van Rijn was disputed. Allegedly the agreement restricted trade between Member States and would therefore be automatically void under EEC Article 85(2). Regulation 17 which sets out the conditions for the prohibition being declared inapplicable pursuant to Article 85(3) had not been adopted at that stage, so that an exemption by the Commission was impossible. The Court then ruled:

'it would be contrary to the general principle of legal certainty — a rule of law to be upheld in the application of the Treaty — to render agreements automatically void before it is even possible to tell which are the agreements to which Article 85 as a whole applies.'[110]

(2)   When Regulation 17 had been adopted notified agreements were assumed to be provisionally valid until the Commission had decided whether the exemption of Article 85(3) could be granted. In the *Portelange Case* this provisional validity was discussed. The Court held:

— 'It would be contrary to the general principle of legal certainty to conclude that, because agreements notified are not finally valid so long as the Commission has made no decision on them under Article 85(3) of the Treaty, they are not completely efficacious.

Although the fact that such agreements are fully valid may possibly give rise to practical disadvantages, the difficulties which might arise from uncertainty in legal relationships based on the agreements notified would be still more harmful.'[111]

§ 69.   The latter example illustrates in particular that legal certainty is not a compelling legal principle which must be safeguarded at all costs. The Court rather regards legal certainty as a desirable end but as one which can be

---

110. *Bosch Case* (13/61), 6 April 1962, [1962] ECR 52; 8 Jur. (1962) 107; 8 Rec. (1962) 104; [1962] CMLR 28; CCH para 8003 (p. 7138).
111. *Portelange Case* (10/69), 9 July 1969, considerations 15, 16, [1969] ECR 316; [1974] 1 CMLR 418; CCH para 8075 (p. 8095).

outweighed by more momentous legal rules or even by considerations of a more pressing economic or practical character.

An important limitation to the principle of legal certainty, which was accepted in the *Portelange Case*, was made in the *Second Brasserie de Haecht Case*, where the Court held that the protection of legal certainty would not necessarily be applicable to agreements made after the entry into force of Regulation 17. With respect to those agreements the claims of interested parties invoking their automatic nullity should also be taken into account. The Court considered that the protection of legal certainty was less important for these new agreements as they could only be implemented at the parties' own risk.[112]

§ 70. In the following paragraphs some specific fields where legal certainty is at stake will be discussed separately, such as the use of time limits, the protection of acquired rights, non-retroactivity and legitimate expectation. The principle of equality before the law and a fair application of the law also promote legal certainty. As their purpose is slightly different (fairness rather than predictability) these notions have been dealt with under separate headings. The use of understandable language is a requirement which perhaps encompasses more elements of fairness than of legal certainty. However, as the Court of Justice has classified this notion under legal certainty the same will be done here.

A separate discussion of various fields of legal certainty does not mean that clearcut distinctions can be drawn. The various fields are closely related to one another and overlap in many respects.

(ii) Time limits

§ 71. Time limits and periods of limitation serve to ensure legal certainty. Uncertainty about the possibility of acts being annulled or of the state of inaction being changed is terminated on the elapse of the prescribed time limit.

For the actions against Community acts and for the actions for damages time limits have been prescribed. They will be discussed in the context of the procedure before the Court in Chapter Five (below § 661-671). But can a time limit be invoked as a general principle of law when no express provisions have been made? The Court of Justice has discussed this question on several occasions.

§ 72. There is no provision which stipulates that an action for failure to act must be initiated within a specific time limit. In the *Steel Subsidies Case* the Court of Justice based the requirement that the exercise of the right to bring the action cannot be indefinitely delayed, on legal certainty (see below § 336).

112. *Second Brasserie de Haecht Case* (48/72), 6 Feb. 1973, considerations 9-13, [1973] ECR 86, 87; [1973] CMLR 302; CCH para 8170.

§ 73. The provisions governing the power of the Commission to impose fines in cases of infringement of the competition rules did not provide for a statute of limitations. When in the *Quinine Cartel Cases* Chemiefarma was fined for acts committed 4–6 years earlier it attempted to invoke such a statute. The Court of Justice flatly refused to apply any statute of limitations, holding:

> 'In order to fulfil their function of ensuring legal certainty limitation periods must be fixed in advance.
> The fixing of their duration and the detailed rules for their applications come within the powers of the Community legislature.
> Consequently the submission is unfounded.'[113]

This may have been too strong a statement. A statute of limitations is not only a regulatory measure; in extreme cases it does provide an element of justice towards the people concerned and may therefore be a compelling legal principle. The Court of Justice acknowledged this in the *Dyestuffs Cases* in which a limitation period was also invoked as a general principle of law. The Court gave the same ruling as in the *Quinine Cartel Cases* but inserted before the last sentence quoted above ('Consequently the submission is unfounded') an additional sentence reading:

> "Although, in the absence of any provisions on this matter, the fundamental requirement of legal certainty has the effect of preventing the Commission from indefinitely delaying the exercise of its power to impose fines, its conduct in the present case cannot be regarded as constituting a bar to the exercise of that power as regards [the violations concerned]'.[114]

The Community legislator finally filled the gap by a Council regulation on limitation periods in proceedings under the rules on transport and competition. Depending on the nature of the infringement this period is three or five years.[115]

§ 74. In the *Riva Case* the Commission had charged a levy for scrap equalization after the passage of an eight year period. Riva submitted that this was against a general principle of legal certainty, but the Court held:

---

113. *Quinine Cartel Cases: AFC Chemiefarma* (41/69), 15 July 1970, considerations 19-21, [1970] ECR 683; CCH para 8083 (p. 7424); *Buchler* (44/69), 15 July 1970, consideration 6, [1970] ECR 750; CCH para 8084; *First Boehringer* (45/69), 15 July 1970, consideration 6, [1970] ECR 795; CCH para 8085.
114. *ICI Case* (48/69), 14 July 1972, considerations 47-50, [1972] ECR 653, [1972] CMLR 621; CCH para 8161; *Francolor Case* (54/69), 14 July 1972, considerations 35-38, [1972] ECR 873; [1972] CMLR 620; CCH para 8166; *Cassella Case* (55/69), 14 July 1972, considerations 25, 26, [1972] ECR 913; [1972] CMLR 619; CCH para 8167; *Hoechst Case* (56/69) 14 July 1972, [1972] ECR 930; [1972] CMLR 627; CCH para 8168; *ACNA Case* (57/69), 14 July 1972, considerations 31-33, [1972] ECR 949, 950; [1972] CMLR 620; CCH para 8169.
115. Council Regulation 2988/74, OJ 24 Nov. 1974, No L 319/1.

'The absence of provisions relating to the barring by time of the powers of organizations competent to draw up estimates on their own authority of the quantities and periods for which undertakings are subject to the duty to contribute to the equalization scheme is explained by the desire of the legislature that in this respect the principle of distributive justice should prevail over that of legal certainty'.[116]

§ 75. In the *Premiums for grubbing fruit trees Case* no time limit had been laid down for the certification required for receiving the premiums. Italy made this certification after a period of two years, in November 1972. The Court of Justice held, in that case, that the time limits were to be deduced *'from the content of [the] Regulations and the aims of the system established by them'.* Due to these aims and to the normal time for grubbing, the certification should have been carried out in the spring of 1971 at the latest. According to the Court:

'It was imperative for the effectiveness of the measures adopted to observe such a time limit.'[117]

§ 76. According to EEC Article 93(3) the Commission shall be informed of any plans to grant or alter State aid favouring certain undertakings or the production of certain goods. If the Commission considers that any such plan is not compatible with the the Common Market, it shall *without delay* institute a specific procedure. The Member State shall not put its proposed measures into effect until this procedure has been completed and a final decision has been arrived at. As the period during which the Commission must take its decision is not defined anywhere, the Court had to rule on the matter for the sake of legal certainty. In the *Lorenz Case* it held:

'In the absence of any Regulation specifying this period, the Member States cannot unilaterally terminate this preliminary period which is necessary for the Commission to fulfil its role.
    The latter, however, could not be regarded as acting with proper diligence if it omitted to define its attitude within a reasonable period.
    It is appropriate in this respect to be guided by Articles 173 and 175 of the Treaty which, in dealing with comparable situations, provide for a period of two months.
    When this period has expired, the Member State concerned may implement the plan, but the requirements of legal certainty involve that prior notice should be given to the Commission.'[118]

116. *Riva Case* (2/70), 3 March 1971, consideration 13, [1971] ECR 109.
117. *Premiums for grubbing fruit trees Case* (30/72), 8 Feb. 1973, considerations 6, 7, [1973] ECR 170, 171; CCH para 8207. See also below § 252.
118. *Lorenz Case* (120/73), 11 Dec. 1973, consideration 4, [1973] ECR 1481; CCH para 8249. The same ruling was given in consideration 4 of the *Markmann Case* (121/73), 11 Dec. 1973, [1973] ECR 1506; CCH para 8250, *the Nordsee Case* (122/73), 11 Dec. 1973, [1973] ECR 1522; CCH para 8251 and the *Lohrey Case* (141/73), 11 Dec. 1973, [1973] ECR 1538; CCH para 8252.

In the *Pfützenreuter Case* the Court held that *force majeure* must be invoked as soon as possible, but it did not indicate a particular time limit, considering that a strict and absolute rule on the matter could not be established.[119]

(iii) Acquired rights[120]

§ 77. An elementary rule of legal certainty is that acquired rights should be respected. In principle, cases must be decided according to the law as it stood at the time of its application.[121]

In the *Klomp Case* the Court had to decide about the regime of privileges and immunities which had been modified in the intervening period between the events which led to the case and the discussion of the case in Court. The Court of Justice held:

'In accordance with a principle common to the legal systems of the Member States, the origins of which may be traced back to Roman law, when legislation is amended, unless the legislature expresses a contrary intention, continuity of the legal system must be ensured.'[122]

In the *Algera Case* the Court of Justice held that a legal act giving rise to substantive rights for a particular party cannot in principle be revoked. The Court stressed the importance of stability which may outweigh the interests of the administration (for quotation, see below § 247).

§ 78. This does not mean, however, that an administrative authority may not interrupt the payment of an allowance if it ascertains that it has been paid erroneously. In the *Simon Case* the Court ruled that the authority may modify its initial decision. It continued:

'Even if in certain cases in view of vested rights withdrawal on grounds of unlawfulness does not have a retroactive effect it always takes effect from the present'[123]

§ 79. The protection of acquired rights does not entitle persons to take advantage of both the old and the new legal situation. The *Fifth Reinarz Case*

---

119. *Pfützenreuter Case* (3/74), 28 May 1974, considerations 24-27, [1974] ECR 599; CCH para 8262.
120. See Günter Püttner, *Der Schutz wohlerworbener Rechte im Gemeinschaftsrecht – insbesondere bei Rücknahme rechtswidriger Verwaltungsakte* – 10 EuR (1975), pp. 218-229.
121. *Henck Cases* (12, 13 and 14/71), 14 July 1971, consideration 5, [1971] ECR 751, 774, 786; CCH para 8145-8147; *Second Deuka Case* (5/75), 25 June 1975, consideration 10, [1975] ECR 771; CCH para 8313.
122. *Klomp Case* (23/68), 25 Feb. 1969, consideration 13. [1969] ECR 50. Another case in which the Court protected acquired rights is the *Belbouab Case* (10/78), 12 Oct. 1978, considerations 7 and 10, [1978] ECR 1924, 1925.
123. *Simon Case* (15/60), 1 June 1961, [1961] ECR 123; 7 Jur. (1961) 246; 7 Rec. (1961) 242. See also *Third Elz Case* (56/75), 24 June 1976, considerations 15-20, [1976] ECR 1108, 1109; See also *Herpels Case* (54/77), 9 March 1978, consideration 38, [1978] ECR 599.

stemmed from a change both in the method of calculating salaries and in the salary scales themselves. In order to prevent the salaries of some officials from being reduced transitional provisions were also made. These different provisions could be interpreted to lead to a situation whereby the cumulation of most favourable rules of each system could be enjoyed simultaneously, but the Court of Justice held:

'A transitional provision issued on the transition to a less generous system does not normally seek to give employees greater rights than they would have had under the system which is revoked.

Such a provision cannot therefore be interpreted as allowing a combination of the more favourable method of calculation of one system with the more favourable salary scale of another.'[124]

(iv) Non-retroactivity

§ 80. Another principle which promotes legal certainty is that of the non-retroactivity of legislative acts.[125] In principle a public act cannot be invoked against a person who has not had a possibility to take cognizance of it.[126] Unless there are specific reasons, regulations may not enter into force immediately, as this would have *'an adverse effect on a legitimate regard for legal certainty.'*[127] In December 1963 the Council of the EEC adopted Regulation 130/63 amending Regulation 3 and 4. Some of the amendments were to enter into force on 1 January 1959. In the *Kalsbeek-van der Veen Case* the Court of Justice held:

'This retroactive effect cannot prejudice in any way the persons whose entitlement to benefit was acquired before the publication of Regulation No 130.[128]

In the *Exportation des Sucres Case* a regulation was involved which provided that it was to enter into force on 1 July 1976. As the regulation was published on 2 July the Court ruled that it could only properly be applied as from 2 July 1976, since there were no factors capable of attributing to it retroactive effect.[129]

124. *Fifth Reinarz Case* (177/73 and 5/74), 11 July 1974, considerations 22, 23, [1974] ECR 829.
125. See e.g. *First Gervais-Danone Case* (77/71), 15 Dec. 1971, consideration 8, [1971] ECR 1137; [1973] CMLR 427; CCH para 8125; on retroactivity see also Mann (*op. cit.*, note 38) pp. 493-499, M. Letemendia, *La rétroactivité en droit communautaire, comparaison avec le droit anglais*, 13 CDE (1977), pp. 518-570 and Advocate-General Warner's opinion in the *IRCA Case* (7/76), 7 July 1976, [1976] ECR 1235-1239.
126. *Second Racke Case* (98/78), 25 Jan. 1979, consideration 15; *Decker Case* (99/78), 25 Jan. 1979, consideration 3.
127. *Neumann Case* (17/67), 13 Dec. 1967, [1967] ECR 456; 13 Jur. (1967) 576; 13 Rec. (1967) 592; CCH para 8059.
128. *Kalsbeek-van der Veen Case* (100/63), 15 July 1964, [1964] ECR 575; 10 Jur. (1964) 1181; 10 Rec. (1964) 1125; [1964] CMLR 559; CCH para 8032. A similar decision was given in the *Second Deuka Case* (5/75), 25 June 1975 considerations 10, 11; [1975] ECR 771; CCH para 8313. See also below § 248.
129. *Exportation des Sucres Case* (88/76), 31 March 1977, [1977] ECR 726.

§ 81. The Court's moves to protect individuals against retroactivity are limited, however. In the first place, retroactive legislation is permitted when there are compelling reasons militating in favour of a retroactive introduction of new rules. Three examples may illustrate this:

(a) Sometimes pressing economic reasons demand retroactive legislation. After revaluations and devaluations, for example, the EEC agricultural prices must be altered. The Court of Justice has always accepted that such adjustments have retroactive effect as from the date of the parity change. In the *First Rewe Case* it held:

'Until a system of aids for German agricultural producers was established it was necessary to avoid any interruption in the maintenance of the level of agricultural prices existing in Germany at the time of the revaluation of the German Mark.

The transitional protective measures authorized by the decision of 30 October 1969 would not have been capable of attaining their objective fully if they had not been applicable from the entry into force of the new parity of the German Mark.

It was thus proper to fix at this same date the point when the protective measures authorized could take effect. The decision of the Commission of 30 October 1969 and those of 31 October and 3 November 1969 which supplemented it are consequently not invalid to the extent to which they have retroactive effect.'[130]

(b) Another compelling reason for accepting retroactivity may be the need for continuity in legal relations. When the Court of Justice annuls a regulation, there may be good reason to replace it by a new one which enters into force with some retroactive effect in order not to create a legal vacuum. In the *First Remunerations Adjustment Case*[131] this was not necessary as the Court had allowed the provisions concerned to remain in effect until replaced, using its powers under EEC Article 174 para 2. But in the *Compensatory Amounts Case*[132] the Court had not availed itself of this power. The Council then tried to remedy the situation by replacing the regulation which was partially annulled by a new one which partially entered into force almost a year prior to its adoption.[133] So far this new regulation has not been contested before the Court of Justice; but it seems reasonable to expect that its retroactivity will be accepted as the evils of a gap between the two regulations on compensatory amounts would be greater than the disadvantages of legal uncertainty arising from the retroactivity of the new regulation.

130. *First Rewe Case* (37/70), 11 Feb. 1971, considerations 15, 16, [1971] ECR 36; [1971] CMLR 254; CCH para 8124.
131. *First Remunerations Adjustment Case* (81/72), 5 June 1973, [1973] ECR 587; [1973] CMLR 658.
132. *Compensatory Amounts Case* (151/73), 21 March 1974, [1974] ECR 285; [1974] 1 CMLR 429; CCH para 8271.
133. EEC Regulation 1428/74, 4 June 1974, OJ 8 June 1974, L 151/2.

The decision that there is indeed a compelling reason militating in favour of the retroactive introduction of a new rule should be made by the legislator, who thereby exercises a large degree of discretion. In the *Neumann Case* the Court ruled that this discretion must be subject to the judicial review of the Court of Justice.[134]

(c) Monetary compensatory amounts charged or paid to overcome the problems caused by the instability of currencies can be established only at the end of the period concerned. In the *IRCA Case* the Court held:

'... with regard to monetary compensatory amounts, the fact that the factors necessary for their calculation are only determined after the period during which the said amounts have become applicable is frequently inherent in the system itself, and cannot therefore be considered, on such grounds, as giving the rules a retroactive effect.'[135]

§ 82. In addition to the compelling reasons for accepting retroactive legislation which have been discussed in § 81 another situation where retroactivity is permissible is the case of the withdrawal of *illegal* provisions. Normally provisions granting rights to individuals cannot be retroactively withdrawn (for the protection of acquired rights, see above § 77-79). The Court of Justice discussed this in the *Second Lemmerz-Werke Case*. Lemmerz-Werke submitted that it had obtained an exemption from making payments to the Scrap Equalization Fund and that this exemption had been retroactively withdrawn, which therefore infringed upon legal certainty. The Court held:

'The legality of the retroactive revocation of a decision granting a benefit to the person to whom it is addressed depends, in the first instance, on the question whether the revoked decision was illegal. This is the position in the present case. In fact no legal provision conferred upon the bodies responsible for the management of the financial machinery of the equalization scheme the authority to grant exemptions.

The High Authority can revoke illegal decisions, even retroactively, provided that in certain exceptional cases proper consideration is given to the principle of legal certainty. Although such consideration is in the first instance a matter for the High Authority, it is, however, subject to review by the Court.'[136]

§ 83. In the *Second Snupat Case* the Court of Justice ruled that particular exemptions from payments to the Scrap Equalization Fund were illegal. It then had to decide whether this illegality would have (retroactive) effect so that previous payments would have to be revised. It was contended that such a revision would be contrary to the principle of legal certainty, but the Court held:

134. *Neumann Case* (17/67), 13 Dec. 1967, [1967] ECR 456; 13 Jur. (1967) 576; 13 Rec. (1967) 592; CCH para 8059.
135. *IRCA Case* (7/76), 7 July 1976, ruling 1, consideration 29, [1976] ECR 1229.
136. *Second Lemmerz-Werke Case* (111/63), 13 July 1965, [1965] ECR 690; 11 Jur. (1965) 953; 11 Rec. (1965) 852; [1968] CMLR 301, 302, 304.

'That allegation disregards the fact that the principle of respect for legal certainty, important as it may be, cannot be applied in an absolute manner, but that its application must be combined with that of the principle of legality; the question which of these principles should prevail in each particular case depends upon a comparison of the public interest with the private interests in question, (...)'

If the administrative act has been adopted on the basis of false or incomplete information provided by the interested person such a balancing is not even necessary. Such an act can always be withdrawn with retroactive effect.[137]

§ **84.**   In the previous cases withdrawal of an illegal act was at stake and the legal certainty provided by that illegal act was sacrificed. But when, for economic reasons, legal certainty is of great importance, the contrary may happen and an illegal situation may be accepted in order to safeguard legal certainty. This occurred in the *Second Defrenne Case* where the Court had ruled that EEC Article 119 on equal pay for men and women had direct effect from 1 January 1962 for the old members and from 1 January 1973 for the new ones. This meant that all unequal pay after those dates would be held to be illegal. As claims for additional pay dating back to the said dates might seriously affect the financial situation of many undertakings and would even drive some of them into bankruptcy, this could lead to great economic distress. As the attitude adopted by the Member States and by the Commission, which did not act against the violations, might have placed the undertakings concerned in a confusing situation, the Court of Justice held:

'In these circumstances, it is appropriate to determine that, as the general level at which pay would have been fixed cannot be known, important considerations of legal certainty affecting all the interests involved, both public and private, make it impossible in principle to reopen the question as regards the past.

Therefore, the direct effect of Article 119 cannot be relied on in order to support claims concerning pay periods prior to the date of this judgment, except as regards those workers who have already brought legal proceedings or made an equivalent claim.'[138]

Before coming to this conclusion, the Court had ruled that EEC Article 119 had direct effect and that unequal pay was, therefore, illegal and had been illegal as from 1 January 1962 (or 1 January 1973, respectively). This would normally mean that the illegality would be subject to legal redress, but — fearing that this would lead to monumental economic disturbances — the Court of Justice chose to extend the protection of legal certainty even to an illegal situation.

137. *Second Snupat Case* (42 and 49/59), 22 March 1961, [1961] ECR 87; 7 Jur. (1961) 162; 7 Rec. (1961) 159.
138. *Second Defrenne Case* (43/75), 8 April 1976, considerations 74, 75, [1976] ECR 481; [1976] 2 CMLR 128; CCH para 8346. See also above § 32.

This is indeed an illustration of the wide scope which legal certainty may have, and an example of the vast discretion which the Court exercises.

§ 85. Apart from compelling reasons and from illegal acts, there are also two more general legal exceptions to the rule of non-retroactivity:

(1) The principle does not apply to interpretations. If a rule is not clear and is clarified by a subsequent rule the clarification inherent in that later rule may be used for cases which occurred prior to it.[139] On 21 June 1971 the EEC Council accepted rules on the interpretation of the Common Customs Tariff which entered into effect on 1 January 1972. The Court of Justice accepted that these rules were applicable to goods imported prior to that date. In the *Osram Case* it held:

> 'There are grounds for considering that these Rules for interpretation were devised with the aim of coordinating, for the tariff as a whole, interpretation practices laid down by special provisions, so that they do not form a legal innovation but apply to imports effected even before 1 January 1972'.[140]

In deciding what questions are questions of interpretation the Court is rather restrictive. A regulation defining the conditions for classifying products under a particular heading of the customs tariff was not considered as an interpretation of that particular heading but as a constitutive act which has no retroactive effect.[141]

(2) The rule of non-retroactivity does not always apply in cases of amendments. Amendments to Community acts may have some retroactive effect. In the *Third Westzucker Case* the Court of Justice held:

> 'According to a generally accepted principle, the laws amending a legislative provision apply, unless otherwise provided, to the future consequences of situations which arose under the former law'.[142]

However, this holds true only for those provisions of a new rule which cover substantially the same ground as the previous rule. New provisions of a regulation which replaces an older regulation cannot be extended to facts which occurred outside the period covered by the new regulation.[143]

139. This rule also exists in national law, see e.g. Bologna Court of Appeals, [1974] ELD, p. 549.
140. *Osram Case* (183/73), 8 May 1974, consideration 8, [1974] ECR 485; [1974] 2 CMLR 367; CCH para 8274. See also *Foral Case*, (36, 37/76), 16 Dec. 1976, [1976] ECR 2018-2021; CCH para 8398.
141. *Biegi Case* (158/78), 28 March 1979, considerations 24, 25.
142. *Third Westzucker Case* (1/73), 4 July 1973, consideration 5, [1973] ECR 729; CCH para 8218; *idem* in *Sopad Case* (143/73), 5 Dec. 1973, consideration 8, [1973] ECR 1441; [1977] 1 CMLR 239; CCH para 8244 and in the *Bauche Case* (96/77), 15 Feb. 1978, consideration 48, [1978] ECR 400; [1978] 3 CMLR 157.
143. *Jansen Case* (104/76), 5 May 1977, consideration 7, [1977] ECR 840.

(v) Legitimate expectations

§ 86.   An important aspect of legal certainty is that the law should not be different from that which could be reasonably expected. In German administrative law this is called *Vertrauensschutz*.

In the *CNTA Case* (see below § 474) the Community had created a system of compensatory payments to overcome disturbances engendered by the changes in the parities of national currencies. On 26 January 1972 the Commission, by Regulation No. 189/72, withdrew this system with effect from 1 February 1972. CNTA contended that this violated the principle of legal certainty in that it ignored the legitimate expectation of persons concerned that the compensatory payments would in fact be maintained for current transactions. The Court of Justice held:

'In the absence of an overriding matter of public interest, the Commission has violated a superior rule of law, thus rendering the Community liable, by failing to include in Regulation No. 189/72 transitional measures for the protection of the confidence which a trader might legitimately have had in the Community rules'.[144]

§ 87.   The Court of Justice protected legitimate expectations in the *First Remunerations Adjustment Case*. On 21 March 1972 the Council had decided to alter over a period of three years the staff remunerations according to a particular formula in order to take into account changes in purchasing power. On 12 December 1972 the Council adjusted the remunerations once again but this time in a more limited way. The Commission appealed against this latter decision, submitting *inter alia* that it violated the principles of confidence and good faith.

The Court held:

'Taking account of the particular employer-staff relationship which forms the background to the implementation of Article 65 of the Staff Regulations, and the aspects of consultation which its application involved, the rule of protection of the confidence that the staff could have that the authorities would respect undertakings of this nature, implies that the Decision of 21 March 1972 binds the Council in its future action.
Whilst this rule is primarily applicable to individual decisions, the possibility cannot by any means be excluded that it should relate, when appropriate, to the exercise of more general powers'.[145]

In the *Second Toepfer Case* the Court of Justice held that the principle of the protection of legitimate expectation forms part of the Community legal order

---

144.   *CNTA Case* (74/74), 14 May 1975, consideration 44, [1975] ECR 550; [1977] 1 CMLR 190; CCH para 8305. On legitimate expectation, see also Advocate-General Trabucchi in the *Transportation Costs for Change of Warehouse Case* (47/75), 4 May 1976, [1976] ECR 582-591; [1977] 1 CMLR 152; CCH para 8360.
145.   *First Remunerations Adjustment Case* (81/72), 5 June 1973, consideration 10, [1973] ECR 584; [1973] CMLR 657.

with the result that any failure to comply with it is an 'infringement of this Treaty or of any rule of law relating to its application' within the meaning of EEC Article 173.[146]

§ 87a. The protection of legitimate expectation is not a compelling principle which always takes priority. It will yield to overriding considerations of public interest.[147] Even when there are no such overriding considerations, the protection of legitimate expectation is possible only under strict conditions. From the Court's case-law Waelbroeck distinguishes six further conditions[148] : (1) the commercial operation for which protection is claimed must be irrevocable[149], (2) the legal rule which caused the expectation must definitely lead to the result expected, a chance is not enough[150], (3) the benefit for which protection is claimed must be a foreseeable result of the previous rules, unforeseen collateral effects are not protected[151], (4) the protected interest must be worth protection[152], (5) the change in legislation should not be foreseeable at the moment when the operation for which protection is claimed was performed[153], (6) transitional provisions of the new legislation must be insufficient.[153a]

(vi) Use of understandable language

§ 88. In the *Farrauto Case* the Court of Justice acknowledged the special problem of legal certainty that is incurred by the stipulation that decisions must be notified to the person concerned in a language which he understands. After having established that several Community rules on social security, which take account of linguistic problems, were not applicable the Court held:

'The national courts of the Member States must nevertheless take care that legal certainty is not prejudiced by a failure arising from the inability of the worker to understand the language in which a decision is notified to him'.[154]

---

146. *Second Toepfer Case* (112/77), 3 May 1978, considerations 18 and 19, [1978] ECR 1032, 1033.
147. See e.g. *Lührs Case* (78/77), 1 Feb. 1978, consideration 6, [1978] ECR 177, 178; CCH para 8468.
148. Michel Waelbroeck, *Examen de Jurisprudence 1971 à 1977*, 22 RCJB (1978), pp. 76, 77.
149. Compare *First Deuka Case* (78/74), 18 March 1975, [1975] ECR 433; CCH para 8302, and *Second Deuka Case*, (5/75), 25 June 1975, [1975] ECR 770, 771.
150. *Third Westzucker Case* (1/73), 4 July 1973. 1973 ECR 730; CCH para 8218.
151. *CAM Case* (100/74), 18 Nov. 1975, [1975] ECR 1405; CCH para 8328.
152. *Second Mackprang Case* (2/75), 27 May 1975, [1975] ECR 616; [1977] 1 CMLR 198; CCH para 8306.
153. *Deuka Cases*, see note 149.
153a *Cooperatives Agricoles Case* (95-98/74, 15 and 100/75), 10 Dec. 1975, [1975] ECR 1641.
154. *Farrauto Case* (66/74), 18 Feb. 1975, consideration 6, [1975] ECR 162; [1976] 2 CMLR 345.

f. EQUALITY

§ 89. In Community law great care is taken to guarantee equality or to prevent discrimination.[155] EEC Article 119 offers a basis for the prohibition of discrimination between the sexes; EEC Article 7 prohibits discrimination on grounds of nationality, as do many regulations. But even if there is no express prohibition at hand, discrimination is illegal as it is contrary to a general principle of Community law. This was underlined inter alia by the Court's wording in the *Frilli Case* in which it was held that the rule of equality of treatment *'is one of the fundamental principles of Community law'*[156] and in the *Third Milac Case* where the Court ruled that the principle of non-discrimination between producers or consumers within the Community is one of the fundamental principles of the Treaty *'which must be observed by any court'.*[157]

In the *Ruckdeschel Case* the Court of Justice held that the prohibition of discrimination *'is merely a specific enunciation of the general principle of equality which is one of the fundamental principles of Community law. This principle requires that similar situations shall not be treated differently unless differation is objectively justified'.*[158]

In the *Sea Fisheries Case* the Court censured Irish legislation which was detrimental to large fishing as discriminatory because of the *factual* circumstance that such large ships were only used by foreign fisherman. The Court held that the rules regarding equality forbid not only overt discrimination by reason of nationality but also all covert forms of discrimination which lead in fact to the same result.[158a]

§ 90. Not all different treatment constitutes discrimination. Equal treatment of unequal subjects or equal treatment under unequal circumstances can be as discriminatory as unequal treatment of equal objects or equal situations.[159] The Court of Justice accepted this in the *Hauts Fourneaux Case* where it held that:

'Pursuant to a principle generally accepted in the legal systems of the Member States, equality of treatment in the matter of economic rules does

---

155. See B. Sundberg-Weitman, *Discrimination on grounds of nationality*, North Holland 1977, 247 pages; Hervé Cassan, *Le principe de non-discrimination dans le domaine social à travers la jurisprudence récente de la Cour de Justice des Communautés européennes*, 12RTDE (1976), pp. 259-270; Clive M. Schmitthoff, *The Doctrines of Proportionality and Non-Discrimination*, 2 ELRev. (1977), pp. 332, 333.
156. *Frilli Case* (1/72), 22 June 1972, consideration 19, [1972] ECR 466; [1973] CMLR 408.
157. *Third Milac Case* (8/78), 13 July 1978, consideration 18, [1978] ECR 1732, 1733.
158. *Ruckdeschel Case* (117/76 and 16/77), 19 Oct. 1977, consideration 7, 1977 ECR 1769; CCH para 8457. *Idem* in *Moulins de Pont-à-Mousson Case* (124/76 and 20/77), 19 Oct. 1977, considerations 16, 17, 1977 ECR 1811; CCH para 8458.
158a. *Sea Fisheries Case* (61/77), 16 Feb. 1978, consideration 78, [1978] ECR 450; [1978] 2 CMLR 516, 517; CCH para 8473.
159. On discrimination see Egbert W. Vierdag, *The Concept of Discrimination in International Law*, The Hague 1973, in particular pp. 50-61.

not prevent different prices being in accordance with the particular situation of consumers or of categories of consumers provided that the differences in treatment correspond to a difference in the situations of such persons.'[160]

Even if there is discrimination, this does not necessarily indicate a violation of Community law. According to the Court of Justice: *'Difference in treatment cannot be regarded as constituting discrimination which is prohibited unless it appears arbitrary.'*[161] There is no discrimination when a difference in treatment is objectively justified.[162]

§ 91. In Community law most attention has been paid to combatting discrimination between Member States, between goods from different Member States or between their nationals. The Court of Justice has repeatedly condemned this kind of discrimination.[163] In addition cases of discrimination which bear no relation to national boundaries have been declared illegal. In the *Fourth Meroni Case* the Court considered that:

'the undertakings subject to the financial arrangements are in competition so that the High Authority must take particular care to ensure that the principle of equality in the field of public charges is always most scrupulously observed; that in such circumstances the High Authority cannot be blamed for having given precedence (...) to the principle of distributive justice rather than that of legal certainty.'[164]

In later cases the Court mentioned as basic principles of the equalization system:

'the principle of the equal liability of all those affected to pay contributions, ..., and the requirement that the scheme be applied impartially to all those subject to it.'[165]

§ 91a. Several Treaty provisions grant favourable treatment to nationals of other Member States. On the basis of the principle of equality Member States are often required to grant similar favourable treatment to those of their own

---

160. *Hauts Fourneaux Case* (8/57), 21 June 1958, [1957-58] ECR 256; 4 Jur. (1958) 265; 4 Rec. (1958) 247.
161. *Union des Minotiers de la Champagne Case* (11/74), 11 July 1974, consideration 22, [1974] ECR 886; [1975] 1 CMLR 86; CCH para 8281.
162. *Kendermann Case* (88/78), 30 Nov. 1978, consideration 12.
163. See e.g. *For Case* (54/72), 20 Feb. 1973, [1973] ECR 204-206; CCH para 8208; *Second Holtz and Willemsen Case* (153/73), 2 July 1974, consideration 13, [1974] ECR 696; [1975] 1 CMLR 108.
164. *Fourth Meroni Case* (14, 16, 17, 20, 24, 26, 27/60 and 1/61), 13 July 1961, [1961] ECR 169; 7 Jur. (1961) 352; 7 Rec. (1961) 338.
165. *Espérance-Longdoz Case* (3/65), 15 Dec. 1965, [1965] ECR 1079; 11 Jur. (1965) 1395; 11 Rec. (1965) 1340; [1966] CMLR 164; *Hainaut-Sambre Case* (4/65), 15 Dec. 1965, [1965] ECR 1110; 11 Jur. (1965) 1434; 11 Rec. (1965) 1377, [1966] CMLR 169.

nationals who are in similar circumstances as nationals of other Member States, for example because they have obtained particular diplomas in another Member State.[166]

§ 92. Also in staff cases the Court of Justice has accepted the *'principles of equality of treatment'* as general principles of law which may not be infringed.[167]

§ 93. EEC Article 48(4) provides that the prohibition of discrimination based on nationality between workers of the Member States is not applicable to employment in the public service. When in Germany foreign workers were admitted to specific public functions, such as the Federal Post Office, but were remunerated with a lower salary than German workers the Court of Justice did not permit such discrimination, holding that the provision of Article 48(4)

'cannot justify discriminatory measures with regard to remuneration or other conditions of employment against workers once they have been admitted to the public service.

The very fact that they have been admitted shows indeed that those interests which justify the exceptions to the principle of non-discrimination permitted by Article 48(4) are not at issue'.[168]

§ 94. In the *Sabbatini Case* the Court of Justice proscribed discrimination between men and women. Prior to that case the Staff Regulations were such that women lost their expatriation allowance when marrying, while men did not. The Court held:

'In this respect, the Staff Regulations cannot however treat officials differently according to whether they are male or female, since termination of the status of expatriate must be dependent for both male and female officials on uniform criteria, irrespective of sex.'[169]

g. FAIR APPLICATION OF THE LAW

(i) Equity, natural justice and fairness

§ 95. It was seen above (§ 64) that the Court in the *Walt Wilhelm Case* referred to 'a general requirement of natural justice', which implies that in determining a penalty, account shall be taken of any prior penal sanction.

166. See, e.g., *Knoors Case* (115/78), 7 Feb. 1979, considerations 5, 15-18; *Auer Case* (136/78), 7 Feb. 1979, considerations 23, 24.
167. See e.g. *Louwage Case* (148/73), 30 Jan. 1974, consideration 12, [1974] ECR 89.
168. *Sotgiu Case* (152/73), 12 Feb. 1974, consideration 4, [1974] ECR 162; CCH para 8257.
169. *Sabbatini Case* (20/71), 7 June 1972, consideration 12, [1972] ECR 351; [1972] CMLR 958. The court used the same wording in the *Bauduin Case* (32/71), 7 June 1972, consideration 12, [1972] ECR 370; [1972] CMLR 958.

The Staff Regulations provide that an appeal to the Court of Justice shall lie only if a complaint has been previously submitted to the appointing authority.[170] The appeal must then be brought within three months after the reply of the appointing authority. In some cases, however, — when for example the action is against the decision of a Selection Board whose decisions cannot be changed by the appointing authority — such previous complaint is not necessary. Strictly speaking, an action should then be brought before the Court of Justice within three months of the dispute arising, rather than within three months after the reply of the appointing authority. The Court has held that it would be *contrary to the rules of fairness* to apply this rule strictly against a staff member for having clearly followed the procedure laid down in the Staff Regulations where he had previously submitted a complaint to the appointing authority even though not being specifically obliged to do so.[171]

In the *Süddeutsche Zucker-Aktiengesellschaft Case* the Court of Justice held that *both logic and equity* lead to the conclusion that sugar sweepings, arising from the production of earlier years on which the production levy has already been imposed, must be deducted from the production subject to the production levy of the current year.[172]

When a text can be interpreted in two ways the Court will normally use the interpretation which is less onerous for the individual concerned. The Court does so for reasons of natural justice.[173] This does not mean that the Court always rules in favour of the individual applicant. Natural justice may also be used against unfair claims which may find some basis in the text of a provision but would lead to unacceptable results.[174]

In the *Welding Case* the Court permitted the Community to use particular methods of calculation on the express condition that they would not *give rise to instance of demonstrable unfairness*', which indicates that the Court will take account of the fairness of provisions and of their application.[175]

Some requirements of natural justice must be honoured by the legislator, for example, exemptions to tax rules. If the legislator abstains from doing so, the Court of Justice feels unable to do so in its place.[176]

(ii) Proportionality[177]

§ 96. Related to the principle of equity is the principle of proportionality according to which the means used by the authorities must be in proportion

170. Staff Regulations, Art. 91 (2), see below § 327, 328.
171. *Costacurta Case* (31/75), 4 Dec. 1975, consideration 5, [1975] ECR 1570. Fairness was also an argument in the *Zerbone Case* (94/77), 31 Jan. 1978, consideration 17, 1978 ECR 114; CCH para 8464.
172. *Süddeutsche Zucker-Aktiengesellschaft Case* (94/75), 5 Feb. 1976, consideration 5, [1976] ECR 159.
173. See, e.g., *Lührs Case* (78/77), 1 Feb. 1978, consideration 13, [1978] ECR 180; CCH para 8468.
174. See, e.g., *Verhaaf Case* (140/77), 9 Nov. 1978.
175. *Welding Case* (87/78), 30 Nov. 1978, consideration 6.
176. *Lührs Case* (78/77), 1 Feb. 1978, consideration 17. [1978] ECR 180.
177. Lord MacKenzie Stuart, *The Court of Justice of the European Communities and the control of executive discretion*, 13 Journal of the Society of Public Teachers of Law

to their purpose. One may not require large sacrifices to be made by some people in order to obtain a result which is of only small importance to others.[178] The Court ruled on proportionality in the *Second Schlüter Case* in which it held:

'In exercising their powers, the Institutions must ensure that the amounts which commercial operators are charged are no greater than is required to achieve the aim which the authorities are to accomplish; however, it does not necessarily follow that that obligation must be measured in relation to the individual situation of any one particular group of operators.

Given the multiplicity and complexity of economic circumstances, such an evaluation would not only be impossible to achieve, but would also create perpetual uncertainty in the law.

An overall assessment of the advantages and disadvantages of the measures contemplated was justified, in this case, by the exceptionally pressing need for practicability in economic measures which are designed to exert an immediate corrective influence; and this need had to be taken into account in balancing the opposing interests'.[179]

§ 97. The principle of proportionality is also important in cases which involve the imposition of penalties. In the *Fédéchar Case* the Court held that a decision in response to a wrongful action by certain enterprises, such as the withdrawal of compensations, *'Must be in proportion to the scale of that action'.*[180] In the *Schmitz Case* the contract of a staff member was not renewed for a reason which the Court considered to be *'clearly exaggerated'.* The Court therefore annulled the decision not to renew the contract.[181]

§ 98. In the *Chinese Mushroom Case* the applicant, Bock, submitted that the Commission had violated the principle of proportionality by using its power to authorize protective measures[182] for blocking an import of a minimal quantity. The Court considered that authorizations under EEC Article 115 are an exception to the normal functioning of the Common Market and should be interpreted and applied restrictively. It held further:

'In these circumstances, the Commission, by extending the authorization at issue to an application relating to a transaction which was insignificant in

(1974), pp. 22-26; Christian Tomuschat, *Le principe de proportionnalité: Quis iudicabit?* 13 CDE (1977), pp. 97-102; Schmitthoff (*op. cit.*, note 155), pp. 332, 333.
178. See also Waelbroeck (*op. cit.*, note 148), pp. 87-89.
179. *Second Schlüter Case* (9/73), 24 Oct. 1973, consideration 22, [1973] ECR 1156; CCH para 8233; *idem* in *First Balkan Case* (5/73), 24 Oct. 1973, [1973] ECR 1112; CCH para 8232.
180. *Fédéchar Case* (8/55), 29 Nov. 1956, [1954-56] ECR 299; 2 Jur. (1955-56) 323; 2 Rec. (1955-56) 304. For the calculation of fines see furthermore the *ALMA Case*, below § 517.
181. *Schmitz Case* (18/63), 19 March 1964, [1964] ECR 97, 98; 10 Jur. (1964) 201; 10 Rec. (1964) 189.
182. EEC Art. 115.

terms of the effectiveness of the measure of commercial policy proposed by the Member State concerned and which in addition had been submitted at a time when the principle of the free circulation of goods applied unrestrictedly to the goods in question, has exceeded the limits of what is 'necessary' within the meaning of Article 115—interpreted within the general framework of the Treaty, following the expiry of the transitional period.

Accordingly, the contested provision must be annulled without its being necessary to consider the other submissions in the application.'[183]

§ 99. In the *Werhahn Case* the applicant alleged that the principle of proportionality had been infringed as a result of the setting of an excessively high level of threshold prices for durum wheat. This, it was pleaded, was unnecessarily burdensome and not in keeping with the task, vested in the Council, namely that of merely protecting the Community market. The Court, in fulfilling a marginal review function (see below § 233) held that *'it does not seem that the Council in its assessment of the level of the threshold price, went beyond what might be considered necessary for achieving the object of the aid system for durum wheat'*. But before coming to this conclusion it carefully considered the facts which might have resulted in disproportionality.[184]

§ 99a. The applicant was more successful in the *Buitoni Case*, in which the legality of Article 3 of Regulation 499/76 of the Commission was disputed.[185] In a previous regulation it was provided that traders who had obtained a certificate of important or a certificate of export and subsequently refrained from importing or exporting would lose the deposit which they had paid when applying for the certificate. Article 3 of Regulation 499/76 extended this sanction to traders who had actually imported or exported, but who failed to furnish the necessary proof thereof within six months. Taking into consideration that it was in the interest of the trader to have his deposit returned as soon as possible, the Court found that the principle of proportionality was violated by imposing the same sanction for the less important breach, of not furnishing proof of importation or exportation in time, as for the far more important one of not importing or not exporting. It declared Article 3 of Regulation 499/76 to be invalid.[186]

(iii) Good faith

§ 100. In the *Lachmüller Case* the Court of Justice held that *'the conduct of an authority, in administrative as in contractual matters, is at all times subject*

183. *Chinese Mushroom Case* (62/70), 23 Nov. 1971, consideration 15, [1971] ECR 909, 910; [1972] CMLR 172; CCH para 8150.
184. *Werhahn Case* (63-69/72), 13 Nov. 1973, considerations 18-20, [1973] ECR 1250, 1251; CCH para 8236. On the proportionality of a processing deposit see *Beste Boter Case* (99, 100/76), 11 May 1977, consideration 11, [1977] ECR 872; CCH para 8420.
185. OJ 1976, no L59, p. 18.
186. *Buitoni Case* (122/78), 20 Feb. 1979, considerations 20-23.

to observance of the principle of good faith'   From this principle was derived the tenet that the dismissal of a staff member may not be arbitrary but must be justified by reference to precise reasons.[187]

§ 101.   In the *First Hoogovens Case* the Court of Justice accepted that persons who by acting in good faith benefit from a Community rule may rely on the principle that the rule will not be retroactively withdrawn. A company which was aware of substantial objections to the rule and of moves afoot to dispute it before the Court was not considered to be behaving in good faith.[188]

(iv)   **Solidarity**

§ 102.   On the relationship between the Member States the Court has accepted a principle of solidarity, meaning that it is encumbent on the States to take account of the repercussions which their acts may have on other Members. In the *Rediscount Rate Case* the Court stressed the importance of solidarity when it held:

'The solidarity *which is at the basis of these obligations as of the whole of the Community system* in accordance with the undertaking provided for in Article 5 of the Treaty, is continued for the benefit of the States in the procedure for mutual assistance provided for in Article 108 where a Member State is seriously threatened with difficulties as regards its balance of payments'.[189]

In the *Premiums for slaughtering cows Case* the Court regarded the disturbance of the equilibrium between advantages and obligations flowing from Community membership as a *'failure in the duty of solidarity accepted by [the] Member States by the fact of their adherence to the Community.*[190]

h.   UNDUE PAYMENT AND UNJUST ENRICHMENT

§ 103.   Staff members are constrained to repay salaries and allowances unduly received, if they are aware, or should have been aware, that there was no due reason for the payment concerned.[191]   In the *Meganck Case* (see below

187. *Lachmüller Case* (48/59), 15 July 1960, [1960] ECR 474, 475; 6 Jur. (1960) 988, 989; 6 Rec. (1960) 956. See also *Fiddelaar Case* (44/59), 16 Dec. 1960, [1960] ECR 547; 6 Jur. (1960) 1140; 6 Rec. (1960) 1099.
188. *First Hoogovens Case* (14/61), 12 July 1962, [1962] ECR 273; 8 Jur. (1962) 544, 545; 8 Rec. (1962) 521; [1963] CMLR 96, 97.
189. *Rediscount Rate Case* (6 and 11/69), 10 Dec. 1969, consideration 16, [1969] ECR 540; [1970] CMLR 65; CCH para 8105 (emphasis added).
190. *Premiums for slaughtering cows Case* (39/72), 7 Feb. 1973, consideration 25 [1973] ECR 116; [1973] CMLR 457; CCH para 8201. The definite article which has been inserted in brackets was used in the other languages, but has been erroneously omitted in the official English translation.
191. See e.g. *Kuhl Case* (71/72), 27 June 1973, considerations 8-16, [1973] ECR 712, 713.

§ 116) the Court broadened the concept of undue payment by the consideration that allowances should be refunded if their payment was due to incorrect
information submitted by the staff member.

§ 104. In the *Danvin Case* the applicant, a staff member, carried out duties
which were classified for a higher rank than that which he actually held. He
applied in vain for a higher salary. He also claimed compensation from the
Commission on the ground of unjust enrichment, since the Commission had
obtained work pertaining to a higher level carried out for too low a payment.
The Court held:

> 'Without prejudice to the question of the applicability to the relationship
> between the Community administration and its officials of the concept of
> unjust enrichment, it cannot, in any case, be accepted that the Commission
> was unjustly enriched by reason of the applicant's activities. Moreover,
> according to a generally accepted principle in the national legal systems, the
> applicant's action would only be well founded if he had suffered loss cor-
> responding to the alleged enrichment of the other party. In this case, the
> applicant has not proved his claim to have suffered prejudice by reason of
> his performing duties of a grade higher than those relating to his own post
> under the Staff Regulations'.[192]

i. FORCE MAJEURE

§ 105. In the *Reich Case* the applicant had on 25 September 1963, delivered
maize to the railways for transport from Mulhouse, on the France-German
frontier in Alsace, to Germany. The railways had delivered the goods in Germany only after 1 October 1963 which meant that Reich had to pay an
additional levy. He invoked *force majeure* submitting that he could not have
foreseen that the railways would take such an extraordinarily long period of
time to transport the goods. Unlike similar regulations on imports from third
States, the regulations concerned did not contain a provision on *force
majeure*. The Court of Justice held that it followed from the regulations
covering trade with third States that to make special provisions for the case of
force majeure is *'justified by reasons of equity'* and that it did not *'appear
that this justification is lacking in the case of imports of cereals from Member
States'.* [193]

In a more general way the Court of Justice accepted an exception for *force
majeure* as one of the principles of Community law in the *Fleischhandelsgesellschaft Case* when it held:

192. *Danvin Case* (26/67), 11 July 1968, [1968] ECR 322; 14 Jur. (1968) 453, 454; 14
Rec. (1968) 473, 474.
193. *Reich Case* (64/74), 20 Feb. 1975, consideration 3, [1975] ECR 268, 269; [1975]
1 CMLR 405; CCH para 8297.

'With regard to the reference to the existence of a general legal principle governing cases of *force majeure*, it is true that the legal systems of the Member States provide, in certain contexts and legal relationships, for the possibility of derogation from the strict requirements of the law, especially from the legal consequences resulting from the non-fulfilment of an obligation, on account of *force majeure*.'[194]

In the same case the Court limited the application of this principle holding:

'Nevertheless, in the relationship between an individual and the public administration, as in the present case, where to exceed the material date does not involve the non-fulfilment of any obligation binding the individual but merely renders the importations in question subject to a system less favourable than that in force before that date, the existence of a general legal principle to the effect alleged is not to be discerned in the national legal systems.'[195]

§ 106. In a number of cases the Court of Justice has defined the notion of *force majeure* in Community law. In the *Schwarzwald Milch Case* the Court had to define the notion *force majeure* as it stands in Article 6 of EEC Regulation 136/64. According to this regulation an importer who has obtained an import licence is obliged to import except in the case of *force majeure*. The Court held:

'As the concept of *force majeure* is not identical in the different branches of law and the various fields of application, the significance of this concept must be determined on the basis of the legal framework within which it is intended to take effect.

Thus, the interpretation of the concept of *force majeure* used in the regulation in question must take into account the particular nature of the relationships in public law between the importers and the national administration, as well as the objectives of that regulation.'

...

'However, recognition of a case of *force majeure* presupposes not only the occurrence of an unusual event but also that the consequences of that event could not be avoided, as for example where an importer could have obtained the goods elsewhere within the period stipulated.

In this respect, too, the importer must be expected to show all due diligence.

This being so, *force majeure* is established if the importer could only have effected the importation within the period stipulated by replacing the goods at an excessive loss taking into account, where necessary, any remedies available to him.

194. *Fleischhandelsgesellschaft Case* (68/77), 14 Feb. 1978, consideration 11, [1978] ECR 370; [1978] 2 CMLR 753; CCH para 8469.
195. *Idem.*

It must, therefore, be concluded that sufficient causal connexion between the circumstances relied on as a case of *force majeure* and the failure to effect the importation must in principle be recognized when delivery in due time by the importer's supplier has become impossible within the meaning of the above definition, and when the importer can only obtain the goods elsewhere at an excessive loss.

Finally, it follows from the scheme of Article 6 of the regulation that it is for the importer to prove the existence of the circumstances necessary to constitute a case of *force majeure*.'[196]

§ 107. In the *Handelsgesellschaft Case* the Court further defined *'force majeure'* in holding:

'It follows from those objectives as well as from the positive provisions of the regulations in question that the concept of *force majeure* is not limited to absolute impossibility but must be understood in the sense of unusual circumstances, outside the control of the importer or exporter, the consequences of which, in spite of the exercise of all due care, could not have been avoided except at the cost of excessive sacrifice. This concept implies a sufficient flexibility regarding not only the nature of the occurrence relied upon but also the care which the exporter should have exercised in order to meet it and the extent of the sacrifices which he should have accepted to that end.'[197]

§ 108. In the *Fleischkontor* and *Pfützenreuter Cases* the Court again added a new element to the notion *force majeure* in holding:

'It is apparent from these objectives, as well as from the actual provisions of the regulations in question, that the concept of *force majeure* is not limited to cases of absolute impossibility, but must be understood in the sense of unusual circumstances, beyond the importer's control and which have arisen despite the fact that the titular holder of the licence has taken all the precautions which could reasonably be expected of a prudent and diligent trader'.[198]

§ 109. On the question of time limits the Court accepted in the *Simet-Feram Case* that an excessively long delay in the delivery of mail can constitute *force majeure*. In that case appeals against ECSC decisions were dispatched from

---

196. *Schwarzwald Milch Case* (4/68), 11 July 1968, [1968] ECR 385, 386; 14 Jur. (1968) 537, 538; 14 Rec. (1968) 562, 563; [1969] CMLR 416, 417; CCH para 8062.
197. *Handelsgesellschaft Case* (11/70), 17 Dec. 1970, consideration 23, [1970] ECR 1137, 1138; [1972] CMLR 286; CCH para 8126; *Köster Case* (25/70), 17 Dec. 1970, consideration 38, [1970] ECR 1177; [1972] CMLR 293, 294; CCH para 8127.
198. *Fleischkontor Case* (186/73), 15 May 1974, consideration 7, [1974] ECR 544; CCH para 8279; *Pfützenreuter Case* (3/74), 28 May 1974, consideration 22, [1974] ECR 599; CCH para 8262. See also *Fourth Kampffmeyer Case* (158/73), 30 Jan. 1974, consideration 8, [1974] ECR 110; CCH para 8261.

Turin in Italy on 21 April 1965. They arrived in Luxembourg on 30 April and
reached the Court on 4 May. The Court accepted *force majeure* to the extent
that it regarded the arrival of the appeal in Luxembourg as the final date,
instead of the delivery at the Court. For Simet this meant that the appeal
came just in time, for Feram that it was one day late and therefore inadmissible.[199]

j. SELF-DEFENCE

§ 110. Closely related to the notion of *force majeure* is the right of self-
defence which was brought up in the *First Modena Case*. Modena was fined
for violation of ECSC Article 60, setting out the rules on faïr competition.
It submitted that it could not have acted otherwise because of prevailing
conditions on the Italian market and of the behaviour of its competitors. It
therefore had acted in self-defence which constituted a lawful justification.
The Court then held:

> 'Legitimate self-protection presupposes an action taken by a person which
> is essential in order to ward off a danger threatening him. The threat must
> be immediate, the danger imminent, and there must be no other lawful
> means of avoiding it. None of these requirements is to be found in the
> present case.'[200]

k. ESTOPPEL

§ 111. The principle of estoppel does not exist in the legal systems of the
Continental Member States. The Court of Justice therefore has not, up to
now, expressly accepted it. In a number of cases, however, it has given expression to very similar principles.

§ 112. Only undertakings engaged in production in the coal or the steel
industry are covered by the ECSC Treaty.[201] The High Authority therefore
pleaded that *Sorema* could not lodge an appeal under ECSC Article 33 against
a decision concerning it. The Court rejected this plea, holding:

> 'The High Authority is however unjustified in raising this plea of inadmis-
> sibility.
>   In fact, by taking a decision concerning the applicant, it has by implica-
> tion recognized the applicant either as an undertaking or as an association
> of undertakings.'[202]

199. *Simet-Feram Case* (25 and 26/65), 2 March 1967, [1967] ECR 42, 43; 13 Jur.
(1967) 52, 53; 13 Rec. (1967) 52, 53.
200. *First Modena Case* (16/61), 12 July 1962, [1962] ECR 303; 8 Jur. (1962) 603, 604;
8 Rec. (1962) 576; [1962] CMLR 246.
201. ECSC Art. 80.
202. *Sorema Case* (67/63), 19 March 1964, [1964] ECR 161; 10 Jur. (1964) 336; 10 Rec.
(1964) 316; [1964] CMLR 360.

§ 113. In the case of a dispute concerning the dismissal of a staff member on grounds of ill health the staff member must be examined by an independent committee of three doctors. The Community and the staff member each appoint one doctor, these two doctors co-opt the third. In the *Alfieri Case* the applicant, a staff member who was dismissed for ill health, had flatly refused to cooperate at all with the selection of the independent committee or the inquiry to be held. Subsequently he pleaded the illegality of his dismissal on the ground that he had not been examined by an independent committee of doctors. The Court of Justice then held:

'This complaint must emphatically be rejected owing to the fact that the applicant refused to appear before the Committee'.[203]

§ 114. In the *Premiums for slaughtering cows Case* the Italian government had submitted that the action brought by the Commission had lost its ground because the situation had become irremediable. The Court held:

'the defendant cannot in any case be allowed to rely upon a *fait accompli* of which it is itself the author so as to escape judicial proceedings'.[204]

§ 115. In the *Continental Can Case* the Court held that the addressee of an act cannot make use of his own refusal to take cognizance of an act in order to plead that the act has not been properly notified to him.[205]

§ 116. In the *Meganck Case* the applicant had for more than three months postponed giving notice to the Community authorities of a change in his domestic circumstances. He therefore had received overpayments which were reclaimed by the Commission. According to the staff regulations overpayments shall be recovered 'if the recipient was aware that there was no due reason for the payment or if the fact of the overpayment was patently such that he could not have been unaware of it'.[206] The applicant, pleading that he had not been aware that the payments had been without reason, appealed for the annulment of the Commission's decision requiring repayment. The Court held that the applicant:

'Thus having placed himself in an irregular situation by his own conduct (...) cannot rely on his good faith to be released from the obligation to return the sums overpaid during this period'.[207]

---

203. *Alfieri Case* (3/66), 14 Dec. 1966, [1966] ECR 451; 12 Jur. (1966) 652; 12 Rec. (1966) 653; [1967] CMLR 121.
204. *Premiums for slaughtering cows Case* (39/72), 7 Feb. 1973, consideration 10, [1973] ECR 112; [1973] CMLR 454; CCH para 8201.
205. *Continental Can Case* (6/72), 21 Feb. 1973, consideration 10, [1973] ECR 241; [1973] CMLR 221; CCH para 8171.
206. Staff Regulations, Art. 85.
207. *Meganck Case* (36/72), 30 May 1973, consideration 17, [1973] ECR 534.

§ 117. To a certain extent the principle of estoppel is less applicable to governmental authorities than to individual persons. When dealing with invest- ments and levies the High Authority had considered parent companies and their subsidiaries as belonging to the same entity. *Klöckner* and others had drawn the conclusion that scrap passing between parent companies and their subsidiaries should qualify as 'own scrap' so that no premiums would have to be paid to the Scrap Equalization Fund. When the High Authority nonetheless charged them to pay such premiums, they claimed that the High Authority could not disregard the position it had previously adopted, that it could not '*venire contra factum proprium*', a notion close to estoppel. The Court re- jected this, considering:

'Moreover the administrative authority is not always bound by its previous actions in its public activities by virtue of a rule which, in relations between the same parties, forbids them to *venire contra factum proprium.* '[208]

§ 118. *Unil-It.* imported cheese from Germany and the Netherlands into Italy shortly after 1 November 1964. According to Regulation 13/64/EEC the Common Market origin of the cheese had to be attested by a certificate DD4. As no such certificate accompanied the cheese the Italian authorities treated it as cheese from third countries and charged *Unil-It.* accordingly. *Unil-It.* demonstrated that at the time of its imports, it was not possible to obtain DD4 certificates; the Court of Justice held:

'(...) the decision of 17 July 1962 (...) entitled the trader to pay the intra- Community levy alone, provided that he proves, by producing certificate DD4, that he has fulfilled the conditions necessary to benefit therefrom, but (...) the Member State which has not adopted substantive measures to implement this decision cannot claim that traders have failed to fulfil the obligations which it involves and must, provisionally, allow other means of proof to be used which are appropriate to the fulfilment of these condi- tions.'[209]

C. CASE-LAW OF THE COURT OF JUSTICE[210]

§ 119. In Continental legal theory a decision of a court, even of a supreme court, only decides the case at issue, and is not binding for future situations. Courts are to *apply* the law and not to make it. When rules are required for general application, they should be made by the legislature. In practice, how- ever, the system is not as strict as one might think. Every application necessi-

208. *Klöckner Case* (17 and 20/61), 13 July 1962, [1962] ECR 342, 8 Jur. (1962) 678; 8 Rec. (1962) 649; *Idem* in the *Third Mannesmann Case* (19/61), 13 July 1962, [1962] ECR 373; 8 Jur. (1962) 736; 8 Rec. (1962) 707.
209. *Unil-It. Case* (30/75), 18 Nov. 1975, consideration 18, [1975] ECR 1428; [1976], CMLR 128 (consideration 25); CCH para 8331.
210. See also J. Mertens de Wilmars, *La jurisprudence de la Cour de justice comme instru- ment de l'intégration communautaire*, 12 CDE (1976), pp. 135-148.

tates interpretation, which means, of course, that rules are somehow refined or supplemented. [211] These supplements entail additional rules which – although theoretically they bind only the parties to the dispute – in practice have a general force of law, since the judiciary will not overrule itself unless cogent reasons are present. Lower courts normally follow the rulings of superior courts unless they have good reason to believe that the superior court may change its opinion. In some specific situations binding force *erga omnes* of a court decision may even be the rule, for example, when the German Constitutional Court has declared a law void.

In practice the cases of the Court of Justice are quoted as precedents which – though not formally binding – are important sources of law. The extent to which the case-law of courts is needed as an additional source of law depends on the legislation involved: the more general the legislation, the more room the courts have for making supplementary rules through interpretation. In the European Communities the principal legislator, the Council of Ministers, hardly operates and the secondary legislator, the Commission, has insufficient powers to fill the gap. The legislation, therefore, is broad and incomplete, with the result that the case-law of the Court of Justice is relatively important.

§ 120. In some fields of Community law where the legislator has left important areas unfilled, the case-law of the Court of Justice may be the most important or even the sole source of law available. Some aspects of the law on competition, such as the provisional validity of certain agreements between undertakings[212] and the relationship between free movements of goods and industrial property rights[213] are almost entirely governed by case-law. It is with respect to this field that Van Gerven speaks of *'creeping legislation'* by the Court of Justice. [214]

Another gap in Community law which has been filled by the case-law of the Court is the absence of a time limit in EEC Article 93(3). The Court ruled that the same time limits should be observed as in EEC Articles 173 and 175 (see above § 76). [215]

---

211. On the law-making function of courts see Van Gerven, *Het beleid van de rechter* (The policy of the judge), Standaard Antwerpen 1973; Mann (*op. cit.*, note 38), Chapter IV; Jean Boulouis, *A propos de la function normative de la jurisprudence; remarques sur l'oeuvre jurisprudentielle de la Cour de Justice des Communautés Européennes*, Mélanges offerts à Marcel Waline, Librairie générale de droit et de jurisprudence, Paris 1974, pp. 149-162.
212. The cases *Bosch* (13/61), 6 April 1962, [1962] ECR 49; [1962] CMLR 25; *Portelange* (10/69), 9 July 1969, [1969] ECR 314; CCH para 8075; *Bilger* (43/69), 18 March 1970, [1970] ECR 134; CCH para 8076; *Rochas* (1/70), 30 June 1970, [1970] ECR 521; [1971] CMLR 115; *Second Brasserie de Haecht* (48/72), 6 Feb. 1973, [1973] ECR 85; [1973] CMLR 301.
213. See Walter van Gerven, *The Recent Case Law of the Court of Justice concerning Articles 30 and 36 of the EEC Treaty*, 14 CMLRev (1977), pp. 5-24.
214. Van Gerven in Europese Monografie No. 16, p. 203.
215. For other examples of gaps filled by the case-law of the Court see Schermers (*op. cit.*, note 51) in particular pp. 459-464; L.A. Geelhoed, *De kwaliteit van het Gemeenschapsrecht*, Europese Monografie No. 19, p. 146.

§ 121. Normally, it is taken for granted that the Court of Justice will follow the precedents it has established and in practice it never expressly overruled its own previous decisions. In the *Da Costa Case* the Court of Justice decided that it is not legally bound by its previous rulings and that national courts are entitled to ask for a new preliminary ruling if they do not wish to follow a ruling given on the same question in a prior case. But the Court also ruled that national courts are free to use previous preliminary rulings without consulting the Court of Justice, even if they are courts ruling in last instance and which are therefore normally obliged to ask for preliminary rulings on all questions of Community law. [216] It apparently attributed to its prior decision some force which extended beyond the case itself.

§ 122. Another early example of express reference to previous case-law is offered by the *Snupat Cases*. Under the ECSC scrap system, steel plants had to pay a levy on all scrap acquired from European sources except from within the plant itself. The High Authority had granted an exemption from the scrap levy to Hoogovens for the scrap obtained from Breedband on the ground that Breedband was so closely affiliated to Hoogovens that its scrap could be considered as equivalent to Hoogovens' own scrap. Snupat asked for a similar exemption for scrap acquired from another company belonging to the same concern as Snupat. The High Authority refused. In the *First Snupat Case*, the Court of Justice, upholding this refusal, decided that no exemption from the scrap levy could be granted for scrap transferred between two different undertakings belonging to the same concern. [217] In the *Second Snupat Case* Snupat disputed the exemption granted to Hoogovens. The Court of Justice then held:

'In its judgment given on 17 July 1959 in Joined Cases 32 and 33/58 (*SNUPAT v High Authority*) the Court decided that an exemption in respect of group scrap was unjustified.

   In these circumstances the abovementioned judgment showed the exemptions in a new light; this should have led, after a fresh examination of their legal basis, to a decision concerning their legality.

   The said judgment must therefore have led the High Authority to re-examine its previous position and to consider whether the disputed exemptions could be retained in view of the principles established by the above-mentioned judgment, since it was required from that time to conform to those principles at the risk of tolerating discrimination interfering with normal competition as provided for by the fundamental rules of the Treaty.' [218]

216. *Da Costa Case* (23-30/62) 27 March 1963, [1963] ECR 37-39; 9 Jur. (1963) 77-79; 9 Rec. (1963) CMLR 237, 238; CCH para 8010 (pp. 7238-7239). See below § 596: See also Peter Hay, *Res Judicata and Precedent in the Court of Justice of the Common Market*, 12 AJCL (1963), pp. 404-408.
217. *First Snupat Case* (32 and 33/58), 17 July 1959, [1959] ECR 142, 143; 5 Jur. (1958-59) 326-328; 5 Rec. (1958-59) 304, 305.
218. *Second Snupat Case* (42 and 49/59), 22 March 1961 [1961] ECR 79; 7 Jur. (1961) 151; 7 Rec. (1961) 150.

In fact, the Court ruled that its decision in the *First Snupat Case* should be binding on all concerns, for there would otherwise be discrimination. According to this ruling most Court decisions have equally binding force for other similar situations, but nonetheless a Court decision never has *direct* effect on other parties than those before the Court. The decision can be construed to mean no more than that there is an obligation on the Community institution to review the position of other parties in a similar situation.

§ 123. Express references to previous cases used to be rare in the case-law of the Court of Justice. In answer to a preliminary question of a national court the Court of Justice sometimes referred to a previous decision by which the same question was decided[219], though prior to 1973 even this was exceptional. Recently, references to previous cases have become more frequent[220], but it is hard to say whether this is because there is more previous case-law to refer to or because since 1973 some of the Court's judges come from a legal system in which the binding force of previous cases is accepted. In the *Matisa Case* the Court was very clear in its reference when it quoted its decision in the *Bakels Case*[221] and then went on:

'Since there is nothing in the present case capable of leading to a different conclusion, it is proper to reply to the same effect.'[222]

In a preliminary ruling in 1978 the Court even sent a copy of a previous decision to a national court which had asked a similar question.[223]

§ 124. Normally the case-law of the Court of Justice is to be regarded as one unit. Decisions taken under the ECSC Treaty are used as precedents for cases under the EEC Treaty and *vice versa*. But, of course, there are exceptions when the provisions of the Treaties read differently. Thus, cases under ECSC

219. See e.g. *Lück Case* (34/67), 4 April 1968, [1968] ECR 250; 14 Jur. (1968) 355; 14 Rec. (1968) 369; CCH para 8071.
220. See e.g. *Lohrey Case* (141/73), 11 Dec. 1973, consideration 8, [1973] ECR 1540; CCH para 8252; *Pastificio Triestino Case* (93/74), 17 June 1975, consideration 5, [1975] ECR 667, 668 CCH para 8323; *Bresciani Case* (87/75), 5 Feb. 1976, consideration 5, [1976] ECR 137; [1976] 2 CMLR 75; CCH para 8347; *Tasca Case* (65/75), 26 Feb. 1976, consideration 5, [1976] ECR 266; [1977] 2 CMLR 200; CCH para 8354; *Fifth Rewe Case* (45/75), 17 Feb. 1976, consideration 9, [1976] ECR 193; [1976] 2 CMLR 22; CCH para 8343; *SADAM Case* (88-90/75), 26 Feb. 1976, consideration 6, [1976] ECR 336; [1977] 2 CMLR 205; CCH para 8355; *Royer Case* (48/75), 8 April 1976, consideration 41 [1976] ECR 514; [1976] 2 CMLR 639, 640; CCH para 8359; *Mazzalai Case* (111/75), 20 May 1976, consideration 11 [1976] ECR 665; [1977] 1 CMLR 116; CCH para 8363; *Dona Case* (13/76), 14 July 1976, considerations 11, 14, [1976] ECR 1340; [1976] 2 CMLR 587; CCH para 8369; *Benedetti Case* (52/76), 3 Feb. 1977, consideration 13, [1977] ECR 180; CCH para 8406; *Greco Case* (37/77), 13 Oct. 1977, consideration 8, [1977] ECR 1717; [1978] 2 CMLR 454; *Boerboom Case* (105/77), 14 March 1978, consideration 8, [1978] ECR 722.
221. See below § 128.
222. *Matisa Case* (35/75) 23 Oct. 1975, consideration 2, (1975) ECR 1210; CCH para 8316.
223. *Schonenberg Case* (88/77), 16 Feb. 1978, consideration 13, [1978] ECR 491; [1978] 2 CMLR 525; CCH para 8474.

Article 88 cannot be used as precedents for cases under EEC Article 169 (see below § 384, 387). Nor can cases under ECSC Article 33(2) be used for establishing direct and individual concern under EEC Article 173(2) (see below § 315-324).

D. CUSTOM

§ 125. The International Court of Justice in the Hague applies as one of its sources of law 'international custom, as evidence of a general practice accepted as law'. Are there any Community customs used as a source of law by the Court of Justice? Perhaps the Communities are still too recently established to have developed customary rules of law. So far, there are no indications that the Court of Justice pays much attention to customary practice. In the *Second Defrenne Case* one of the arguments pleaded against the grant of direct effect to EEC Article 119 was that the Member States had considered the Article not to have direct effect for a lengthy period of time, whilst the Commission could be deemed to have tacitly accepted this in that it had not acted against the Member States. This argument might be seen as invoking a rule of custom. The Court of Justice held however:

'The effectiveness of this provision cannot be affected by the fact that the duty imposed by the Treaty has not been discharged by certain Member States and that the joint institutions have not reacted sufficiently energetically against this failure to act.

To accept the contrary view would be to risk raising the violation of the right to the status of a principle of interpretation, a position the adoption of which would not be consistent with the task assigned to the Court by Article 164 of the Treaty.'[224]

This reasoning demonstrates that the Court of Justice will not accept as customary law any negligence to apply any written obligations. The latter conclusion is not weakened by the fact that the Court finally accepted the practice engaged in by the Member States by a different process of reasoning (see above § 84).

In many other cases rules which have become customary could probably be applied as general rules native to the Community legal order (see above § 36).

E. OTHER LEGAL ORDERS

1. Other legal orders as a source of Community law

§ 126. The sources of Community law mentioned so far are subject to the authority of the Community legal system. The Community legislator may

224. *Second Defrenne Case* (43/75), 8 April 1976, considerations 33, 34, [1976] ECR 475; [1976] 2 CMLR 124, 125; CCH para 8346.

amend them at his own discretion: he can alter Community acts and, by making express provisions, can set aside both the case-law of the Court, customary law and most general principles common to the laws of the Member States. In practice, some exceptions may, perhaps, be made for the compelling legal principles (see above § 34) which, though in theory subject to possible amendment by the legislator, are very hard to amend in practice, and for the Community Treaties themselves which are also difficult to amend, though in theory amendment is possible by a Community legislator as personified by the Community institutions and the national institutions acting together.

Community law is not isolated from other law. On the one hand it is related to international law, on the other to the national legal orders of the Member States. Does that mean that international law and the national laws of the Member States are sources of Community law? Strictly speaking it does not. International and national law are not subject to the Community legislator; they cannot be amended or withdrawn at its discretion. For this reason one could say that the Court of Justice applies legal orders other than the Community legal order without these legal orders being construed as part of the Community legal order. This would mean, however, that national courts, whenever they are obliged to apply Community law, would not be compelled to incorporate the rules of international and national law which the Court of Justice would normally apply into that Community law. If, for example, the Court of Justice were to find that specific rules made under the General Agreement on Tariffs and Trade (GATT), or particular parts of the European Convention on Human Rights, are directly binding on the Communities, it may therefore set aside or amend provisions of Community regulations. Would it then be possible for a British court to rule that the GATT provisions or the European Convention are not directly applicable in the United Kingdom and, therefore, should not be taken into consideration when a British court applies Community law? Such an inconsistency in the application of international law would lead to a disparity in the effect of Community law and must therefore be held to be unacceptable.

It may, therefore, be submitted that international law as well as the national laws of the Member States, in so far as they have been incorporated into the Community legal order, must be treated ás sources of Community law, even though these sources may be of such a nature as to be different from the other sources mentioned above.

2. International law[225]

a. GENERAL RULES

§ 127.   Many rules of international law are not of a compulsory nature. They are applied as rules of customary law or as general principles of law and are,

---

225. Albert Bleckmann, *Die Position des Völkerrechts im inneren Rechtsraum der Europäischen Gemeinschaften, Monimus oder Dualismus der Rechtsordnungen*, 18 Jahrbuch

therefore, very similar to the sources of Community law described above. In some cases where the Court of Justice did not consider itself bound to apply international law, it has used international law as a source of Community law. Thus the Court held in the *Interfood Case*:

> 'Since agreements regarding the Common Customs Tariff were reached between the Community and its partners in GATT the principles underlying those agreements may be of assistance in interpreting the rules of classification applicable to it.
>
> Consequently account should be taken of the content of agreements concluded in the course of the Tariff Conference of 1960 to 1961 (...)'[226]

§ 128. A similar reference was made in, *inter alia*, the *Bakels* and *Matisa Cases* with respect to the so called 'Brussels Nomenclature' established by a customs convention of 1950 and by a series of explanatory notes provided thereto. On these the Court held:

> 'In the absence of relevant Community provisions, the explanatory notes and the classification opinions provided for by the Convention on Nomenclature for the Classification of Goods in Customs Tariffs are an authoritative source for the purpose of the interpretation of the headings to the Common Customs Tariff'.[227]

§ 129. In the *Second Nederlandse Spoorwegen Case* the Court proceeded a step further by accepting that the EEC has succeeded its Member States as a member of the Customs Cooperation Council, and by subsequently holding:

> 'It is true that these classification opinions do not bind the Contracting Parties but they have a bearing on'interpretation which is all the more decisive because they emanate from an authority entrusted by the Contracting Parties with ensuring uniformity in the interpretation and application of the nomenclature.
>
> When, furthermore, such an interpretation reflects the general practice followed by the Contracting States, it can be set aside only if it appears incompatible with the wording of the heading concerned or goes manifestly beyond the discretion conferred on the Customs Co-operation Council.'[228]

(1975), pp. 300-319; Karl M. Meessen, *The Application of Rules of Public International Law within Community Law*, 13 CMLRev (1976), pp. 485-501. Robert Kovar, *La Contribution de la Cour de justice au développement de la condition internationale de la Communauté européenne*, 14 CDE (1978), pp. 527-573.
226. *Interfood Case* (92/71), 26 April 1972, consideration 6, [1972] ECR 242; [1973] CMLR 576; CCH para 8180.
227. *Bakels Case* (14/70), 8 Dec. 1970, consideration 11, [1970] ECR 1009; [1971] CMLR 200; CCH para 8118; *Matisa Case* (35/75), 23 Oct. 1975, consideration 2, [1975] ECR 1210; CCH para 8316. See also *Carstens Keramik Case* (98 and 99/75), 18 Feb. 1976, consideration 11, [1976] ECR 252; CCH para 8348.
228. *Second Nederlandse Spoorwegen Case* (38/75), 19 Nov. 1975, considerations 24, 25, [1975] ECR 1451; [1976] CMLR 179; CCH para 8327.

In the *Dittmeyer Case* the Court of Justice repeated that the opinions of the Committee on Common Customs Tariff Nomenclature constitute an important means of ensuring the uniform application of the Common Customs Tariff. It added that such opinions do not have legally binding force so that, where appropriate, it may be necessary to consider whether their content is in accordance with the actual provisions of the Common Customs Tariff.[229]

§ 130. In the *Rutili Case* the Court of Justice used the European Convention on Human Rights as an argument for establishing a general principle of law. In that case it decided that the words 'subject to limitations justified on grounds of public policy' in EEC Article 48(3) do not grant full discretion to the Member States to make any restrictions to the freedom of movement provided for in the article. As one of its reasons the Court considered:

'Taken as a whole, these limitations placed on the powers of Member States in respect of control of aliens are a specific manifestation of the more general principle, enshrined in Articles 8, 9, 10 and 11 of the Convention for the Protection of Human Rights and Fundamental Freedoms, signed in Rome on 4 November 1950 and ratified by all the Member States, and in Article 2 of Protocol No 4 of the same Convention, signed in Strasbourg on 16 September 1963, which provide, in identical terms, that no restrictions in the interests of national security or public safety shall be placed on the rights secured by the above-quoted articles other than such as are necessary for the protection of those interests "in a democratic society" '.[230]

§ 131. In some other cases the Court of Justice has not only used international law as a model, but has actually applied it. In the *Radio Tubes Case* the Court applied the principle of international law that *'by assuming a new obligation which is incompatible with rights held under a prior treaty a State ipso facto gives up the exercise of these rights to the extent necessary for the performance of its new obligations'.*[231]

In the *Van Duyn Case* the Court held that *'it is a principle of international law, which the EEC Treaty cannot be assumed to disregard in the relations between Member States, that a State is precluded from refusing its own nationals the right of entry or residence'.*[232]

229. *Dittmeyer Case* (69, 70/76), 15 Feb. 1977, consideration 4, [1977] ECR 238; CCH para 8408.
230. *Rutili Case* (36/75), 28 Oct. 1975, consideration 32, [1975] ECR 1232; [1976] 1 CMLR 155; CCH para 8322.
231. *Radio Tubes Case* (10/61), 27 Feb. 1962, [1962] ECR 10; 8 Jur. (1962) 22; 8 Rec. (1962) 22; [1962] CMLR 203; CCH para 8002. The quoted principle of international law has since been codified in Art. 30 of the Vienna Convention on the Law of Treaties. See also Art. 41 of that Convention.
232. *Van Duyn Case* (41/74) 4 Dec. 1974, consideration 21/23, [1974] ECR 1350, 1351; [1975] CMLR 17, 18; CCH para 8283.

b. TREATY OBLIGATIONS[233]

(i) Prior treaties concluded by Member States

§ 132.   EEC Article 234 provides that the rights and obligations arising from treaties concluded between Member States and third States, prior to the Communities, 'shall not be affected by the provisions of this Treaty'. Although this excludes making such prior treaties part of the Community legal order, it does not mean that they will not affect Community law and therefore are of no relevance to it. This will be particularly true in the case of multilateral treaties to which all Member States are parties and even more so when such treaties cover a field related to one regulated by the Communities. The question has been posed whether such multilateral treaties should not be uniformly applied throughout the Member States of the Communities and whether, therefore, the Court of Justice should not be entitled to give preliminary rulings on their interpretation (see below § 604-607).

A similar position has been attributed to Benelux and BLEU agreements. They have been granted priority over the EEC Treaty 'to the extent that the objectives of these regional unions are not attained by the application of the EEC Treaty.'[234]   This means that in the interpretation and application of Community law these agreements should be taken into account.

(ii) Treaty obligations of the Community

§ 133.   In the *Third International Fruit Company Case*, the validity of an EEC act was contested on the ground that it violated Article XI of the General Agreement on Tariffs and Trade (GATT). As the GATT entered into force before the EEC Treaty, the Court could have decided the question under EEC Article 234 but it did not do so. It preferred to look at the question in a wider context, taking account of the international obligations of the Community itself. It considered that the obligations of GATT have generally been transferred to the Community itself so that the Community is bound by the GATT Treaty.[235]   In the same case the Court held that Community acts would be void if incompatible with the treaty obligations of the Community.

In the *Second Nederlandse Spoorwegen Case* a Dutch court had asked whether under Dutch (and international) law it was not obliged to apply GATT provisions even though it might thereby come into conflict with Community law. The Court of Justice further developed the reasoning which it had given in the *Third International Fruit Company Case* that the international obligations under GATT have shifted from the Member States to the Community by holding:

---

233. Jean Paul Pietri, *La valeur juridique des accords liant la Communauté économique européenne*, 12 RTDE (1976), pp. 51-75, 194-214; Hans Krück, *Völkerrechtliche Verträge im Recht der Europäischen Gemeinschaften*, Springer Verlag 1977, 210 pages.
234. EEC Art. 233.
235. *Third International Fruit Company Case* (21-24/72), 12 Dec. 1972, considerations 14-18, [1972] ECR 1227; CCH para 8194.

'Similarly, since so far as fulfilment of the commitments provided for by GATT is concerned, the Community has replaced the Member States, the mandatory effect, in law, of these commitments must be determined by reference to the relevant provisions in the Community legal system and not to those which gave them their previous force under the national legal systems.'[236]

In the same case the Court ruled that, just as in the case of commitments arising from GATT, the Community had replaced the Member States in commitments arising from the Convention of 15 December 1950 on the Nomenclature for the Classification of Goods in Customs Tariffs and from the Convention of the same date establishing a Customs Co-operation Council, and is bound by the said commitments.[237]

§ 134. After the *Third International Fruit Company Case* it may reasonably be expected that the Court of Justice will apply the European Convention on Human Rights to which all Member States are parties as of 3 May 1974. As yet the Court has not expressly accepted this convention as binding on the European Communities, but it has twice referred to it in a way which suggests that it may soon do so. In the *Second Nold Case* it held that *international treaties for the protection of human rights on which the Member States have collaborated or of which they are signatories, can supply guidelines which should be followed within the framework of Community Law*'. (see above § 54). In the *Rutili case* it expressly referred to the Convention and subsequently applied a provision from it in the Community legal order without stating, however, that the Community was bound by that provision (see above § 130).

Even if the Community is considered bound by the European Convention on Human Rights, this does not necessarily mean that the Community institutions, or even the Member States when acting on behalf of the Community, may be brought before the Commission of Human Rights or the Court of Human Rights in Strasbourg. When the Confédération Française Démocratique du Travail (CFDT) had been refused a seat in the Consultative Committee of the ECSC and an action brought before the Court of Justice had been declared inadmissible[238], the CFDT brought an action before the Commission of Human Rights against the Community as well as against eight of its Member States (the ninth, France, has not accepted the right of individual petition). These actions, however, were declared inadmissible by decision of the European Commission of Human Rights of 10 July 1978. With respect to the action against the Communities the Commission held that the Communities have separate legal personality and are not parties to the European Convention on Human Rights. For these reasons the complaint fell outside the jurisdiction *ratione personae* of the Commission.[239]

236. *Second Nederlandse Spoorwegen Case* (38/75), 19 Nov. 1975, consideration 16, [1975] ECR 1450; [1976] 1 CMLR 178; CCH para 8327.
237. *Idem*, consideration 21.
238. *CFDT Case* (66/76), 17 Feb. 1977, [1977] ECR 311; [1977] 1 CMLR 596.
239. Decision of 10 July 1978 in Case No. 8030/77. See also below § 567.

§ **135.** Some international agreements have been concluded by the Communities in their own right. In the *Second Haegeman Case* the Court of Justice held, when requested to interpret an international agreement to which the EEC was a party (the Association Agreement with Greece):

'The Athens Agreement was concluded by the Council under Articles 228 and 238 of the Treaty as appears from the terms of the decision dated 25 September 1961.

This agreement is therefore, in so far as concerns the Community, an act of one of the institutions of the Community within the meaning of sub-paragraph (b) of the first paragraph of Article 177. The provisions of the Agreement, from the coming into force thereof, form an integral part of Community law.'[240]

§ **136.** From the abovementioned cases it may be concluded that treaties are to be applied as part of Community law whenever the Communities can be considered to be parties to them, either because they succeeded their Members as parties, or because they became parties in their own right.[241]

The application of such treaties as part of Community law means that they are incorporated into the Community legal order without, however, being subject to that legal order. They play the same independent role in Community law as Community law plays in the legal orders of the Member States (see below § 145-148).

The EEC Treaty offers some indication that the relationship between Community law and international law is a monist one (see below § 148, 155). It requires no transformation, but provides that agreements concluded by the Community 'shall be binding on the institutions of the Community and on Member States'.[242] There is good reason for such a monist relationship as the main argument for transformation, that is to secure the influence of the parliament, does not apply to the Communities. The European Parliament has as little influence on the Community's implementing act as it has on treaty-making.

Community practice, however, seems rather dualist. Treaties concluded by the Community are enacted in regulations which are published in the Official Journal of the Communities[243], the Court of Justice interprets them as Community acts (see above § 135). This may only be a matter of form. The problems for which the question of transformation is relevant, namely a conflict between the treaty text and the transforming act or a conflict between

---

240. *Second Haegeman Case* (181/73), 30 April 1974, considerations 3-6, [1974] ECR 459, 460; [1975] 1 CMLR 530; CCH para 8273. The Court interpreted the Yaounde Convention in the *Bresciani Case* (87/75), 5 Feb. 1976, considerations 16-29, [1976] ECR 140-142; [1976] 2 CMLR 77-79; CCH para 8347.
242. EEC Art. 228 (2).
243. See Theo Öhlinger, *Rechtsfragen des Freihandelsabkommens zwischen Österreich und der EWG*, 34 ZaöRV (1974), p. 659.
241. Advocate-General Trabucchi doubts whether it is appropriate to grant to international law a similar status as to Community law, see his opinion in the *Bresciani Case* (87/75), 5 Feb. 1976, [1976] ECR 148; [1976] 2 CMLR 71; CCH para 8347.

the transforming act and a later inconsistent act of the Community, have not occurred yet.

c. BINDING DECISIONS OF INTERNATIONAL ORGANIZATIONS

§ 137. Under the Charter of the United Nations the Security Council may take decisions binding upon all UN Members, and even having effect on non-Members. [244] Such decisions will also bind the Communities as the Nine are all UN Members.

The only binding resolutions taken by the Security Council were those which imposed economic sanctions against Rhodesia. [245] These sanctions are binding in international law and must therefore be considered to be incorporated within the Community legal order.

Apart from the decisions taken by the Security Council international organizations may also adopt binding rules in some technical fields such as fishing on the high seas or concerning air navigation.

d. PEREMPTORY NORMS OF INTERNATIONAL LAW

§ 138. Peremptory norms of international law invalidate treaties and *a fortiori* acts made under treaties. [246] There are not many peremptory norms of international law but they are rapidly developing. Under modern international law it may well be submitted that, for instance, the prohibition of racial discrimination is a peremptory norm. This means that treaties and any rules derived from treaties which lead to racial discrimination are void. The peremptory norms of international law must be considered as being incorporated in all other legal orders, including that of the European Communities.

3. National laws of the Member States [247]

a. EXPRESS REFERENCES

§ 139. Sometimes Community provisions expressly refer to the national laws of the Member States. Thus companies and firms must be formed in accordance with the laws of the Member States [248] ; enforcement of EEC decisions is governed by the rules of civil procedure in force in the State in which they

---

244. UN Charter Art. 2(5), (6) and 25.
245. Security Council Resolutions 232 (1966) and 235 (1967).
246. Vienna Convention on the Law of Treaties, Artt. 42-53.
247. Detlef Schumacher, *Die Berücksichtigung nationalen Rechts durch Organe der Europäischen Gemeinschaften*, NJW 1970, pp. 980-984; John A. Usher, *The Influence of National Concepts on Decisions of the European Court*, 1 ELRev. (1976), pp. 359-374.
248. EEC Art. 58.

must be carried out[249]; lawyers may represent before the Court of Justice only if they are qualified to practise before national courts[250]; periods assimilated to insurance periods for migrant workers are to be calculated as defined in the legislation under which they were completed[251]; the contractual liability of the Community is governed by different national laws depending on the State involved.[252]

In such cases the notions of national law have been incorporated into the Community legal order. Thus the uniformity of Community law is affected to the extent that there will be divergencies in the application of Community law in each Member State. The Community legislator has accepted, for example, that University professors are entitled to represent parties from some Member States, but not from others; they have accepted that some periods may be assimilated to insurance periods in one Member State whilst a similar period cannot be assimilated in others.

b. IMPLICIT REFERENCES

§ 140. Community law uses a large number of legal notions such as 'persons', 'services', 'capital', 'workers', 'undertakings', etc. which are not further defined. Should such notions be understood as regulated by the national law involved, or should they be interpreted uniformly throughout the Community as part of Community law? Against the latter solution one cannot make the objection that Community law does not cover such notions, for the acceptance of 'general principles common to the laws of the Member States' as a source of Community law (see above § 35 ff) makes it possible for almost any legal notion to become part of Community law.

The Court of Justice avails itself of both solutions: sometimes it refers to national law, on other occasions it refuses to do so and formulates a common notion under Community law. In his private writings Judge Pescatore submits that the latter solution is the normal one: 'the Communities aim at unity, and not simply at a coordination'.[253] This view was supported by the Court of Justice when it held, with reference to the words 'correct offer', in the *Hagen Case* that:

'Terms used in Community law must be uniformly interpreted and implemented throughout the Community, except when an express or implied reference is made to national law'.[254]

---

249. EEC Art. 192.
250. EEC Statute Art. 17 (2).
251. EEC Regulation No. 3 of 25 Sept. 1958, Art. 1 (2); *Murru Case* (2/72), 6 June 1972, consideration 9, [1972] ECR 337; [1972] CMLR 895.
252. EEC Art. 215 (1). The Court of Justice applied this article in the *Pelligrini Case* (23/76), 7 Dec. 1976, [1976] ECR 1819.
253. Pierre Pescatore, *L'ordre juridique des Communautés européennes*, second edition, Presses Universitaires de Liège, 1973, p. 170.
254. *Hagen Case* (49/71), 1 Feb. 1972, consideration 6, [1972] ECR 34; [1973] CMLR 71.

76

On the other hand, if one also takes into account all legal notions which may be of only indirect relevance to the cases before the Court of Justice — such as the legal personality of the undertakings involved, the validity of contracts made, the powers of directors, etc. — the implicit references to national law probably outnumber the common notions.

§ 141. Some cases which have come before the Court of Justice may further illustrate the problem:

(1) In the *First Nold Case* the applicant's right of appeal was disputed on the grounds that the company lacked legal personality, being in liquidation, and that it was illegally represented by Erich Nold. The Court of Justice then decided that these questions had to be decided by the rules of the municipal law concerned.[255]

In the *Sixth Rewe* and *Comet Cases* the Court of Justice held that the domestic legal systems must determine the procedural conditions governing actions at law intended to ensure the protection of the rights which citizens have from the direct effect of Community law. Such conditions cannot, however, be less favourable than those relating to similar actions of a domestic nature. EEC Articles 100-102 and 235 enable appropriate measures to be taken if the differences between the national provisions are likely to distort or harm the functioning of the Common Market.[256]

In the *Santa Anna Case* the Court of Justice held that there is no uniform Community definition of 'agricultural holding', which means that national courts will use their domestic definitions of this concept.[257] A similar decision was taken in the *Denkavit Case* with respect to 'agricultural undertaking'.[258]

(2) In the *Hoekstra Case* the applicant claimed benefits accorded to 'wage-earners and comparable workers' by EEC Regulation No 3. According to the rules of municipal law Mrs. Hoekstra was not a 'wage-earner' nor a 'comparable worker'. For that reason the Dutch authorities had initially refused to apply the regulation. The Court of Justice, however, held:

255. *First Nold Case* (18/57), 20 March 1959, [1959] ECR 48, 49; 5 Jur. (1958-59) 115; 5 Rec. (1958-59) 110, 111. Other issues decided according to national law were, *inter alia*, duties of maintenance for civil servants, *Meinhardt Case* (24/71), 17 May 1972, consideration 6, [1972] ECR 276, 277, timelimits for social security payments relevant both to national and to Community law, *Mutualités Chrétiennes Case* (35/74), 12 Nov. 1974, consideration 13, [1974] ECR 1248; [1975] CMLR 282.
256. *Sixth Rewe Case* (33/76), 16 Dec. 1976, consideration 5, [1976] ECR 1997, 1998; [1977] 1 CMLR 550; CCH para 8382; *Comet Case* (45/76), 16 Dec. 1976, considerations 12-17, [1976] ECR 2053; [1977] 1 CMLR 553; CCH para 8383. See also Robert Kovar, *Droit communautaire et droit procedural national*, 13 CDE (1977), pp. 230-244; Derrick Wyatt, *National periods of limitation as a bar to Community rights*, 2 ELRev. (1977), pp. 122-125.
257. *Santa Anna Case* (85/77), 28 Feb. 1978, considerations 8, 9, 14, [1978] ECR 540, 541; [1978] 3 CMLR 79, 80; CCH para 8472.
258. *Denkavit Case* (139/77), 13 June 1978, consideration 11, [1978] ECR 1331, 1332; [1979] 1 CMLR 123.

'Articles 48 to 51 of the Treaty, by the very fact of establishing freedom of movement for "workers", have given Community scope to this term.

If the definition of this term were a matter within the competence of national law, it would therefore be possible for each Member State to modify the meaning of the concept of "migrant worker" and to eliminate at will the protection afforded by the Treaty to certain categories of person.

Moreover nothing in Article 48 to 51 of the Treaty leads to the conclusion that these provisions have left the definition of the term "worker" to national legislation. On the contrary, the fact that Article 48(2) mentions certain elements of the concept of "workers", such as employment and remuneration, shows that the Treaty attributes a Community meaning to that concept. Article 48 to 51 would therefore be deprived of all effect and the abovementioned objectives of the Treaty would be frustrated if the meaning of such a term could be unilaterally fixed and modified by national law.

The concept of "workers" in the said Articles does not therefore relate to national law, but to Community law.'[259]

In the *Rutili Case* the Court of Justice held:

'The concept of public policy must, in the Community context and where, in particular, it is used as a justification for derogating from the fundamental principles of equality of treatment and freedom of movement for workers, be interpreted strictly, so that its scope cannot be determined unilaterally by each Member State without being subject to control by the institutions of the Community.'[260]

In other cases the Court held that 'importation'[261], 'capital goods'[262] and 'persons associated in business'[263] are expressions of Community law, at least for the cases concerned. Their interpretation cannot be left to the discretion of each Member State. The question whether an application for an import licence can be void on the ground of mistake is also a question of Community law.[264]

Under the Convention of 27 September 1968 on Jurisdiction and the Enforcement of Judgement in Civil and Commercial Matters the Court of Justice ruled that the expression 'ordinary appeal' must be determined by Commu-

---

259. *Hoekstra Case* (75/63), 19 March 1964, [1964] ECR 184; 10 Jur. (1964) 384, 385; 10 Rec. (1964) 361, 362, 363; [1964] CMLR 330, 331; CCH para 8022 (p. 7377).
260. *Rutili Case* (36/75), 28 Oct. 1975, consideration 27, [1975] ECR 1231; [1976] 1 CMLR 155; CCH para 8322.
261. *Pfützenreuter Case* (3/74), 28 May 1974, consideration 9, [1974] ECR 597; CCH para 8262.
262. *Capital Goods Case* (51/76), 1 Feb. 1977, consideration 11, [1977] ECR 125; [1977] 1 CMLR 427; CCH para 8409.
263. *Second Hoechst Case* (82/76), 17 Feb. 1977, considerations 6-8, [1977] ECR 346, 347; CCH para 8393.
264. *Hirsch Case* (85/78), 12 Dec. 1978, consideration 12.

nity law and not by the law of any individual Member State.[265] Under the same convention it was held that there should be an independent Community concept of 'the contract of sale on instalment terms'.[266]

§ 142. From these cases two conclusions can be drawn: first, that it is the Court of Justice which decides according to the principle of Community law and the interests of the Communities whether to apply national law or not, and second that national law cannot be applied to those notions contained in EEC provisions which are essential to the purpose for which the provisions were made.

The second conclusion creates a distinction between the essential and the less essential provisions of Community law: in a regulation on workers the notion 'worker' must be defined as a uniform Community concept. On the other hand, concepts such as the legal personality of undertakings involved in a case can be judged according to national law.

It goes without saying that this distinction is vague. For the really uniform application of a law all the notions pertaining to it should be uniformly interpreted. This conclusion reveals that, in practice, minor divergences in the application of Community law are accepted for practical reasons: it would be impossible to replace all the notions used in Community law by uniform Community concepts. As long as there are differences between national legal orders such minor discrepancies must be accepted, as it must be accepted, for instance, that undertakings are subject to different levels of taxation.

Furthermore, the distinction drawn between notions which are essential to Community law and those which are not is unreliable and lacks permanency as issues which are not essential today may become so tomorrow.

§ 143. A special situation where national law must be taken into account arose from the *Walt Wilhelm Case* in which the Court of Justice ruled that both the national courts and the Community court must take account of prior penal sanctions imposed by other courts (see above § 64 and below § 549). This means that the Court of Justice will have to take national case-law on penal sanctions into consideration.

§ 144. The Court of Justice will not apply national law which conflicts with Community law. Though according to the law of her domicile *Jeanne Airola* was of Italian nationality the Court considered her to be Belgian for the sake of the expatriation allowance granted to Community staff members. In doing so the Court held:

'In the present case the applicant, on her marriage, had the nationality of her husband conferred on her without the right to renounce it but by an express declaration she retained her Belgian nationality of origin.

265. *Industrial Diamond Supplies Case* (43/77), 22 Nov. 1977, consideration 28, [1977] ECR 2188: [1978] 1 CMLR 365; CCH para 8453.
266. *Bertrand Case* (150/77), 21 June 1978, consideration 19, [1978] ECR 1446; [1978] 3 CMLR 509.

Consequently, in applying the provision in question, the applicant's Italian nationality has not to be taken into account.'[267]

III. INCORPORATION IN THE NATIONAL LEGAL ORDER

A. NEED FOR INCORPORATION

§ 145. An individual lives in different communities, large and small, at the same time. He forms part of local, provincial, national, supranational and universal groups of people. Each of these groups need their own rules of law. Some subjects can be best regulated at the local level, others at the provincial, national or supranational level. With the rapid development of better communications there is an increasing need to make rules for larger communities. For example, problems relating to air-traffic and space communications can only be sensibly regulated on the universal plane.[268]

One could envision that each of these communities has its own legal system with a complete set of legal rules and with courts for the interpretation and application of those rules. Our social organisation, however, is not that perfect. One can indeed find final rules for each of the levels mentioned, but barring a few minor exceptions, there is only one judicial system for their interpretation and application: the system at the national level. Local and provincial courts form part of the national court system. The universal court — the International Court of Justice in The Hague — has so little power that it cannot properly perform the function of applying universal rules of law. When a universal rule of law is to be applied in a dispute between individuals, the national courts will take this upon themselves and in practice will autonomously interpret the universal rules involved.

National courts apply a range of legal orders. The examination of local and provincial rules by national courts causes no great problems, but the subjection of rules of wider legal orders to national courts is illogical and therefore problematic. How can a court apply rules of law which pertain to a larger body of people than the court itself? The answer much depends on the role which is to be attributed to courts. If a court is to be construed as a national instrument charged with the enforcement of the national legal order and in any way directly answerable to the national State, then a problem is indeed engendered. If a court is, on the other hand, an instrument of 'the Law', charged with doing justice independently of any governmental authority, then it is much less problematical to entrust that court with the application and interpretation of rules stemming from a wider legal order.

§ 146. The national courts, as has been stated above, have to apply a number of legal orders. As local, provincial and national legal orders are hierarchically

---

267. *Airola Case* (21/74), 20 Feb. 1975, considerations 4, 5, 9-14, [1975] ECR 228, 229.
268. See H.G. Schermers, *Problemen van bovennationaal bestuur*, Kluwer 1965.

connected they may be regarded as one; but the Community legal order and the international legal order are clearly distinct.

For a court it may be difficult to apply different legal orders at the same time. In all national legal systems the attempt has therefore been made to link these legal orders together, either into one integrated whole or at least into a clear hierarchical system. As the application of the national legal order is by far the most important function of all national judiciaries, the approach has been to try in some way or other to incorporate the application of the other legal orders into the national one.

Such incorporation of international law into the national legal order does not subject international law to national law. The national legal order cannot change the incorporated international provisions, which remain independent and superior rules of law. Incorporation is only for the sake of the execution of the international rules.

For international law, and in this respect this includes Community law, the fact of incorporation in the national legal order is of vital importance. It provides the means for the public and individuals to invoke the rules of those legal orders before a court, which would otherwise be impossible.

§ 147. The manner in which international and Community law has been incorporated into the national legal orders is quite different. This is a result of the different solutions which were found for creating legal rules during the historical development of each legal order.

In early times, the King or some equivalent authority in Republics made the laws both on internal and on external matters. Royal edicts were binding and were applied by the courts irrespective of the question whether the rules in question had been formulated solely for the realm or, in collaboration with other Kings, for a larger body of subjects. No distinction was needed, or made, between national and international law.

During the last century, however, absolute power enjoyed by monarchs has gradually faded away as far as domestic legislation is concerned. National parliaments succeeded in acquiring greater influence, and nowadays no domestic law can be made without the approval of parliament. As far as external relations are concerned, however, Kings, who were gradually to be replaced by the executive branch of Governments, have retained their powers for much longer, and parliamentary influence over international affairs is still considerably weaker than that over domestic affairs. No problems arise in the case of international arrangements of a purely intergovernmental nature, but when international arrangements impinge upon domestic legislation, conflicts may accur. Let it be assumed that the government wants a specific law on the Statute book but is not certain of parliamentary support. Can the government then incorporate such a law into a treaty with other States and thus make it binding within the national legal order?

§ 148. The Member States of the Communities have coped with this problem in different ways. There exists among them two schools which divide international and national law into two separate legal orders. They are therefore called *dualist*. Then there is a third school considering that national law and international law form part of the same legal system; it is therefore called *monist*.

B. TRADITIONAL SYSTEMS OF INCORPORATION

1. Dualism

§ 149. None of the Member States of the European Communities has a completely dualist system in the sense that international law has no effect within the national legal system. Customary international law forms part of the law of the land in all Member States.[269] But in *Britain, Denmark,* and *Ireland* international treaties are not directly applicable. The government may conclude all sorts of international arrangements (only in Denmark is prior parliamentary approval usually required) but in all the States cited they cannot be immediately applied within the national legal order (again there are some exceptions with respect to Denmark[270]). The Irish constitution defines this most clearly:

'The sole and exclusive power of making laws for the State is hereby vested in the Oireachtas: no other legislative authority has power to make laws for the State.'[271]
'No international agreement shall be part of the domestic law of the State save as may be determined by the Oireachtas'.[272]

Under this system the governments cannot make international agreements with binding effect in the national legal order. If such effect is desired, they must introduce national legislation. In any international agreement they must either not engage themselves fully − by merely promising that they will *try* to incorporate the international rules into their national legal orders − or they must postpone ratification of the international agreement until the necessary national legislation has been passed.

In order to introduce an international rule into national law it has to be *transformed* into a national legal rule.

§ 150. The main advantage of this system is that the national parliament retains an unfettered freedom to act. It can autonomously decide whether, and to what extent, it should incorporate the international rule into the national legal order. It can give an absolute refusal or it can make amendments. National parliamentary sovereignty is thereby fully safeguarded.

269. For Britain see Oppenheim-Lauterpacht, *International Law*, 8th Edition, pp. 39-41.
270. See Brinkhorst-Schermers (*op. cit.*, note 83), pp. 175-177.
271. Constitution of the Republic of Ireland, Art. 15 (2), Amos J. Peaslee, *Constitutions of Nations*, Vol. III, Nijhoff 1968, pp. 469.
272. *Idem*, Art. 29 (6), *Idem*, p. 483.

§ 151. The disadvantages are to be felt in the international field:

(1) Transformation takes time. The fact that international rules can only be effective within the national legal order *after* the necessary national legislation has been enacted causes an extra delay of many months to the international treaty-making process which already is inherently too slow.

(2) Parliamentary amendments may change the text as adopted in the international agreement. This leads to discrepancies where uniformity has been the aim.

(3) The international rule has no status of its own in the national legal order. Any future national law will take priority over the law which incorporated the international rule into the national legal order. This is to the detriment of international cooperation as it carries the additional risk of the treaty being violated, even if involuntarily. It may also cause legal uncertainty as regards the faithful application of the international rule of law.

(4) The system cannot be implemented for transforming binding decisions issued by international organizations; first, because they do not usually allow sufficient time for national legislation and second because parliamentary approval of binding decisions is logically inconsistent as parliaments would have no option: they may not amend, they may not even disapprove. Such international decisions are binding irrespective of what any national parliament might decide. This fourth drawback with the system of transformation is of great importance for Community law. It presents one of the strongest arguments militating in favour of why the monist solution is the only acceptable one for Community law.

2. Mitigated dualism

§ 152. In the *Federal Republic of Germany* and in *Italy* the government is not free to adhere to international treaties. Before doing so they must obtain parliamentary approval. Such approval is given by law.

In both these States the general rules of international law are binding and take priority over national legislation[273], but in the field of treaty law they are traditionally dualist. As general rules of international law play only a minor role in international legislation one may still designate both States as dualist. The effects of dualism are mitigated, however, by the rule that the law approving the treaty simultaneously incorporates it into the national legal order.

The Danish constitution also requires parliamentary approval of important treaties[274], but the approval does not incorporate the treaty into Danish law.

The mitigated dualism of Germany and Italy reveals two differences from the British system:

(a) Parliament cannot amend the text which is incorporated in the na-

---

273. Constitution of the Federal Republic of Germany, Art. 25; Constitution of Italy, Art. 10.
274. Constitution of Denmark, Art. 19.

tional legal order. Its only choice is to approve or to reject the text as it stands. If it grants the approval the treaty becomes part of national law and the government is entitled to ratify it; if it does not, the State cannot become a party to the treaty.

(b) As soon as it is adopted, the international engagement forms part of the domestic legal order.

Of the disadvantages mentioned in § 151 the second is precluded whilst the first is greatly diminished. The order two hold true as for the British system.

§ 153. In practice, there is another problem encountered by the mitigated dualist system as applied in Germany and Italy. These two Member States have a Constitutional Court entitled to annul laws which are considered to be in violation of the Constitution. As international agreements have the same status as domestic laws, they are in the same manner subject to constitutional review. [275] This could cause international problems as annulment of an international agreement by the Constitutional Court would normally lead to a breach of an international obligation.

3. Monism

§ 154. France and the Benelux-countries have a monist system. In their constitutional framework international law is part of the legal system which national courts must per se apply. No national measures of transformation are required. This does not necessarily mean that the rules of international law take priority over conflicting rules of national law. They will do so if they are the more recent of the two, but if they are succeeded by subsequent legislation, one of two approaches is possible:

(a) The attitude taken in the *Belgian Fromagerie 'Le Ski' Case* quoted below (§ 165) that the pre-eminence of the international rule is to be derived from the very nature of international law. This notion is so widely adhered to that it almost forms an intrinsic part of the monist system.

(b) The national legislature is the institution most competent to solve conflicts arising between the national and the international legal orders. If it thinks fit to make national provisions which overrule international ones, then the judiciary should not subject this to its review. It must follow the legislature and apply the more recent rule of national law.

§ 155. In *France* where the judiciary is traditionally not entitled to control the legislature the second concept is still occasionally adhered to[276], notwithstanding the system of the French Constitution which provides:

275. See Hans G. Rupp, *Judicial Review of International Agreements: Federal Republic of Germany*, 25 AJCL (1977), pp. 286-302.
276. *See French Semoules Case, Conseil d'Etat*, 1 March 1968, Rec. D 1968, Jurisprudence, p. 285; RTDE 1968, pp. 388-399 and the annotation by Lagrange in Rec. D, 10 April 1968, p. 286, English translation in Brinkhorst-Schermers (*op. cit.*, note 83), pp. 197, 198.

'Treaties or agreements duly ratified or approved shall, upon their publication, have an authority superior to that of laws, subject, for each agreement or treaty, to its application by the other party'.[277]

In *Belgium* the situation was not clear until 1971. In May of that year the Belgian Supreme Court, *Court de Cassation*, opted for the monist system. (see below § 165).

According to the *Luxembourg* Supreme Court (Cour Supérieure de Justice):

'Though it is true that in principle the date of entry into force determines the effect of successive laws, subsequent provisions abrogating previous contrary ones, this cannot be so where the two laws are of different status, that is, where one of them is an international treaty incorporated by enactment into the domestic legislation; such a treaty indeed ranks higher as it derives from a source higher than the will of a municipal body; consequently, where there is a conflict between the provisions of an international treaty and those of a subsequent municipal law, the former must prevail.'[278]

According to the *Dutch* constitution:

'Legal regulations in force within the Kingdom shall not apply if this application should be incompatible with directly effective provisions of agreements entered into either before or after the enactment of the regulations.[279]

§ 156. None of the four States mentioned have so far demonstrated that they are completely monist. In the Netherlands the priority of treaties is limited to those which have direct effect. This may mark a drawback with the system. On the other hand the Dutch Constitution is the only one which provides that international treaties also take priority over provisions of the national Constitution.[280] This priority is not as important as it might seem, however. None of the four States mentioned have provisions for constitutional review by courts. The parliaments have, of course, to take the Constitution into account when they make laws, but once the laws have been enacted, their constitutionality cannot be challenged before the courts. The courts must apply the laws. They have no competence to declare laws unconstitutional. The same will hold for international agreements.

---

277. Constitution of France, Art. 55, Peaslee (*op. cit.*, note 271), p. 323.
278. *Luxembourg Chambre des Métiers Case*, 14 July 1954, Pasicrie Luxembourgeoise XVI p. 150; Brinkhorst-Schermers (*op. cit.*, note 83), pp. 221, 222.
279. Constitution of the Netherlands, Art. 66, Peaslee (*op. cit.*, note 271) p. 660. On this article see L.J. Brinkhorst and J.G. Lammers, *The impact of international law, including European Community law on the Netherlands' legal order*, in *Introduction to Dutch law for foreign lawyers*, Kluwer 1978, pp. 561-584.
280. Constitution of the Netherlands, Art. 60, idem p. 659.

§ 157. The main advantages of the monist system are its greater logic — the legal rules of a larger community should always prevail over those of its parts — and its reinforcement of international law. As international law has effectively no judiciary of its own, its success and progress depend on its application within the national legal orders. Its one defect is the undemocratic way in which international law is formed. Decisions of democratically elected parliaments may be set aside by rules established by bureaucratic entities. The European Communities are trying to cope with this shortcoming by strengthening the role of the European Parliament in making Community law.

C. THE INCORPORATION OF COMMUNITY LAW[281]

1. Treaty provisions

§ 158. The Community Treaties do not expressly provide how they were subsequently to be incorporated into the national legal orders of the Member States. At the time of their drafting this was left to the discretion of the legal systems of the Member States. For regulations it was expressly provided, however, that they shall be binding in their entirety and '*directly applicable*' in all Member States. [282] The words 'directly applicable' must mean that no transformation measures are allowed. Each of the national legal orders must accept them as immediately binding even though they stem from an external source. For regulations the Treaties prescribe a monist system. The Court of Justice expressed this in the *Tasca Case* in which it held:

'According to the second paragraph of Article 189 of the Treaty a regulation "shall have general application" and "shall be directly applicable in all Member States". Accordingly, by reason of its very nature and its function in the system of the sources of Community law it produces immediate effects and as such is capable of conferring on parties rights which the national courts must protect'. [283]

2. Attitude of the Court of Justice

§ 159. The Court of Justice has repeatedly ruled that it considers the relationship between national law and Community law to be monist. There can be

281. See also J.P. Warner, *The Relationship between European Community Law and the National Laws of Member States*, 93 LQR (1977), pp. 349-366; G.M. Borchardt, *Structures d'accueil, Beschouwingen over de verhouding nationaal recht — gemeenschapsrecht in de zes oude Lid-Staten van de Europese Gemeenschappen*, No. 3/78 Studentenscripties, Asser Instituut, the Hague 1977; Dominique Carreau, *Droit communautaire et droits nationaux; concurrence ou primauté?* 14 RTDE (1978), pp. 381-418.
282. EEC Art. 189 (2).
283. *Tasca Case* (65/75), 26 Feb. 1976, consideration 16, [1976] ECR 308; [1977] 2 CMLR 203; CCH para 8354.

no transformation of Community law into national law. It must be of direct use to Community citizens within their national legal orders, and in the case of a conflict arising Community law must take priority over national law irrespective of the date when the latter legislation was adopted.[284]

§ 160. In the *Van Gend en Loos Case* the Court of Justice held:

'The objective of the EEC Treaty, which is to establish a Common Market, the functioning of which is of direct concern to interested parties in the Community, implies that this Treaty is more than an agreement which merely creates mutual obligations between the contracting states. This view is confirmed by the preamble to the Treaty which refers not only to governments but to peoples. It is also confirmed more specifically by the establishment of institutions endowed with sovereign rights, the exercise of which affects Member States and also their citizens. Furthermore, it must be noted that the nationals of the states brought together in the Community are called upon to cooperate in the functioning of this Community through the intermediary of the European Parliament and the Economic and Social Committee.

In addition the task assigned to the Court of Justice under Article 177, the object of which is to secure uniform interpretation of the Treaty by national courts and tribunals, confirms that the states have acknowledged that Community law has an authority which can be invoked by their nationals before those courts and tribunals.

The conclusion to be drawn from this is that the Community constitutes a new legal order of international law for the benefit of which the states have limited their sovereign rights, albeit within limited fields, and the subjects of which comprise not only Member States but also their nationals. Independently of the legislation of Member States, Community law therefore not only imposes obligations on individuals but is also intended to confer upon them rights which become part of their legal heritage. These rights arise not only where they are expressly granted by the Treaty, but also by reason of obligations which the Treaty imposes in a clearly defined way upon individuals as well as upon the Member States and upon the institutions of the Community'.[285]

§ 161. *The Costa Enel Case* involved an Italian nationalization law which was adopted after the law approving the EEC Treaty. When the Justice of the Peace in Milan requested a preliminary ruling on the question whether the EEC Treaty permitted such a nationalization law the Italian government intervened submitting that the request for a preliminary ruling was 'absolutely

---

284. *Pigs Marketing Case* (83/78), 29 Nov. 1978, consideration 69, [1979] 1 CMLR 204. On the question of priority see also Peter Hay and Vicki Thomson, *The Community Court and Supremacy of Community Law: a progress report*, 8 Vanderbilt Journal of Transnational Law (1975), pp. 651-670.
285. *Van Gend en Loos Case* (26/62), 5 Feb. 1963, [1963] ECR 12; 9 Jur. (1963) 22-24; 9 Rec. (1963) 22-24; [1963] CMLR 129, 130; CCH para 8008 (pp. 7214-7215).

inadmissible' as the Italian Court could not apply the Italian law approving the EEC Treaty and could, therefore, not request a preliminary ruling, since the nationalization law was of a more recent date. If the latter law violated the EEC Treaty then the Commission should act under EEC Article 169. The Italian court had no choice; under Italian law it had to apply the more recent of the two laws.

The Court of Justice replied:

'The Italian Government submits that the request of the Giudice Conciliatore is "absolutely inadmissible", inasmuch as a national court which is obliged to apply a national law cannot avail itself of Article 177.

By contrast with ordinary international treaties, the EEC Treaty has created its own legal system which, on the entry into force of the Treaty, became an integral part of the legal systems of the Member States and which their courts are bound to apply.

By creating a Community of unlimited duration, having its own institutions, its own personality, its own legal capacity and capacity of representation on the international plane and, more particularly, real powers stemming from a limitation of sovereignty or a transfer of powers from the States to the Community, the Member States have limited their sovereign rights, albeit within limited fields, and have thus created a body of law which binds both their nationals and themselves.

The integration into the laws of each Member State of provisions which derive from the Community, and more generally the terms and the spirit of the Treaty, make it impossible for the States, as a corollary, to accord precedence to a unilateral and subsequent measure over a legal system accepted by them on a basis of reciprocity. Such a measure cannot therefore be inconsistent with that legal system. The executive force of Community law cannot vary from one State to another in deference to subsequent domestic laws, without jeopardizing the attainment of the objectives of the Treaty set out in Article 5(2) and giving rise to the discrimination prohibited by Article 7.

The obligations undertaken under the Treaty establishing the Community would not be unconditional, but merely contingent, if they could be called in question by subsequent legislative acts of the signatories. Wherever the Treaty grants the States the right to act unilaterally, it does this by clear and precise provisions (for example Articles 15, 93(3), 223, 224 and 225). Applications, by Member States for authority to derogate from the Treaty are subject to a special authorization procedure (for example Articles 8(4), 17(4), 25, 26, 73, the third subparagraph of Article 93(2), and 226) which would lose their purpose if the Member States could renounce their obligations by means of an ordinary law.

The precedence of Community law is confirmed by Article 189, whereby a regulation "shall be binding" and "directly applicable in all Member States". The provision, which is subject to no reservation, would be quite meaningless if a State could unilaterally nullify its effects by means of a legislative measure which could prevail over Community law.

It follows from all these observations that the law stemming from the Treaty, an independent source of law, could not, because of its special and original nature, be overridden by domestic legal provisions, however framed, without being deprived of its character as Community law and without the legal basis of the Community itself being called into question.

The transfer by the States from their domestic legal system to the Community legal system of the rights and obligations arising under the Treaty carries with it a permanent limitation of their sovereign rights, against which a subsequent unilateral act incompatible with the concept of the Community cannot prevail. Consequently Article 177 is to be applied regardless of any domestic law, whenever questions relating to the interpretation of the Treaty arise.'[286]

§ 162.   The monist view espoused by the Court of Justice means that Community law must be applied directly within the national legal order in so far as it has direct effect. The entry into force and the application of a directly effective Community rule are independent of any measure of reception into national law. In particular, such measure cannot have any influence on the date from which the Community rule becomes operative.[287] Member States may neither adopt, nor allow national organizations having legislative power to adopt any measure which would conceal the Community nature and effect of any such provision from the persons to whom it applies.[288] Community rules must apply *as such* and therefore without any transformation into a national legislative act.

The Court of Justice is strict in its requirements that Community law must be applied with priority over national law without any restriction. The Italian Constitutional Court has accepted the direct application, without transformation, of Community law within the Italian legal order, and its priority over national law.[289] But it could not accept that Italian judges might refuse to apply Italian laws, for whatever reason, without prior reference to the Constitutional Court. Under the Italian constitution the control of the validity of laws is the express task of the Constitutional Court. This Court therefore ruled that Italian judges who consider that an Italian law may conflict with a rule of Community law, must being the question of the validity of the Italian law before the Constitutional Court.[290] In such a situation an Italian Court,

286. *Costa Enel Case* (6/64), 15 July 1964, [1964] ECR 593, 594; 10 Jur. (1964) 1218-1220; 10 Rec. (1964) 1158-1160; [1964] CMLR 455, 456; CCH para 8023 (pp. 7390, 7391). For transformation of regulations see also below § 288.
287. *Variola Case* (34/73), 10 Oct. 1973, consideration 15, [1973] 2 ECR 992; CCH para 8226.
288. *Amsterdam Bulb Case* (50/76), 2 Feb. 1977, consideration 7, [1977] ECR 146; [1977] 2 CMLR 225; CCH para 8391; *Zerbone Case* (94/77), 31 Jan. 1978, consideration 26, [1978] ECR 116; CCH para 8464.
289. *Italian Frontini Case* (no. 183), *Corte Costituzionale*, 27 Dec. 1973, [1974] 2 CMLR 383-390; Brinkhorst-Schermers (*op. cit.*, note 83), pp. 213-217.
290. *Italian ICIC Case* (no. 232 GC III) *Corte Costituzionale*, 22, 23 Oct. 1975, Brinkhorst-Schermers (*op. cit.*, note 83) pp. 217-220; EuR 1976, pp. 246-253; RTDE 1976, pp. 396-403; CMLRev 1976, pp. 530-536.

however, requested a preliminary ruling of the Court of Justice on the question whether national laws in conflict with Community law must be forthwith disregarded without waiting for a decision of the Constitutional Court, in particular because such decision would, under Italian law, have no retroactive effect. The Court of Justice held that every national court must set aside any provision of national law which may conflict with it, whether prior to or subsequent to the Community rule, and that any national provision witholding the power to do so from a national court is incompatible with those requirements which are the very essence of Community law. The Italian Court should not wait for a decision of the Italian Constitutional Court. [291]

This unrestricted priority only exists with respect to those provisions that do not require further legislation. It is of the greatest importance, therefore, whether individual provisions of the Treaties and of Community acts have direct effect or not (see below § 175-192).

3. Attitude of national judiciaries [292]

a. FRANCE, LUXEMBOURG, NETHERLANDS

§ 163. For the national courts in the monist Member States (see above § 154) acceptance of the abovementioned view of the Court of Justice caused no great problems. [293] As all rules of international law were accepted in the national legal order without requiring any specific national measure and as priority was granted to them over national law, the acceptance of Community law as part of the national legal system and the granting of priority to Community law over national law was nothing new or revolutionary. Only in France have problems occasionally arisen due to the reluctance of the courts to leave statutes unapplied even if they are contrary to Community law. As the courts are traditionally not permitted to question the legality of statutes approved by parliament they find it difficult to set them aside in the event of a conflict with Community law. [294]

§ 163a. Generally the judiciaries of France, Luxembourg and the Netherlands loyally apply Community law, with one serious exception: the French Conseil d'Etat. Being used to supervising all French administrative courts and

291. *Second Simmenthal Case* (106/77), 9 March 1978, considerations 21-24, [1978] ECR 644. On this case, see Neville March Hunnings, *Rival Constitutional Courts*, CMLRev (1978), pp. 479-487.
292. See also Gerhard Bebr, *How supreme is Community law in the national courts*, 11 CMLRev (1974), pp. 3-37.
293. See Eric E. Bergsten, *Community Law in the French Courts*, Nijhoff, The Hague 1973; Manfred Simon, *Enforcement by French Courts of European Community Law*, The Law Quarterly Review 1974, pp. 467-485 and the national reports to the Sixth Congress of FIDE, Luxembourg 24-26 May 1973.
294. But the Cour de Cassation did accept the primacy of the Community Treaties over subsequent statutes, see *French Weigel Case*, 24 May 1975, Rec. D 1975, p. 497; 1 ELRev (1976), p. 256. See Dirk Baumgartner, *Der Vorrang des Gemeinschaftsrechts vor französischem Recht*, 92 Deutscher Verwaltungsblatt (1977), pp. 70-76.

tribunals this court seems to consider itself entitled to supervise the Court of Justice of the European Communities as well. In the *French Cohn Bendit Case* is disagreed with the Court of Justice that directives under EEC Article 56 may have direct effect and it annulled a decision of the administrative tribunal in Paris which requested a preliminary ruling on the intergration of such a directive. It founded this annulment on the ground that in its opinion the directive could not have direct effect and could, therefore, not be invoked before a French court. For this reason Community law was not applicable in the case at hand and the request for a preliminary ruling was unfounded.[295]

§ 164. Another problem which the French courts encountered was the restriction laid down in the French Constitution that the priority of treaties is subject to their application by the other party. For the application of Community law this restriction was set aside in the *French Cafés Jaques Vabre Case* in which the *Cour de Cassation* held:

'But in the Community legal order the failure of a Member State of the EEC to comply with its obligations under the Treaty of 25 March 1957 is subject to the procedure laid down by Article 170 of that Treaty and so the plea of lack of reciprocity cannot be made before the national courts.'[296]

b. BELGIUM

§ 165. The situation in Belgium was not entirely clear when the Communities were established. Many authors and courts considered Belgium to adhere to the mitigated dualist system, but there was no recent case of the Supreme Court confirming that supposition. It was only in 1971 that the Belgian Supreme Court, the *Cour de Cassation*, took a clear position. In the *Belgian Fromagerie 'Le Ski' Case* it held:

'Even if assent to a treaty, as required by Article 68(2) of the Constitution, is given in the form of a statute, the legislative power, by giving this assent, is not carrying out a normative function. The conflict which exists between a legal norm established by an international treaty and a norm established by a subsequent statute, is not a conflict between two statutes.

The rule that a statute repeals a previous statute in so far as there is a conflict between the two, does not apply in the case of a conflict between a treaty and a statute.

In the event of a conflict between a norm of domestic law and a norm of international law which produces direct effects in the internal legal system, the rule established by the treaty shall prevail. The primacy of the treaty results from the very nature of international treaty law.

295. *French Cohn Bendit Case*, No. 11 604, 22 Dec. 1978.
296. *French Cafés Jacques Vabre Case, Cour de Cassation*, 24 May 1975, [1975] CMLR 369; 13 CMLRev (1976) pp. 128-132 with note by Gerhard Bebr; Brinkhorst-Schermers (*op. cit.*, note 83), pp. 202, 203.

This is *a fortiori* the case when a conflict exists, as in the present case, between a norm of internal law and a norm of Community law.

The reason is that the treaties which have created Community law have instituted a new legal system in whose favour the Member States have restricted the exercise of their sovereign powers in the areas determined by those treaties.'[297]

In this case the Belgian Supreme Court opted for the monist system, not only as regards the relationship between national law and Community law, but also as a general rule for applying international law within the Belgian legal order.

c. GERMANY AND ITALY

(i) Priority

§ 166. The two original Member States which had a mitigated dualist system recognised the special position of the Community legal order as distinct from traditional international law. In the *German Handelsgesellschaft Case* the German Constitutional Court, the *Bundesverfassungsgericht*, held:

'This Court — in this respect in agreement with the law developed by the European Court of Justice — adheres to its settled view that Community law is neither a component part of the national legal system nor international law, but forms an independent system of law flowing from an autonomous legal source.

...

In principle, the two legal spheres stand independent of and side by side one another in their validity, and, in particular, the competent Community organs, including the European Court of Justice, have to rule on the binding force, construction and observance of Community law, and the competent national organs on the binding force, construction and observance of the constitutional law of the Federal Republic of Germany.'[298]

In Germany the direct applicability of Community law, which obviates the need for transformation, and its priority have been based on Article 24(1) of the German Constitution which provides that sovereign powers can be transferred to intergovernmental organizations. In the *German Lütticke Case* the German Constitutional Court, the *Bundesverfassungsgericht*, held:

'For by ratification of the EEC Treaty, in accordance with Article 24, para. 1, of the Basic Law, an independent legal order of the EEC has come

297. *Belgian Fromagerie 'Le Ski' Case, Cour de Cassation*, 21 May 1971, [1972] CMLR 373; Brinkhorst-Schermers (*op. cit.*, note 83), pp. 173-175.
298. *German Handelsgesellschaft Case, Bundesverfassungsgericht*, 29 May 1974, [1974] 2 CMLR 549; Brinkhorst-Schermers (*op. cit.*, note 83); pp. 186-191.

into being which has effects on the domestic legal order and is to be applied by the German courts.

The decision of the European Court of Justice interpreting Article 95 of the Treaty, pronounced within the scope of its competence according to Article 177 of the EEC Treaty, was binding on the Bundesfinanzhof. Article 24, para. 1, of the Basic Law, when correctly interpreted, lays down not only that the delegation of sovereign powers to international institutions is admissable, but also that the sovereign acts of their organs, as in this case the judgement of the European Court of Justice, are to be recognised by the originally exclusive holder of sovereignty.

Proceeding from this legal situation, the German courts, since the coming into effect of the Common Market, must apply also those rules of law which, though attributable to an independent, supranational sovereign power, nevertheless display direct effect in the domestic sphere and overrule and set aside incompatible national law on the basis of their interpretation by the European Court of Justice; for only in this way can the subjective rights accorded to the citizens of the Common Market be realised.'[299]

§ 167. Similarly in Italy, where the transfer of sovereignty to the Community is founded on Article 11 of the Constitution, the Constitutional Court, the *Corte Costituzionale*, held in the *Italian Frontini Case*:

'Fundamental requirements of equality and legal certainty demand that the Community norms, which cannot be characterised as a source of international law, nor of foreign law, nor of internal law of the individual States, ought to have full compulsory efficacy and direct application in all the Member States, without the necessity of reception and implementation statues, as acts having the force and value of statue in every country of the Community, to the extent of entering into force everywhere simultaneously and receiving equal and uniform application to all their addressees'.

The Constitutional Court continued by saying that Community law should not be '*the subject of state-issued provisions which reproduce them*' in national law.[300]

§ 168. The position of the two Constitutional Courts means that in Germany as well as in Italy Community law is applied directly and cannot be set aside by subsequent national laws. The two Constitutional Courts differ, however, as to the effect of such subsequent national laws. In Germany every court is entitled not to apply national laws which are contrary to Community law. In

---

299. *German Lütticke Case, Bundesverfassungsgericht*, 9 June 1971, AWD 1971, pp. 418-420; Brinkhorst-Schermers (*op. cit.*, note 83), pp. 185, 186. This was confirmed in the *German Handelsgesellschaft Case*, 29 May 1974, [1974] 2 CMLR 549.
300. *Italian Frontini Case* (no. 183), *Corte Costituzionale*, 27 Dec. 1973, [1974] 2 CMLR 386, 387; Brinkhorst-Schermers (*op. cit.*, note 83), pp. 213-217.

case of doubt it is to ask for a preliminary ruling on the interpretation of Community law (see below § 554-625). In Italy, on the other hand, laws must be applied unless the Constitutional Court decides otherwise. In the case of a conflict with Community law the Italian courts must bring the question of the legitimacy of the national law before the Constitutional Court, which then decides. The Court of Justice rejected this system for the case of conflicts with rules of Community law (see above § 162).

(ii) **Constitutionality** [301]

§ **169.** In Germany and Italy there also arises the question of constitutional review (see above § 153). Can Community law be set aside if it violates the Constitution?

In Germany constitutional complaints, *Verfassungsbeschwerden*, can be raised against any government act allegedly violating the Constitution by anybody whose rights are directly affected. [302] In the *German Constitutional Rights Case* the German Constitutional Court held that constitutional complaints can be raised only against acts of German public authorities and not against acts of the Communities. [303] This procedure therefore cannot affect Community law.

The Italian Constitutional Court expressed the same opinion when it held in the *Italian Frontini Case*:

'The constitutional provisions govern solely the legislative activity of the organs of the Italian State, and by their nature are not referable or applicable to the activity of the Community organs, which are governed by the Rome Treaty, which constitutes the constitution (*lo statuto fondamentale*) of the Community'. [304]

§ **170.** There remains the question of the control of the constitutionality of laws, the *Konkrete Normen Kontrolle*. Can national courts dispute the validity of Community law if they consider it to be contrary to the national constitution? On this question the Italian Constitutional Court held:

'It should, on the other hand, be mentioned that the legislative competence of the organs of the EEC is laid down by Article 189 of the Rome Treaty as limited to matter concerning economic relations, *i.e.* matter with regard to

301. For a survey of literature, see Manfred Zuleeg, *Neuere Literatur zum Europarecht: Die Europäischen Gemeinschaften und nationales Verfassungsrecht*, 102 AöR (1977), pp. 298-316.
302. *Grundgesetz*, Art. 93(1) No. 4a. See Fuss (*op. cit.*, note 82), p. 65. See also Jürgen Jekewitz, *Verfassungsbeschwerden wegen Verstoßes auch gegen Gemeinschaftsrecht?* 13 EuR (1978), pp. 26-31.
303. *German Constitutional Rights Case, Bundesverfassungsgericht* 18 Oct. 1967, AWD 1967, pp. 477, 478; Eur 1968, pp. 134-137; 5 CMLRev. (1967-68) pp. 483, 484; Brinkhorst-Schermers (*op. cit.*, note 83) p. 183. This ruling was confirmed in the *German Handelsgesellschaft Case, Bundesverfassungsgericht* 29 May 1974, see below § 171.
304. *Italian Frontini Case* (No. 183), *Corte Costituzionale*, 27 Dec. 1973, [1974] 2 CMLR 386, 387; Brinkhorst-Schermers (*op. cit.*, note 83), p. 216.

which our Constitution lays down the statute monopoly (*riserva di legge*) or the reference to statute (*rinvio alla legge*), but the precise and exact provisions of the Treaty provide a safe guarantee, so that it appears difficult to form even abstractly the hypothesis that a Community regulation can have an effect in civil, ethico-social, or political relations through which provisions conflict with the Italian Constitution. It is hardly necessary to add that by Article 11 of the Constitution limitations of sovereignty are allowed solely for the purpose of the ends indicated therein, and it should therefore be excluded that such limitations of sovereignty, concretely set out in the Rome Treaty, signed by countries whose systems are based on the principle of the rule of law and guarantee the essential liberties of citizens, can nevertheless give the organs of the EEC an unacceptable power to violate the fundamental principles of our constitutional order or the inalienable rights of man. And it is obvious that if ever Article 189 had to be given such an aberrant interpretation, in such a case the guarantee would always be assured that this Court would control the continuing compatibility of the Treaty with the above-mentioned fundamental principles. But it should be excluded that this Court can control individual regulations, given that Article 134 of the Constitution relates solely to the review of constitutionality of statutes and acts having statutory force of the state and of the regions, and Community regulations, in the present context, are not such.'[305]

§ 171.   The German Constitutional Court was more hesitant. In the *German Handelsgesellschaft Case* it held:

'The part dealing with fundamental rights is an inalienable essential feature of the current Constitution of the Federal Republic of Germany and one which forms part of its basic constitutional structure. Article 24 of the Constitution (which permits transfer of sovereignty to international organizations) does not without reservation allow it to be subjected to qualifications. In this, the present state of integration of the Community is of crucial importance. The Community still lacks a democratically legitimated parliament directly elected by general suffrage which possesses legislative powers and to which the Community organs empowered to legislate are fully responsible on a political level; it still lacks in particular a codified catalogue of fundamental rights, the substance of which is reliably and unambiguously fixed for the future in the same way as the substance of the Constitution and therefore allows a comparison and a decision as to whether, at the time in question, the Community law standard with regard to fundamental rights generally binding in the Community is adequate in the long term measured by the standard of the Constitution with regard to fundamental rights (without prejudice to possible amendments) in such a way that there is no exceeding the limitation indicated, set by Article 24 of the Constitution. As long as this legal certainty, which is not guaranteed

305.   *Idem*, p. 389, respectively pp. 216, 217.

merely by the decisions of the European Court of Justice, favourable though these have been to fundamental rights, is not achieved in the course of the further integration of the Community, the reservation derived from Article 24 of the Constitution applies. What is involved is, therefore, a legal difficulty arising exclusively from the Community's continuing integration process, which is still in flux and which will end with the present transitional phase.

Provisionally, therefore, in the hypothetical case of a conflict between Community law and a part of national constitutional law or, more precisely, of the guarantees of fundamental rights in the Constitution, there arises the question of which system of law takes precedence, that is, ousts the other. In this conflict of norms, the guarantee of fundamental rights in the Constitution prevails as long as the competent organs of the Community have not removed the conflict of norms in accordance with the Treaty mechanism.'[306]

§ 172. From the opinion expressed in the above quotation the German Constitutional Court drew the following conclusion with regard to the jurisdiction of the European Court of Justice and of the German Constitutional Court:

'In the framework of this jurisdiction, the European Court determines the content of Community law with binding effect for all the Member States. Accordingly, under the terms of Article 177 of the Treaty, the courts of the Federal Republic of Germany have to obtain the ruling of the European Court before they raise the question of the compatibility of the norm of Community law which is relevant to their decision with guarantees of fundamental rights in the Constitution.

As emerges from the foregoing outline, the Bundesverfassungsgericht never rules on the validity or invalidity of a rule of Community law. At most, it can come to the conclusion that such a rule cannot be applied by the authorities or courts of the Federal Republic of Germany in so far as it conflicts with a rule of the Constitution relating to fundamental rights.'[307]

Three of the eight judges who decided the case dissented. In Community circles the *German Handelsgesellschaft Case* has not been well received.[308]

The Commission has written in its Eighth General Report:

'This ruling is contrary to Community law — and in particular to the principle of its autonomy and of its primacy over national law, including constitutional law — and to all the relevant case law of the European Court.

---

306. *German Handelsgesellschaft Case, Bundesverfassungsgericht*,29 May 1974, [1974] 2 CMLR 551, 552; Brinkhorst-Schermers (*op. cit.*, note 83), p. 189.
307. *Idem.*
308. For an extensive commentary on the case see Fuss (*op. cit.*, note 82) pp. 126-200; for a shorter one see Hans Peter Ipsen, *BverfG versus EuGH re 'Grundrechte'*, 10 EuR (1975) pp. 1-19; Meinhardt Hilf, Eckart Klein and Albert Bleckmann, *Sekundäres Gemeinschaftsrecht und deutsche Grundrechte, zum Beschluß des Bundesverfassungsgerichts vom 29. Mai 1974*, 35 ZaöRV (1975), pp. 51-107.

Accordingly it is a dangerous threat to the unity of Community law and creates uncertainty as to the latter's uniform application.

By claiming the power to verify the compatibility of Community secondary legislation with the fundamental rights in the Basic Law, the Constitutional Court is impugning the exclusive jurisdiction of the Court of Justice to ensure that in the interpretation and application of the treaties the law is observed (Article 164 of the EEC Treaty).

The Commission has informed the German Government of its grave concern.'[309]

§ 173. The Court of Justice will not be easily moved to interpret Community law in such a way that it could violate a fundamental rule of the German Constitution (see above § 47). In practice, the harm done by the *German Handelsgesellschaft Case* will therefore not so much relate to the non application of Community law in Germany, but, what is of greater practical significance, to the possibility that parties to a case will challenge the constitutionality of Community law. German courts will then discuss the question in order to decide whether or not they should bring the matter before the Constitutional Court.[310] This will delay the full application of Community law in Germany and it will detract from its authority.

d. BRITAIN, DENMARK, IRELAND

§ 174. At the time of their accession to the Communities the new Member States enacted several constitutional or legal provisions which grant a specific status to Community law.

Ireland provided the most unequivocal support for Community law by amending Article 29 of its Constitution which, after stipulating that Ireland should be a Member of the Communities, now provides:

'No provision of the Constitution invalidates laws enacted, acts done or measures adopted by the State necessitated by the obligations of membership of the Communities or prevents laws enacted, acts done or measures adopted by the Communities, or institutions thereof, from having the force of law in the State.'[311]

The Danish Constitution provides for a delegation of powers to international authorities and therefore offers a similar basis for the superiority of the Community legal order as the constitutions of Germany and Italy.[312]

In Britain Article 2(1) of the European Communities Act provides:

309. Eighth General Report on the Activities of the European Communities (1974), para 465, p. 270.
310. See, e.g. , *German Balkan Case, Finanzgericht Berlin*, 27 Feb. 1976.
311. Third Amendment to the Irish Constitution (1972).
312. Constitution of Denmark, Art. 20.

'All such rights, powers, liabilities, obligations and restrictions from time to time created or arising by or under the Treaties, and all such remedies and procedures from time to time provided for by or under the Treaties, as in accordance with the Treaties are without further enactment to be given legal effect or used in the United Kingdom shall be recognised and available in law, and be enforced, allowed and followed accordingly.'[313]

This provision grants to Community law a strong position in English law. English courts will not easily accept an interpretation of a statute which causes a conflict with Community law. So far there has been no clear indication that in such a case the position of Community law would differ from that of international law. In the *English Felixtowe Dock Case* before the Court of Appeal the Master of the Rolls stated in an *obiter dictum*:

'Once the Bill is passed by Parliament and becomes a Statute, that will dispose of all this discussion about the [EEC] Treaty. These courts will then have to abide by the Statute without regard to the Treaty at all.'[314]

D. PROVISIONS HAVING DIRECT EFFECT

1. The notion 'direct effect'[315]

§ 175. Many legal rules are of a preparatory or general nature and need further legislation before they can be applied to individual citizens. Neither in the national, nor in the international, nor in the Community legal order are such legal rules capable of directly regulating the legal position of parties before courts. This does not preclude their indirect effect. In coming to decisions courts should pay attention to all relevant rules of law even when they do not directly govern the situation at hand.

Other legal rules need no further legislation and are therefore called '*directly effective*'. (In this context the expression 'directly applicable' has been deliberately avoided as that has been used for a different purpose in EEC Article 189 — see above § 158 — with respect to all EEC regulations including those which have no direct effect). It is the *need* for further legislation that is decisive. Sometimes further legislation has been enacted although it was not needed, sometimes it was even passed with the purpose of postponing the

---

313. See Mitchell, Kuipers and Gall in 9 CMLRev. (1972) pp. 141-144; Philip Allott, *Le Royaume Uni et le droit des Communautés Européennes*, 19 AFDI (1973), pp. 36-101.
314. *English Felixtowe Dock Case*, 29 July 1976, [1976] 2 CMLR 664, 665. See also Lawrence Collins, *Remedies in the United Kingdom: Some Practical Problems of Direct Applicability* in Jacobs (*op. cit.*, note 82), pp. 161-179.
315. A. Bleckmann, *L'effet direct des normes et décisions de droit européen*, in: Les recours des individus devant les instances nationales en cas de violation du droit européen, Colloque Bruxelles, 24 et 25 Avril 1975; Walter van Gerven, *The Legal Protection of Private Parties in the Law of the European Economic Community*, in Jacobs (*op. cit.*, note 82), pp. 4-9; Marc Maresceau, *De directe werking van het Europese Gemeenschapsrecht*, Europese Monografie No 24, Kluwer 1978.

direct effect of a Treaty provision. The Court of Justice takes the view that such unnecessary further legislation cannot alter the direct effect of a Treaty provision. [316]

Whether a rule has direct effect or not may depend on the person involved. Many rules have direct effect for the Member States (e.g. obliging them to pass particular legislation) whilst they have no such direct effect for individuals. In fact the question whether a rule has direct effect or not depends as much on the persons involved as on the rules themselves. In Community law, however, the notion 'direct effect' is usually construed in a narrow sense, covering only those provisions which have direct effect for all citizens, who may, in factual terms, be affected. This makes the notion into an absolute one: a provision has either direct effect for everybody, or it has no direct effect at all. In principle we will use the notion in this sense, lending support to the opinion of Van Gerven, namely that: *the direct effect of a provision depends mainly on whether the courts, and finally the Court of Justice, feel able and sufficiently equipped to apply the provision without any further act by the authorities of the Community or of its Member States.* [317] We will see, however, that even when a rule is capable of being applied by the courts without any such further act, the circumstances may not be such that it can be applied equally with respect to all persons affected by it. The questions whether a person knows the rule, or should have been able to know it, will, for example, be relevant.

§ 176. Though the question whether a particular rule of law has direct effect or not may be met in any — national or international — legal order, it is of special relevance to the relationship between Community law and national law. When the former is incorporated into the national legal orders of the Member States, the directly effective rules are the ones which are imposed upon the national legal orders. They must be applied as part of those legal orders and with priority over the national legal rules.

The directly effective provisions of Community law are the backbone of the Community legal system and the most important remnant of the supranational ideals of the Community's 'founding fathers'. Governments faced with the need of dealing with pressing problems of the day tend to accord overriding importance to their solution; they are often prepared to clear them up at any cost even if the solution thereby leads to a violation of international obligations. International law offers many examples of obligations entered into, and subsequently not fulfilled due to some supposed urgent national interest. As there is no recourse to sanctions and other Governments are equally negligent, the international community has insufficient means of pro-

---

316. See e.g. *Manghera Case* (59/75), 3 Feb. 1976, considerations 20, 21, [1976] ECR 102; [1976] 1 CMLR 568; CCH para 8342. *Second Defrenne Case* (43/75), 8 April 1976, considerations 57, 64, [1976] ECR 478, 479; [1976] 2 CMLR 127; CCH para 8346.
317. W. van Gerven, *De niet-contractuele aansprakelijkheid van de Gemeenschap wegens normatieve handelingen*, SEW 1976, p. 28 (*My translation* H.G.S.).

tecting itself against any illegal conduct engaged in by the national governments.[318]

Membership of the European Communities has not brought about a fundamental change in this the attitude on the part of the national governments. As
long as they remain empowered to do so they will still violate their obligations
if they consider this to be justified by some all-important national interest.
Let us assume that there is a sudden shortage of potatoes in a Member State.
In order to prevent a steep rise in prices the Government may want to prohibit all exports. It is not entitled to do so under the EEC Treaty, and, seen
from a wider perspective such an export ban may not even be good policy.
But faced with the need to solve the problem, any Government in the Communities might wish to prohibit exports. It would not be prevented from
doing so by the Community procedure available for use against Treaty violations (see below § 383-432). This procedure takes so much time that the new
harvest would be in and the ban could be lifted long before the procedure
became operative. The strongest reason actually persuading governments
against committing such violations is that they know full well that exporters
would ignore such prohibitions and, if brought before a court, would successfully invoke EEC Article 34 which prohibits all quantitative restrictions on
exports, and would rely on the fact that it has direct effect and cannot be set
aside by any government measures. The Governments know that their measures would be stripped of their effect and that exporters may even successfully claim damages from the Government before their national courts on
ground of the illegality of the measures. This knowledge constitutes the most
effective sanction against Treaty violations.[319]

§ 177.   The question whether or not a provision of Community law has direct
effect is a question of interpretation of Community law and should, therefore,
be decided by the Court of Justice.[320] Thus, uniformity is ensured throughout the Community on the question whether national courts must apply a
particular rule of Community law in cases brought before them by individuals.
This also secures uniformity in the way in which Community law is to be
interpreted. This does not, however, amount to a guarantee of complete uniformity in the application of Community law since it is entirely up to the
national legal systems to decide whether the individual may bring his case
before any national court in the first place. If there is no national remedy
against an allegedly invalid national act then the national court cannot set that
act aside on the ground that it is contrary to Community law. The possibilities

---

318. See also Pierre Pescatore, *L'effet direct du droit Communautaire*, Pasicrie Luxembourgeoise 1972, Nos. 5 and 6, first part, pp. 11-15, and *Rôle et chance du droit et des
juges dans la construction de l'Europe*, Rapport inaugural au VIe Congres de la FIDE,
Luxembourg 1973, Revue international de droit comparé, 1974, pp. 5-19, in particular
pp. 8-10.
319. This has actually happened, see Schermers (*op. cit.*, note 55).
320. The Dutch Supreme Court, the *Hoge Raad*, accepted this in the *Netherlands Bosch
Case*, 18 May 1962, N.J. 1965 No. 115; 12 NTIR (1965) pp. 318-322; Brinkhorst-Schermers (*op. cit.*, note 83) p. 225.

of appealing against invalid acts in national sphere vary a great deal. It cannot be purely accidental that all the questions brought before the Court of Justice on the classification of products under the Common Customs Tariff have come from German courts, with a few exceptions where they have come from Dutch courts. This must be explained from the fact that in the other Member States such actions are either impossible or so difficult that importers and exporters are never induced to bring them.

§ 178. Whether a rule has direct effect or not will often be demonstrated by its formulation. A particular formulation usually expresses a particular intention as to the effect, and that intention is relevant for the interpretation. Rules formulated in a way clearly granting rights to individuals or imposing obligations upon them will normally be directly effective. No previous acts of national or other authorities are involved. Waelbroeck therefore, speaks of 'immediacy' (*immédiaté*) or of 'positive direct effect'.[321] Such rules will only rarely cause problems.

Difficulties more easily arise when rules are addressed to one party, usually a Member State, and create − in a more indirect way − rights or obligations for others. Are such rights or obligations directly effective? In practice, this question has arisen only in cases when individuals could derive *rights* from obligations imposed upon others, not when they derive *obligations* from such provisions. Rules which impose rights or obligations in an indirect way will usually infringe an essential procedural requirement because they are not correctly published or notified to the persons to whom they apply. In the case of rights indirectly granted this ground of illegality will not be invoked, but in the case of an obligation it certainly will.

2. Direct effect of Treaty provisions

§ 179. The *Treaties* have been incorporated into the national legal orders and the rights given by them to individuals as well as the obligations imposed on individuals must therefore be applied by the national judiciary.

The first case in which the Court of Justice had to answer the question whether individual citizens could invoke Treaty provisions imposing obligations on States, concerned EEC Article 12. The article reads: '*Member States shall refrain from introducing ... new customs duties ...*' and when *Van Gend en Loos* invoked it before his national court the Dutch government submitted that the article was addressed to the Member States and could therefore not be invoked by private individuals. The Court of Justice, however, held:

'The wording of Article 12 contains a clear and unconditional prohibition which is not a positive but a negative obligation. This obligation, moreover, is not qualified by any reservation on the part of states which would make

321. See also Michel Waelbroeck, *L'immédiaté communautaire, caractéristique de la upranationalité: quelques conséquences pour la pratique*, Le droit international demain, Neuchâtel 1974 (25th Congress of the AAAA), pp. 87, 88.

its implementation conditional upon a positive legislative measure enacted under national law. The very nature of this prohibition makes it ideally adapted to produce direct effects in the legal relationship between Member States and their subjects.

The implementation of Article 12 does not require any legislative intervention on the part of the states. The fact that under this Article it is the Member States who are made the subject of the negative obligation does not imply that their nationals cannot benefit from this obligation.'[322]

§ 180.   The *Second Lütticke Case* concerned EEC Article 95 which provides in its first paragraph: *'No Member State shall impose ... on the products of other Member States any internal taxation ... in excess of that imposed ... on similar domestic products'* and in its last paragraph: *'Member States shall not later than at the beginning of the second stage repeal or amend any provisions existing when this Treaty enters into force which conflict with the preceding rules'*. Here the obligation on the Member States seems less specific in two ways:

(1) the last paragraph demonstrates that the provision was not immediately applicable and (2) the obligation does not prohibit internal taxation of foreign products; it only requires Member States to harmonize it with the taxation of domestic products; the governments seem free to decide how and on what level they wish to set the fiscal burden. Still the Court of Justice held that *Lütticke* could invoke this provision before his national court as from the beginning of the second stage (1 January 1962). The Court held:

'Article 95 thus contains a general rule provided with a simple suspensory clause with regard to provisions existing when it entered into force. From this it must be concluded that on the expiry of the said period the general rule emerges unconditionally into full force.

...

The first paragraph of Article 95 contains a prohibition against discrimination, constituting a clear and unconditional obligation. With the exception of the third paragraph this obligation is not qualified by any condition or subject, in its implementation or effects, to the taking of any measure either by the institutions of the Community or by the Member States. This prohibition is therefore complete, legally perfect and consequently capable of producing direct effects on the legal relationships between the Member States and persons within their jurisdiction. The fact that this Article describes the Member States as being subject to the obligation of non-discrimination does not imply that individuals cannot benefit from it.

...

It follows from the foregoing that, notwithstanding the exception in the third paragraph for provisions existing when the Treaty entered into force until January 1962, the prohibition contained in Article 95 produced

322.   *Van Gend en Loos Case* (26/62), 5 Feb. 1963, [1963] ECR 13; 9 Jur. (1963) 24; 9 Rec. (1963) 24; [1963] CMLR 130; CCH para 8008.

direct effects and creates individual rights of which national courts must take account.'[323]

§ 181. Though EEC Article 95(1) does not contain a clear-cut prohibition, the Court's interpretation in the *Second Lütticke Case* is based on the submission that, for all practical purposes, the Article is equivalent to a prohibition on the imposition of any taxes on products from other Member States in addition to those imposed on national products. As it is easy to establish the nullity of acts or rules violating a prohibition addressed to the State concerned, the *Van Gend en Loos* and *Second Lütticke Cases* might suggest that only those provisions have direct effect that can be applied without any latitude of judgement or discretion. This, however, is not the case. EEC Article 95(2), for example, contains a prohibition of internal taxation of such a nature that it affords indirect protection to other products. Whether, in a specific case, there is protection or not necessitates an assessment of economic factors. The German Government therefore submitted in the *Fink-Frucht Case* that EEC Article 95(2) could have no direct effect. The Court of Justice held, however:

'This provision contains a straightforward prohibition against protection which is the necessary complement to the prohibition set out in the first paragraph of the article. The obligation which results from that prohibition is unconditional, and no action is required on the part of the institutions of the Community or the Member States for its implementation or its entry into force. The prohibition is therefore self-sufficient and legally complete and is thus capable of having direct effects on the legal relationships' between Member States and those subject to their jurisdiction. Although this provision involves the evaluation of economic factors, this does not exclude the right and duty of national courts to ensure that the rules of the Treaty are observed whenever they can ascertain, (...), that the conditions necessary for the application of the article are fulfilled.'[324]

Commenting on the last sentence of this quotation Pescatore (one of the Judges in the case) explained that the Court of Justice wished to say that the national judge does not simply automatically apply Community law. The Court of Justice was of the opinion that it falls upon a judge when meeting specific situations, to further determine legal notions of a more general nature.[325]

§ 182. In the *Fifth Rewe Case* the Court of Justice gave a general ruling on Treaty articles abolishing discrimination when it held:

323. *Second Lütticke Case* (57/65), 16 June 1966, [1966] ECR 210, 211; 12 Jur. (1966) 354, 355; 12 Rec. (1966) 302, 303; [1971] CMLR 684, 685; CCH para 8045 (pp. 7611, 7612).
324. *Fink-Frucht Case* (27/67), 4 April 1968, [1968] ECR 232; 14 Jur. (1968) 328; 14 Rec. (1968) 341, 342; [1968] CMLR 230; CCH para 8069.
325. Pescatore (*op. cit.*, note 318), pp. 8, 9.

'The provisions of the Treaty requiring Member States to abolish all discrimination within a specific period become directly applicable even where the duty has not been discharged before the expiry of that period.'[326]

The prohibition of discrimination is directly effective for several subjects regulated by the Treaty.[327]

§ 183. The effect on individuals of obligations addressed to Member States is less direct than the effect of rights and obligations imposed upon the individuals themselves. In consequence thereof individuals cannot always invoke obligations imposed on Member States. This is possible only when five conditions have been fulfilled:

a) The provision must contain a clear obligation on the Member State.

b) The content of the provision must be such that it can cause direct effect.

c) No further acts either by Community institutions or by Member States must be needed for the obligation to realise its aim.

d) The provision must be either unconditional, or the conditions must have been fulfilled.

e) The Member State should have no discretion in the execution of the obligation.[328]

§ 184. When is a provision unconditional? EEC Article 48 places a clear obligation upon the Member States to permit freedom of movement for workers. No further acts are needed and the Member States have no discretion. But then there is that short but important phrase in para 3: *'subject to limitations justified on grounds of public policy, public security or public health.'* Is that a condition sufficient to prevent direct effect? In the *Van Duyn Case* the Court of Justice considered that it is not, holding:

'The application of these limitations is, however, subject to judicial control, so that a Member State's right to invoke the limitations does not prevent the provisions of Article 48, which enshrine the principle of freedom of movement for workers, from conferring on individuals rights which are enforceable by them and which the national courts must protect.'[329]

This sort of condition does not prevent the courts from feeling able and sufficiently equipped to apply the article (see above § 175).

326. *Fifth Rewe Case* (45/75), 17 Feb. 1976, consideration 24, [1976] ECR 198; [1976] 2 CMLR 25; CCH para 8343.
327. See Maresceau (*op. cit.*, note 315), pp. 99-105; *Kenny Case* (1/78), 28 June 1978, consideration 12, [1978] ECR 1497; [1978] 3 CMLR 667.
328. P.J.G. Kapteyn and P. VerLoren van Themaat, *Inleiding tot het recht van de Euro pese Gemeenschappen*, 2nd ed. Kluwer 1974, p. 176, see also the English translation of the first edition, Kluwer 1973, pp. 182-188; R.H. Lauwaars in SEW 1976, p. 75.
329. *Van Duyn Case* (41/74), 4 Dec. 1974, consideration 7, [1974] ECR 1347; [1975] CMLR 15; CCH para 8283; see also *Rutili Case* (36/75), 28 Oct. 1975, considerations 19-21, [1975] ECR 1230; [1976] 1 CMLR 154; CCH para 8322.

§ 185. In the *Second Defrenne Case* one of the arguments advanced against the direct effect of EEC Article 119 was that the article contains the wording '*the principle* that men and women should receive equal pay'. It was submitted that this wording indicates a general aim, rather than a right. The Court held, however:

'in the language of the Treaty this term is specifically used in order to indicate the fundamental nature of certain provisions, as is shown, for example, by the heading of the first part of the Treaty which is devoted to "Principles" and by Article 113, according to which the commercial policy of the Community is to be based on "uniform principles".'[330]

§ 186. When the obligation imposed upon a Member State has direct effect, that Member State is no longer entitled to adopt or to apply national legislation contrary to that obligation. National courts should refuse to apply such legislation due to its illegality, thus giving priority to Community law. In the *Rutili Case* several Community provisions on the freedom of movement for workers were invoked in order to demonstrate that some French measures restricting this freedom were illegal. The Court of Justice held:

'The effect of all these provisions, without exception, is to impose duties on Member States and it is, accordingly, for the courts to give the rules of Community law which may be pleaded before them precedence over the provisions of national law if legislative measures adopted by a Member State in order to limit within its territory freedom of movement or residence for nationals of other Member States prove to be incompatible with any of those duties.

Inasmuch as the object of the provisions of the Treaty and of secondary legislation is to regulate the situation of individuals and to ensure their protection, it is also for the national courts to examine whether individual decisions are compatible with the relevant provisions of Community law.'[331]

§ 187. In its case-law the Court of Justice has established that at least the following articles of the EEC Treaty, imposing obligations on the Member States, have direct effect for individual citizens[332]:
Article 7 (for some subject matters)[333]
Article 12[334]
Article 13(2)[335]

---

330. *Second Defrenne Case* (43/75), 8 April 1976, consideration 28, [1976] ECR 474; [1976] 2 CMLR 124; CCH para 8346.
331. *Rutili Case* (36/75), 28 Oct. 1975, considerations 16, 17, [1975] ECR 1229; [1976] 1 CMLR 153, 154; CCH para 8322.
332. On the relevant cases see Derrick Wyatt, *Directly Applicable Provisions of EEC Law*, New Law Journal 1975, pp. 458-460; 575-578; 669-672; 793, 794.
333. See above § 182.
334. *Van Gend en Loos Case*, quoted above § 179.
335. *Capolongo Case* (77/72), 19 June 1973, consideration 11, [1973] ECR 623; [1974]

Article 16 [336]
Article 30 [337]
Article 31 and 32(1) [338]
Article 37(1) [339]
Article 37(2) [340]
Article 48 [341]
Articles 48-66 [342]
Article 52 [343]
Article 53 [344]
Articles 59 and 60 [345]
Article 85(1) [346]
Article 86 [347]
Article 90(1) [348]

Article 93(3) last sentence 'the prohibition of State aids which have not been notified to the Commission or in regard to which the Commission has initiated a procedure under' Article 93(3)[349]

CMLR 245; CCH para 8213; *IGA V Case* (94/75), 18 June 1975, consideration 22, [1975] ECR 711; [1976] 2 CMLR 54 (there it is consideration 12); CCH para 8311. See also *SACE Case* 33/70), 17 Dec. 1970, consideration 10, [1970] ECR 1222; [1971] CMLR 132.
336. *Eunomia Case* (18/71), 26 Oct. 1971, [1971] 2 ECR 816; [1972] CMLR 10, 11; *Second Art Treasurers Case* (48/71), 13 July 1972, [1972] 2 ECR 532; [1972] CMLR 707, 708; *Comet Case* (45/76), 16 Dec. 1976, consideration 11, [1976] ECR 2052; [1977] 1 CMLR 553; CCH para 8383.
337. *Iannelli Case* (74/76), 22 March 1977, consideration 13, [1977] ECR 575; [1977] 2 CMLR 715; CCH para 8401.
338. *Salgoil Case* (13/68), 19 Dec. 1968, [1968] ECR 460, 461; 14 Jur. (1968), 642, 644; 14 Rec. (1968) 673, 674; [1969] CMLR 194, 195; CCH para 8072.
339. *Manghera Case* (59/75), 3 Feb. 1976, considerations 16-18 [1976] ECR 101, 102; [1976] 1 CMLR 567; CCH para 8342. See also *Hansen Case* (91/78), 13 March 1979, consideration 16.
340. *Costa Enel Case* (6/64), 15 July 1964, [1964] ECR 597, 10 Jur. (1964) 1224; 10 Rec. (1964) 1164; [1964] CMLR 459; CCH para 8023.
341. *Van Duyn Case* (41/74), 4 Dec. 1974, considerations 4-8; [1974] ECR 1346, 1347 [1975] 1 CMLR 14, 15; CCH para 8283. See also *Marine Labour Code Case* (167/73), 4 April 1974, consideration 41, [1974] ECR 372; [1974] 2 CMLR 230; CCH para 8270.
342. In the *Watson Case* (118/75), 7 July 1976, the Court held in a more general way that EEC Articles 48-66 and the measures adopted by the Community in application therefore have direct effect. See [1976] ECR 1196-1200; [1976] 2 CMLR 569-573; CCH para 8368
343. *Reyners Case* (2/74), 21 June 1974, consideration 32; [1974] ECR 652; [1974] 2 CMLR 327; CCH para 8256.
344. *Costa Enel Case* (6/64), 15 July 1964, [1964] ECR 596; 10 Jur. (1964) 1223; 10 Rec. (1964) 1162; [1964] CMLR 458; CCH para 8023.
345. *Van Binsbergen Case* (33/74), 3 Dec. 1974, consideration 27; [1974] ECR 1312 [1975] 1 CMLR 314; CCH para 8282. On Art. 59 see also *Van Wesemael Case* (110 111/78), 18 Jan. 1979, consideration 16.
346. *BRT-Sabam Case* (127/73), 30 Jan. 1974, consideration 16, [1974] ECR 62; [1974 2 CMLR 271; CCH para 8268, 8269.
347. *Sacchi Case* (155/73), 30 April 1974, consideration 18, [1974] ECR 430; [1974] 2 CMLR 204; CCH para 8267.
348. *Pigs Marketing Case* (83/78), 29 Nov. 1978, implied in the reasoning of the Court, in particular considerations 43, 44, 66, [1979] 1 CMLR 201, 204.
349. *Costa Enel Case* (6/64), 15 July 1964, [1964] ECR 596; [1964] CMLR 457; CCH para 8023; *Capolongo Case* (77/72), 19 June 1973, consideration 6, [1973] ECR 621 [1974] 1 CMLR 244, 245; CCH para 8213; Maresceau (*op. cit.*, note 315), pp. 75-79, 96.

Article 95(1)[350]
Article 119[351]
The articles which have no direct effect can usually be recognized from the fact that their texts leave some discretion to Member States or to Community institutions. The Court has expressly stated that no direct effect should be granted to Articles 32(2) and 33[352], to Article 90(2)[353], Article 92(1)[354], nor to Article 97.[355]

§ 188. The direct effect of Treaty provisions is not limited to the relationship between individuals and Member States. The Court of Justice has repeatedly ruled that Treaty articles have equal effect in the mutual relationship between individuals.[356] In the *Walrave Case* the Court of Justice held that the prohibition of discrimination on the ground of nationality does not only apply to the action of public authorities but extends likewise to associations and organizations of a private character.[357] In the *Second Defrenne Case* the Court held that EEC Article 119 on equal pay for men and women can be invoked against private employers as well as against public authorities.[358]

3. Direct effect of secondary Community law

§ 189. *Regulations* have general application, they are binding in their entirety and are directly applicable in all Member States.[359] This does not necessarily mean that they have direct effect and can therefore be invoked by individuals. Many regulations need further legislation before they will realise their aim. However, it does mean that regulations must be applied by national courts whenever their contents grant rights to individuals or impose obligations on them.[360] The Court of Justice has repeatedly stated that the direct

---

350. *Second Lütticke Case*, quoted above, note 323.
351. *Second Defrenne Case* (43/75), 8 April 1976, considerations 24, 40, [1976] ECR 474, 476; [1976] 2 CMLR 124, 125; CCH para 8346.
352. *Salgoil Case* (13/68), 19 Dec. 1968; [1968] ECR 461; 14 Jur. (1968) 644; 14 Rec. (1968) 674; [1969] CMLR 195; CCH para 8072.
353. *Hein-Müller Case* (10/71), 14 July 1971, consideration 16, [1971] ECR 730; CCH para 8140.
354. *Capolongo Case* (77/72), 19 June 1973, considerations 4-6, [1973] ECR 621; [1974] 1 CMLR 244, 245; CCH para 8213.
355. *Molkerei-Zentrale Case* (28/67), 3 April 1968, [1968] ECR 156; 14 Jur. (1968) 222; 14 Rec. (1968) 230, 231; [1968] CMLR 221; CCH para 8064.
356. See W. van Gerven, *Contribution de l'arrêt Defrenne au dévelopment du droit communautaire*, 13 CDE (1977), pp. 138-143.
357. *Walrave Case* (36/74), 12 Dec. 1974, considerations 17-19, [1974] ECR 1418, 1419; [1975] 1 CMLR 332, 333; CCH para 8290.
358. *Second Defrenne Case* (43/75), 8 April 1976, consideration 22, [1976] ECR 474; [1976] 2 CMLR 124; CCH para 8346.
359. EEC Art. 189.
360. See e.g. *Politi Case* (43/71), 14 Dec. 1971, consideration 9, [1971] ECR 1048, 1049; [1973] CMLR 70; CCH para 8159; *Marimex Case* (84/71), 7 March 1972, consideration 5, [1972] ECR 96; (1972) CMLR 915; CCH para 8176; *Leonesio Case* (93/71), 17 May 1972, considerations 5, 22, [1972] ECR 293, 295, 296; [1973] CMLR 352, 354; CCH para 8175; *Variola Case* (34/73), 10 Oct. 1973, consideration 8, [1973] ECR 990; CCH para 8226.

application of a regulation means that its entry into force and its application in favour or against individuals are independent of any measure of reception into national law. [361]

§ 190. *Decisions* addressed to individuals will have direct effect on them. This is a necessary consequence of the binding force granted to decisions by EEC Article 189, ECSC Article 14 and Euratom Article 161.

§ 191. Decisions addressed to other persons than those invoking them and *directives* — which are a species of decisions addressed to Member States as they could be replaced by decisions ordering Member States to achieve specific results — are in this respect in a similar position as Treaty articles addressed to others. [362]

Individuals have frequently claimed rights derived from obligations imposed upon their States by directives or decisions. In principle they are entitled to do so. The Court of Justice has repeatedly held that it would be incompatible with the binding effect attributed to decisions and directives by EEC Article 189 to exclude in principle the possibility that persons affected may invoke the obligation imposed upon others. The useful effect of such acts would be weakened if individuals were prevented from relying on them before their national courts and if the latter were prevented from taking them into consideration as elements of Community law.

On these grounds the Court of Justice has accepted the direct effect of decisions addressed to others in the *Grad Case* [363] , and the direct effect of directives *inter alia* in the *Van Duyn* and *Capital Goods Cases.* [364]

As in the case of Treaty obligations, the negative obligations (those to abstain from acting or to abolish acts) are most susceptible of giving rise to direct effect for citizens. Positive obligations usually leave a margin of discretion to the Member State as to the manner in which the acts are to be made and are therefore often not unconditional, clear and precise. When there is no such margin of discretion — which is to be decided by the Court of Justice — positive obligations imposed by directives and decisions may have direct effect as well. [365] An example of this can be found in the *Ratti Case*. A

---

361. *Variola Case* (34/73), 10 Oct. 1973, consideration 10, [1973] ECR 990; CCH para 8226 and, e.g. *Zerbone Case* (94/77), 31 Jan. 1978, consideration 23, [1978] ECR 115; CCH para 8464; *Bussone Case* (31/78), 30 Nov. 1978, consideration 30.
362. K.R. Simmonds, *Van Duyn v. Home Office: the direct effectiveness of directives,* 24 ICLQ (1975), pp. 419-437; C.W.A. Timmermans, *Need directives have direct effect to cause effects within the national legal systems?* 16 CMLRev (1979).
363. *Grad Case* (9/70), 6 Oct. 1970, consideration 5, (1970) ECR 837; [1971] CMLR 23; CCH para 8107.
364. *Van Duyn Case* (41/74), 4 Dec. 1974, considerations 12, 15; (1974) ECR 1384, 1349; [1975] 1 CMLR 16; CCH para 8283; *Capital Goods Case* (51/76), 1 Feb. 1977, considerations 22-24; [1977] ECR 126, 127; [1977] 1 CMLR 429; CCH para 8409. See also *Delkvist Case* (21/78), 29 Nov. 1978, considerations 20, 21; [1979] 1 CMLR 383, and Yves Crétien, *L'application directe des dispositions de certaines directives,* 14 RMC (1971), pp. 231-237; Eberhard Grabitz, *Entscheidungen und Richtlinien als unmittelbar wirksames Gemeinschaftsrecht,* 6 EuR (1971), pp. 1-22.
365. *Enka Case* (38/77), 23 Nov. 1977, consideration 17, [1977] ECR 2213; [1978] 2 CMLR 230; CCH para 8443.

directive on the packaging of products had not been introduced into the Italian legal order. Mr. Ratti nonetheless applied the directive and thus violated an old Italian rule of Law. The Court in which he was prosecuted for this violation requested a preliminary ruling of the Court of Justice held that after the date on which a directive should have been introduced a Member State may not apply to a national law which has not been adapted to that directive on an individual who acts in conformity with the directive. The penal sanction of the old Italian rule of law could not, therefore be applied to Mr. Ratti. [365a]

§ 192. In one respect directives and decisions addressed to others differ fundamentally from Treaty provisions: they are less accessible. One may expect individuals to be familiar with the Treaties or at least have access to them. For example, individuals may know of the requirement of equal pay for men and women contained in EEC Article 119, even if it is addressed to the Member States. It is more difficult to assume that individuals will know the contents of directives and decisions addressed to others. This may be unfair when such directives or decisions create *rights* for individuals: the well-informed will be in a better position than those who are less knowledgeable.

But it is far worse still in the case of directives or decisions which create *obligations* for individuals: one cannot oblige individuals to perform obligations which they do not know of nor could be expected to know of. [366] For this reason it is unlikely that courts can be legally obliged to give direct effect to all directives and decisions. This may cause problems, for example, when a Community directive obliges all Member States to introduce some particular burden (e.g. a tax or a levy) on a specific group of producers. In the *Leonesio Case* the Court considered that individuals of one Member State should not be placed in a less favourable position than those of the other States. [367] In the *Kohlegesetz Case,* quoted in § 404, the Court held that advantages for individuals arrived at illegally should be compensated. In line with these cases it could be submitted that an illegal advantage won for the inhabitants of one, or more, States derived from the failure to levy an obligatory tax or levy is a violation of the Treaty obligations encumbent upon that State. On this account the State could then be compelled to levy the Taxes even without a national provision to this end.

Another situation which would cause problems is when provisions entailing obligations for individuals are withdrawn by a directive which at the same time introduces other obligations. It might be difficult to grant direct effect to the nullification of the old obligations whilst refraining from recognizing the direct effect of the fresh obligations. [368]

Such problems should be solved, however, by the legislator rather than by the judiciary.

365a. *Ratti Case* (148/78), 5 April 1979, considerations 18-24.
366. A.J. Easson, *Can directives impose obligations on individuals?* 4 ELRev. (1979), pp. 67-79.
367. *Leonesio Case* (93/71), 17 May 1972, consideration 21, [1972] ECR 295; [1973] CMLR 354; CCH para 8175.
368. See Henry G. Schermers, *Indirecte obligations, Four questions in respect of EEC obligations arising from rights or obligations of others,* 24 NTIR (1977), pp. 260-273.

CHAPTER TWO

Judicial review

I. THE NEED FOR JUDICIAL REVIEW

§ 193. The three Community Treaties all begin with assigning far-reaching tasks to the newly established Communities, tasks which are delineated precisely throughout the Treaties. The methods of implementation which may be used and the kinds of decisions to be taken are narrowly prescribed. The tasks entrusted to the Communities must be carried out by the four Institutions, each acting within the limits of the powers conferred upon them by the Treaties. It is of great importance for the Member States which transferred sovereignty to the Communities, for the Institutions, each of which has its own responsibilities, and for the citizens of the nine in whose interest the Communities are to work, that all Community decisions respect the requirements set out in the Treaties and that no powers are exercised unless expressly founded in the Treaties. Without some guarantee that the limits of the Treaties should be respected the Member States might not have been willing to transfer such wide-ranging powers to the Communities at all.

It is the task of the Court of Justice to ensure that in the interpretation and application of the Treaties the law is observed.[1] This entails the review of the legality of Community acts and of the failure of the Communities to act.

§ 194. The aims of the Communities can only partly be realized by acts of Community Institutions. Frequently acts by Member States are required. This points out the dual rôle of the Member States: on the one hand they are essential elements of the Communities, on the other they are their most important counterparts.[2] To the Member States, as counterparts, the Communities address decisions and directives, ordering them to follow particular policies. From the Member States, as counterparts, the Communities continuously try to draw the necessary powers and sovereignty. If, however, the Member States consider themselves mainly as constituting the opposing pole to the Communities, against which they must defend their national interests, the progress in the Communities will be impeded. Such an attitude is intrinsically wrong, as the Communities and their Members are not opponents, they have the common goal of increasing the prosperity of the population. In the

1. EEC Art. 164; ECSC Art. 31.
2. Schermers, *International Institutional Law*, Sijthoff, Leiden 1972. Vol. I pp. 65, 66, second edition to be published in 1979.

development of the Communities the Member States must play an important rôle, as they are the most important elements which compose the Communities.

Whilst functioning in their capacity as elements of the Communities, the acts of the Member States form part of the legal order of the Communities; these acts are of as great an importance as the acts of the Community institutions. The legal control of the acts of the Member States, as elements of the Communities, is therefore basically of the same nature as the legal control of Community acts. In many cases the acts of the institutions and those of the Member States are interwoven, such as in the case of Article 10 of Regulation 1041/67, according to which 'refunds are payable by the Member State in whose territory the export customs formalities have been completed'. This means that the application of the regulation is carried out in accordance with the administrative and procedural principles of national law, but it means at the same time that the requirement of uniform application of Community law must be complied with, in order to avoid exporters being treated differently according to the frontier across which their products are exported.[3] This relationship was also demonstrated by the Court of Justice which censured an article of an EEC Regulation in the *Rey Soda Case* and national intervention measures in the *Cucchi Case* on the same grounds of Community law.[4]

Because of this close connection between the acts of the Member States and the acts of the Communities we will discuss the Court's review of treaty violations by Member States under the same heading as the Court's review of Community acts.

§ 195. Judicial review of the legality of acts of the Community institutions and of the Member States is made possible due to the basic similarity — notwithstanding all the differences — of the legal systems of the Member States.[5] They all share a common tradition, based on the rule of law, granting rights to their citizens even vis-à-vis the government and preventing the enjoyment of absolute power. In all Member States the exercise of government power is controlled, though not in the same way. In those Member States with strong parliamentary traditions, control by parliament is of greater importance than that by the courts; in Member States where parliaments have been weaker, the rôle played by the courts is predominant.

In the Communities the control by the parliamentary organ is extremely weak, weaker than in any of the Member States. This makes the control by the Court of Justice more important than that of any administrative court in the Member States. The control of the executive is almost entirely in the hands of the Court.

---

3. *First Schlüter Case* (94/71), 6 June 1972, considerations 10, 11, [1972] ECR 318, 319; [1973] CMLR 129, 130; CCH para 8186.
4. See *Cucchi Case* (77/76), 25 May 1977, considerations 30-32, [1977] ECR 1008, 1009; CCH para 8422.
5. See Z.M. Nedjati and J.E. Trice, *English and Continental Systems of Administrative Law*, North Holland 1978.

II. JUDICIAL REVIEW OF COMMUNITY ACTS

A. WHAT ACTS ARE SUSCEPTIBLE TO JUDICIAL REVIEW?

1. Binding acts contemplated by the Treaties

a. ECSC ART. 14 AND EEC ART. 189

§ 196. The ECSC Treaty enumerates two sorts of binding acts: *'decisions'* which bind in their entirety and *'recommendations'* which bind as to the aims to be pursued but leave the choice of the appropriate methods for achieving these aims to those to whom the recommendations are addressed.[6]

Neither of the names is appropriate. The name 'decision' is too vague as it covers both the acts which provide for general rules of law and those which are individually addressed to specific persons. In later articles the Treaty therefore distinguishes between 'general decisions' and 'individual decisions'.[7] The name 'recommendation' is generally used in international law for non-binding resolutions and is, therefore, misleading.

§ 197. In the EEC and Euratom Treaties a more appropriate terminology is used[8] : *'regulations'* for acts of general application which are binding in their entirety and directly applicable in all Member States (the general decision of ECSC); *'decisions'* which are binding in their entirety upon those to whom they are addressed (the individual decision of ECSC); and *'directives'* which are binding, as to the result to be achieved, upon each Member State to which they are addressed, but leave to the national authorities the choice of form and method. The EEC directive is about the same as the ECSC recommendation, but it can only be addressed to Member States, while ECSC recommendations may also be directed to coal and steel undertakings, or associations.

b. THE DISTINCTION BETWEEN GENERAL AND INDIVIDUAL ACTS

(i) Distinguishing criteria

§ 198. The right to bring an action against general acts is more restrictive than that against individual ones. It is, therefore, important to know what constitutes an individual act. The Court of Justice has repeatedly decided that the nature of an act does not depend on its form, but on its content. The title therefore cannot be decisive. Under the ECSC Treaty the Court held:

---

6. ECSC Art. 14.
7. See e.g. ECSC Art. 33.
8. EEC Art. 189, Euratom Art. 161.

112

'In order to ascertain whether a decision of the High Authority is general
or individual its content must in particular be examined to establish whether
its provisions are likely to affect directly and individually the situation of
the persons to whom they apply.'[9]

§ 199.   In the *First Simet Case*, decided five years earlier, the Court gave a
number of criteria for its decision as to why an act was general in nature: the
act laid down normative principles; it specified in an abstract manner the
conditions for their application; it established general organizational rules
which regulated in an identical way an indeterminate number of cases; its
rules were applicable to any situation which is or will come within the conditions specified for their application.[10] In the same case the Court held that an
act amending a general decision is also general itself.[11]

§ 200.   Under the EEC Treaty the Court came to a similar conclusion in the
Fruit and Vegetables Case, when it considered:

'In examining this question, the Court cannot restrict itself to considering
the official title of the measure, but must first take into account its object
and content.

Under the terms of Article 189 of the EEC Treaty, a regulation shall
have general application and shall be directly applicable in all Member
States, whereas a decision shall be binding only upon those to whom it is
addressed. The criterion for the distinction must be sought in the general
'application' or otherwise of the measure in question.

The essential characteristics of a decision arise from the limitation of the
persons to whom it is addressed, whereas a regulation, being essentially of a
legislative nature, is applicable not to a limited number of persons, defined
or identifiable, but to categories of persons viewed abstractly and in their
entirety. Consequently, in order to determine in doubtful cases whether
one is concerned with a decision or a regulation, it is necessary to ascertain
whether the measure in question is of individual concern to specific individuals.

In these circumstances, if a measure entitled by its author a regulation
contains provisions which are capable of being not only of direct but also
of individual concern to certain natural or legal persons, it must be admitted, without prejudice to the question whether that measure considered in
its entirety can be correctly called a regulation, that in any case those
provisions do not have the character of a regulation and may therefore be

9.   *Second Modena Case* (55-59 and 61-63/63), 9 June 1964, [1964] ECR 227, 228; 10
Jur. (1964) 474; 10 Rec. (1964) 447; [1964] CMLR 413.
10.   *First Simet Case* (36-38, 40 and 41/58), 17 July 1959, [1959] ECR 166, 167; 5 Jur.
(1958-59) 379, 380; 5 Rec. (1958-59) 352; See also Jean-Victor Louis, *Les Règlements de
la Communauté Economique Européenne*, Presses Universitaires de Bruxelles 1969, p. 225.
11.   *First Simet Case*, see note 10. In Dutch law this is not always the case, see CHF Polak,
Het begrip 'beschikking' in BAB en AROB, 52 NJB (1977), p. 96.

impugned by those persons under the terms of the second paragraph of Article 173.'

...

'It is possible without doubt for a decision also to have a very wide field of application. However, a measure which is applicable to objectively determined situations and which involves immediate legal consequences in all Member States for categories of persons viewed in a general and abstract manner cannot be considered as constituting a decision, unless it can be proved that it is of individual concern to certain persons within the meaning of the second paragraph of Article 173.'[12]

§ 201.   In practice it may be difficult to distinguish whether an act has general application or only affects a limited group of addressees.

In the *Fédéchar Case* the High Authority had ordered a reduction of Belgian coal prices by Decision 22/55.[13] The amount of the reduction depended on the size and quality of the coal. The effect of the decision on the three mines in the Kempen district was different from that on the other Belgian mines. *Fédéchar* therefore submitted that the decision was of an individual nature, while the High Authority claimed that it was a general one. The Court of Justice rejected the applicant's argument that the variations in the effects of the price list determined the nature of Decision No 22/55.

It held:

'That decision was adopted within the context of a special system provided for in relation to Belgium for the duration of the transitional period by Article 26 of the Convention which applies in accordance with specific rules, however detailed and varied they may be, to all undertakings and transactions governed by that system.

Within the context of that system the decision concerns the undertakings only in so far as they are producers of coal and it in no way identifies them. If new deposits were discovered in Belgium the company working them would be bound to sell at the prices fixed by the decision. Furthermore, the territorial limitation does not imply individual identification and is justified by the fact that the Belgian industry is in need of equalization.

The fact that Decision No 22/55 lays down specific and detailed rules which are applicable in different situations does not conflict with the general nature of the decision. Article 50(2) of the Treaty in fact provides that the mode of assessment and collection shall be determined by a general decision of the High Authority, which shows that the fact that such a decision has specific consequences which are individual and varied does not affect its nature as a general decision.'[14]

---

12. *Fruit and Vegetables Case* (16 and 17/62), 14 Dec. 1962, [1962] ECR 478, 479, 8 Jur. (1962) 958, 959; 8 Rec. (1962) 919; [1963] CMLR 173, 174; CCII para 8005.
13. High Authority Decision 22/25 of 28 May 1955, OJ 31 May 1955.
14. *Fédéchar Case* (8/55), 16 July 1956, [1954-56] ECR 256; 2 Jur. (1955-56) 234, 235; 2 Rec. (1955-56) 223, 224.

§ 202. Under the EEC Treaty the question whether a regulation was really of general nature was brought up in the *First International Fruit Company Case*. There the Court came to a different conclusion from that in the *Fédéchar Case*. The Commission had drawn up various rules for the import of apples, which required the Member States to collect all applications for import licences on a weekly basis, and to totalise the quantity of imports requested, thus allowing the Commission to decide how many licences could be granted. [15] In a subsequent regulation, the Commission decided what percentage of import licences requested by 20 March 1970 could be met. [16] The latter regulation had to be extended several times to cover applications received in subsequent weeks. The last extention was by Regulation 983/70. [17] The national authorities subsequently issued import licences based on the Commission regulations. The *International Fruit Company* brought an action against the refusal of the competent Dutch authority to grant an import licence. It blamed the Commission since the Dutch authority had no discretionary power. The Court admitted the action considering:

'It is obvious that Regulation No. 983/70 was adopted with one eye on the state of the market, and the other on the quantities of dessert apples for which import licences had been applied for in the week ended 22 May 1970. It follows that at the moment of adoption of the said Regulation the number of applications which could be affected by it was fixed. No new applications could be added.

To what extent, in percentage terms, the applications could be granted, depended on the total quantity, for which applications had been submitted. Accordingly, the Commission, by deciding that the system introduced by Article 1 of Regulation No. 565/70 should be maintained in the relevant period, decided to grant every application submitted, albeit by merely taking note of the quantities requested.

Consequently, Article 1 of Regulation No. 983/70 is not a provision of general application within the meaning of the second paragraph of Article 189 of the Treaty, but must be regarded as a bundle of individual decisions taken by the Commission under Article 2(2) of Regulation No. 459/70, each of which, although taken in the form of a regulation, affects the legal position of one of the applicants.' [18]

§ 203. The general nature of a regulation was also disputed in the *Watenstedt Case*. In a regulation on sugar the Council had made an exception for raw beet sugar. The *Zuckerfabrik Watenstedt*, which produced raw beet sugar, together with a limited number of other factories, challenged this exception, submitting that it was of individual concern to the producers of raw beet sugar.

---

15. Regulation 459/70, 1 March 1970, OJ L 57 of 12 March 1970, pp. 20-22.
16. Regulation 565/70, 25 March 1970, OJ L 69 of 26 March 1970, pp. 33-35.
17. Regulation 983/70, 28 May 1970, OJ L 116 of 29 May 1970, p. 35.
18. *First International Fruit Company Case* (41-44/70), 13 May 1971, considerations 16-21, [1971] ECR 421, 422; CCH para 8142.

Unlike the Advocate-General, the Court did not accept this submission, holding that:

> 'Moreover, a measure does not lose its character as a regulation simply because it may be possible to ascertain with a greater or lesser degree of accuracy the number or even the identity of the persons to which it applies at any given time as long as there is no doubt that the measure is applicable as the result of an objective situation of law or of fact which it specifies and which is in harmony with its ultimate objective. Furthermore, the fact that a legal provision may have different practical effects on the different persons to whom it applies in no way contradicts its nature as a regulation provided that the situation to which it refers is objectively determined.'[19]

§ 204.   According to their definition (EEC Article 189) regulations have *general* application and are directly applicable in all Member States. This does not mean, however, that a general act could not qualify as a regulation if it is applicable in only one Member State. Even then it must be termed a regulation as long as it applies to an abstract group of persons.[20]

(ii)   Individual provisions in general rules

§ 205.   In the penultimate paragraph of the extract quoted, above, (§ 200) from the *Fruit and Vegetables Case*, the important statement is made that an individual provision incorporated in a general rule can be isolated from that rule, and be separately impugned as an individual act.

When discussing the question whether a plaintiff is individually affected by a *decision* addressed to someone else (below § 314-324) we shall see that the Court of Justice has accepted such individual effect when a decision is made retroactively for a period which is entirely in the past (*First Toepfer Case*, see below § 318). In the case of such a period the group of enterprises affected is fixed without the possibility of later additions so that the Communities would be in a position to identify by name which enterprises would be concerned. As for the question whether a provision of a regulation is of an individual nature, the issue is slightly more complicated. Even if such a provision exclusively covers a period in the past, with the result that the persons affected by it may be identified, it can still not be separately challenged if the provision is an integral part of the general rule and if the general rule could not operate properly without such specific provisions for specific cases.

§ 206.   In the *Compagnie Française Case* the Court of Justice had to consider a separate appeal against a provision of a regulation which formed an inseparable unity with that regulation even though the individuals affected by the specific provision could have been identified. Had the Communities not acted

---

19. *Watenstedt Case* (6/68), 11 July 1968, [1968] ECR 415; 14 Jur. (1968) 579; 14 Rec. (1968) 605, 606; [1969] CMLR 37; CCH para 8063 (p. 1970).
20. See e.g. *Molitoria Impolese Case* (30/67), 13 March 1968, [1968] ECR 121; 14 Jur. (1968) 173; 14 Rec. (1968) 181; CCH para 8060.

after the French devaluation of 8 August 1969, the prices of French agricultural produce would have suddenly risen, due to the fact that these prices were fixed in terms of Units of Account which would, as a result of the devaluation, have rendered a corresponding increase in the prices expressed in French francs. Desirous of mitigating the serious effects of this, the EEC allowed France to temporarily maintain the prices, expressed in French francs, as they were before the devaluation (this meant a substantial lowering of the prices expressed in Units of Account). In order to prevent disturbances on the EEC market, several measures were taken with respect to trade with other Member States. One of these was a Council regulation of 1 August 1969, permitting France to introduce import subsidies and export charges in its trade with its EEC partners. Another regulation, passed by the Commission on 22 August, further refined the Council regulation to apply to contracts concluded before 1 August but executed after that date. It was against two provisions of this latter regulation that the *Compagnie Française* appealed. It submitted that the provisions concerned contracts concluded in the past and that it was therefore possible to identify the enterprises concerned. For that reason the provisions were of an individual nature and could be separately appealed. The Court did not accept this submission, reasoning:

'Where a measure has the character of a regulation that character is not called in issue by virtue of the fact that the number and even the identity of the persons to whom it applies at a given moment may be determined more or less precisely, provided that it is clear that this application depends on an objective legal or factual situation defined by the measure with reference to its purpose.

The fact that a transitional provision is applicable only to certain situations arising before a date fixed by it and, therefore, often established before it comes into force, does not prevent that provision from being an integral part of the former and new provisions which it is designed to reconcile and, consequently, from partaking of their general nature.' [21]

§ 207.   In the *Second Toepfer Case* an article of a regulation was challenged by an individual. The Court of Justice on its own motion studied the question whether the article was in substance a decision and only when it was demonstrated to be so was the case declared admissible (see below § 313).

(iii)   Acts which are general for some parties but individual for others

§ 208.   In the *First Nold Case*, the Court was faced with the question of whether a decision can be individual for some parties and general for others.

In a number of individual decisions, the High Authority had authorized German sales agencies for Ruhr coal to impose specific conditions upon traders that had to be fulfilled if they were to be accepted as wholesalers for

---

21. *Compagnie Française Case* (64/69), 16 April 1970, considerations 11, 12 [1970] ECR 226, 227; [1970] CMLR 385; CCH para 8091.

Ruhr coal. As a result of these conditions, some smaller traders were no longer classified as wholesalers and could therefore no longer obtain their coal directly from the mines. One of these smaller traders, Nold, brought an action against the authorizing decision. The question to be solved was whether in respect of traders these decisions were of a general nature or not, as they formulated general rules of what constituted a wholesaler. The Court considered:

'From this it is clear that the authorizations in question are individual in character in relation to the undertakings concerned.

Although the Treaty is silent on the matter a decision which is individual in character in relation to the undertakings to which it is directed cannot at the same time be regarded as a general decision in relation to third parties.

Moreover, general decisions are quasi-legislative measures which issue from a public authority and have a legislative effect *erga omnes*.' [22]

Therefore, the act was considered individual with respect to Nold, once it had been established that it was individual for its addressee.

§ **209.** Can a general act be individual for an association comprising all its addressees? Under the ECSC Treaty this question arose in the *Fédéchar Case*. Fédéchar was the federation of all the Belgian coal mines, to which Decision 22-55 had been addressed. Fédéchar submitted that the decision was therefore an individual one with respect to it. The Court did not accept this submission, considering:

'The fact that all the undertakings referred to by the decision — and only they — are grouped within the applicant association does not lead to a different result. If it were otherwise not even a decision applying to all the undertakings of the Community could be held to be general in nature if those undertakings were grouped within one single association. The question whether a decision is individual or general in nature must be decided on the basis of objective criteria, with the result that it is impossible to draw distinctions according to whether the applicant is an association or an undertaking.' [23]

§ **210.** Under the EEC Treaty the same question was raised in the *Fruit and Vegetables Case*. Again the Court rejected the submission, holding:

'one cannot accept the principle that an association, in its capacity as the representative of a category of businessmen, could be individually concerned by a measure affecting the general interests of that category.

22. *First Nold Case* (18/57), 20 March 1959, [1959] ECR 50; 5 Jur. (1958-59) 117; 5 Rec. (1958-59) 112, 113.
23. *Fédéchar Case* (8/55), 16 July 1956, [1954-56] ECR 256; 2 Jur. (1955-56) 235; 2 Rec. (1955-56) 223, 224.

Such a principle would result in the grouping, under the heading of a single legal person, of the interests properly attributed to the members of a category, who have been affected as individuals by genuine regulations, and would derogate from the system of the Treaty which allows applications for annulment by private individuals only of decisions which have been addressed to them, or of acts which affect them in a similar manner.

In these circumstances, it cannot be admitted that the provision in dispute is of individual concern to the applicants'. [24]

§ 211.   Similarly the Court held in the *Second Civil Servants Unions Case* that:

'An organization formed for the protection of the collective interests of a category of persons cannot be considered as being directly and individually concerned by a measure affecting the general interests of that category'. [25]

In this case the organizations concerned were somewhat more closely connected with the disputed regulation as they had taken part in the discussions preceding it. The Court considered this insufficient for granting them the right to bring an action. [26]

(iv)   Individual nature of decisions addressed to States

§ 212.   In the *Plaumann Case*, the Commission submitted that the decisions addressed to Member States could be acts of a general nature. Often such decisions are of a more general character than decisions addressed to private parties since they are to have a general effect within the Member State concerned. Therefore, so the Commission argued, such decisions should not be subject to action by private parties. EEC Article 173(2) was invoked to support this submission since, although it provides that individuals may bring an action against decisions addressed to another person, the Commission argued that the word 'person' could not include a Member State in its capacity as a public authority. The Court did not accept this submission, considering:

'the second paragraph of Article 173 does allow an individual to bring an action against decisions addressed to "another person" which are of direct and individual concern to the former, but this Article neither defines nor limits the scope of these words. The words and the natural meaning of this provision justify the broadest interpretation. Moreover provisions of the

24.   *Fruit and Vegetables Case* (16 and 17/62), 14 Dec. 1962, [1962] ECR 479, 480, 8 Jur. (1962) 960; 8 Rec. (1962) 920; [1963] CMLR 175; CCH para 8005.
25.   *Second Civil Servants Unions Case* (72/74), 18 March 1975, consideration 17; [1975] ECR 410; [1975] 2 CMLR 193.
26.   *Idem*, consideration 19. See also the *First Civil Servants Unions Case* (175/73), 8 Oct. 1974, consideration 17, 18; [1974] ECR 925, 926; [1975] 1 CMLR 140.

Treaty regarding the right of interested parties to bring an action must not be interpreted restrictively.

...

The defendant further contends that the contested decision is by its very nature a regulation in the form of an individual decision and therefore action against it is no more available to individuals than in the case of legislative measures of general application.

It follows however from Articles 189 and 191 of the EEC Treaty that decisions are characterized by the limited number of persons to whom they are addressed. In order to determine whether or not a measure constitutes a decision one must enquire whether that measure concerns specific persons. The contested Decision was addressed to the government of the Federal Republic of Germany and refuses to grant it authorization for the partial suspension of customs duties on certain products imported from third countries. Therefore the contested measure must be regarded as a decision referring to a particular person and binding that person alone.' [27]

2. Justiciable versus non-existent acts

a. THE PROBLEM OF NON-EXISTENT ACTS

§ 213. As the conduct of government authorities is assumed to be valid, the validity of their acts can be challenged only under certain conditions. In the case of an action for annulment in the European Communities the most important condition is that it must be lodged within a strict time limit, usually within two months. If the validity of an act cannot, or can no longer, be challenged, the validity of the authority's conduct is final.

These limitations imposed on the possibility of challenging official acts stress the need for a separate category of non-existent acts, which can never be applied even if they cannot, or can no longer, be impugned.

In this thorough study of the non-existent acts in Community law [28] Van Empel distinguishes two groups of legally non-existent acts:

(a) acts non-existent in fact, such as acts which have not entered into force, so that the project exists only on paper; or acts which clearly emanate from persons not vested with the necessary competence, such as a member of the clerical staff, and

(b) acts which lack all legal foundation. The latter group includes acts which exist, but are so flagrantly illegal that they ought not be applied even though unchallenged within the time limits provided for. This group is clearly differentiated by German administrative law, which permits a *Feststellungs-klage* [29] against them, but is less acceptable in the laws of other Member

27. *Plaumann Case* (25/62), 15 July 1963, [1963] ECR 106, 107; 9 Jur. (1963) 231; 9 Rec. (1963) 222; [1964] CMLR 46; CCH para 8013.
28. Martijn van Empel, *L'acte public inexistant et le droit communautaire*, 1971 CDE pp. 251-283.
29. *Verwaltungsgerichtsordnung*, para 43.

States such as Belgium and Luxembourg. The possibility of the *Feststellungs-klage* would counteract the over-rigidity of the provision whereby Community acts are final unless challenged within the period of two months. On the other hand, it affects legal certainly and should therefore be narrowly interpreted.

The need for a legal construction permitting an intermediary group of acts, between non-existent acts and justiciable acts, is not very strongly felt in Community law. By means of the plea of illegality (see below § 356-365) the legality of regulations can be disputed after the expiry of the time limit for the action for annulment; and under EEC Article 177 (see below § 366-378) national courts may ask a ruling of the Court of Justice on the validity of any rule of Community law at any time.

§ 214.   So far the Court of Justice has not recognized a separate group of acts without legal foundation. It has ruled a few times on the question of the non-existence or the absolute nullity of an act, but it does not easily accept such non-existence. In the *Algera Case* the Court considered:

'In the opinion of the Court, the unlawful nature of an individual admini-strative measure entails its complete nullity only in certain circumstances which do not occur in the present action. Apart from those exceptional cases, the theoretical writing and the case-law of the Member States allow only of voidability and revocability. The adoption of an administrative measure creates a presumption as to its validity. That validity can be set aside only by means of annulment or withdrawal, in so far as those mea-sures are permissible.' [30]

The last two sentences lead us to the heart of the administrative appeal: there is no equality of the parties before an administrative court. The act is presumed to be valid and can only be challenged when the right to bring an action is provided for, and on the conditions (standing before the court, time limits, grounds of illegality) under which the action is admitted; acts remain in force until repealed or annulled.

§ 215.   The Court gave further consideration to the problem of non-existence in the *Schots-Kortner Case*. On 7 July 1972 it had decided in the *Sabbatini Case* that Article 4(3) of Annex VII of the Staff Regulations was illegal since it discriminated between men and women (women lost their expatriation allowance when they married, while men did not). The Court had therefore annulled the decision by which Mrs. Sabbatini's expatriation allowance was withdrawn on the occasion of her marriage. [31] After this case, a large number of married women appealed against the decisions by which their expatriation allowance had been withdrawn. They could not avail themselves of the normal

30. *Algera Case* (7/56 and 3-7/57), 12 July 1957, [1957-58] ECR 60, 61; 3 Jur. (1957) 128, 3 Rec. (1957) 122.
31. *Sabbatini Case* (20/71), 7 June 1972, [1972] ECR 351; [1972] CMLR 959; see also *Bauduin Case* (32/71), 7 June 1972, [1972] ECR 370; [1972] CMLR 959.

actions since the time limit of two months had long passed. Therefore, they claimed that Article 4(3) of Annex VII of the Staff Regulations was legally non-existent. The Court of Justice replied:

'In any event the provisions of Article 4(3) of Annex VII to the Staff Regulations cannot be termed "non-existent", originating as it does with the competent authority and taken with due regard to the procedural and formal conditions laid down by the Treaties'. [32]

The reasoning of the Court demonstrates that 'non-existence' will not easily be accepted for decisions adopted in accordance with the normal procedure.

§ 216. A third case in which non-existence was invoked was the *Rediscount Rate Case*. The Commission acted against France for non-compliance with one of its decisions.

France had not brought an action against the decision but submitted that it was non-existent since it was taken in a field which was beyond the competence of the Commission. The Court considered:

'If this allegation were valid, the abovementioned decision would lack all legal basis in the Community legal system and in proceedings where the Commission in the interest of the Community is taking action for failure by a State to fulfil its obligations, it is a fundamental requirement of the legal system that the Court should investigate whether this is the case.'

Subsequently the Court concluded that the Commission was competent and continued to state that,

'In view of the definitive nature of the decision in question it is not necessary to consider the other submissions which the French Government has put forward outside the procedures and time-limits laid down in the Treaty and the observance of which is required in the interest both of the States themselves and of the Community.' [33]

The Court apparently considered the question whether the decision was non-existent, but concluded that such was not the case. It has been disputed whether the Court considered this question only because the case was brought under Article 169 (France was accused of violating the Treaty) or whether it did so because the submission of absolute incompetence was thought so important that it had to be considered.[34] Probably, both considerations played a role.

32. *Schots-Kortner Case* (15-33/73 etc.), 21 Feb. 1974, consideration 33, [1974] ECR 191.
33. *Rediscount Rate Case* (6 and 11/69), 10 Dec. 1969, considerations 13 and 24, [1969] ECR 539, 540; [1970] CMLR 65, 66; CCH para 8105.
34. *See* notes on the *Rediscount Rate Case* by Schermers in 19 AA (1970), pp. 174, 175; and by Brinkhorst in 7 CMLRev. (1970), 485.

§ 217.   Apart from the cases where letters were not accepted as decisions (see below § 225, 226) the only case in which the Court considered a decision to be non-existent is the *Tubes de la Sarre Case*. The High Authority had taken an act which the Court accepted 'had undoubtedly been meant as an opinion in the sense of ECSC Article 54, para 4' (which is an opinion with legal effect). Nonetheless, the Court did not recognize the act as such, because it was not reasoned.

The Court considered:

'Several of the conditions laid down by the Treaty have not been fulfilled; although some of them are formal requirements which cannot affect the character or the existence of an act, it is clear that a statement of reasons for an opinion is not only required by Articles 5 and 15 and the fourth paragraph of Article 54 of the Treaty but that it is an essential, indeed constituent element of such an act, with the result that in the absence of a statement of reasons the act cannot exist. In consequence, the letter of 19 December 1956 does not constitute an opinion within the meaning of the fourth paragraph of Article 54 of the Treaty and Application 1/57 is inadmissible for want of subject-matter since the act which it impugns is, in law, non-existent.' [35]

It must be taken into consideration that ECSC Article 54(4) speaks of a 'reasoned opinion', which strengthens the argument that a non-reasoned opinion can never come under the scope of this article. On the other hand, the Court referred to ECSC Article 15 which contains the general provision that decisions, recommendations and opinions shall state the reasons on which they are based. This could indicate that the Court wanted to express a general rule. [36] If the latter hypothesis is correct, the Court has subsequently changed its position. In other cases, the Court did not follow the same line that a total absence of reasoning meant non-existence of the act. In the *First Nold Case*, although the Court ruled that insufficient reasoning is tantamount to no reasoning at all, it did not conclude that the act concerned was non-existent. Rather, it annulled the act according to the normal procedure of ECSC Article 33. [37] In the *First Cement Convention Case* the Court allowed an action against a letter since the letter had legal effect. The letter contained no reasoning and was, therefore, annulled according to the procedure contained in EEC Article 173. It was not, however, declared non-existent. [38]

§ 218.   Advocate-General Roemer recommended that the Court should consider an act non-existent in the *First Fives Lille Cail Case*. He based his

---

35.   *Tubes de la Sarre Case* (1 and 14/57), 10 Dec. 1957, [1957-58] ECR 112, 113; 3 Jur. (1957) 233, 234; 3 Rec. (1957) 219, 220.
36.   Van Empel (*op. cit.*, note 28) p. 273.
37.   *First Nold Case* (18/57), 20 March 1959, [1959] ECR 53; 5 Jur. (1959) 121; 5 Rec. (1959) 116.
38.   *First Cement Convention Case* (8-11/66), 15 March 1967, [1967] ECR 90-93; 13 Jur. (1967) 114-116; 13 Rec. (1967) 116-119; [1967] CMLR 102-105; CCH para 8052 (pp. 7784-7786). See below § 245.

suggestion on a comparison of the national legal systems. [39] In the *First Cement Convention Case* the same Advocate-General was of the opinion that the act concerned was an informal letter of a civil servant, and for that reason was not a challengeable Community act. [40]

Advocate-General Lagrange in a similar case, expressed the opinion that a letter written by a civil servant who could not be considered competent to take a decision should, nonetheless, be considered as a decision, but as constituting an illegal one which should be annulled. He preferred this solution to the one proposed by Advocate-General Roemer as legally more correct. [41]

§ 219. The strongest argument militating in favour of Lagrange's solution is the costs of the proceedings. In the event of illegality the applicant will win his case and the Community institution concerned will bear the costs of the proceedings. When non-existence is established, the action will be declared inadmissible (one cannot challenge an act which does not exist), with the result that the applicant will have to bear the costs. [42]

In exceptional cases the Court may order the parties to bear their own costs and may order a successful party to pay the costs which it considers that party to have unreasonably caused. [43] This would enable the Court to rule that even in the case of a non-existent act the Community institution concerned should bear at least part of the costs of the proceedings.

In the *Tubes de la Sarre Case* where the Court accepted the non-existence of an act, the action was declared inadmissible and the applicant was ordered to pay all costs. [44]

In the *First Lemmerz-Werke Case*, the *Henricot Case* and the *Second Hoogovens Case* the actions were brought against letters which the Court did not accept as decisions (see below § 225). Thus, in these cases also there were no judiciable acts. On the question of costs, the Court considered:

'The peremptory tone of the letter involved in these proceedings, accentuated by the mode of despatch, and the setting of a time-limit for payment, were capable in themselves of creating uncertainty in the applicant's mind about the nature of the said letter. The High Authority, having by its own conduct induced the applicant to institute proceedings in order to safeguard its rights, must bear the greater part of the costs. It is appropriate that these should be consolidated and that the High Authority should bear three-quarters thereof and the applicant one-quarter.' [45]

39. *First Fives Lille Cail Case* (19, 21/60, 2, 3/61) 15 Dec. 1961, Opinion, [1961] ECR 307; 7 Jur. (1961) 648; 7 Rec. (1961) 612, 613. See below § 453.
40. *First Cement Convention Case* (8-11/66), 15 March 1967, Opinion, [1967] ECR 107-109; 13 Jur. (1967) 133, 134; 13 Rec. (1967) 136-138; [1967] CMLR 96-98; CCH para 8052. For the legality of letters by civil servants, see below § 226.
41. *Knutange Case* (15, 29/59), 12 Feb. 1960, Opinion, [1960] ECR 12; 6 Jur. (1960) 34; 6 Rec. (1960) 34. See also below § 226.
42. Rules of Procedure of the Court of Justice, Art. 69 (2).
43. *Idem* Art. 69 (3), see below § 705.
44. *Tubes de la Sarre Case* (1 and 14/57), 10 Dec. 1957, [1957-58] ECR 115; 3 Jur. (1957) 238; 3 Rec. (1957) 224.
45. *Second Hoogovens Case* (28/63), 5 Dec. 1963, [1963] ECR 236; 9 Jur. (1963) 504; 9

b. ACTS WHICH MIGHT BE CONSIDERED NON-EXISTENT

(i) Acts not contemplated by the Treaties

§ 220. ECSC Article 33 provides for an action only against general decisions (termed 'regulations' by the other Communities), individual decisions ('decisions' in the other Communities) and recommendations ('directives' in the other Communities). EEC Article 173 permits actions against 'acts of the Council and the Commission other than recommendations or opinions'. If no acts existed other than those enumerated by ECSC Article 14 and EEC Article 189, both treaty systems would lead to the same result: binding acts may be challenged, non-binding ones may not. In the *ERTA Case*, however, the Court accepted other types of acts (in that case political consultations) as being subject to Court proceedings. In the *Second Haegeman Case* the Court confirmed this, when it considered that an international agreement concluded with a third State (Greece) is *'in so far as it concerns the Community, an act of one of the Institutions'*. [46] The fact that there are other acts of the institutions than those enumerated in EEC Article 189 leads, theoretically, to a distinction being drawn between the two systems: in the ECSC such other acts could not be challenged, while in the EEC actions are admissible. In practice, there is no noticeable distinction. Under the ECSC Treaty, the Court has never accepted the existence of 'other acts'; on the contrary, it considered several times that:

> 'An act of the High Authority constitutes a decision when it lays down a rule capable of being applied, in other words, when by the said act the High Authority unequivocally determines the position which it decides to adopt if certain conditions are fulfilled.' [47]

It may safely be assumed that the Court will classify any binding acts of the ECSC as decisions in the sense of ECSC Article 14, with the result that these acts may be subject to an application for annulment.

§ 221. In deciding the *ERTA Case* under the EEC Treaty, the Court took care to safeguard the right to institute proceedings against all ECC acts which have legal effect.

The Court stated:

Rec. (1963) 481, 482; [1964] CMLR 128. In the two other cases the High Authority had not asked the Court to order the applicant to pay the costs of the proceedings. The Court therefore ordered the High Authority to bear its own costs in full and three-quarters of the costs of the applicants. *First Lemmerz-Werke Case* (53 and 54/63), 5 Dec. 1963, [1963] ECR 249; 9 Jur. (1963) 531; 9 Rec. (1963) 508; [1964] CMLR 400; *Henricot case* (23, 24 and 52/63), 5 Dec. 1963, [1963] ECR 225; 9 Jur. (1963) 477, 478; 9 Rec. (1963) 456, 457; [1964] CMLR 123, 124.
46. *Second Haegeman Case* (181/73), 30 April 1974, consideration 4 (quoted above in § 135) [1974], ECR 459; [1975] 1 CMLR 530; CCH para 8273.
47. *Tubes de la Sarre Case* (1 and 14/57), 10 Dec. 1957, [1957-58] ECR 114; 3 Jur. (1957) 236; 3 Rec. (1957) 222; see also *Fédéchar Case* (8/55), 16 July 1956, [1955-56] ECR 257; 2 Jur. (1956) 236; 2 Rec. (1956) 225.

'Under Article 173, the Court has a duty to review the legality 'of acts of the Council ... other than recommendations or opinions'.

Since the only matters excluded from the scope of the action for annulment open to the Member States and the institutions are 'recommendations or opinions' — which by the final paragraph of Article 189 are declared to have no binding force — Article 173 treats as acts open to review by the Court all measures adopted by the institutions which are intended to have legal force.

The objective of this review is to ensure, as required by Article 164, observance of the law in the interpretation and application of the Treaty. It would be inconsistent with this objective to interpret the conditions under which the action is admissible so restrictively as to limit the availability of this procedure merely to the categories of measures referred to by Article 189.

An action for annulment must therefore be available in the case of all measures adopted by the institutions, whatever their nature or form, which are intended to have legal effects.'[48]

This opinion of the Court leaves no doubt with respect to the EEC and Euratom Treaties. Its reasoning supports the proposition that the Court will accept 'other binding acts' in the ECSC as decisions, if ever a similar situation were to present itself under the ECSC Treaty.

§ 222. The most important acts, not forseen by the Treaties, are the *decisions and agreements adopted by the Representatives of the Governments of the Member States meeting within the Council.*[49] These decisions and agreements have no formal legal connection with Community law. They are taken by the members of the Council — who must be members of the Governments of the Member States[50] and often are Ministers for Foreign Affairs — in their capacity as representatives of States, in cases when the Council is not considered competent to decide. Though the topics covered are matters related to Community law (that is why the decisions are taken when the representatives meet within the Council), their form is that of an international agreement concluded by competent delegates of independent States. Under international law Ministers for Foreign Affairs are considered competent to engage their States without having to produce full powers.[51] But in some national legal

---

48. *ERTA Case* (22/70), 31 March 1971, considerations 38-42, [1971] ECR 276, 277; [1971] CMLR 357; CCH para 8134.
49. On these decisions and agreements see Gerhard Bebr, *Acts of representatives of the Governments of Member States*, 14 SEW (1966) pp. 529-545; Henry G. Schermers, *Besluiten van de vertegenwoordigers der Lid Staten; Gemeenschapsrecht?* 14 SEW (1966) pp. 545-579; Burger Report to the European Parliament, 12 March 1969, document 215 and the debates thereon on 8 May 1969; Jean Victor Louis, *Les décisions des représentants des Gouvernements des Etats Membres*, in Les Novelles, droit des Communautés européennes, Maison Ferdinand Larcier, Brussels 1969, pp. 427-435.
50. Merger Treaty, Art. 2.
51. Vienna Convention on the Law of Treaties, Artt. 7 (2).

systems problems may arise, for instance, under the Dutch constitution all international agreements require parliamentary approval. [52] As the decisions and agreements adopted by the Representatives of the Governments of the Member States meeting within the Council have not been presented to Parliament some parliamentary questions have been directed at the Dutch Prime Minister. In his answer the Prime Minister (then also Minister of Foreign Affairs *ad interim*) replied that most of these decisions cannot be qualified as international agreements within the meaning of the Dutch constitution, but that those which can be qualified as such will be subjected to parliamentary approval. [53]

For recent decisions and agreements, adopted by the Representatives of the Governments of the Member States meeting within the Council, parliamentary approval is facilitated by the addition of the provision that: the 'Member States shall adopt all the measures necessary for the implementation' of the decision or agreement. [54] This opens up the possibility for the individual Governments to bring the decisions and agreements before their parliaments. Factual circumstances, however, often do not permit national parliaments to discuss these decisions or agreements. [55]

§ 223. As decisions and agreements must be adopted either under international law or under Community law, the reply by the Dutch Prime Minister — that most of the decisions and agreements, adopted by the Representatives of the Governments of the Member States meeting within the Council, are not agreements under international law — means that they have to be considered as part of Community law. In international institutional law the collective membership is often seen as a special institution of the organization to which tasks can be attributed. [56] The Community Treaties in several articles expressly charge the Member States to take collective decisions, for example in EEC Article 167 requiring the Governments of the Member States to appoint 'by common accord' the Judges and the Advocate-General. [57]

Even if they are not expressly required by the Treaties many decisions and agreements adopted by the Representatives of the Governments of the Member States meeting within the Council can be considered as part of the body of Community law, due to the matters they regulate. According to Pescatore they can thus be brought under the jurisdiction of the Court on the basis of

---

52. Netherlands' Constitution Art. 60-62.
53. Questions by Mr. Vredeling and Mr. Blaise of 5 July 1966 and reply by Prime Minister Cals of 26 July 1966, *Aanhangsel tot het Verslag van de Handelingen der Tweede Kamer* 1965-1966, p. 1233.
54. See, e.g., the decision of the Representatives of the Governments of the Member States of the European Coal and Steel Community, meeting within the Council, of 26 June 1975 (on tariff preferences for products from Israel), OJ 28 June 1975 No. L 165, p. 76.
55. See the decision quoted above, in note 54, which entered into force five days after its adoption.
56. Schermers (*op. cit.*, note 2). Vol. I, pp. 66-69; Vol. II p. 704.
57. Up to 1966 half of the agreements of the Representatives of the Governments of the Member States meeting within the Council were based on such specific Treaty instructions, see Schermers (*op. cit.*, note 49) p. 554.

EEC Article 5 whereby it is incumbent on the Member States to take all appropriate measures to ensure fulfilment of the obligations arising out of the Treaty. The obligation contained in this Article may be seen as the basis on which the Member States have made the decisions and agreements concerned.[58] Due to the fact that these decisions and agreements are clearly adopted by the Member States in their capacity as elements of the Communities (see above § 194) no problem is engendered by accepting these measures as part of Community law. Since they originate from the Member States, however, they fall under the more limited control exercised by the Court of Justice over the Member States under EEC Article 169 (see below § 380-432) and do not constitute acts subject to an application for annulment.

§ 224. The decisions and agreements adopted by the Representatives of the Governments of the Member States meeting within the Council have been recognized as part of Community law by the express reference to them in Article 3 of the Act of Accession. According to this article, the new Member States accede to these decisions and agreements. As the jurisdiction of the Court of Justice applies in respect of the Act of Accession [59] the Court's obligation to ensure that the law is observed [60] will also cover the interpretation and application of decisions and agreements adopted by the Representatives of the Governments of the Member States meeting within the Council which were adopted before the accession.

(ii) Letters

§ 225. The procedural requirements of Community acts will be discussed below in conjunction with the grounds of illegality (§ 254-297). The question which must now be considered is whether a letter written by a civil servant of the Communities is a Community act subject to an application for annulment or rather an informal opinion or even a non-existent act. This question arose in the *First Lemmerz-Werke Case*, where a director-general in the staff of the High Authority addressed a letter to *Lemmerz-Werke*, requesting payment of a levy. *Lemmerz-Werke* instituted proceedings against the letter, but the High Authority denied that the letter was a binding act subject to annulment. It referred to its Decision 22/60 in which it had ruled that all decisions would be issued in a specific form: they would bear the title 'Decision', would refer to the Treaty articles on which they were based, would subsequently mention the considerations as to why they were taken, would be presented in the form of articles and signed by a member of the High Authority. [61] Since the letter to *Lemmerz-Werke* did not correspond to the abovementioned form, it should not be considered as a binding act of the High Authority.

The Court did not accept this view. On the contrary, it ruled that,

---

58. Pierre Pescatore, *L'ordre Juridique des Communautés Européennes*, 2nd ed., Liège 1973, p. 141.
59. Accession Treaty Art. 1, paras 2 and 3.
60. EEC Art. 164.
61. High Authority Decision 22/60, OJ 1248/60.

'Although it is desirable to ensure observance of the requirements prescribed in the appropriate manner by the High Authority, which enable governments, institutions and undertakings to identify decisions from their actual form, it does not follow that a measure should not be considered a decision, merely because it fails to comply with some inessential requirement of form if the fundamental conditions underlying the concept of a decision within the meaning of the Treaty are otherwise satisfied.' [62]

Nevertheless, the Court did not accept the letters as decisions. It continued, reasoning:

'According to Article 14, decisions shall be taken by the High Authority, that is to say by its members sitting as a body. As such decisions are "binding in their entirety" however, they must show that they are intended to have legal effects upon those to whom they are addressed.

It follows from the natural meaning of the word that a decision marks the culmination of procedure within the High Authority, and is thus the definitive expression of its intentions.

Finally, it is necessary for the legal protection of all those affected that they should be able to identify by its very form a decision which involves such serious legal consequences, in particular a compulsory time-limit for exercising the right of instituting proceedings against it. In particular, for a measure to amount to a decision, those to whom it is addressed must be enabled clearly to recognize that they are dealing with such a measure.

It follows therefore from all these considerations that a decision must appear as a measure taken by the High Authority, acting as a body, intended to produce legal effects and constituting the culmination of procedure within the High Authority, whereby the High Authority gives its final ruling in a form from which its nature can be identified.

Any measure, therefore, which in particular, does not appear to have been debated and adopted by the High Authority and authenticated by the signature of one of its members, cannot be regarded as a decision.' [63]

Since the letter did not fulfil these conditions, it could not be considered a decision.

§ 226. The last paragraph of the above opinion is the conclusion drawn from the penultimate one which contains the requirements. The conclusion was that the letter was not a decision since it was neither discussed by the High Authority nor signed by one of its members. The two requirements should

---

62. *First Lemmerz-Werke Case* (53 and 54/63), 5 Dec. 1963, [1963] ECR 247, 248; 9 Jur. (1963) 529; 9 Rec. (1963) 506; [1964] CMLR 399. The same consideration has been given in the *Henricot Case* (23, 24 and 52/63), 5 Dec. 1963 [1963] ECR 223; 9 Jur. (1963) 475; 9 Rec. (1963) 454; [1964] CMLR 122, 123 and in the *Second Hoogovens Case* (28/63), 5 Dec. 1963, [1963] ECR 235; 9 Jur. (1963) 502, 503; 9 Rec. (1963) 480, 481; [1964] CMLR 127, 128.
63. *Idem.*

not be read cumulatively. If it is clear that an act has been discussed by the High Authority it need not also be signed by one of its members. In the *Knutange Case* the Court had already considered:

'In the letter of 27 February 1959, signed by an official of the High Authority and contested in Application 15/59, it is stated that 'after inquiry, the High Authority has found that the terms of the above-mentioned decisions do not allow such exoneration to be granted to you'. Thus, that letter constituted notification of a decision which had apparently been taken by the High Authority.' [64]

Also in the *First Cement Convention Case*, a letter was disputed in which an employee had communicated the Commission's viewpoint to the applicant. Again, the Court recognized the letter as a decision. [65] Five years later, in the *ICI Case*, the Court accepted that the Commission may delegate signatory authority to particular employees. [66] A letter by a Head of Division to a staff member concerning her expatriation allowance has also been accepted by the Court as a decision of the Commission. [67]

For letters preliminary to acts see below § 244, 245; for letters containing an interpretation of acts see below § 246.

In staff cases even the monthly salary statement may be considered as an act subject to an application for annulment if it clearly shows the decision taken. [68]

3. Recommendations, resolutions and opinions

§ 227. EEC Article 173 provides that the Court of Justice shall review the legality of acts of the Council and the Commission 'other than recommendations and opinions'. Resolutions as such are not foreseen as a special form of acts. They are normally understood as having the same force as recommendations, so that they must follow the same rules as recommendations and opinions. As Article 173 governs the action for annulment (see below § 300-328), it is beyond doubt that the annulment of recommendations and opinions cannot be asked of the Court; but it is less clear whether this prohibition would also apply to the review of legality of recommendations and opinions as provided for in other articles. The plea of illegality (see below § 356-365) is limited to regulations, but neither the action against failure to act (EEC Article 175, see below § 329-355) nor the request by a national court for a

64. *Knutange Case* (15 and 29/59), 12 Feb. 1960, [1960] ECR 7; 6 Jur. (1960) 24; 6 Rec. (1960) 24.
65. *First Cement Convention Case* (8-11/66), 15 March 1967, [1967] ECR 90-93; 13 Jur. (1967) 113-116; 13 Rec. (1967) 116-119; [1967] CMLR 102-105; CCH para 8052 (pp. 7784-7786). See below § 245.
66. *ICI Case* (48/69), 14 July 1972, consideration 13, [1972] ECR 650; [1972] CMLR 618; CCH para 8161.
67. *Goeth Case* (56/72), 8 Feb. 1973, [1973] ECR 186.
68. *Wack Case* (1/76), 15 June 1976, consideration 5, [1976] ECR 1023.

preliminary ruling on the validity of acts of the institutions (EEC Article 177, see below § 366-379) is expressly limited to binding acts. For both actions there may be good reasons not to exclude recommendations and opinions. When an institution is obliged under Community law to issue a recommendation or opinion, it is in the interest of the legal system that a failure to do so can be judicially reviewed. For the interpretation of national measures recommendations and opinions of the Communities may be relevant. In the *Thieffry Case* the Court of Justice held that the General Programma for the abolition of restrictions on freedom of establishment [69] provides useful guidance for the implementation of the relevant provisions of the EEC Treaty. [70] Likewise non-binding acts may provide useful guidelines for national courts if properly interpreted by the Court of Justice.

§ 228. Under the ECSC Treaty an action can be brought for the annulment of decisions and recommendations. [71] However, an ECSC recommendation is not a recommendation in the proper sense: it is binding as to the aims pursued [72] and should therefore more properly be called a 'directive', in the EEC terminology. In their normal meaning of legally non-binding acts recommendations, resolutions and opinions cannot be challenged, for the purpose of annulment, in the ECSC. In the ECSC the action against failure to act and the plea of illegality are both limited to binding acts; preliminary rulings can, however, be given on the validity of any act [73]; furthermore in a suit for damages, the legality of any act could be brought into discussion.

§ 229. In most cases the judicial review of recommendations, resolutions and opinions appears limited, a state of affairs which is to be deplored as recourse is increasingly made to these acts to further develop Community law. [74] Frequently this can exert substantial influence on the legal position of Member States and individuals [75]:

(a) A recommendation or resolution may initiate new spheres of activity on the part of the Communities. Even though States cannot be compelled to participate in such initiatives they will be under some political pressure to do so.

(b) By means of a recommendation the Communities may suggest detailed rules to be adopted by the Member States. Although they are free either to adopt or not to adopt such rules, amendment of the rules may, in practice,

69. O.J. English Special Edition, Second Series, IX, p. 8.
70. *Thieffry Case* (71/76), 28 April 1977, consideration 14, [1977] ECR 777; [1977] 2 CMLR 403; CCH para 8396.
71. ECSC Art. 33.
72. ECSC Art. 14.
73. ECSC Art. 41.
74. Charles-Albert Morand pleads that the Court of Justice should admit the action for annulment against recommendations due to their great importance, but offers no legal ground for this plea, *Les recommendations, les résolutions et les avis du droit communautaire*, 1970 CDE pp. 623-644, at p. 631.
75. On the effect of recommendations of international organizations: see Schermers (*op. cit.*, note 2) Vol. II, pp. 492-506.

prove to be difficult. To a certain extent, the recommendation predetermines the actual details of the final texts, in particular when uniformity is in the interest of all Member States.

(c) Inferior organs of the organization are bound by the resolutions emanating from superior ones.

(d) Acceptance of a recommendation by a Member State creates an agreement between that State and the Community, entailing legal consequences. [76]

(e) Compliance by some Member States may compel others to take account of a recommendation, for instance, when the Communities recommend the use of particular documents in internal Community trade with the result that other Member States do not accept goods without such documents, a Member State has practically no other choice but to comply.

§ 230. Due to the restrictive nature of the texts of the Treaties, recommendations, resolutions and opinions will not easily come before the Court of Justice. Apart from the action against failure to act, under the EEC Treaty preliminary rulings on these acts seem to be the only court rulings feasible. Even though it can be disputed whether preliminary rulings can be asked on the validity of non-binding acts, they are certainly possible as regards their interpretation. [77] It may not always be possible to obtain a *uniform* interpretation of these acts, however. Unlike other community acts recommendations, resolutions and opinions can be accepted by the Member States with reservations. [78]

The Court of Justice has been reluctant in accepting the legal consequences of recommendations, resolutions and opinions. In the *Dairy-Products Case* it refused to grant legal effect to the time limits set by a resolution of the Council. The Court considered that the use of a different form of act from those mentioned in EEC Article 189, indicated that less binding effect was intended. [79]

In the *Second Schlüter Case*, the Court of Justice refused to take account of the Resolution adopted by the Council and Government Representatives on the establishment of an economic and monetary union considering:

'Moreover, the Council Resolution of 22 March 1971, which is primarily an expression of the policy favoured by the Council and Government Representatives of the Member States concerning the establishment of an economic and monetary union within the next ten years following 1 January 1971, cannot for its part, either, by reason of its content, create legal consequences of which parties might avail themselves in court'. [80]

§ 231. Sometimes individuals are interested in obtaining the advice of the Commission or in the Commission issuing advice to a third party. They may

---

76. Morand (*op. cit.*, note 74) p. 630.
77. See also Gerhard Bebr in CDE 1975, p. 391.
78. See Morand.(*op. cit.*, note 74) p. 630.
79. *Dairy-Products Case* (90, 91/63), 13 Nov. 1964; [1964] ECR 631; 10 Jur. (1964) 1293; 10 Rec. (1964) 1232; [1965] CMLR 72; CCH para 8028.
80. *Second Schlüter Case* (9/73), 24 Oct. 1973, [1973] ECR 1161; CCH para 8233.

then officially request the Commission to render advice. An express ref[
the Commission to do so is not accepted by the Court as a judiciable act. -

When, of course, recommendations, resolutions or opinions have binding effect, the Court will disregard their actual title and consider them as regulations, decisions or directives (see above § 220, 225). The reasoned opinion mentioned in ECSC Article 54(5) has the force of a decision and can, therefore, be subject to an application for annulment. [82]

4. Internal directives

§ 232. To what extent can an internal directive be subject to an application for annulment? In the *Phoenix-Rheinrohr Case* the Court held that a letter of an internal nature, circulated by a chief executive to the departments under his control, and intended to guide the working of those departments, can only give rise to obligations on the part of those administrative bodies receiving it. Such a letter is therefore not a decision within the meaning of the ECSC Treaty and cannot be challenged. [83]

In the *Louwage Case* an internal directive provided that officials who had been authorized to move their domicile, but had not done so during the year subsequent to their appointment, were entitled to a daily subsistence allowance. The Commission had not applied this internal directive to the applicant. When Louwage invoked the directive in court, the Court of Justice replied:

'Although an internal directive has not the character of a rule of law which the administration is always bound to observe, it nevertheless sets forth a rule of conduct indicating the practice to be followed, from which the administration may not depart without giving the reasons which have led it to do so, since otherwise the principles of equality of treatment would be infringed'. [84]

The latter formula suggests that internal directives may bring an alteration in the legal position of individuals; this could be a reason for allowing actions against them (see the *First Cement Convention Case*, below § 245).

5. Evaluation of a situation [85]

§ 233. According to ECSC Article 33, the Court may not normally 'examine the evaluation of the situation resulting from economic facts or circumstan-

81. See *Chevalley Case* (15/70), 18 Nov. 1970, [1970] ECR 980; CCH para 8115; *First Lütticke Case* (48/65), 1 March 1966, [1966] ECR 27; 12 Jur. (1966) 39; 12 Rec. (1966) 39; [1966] CMLR 386, 387; CCH para 8044.
82. ECSC Art. 54 (5); *Tubes de la Sarre Case* (1 and 14/57), 10 Dec. 1957, [1957-58] ECR 114; 3 Jur. (1957) 236; 3 Rec. (1957) 222.
83. *Phoenix-Rheinrohr Case* (20/58), 17 July 1959, [1959] ECR 82; 5 Jur. (1958-59) 192; 5 Rec. (1958-59) 181; see also below § 246.
84. *Louwage Case* (148/73), 30 Jan. 1974, consideration 12, [1974] ECR 89.
85. See also Bernard Asso, *Le contrôle de l'opportunité de la décision économique devant la Cour européenne de justice*, 12 RTDE (1976), pp. 21-50.

ces, in the light of which the High Authority took its decisions or made its recommendations, save where the High Authority is alleged to have misused its powers or to have manifestly failed to observe the provisions of this Treaty or any rule of law relating to its application.' [86] This provision stems from a compromise between the French and the German delegations at the time of the establishment of the Community. [87] The French delegation feared that since the ECSC Treaty contained many broad and rather vague rules, the Court of Justice would have broad discretion to enter into a subjective judgment of the economic background of ECSC acts if it had the freedom to annul on the grounds of any violation of the Treaty. It therefore wanted to exclude 'infringement of the Treaty' as a ground of illegality. The other delegations, in particular that of the Federal Republic of Germany did not want the Court's power of review to be curtailed to that extent and, therefore, the compromise reached was to include 'infringement of the Treaty' as a ground of illegality but to add, at the same time, the limitation on economic facts or circumstances.

As a result of this provision the Court will not examine economic facts and circumstances whenever the evaluation of the Commission (High Authority) seems reasonably tenable. The Court will review economic facts and circumstances only when such evaluation is manifestly wrong. [88] In Dutch law this is called a 'marginal review function', as the Court only reviews when the executive operates outside reasonable margins.

§ 234.   The Court confirmed this interpretation of ECSC Article 33(1) in the *Coal Price Case* where it held:

'The term 'manifest' presupposes that a certain degree is reached in the failure to observe legal provisions so that the failure to observe the Treaty appears to derive from an obvious error in the evaluation, having regard to the provisions of the Treaty, of the situation in respect of which the decision was taken. In the present instance the 'manifest' failure to observe the Treaty can only result from the finding by the Court of the existence of an economic situation which *prima facie* reveals no necessity for the contested measure in the pursuit of the objectives set out in Article 3 of the Treaty, in particular paragraph (c).' [89]

---

86. ECSC Art. 33 (1).
87. See C.W.A. Timmermans, *De Administratieve Rechter en Beoordelingsvrijheden van Bestuursorganen*, Thesis Leiden 1973, pp. 114, 115.
88. See B. van der Esch, *Pouvoirs discrétionnaires de l'Exécutif européen et contrôle juridictionnel*, Europese Monografie No. 12, Kluwer 1968, in particular pp. 36-70. See also *Second Racke Case* (98/78), 25 Jan. 1979, consideration 5.
89. *Coal Price Case* (6/54), 21 March 1955, [1954-56] ECR 115; 1 Jur. (1954-55) 241, 242; 1 Rec. (1954-55) 225. For examples where the Court refused to review the system established by the High Authority for the reason that such review would exceed the limits of its judicial review, see *Knutange Case* (15 and 29/59), 12 Feb. 1960, [1960] ECR 10; 6 Jur. (1960) 27, 28; *Klöckner Case* (17 and 20/61), 13 July 1962, [1962] ECR 346; 8 Jur. (1962) 683; 8 Rec. (1962) 653.

Similarly, in the *Barge Case* the Court held:

'These explanations, contested only as to certain details by the applicant, appear pertinent. In adopting Article 10 (b) and (d) of Decisions Nos 2/57 and 16/58, the High Authority *may have considered that* a correct application of Articles 3, 4 and 5 of the Treaty required the exclusion of the said types of ferrous scrap from the equalization scheme and there is nothing to indicate that in so doing it distorted the scheme.' [90]

§ 235.   There is no provision similar to ECSC Treaty Article 33 in the EEC or the Euratom Treaties. Undoubtedly, the experience gained under the ECSC Treaty taught the drafters that it was more expedient to allow the Court to delineate the extent of its control over the legality of Community acts. [91]

In practice, the Court acts in much the same way as under the ECSC Treaty. Once again, the Court only annuls when the evaluation of the economic situation is manifestly wrong. [92] In both *Deuka Cases* the Court considered that the Commission had considerable freedom in adjusting the denaturing premium for wheat when the balance of the market in cereals was likely to be disturbed. Then the Court proceeded:

'When examining the lawfulness of the exercise of such freedom, the courts cannot substitute their own evaluation of the matter for that of the competent authority, but must restrict themselves to examining whether the evaluation of the competent authority contains a patent error or constitutes a misuse of powers'. [93]

§ 236.   Other examples of 'marginal review' (see 233) under the EEC Treaty can be found in the *Second Schlüter Case* where the Court of Justice held that it was not satisfied that in adopting a particular system of monetary compensatory amounts the Council imposed burdens on traders 'which were *manifestly* out of proportion to the object in view' [94] and in the *Third Roquette Case* where the Court of Justice held, again with respect to monetary compensatory amounts:

90.   *Barge Case* (18/62), 16 Dec. 1963, [1963] ECR 281; 9 Jur. (1963) 591, 592; 9 Rec. (1963) 568; [1965] CMLR 345 (italics added). The italicized words read in French ... que a Haute Autorité *a pu estimer que* ...
91.   Timmermans (*op. cit.*, note 87) p. 119. He refers to further literature on pp. 114 and 116.
92.   See e.g. *Electric Refrigerators Case* (13/63), 17 July 1963, [1963] ECR 178; 9 Jur. 1963) 377; 9 Rec. (1963) 362; [1963] CMLR 312; CCH para 8014; *Customs duties on Silk Case* (32/64), 17 June 1965, [1965] ECR 375; 11 Jur. (1965) 655; 11 Rec. (1965) 486; [1967] CMLR 221; CCH para 8036; *Second Balkan Case* (55/75), 22 Jan. 1876, consideration 8, [1876] ECR 30; CCH para 8340.
93.   *First Deuka Case* (78/74), 18 March 1975, consideration 9, [1975] ECR 432; [1975] 2 CMLR 43; CCH para 8302; *Second Deuka Case* (5/75), 25 June 1975, consideration 4, 1975] ECR 769; CCH para 8313. The word 'courts' is used in plural to take account of the role of national courts in this matter.
94.   *Second Schlüter Case* (9/73), 24 Oct. 1973, consideration 23, [1973] ECR 1156; CCH para 8233 (*italics added*).

'As the evaluation of a complex economic situation is involved, the Commission and the Management Committee enjoy, in this respect, a wide measure of discretion.

In reviewing the legality of the exercise of such discretion, the Court must confine itself to examining whether it contains a manifest error or constitutes a misuse of power or whether the authority did not clearly exceed the bounds of its discretion.' [95]

§ 237. Under EEC Article 115 the Commission may authorize a Member State to withhold Community treatment from imported products from third States where that State has restricted such imports. The Article leaves wide discretion to the Commission but determines the purpose for which the authorization may be granted and provides that the Commission shall determine the conditions and details. In the *Bock and Kaufhof Cases* the Commission had granted authority to the Federal Republic of Germany not to admit the import of certain foodstuffs from the People's Republic of China which were in free circulation in other Member States. The Commission had given the authorization without any serious study of the question whether these German measures were really necessary. Could the Court review the Commission's act? In the *Kaufhof Case* the Court held:

'By failing to review the reasons put forward by the Member State concerned in order to justify the measures of commercial policy which it wishes to introduce, the Commission was in breach of its duty under Article 115 to examine whether the measures have been 'taken in accordance with this Treaty' and whether the protective measures sought are necessary within the meaning of the same provision.

By extending the authorization to applications already received, without taking account of the size or insignificance of the quantity in question in these applications, the Commission has also exceeded the limits of its discretion.' [96]

There is some indication that in its recent case law the Court is more willing to evaluate a situation than it used to be in its earlier days. [97]

§ 238. In several civil servant cases the Court refused to replace opinions formed by the Commission on the abilities of candidates by the Court's own assessment. [98]

---

95. *Third Roquette Case* (29/77), 20 Oct. 1977, considerations 19, 20, [1977] ECR 1843; CCH para 8440.
96. *Kaufhof Case* (29/75), 8 April 1976, consideration 6, [1976] ECR 443; CCH para 8357. See also *Chinese Mushroom Case* (Bock), (62/70), 23 Nov. 1971, consideration 15, [1971] ECR 905, 910; [1972] CMLR 172; CCH para 8150.
97. See, e.g. *Fifth Kampffmeyer Case* (56-60/74), 2 June 1976, considerations 15-19 [1976] ECR 744-746; CCH para 8392.
98. See e.g. *Leroy Case* (35/62 and 16/63), 5 Dec. 1963, [1963] ECR 206, 207; 9 Jur (1963) 436, 437; 9 Rec. (1963) 420.

6. Other acts, the identity of which has been disputed before the Court of Justice

a. PARTS OF ACTS

§ 239. EEC Article 174(2) provides that the Court may state which of the effects of a regulation which it has declared void shall be considered as definitive (see below § 379a). This enables the Court to annul part of a regulation while leaving other parts in force.

§ 240. Article 174(2) is a qualification to the main provision of Article 174(1) that the Court shall declare the act concerned to be void if the action is well founded. Does this mean that decisions must either be declared valid or annulled in their entirety or is it possible to bring an action against a part of the decision without bringing the other parts into dispute? From the beginning the Court of Justice has taken the latter view. Its very first case concerned the annulment of specific articles of some ECSC decisions. [99]

Is it also possible to challenge seperate articles when the decision-making institution objects to the separation of a particular article from the act as a whole? Under the ECSC Treaty this question arose at the formation of the *Geitling* cartel for the sale of Ruhr valley coal. The authorization of the High Authority, required under ECSC Article 65, was granted by Decision 5-56. [100] Article 8 of this decision contained a number of conditions which Geitling considered illegal. Since it did not want to risk the annulment of the entire authorization it appealed against Article 8 only. The High Authority objected, but the Court accepted the appeal. It saw no objection to a possible annulment of a single article since the High Authority was free to subsequently amend the original decision, taking account of the annulment of the article. [101]

Under the EEC Treaty a similar decision was given in the *Transocean Marine Paint Case*. In that case, which also concerned an unfavourable provision in a favourable decision, the applicant appealed for the annulment of a part of the Commission's decision granting exemption under EEC Article 85(3). The Court annulled a subparagraph of an article and referred the case back to the Commission. [102]

In one of the *Bearings Cases* the applicant had challenged only one article of EEC Regulation 1778/77. The Court annulled that article, but held, in an obiter dictum: *'that there is nothing to prevent this regulation's being annulled in its entirely'* and *'that Regulation No 1778/77 is unlawful'.* [103]

99. *First Monnet-Rabat Case* (1/54), 21 Dec. 1954, [1954-55] ECR 3, 17; 1 Jur. 1954-55) 15, 36; 1 Rec. (1954-55) 15, 34.
00. Decision 5-56 of 15 Feb. 1956, OJ 13 March 1956, p. 29 ff.
01. *Geitling Case* (2/56), 20 March 1957, [1957-58] ECR 14, 15; 3 Jur. (1957) 37; 3 Rec. (1957) 35.
02. *Transocean Marine Paint Case* (17/74), 23 Oct. 1974, [1974] ECR 1082; [1974] 2 MLR 479; CCH para 8241.
03. *NTN Toyo Case* (113/77), 29 March 1979, considerations 26, 27.

§ **241.** The annulment of specific articles of a Community act is not always possible. It will not be granted if the disputed article forms an inseparable part of the act, so that without the article the act has no legal effect. [104]

If a party has requested the annulment of a part of an act and the Court considers that part so intimately linked with the rest of the act that it cannot separately annul the disputed part, the question arises whether the Court should annul the entire act or declare the action inadmissible. In the *Jamet Case* the Court opted for the latter, reasoning:

'Furthermore, if the Court were to annul the entire measure this would constitute a ruling *ultra petita* since the application against the contested decision does not concern public policy'. [105]

b. GROUPS OF ACTS

§ **242.** In the very first case before it, the Court of Justice accepted an action against (some articles of) three decisions taken on the same date. [106] This is quite acceptable. The situation, however, is more difficult when two contemporaneous decisions are interconnected and the action, although brought against one of them, is applicable to both. This occurred in the *Simet Feram Case*. Two decisions were addressed to Simet: one established the amount of scrap used by the Italian steel plant; in the other, Simet was ordered to pay the scrap levy. Simet brought an action only against the latter decision but this action also contested the amount established by the former one. The Court considered that the two decisions were so closely related that for practical purposes they should be accepted as constituting a single whole. It was clearly the applicant's intention to challenge both decisions. Furthermore, the High Authority was under no misapprehension on this point and its rights of defence were in no way prejudiced. [107]

§ **243.** An even more difficult problem arises with respect to actions brought against a string, or 'chain', of decisions, but where the action is directed only against the last link of the chain. The question then is whether the time limit for attacking the previous links has passed, thereby precluding the possibility of legal action. This situation often occurs with staff cases, such as the *Ley Case*, where the Commission advertised a vacancy and declared in an announcement of 29 October 1962, that it should be filled by means of internal promotion. Subsequently, it decided by a decision of 26 February 1964 to fill the vacancy in another manner. Ley brought an action against both communications. The Commission submitted that the action against the notification of 29 October 1962 was tardy, but the Court held:

104. See e.g. *Jamet Case* (37/71), 28 June 1972, considerations 10, 11, [1972] ECR 489
105. *Idem*, consideration 12.
106. *First Monnet-Rabat Case* (1/54), 21 Dec. 1954, [1954-56] ECR 6; 1 Jur. (1954) 20
1 Rec. (1954) 19, 20.
107. *Simet Feram Case* (25 and 26/65), 2 March 1967, [1967] ECR 43; 13 Jur. (1967) 53; 13 Rec. (1967) 53.

'Since the recruitment procedure comprises several interdependent measures, this objection would be tantamount to requiring persons concerning to bring as many actions as the number of acts adversely affecting them contained in the said procedure. Having regard to the close connection between the different measures comprising the recruitment procedure, it must be accepted that in an action contesting later steps in such a procedure, the applicant may contest the legality of earlier steps which are closely linked to them.

The grounds of complaint invoked by the applicant against the disputed notice and notification may therefore be taken into consideration by the Court in its appraisal of the legality of the decisions of 26 February 1964 which constitute the main subject-matter of the application.' [108]

In the *Oslizlok Case* the Court of Justice admitted an action against a decision even though the decision was not expressly challenged. It held:

'Although the applicant does not make any submission *expressis verbis* against the decision relating to the reorganization of the Directorate General for Regional Policy, it appears from the arguments put forward in support of the third submission that it is also directed against that decision'. [109]

It is therefore possible to bring an action against a 'chain' of decisions; however, the relationship between the links must be close. It is not permitted, for example, to challenge all nominations to a particular grade to which the appellant seeks promotion. [110]

c. PRELIMINARY ACTS

§ 244. The formulation of decisions is preceded by consultations and the collection of data in which the future addressee himself may be involved. To what extent can an action be brought against these preliminary acts? According to past Court decisions, letters stating that the subject is under consideration [111] or asking for patience [112] are not official acts, have no legal effect and cannot be challenged in Court. For staff members, only decisions made by the competent authority are decisions, whereas communications issued by a senior staff member are not. [113]

108. *Ley Case* (12 and 29/64), 31 March 1965, [1965] ECR 118; 11 Jur. (1965) 158; 11 Rec. (1965) 158, 159.
109. *Oslizlok Case* (34/77), 11 May 1978, consideration 5, [1978] ECR 1111.
110. *Lacroix Case* (30/68), 28 May 1970, [1970] ECR 309-312.
111. *Second Snupat Case* (42 and 49/59), 22 March 1961, [1961] ECR 72; 7 Jur. (1961) 142; 7 Rec. (1961) 142; *Second Richez Paris Case* (40/71), 17 Feb. 1972, considerations 3, 9, [1972] ECR 79.
112. *Müllers Case* (79/70), 7 July 1971, considerations 10, 17, [1971] ECR 697, 698.
113. *First Guillot Case* (53/72), 11 July 1974, consideration 2, [1974] ECR 802; [1975] CMLR 176.

§ 245. The question of the legal force of preliminary acts is best illustrated by the *First Cement Convention Case*. Under Article 15(2) (a) of Regulation No. 17, undertakings which violate EEC competition law are liable to heavy fines. However, no fine shall be imposed in respect of agreements which have been notified to the Commission as long as the Commission has not ruled on their validity and on the possibility of exempting them (Article 15(3)). There is, however, an exception to this safeguard. If, after preliminary examination the Commission is of opinion that Article 85(1) of the Treaty applies, and that the granting of an exemption is not to be justified, it can communicate this to the parties concerned. This communication has the effect of removing the protection against fines (Article 15(6)). Apparently, the latter provision was added to prevent the enjoyment of temporary validity bestowed during the time-consuming procedures of the Commission from being applicable to agreements which are manifestly contrary to the aims of the Treaty.

Under the terms of the Cement Convention, 74 enterprises had divided the market between themselves. The Convention was duly notified and the Commission concluded after preliminary examination that the agreement violated EEC competition law. This conclusion was communicated to each of the enterprises by letter expressly referring to Regulation 17, Article 15(6). The enterprises brought an action against those letters. The Commission argued that the action should not be allowed since a communication under Article 15(6) was not a decision but rather a preliminary opinion.

The Court of Justice considered that as a result of the letters:

'The undertakings ceased to be protected by Article 15(5) which exempted them from fines, and came under the contrary rules of Article 15(2) which thenceforth exposed them to the risk of fines. This measure deprived them of the advantages of a legal situation which Article 15(5) attached to the notification of the agreement, and exposed them to a grave financial risk. Thus the said measure affected the interests of the undertakings by bringing about a distinct change in their legal position. It is unequivocally a measure which produces legal effects touching the interests of the undertakings concerned and which is binding on them. It thus constitutes not a mere opinion but a decision.

...

Neither the fact that the word "decision" is not used in Article 15(6) nor the fact that the procedure provided for therein is of a preliminary nature justifies the conclusion that the Commission is empowered to proceed by a mere opinion, especially since the words "deliver an opinion" are not found in the said provision either. The silence of the text in a matter which affects the protection of the rights of individuals cannot be construed in the manner most unfavourable to them. Notwithstanding its preliminary nature, the measure by which the Commission takes a decision in such a case constitutes the culmination of a special procedure which is distinct from the procedure under which, after Article 19 has been applied, a decision on the substance of the case can be taken. Therefore it is not possible to find, either in the absence of any express reference in Arti-

140

cle 15(6) to one of the measures set out in Article 189 of the Treaty or in the preliminary nature of the Commission's examination, sufficient grounds for excluding the necessity for a decision.' [114]

The legal effect apparently is considered to be the most important criterion. The above case illustrates that an action may be brought against preliminary acts provided that these acts have legal effect for the appellant.

d. INTERPRETATIONS

§ 246. The question whether preparatory acts can be challenged (see above § 244) concerns actions prior to an act being taken. It may also happen, that after an act has been taken, further clarification is given. Can such a clarification be challenged?

In the *Phoenix-Rheinrohr Case* the High Authority had, by letter of 18 December 1957, further explained the notion of 'own resources of scrap' as used in general decisions 22-54, 14-55 and 2-57. The letter was published in the Official Journal.[115] Some German scrap users formally asked the High Authority whether this letter was a decision or not and received a reply from the 'Market Devision' stating that the letter was, indeed, a decision. The Court nonetheless declared *Phoenix-Rheinrohr's* action inadmissible on the ground that the letter did not constitute a decision. It considered that the High Authority *'had merely reaffirmed the principles which it considered rightly or wrongly, to follow logically from the basic Decision 2-57'.* The letter to the German scrap users could not affect this position as it only *'expresses the position of an official of the High Authority, and does not necessarily, in itself alone and in the present case, convey the intentions of the High Authority.'* [116]

e. WITHDRAWAL OF ACTS

§ 247. Normally, acts are withdrawn by other acts. Such further acts can be challenged in the same way and under the same conditions as acts instituting new rules.

The repeal of a general act is of a general nature and falls under the same requirements for Court action as the original act itself. In respect to withdrawal, a particular question arises: may acts which have granted rights to persons

---

114. *First Cement Convention Case* (8-11/66), 15 March 1967, [1967] ECR 9, 92; 13 Jur. (1967) 114 and 116; 13 Rec. (1967) 116-119; [1967] CMLR 102-104; CCH para 8052.
115. OJ 1 Feb. 1958, p. 45 ff.
116. *Phoenix-Rheinrohr Case* (20/58), 17 July 1959, [1959] ECR 82; 5 Jur. (1958-59) 191, 192; 5 Rec. (1958-59) 180, 181. The same reasoning was followed in the *First Snupat Case* (32, 33/58), 17 July 1959, [1959] ECR 139-141; 5 Jur. (1958-59) 323, 324; 5 Rec. (1958-59) 301, 302, in the *Felten Case* (21/58), 17 July 1959, [1959] ECR 105; 5 Jur. (1958-59) 242; 5 Rec. (1958-59) 227 and the *First Mannesmann Case* (23/58), 17 July 1959, [1959] ECR 124; 5 Jur. (1958-59) 289; 5 Rec. (1958-59) 270. See also above § 232.

be revoked without their consent or would such withdrawal be an illegal act subject to challenge before the Court of Justice? [117]

This question came before the Court in the *Algera Case*. The applicants in that case were appointed as civil servants by decision of 12 December 1955. By a later decision that decision was repealed and replaced by the Staff Regulations adopted in 1956 for all four institutions. Miss Algera submitted that the rights she had acquired by the decision of 12 December could not be withdrawn without her approval.

The Court held:

'It emerges from a comparative study of this problem of law that in the six Member States an administrative measure conferring individual rights on the person concerned cannot in principle be withdrawn, if it is a lawful measure; in that case, since the individual right is vested, the need to safeguard confidence in the stability of the situation thus created prevails over the interests of an administration desirous of reversing its decision. This is true in particular of the appointment of an official.

If, on the other hand, the administrative measure is illegal, revocation is possible under the law of all the Member States. The absence of an objective legal basis for the measure affects the individual right of the person concerned and justifies the revocation of the said measure. It should be stressed that whereas this principle is generally acknowledged, only the conditions for its application vary.'

Furthermore, after a comparative study of the national legal systems it concluded:

'Thus the revocability of an administrative measure vitiated by illegality is allowed in all Member States.
In agreement with the Advocate-General's opinion, the Court accepts the principle of the revocability of illegal measures at least within a reasonable period of time, such as that within which the decisions in question in the present dispute occurred.' [118]

§ 248. In the *Second Snupat Case* the Court of Justice considered that in the law of all Member States administrative acts can be withdrawn retroactively if based on incorrect or incomplete information supplied by the persons concerned. In the case before the Court the question whether such retroactive withdrawal would be justified was left to the judgment of the High Authority (see above § 83). [119]

---

117. On this question see W. Wiesner, *Der Widerruf individueller Entscheidungen der Hohen Behörde der EGKS*, Hamburg 1966.
118. *Algera Case* (7/56 and 3-7/57), 12 July 1957, [1957-58] ECR 55, 56; 3 Jur. (1957) 121, 122; 3 Rec. (1957) 115, 116.
119. *Second Snupat Case* (42 and 49/59), 22 March 1961, [1961] ECR 87; 7 Jur. (1961) 162, 163; 7 Rec. (1961) 160, 161.

In the *First Hoogovens Case* the Court accepted that illegal acts may be withdrawn with retroactive effect, but considered that:

'However, the foregoing consideration does not mean that, even in these cases, the time factor has not a part to play; the competent authority can withdraw an exemption with retroactive effect only by taking into account the fact that the beneficiaries of the revoked Decision could assume in good faith that they would not have to pay contributions on the ferrous scrap in question, and could arrange their affairs in reliance on the continuance of this situation.' [120]

f. ACTS CONFIRMED BY TREATY

§ 249. In the *König Case* the legality of EEC Regulation 7a/59 of the Council was challenged. [121] The Council then submitted that the regulation was, at all events, validated by Article 1 of the Treaty of Accession, which provides that the acceding States become Parties to the Treaties establishing the Communities 'as amended or supplemented.'

The Court of Justice rejected this submission, holding that:

'Although certain clauses in these Acts, such as Article 3 of the Treaty of Accession, may be considered as a recognition, by all the parties, of the binding character of decisions taken or agreements reached within the general system of Community law, no provision in the Treaty of Accession or in the Acts accompanying it can be construed as validating measures, whatever their form, which are incompatible with the Treaties establishing the Communities.' [122]

7. Failure to act

§ 250. Community law often obliges the institutions or the Member States to act. In such cases, a failure to act may be the root of as great an injustice as the execution of an illegal act and may cause as great a harm to the Community or to others. For that reason, the judicial review of the Court of Justice has also been extended to cover a failure to act (an act which does not exist, but should have been taken).

In the case of a failure to act there is neither an act, nor a document, to attack. This entails a practical problem which has been solved in the Communi-

---

120. *First Hoogovens Case* (14/61), 12 July 1962; [1962] ECR 273; 8 Jur. (1962) 544; 8 Rec. (1962) 521; [1963] CMLR 96. This ruling was confirmed in the *Second Lemmerz Werke Case* (111/63), 13 July 1965; [1965] ECR 690; 11 Jur. (1965) 953; 11 Rec. (1965) 852; [1968] CMLR 301.
121. Regulation of 18 Dec. 1959, O.J. 1961, p. 71.
122. *König Case* (185/73), 29 May 1974, consideration 3, [1974] ECR 616; CCH para 8275.

ties by the instrument of a special action against failure to act. Under this system, the negligent institution can be officially requested to act and in case of failure to do so, the official request can be used as a basis for the action (see below § 333, 334).

§ 251. *When is a failure to act susceptible to judicial review?* Applications to courts should be based on positive rules of law. In the case of an action for annulment the disputed act of the institution concerned is the positive rule. Should that rule be *binding* then the action is permitted; if it is a recommendation or a preparatory act then there is either no right to challenge the act or the action should wait until the preparations have culminated in a binding act which can then be challenged. In the case of an action against failure to act the positive rule of law available is the rule which provides for the act to be taken. There should be a right of instituting proceedings if that rule is binding, in other words when it *obliges* institutions or Member States to act. When the rule only *entitles* them to act, then there should be no right of instituting proceedings in a legal system which does not grant an action against recommendations. The actual form of the act to be taken should not be relevant. When an institution is obliged to take a non-binding act and fails to do so, there should be an action against failure to act as the positive rule of law concerned is a binding one. This would be in accordance with the system which grants an action for annulment against a binding act irrespective of the question as to what is the obligation contained in the act.

§ 252. *When does a failure to act become reproachable?* Obligations under Community law may have to be fulfilled before a certain date. In that case the inaction is illegal as from that date. But often no date is expressly set. A time limit may, however, be implied from the details contained in the obligation and from the aim of the system under which it is established.[123] In the *Premiums for Grubbing Fruit Trees Case* the Court of Justice considered that the normal time for grubbing is between autumn and spring and that therefore the Italian Republic should have taken the required measures in the spring of 1971, at the latest. The Court then went on to proclaim:

> 'It was imperative for the effectiveness of the measures adopted to observe such a time limit, as they would only have been able fully to achieve their objective on condition that they were implemented simultaneously in all Member States'. [124]

When a failure to act has become reproachable, this can be officially established by a formal invitation to act. (see below § 333, 336).

---

123. *Premiums for Grubbing Fruit Trees Case* (30/72), 8 Feb. 1973, consideration 6 (3), [1973] ECR 170; CCH para 8207. See also above, § 75.
124. *Idem*, consideration 7 (5). See also Ami Barav, *Failure of Member States to fulfil their obligations under Community law*, 12 CMLRev., 1975, pp. 369-383 at 373.

§ 253. In a few cases which are expressly mentioned in the Treaties a failure to act cannot be brought before the Court of Justice, but must be brought before another, executive, institution. [125] The most important of these are the civil servant cases, which must be brought before the appointing authority. If at the end of a period of four months no reply has been received, this shall be deemed to constitute an implied decision rejecting the request. Civil servants may lodge a complaint against that rejection in accordance with the normal procedure for staff complaints. This means that again the appointing authority must be called upon to make a decision. If it refuses to annul the implied negative decision, then the civil servant may bring his case before the Court of Justice. [126]

B. GROUNDS OF ILLEGALITY

§ 254. In administrative law, there is no equality of the parties (see below § 444). Government acts are assumed to be valid, unless the opponent demonstrates that the conditions required for assessing their invalidity are fulfilled. What these conditions are depends on the legal system. One system may provide that government acts remain valid unless some obvious injustice has been demonstrated; others hold that government acts are void when even a procedural error is discovered.

The Community Treaties enumerate the grounds of illegality in the articles governing the most direct action against the validity of Community acts (the action for annulment, see below § 300-328). As it seems impossible to accept that a Community act should be considered valid if challenged under one form of proceedings, and invalid if challenged under another, it must be assumed that the same grounds of illegality apply for the other methods established for challenging Community acts (see below § 329-379). For the plea of illegality and the action against failure to act there can be no doubt as to this since explicit [127] or implicit [128] reference is made to the action for annulment. Only in the case of preliminary questions raised by national courts on the validity of a Community act and in the case of disputes on the validity of an act in an action for damages could the grounds for illegality accepted by the Court of Justice be slightly different. The possibility of disputing the legality of an act after a lengthy period of time could justify a more severe attitude by the Court. Such differences will be mentioned when discussing the separate grounds for illegality.

The five grounds of illegality enumerated by the Treaties are:
(1) lack of competence;
(2) infringement of an essential procedural requirement;
(3) infringement of the Treaty;

---

125. See ECSC, Artt. 58(1), 59(1), 61(3).
126. Staff Regulations, Art. 90(1), (2).
127. ECSC Art. 36; EEC Art. 184; Euratom Art. 156.
128. ECSC Art. 35; Euratom Art. 148; EEC Art. 175, as interpreted by the Court of Justice, see below § 344.

(4) infringement of any rule of law relating to the application of the Treaty;
(5) misuse of powers.

§ 255. These grounds of illegality have gradually lost their individual importance. Recent annulment proceedings indicate that the Court is not concerned
with the specific ground of illegality. Most causes of illegality come under the
heading of 'violations of the Treaty or of any rule of law relating to its application'. However, it is useful to discuss each of the five grounds and the manner
in which they have developed, in particular since this development indicates
how the Court has clarified the distinction between legal and illegal acts.
    The grounds of illegality must have been present at the time the decision
was taken. '*The legality of a Community act cannot depend on retrospective
considerations of its efficiency*' said the Court in the *Schroeder Case*. [129]
    The illegality of an act will normally mean that the act is invalid and no
longer applicable. However, this is not necessarily the case. There may be
situations in which an illegal act is better than no act at all or where the
illegality is caused by the absence of a provision rather than by an improper
provision, so that invalidity does not provide a solution. The court may then
leave the act in existence and rule that the Community must adopt the measures necessary to correct the illegality. [130]

1. Lack of competence

§ 256. The institutions of the Communities have no general competence as is
the case with national governments. They may act only in those fields where
the Treaties expressly attribute competence to them. [131] Even though one
may assume that the Court of Justice will not be over-strict in its interpretation of the provisions attributing powers to the Council or the Commission [132] the resulting limitation or division of powers seriously restricts the
latitude for decision-making. Competence will be lacking when the Council or
the Commission acts in a field not covered by the Treaties or when either acts
in a field expressly reserved to the other.
    In practice, of course, no institution will ever state that it is acting in a field
entirely outside the Communities' competence. If it were to do so, the act in
question would probably be considered non-existent (see above § 213-226).
What is more likely is that it will claim that a particular provision includes an
implied grant of competence. The dispute will then turn on the question of
whether that particular provision has been violated, rather than on the ground

---

129. *Schroeder Case* (40/72), 7 Feb. 1973, consideration 14, [1973] ECR 142; CCH
para 8206. See also *Compagnie d'Approvisonnement Case* (9 and 11/71), 13 June 1972,
consideration 39. [1972] ECR 407; CCH para 8177.
130. See, e.g.,*Moulins de Pont-à-Mousson Case* (124/76 and 20/77), 19 Oct. 1977, considerations 24, 28, [1977] ECR 1812, 1813.
131. See e.g. EEC Treaty Art. 4.
132. Pescatore (*op. cit.*, note 58) p. 72; *Massey-Ferguson Case* (8/73), 12 July 1973,
consideration 4. [1973] ECR 908; CCH para 8221.

of 'lack of competence'. Lack of competence, therefore, is very rarely used as a ground for declaring a Community act void.

In the Court's case law, three issues concerning competence have played a role: (a) delegation of powers, (b) the principle of implied powers, and (c) jurisdiction beyond the territory of the Common Market.

a. DELEGATION OF POWERS

§ 257. In the case of an illegal delegation of powers, the body to which the powers have been delegated will be incompetent to exercise them. In the *First Meroni Case*, the Court of Justice made an important statement about the legality of a delegation of powers. Meroni contested Decision 14-55 by which the High Authority had partly transferred competence to the Common Bureau of Scrap Iron Consumers and the Equalisation Fund for Imported Scrap Iron, both private institutions in Brussels. The Court admitted the application and declared the transfer of competence illegal. It may be thus concluded that the decisions of these private institutions, taken in execution of the transferred competence were invalid on the ground of lack of competence.

The following considerations of the Court are of general interest:
'If the High Authority had itself exercised the powers the exercise of which is conferred by Decision No 14/55 on the Brussels agencies, those powers would have been subject to the rules laid down by the Treaty and in particular those which impose upon the High Authority:

The duty to state reasons for its decisions and to refer to any opinions which were required to be obtained (Article 15);

The duty to publish annually a general report on its activities and its administrative expenses (Article 17);

The duty to publish such data as could be useful to governments or to any other parties concerned (Article 47).

On the same supposition, its decisions and recommendations would have been subject to review by the Court of Justice on the conditions laid down by Article 33.

Decision No 14/55 did not make the exercise of the powers which it conferred upon the Brussels agencies subject to any of the conditions to which it would have been subject if the High Authority had exercised them directly.

Even if the delegation resulting from Decision No 14/55 appeared as legal from the point of view of the Treaty, it could not confer upon the authority receiving the delegation powers different from those which the delegating authority itself received under the Treaty.

The fact that it is possible for the Brussels agencies to take decisions which are exempt from the conditions to which they would have been subject if they had been adopted directly by the High Authority in reality gives the Brussels agencies more extensive powers than those which the High Authority holds from the Treaty.

In not making the decisions of the Brussels agencies subject to the rules to which the decisions of the High Authority are subject under the Treaty, the delegation resulting from Decision No 14/55 infringes the Treaty.

A delegation of powers cannot be presumed and even when empowered to delegate its powers the delegating authority must take an express decision transferring them.

Article 3 lays down no fewer than eight distinct, very general objectives, and it is not certain that they can all be simultaneously pursued in their entirety in all circumstances.

In pursuit of the objectives laid down in Article 3 of the Treaty, the High Authority must permanently reconcile any conflict which may be implied by these objectives when considered individually, and when such conflict arises must grant such priority to one or other of the objectives laid down in Article 3 as appears necessary having regard to the economic facts or circumstances in the light of which it adopts its decisions.

Reconciling the various objectives laid down in Article 3 implies a real discretion involving difficult choices, based on a consideration of the economic facts and circumstances in the light of which those choices are made.

The consequences resulting from a delegation of powers are very different depending on whether it involves clearly defined executive powers the exercise of which can, therefore, be subject to strict review in the light of objective criteria determined by the delegating authority, or whether it involves a discretionary power, implying a wide margin of discretion which may, according to the use which is made of it, make possible the execution of actual economic policy.

A delegation of the first kind cannot appreciably alter the consequences involved in the exercise of the powers concerned, whereas a delegation of the second kind, since it replaces the choices of the delegator by the choices of the delegate, brings about an actual transfer of responsibility.

In any event under Article 53 as regards the execution of the financial arrangements mentioned therein, it is only the delegation of those powers 'necessary for the performance of the tasks set out in Article 3' which may be authorized. Such delegations of powers, however, can only relate to clearly defined executive powers, the use of which must be entirely subject to the supervision of the High Authority.

The objectives set out in Article 3 are binding not only on the High Authority, but on the 'institutions of the Community ... within the limits of their respective powers, in the common interest'.

From that provision there can be seen in the balance of powers which is characteristic of the institutional structure of the Community a fundamental guarantee granted by the Treaty in particular to the undertakings and associations of undertakings to which it applies.

To delegate a discretionary power, by entrusting it to bodies other than those which the Treaty has established to effect and supervise the exercise of such power each within the limits of its own authority, would render that guarantee ineffective.' [133]

148

§ **258.** The principle was established by the *First Meroni Case* that discretionary powers may not be delegated. Meroni's case concerned delegation of powers to a private institution, but the Court followed the same principle in the *Rey Soda Case* for delegation to a Member State. Under Council Regulation 1009 the Commission was charged to adopt according to the so-called Management Committee procedure the requisite provisions to prevent the sugar market from being disturbed. By Article 6 of Commission Regulation 834/74 the Commission provided that Italy should take the necessary measures to prevent disturbances on the Italian sugar market. [134] The validity of this delegation by the Commission was disputed. The Court held:

'Nevertheless Article 37(2) of the basic regulation enabling the Commission to take, in accordance with the consultation procedure of the Management Committee, measures directly applicable in a Member State, cannot be interpreted as enabling the Commission to impose upon a Member State the obligation to draw up, under the guise of implementation measures, essential basic rules which would not be subject to any control by the Council.

...

In addition, by not specifying the bases of the calculation of the tax in the provision in question and leaving Italy to choose them, the Commission discharged itself of its own responsibility to adopt the basic rules and to submit them by way of the Management Committee procedure to the approval if need be of the Council.

There fore the answer to the first two questions from the national court must be that Article 6 of Regulation No 834/74 is invalid.' [135]

§ **259.** There is one important exception to the rule that discretionary powers may not be delegated. EEC Article 155 provides *inter alia*: 'the Commission shall exercise the powers conferred on it by the Council for the implementation of the rules laid down by the latter.' [136] The Court of Justice explained this rule in the *Köster Case*, where it held:

'Both the legislative scheme of the Treaty, reflected in particular by the last indent of Article 155, and the consistent practice of the Community institutions establish a distinction, according to the legal concepts recognized in all the Member States, between the measures directly based on the Treaty itself and derived law intended to ensure their implementation. It cannot therefore be a requirement that all the details of the regulations concerning the common agricultural policy be drawn up by the Council according to the procedure in Article 43. It is sufficient for the purposes of that provi-

---

133. *First Meroni Case* (9/56), 13 June 1958, [1957-58] ECR 149-152; 4 Jur. (1958) 41-46; 4 Rec. (1958) 40-44.
134. O.J. 1974, L99, p. 15.
135. *Rey Soda Case* (23/75), 30 Oct. 1975, considerations 25, 48, 49; [1975] ECR 1302, 1306; [1976] 1 CMLR 210, 212; CCH para 8321.
136. EEC Art. 155, last paragraph.

sion that the basic elements of the matter to be dealt with have been adopted in accordance with the procedure laid down by that provision. On the other hand, the provisions implementing the basic regulations may be adopted according to a procedure different from that in Article 43, either by the Council itself or by the Commission by virtue of an authorization complying with Article 155.' [137]

In the *Rey Soda Case* the Court held that it followed from the context of the Treaty in which the above quotation of EEC Article 155 must be placed, and also from practical requirements, that the concept of implementation must be given a wide interpretation. [138]

§ 260. The power to sign letters on behalf of the Commission may be delegated. In the *ICI Case* the Court held:

'The applicant asserts that the notice of objections, for which Article 2 of Regulation No 99/63 of the Commission makes provision, is irregular because it is signed by the Director-General for Competition *per procurationem* although, according to the applicant, no such delegation of powers on the part of the Commission is permitted.

It is established that the Director-General for Competition did no more than sign the notice of objections which the Member of the Commission responsible for problems of competition had previously approved in the exercise of the powers which the Commission had delegated to him.

Therefore that official did not act pursuant to a delegation of powers but simply signed as a proxy on authority received from the Commissioner responsible.

The delegation of such authority constitutes a measure relating to the internal organization of the departments of the Commission, in accordance with Article 27 of the provisional Rules of Procedure adopted under Article 16 of the Treaty of 8 April 1965 establishing a single Council and a single Commission.

Therefore this submission is unfounded.' [139]

§ 261. Predominantly in agriculture, but also in other fields, the Council has delegated powers to the Commission with the stipulation that in exercising these powers, the Commission must consult a *Management Committee*. In case of disagreement between the Commission and the Management Committee, the Council itself can decide. Thus, the Management Committees play an important role, although this is not provided for in the Treaties.

---

137. *Köster Case* (25/70), 17 Dec. 1970, consideration 6, [1970] ECR 1170; [1972] CMLR 289; CCH para 8127.
138. *Rey Soda Case* (23/75), 30 Oct. 1975, consideration 10, [1975] ECR 1300; [1976] 1 CMLR 208; CCH para 8321.
139. *ICI Case* (48/69), 14 July 1972, considerations 11-15, [1972] ECR 649, 650; [1972] CMLR 618; CCH para 8161.

For this reason it was submitted in the *Köster Case* that powers had been unlawfully delegated. The Court held:

'Article 155 provides that the Commission shall exercise the powers conferred on it by the Council for the implementation of the rules laid down by the latter. This provision, the use of which is optional, enables the Council to determine any detailed rules to which the Commission is subject in exercising the power conferred on it. The so-called Management Committee procedure forms part of the detailed rules to which the Council may legitimately subject a delegation of power to the Commission. It follows from an analysis of the machinery set up by Articles 25 and 26 of Regulation No 19 that the task of the Management Committee is to give opinions on draft measures proposed by the Commission, which may adopt immediately applicable measures whatever the opinion of the Management Committee. Where the Committee issues a contrary opinion, the only obligation on the Commission is to communicate to the Council the measures taken. The function of the Management Committee is to ensure permanent consultation in order to guide the Commission in the exercise of the powers conferred on it by the Council and to enable the latter to substitute its own action for that of the Commission. The Management Committee does not therefore have the power to take a decision in place of the Commission or the Council. Consequently, without distorting the Community structure and the institutional balance, the Management Committee machinery enables the Council to delegate to the Commission an implementing power of appreciable scope, subject to its power to take the decision itself if necessary.

The legality of the so-called Management Committee procedure, as established by Articles 25 and 26 of Regulation No 19, cannot therefore be disputed in the context of the institutional structure of the Community.' [140]

§ 262. According to Article 7(3) of Annex IX of the Staff Regulations the appointing authority must hear an official before taking a disciplinary measure against him. By reason of the gravity of a disciplinary action and having regard to the form of words employed in Article 7 the Court of Justice ruled in the *First van Eick Case* that this provision must be considered as a *'peremptory legal requirement'*. The appointing authority itself must therefore perform this function. The task of hearing the official may only be delegated to one or more members of the appointing authority for reasons of good administration of the service and only under conditions which fully guarantee the rights of the official involved. [141]

---

140. *Köster Case* (25/70), 17 December 1970, considerations 9, 10, [1970] ECR 1171; [1972] CMLR 289, 290; CCH para 8127.
141. *First van Eick Case* (35/67), 11 July 1968, [1968] ECR 344, 345; 14 Jur. (1968) 483; 14 Rec. (1968) 503, 504.

§ 263.   In the *First Snupat Case* the High Authority had lawfully delegated powers to the Equalization Fund for Imported Scrap Iron. It had, however, not provided for any procedure for bringing an appeal on the decisions of the Fund, to the High Authority itself. The Court of Justice held that in that case the decisions of the Fund were to be considered as decisions of the High Authority itself, as far as applications to the Court were concerned. [142]

b. IMPLIED POWERS [143]

§ 264.   Not all the powers of the Communities are expressly enumerated in the Treaties. Many powers are to be drawn by implication from others. The power to establish a Common Customs Tariff, for example, implies the power to classify products in particular categories and the power to make rules governing their control. The Court of Justice accepted the theory of implied powers in Community law in the *Fédéchar Case* in which it held:

'The Court considers that without having recourse to a wide interpretation it is possible to apply a rule of interpretation generally accepted in both international and national law, according to which the rules laid down by an international treaty or a law presuppose the rules without which that treaty or law would have no meaning or could not be reasonably and usefully applied.' [144]

§ 265.   The Court accepted the existence of implied powers of the Community also in the *ERTA Case* where it was disputed whether the EEC had authority to enter into international agreements on subjects for which such authority had not been expressly granted. The Court then held:

'Such authority arises not only from an express conferment by the Treaty — as is the case with Articles 113 and 114 for tariff and trade agreements and with Article 238 for association agreements — but may equally flow from other provisions of the Treaty and from measures adopted, within the framework of those provisions, by the Community institutions.' [145]

---

142. *First Snupat Case* (32 and 33/58), 17 July 1959, [1959] ECR 137; 5 Jur. (1958-59) 320, 321; 5 Rec. (1958-59) 298.
143. See R.H. Lauwaars, *Lawfulness and Legal Force of Community Decisions*, Sijthoff Leiden 1973, pp. 94-104; Clarence J. Mann, *The Function of Judicial Decision in European Economic Integration*, Nijhoff, The Hague 1972, pp. 288-299; Gert Nicolaysen, *Zur Theorie von den Implied Powers in den Europäischen Gemeinschaften*, Europarecht 1966, pp. 129-142.
144. *Fédéchar Case* (8/55), 29 Nov. 1956, [1954-56] ECR 299; 2 Jur. (1955-56) 323, 324; 2 Rec. (1955-56) 305. For other similar decisions, see the *Publication of Transport Tariffs Cases* (20/59), 15 July 1960, [1960] ECR 336; 6 Jur. (1960), 707; 6 Rec. (1960) 688 and (25/59), 15 July 1960, [1960] ECR 372; 6 Jur. (1960) 781; 6 Rec. (1960) 757.
145. *ERTA Case* (22/70), 31 March 1971, considerations 16-19; [1971] ECR 274; [1971] CMLR 354, 355; CCH para 8134.

§ 266. The acceptance by the Court of the theory of implied powers does not settle the problem, which concerns principally the extent of the powers rather than the fact of their existence. Under the widest theory of interpretation the attribution of a specific task in the initial articles of the Treaties would imply the grant of all the powers necessary to fulfill that task. Acceptance of this theory would mean that the Communities are in the same position as national governments which are entitled to exercise all powers benefiting the general public. The rules and limitations, expressed throughout the remainder of the Treaties, clearly indicate that such extensive implied powers were not intended. No fixed limits can be set, however. It should be accepted that when circumstances change over the years, and detailed provisions of the Treaties become outdated, then the general articles at the beginning of the Treaties will assume importance and recourse to implied powers will become increasingly acceptable.

§ 267. It may not always be clear in international organizations which organ is competent to exercise the implied powers of the organization itself. For the EEC this problem has been settled by EEC Article 235 which provides that the Council shall act unanimously on a proposal of the Commission and after consulting the European Parliament, 'if action by the Community should prove necessary to attain, ..., one of the objectives of the Community and this Treaty has not provided the necessary powers.' In this article the Treaty accepts that the Community has an implied power to act when action is necessary to attain the Community's objectives. [146]

EEC Article 235 concerns the implied powers of the *Community*. It does not exclude the possibility that individual institutions may have implied powers of their own. The powers expressly granted to the Commission may also imply further powers, which the Commission may exercise. Acts of the Commission, therefore, need not be void for the sole reason that the necessary competence has not been expressly granted to the Commission.

c. JURISDICTION BEYOND THE TERRITORY OF THE COMMON MARKET

§ 268. On several occasions, non-European companies operating within the Common Market, but with their seats outside, have been fined by the Commission for violating EEC competition law in respect of their trade within the Common Market. These companies contended that the Commission lacked the competence to impose such fines. The Court, however, did not accept these contentions since it considered that the actions for which the fine had been imposed constituted practices carried out within the Common Market

---

146. On EEC art. 235 see Ivo E. Schwarz, *Article 235 and Law-Making Powers in the European Community*, 27 ICLQ (1978), pp. 614-628 and Everling, Schwarz and Tomuschat, *Die Rechtsetzungsbefugnisse der EWG in Generalermächtigungen, insbesondere in Art. 235 EWGV*, EuR Sonderhaft 1976, pp. 2-76.

and therefore within the jurisdiction of the Communities. It was considered irrelevant that the seat of the companies was outside Community territory. [147]

It has not been disputed that the Community institutions cannot extend their powers outside Community territory.

2. Infringement of an essential procedural requirement

§ 269. As mentioned above (§ 225), the High Authority adopted a decision which carefully regulates how future acts of the High Authority should be issued. The other Community institutions did the same. [148] These rules certainly contain procedural requirements, but they are not *essential* procedural requirements in the sense of EEC Article 173 or ECSC Article 33. Acts which do not fulfill the conditions of these decisions have been accepted as Community acts (see § 225) and if no other requirements have been violated, they are valid acts. Other procedural requirements, in particular those contained in the Rules of Procedure of the Court, concern the *admissibility* of actions. Applications which are not in accordance with these rules will be declared inadmissible. [149] For the *annulment* of acts three procedural requirements must be maintained as essential: (a) the required advice must have been sought, (b) the acts must be reasoned, and (c) the acts must be published.

a. CONSULTATION [150]

§ 270. Several articles of the Treaties require that other organs — such as the European Parliament or the Consultative Committee of the ECSC — must be consulted before action is taken. [151] In some early cases, the Court ruled that the consultations formed an essential procedural requirement. [152] Since the Court ruled in each of these early cases that the consultation was sufficient, it did not annul the contested decisions on the ground of violation of an essential procedural requirement.

The Court was not very formalistic in this respect, 'as it allowed the High Authority to consult the records of the Consultative Committee of the ECSC without actually waiting for official advice. [153]

---

147. See e.g. *ICI case* (48/69), 14 July 1972, considerations 126-142; [1972] ECR 661-663; [1972] CMLR 628, 629; CCH para 8161. See also below § 289.
148. See e.g. Provisional Rules of Procedure of the Council, Rules 9-14.
149. *Customs Duties on Silk Case* (32/64), 17 June 1965, [1965] ECR 372; 11 Jur. (1965) 652; 11 Rec. (1965) 484; CCH para 8036.
150. R.H. Lauwaars, (*op. cit.*, note 143) pp. 111-117, 150-151.
151. See e.g. Articles 43, 49, 54, 63, 75 and 87; ECSC Articles 50(2), 53, 55(2), 58, 59, 60.
152. *First Monnet Rabat Case* (1/54), 21 Dec. 1954, [1954-56] ECR 15; 1 Jur. (1954-55) 33; 1 Rec. (1954-55) 31; *Second Monnet Rabat Case* (2/54), 21 Dec. 1954, [1954-56] ECR 52; 1 Jur. (1954-55) 107, 108; 1 Rec. (1954-55) 99, 100; *Coal Price Case* (6/54), 21 March 1955, [1954-56] ECR 112; 1 Jur. (1954-55) 237; 1 Rec. (1954-55) 221.
153. *Second Monnet Rabat Case* quoted above (note 152).

§ 271. Consultation is required at the stage of drawing up the draft of an act. A problem arises if, during subsequent proceedings, the draft is substantially changed. Is it necessary to repeat the consultation procedure? Here again, the Court has not been rigid. In one of the *Quinine Cartel Cases*, the applicant submitted that the delegation of powers provided for in Article 24 of Regulation 17 was illegal because it did not form part of the original draft as presented to the European Parliament. The Parliament, therefore, had not formulated an opinion on that particular provision. The Court rejected the argument, considering 'that the draft which was the object of a favourable advice of the Parliament contained in its Article 20 a provision which was *substantially identical* to that of Article 24 of Regulation No. 17.' [154] In his report to the Legal Committee of the European Parliament, Jozeau-Marigné concludes that 'the consultation with the European Parliament is in conformity with the Treaty and legally correct, only if it is complete, which means that it must cover *all essential issues of the provisions proposed* by the Commission or accepted by the Council.' [155]

Neither the Court nor the Parliament requires every detail of the final text to have been reviewed by the European Parliament. Consultation is deemed to be sufficient when the essential issues at stake in the act have formed part of the draft presented to the consulted organs.

§ 272. If the European Parliament dislikes a proposed regulation, it could refuse to tender its advice. Since the Treaty articles concerned require *consultation* of the European Parliament and not its *agreement*, such a refusal could not prevent the Council from deciding on the issue. The consultation should be considered as sufficient if, after a reasonable delay, no reply is received. [156] There is no case law on the question of what is a reasonable delay. Where complicated matters are involved the European Parliament and the Economic and Social Committee may demand a considerable amount of time for studying the proposal and thereby cause considerable delay. By this, they are able to exert some pressure in the case of technically involved topics, which the Council considers urgent, by threatening to delay the procedure unless the Council is prepared to meet their wishes. That the European Parliament and the Economic and Social Committee can, in fact, delay the passage of Community acts on which their advice is needed was demonstrated by the answer of the Commission to parliamentary question 289/75 in which the Commission stated:

154. *Quinine Cartel Case (AFC Chemiefarma)* (41/69), 15 July 1970, consideration 69, [1970] ECR 689 (italics added); CCH para 8083. The advice of the European Parliament was published in O.J. 1961, p. 1416.
155. European Parliament, doc. 110/1967-68, para 21 (italics added). See also S. Patijn, *De uitbreiding van de bevoegdheden van het Europese Parlement*, Rotterdam 1973, pp. 100-102; Louis, *Les réglements de la Communauté (op. cit.*, note 10), p. 12; Lauwaars (*op. cit.*, note 143) pp. 122-125.
156. H.G. Schermers, *De middelen waarmee een beroep voor het Hof van Justitie van de Europese Gemeenschappen kan worden ingesteld*, Europese Monografie no. 1, Kluwer 1964, p. 36.

'On 17 June 1975 the Council examined a second Directive ... A general discussion could not, however, be held on the proposed Directive as the Economic and Social Committee had not delivered its Opinion. The proposal is to be entered on the agenda for the next Council meeting on social affairs as the Economic and Social Committee's Opinion is expected in the autumn.' [157]

b. STATEMENT OF REASONS [158]

(i) Why is reasoning needed?

§ 273. Since each Community Treaty provides that binding Community acts must state the reasons on which they are based [159], a lack of reasoning will violate the Treaty. The Court has also accepted the obligation to give reasons as an essential procedural requirement, and in the case of insufficient reasoning, will annul the act on that ground. Reasoning as an 'essential procedural requirement' refers to its formal aspects: it must be made clear why and how the act has been taken, while the ground 'violation of the treaty' will be applicable if the reasoning demonstrates that the grounds on which the act is based are wrong or insufficient, or if the reasoning, though clear and consistent, is erroneous. [160] On many occasions, the Court has expressed the justification for reasoning in the following or similar wording:

'In imposing upon the Commission the obligation to state reasons for its decisions, Article 190 is not taking mere formal considerations into account but seeks to give an opportunity to the parties of defending their rights, to the Court of exercising its supervisory functions and to Member States and to all interested nationals of ascertaining the circumstances in which the Commission has applied the Treaty.' [161]

§ 274. In this quotation the Court expresses three considerations behind the requirements for reasoning of Community acts: (1) the parties involved must know their rights, (2) the Court of Justice must be able to exercise its judicial review, and (3) the Member States, as well as those of its nationals that may

---

157. Answer to written question No. 289/75 by Mr. Cousté, 2 Oct. 1975, O.J., 18 Nov. 1975 No. C 264, p. 15.
158. Lauwaars (*op. cit.*, note 143) pp. 151-165; Hans-Hermann Scheffler, *Die Pflicht zur Begründung von Massnahmen nach den europäischen Gemeinschaftsverträgen*, Berlin 1974, 227 pages; C.D. Ehlermann and D. Oldekop, *Due Process in Administrative Procedure*, FIDE, Copenhagen 1978, Volume 3, pp. 11/17-11/19, Christian Hen, *La motivation des actes des institutions communautaires*, 13 CDE (1977), pp. 49-91.
159. EEC Art. 190, Euratom Art. 162, ECSC Art. 15.
160. *Second Oranges Case* (34/62), 15 July 1963, [1963] ECR 142; 9 Jur. (1963) 308; 9 Rec. (1963) 294, 295; [1963] CMLR 389, 390; CCH para 8016; *Brescia Case* (31/59), 4 April 1960, [1960] ECR 82; 6 Jur. (1960) 179; 6 Rec. (1960) 175.
161. *Brennwein Case* (24/62), 4 July 1963; [1963] ECR 69; 9 Jur. (1963) 149; 9 Rec. (1963) 143; [1963] CMLR 367; CCH para 8012 (p. 7254).

be concerned, must know how the Commission applies the Treaty. The last consideration may be formulated too strictly. Not only the Member States, but also another Community institution (the Council or the Commission as the case may be) may want to appeal and the European Parliament has an interest in learning the reasons behind all Community acts in order that it may exert its political control effectively.

In the *ERTA Case* the Court of Justice took account of only the first of these three considerations. Under contention was an act of a special type; the claimant (the Commission) was fully informed of its background. It had actively participated in the formulation of the act and therefore did not require any reasoning. Apparently the Court did not feel that the other two considerations for reasoning were sufficiently important for that special kind of act to warrant an annulment because of a total lack of reasoning. [162]

(ii) What constitutes reasoning?

§ 275. Normally, the reasoning of acts is contained in the recitals which are published as part of the act. However, recitals are not required in all cases. The reasons on which a piece of legislation is based may appear also from the whole body of the legal rules governing the field under consideration. [163] Not every act needs an independent reasoning of its own. Reference may be made to the reasoning of previous acts [164], provided such reference is clear and complete. [165]

§ 276. In the *Geitling Case*, the Court considered that both the factual matters upon which the legal justification of the act depends and the considerations which have led to the act must be set out.

Then it continued:

'In general terms, it was not necessary in the present case to state independent and exhaustive reasons for the contested article, as an element of a complex decision. Sufficient reasons can be deduced from the context of all the findings stated in support of the decision as a whole.'[166]

§ 277. A civil servant who seeks to challenge a decision concerning his position must first bring his case before his superiors who must take a reasoned

162. *ERTA Case* (22/70), 31 March 1971, considerations 98, 99; [1971] ECR 283; [1971] CMLR 362; CCH para 8134.
163. *An Bord Bainne Case* (92/77), 23 Feb. 1978, consideration 36, [1978] ECR 515; [1978] 2 CMLR 585; CCH para 8471.
164. *Tubes de la Sarre Case* (1 and 14/57), 10 Dec. 1957, [1957-58] ECR 113; 3 Jur. (1957) 234; 3 Rec. (1957) 220; *Schwarze Case* (16/65), 1 Dec. 1965, [1965] ECR 887, 888; 11 Jur. (1965) 1118; Rec. (1965) 1096; [1966] CMLR 187; CCH para 8039 (p. 7556); *First Deuka Case* (78/74), 18 March 1975, consideration 6, [1975] ECR 431; [1975] 2 CMLR 42; CCH para 8302.
165. *Second Dalmas Case* (1/63), 16 Dec. 1963, [1963] ECR 313; 9 Jur. (1963) 667; 9 Rec. (1963) 636; [1964] CMLR 236.
166. *First Geitling Case* (2/56), 20 March 1957, [1957-58] ECR 15; 3 Jur. (1957) 38; 3 Rec. (1957) 36; See also *Barge Case* (18/62), 16 Dec. 1963; [1963] ECR 2850.

decision (see below § 510). Against that reasoned decision the civil servant may bring an action (see below § 325-328). If the superiors fail to take the reasoned decision that failure is to be interpreted as an implied negative decision (Staff Regulations, Article 90). Such an implied negative decision is of course, not reasoned. However, it is not void on that ground. The Court of Justice considers that the reasoning of the act against which the civil servant objects is also the reasoning of the implied decision rejecting the complaint.[167]

(iii) How extensive should reasoning be?

§ 278. Not all acts require detailed reasoning. In the *Brennwein Case*, the Court continued after the paragraph quoted above (§ 273):

> 'To attain these objectives, it is sufficient for the Decision to set out, in a concise but clear and relevant manner, the principal issues of law and of fact upon which it is based and which are necessary in order that the reasoning which has led the Commission to its Decision may be understood'. [168]

§ 279. In other cases the Court of Justice further specified the conditions for sufficient reasoning: *'The extent of the requirement to state the reasons on which measures are based, depends on the nature of the measure in question.'*[169] *'The requirements of a statement of reasons vary according to whether one is concerned with general decisions having the character of regulations, or with decisions which do not have that character.'*[170] *'In the case of a regulation, that is to say, a measure intended to have general application, the reasoning may be confined to indicating the general situation which led to its adoption on the one hand, and the general objectives which it is intended to achieve on the other.* [171] *'A specific statement of reasons in support of all the details which might be contained in a regulation cannot be required, provided such details fall within the general scheme of the measure as a whole.'*[172] *'Although a decision which fits into a well-established line of decisions may be reasoned in a summary manner, for example by a reference to those decisions, if it goes appreciably further than the previous decisions, the Commission must give an account of its reasoning.'*[173]

---

167. *Moli Case* (14/76), 27 Oct. 1977, consideration 12, [1977] ECR 1978; *Mollet Case* (75/77), 13 April 1978, consideration 12, [1978] ECR 906.
168. *Brennwein Case* (24/62), 4 July 1963, [1963] ECR 69; 9 Jur. (1963) 150; 9 Rec. (1963) 143; [1963] CMLR 367; CCH para 8012 (p. 7254).
169. *Beus Case* (5/67) 13 March 1968, [1968] ECR 95; 14 Jur. (1968) 135; 14 Rec. (1968) 143; [1968] CMLR 145; CCH para 8061.
170. *Barge Case* (18/62), 16 Dec. 1963, [1963] ECR 280; 9 Jur. (1963) 591; 9 Rec. (1963) 567.
171. *Beus Case*, quoted above, note 169; also in *Welding Case* (87/78), 30 Nov. 1978, consideration 11.
172. *Second Lassie Case* (80/72), 20 June 1973, consideration 25, [1973] ECR 651; CCH para 8215. See also *Danhuber Case* (134/78), 22 March 1979, consideration 6.
173. *Papier Peints Case* (73/74), 26 Nov. 1975, consideration 31, [1975] ECR 1514; [1976] 1 CMLR 614; CCH para 8335.

These quotations demonstrate that not all individual provisions of an act need to be separately reasoned, provided that all parties involved, as well as the Court, are aware of the reasons why the act was taken. This must be clear, either from the act itself, or from the context in which it is promulgated. However, when an act is composed of several different elements, each of those elements needs separate reasoning. [174]

§279a. Less reasoning may be required when the addressee of the act has participated in its formulation. In the *Food Gifts Case* the Court considered:

'The extent of the duty to state reasons, laid down by Article 190 of the Treaty, depends on the nature of the act in question and on the context in which it is adopted.

In the present case, it is not disputed that the Netherlands Government was closely involved in the process of making the contested decision and was therefore aware of the reason why the Commission did not consider that it should accede to the demand for reimbursement by the said Government, insofar as it referred to expenses incurred under a food aid programme.

In these circumstances, the contested decision must be held to be sufficiently reasoned.' [175]

(iv) Acts which may require less reasoning

§ 280. Some acts need not to be fully reasoned. When the purpose of a specific article of a regulation (in casu the article on its entry into force) is perfectly clear, it needs no special reasoning. [176]

In one case, where the High Authority requested information, the Court held that no detailed reasoning was required in order to explain why the information was needed because such details would only come to light during the research for which the information was asked. [177]

In cases where payment is ordered from the addressees, the Court requires more detailed information on how the amount has been established. [178]

§ 281. Some acts must be taken frequently and at short notice. Fast decisionmaking may be hampered by over-stringent requirements of detailed reasoning. An example of this problem is presented by the *Schwarze Case*.

Under Regulation 89 the Commission was obliged to fix some 220 agricul-

---

174. *Salerno Case* (4, 19, 28/78), 30 Nov. 1978, considerations 26-30.
175. *Food Gifts Case* (13/72), 11 Jan. 1973, consideration 11-13, [1973] ECR 39; CCH para 8200. See also *ERTA Case* quoted above, note 162.
176. *Second Westzucker Case* (57/72), 14 March 1973, consideration 19, [1973] ECR 342; CCH para 8211.
177. *Brescia Case* (31/59), 4 April 1960, [1960] ECR 81; 6 Jur. (1960) 177; 6 Rec. (1960) 173.
178. *First Meroni Case* (9/56), 13 June 1958, [1960] ECR 143; 4 Jur. (1958) 31; 4 Rec. (1958) 30; *Second Dalmas Case* (1/63), 16 Dec. 1963, [1963] ECR 312, 313; 9 Jur. (1963) 666, 667; 9 Rec. (1963) 636, 637; [1964] CMLR 235.

tural prices every Friday on the basis of information received on the previous day by telex from the Member States. The Permanent Representatives had to be consulted and the operation had to be carried out within twenty four hours, as swift and frequent price fixing is one of the necessary conditions for the efficient operation of the agricultural system. Schwarze submitted that one of the decisions taken under this sytem was insufficiently reasoned in particular because it did not give the concrete facts on which it was based. The Commission replied that they only had time for calculating the prices, and that they could not possibly pay attention to a detailed reasoning for each decision. Moreover, the general system being clear enough, no such reasoning would be required. The Court held:

'The degree of precision of the statement of reasons for such a decision must be weighed against practical realities and the time and technical facilities available for making such a decision. A specific statement of reasons for each individual decision fixing a free-at-frontier price as envisaged by the Finanzgericht would mean the publication and technical evaluation of all the facts submitted by the exporting Member State or gathered by the Commission's staff for several hundreds of prices requiring to be fixed. In view, first, of the time available for the issue of the decisions and, secondly of the number of prices to be fixed, the requirement of such a specific statement of reasons would be incompatible with the proper functioning of the machinery provided for in Regulation No. 19 of the Council and Regulation No. 89 of the Commission. The preparation and drafting of this kind of statement of reasons would take up so much time that the determination of prices would run the risk of being, to some extent, out of date by the time it was issued.

Moreover a comparison of the free-at-frontier prices as fixed with the general criteria published is sufficient to inform persons with a legitimate interest of the character of the data on the basis of which the decision was taken and of the conclusions to be drawn therefrom. The need to protect the parties to whom the decision is addressed and nationals of Member States affected by the decision, as also the need for proper judicial review, is sufficiently met as long as the Commission, as here, puts at the disposal of the parties the technical data used by it in fixing the free-at-frontier prices whenever the decision is challenged before a court having the appropriate jurisdiction.'[179]

§ 282. Sometimes Community institutions have wide discretion in taking their decisions. In such cases, it could be argued that less reasoning is required, as no detailed information is needed to demonstrate that the act is within the competence attributed. However, the Court has not adopted this position. In a case where the powers of the High Authority were rather broad (Art. 65(2))

---

179. *Schwarze Case* (16/65), 1 Dec. 1965, [1965] ECR 888, 889; 11 Jur. (1965) 1119, 1120; 11 Rec. (1965) 1096, 1097; [1966] CMLR 188; CCH para 8039. On the requirement of reasoning in general and on the *Schwarze Case* in particular see G. le Tallec and C.D. Ehlermann, *La motivation des actes des Communautés européennes*, 1966 RMC, pp. 179-187.

the Court required extensive reasoning. [180] It is in the interest of the individuals concerned that the Community institutions carefully document the decisions they take, particularly when the Treaty gives them extensive freedom in reaching their decisions. [181]

In the *Racke Case* a Commission regulation was contested by which the monetary compensatory amounts for certain products were discontinued for most Member States, but not for Germany, without stating the reasons why this measure could not be applied to Germany as well. The Court held, that in this case no reasoning was required since, with regard to Germany, the existing rules would remain in force, which were still based on the original grounds.[182]

When, in a reasoned decision, the Commission decided to conclude a contract with a particular firm, it was not obliged to separately state the reasons for the rejection of someone else's tender. [183]

§ 283. In some civil servants cases the Court required less reasoning than in others. In 1977 the Court ruled that when a staff member has been previously informed of the reasons for a transfer decision then the decision itself need not contain these same reasons. [184]

In a case where a candidate for appointment as an official was refused on account of physical unfitness the Court held that the duty to state reasons must be reconciled with the requirements of professional secrecy which normally leave it to the individual doctor to decide whether to communicate the nature of the condition of the candidate. [185]

The appointing authority has no duty to provide a statement of the reasons on which a decision not to accept an application for a post was based since the recital of such a statement of reasons might be prejudicial to the candidate. [186] Likewise the termination of the employment of temporary staff need not be reasoned. [187]

(v) Consequence of insufficient reasoning

§ 283a. In the *First Nold Case*, the Court, after considering that the obligation to give reasons has been prescribed not only for the benefit of the parties concerned but also to help the Court to exercise the powers of judicial review which the Treaty confers upon it, held that a failure to give reasons which

---

180. *Second Ruhrkohlen Case* (36-38 and 40/59), 15 July 1960, [1960] ECR 439; 6 Jur. (1960) 927-929; 6 Rec. (1960) 897, 898. See also *Transocean Marine Paint Case* (17/74), 23 Oct. 1974, consideration 16, [1974] ECR 1080; [1974] 2 CMLR 477, 478; CCH para 8241.
181. Timmermans (*op. cit.* note 87) pp. 94, 95.
182. *First Racke Case* (136/77), 25 May 1978, considerations 8, 9, [1978] ECR 1257; [1978] 3 CMLR 624, 625.
183. *Temporary Staff Suppliers Case* (56/77), 23 Nov. 1978, consideration 13.
184. *Geist Case* (61/76), 14 July 1977, consideration 23, [1977] ECR 1432; *Ditterich Case* (86/77), 12 Oct. 1978, consideration 39, [1978] ECR 1867.
185. *Moli Case* (121/76), 27 Oct. 1977, consideration 14, [1977] ECR 1978.
186. *Ganzini Case* (101/77), 13 April 1978, consideration 10, [1978] ECR 920.
187. *Schertzer Case* (25/68), 18 Oct. 1977, consideration 39, [1977] ECR 1744.

hinders this judicial review may be, and must be, reviewed by the Court of its own motion. [188]

In the *Tubes de la Sarre Case*, the Court considered a 'reasoned opinion' under ECSC Article 54(4), which was not reasoned, as a non-existent act (see above § 217). Though the Court's wording might suggest that a total absence of reasoning would lead to the non-existence of the act in other cases as well, the Court did not follow this line in its subsequent case-law, so that we may safely assume that a total absence of reasoning will not be adequate to deprive an act of all legal force, but it will be a ground for annulment by the Court of Justice.

§ 284.   The reasoning of an act has no binding force of its own. There is no action against the reasoning if it expresses intentions for a further policy which appears contrary to the Treaties. In such a case one has to wait until such policies are being realized. [189]

c.   THE RELATIONSHIP BETWEEN CONSULTATION AND REASONING

§ 285.   The purpose of consultation is to give some influence over decisions to the consulted organ. The requirement to seek the opinion of the Advisory Committee or the Council in ECSC or of the European Parliament or the Economic and Social Committee in EEC would make no sense if the consulting organ had no obligation to read the opinion.

In order to give full weight to the opinions of the consulted organs the Council and the Commission might have been obliged not only to mention these opinions in their decisions but also to argue why they have not been followed.

EEC Article 190 and ECSC Article 15 (1) provide that binding Community acts must *refer* to the opinions which were required to be obtained pursuant to the Treaty. In particular, for the European Parliament, an extensive interpretation of this obligation would have been valuable and it could be submitted that the Court, looking at the purpose of the provision, ought to rule that the reference should include some demonstration that the opinions have been studied and express reasoning why particular proposals of the Parliament have not been followed.

§ 286.   With respect to the opinions of the European Parliament, the extensive interpretation suggested above has never been invoked before the Court, since the Court had clearly rejected it in respect of the advisory organs of ECSC. In the *ISA Case* it held:

---

188. *First Nold Case* (18/57), 20 March 1959, [1959] ECR 52; 5 Jur. (1958-59) 119; 5 Rec. (1958-59) 114, 115.
189. *First Ruhrkohlen Case* (16-18/59), 12 Feb. 1960, [1960] ECR 25; 6 Jur. (1960) 61-64; 6 Rec. (1960) 61-64.

'The applicant regards as a departure from the rules of sound administration and in consequence as evidence tending to establish a misuse of powers the fact that, in stating the reasons on which the contested decisions were based, the High Authority failed to comment on the divergent opinions expressed within the consultative bodies. The Court does not share this view. Under Article 15 of the Treaty, the High Authority is bound to 'state the reasons' on which its decisions are based and to 'refer to' any opinions which were required to be obtained. It follows from this that it must state the reasons for which it decided to promulgate the rules in question and that it is bound to refer to the fact that the opinions required by the Treaty have been obtained. On the other hand, the Treaty does not require that it should mention, still less that it should try to refute, the divergent opinions expressed by the consultative bodies or by some of their members.'[190]

d. PUBLICATION AND NOTIFICATION

§ 287. EEC Article 191(1) requires that regulations shall be published in the Official Journal of the Community. If it is not otherwise provided, they enter into force on the twentieth day following their publication. What is the day of publication? Is it the date borne by the issue of the Official Journal containing the regulation, the date on which that Official Journal actually appeared, or the date on which the Official Journal was available in the Member State concerned? The Court of Justice held that uniform application of Community law requires that regulations enter into force throughout the entire Community on the same date. This means that availibility in the Member State cannot be taken into account. As the Council has instructed the Office of Publication to assure that the date printed on each Official Journal corresponds with the actual date of appearance, the Court accepted the date borne by the issue of the Official Journal containing the text of the regulation as the date of publication of that regulation, unless it is proved that the actual publication was on a later date.[191]

It is probable that the Court of Justice would consider a regulation which has not been published as invalid. In the *Drescig Case* rules concerning Community personnel which had been issued by a decision of the Commission were involved. The Court of Justice considered this decision to be an internal rule and declared that:

'The fact that this is the nature of the Decision of 26 February 1971 is confirmed by the fact it was published by the Commission not in the Official Journal, but in an information bulletin intended for the staff.'[192]

190. *ISA Case* (4/54), 11 Feb. 1955, [1954-55] ECR 100; 1 Jur. (1954-55) 210, 211; 1 Rec. (1954-55) 196.
191. *Second Racke Case* (98/78), 25 Jan. 1979, considerations 16, 17; *Decker Case* (99/78), 25 Jan. 1979, considerations 4, 5.
192. *Drescig Case* (49/72), 30 May 1973, consideration 11, [1973] ECR 571.

This indicates that the Court takes account of the method of publication in establishing the nature of an act.

When Community law requires that an act be taken before a certain date, then the date of its adoption is decisive. The act is valid, if it is adopted in time, even if it is published after the required date.[193] However, a regulation cannot be applied before its publication, unless there are special reasons for granting retroactive effect to it. A delay in the publication of the Official Journal is not such a special reason and therefore entails a delay in the entry into force. [194]

§ 288.   The Court has ruled on the publication of Community regulations by national decree. It rejected the reproduction of the provisions of Community Regulations in national decrees in the *Premiums for Slaughtering Cows Case* where it held:

'By following this procedure, the Italian Government has brought into doubt both the legal nature of the applicable provisions and the date of their coming into force.

According to the terms of Article 189 and 191 of the Treaty, Regulations are, as such, directly applicable in all Member States and come into force solely by virtue of their publication in the *Official Journal* of the Communities, as from the date specified in them, or in the absence thereof, as from the date provided in the Treaty.

Consequently, all methods of implementation are contrary to the Treaty which would have the result of creating an obstacle to the direct effect of Community Regulations and of jeopardizing their simultaneous and uniform application in the whole of the Community.' [195]

§ 289.   EEC Article 191 (2) provides that *'directives and decisions shall be notified to those to whom they are addressed and shall take effect upon such notification'*. In practice, all directives and all decisions which are of importance to others than the addressee are published in the Official Journal. [196] As an action for annulment must be instituted within two months of the publication of the measure, or of its notification to the plaintiff, the publication of these acts is important for the commencement of time limits (see below § 665, 666). The entire act must be published, including, for example, the extent of subsidies granted and consequently their effect upon the economic sector concerned. [197]

193. *König Case* (185/73), 29 May 1974, consideration 6, [1974] ECR 617; CCH para 8275.
194. *Exportation des Sucres Case* (88/76), 31 March 1977, considerations 17, 18, [1977] ECR 726; CCH para 8418.
195. *Premiums for Slaughtering Cows Case* (39/72), 7 Feb. 1973, [1973] ECR 114; CCH para 8201.
196. A.G. Toth, *Legal Protection of Individuals in the European Communities*, North Holland, 1978, Vol. 1, pp. 72-76.
197. Advocate-General Roemer in the *Eridania Case* (10, 18/68), 10 Dec. 1969, [1969] ECR 488. See also Peter Oliver, *Limitation of Actions before the European Court*, 3, ELRev. (1978), p. 8.

It has been disputed whether the provision that decisions must be notified is an essential procedural requirement, which would mean that without proper notification a decision would be void. In Article 4 of a decision of 24 July 1969 addressed to *Imperial Chemical Industries Ltd. (ICI)* in England, the Commission stated that the notification could be effected at the registered office of a subsidiary established within the Common Market. Thereupon a notification decision addressed to ICI at its German subsidiary's office was posted and ICI regarded it as an infringement of an essential procedural requirement.

The Court considered that such a decision could not change EEC Article 191 and therefore could not effect ICI's rights.

It then continued:

'Irregularities in the procedure for notification of a decision are extraneous to that measure and cannot therefore invalidate it.

In certain circumstances such irregularities may prevent the period within which an application must be lodged from starting to run.

The last paragraph of Article 173 of the Treaty provides that the period for instituting proceedings for the annulment of individual measures of the Commission starts to run from the date of notification of the decision to the applicant or, in the absence thereof, from the day on which it came to the knowledge of the latter.

In the present case it is established that the applicant has had full knowledge of the text of the decision and that it has exercised its right to institute proceedings within the prescribed period.

In these circumstances the question of possible irregularities concerning notification ceases to be relevant.

Therefore the abovementioned submissions are inadmissible for want of relevance.' [198]

The Court of Justice gave a further definition of notification in the *Continental Can Case*, where it held: '*A decision is properly notified within the meaning of the Treaty, if it reaches the addressee and puts the latter in a position to take cognizance of it.*' [199] On notification see also below § 665.

3. Infringement of the Treaty

§ 290. The most important ground of illegality is 'violation of the Treaty'. The Treaty grants power to institutions, expresses the purpose for which the

---

198. *ICI Case* (48/69), 14 July 1972, considerations 39-44, [1972] ECR 652, [1972] CMLR 620; CCH para 8161.
199. *Continental Can Case* (6/72), 21 Feb. 1973, consideration 10, [1973] ECR 241; CCH para 8171.

power has been given, and regulates how it should be exerted. This means that virtually any error by a Community institution can be viewed as a Treaty violation. This ground of illegality is therefore invoked in all actions, and it is the one which is most often successful.

The Court has accepted that not only those articles of the Treaty on which the act is directly founded are relevant. All articles and, in particular, the general articles at the beginning of the Treaties should be respected.

ECSC Article 53 expressly refers to ECSC Article 3. In the *Hauts Fourneaux Case*, where an act based on Article 53 was disputed, the Court held:

'The express reference made to Article 3 does not release the High Authority from its duty to observe the other articles of the Treaty and in particular Articles 2, 4 and 5 which, together with Article 3, must always be observed because they establish the fundamental objectives of the Community. Those provisions are binding and must be read together if they are to be properly applied. These provisions can stand by themselves and accordingly, in so far as they have not been adopted in any other provision of the Treaty, they are directly applicable. If they have been adopted or are governed by other provisions of the Treaty words relating to the same provision must be considered as a whole and applied together. In practice it will always be necessary to reconcile to a certain degree the various objectives of Article 3 since it is clearly impossible to attain them all fully and simultaneously as those objectives constitute general principles which must be observed and harmonized as far as possible.' [200]

§ 291. Rules of law are made to cover particular facts. A miscalculation of the facts may therefore lead to an improper application of the law or an infringement of the Treaty. In his study of the case law of the Court of Justice, Waelbroeck mentions the following examples as decisions annulled due to a false evaluation of the underlying facts [201]:

In the *Barge Case* the High Authority estimated the amount of scrap used by the applicant on the basis of his electricity bills. When it was demonstrated that the estimates were incorrect the Court of Justice annulled the decision concerned. [202]

In the *Raponi, Bernusset* and *De Pascale Cases* the Court annulled certain nominations of civil servants for the reason that the applications submitted by other candidates had been insufficiently examined, with the result that the Commission had based its decisions on incomplete facts. [203]

---

200. *Hauts Fourneaux Case* (8/57), 21 June 1958, [1957-58] ECR 253; 4 Jur. (1958) 259, 260; 4 Rec. (1958) 242.
201. Michel Waelbroeck, *Examen de Jurisprudence 1955 à 1971, Communautés Européennes*, RCJB 1971, pp. 541, 542.
202. *Barge Case* (18/62), 16 Dec. 1963, [1963] ECR 278-279; 9 Jur. (1963) 588, 589; 9 Rec. (1963) 564-566; [1965] CMLR 343, 344.
203. *Raponi Case* (27/63), 19 March 1964, [1964] ECR 138, 139; 10 Jur. (1964) 287, 288; 10 Rec. (1964) 268, 269; *Bernusset Case* (94 and 96/63), 9 June 1964, [1964] ECR 309, 313; 10 Jur. (1964) 641, 645; 10 Rec. (1964) 612-616; *De Pascale Case* (97/63), 7 July 1964, [1964] ECR 527, 528; 10 Jur. (1964) 1087, 1088; 10 Rec. (1964) 1036-1038.

Waelbroeck comes to the conclusion that the extent of the supervision of the facts by the Court of Justice varies from case to case. If special technical knowledge is needed, for example, for the authorization of an agreement under EEC Article 85 (3), or if the decision concerns the assessment of human factors such as the qualifications of a person for a post, the Court leaves much freedom to the decision-making institution. The control exercised by the Court is more strict if the facts in issue are such that the Court can interpret them itself. [204]

4. Infringement of any rule of law relating to the application of the Treaty

§ 292.   This ground which, in the text of ECSC Article 33 and EEC Article 173, forms part of the ground 'infringement of the Treaty or of any rule of law relating to its application' is in fact the only ground which plays a role independent of the ground 'infringement of the Treaty'. An infringement of any other ground is simultaneously an infringement of the Treaty, but this is additional to it.

What are the rules of law relating to the application of the Treaty? One might think of the Protocols annexed to the Treaties, but as they form an integral part of the Treaties themselves [205], no special reference in respect of them was necessary. The Treaty drafters seem to have thought of the regulations executing the Treaties, because they wrote in the Dutch text 'infringement of any rule executing the Treaty' (enige uitvoeringsregeling daarvan). The Court of Justice has expressly qualified the infringement of a regulation as an infringement of a rule of law relating to the application of the Treaty. [206]   But this sort of infringement does not add anything to the other grounds of illegality as a violation of a regulation would at the same time be a violation of the Treaty which provides that regulations are binding and should be applied. [207]

One set of rules of law remains: those underlying the Treaties. Treaties are concluded under international law and therefore the rules of international law should be taken into account when the content of a treaty is expanded on by Community acts. Community acts made in violation of binding rules of international law are, therefore, illegal. The Court of Justice confirmed this in the *Third International Fruit Company Case*, in which it held:

'Before the incompatibility of a Community measure with a provision of international law can affect the validity of that measure, the Community must first of all be bound by that provision.' [208]

---

204. Waelbroeck, (*op. cit.*, note 201), p. 544.
205. EEC Art. 239; ECSC Art. 84.
206. *Fourth Simmenthal Case* (92/78), 6 March 1979, consideration 106.
207. EEC Art. 189; ECSC Art. 14.
208. *Third International Fruit Company Case* (21-24/72), 12 Dec. 1972, consideration 7, [1972] ECR 1226; CCH para 8194.

For a survey of the rules of international law to which the Communities are bound, see above § 127-138.

Apart from international law, the other rules of law underlying the Treaties are the general principles of law. In order to serve as a ground of illegality a general principle of law must be compulsory. The most important compulsory principle of law is respect for fundamental rights, of which the Court of Justice said in the *Handelsgesellschaft Case*: *'respect for fundamental rights forms an integral part of the general principles of law protected by the Court of Justice.'* [209] For a further survey of general principles of law, see above § 33-118.

5. Misuse of powers [210]

§ 293. Powers have often been granted to Community institutions for specific purposes. Should they use these powers for other purposes, then the acts taken could be annulled on the ground of misuse of powers. Misuse of powers is also applicable when an institution uses a particular form of act with the intention of circumventing a procedure specially provided by the Treaty. [211]

Misuse of powers is of special importance under the ECSC Treaty, since private persons are limited to this ground in actions against general decisions (see below § 307-309).

In the *First Assider Case*, Advocate-General Lagrange surveyed the notion of 'misuse of powers' in the national laws of each of the (original) Member States, which revealed considerable differences. [212] Therefore, the national definitions of 'misuse of powers' cannot be applied in Community law. The case-law of the Court of Justice must be used for guidance. In the *Fédéchar Case*, the same Advocate-General defined the boundary between 'misuse of powers' and other grounds of appeal. He concluded – and the Court seemed to concur – that the improper use of clearly defined powers can still be contested on the ground 'misuse of powers' and need not be brought under 'violation of the treaty' (i.e. the article defining the powers). [213]

'Misuse of powers' can only be committed by an organ vested with discretionary powers. If there is no choice, then the delegated power cannot be used for another purpose than for which it has been granted. An organ charged with collecting fixed sums of money, for example, cannot misuse those pow-

---

209. *Handelsgesellschaft Case* (11/70), 17 Dec. 1970, consideration 4, [1970] ECR 1134; [1972] CMLR 283; CCH para 8126.
210. Friedrich Clever, *Ermessensmissbrauch und détournement de pouvoir nach dem Recht der Europäischen Gemeinschaften*, Duncker & Humblot, Berlin 1967, 185 pages; Hermann Soell, *Das Ermessen der Eingriffsverwaltung*, Universitätsverlag Heidelberg, pp. 286-365; *Idem, Das Ermessen der Eingriffsverwaltung*, Heidelberg 1973, pp. 286-365.
211. *Hauts Fourneaux Case* (8/57) 21 June 1958, [1957-58] ECR 255; 4 Jur. (1958) 263; 4 Rec. (1958) 245.
212. *First Assider Case* (3/54), 11 Feb. 1955, Opinion of the Advocate-General, [1954-56] ECR 75-85; 1 Rec. (1954-55) 149-169.
213. *Fédéchar Case* (8/55), 16 July 1956, Opinion of the Advocate-General, [1954-56] ECR 273; 2 Rec. (1955-56) 255.

ers. [214] It is incompetent to collect other sums and it violates its obligations if it does not collect any at all.

§ 294.   In the *First Monnet Rabat Case* the French government invoked 'misuse of powers' for the reason that the High Authority had taken its decision not only for the purpose for which the powers had been granted, but also for other purposes. The Court held:

> 'In any case, it is obvious that the decisions were above all intended to further the Treaty's aims. Even if the grounds for the High Authority's decisions included, in addition to proper grounds, the improper one of avoiding subjecting guilty undertakings to penalties, this would not make the decisions invalid for misuse of powers, in so far as they do not detract from the main aim, which is the prohibition of unfair competitive practices and discrimination.' [215]

§ 295.   In the *Fédéchar Case* 'misuse of powers' was claimed on the ground that the decision had been based on incorrect data. The Court, although agreeing that some data had been incorrect, denied misuse of powers, holding:

> 'Even if the defendant has committed certain errors in selecting the basis for its calculations, as is the case with regard to selection of the reference year and perhaps also with regard to amortization and the grouping of categories of coal, it is not to be held that its errors constitute *ipso facto* proof of misuse of powers unless it has also been established objectively that the High Authority pursued in this case, through a serious lack of care or attention amounting to a disregard for the lawful aim, purposes other than those for which the powers provided for in Article 26 (2) (a) were conferred.' [216]

§ 296.   In the *Second Chasse Case*, the High Authority based a decision on ECSC Article 53 (b). The applicant maintained that it should have been based on ECSC Article 59 and that the action of the High Authority indicated an intent to avoid the guarantees contained in Article 59. The Court held:

> 'In this connexion it must be recognized that there might have been a misuse of powers if the High Authority had been faced with a situation covered by the procedure in Article 59 and, in order to evade the safeguards provided for in Article 59, had nevertheless deliberately decided to make use of Article 53 (b) and of the financial arrangements provided for therein. But it has not been established that, when the basic decisions were taken, the High Authority was faced with such a situation. In the circum-

214. *Idem*, 272; 254.
215. *First Monnet Rabat Case* (1/54), 21 Dec. 1954, [1954-56] ECR 16; 1 Jur. (1954-55) 34; 1 Rec. (1954-55) 32, 33.
216. *Fédéchar Case* (8/55), 29 Nov. 1956, [1954-56] ECR 303; 2 Jur. (1955-56) 329; 2 Rec. (1955-56) 309, 310.

stances, there is no evidence that the introduction of the equalization system by way of a financial arrangement established pursuant to Article 53 (b) was vitiated by misuse of powers. The complaint is without foundation.' [217]

§ 297.   In practice, 'misuse of powers' is not an important ground of illegality. This may be partly because the other grounds sufficiently cover all cases of illegality and partly because of problems of proof. [218]   In the *First Chasse Case* the Court ruled:

'To prove a misuse of powers the applicant would have had to demonstrate that the decision itself was in fact pursuing an objective other than that for the purposes of which the High Authority was entitled to act.' [219]

Misuse of powers can be proven by witnesses [220]   as well as by using documents and preliminary discussions preceding the act. [221]   Only rarely has the Court annulled a decision on the ground 'misuse of powers'. In one case, a staff member had been transferred 'in the interest of the service' whilst actually, the transfer was a disciplinary measure. [222]   In another case an internal competition for the recruitment of staff member was organized for the sole purpose of appointing a particular official to the post declared vacant. The Court of Justice annulled the appointment on the ground of misuse of powers. [222a]

C. WAYS OF CHALLENGING COMMUNITY ACTS

§ 298.   If a Community act lacks all legal basis, it may be considered non-existent (see above § 213-226). In such extreme cases, there is no act and therefore no act can be challenged. The non-existent act can be simply ignored and its non-existence can be invoked at any time, by anybody and before any court, tribunal or authority. It was noted above that the occurrence of non-existence is rare and should be limited to exceptional situations.

---

217. *Second Chasse Case* (15/57), 13 June 1958, [1957-58] ECR 231; 4 Jur. (1958) 205; 4 Rec. (1958) 193, 194.
218. Waelbroeck (*op. cit.*, note 201), p. 546 and Timmermans (*op. cit.*, note 87), p. 162.
219. *First Chasse Case* (2/57), 13 June 1958, [1957-58] ECR 207; 4 Jur. (1958) 155; 4 Rec. (1958) 148.
220. *Fiddelaar Case* (44/59), 16 Dec. 1960, [1960] ECR 545-547; 6 Jur. (1960) 1138-1140; 6 Rec. (1960) 1097.
221. *Coal Price Case* (6/54), 21 March 1955, [1954-56] ECR 116; 1 Jur. (1954-55) 243; 1 Rec. (1954-55) 226.
222. *Gutmann Case* (18 and 35/65), 1st judgment, 5 May 1966, [1966] ECR 118; 12 Jur. (1966) 173; 12 Rec. (1966) 171. [According to Waelbroeck (*op. cit.*, note 201), p. 546 and Timmermans (*op. cit.*, note 87) p. 164, this was the only case in which the Court had done so up to 1971 and 1973, respectively. In 1979 the Court annulled a regulation partly on misuse of powers. See *Fourth Simmenthal Case* (92/78), 6 March 1979, consideration 106.]
222a. *Giufrida Case* (105/75), 29 Sept. 1976, considerations 10-13, 18, [1976] ECR 1403, 1404.

In all other cases Community acts are to be considered valid until the Court of Justice has decided to the contrary. In order to establish its nullity an act must be challenged before the Court of Justice.

§ 299. There are five methods in which this can be done, each one serving a different purpose and therefore applicable to different situations. (1) The action for annulment is a direct attack on the act, aiming at its total destruction. In the interests of legal certainty it may only be brought during a short period of time. (2) The action against failure to act has been created for the purpose of challenging the failure to act of Community institutions. Its aim is to provoke action by the Community authorities. (3) The plea of illegality is designed to prevent the application of an illegal act from being used as a legal basis for further action. It can be invoked before the Court of Justice when the validity of such further action is disputed. (4) A request for a preliminary ruling on the validity of a Community act can be brought by national courts when they have to apply a Community act whose validity is doubted. It obviates the situation where national courts would otherwise be obliged to apply invalid rules of Community law. (5) In a suit for damages caused by an illegal act the Court of Justice may establish such illegality. The methods mentioned under (3), (4) and (5) do not result in the nullity of Community acts; they only prevent them from being applied in particular cases.

As a sixth method of challenging the validity of Community acts, it could be conceived that the Court of Justice would be prepared to review the legality of an act whenever a Member State, accused of its breach, is sued before the Court for non fulfilment of its obligations. At this stage, however, the Court has not been willing to discuss the question of legality in such cases. (see below § 386).

1. The action for annulment

a. SCOPE OF THE ACTION FOR ANNULMENT [223]

§ 300. The action, or appeal, for annulment is a direct challenge upon the validity of Community acts. On any of the grounds mentioned above (§ 254-297) the illegality of a Community act can be pleaded before the Court of Justice with the sole purpose of getting the act annulled. In the annulment proceedings the Court has no other option than to annul or not to annul. It cannot replace the act by another one or make amendments to it. [224] At the most, the Court may indicate what changes are needed for legalising the act.

223. See Michel Fromont, *L'influence du droit français et du droit allemand sur les conditions de recevabilité du recours en annulation devant la Court de Justice des Communautés européennes*, 2 RTDE (1966), pp. 47-65; A.G. Toth, *The Individual and European Law*, 24 ICLQ (1975), in particular pp. 672-681.
224. See e.g. *Second Limburg Coalmines Case* (30/59), 23 Feb. 1961, [1961] ECR 17; 7 Jur. (1961) 37; 7 Rec. (1961) 36. For further examples, see Waelbroeck (*op. cit.*, note 201) p. 542.

There is one exception to this rule: when a regulation is declared void, the Court may decide that particular effects accomplished by it shall remain valid [225], or shall remain valid temporarily (see below § 379a).

Until 31 December 1978 the action for annulment was instituted 214 times under the EEC Treaty (26 times by Governments, 3 times by Community institutions and 185 times by individuals) [226], which is about one fifth of the total number of cases brought before the Court if staff cases are excluded. Under the ECSC Treaty 300 cases for annulment have been brought (22 by Governments, one by an institution and 277 by individuals)[227], which is, again apart from staff cases, more than 95 percent of all cases brought under the ECSC Treaty.

The action for annulment does not have suspensory effect, but the Court may, if it considers that circumstances so require, order that application of the contested act should be suspended (see below § 672-676).

If the action for annulment succeeds, the annulment has general effect. When *Assider* instituted proceedings for the annulment of Article 1 of ECSC Decision 2-54, the Court replied:

'Since Article 1 of Decision No 2/54 of the High Authority was for all purposes annulled by judgment of 21 December 1954 in the case of the *French Government v The High Authority*, this application for annulment has on this point no longer any purpose.' [228]

§ 301. The ECSC action for annulment is governed by ECSC Article 33 which grants jurisdiction to the Court of Justice to annul binding acts of the High Authority. ECSC Article 38 contains a similar provision for acts of the European Parliament and the Council.

Under EEC Article 173 the Court is entitled to review the legality of the binding acts of the Council and the Commission. Apart from civil servants in staff cases, individuals may not challenge acts of the Court of Justice or the European Parliament. [229] Against court decisions actions may be brought as application for revision (see below § 716). As the European Parliament originally had very limited powers judicial review of its acts was hardly conceivable before the two budgetary treaties of 1970 and 1975. The dispute between the European Parliament and the Council about the legality of the 1979 budget demonstrated that there may now be reason for judicial review. Such review is possible through the other ways of challenging Community acts, discussed below (see § 329-379), but not through the action for annulment. This seems an anomaly which needs correction. [230]

---

225. EEC Art. 174.
226. Twelfth General Report, p. 368, table 2.
227. *Idem*, table 3. Four cases under ECSC article 88 are to be deducted from this total.
228. *First Assider Case* (3/54), 11 Feb. 1955, [1954-56] ECR 70; 1 Jur. (1954-55) 148; 1 Rec. (1954-55) 139.
229. *De Lacroix Case* (91/76), 3 Feb. 1977, consideration 8, [1977] ECR 229.
230. See Editional Comments, 16 CMLRev. (1979), pp. 175-177.

§ 302. In each of the Communities there are two important restrictions to the action for annulment: (a) as in any other system administrative law an action for annulment must be lodged within a limited period of time in order to prevent a long period of uncertainty arising about the binding character of the act; (b) the right to bring an action for annulment has been granted to a strictly delimited group of persons, as the drafters of the Community Treaties feared that a flood of actions would hamper the functioning of the Communities.

Time limits will be discussed in Chapter Five on procedure (see below § 661). Here specific attention must be paid to the capacity to bring the action.

b. CAPACITY TO BRING THE ACTION

(i) Actions by Member States and Institutions

§ 303. Actions for annulment may be brought by the Member States, by the Council and by the Commission, in other words by those involved in the formulation of Community law. The institutions charged with the task of control (the European Parliament and the Court of Justice) have no right to bring an action against Community acts. Member States, the Council and the Commission may challenge all binding acts; they need not be of special interest to them.

(ii) Actions by private parties under the ECSC

α. Undertakings entitled to bring an action under ECSC

§ 304. Under the ECSC Treaty private parties, other than staff members for staff cases, may not institute proceedings against acts of the Council or the European Parliament. [231] As almost all rules affecting individuals are made by the High Authority this limitation is of little practical importance. The fact that individuals may not challenge acts of the Council in a direct action does not exclude the possibility that the Court of Justice may rule on their validity in preliminary rulings at the request of national courts (see below § 554-625). [232]

ECSC Article 33 limits the right of bringing an action against the High Authority to *undertakings* and associations referred to in Article 48. ECSC Article 80 defines 'undertakings' to mean those 'engaged in production in the coal or the steel industries within the European territories of the Member States'. [233] For the purposes of Articles 65 and 66, concerning agreements

---

231. ECSC Art. 38.
232. See *CFDT Case* (66/76), 17 Feb. 1977, consideration 12, [1977] ECR 309, 310; [1977] 2 CMLR 595.
233. Some European territories are excepted by Article 79, para 2, which was added by the Act of Accession (Faroe Islands, Bases in Northern Ireland and Cyprus, to some extent the Channel Islands and the Isle of Man).

and concentrations, undertakings and agencies regularly engaged in distribution other than the retail trade are included in the definition.[234] Article 48 provides that the above mentioned undertakings may form associations and that such associations have rights and duties under the Treaty. In the *Coal Consumers in Luxembourg Case* the Court decided that associations are to be formed of undertakings in the sense of Article 80 so that an association composed of five members, of which only one is covered by the definition of Article 80, has no right to institute proceedings.[235]

Private parties other than the above-mentioned ones cannot challenge ECSC decisions.

§ 305. May a steel undertaking challenge a decision concerning coal and *vice versa*? The Luxembourg government disputed this assertion in the *Steel Industries in Luxembourg Case*, but the Court held:

> 'In the opinion of the Advocate General, there is no provision of the Treaty which requires that the speciality of the producers must be linked to the special field of the dispute.
>
> The silence of the Treaty on this point cannot be interpreted to the disadvantage of the undertakings and associations.
>
> For this reason the applicant's right to institute proceedings before the Court cannot in this instance be contested.'[236]

§ 306. Not every undertaking involved in the production of coal and steel may institute proceedings against any decision of the High Authority. *Vloeberghs* imported coal which it broke, screened and washed, and also manufactured briquettes. He instituted an action against the High Authority's failure to act concerning a decision on the import of coal. As an importer, he had no right to institute proceedings. According to the Court, breaking, screening and washing did not qualify him either:

> 'To decide whether a particular activity constitutes a 'production' activity it is necessary to refer to the nomenclature of Annex-I to the Treaty. If the activity involves a certain degree of processing of the raw material, the decisive criterion is in particular whether after the processing operation the product in question falls within the said nomenclature under a heading different from that under which it appeared previously.'

This was not the case. Furthermore, as a manufacturer of briquettes, Vloeberghs was not allowed to bring an action. On this point the Court held:

234. The Court confirmed that these undertakings are entitled to bring an action. See *First Nold Case* (18/57), 4 Dec. 1957, [1957-58] ECR 123; 3 Jur. (1957) 255; 3 Rec. (1957) 241.
235. *Coal Consumers in Luxembourg Case* (8 and 10/54), 23 April 1956, [1954-56] ECR 239, 240; 2 Jur. (1955-56) 195-197; 2 Rec. (1955-56) 186, 187.
236. *Steel Industries in Luxembourg Case* (7 and 9/54), 23 April 1956, [1954-56] ECR 191; 2 Jur. (1955-56) 90; 2 Rec. (1955-56) 86.

'Although it is true that the applicant carries on production activities as a manufacturer of briquettes, that capacity has not been taken into account in the present case in which the applicant has instituted proceedings in its capacity as an importer and exporter of, and therefore as a dealer in, coal originating in third countries, whilst its capacity as manufacturer of briquettes plays no role either directly or indirectly in relation to the subject-matter of the dispute.'[237]

β. *Actions against general decisions under ECSC*

§ 307. For the distinction between general and individual acts, see above § 198-212. Private parties may institute proceedings against general decisions (regulations) of the High Authority[238], but not against general decisions of other ECSC institutions (see above § 304). The other limitation on the right of private parties to bring an action against general decisions is far more restrictive: they may apply for annulment only when they consider the decision to involve a misuse of powers affecting them. It seems probable that the drafters of the Treaty made this exception with an eye to individual decisions disguised as general ones. Due to the fairly small number of undertakings involved, it would be easy for the High Authority to frustrate the right to institute proceedings by issuing a general decision instead of addressing an individual one to the undertaking concerned. The general decision could be so detailed and specific that, in practice, only one undertaking would be affected, e.g.: 'all coal mines, mining in soil containing so much chalk, at a depth of so many feet, with so many personnel, shall ...' This would constitute a misuse of powers and against such misuse the Treaty permits a Court action. This explains why only the ground of 'misuse of powers' is permitted and not the other grounds, while in general 'violation of the Treaty' constitutes a more important ground for annulment.

When the High Authority brought this reasoning up in the *Fédéchar Case*, however, it was not accepted, as the Court replied:

'That argument must be rejected. A disguised individual decision remains an individual decision, since its nature depends on its scope rather than on its form. Furthermore, such an interpretation of Article 33 and especially of the words 'affecting them' cannot be accepted, since the phrase 'affecting them' can be understood only in the sense of the words which express it, that is, where it concerns an undertaking which is the subject or at any rate the victim of the misuse of powers alleged by that undertaking. The Court considers that Article 33 clearly states that associations and undertakings may contest not only individual decisions but also general decisions in the true sense of the term.'[239]

237. *Vloeberghs Case* (9 and 12/60), 14 July 1961, [1961] ECR 212; 7 Jur. (1961) 445, 446; 7 Rec. (1961) 422-424.
238. ECSC Art. 33.
239. *Fédéchar Case* (8/55), 16 July 1956, [1954-56] ECR 257-258; 2 Jur. (1955-56) 237; 2 Rec. (1955-56) 226.

§ 308. Once it was established that the ground of illegality 'misuse of powers' can be used against all general decisions of the ECSC, the question arose whether 'misuse of powers' must be proved before the case can be admitted before the Court.

The Court did not require such proof in the Assider Case in which it held:

'The Court rejects the defendant's argument that the admissibility of proceedings brought by undertakings or associations of undertakings against general decisions is subject to proof of the existence of a misuse of powers affecting them. Under the provisions of the second paragraph of Article 33 of the Treaty, undertakings or associations of undertakings 'may ... institute proceedings ... against general decisions ... which they *consider* to involve a misuse of powers affecting them.' From this wording, which is perfectly clear, for an application to be admissible it is enough for the applicant formally to allege that there has been a misuse of powers affecting it just as it is sufficient, as regards the admissibility of an application from a State, for it to allege the existence of one of the four grounds for annulment set out in the first paragraph of Article 33 of the Treaty. The allegation must indicate the reasons for which the applicant considers that there has been a misuse of powers affecting it.' [240]

§ 309. Once misuse of powers has been alleged, the case is admissible and comes before the Court. Once there, the question arises whether it would then be possible to invoke other grounds of illegality. Following the suggestion of Advocate-General Lagrange in the *First Assider case* [241], Fédéchar submitted that it had such a right, but the Court replied:

'That argument must be dismissed. If the Treaty provides that private undertakings are entitled to seek the annulment of a general decision on the ground of misuse of powers affecting them, that is because they have no right of action on any other ground.

If the applicant's argument were correct, undertakings would have a right of action as extensive as that of the States and the Council and it would be difficult to explain why, instead of simply treating actions brought by undertakings in the same way as those brought by States or the Council, Article 33 introduced a clear distinction between individual decisions and general decisions, while restricting the annulment of general decisions in the case of undertakings to the submission of misuse of powers affecting them. The phrase 'under the same conditions' cannot be interpreted as meaning that, after establishing a case of misuse of powers affecting them, undertakings are entitled to put forward in addition the other grounds for annulment, since once the misuse of powers affecting them is established the

240. *First Assider Case* (3/54), 11 Feb. 1955, [1954-56] ECR 69; 1 Jur. (1954-55) 146, 147; 1 Rec. (1954-55) 138, 139. See also *Fédéchar Case* (8/55), 16 July 1956, [1954-56] ECR 257; 2 Jur. (1955-56) 236, 237; 2 Rec. (1955-56) 226.
241. *First Assider Case* (3/54), 11 Feb. 1955, [1954-56] ECR 74; 1 Rec. (1954-55) 148.

decision in question is annulled, and that annulment does not have to be pronounced again on other grounds.' [242]

γ. Actions against individual decisions under ECSC

§ 310. Undertakings may challenge decisions addressed to them by the High Authority (Commission). [243] They may also institute proceedings against decisions addressed to others, provided that they *'concern them'*. In contradistinction to the EEC Treaty this concern need not be individual or direct. The interpretations of the Court of Justice have not been restrictive in accepting that a decision 'concerned' others.

In the *Second Limburg Coalmines Case* the High Authority had decided not to object to a special premium paid by the German government to the German miners. The Limburg mines alleged that the premium affected their competitive position and that therefore the decision not to object, taken by the High Authority concerned them. The High Authority submitted that its (negative) decision did not concern the Limburg coal mines since it did not directly affect their legal position nor had the mines a direct and special interest in the matter. The Court held:

'For an application for annulment of a decision which is individual in character, submitted by an undertaking, to be admissible it is enough that the applicant claims that the decision concerns it and supports its claim by an appropriate statement explaining the interest which it has in having the decision declared void.

...

Contrary to the contention of the defendant, to enable an undertaking to institute proceedings against a decision concerning it which is individual in character, it is not necessary that it should be the only, or almost the only, party concerned by the decision.' [244]

The Second Limburg Coalmines Case confirmed a prior decision of the Court in the *Chambre Syndicale de l'Est de la France Case*, in which the Court also ruled that a competitor was sufficiently concerned to have standing to bring an action. [245]

---

242. *Fédéchar Case* (8/55), 16 July 1956, [1954-56] ECR 258; 2 Jur. (1955-56) 238; 2 Rec. (1955-56) 227.
243. They have no action against acts of other institutions (ECSC Art. 38), but in practice such acts do not exist.
244. *Second Limburg Coalmines Case* (30/59), 23 Feb. 1961, [1961] ECR 16, 17; 7 Jur. (1961) 36; 7 Rec. (1961) 34-36.
245. *Chambre Syndicale et de l'Est de la France Case* (24 and 34/58), 15 July 1960, [1960] ECR 292; 6 Jur. (1960) 614; 6 Rec. (1960) 589.

(iii) Actions by private parties under the EEC and Euratom [246]

§ 311. Unlike the ECSC Treaty, the EEC and Euratom Treaties contain no limitations as to the parties competent to institute proceedings: any natural or legal person may do so when the other conditions for bringing the action have been fulfilled.

α. *Actions challenging regulations*

§ 312. The possibility of challenging general provisions in the case of misuse of powers, provided for in the ECSC Treaty (see above § 307), does not exist in the EEC and Euratom. The exception for individual decisions disguised as general rules was no longer required as the drafters of the more recent Community Treaties took cognizance of the fact that the Court would accept such disguised decisions as individual ones.

EEC Article 173(2) grants individuals a right of appeal only against *decisions*. In the *Fruit and Vegetables Case* one of the applicants suggested that the word 'decision' in this article could be construed to cover acts of a general nature and thus to extend to any act, including the decisions which are expressly mentioned in EEC Article 189 as well as other forms of decisions such as regulations. This submission – untenable in the German or Dutch versions of the Treaty where a technical term, *Entscheidung* or *Beschikking*, is used for the more specific decision, both in Article 189 and in Article 173 – was not upheld by the Court.

It held:

'The Court is unable in particular to adopt the interpretation suggested by one of the applicants during the oral procedure, according to which the term "decision", as used in the second paragraph of Article 173, could also cover regulations. Such a wide interpretation conflicts with the fact that Article 189 makes a clear distinction between the concept of a "decision" and that of a "regulation". It is inconceivable that the term "decision" would be used in Article 173 in a different sense from the technical sense as defined in Article 189'. [247]

§ 313. Under EEC Article 173(2) individuals cannot bring an action against regulations. There is one exception to this rule: when an act, though presented as a regulation, is in fact an individual decision or a bundle of individual decisions (see above § 202). Then that individual decision or bundle of decisions can be challenged *even if it is one of a number of provisions having a legislative function.* [248] In the *CAM case* as well as in the *Exportation des*

---

246. See Robert Kovar and Ami Barav, *Le recours individuel en annulation*, 12 CDE 1976, pp. 68-109.
247. *Fruit and Vegetables Case* (16 and 17/62), 14 Dec. 1962, [1962] ECR 478, 8 Jur. (1962) 958, 959; 8 Rec. (1962) 919; [1963] CMLR 173, 174; CCH para 8005.
248. See *CAM case* quoted below, § 320.

Sucres Case the Court took up the questions of direct and individual concern, without previously considering whether the act indeed was a decision. When it had established that there was individual concern, it declared the case admissible, apparently implying that in a case of individual concern the act must be a decision. [249] In both cases this could hardly be doubted because they concerned actions against entire regulations. When an entire regulation individually affects specific persons, it must in fact be a decision against that person. In the *UNICME Case* the Court ruled in a similar situation: *'It is unnecessary to consider whether the contested measure may be regarded as a regulation and it is sufficient to establish whether it is in fact of direct and individual concern to the applicants'.* [250]

The situation is different, however, when an action is brought against *part* of a regulation. Even when it is of direct and individual concern to the applicant, a part of a regulation may retain its regulatory nature. This was the case in the *Compagnie Française Case* where the Court first held that the disputed act had the character of a regulation and then refused to discuss the question of direct and individual concern (see above § 206). Similary in the *First Scholten Honig Case* the Court first studied the nature of the contested measures. The question of concern to the applicant was discussed only to establish the regulatory nature of the act. As soon as it was established that the act was a regulation, the action was declared in admissible. [251] In the *Second Toepfer Case* an action was brought against an article of a regulation. The Commission did not challenge the admissibility, but the Court held on its own motion that: *'although the provision was in a regulation, it amounted in substance to a decision of just the same direct and individual concern to holders of export licences, such as the applicant, as if it had been addressed to them'.* Therefore the application was admissible. [252]

In the *Bearings Cases* as well the Court first studied whether the act concerned was of a regulatory nature or not. It admitted an action by an individual against Article 3 of Council Regulation 1778/77 after finding that that article constituted a *'collective decision relating to named addressees'.* [253]

The conclusion must be that individuals cannot bring an action against provisions which form an integral part of a general normative rule but that it is possible to challenge provisions of regulations which may be seen as separate individual acts.[254]

---

249. *CAM Case* and *Exportation des Sucres Case* (88/76), 31 March 1977. considerations 8-12, [1977] ECR 725, 726; CCH para 8418.
250. *UNICME Case* (123/77), 16 March 1978, consideration 7, [1978] ECR 851; CCH para 8482.
251. *First Scholten Honig Case* (101/76), 5 May 1977, consideration 10, [1977] ECR 806; CCH para 8413.
252. *Second Toepfer Case* (112/77), 3 May 1978, consideration 9, [1978] ECR 1030.
253. *NTN Toyo Case* (113/77), 29 March 1979, consideration 11; *ISO Case* (118/77), 29 March 1979, considerations 14, 22; *Nippon Seiko Case* (119/77), 29 March 1979, consideration 14; *Koyo Seiko Case* (120/77), 29 March 1979, considerations 13, 21; *Nachi Case* (121/77), 29 March 1979, consideration 11.
254. See also *Usines de Beaufort Case* (103-109/78), 18 Jan. 1979, considerations 16, 17 and Kovar and Barav, (*op. cit.*, note 246), pp 68-109.

β. Actions challenging decisions [255]

§ 314. As under the ECSC Treaty, individuals may always challenge decisions which are addressed to them. An action against decisions addressed to other persons may be brought only if they are of individual and direct concern to the applicant. By the imposition of this cumulative precondition the drafters of the Treaty expressed their wish to restrict the individual's possibility of availing himself of this form of action [256], given the rather wide interpretation attributed to ECSC Article 33 by the Court of Justice (see above § 310). This precondition considerably restricts any resort to this action by individuals. In several of the Member States secondary legislation is subject to challenge by private persons establishing merely a direct interest in the matter. The Court of Justice and the Commission have suggested that, in future, the right of individual action might be developed in a similar manner in the Communities so that a direct interest would be sufficient for individuals to challenge acts addressed to others. [257]

At present, however, acts can only be challenged if they are of individual as well as of direct concern to the applicant. Both notions have been further defined in the Court's case law.

§ 315. (1) *Individual concern.* Plaumann, an importer of clementines, instituted proceedings against a decision addressed to the German government by which the Commission refused to authorize the Federal Republic of Germany to suspend the collection of import duties on clementines (EEC Article 25(3)). Plaumann, who actually had to pay the duties, claimed that the decision concerned him. The Court, in considering that Plaumann was not individually concerned, held:

'Persons other than those to whom a decision is addressed may only claim to be individually concerned if that decision affects them by reason of certain attributes which are peculiar to them or by reason of circumstances in which they are differentiated from all other persons and by virtue of these factors distinguishes them individually just as in the case of the person addressed. In the present case the applicant is affected by the disputed Decision as an importer of clementines, that is to say, by reason of a

---

255. See CSP Harding, *Decisions addressed to Member States and Article 173 of the Treaty of Rome*, 25 ICLQ (1976), pp. 15-34; Eric Stein and G. Joseph Vining, *Citizen Access to Judicial Review of Administrative Action in a Transnational and Federal Context*, 70 AJIL (1976) pp. 219-241.
256. It is hard to prove that this was the intention of the Treaty-making Powers. Weinhardt, — mentioning a considerable number of authors who, shortly after the drafting of the EEC Treaty, held that this was the case — comes to the conclusion that at the time of ratification, the Member States were not of the opinion that EEC Art. 173 was in this respect more restrictive than ECSC Art. 33. See Dieter Weinhardt, *Die Klagebefugnis des Konkurrenten*, Göttingen 1973, pp. 171, 172.
257. *Suggestions of the Court of Justice on European Union*, Bulletin of the European Communities, Supplement 9/75, p. 18; *Report on European Union by the Commission*, Bulletin of the European Communities, Supplement 5/75, p. 37. The suggestion was acknowledged in the *Tindemans Report*, Chapter V E.

commercial activity which may at any time be practised by any person and is not therefore such as to distinguish the applicant in relation to the contested Decision as in the case of the addressee.

For these reasons the present action for annulment must be declared inadmissible'. [258]

§ 316. The Belgian Company *Glucoseries Réunies* had to suffer the disadvantage of a French levy imposed on the import of glucose, and authorized by the EEC Commission. The Company appealed against the authorization, submitting individual concern based on the fact of its being the sole Belgian exporter of glucose to France. The Court repeated the first consideration, quoted in the *Plaumann Case* above and added that the authorization not only affected imports into France from Belgium; but that imports from other Member States also had to be taken into consideration. In declaring the action by *Glucoseries Réunies* inadmissible, the Court added the following consideration:

'In view of the general economic scope of the contested Decision, it is not of individual concern to the applicant even if the latter does occupy the position which it claims on the Belgian market in respect of glucose exports to France.' [259]

§ 317. The facts of the German *Getreide-Import Case* seemed to indicate a more specific connection with the applicant. According to Regulation No. 19, (on cereals), the Commission periodically established the relevant world market price for wheat on a particular day, on the basis of which the levy importers had to pay was determined. By a decision of 25 June 1964, the Commission established a price for 26 June, which, in the opinion of Getreide-Import, resulted in an excessive levy. Getreide-Import was the only importer who applied for an import licence on 26 June. Therefore, it submitted that the decision of 25 June, establishing the price for 26 June, was of individual concern.

The Court did not, however, accept this submission. It held Getreide's appeal inadmissible, using the same reasoning as in the *Plaumann Case*, to which it added:

'Moreover, the purely fortuitous fact that after the contested Decision was made only the applicant considered it advisable to apply for an import licence on the date in question is not sufficient to differentiate it from the other importers and to distinguish it individually as required by Article 173 of the Treaty.' [260]

258. *Plaumann Case* (25/62), 15 July 1963, [1963] ECR 107, 108; 9 Jur. (1963) 232; 9 Rec. (1963) 224; [1964] CMLR 47; CCH para 8013.
259. *Glucoseries Réunies Case* (1/64), 2 July 1964, [1964] ECR 417; 10 Jur. (1964) 862; 10 Rec. (1964) 824; [1964] CMLR 603; CCH para 8024 (p. 7407).
260. *First Getreide-Import Case* (38/64), 1 April 1965, [1965] ECR 208; 11 Jur. (1965) 424, 425; 11 Rec. (1965) 270, 271; [1965] CMLR 283; CCH para 8033.

§ 318. This was followed by the *First Toepfer Case*, which also concerned the establishment of cereals prices for the purpose of the import levy. On this occasion, the Commission committed an error in failing to take account of the new harvest and fixed a price for maize for 1 October 1963 reducing the levy to nil. Thereupon fourteen importers applied for import licenses for large quantities of maize. Alarmed by this, the German government suspended the issue of all import licenses, maintaining it was taking safeguard measures. Regulation 19 did provide for safeguard measures but required the approval of the Commission. The German government immediately consulted the Commission, which established a new price from 2 October and, by decision of 4 October 1963, retroactively authorized the German government to take safeguard measures for 1 October. Toepfer brought an action against this authorization.

In this case the Court agreed that the authorization was of individual concern to Toepfer. It held:

> 'The only persons concerned by the said measures were importers who had applied for an import licence during the course of the day of 1 October 1963. The number and identity of these importers had already become fixed and ascertainable before 4 October, when the contested decision was made. The Commission was in a position to know that its decision affected the interests and the position of the said importers alone.
>
> The factual situation thus created differentiates the said importers, including the applicants, from all other persons and distinguishes them individually just as in the case of the person addressed.' [261]

§ 319. In the *Chinese Mushroom Case*, the essential element was the same as in the *Toepfer Case*: the applicant could be singled out because the rule related to a period of time in the past. The most important difference was that in the Mushroom Case, the retroactive rule comprised only part of the decision. Bock, an importer of mushrooms, applied for an import licence for 65.5 tons of Chinese Mushrooms. The German government was necessitated to grant this type of licence as long as the Commission had not authorized a refusal. As the German government did not want to permit the import on policy grounds, they delayed their decision and asked the Commission for an authorization to prohibit this kind of import. The Commission granted the authorization not only for future cases but also for applications 'at present and duly pending before the German authorities'. Bock appealed against the latter specific provision of the authorization. The Commission maintained that the decision did not concern the applicant firm individually, but referred in an abstract manner to all market participants who intended to import the goods in question into Germany during the period of validity of the decision.

The Court declared the application admissible considering:

---

261. *First Toepfer Case* (106 and 107/63), 1 July 1965, [1965] ECR 411, 412; 11 Jur. (1965) 517; 11 Rec. (1965) 532; [1966] CMLR 142; CCH para 8031 (p. 7460).

'However, the applicant has challenged the decision only to the extent to which it also covers imports for which applications for import licences were already pending at the date of its entry into force. The number and identity of importers concerned in this way was already fixed and ascertainable before that date. The defendant was in a position to know that the contested provision in its decision would affect the interests and situation of those importers alone. The factual situation thus created differentiates the latter from all other persons and distinguishes them individually just as in the case of the person addressed.' [262]

§ 320. In the *CAM Case* exporters were involved who had entered into contracts at a time prior to the date of the measure concerned. The Commission had distinguished them from other exporters. The Court held:

'By adopting these distinguishing criteria the contested measure affects a fixed number of traders identified by reason of the individual course of action which they pursued or are regarded as having pursued during a particular period.
    Such a measure, even if it is one of a number of provisions having a legislative function, individually concerns the persons to whom it applies in that it affects their legal position because of a factual situation which differentiates them from all other persons and distinguishes them individually [in a similar way as an addressee].
    The application is admissible.' [263]

§ 320a. The possibility of determining more or less precisely the number or even the identity of the persons to whom a measure applies is not enough. This *'by no means implies that it must be regarded as being of individual concern to them'*. [264] The concern must also be established in an individual capacity and not as a member of a group for which the rules were made.

§ 321. Undertakings have on occasion submitted that measures of benefit to their competitors were of direct and individual concern to them. Under the ECSC Treaty, competitors may indeed bring an action (see above § 310). Under the EEC Treaty however, this is not the case. The Court held in the *Eridania Case*:

'The mere fact that a measure may exercise an influence on the competitive relationships existing on the market in question cannot suffice to allow any trader in any competitive relationship whatever with the adressee of the

262. *Chinese Mushroom Case* (62/70), 23 Nov. 1971, consideration 10, [1971] ECR 908; [1972] CMLR 170, 171; CCH para 8150.
263. *CAM Case* (100/74), 18 Nov. 1975, considerations 18-20, [1975] ECR 1403; CCH para 8328. The part between brackets reads in the official English text: 'just as in the case of the person addressed'. The authentic French text is: *'Une manière analogue à celle d'un destinataire'*.
264. *UNICME Case* (123/77), 16 March 1978, consideration 16, [1978] ECR 852; CCH para 8482.

measure to be regarded as directly and individually concerned by that measure.

Only the existence of specific circumstances may enable a person subject to Community law and claiming that the measure affects his position on the market to bring proceedings under Article 173.' [265]

§ 322. Reading these cases in conjuction, it can be concluded that a natural or legal person can successfully claim individual concern only when he disputes an act, concerning a period in the past and therefore affecting an identifiable group of persons, to which the applicant belongs.

§ 323. (2) *Direct concern.* A decision addressed to another person should not only be of *individual* but also of *direct* concern to the applicant. Otherwise he cannot bring an action. The Court of Justice interprets direct concern to mean that the adressee is left no latitude of discretion, that is that the decision affects the applicant without the addressee being necessitated to take any decision himself.

Toepfer was directly concerned by the decision addressed to Germany, as the decision in question had direct effect. The German government could not alter its application. [266] In the *Bearings Cases* the Court established direct concern because the national implementing measures were '*purely automatic and, moreover, in pursuance not of intermediate national rules but of Community rules alone*'. [267] In the *Alcan Case* the applicant was not directly concerned because the decision, addressed to Belgium and Luxembourg, left discretionary powers in the hands of these member States. It was therefore not at all certain that the regime permitted by the decision would have any consequence for the applicant. [268]

In the *First International Fruit Company Case* no discretionary powers were ascribed to the Member States, as they were required to pass on the necessary data to the Commission to enable it to decide on the quantity of apples which could be imported from third countries. On the basis of this, licences were issued in accordance with conditions dictated by the Commission. The decision in which the Commission established a percentage of requests for imports which could be granted, although addressed to the Member States, was therefore of direct concern to the International Fruit Company. [269]

---

265. *Eridania Case* (10 and 18/68), 10 Dec. 1969, consideration 7, [1969] ECR 481; CCH para 8099. The Advocate-General was of a different opinion.
266. *First Toepfer Case* (106 and 107/63), 1 July 1965, [1965] ECR 411, 412; 11 Jur. (1965) 517; 11 Rec. (1965) 532, 533; [1966] CMLR 141, 142; CCH para 8031.
267. *NTN Toyo Case* (113/77), 29 March 1979, consideration 11; *ISO Case* (118/77), 29 March 1979, consideration 26; *Nippon Seiko Case* (119/77), 29 March 1979, consideration 14; *Koyo Seiko Case* (120/77), 29 March 1979, consideration 25; *Nachi Case* (121/77), 29 March 1979, consideration 11.
268. *Alcan Case* (69/69), 16 June 1970, [1970] ECR 394; [1970] CMLR 346; CCH para 8110.
269. *First International Fruit Company Case* (41-44/70), 13 May 1971, considerations 23-29; [1971] ECR 422, 423; [1975] 2 CMLR 535; CCH para 8142.

In the *Chinese Mushroom Case*, the decision in dispute contained an authorization which the German government could either make use of or not. On this account the Commission submitted that the decision was not of direct concern to the applicant, Bock. In this respect, the situation was the same as in the *Alcan Case*, mentioned above. The Court considered, however:

> 'The appropriate German authorities had nevertheless already informed the applicant that they would reject its application as soon as the Commission had granted them the requisite authorization. They had requested that authorization with particular reference to the applications already before them at that time.
>
> It follows therefore that the matter was of direct concern to the applicant.' [270]

In the *CAM Case* the Member States were required to pay the export refunds fixed by the Commission. Therefore, the Commission's measure establishing that no refunds were to be paid to the exporters involved concerned the exporters directly even though the measure was not addressed to them. [271]

In the *Fourth Simmenthal Case* the Commission admitted that a decision addressed to Italy was of individual and direct concern to Simmenthal. Nonetheless, the Court examined of its own motion whether Simmenthal should not have challenged the Italian act, executing the Commission's decision, before an Italian court rather than to bring an action against the Commission's decision before the Court of Justice. The Court held that Simmenthal's action against the Commission's decision was admissible in so far as the Italian authorities had no discretion when adopting the Italian act. Questions which the Italian authorities could decide and the question whether the Italian act was in conformity with Community law fell outside the competence of the Community institutions and should, therefore, be brought before an Italian court. [272]

§ 324. The notion 'direct concern' somewhat resembles the notion 'direct effect' (see above § 175). [273] In both cases the intermediary Government has no discretion and the act is of direct legal relevance to individuals who need not necessarily be the addressees stated in it. The two notions however do not completely coincide. In the case of an unconditional prohibition, there will usually be direct effect: individuals may invoke the prohibition, and national measures taken contrary to it cannot be applied by the national courts. In the case of direct concern, on the other hand, a negative is assimilated to a positive decision which could have been taken instead. Thus, the Court held in the *Alcan Case*:

270. *Chinese Mushroom Case* (Bock) (62/70), 23 Nov. 1971, considerations 6-8, [1971] ECR 908; [1972] CMLR 170; CCH para 8150.
271. *CAM Case* (100/74), 18 Nov. 1975, consideration 14, [1975] ECR 1402, 1403; CCH para 8328.
272. *Fourth Simmenthal Case* (92/78), 6 March 1979, considerations 22, 26, 28-30.
273. See Kovar and Barav (*op. cit.*, note 246) pp. 94-109.

'The decision rejecting the request does not therefore concern the applicants in any other manner than would the positive decision which they wished to obtain'. [274]

and in the *Nordgetreide Case*, the Court stated:

'Since the definition by the Commission of its position amounts to a rejection it must be appraised in the light of the object of the request to which it constituted a reply'. [275]

§ 324a. EEC Regulation No. 17 on competition allows natural and legal persons who claim a legitimate interest to make an application to the Commission for finding that particular undertakings infringe EEC competition rules. In the *Second Metro Case* the Court of Justice held that individuals who have made such an application must be considered to be directly and individually concerned by a decision which the Commission later addresses to the undertakings concerned. [276] It may be submitted that other individuals who had a right to send a similar application but abstained from doing so are equally concerned by the Commission's decision.[277]

(iv) Actions by civil servants [278]

§ 325. Actions by civil servants represent almost a third of all cases brought before the Court of Justice (see below § 509).

Civil servants of the Communities are either officials or 'other servants'. Officials of the Communities are all individuals who have been appointed to established posts on the staff of one of the institutions by written decision of the appointing authority. Their conditions of employment are laid down in the Staff Regulations [279] of which Title VII, Articles 90 and 91 cover their right to bring actions. Other servants include temporary staff, auxiliary and local staff, special advisers and the establishment staff of the joint Nuclear Research Centre of Euratom. Disputes arising between an institution of the Communities and a member of the local staff are to be submitted to the competent court in accordance with the laws in force in the place where the servant performs his duties [280], but the right to bring proceedings of all other

---

274. *Alcan Case* (69/69), 16 June 1970, consideration 15, [1970] ECR 394; [1970] CMLR 346; CCH para 8110.
275. *Nordgetreide Case* (42/71), 8 March 1972, consideration 5, [1972] ECR 110; [1973] CMLR 187; CCH para 8174.
276. *Second Metro Case* (26/76), 25 Oct. 1977, consideration 13, [1977] ECR 1901.
277. See James Dinnage, *Locus standi and Article 173 EEC: the effect of Metro SB Grossmärkte v. Commission*, 4 ELRev. (1979), pp. 15-34.
278. See also L. Neville Brown and Francis G. Jacobs, *The Court of Justice of the European Communities*, Sweet & Maxwell 1977, pp. 124-130.
279. Supplement to the Official Journal No. C12 of 24 March 1973. The amendments adopted after that date do not affect Title VII.
280. Conditions of Employment of Other Servants of the Communities, Art. 81 OJ No. C12 of 24 March 1973, p. 78.

'other servants' is covered by Title VII of the Staff Regulations. Therefore, this right is the same for all civil servants except for the local staff.

The *Mills Case* was brought by a servant of the European Investment Bank. The Court held '*that by the words "any dispute between the Community and its servants" EEC Article 179 is not restricted exclusively to the institutions of the Community and their staff but also includes the Bank as a Community institution established and with a legal personality conferred by the Treaty.*' [281]

§ 326. Various powers have been attributed to the '*appointing authority*'. Each institution determines which officials within it shall exercise these powers. [282] The Commission acts as the appointing authority for its officials in the ranks A1, A2 and A3. One of the members of the Commission, charged with personnel matters, is the appointing authority for other officials in the A ranks. For the officials of the B category the directors of personnel in Brussels and Luxembourg are the appointing authorities; for those of the C and D level, the head of the section for recruitment.

§ 327. Civil servants of the European Communities may not directly challenge Community acts before the Court of Justice, including decisions individually addressed to them. [283] They must submit their complaints to the appointing authority through their immediate superiors. The object of his provision is to enable and encourage an amicable settlement of dispute. [284] The acts which are subject to such complaints are not narrowly defined. A civil servant may bring an action against any act '*adversely affecting him*' including, for example, decisions as a result of which people other than the applicant were appointed, or the announcement of a vacancy if the conditions for appointment to the post are such that he is excluded. [285] In general the requirements for admissibility are more lenient than in the case of the normal action for annulment. [286] The act must, of course, still exist at the date when the application is made. [287]

The Court makes an exception to the requirement that civil servants must first submit their complaints to the appointing authority for decisions of a selection board, in view of the fact that the appointing authority has no power to annul or amend those decisions. [288]

281. *Mills Case* (110/75), 15 June 1976, consideration 14, [1976] ECR 968.
282. Staff Regulations, Art. 2. On the question of further sub-delegation see Advocate-General Trabucchi's opinion in the *Second De Greef Case* (46/72), 30 May 1973, [1973] ECR 559-561.
283. For an example of a case declared inadmissible on this ground, see *Wack Case* (1/76), 15 June 1976, consideration 9, [1976] ECR 1024.
284. *Sergy Case* (58/75), 1 July 1976, consideration 5, [1976] ECR 602.
285. *First Küster Case* (79/74), 19 June 1975, consideration 6, [1975] ECR 730.
286. See e.g. *De Dapper Case* (54/75), Second judgement 29 Sept. 1976, [1976] ECR 1386-1390.
287. *Hebrant Case* (66/75), 20 May 1976, consideration 5, [1976] ECR 602.
288. *Salerno Case* (4, 19, 28/78), 30 Nov. 1978, consideration 9.

§ 328. After receiving the complaint the appointing authority must notify the civil servant of its reasoned decision (within four months). [289] Against that reasoned decision, which necessarily constitutes an individual act, the civil servant can institute proceedings before the Court of Justice which usually decides the case in Chamber (see below § 649, 650). The question has arisen to what extent the action before the Court must be identical to the one brought before the authorities. Is it permissible to raise additional arguments before the Court? The Court of Justice held that it is essential that the administration is in a position to know what are the complaints made but that new arguments may be brought before the Court, provided that they do not alter the claim. [290] For example it is permitted to add in the case before the Court of Justice a claim for damages caused by an alledgedly illegal act if the legality of the act was disputed before the authorities. [291] However, it is not permitted to bring an independent action for damages before the Court of Justice, without prior appeal to the administration. [292]

The action by civil servants is not fundamentally different from actions brought by others, with two exceptions: (1) the Court of Justice has unlimited jurisdiction in disputes of a financial character (see below § 509, 510); this means that the Court may not only uphold or annul the decision concerned but may also modify allowances or other sums of money; (2) the time limit for bringing the case before the Court of Justice is three months instead of two (in the EEC) or one (in the ECSC).

2. The action against failure to act

a. PURPOSE OF THE ACTION AGAINST FAILURE TO ACT

§ 329. The action against failure to act, often called the *appeal against inaction*, is not very frequently used. Under the EEC Treaty it was brought eleven times up to 31 December 1978 [293], which is less than one per cent of all EEC cases excluding those brought by staff members. The action is used when the Council or the Commission fails to act in cases where they are obliged to do so. [294] The Court of Justice may consequently be asked to declare the inaction illegal. In the action for annulment a similar declaration brings about a legal change. It has the effect that the act is retroactively annulled and ceases

---

289. Staff Regulations, Art. 90 (2) and (3).
290. *Sergy Case* (58/75), 1 July 1976, considerations 32-36 [1976] ECR 1152, 1153.
291. *Herpels Case* (54/77), 9 March 1978, considerations 16-19, [1978] ECR 596, 597.
292. *Sixth Reinarz Case* (48/76), 17 Feb. 1977, considerations 4-12, [1977] ECR 297, 298.
293. Twelfth General Report, p. 368, table 2.
294. EEC Art. 175, ECSC Art. 35. On this action, see Ami Barav, *Considérations sur la spécificité du recours en carence en droit communautaire*, 1975 RTDE pp. 53-71; A.G. Toth, *The law as it stands on the appeal for failure to act*, LIEI 1975/2, pp. 65-93 and *op. cit.* note 196, Vol 2, pp. 97-117; Emile Reuter, *Le recours en carence de l'Article 175 du Traité de la CEE dans la jurisprudence de la Cour de Justice des Communautés Européennes*, 8 CDE (1972) pp. 159-174.

to exist. In an action against failure to act no such change in the legal status can be achieved. The Court cannot create the act that should have been promulgated. Its declaration that the inaction is illegal creates an obligation on the part of the institution concerned to issue an act. At the most the Court may indicate what sort of act is required. The actual discretion as to the content and form of the act is exercised, however, by the Council or the Commission. [295]

§ 330. Actions against failure to act can aim at the bringing about of three different forms of acts. Sometimes the Community institutions are obliged to take a specific act (e.g. to grant a specific subsidy to a particular undertaking); on other occasions they are obliged to take a binding act but the form of the act is left to their discretion; finally the institutions may be obliged to take nonbinding acts. To a certain extent the right to institute proceedings against failure to act and the result of the proceedings may vary according to such differences in the acts sought to be obtained (see above § 251).

b. PRECONDITIONS OF THE ACTION AGAINST FAILURE TO ACT

(i) Obligation to act

§ 331. When discussing the acts susceptible to review (above § 250) it was submitted that inaction (the 'non-act') should be challenged in any case where the *obligation* to act had not been fulfilled. In principle it is irrelevant what sort of act the obligation entails: the obligation to make a recommendation or a proposal is as legally definitive as the obligation to take a decision.

There is good reason to bring any obligation to act under the judicial review of the Court. In particular, the obligation to initiate action is of great importance, as it is from the Commission that the proposal for action by the Council stems. If this obligation is performed incorrectly and leads to the wrong act being taken then the action for annulment must wait until the wrong act finally enters into force. On the other hand, if the obligation to initiate action is not fulfilled, then an action against failure to act presents the only remedy possible.

Under the EEC and Euratom Treaties the Member States and the Institutions may lodge the action against any failure to act[296], individuals may only challenge the failure to take a *binding* act. [297] Under the ECSC Treaty all action against failure to act is limited to the failure to take binding acts. [298]

---

295. *Second Snupat Case* (42 and 49/59), 22 March 1961, [1961] ECR 88; 7 Jur. (1961) 163; 7 Rec. (1961) 160, 161. See also Advocate-General Roemer in the *Steel Industries in Luxembourg Case* (7 and 9/54), 23 April 1956, 2 *Sammlung der Rechtsprechung des Gerichtshofs* (1955-56) p. 112; [1954-56] ECR 207; 2 Jur. (1955-56) 121; 2 Rec. (1955-56) 114, 115.
296. EEC Art. 175(1); Euratom Art. 148(1).
297. EEC Art. 175(3); Euratom Art. 148(3).
298. ECSC Art. 35.

The Court of Justice confirmed this limitation in the *Borromeo Case*. Borromeo had asked the Commission for advice on a conflict between an Italian draft bill and a rule of Community law; the advice was not given and Borromeo appealed against the failure to act. The Court could have rejected his application on the ground that the Commission was not obliged to act, but it expressly did so on the ground that the act, if taken, would have been a non-binding act. [299]

§ 332.   The EEC and Euratom Treaties do not refer to inaction in violation of 'an obligation', but to inaction *'in infringement of this Treaty'*. [300] Under the ECSC Treaty the act must be *'required by this Treaty, or by rules laid down for the implementation thereof'*. [301] These provisions appear to restrict the action against failure to act to the non-fulfilment of only those obligations which are enumerated in the treaties. But in practice any obligation incumbent upon the Community institutions can be based on the Treaties so that there is virtually no restriction engendered by this formulation of words.

The institution must be obliged to act. Normally no failure will be deemed to exist if it is left to the discretion of the institution in question to decide whether it should act or not. Unlike the other Community Treaties, the ECSC Treaty admits the action against failure to act also where the Commission is empowered to act, but abstains from doing so and such abstention constitutes a misuse of powers. [302] In practice this provision has played no significant role at all and it is hardly conceivable that it ever will do so. When a misuse of powers has been committed there will usually be an act performed, in violation of the Treaty or of some other rule of Community law, which can be challenged by an action for annulment.

(ii) Calling upon the institution to act

§ 333.   Before an action against failure to act can be lodged the institution concerned must be called upon to act. This allows the institution to define its position and to take the requested act if its inaction was the result of negligence. It also provides a legal document upon which further action can be based. This document determines the subject matter of the action and marks the starting point for the time limits. If the institution remains negligent for the duration of two months, then the action can be brought in a manner similar to the action for annulment.

The invitation to the institution to take action is a formal act; not every letter to the Commission will qualify as such. [303] It must clearly indicate what

---

299. *Borromeo Case* (6/70), 15 July 1970, consideration 6, 7, [1970] ECR 819; [1970] CMLR 441, 442; CCH para 8114. The same decision was given in the *Chevalley Case* (15/70), 18 Nov. 1970, considerations 8-11, [1970] ECR 979, 980; CCH para 8115.
300. EEC Art. 175; Euratom Art. 148.
301. ECSC Art. 35(1).
302. ECSC Art. 35(2).
303. Advocate-General Roemer in *Komponistenverband Case* (8/71), 13 July 1971, [1971] ECR 716; CCH para 8143; [1973] CMLR 908, 909. See also Court of Justice in *Angelini Case* (31/72), 4 April 1973, consideration 3, [1973] ECR 408.

specific measures are requested and that proceedings will be instituted if the institution does not act.[304] A request 'to take sufficient and appropriate measures with a view to re-establishing and guaranteeing normal conditions' is insufficient.[305] The applicant must be identifiable. Claimants who have not taken part in the invitation calling upon the institution to act may not later participate in the action before the Court.[306] The subsequent claim before the Court can only be based upon *'the refusal of the High Authority to take the decision which it was called upon to adopt*[307]*,'* nor can it be based on other legal grounds.[308]

§ 334. The requirement asked of the institution to take a position is not the same under the ECSC and EEC Treaties. Under the former treaty the Commission must take a *'decision'*, while under the latter the mere adoption of a *position* is sufficient. Under the ECSC Treaty the Court did not accept that a letter, stating that the question was the subject of further examination, satisfied the requirement of taking a decision.[309] Nor did it accept as a decision on an exemption a letter which, after explaining the position of the High Authority on the system from which exemption was requested, contained the proviso *'that further and better information would be supplied'*.[310]

On account of the different wording of EEC Article 175 it may be expected that the Court will more easily accept that the Community institution has adopted a position, which will prevent an action against a failure to act being pursued and will oblige the applicant to institute proceedings against the act on which the position was taken.

(iii) Ground of illegality

§ 335. EEC Article 175 provides that an action may be brought if the Council or the Commission fails to act 'in infringement of this Treaty'. It might be deduced that the express references to an infringement of the Treaty rather than to a more general failure to fulfil an obligation, could refer to a particular ground of illegality which must be used. The action against failure to act might then be lodged on only one of the grounds of illegality required for challenging Community acts (see above § 254-297). But in fact the words do

---

304. See e.g. *First Limburg Coalmines Case* (17/57), 4 Feb. 1959, [1959] ECR 8; 5 Jur. (1958-59) 27; 5 Rec. (1958-59) 26; *First Elz Case* (22, 23/60), 13 July 1961, [1961] ECR 188; 7 Jur. (1961) 393, 394; 7 Rec. (1961) 375.
305. *Hake Case* (75/69), 8 July 1970, consideration 4, [1970] ECR 542; [1970] CMLR 432, 433.
306. Advocate-General Roemer in the *Chambre Syndicale de l'Est de la France Case* (24, 34/58), 15 July 1960, [1960] ECR 306; 6 Jur. (1960) 641; 6 Rec. (1960) 625.
307. *Chambre Syndicale de l'Est de la France Case* (24, 34/58), 15 July 1960, [1960] ECR 299; 6 Jur. (1960) 625; 6 Rec. (1960) 609.
308. *Hamborner Bergbau Case* (41 and 50/59), 16 Dec. 1960, [1960] ECR 504, 505; 6 Jur. (1960) 1052, 1053; 6 Rec. (1960) 1016.
309. *Second Snupat Case* (42 and 49/59), 22 March 1961; [1961] ECR 73, 74; 7 Jur. (1961) 144; 7 Rec. (1961) 143.
310. *Fifth Meroni Case* (21-26/61), 6 April 1962, [1962] ECR 77; 8 Jur. (1962) 156; 8 Rec. (1962) 154.

not lead to any practical restriction for, as was discussed above (§ 290), the Court interprets 'infringement of the treaty' widely. Misuse of powers would undoubtedly be considered as an infringement of the Treaty. On the other hand, infringement of an essential procedural requirement or lack of competence manifestly cannot be submitted in the case of inaction. The only ground of illegality which may give rise to doubt is the ground 'infringement of any rule of law relating to the application of the Treaty', and, in particular, the infringement of general principles of law (see above § 292). One could imagine situations where inaction by the Commission could, for instance, endanger basic human rights although there was no concomitant clear Treaty provision obliging the Commission to act. In such cases, inaction would infringe a general principle of law and the question would arise whether this eventually would be covered by ECSC Article 35 or EEC Article 175. There is no case-law on this question but several arguments plead that it would. (1) ECSC Article 35 and EEC Article 175 do not refer to infringement of the Treaty specifically as a ground of illegality. One may therefore submit that a more general reference is meant [311], thereby implying a reference to all grounds of illegality provided for in the Treaties. (2) The development of Community law is clearly moving in the direction towards accepting the violation of general principles of law, as far as is possible, as a ground of illegality.

c.　TIME LIMITS

§ 336.　There is no time within which the institution must be called upon to act. For the action for annulment it was possible to provide that the application must be brought within two months of the decision being notified or published (in the ECSC this is one month, in staff cases three months). But the moment when a failure to act becomes reproachable is so difficult to establish that no time limits have been provided for calling upon the institution to act. This does not mean, however, that the applicant may wait for an indefinite period of time.

In December 1968 the Commission had informed the Netherlands Government that it would not take certain measures under the ECSC Treaty. When 18 months later, in June 1970, the Netherlands Government brought an action against the failure to act the Court considered the delay unreasonable, the more so because the position of the Commission had been clear even before December 1968. The action was declared inadmissible on the following grounds:

'It follows, however, from the common purpose of Articles 33 and 35 that the requirements of legal certainty and of the continuity of Community action underlying the time-limits laid down for bringing proceedings under Article 33 must also be taken into account — having regard to the special difficulties which the silence of the competent authorities may involve for the

311.　Most authors seem to do so, see Barav (op. cit., note 294) p. 70.

interested parties – in the exercise of the rights conferred by Article 35.

These requirements may not lead to such contradictory consequences as the duty to act within a short period in the first case and the absence of any limitation in time in the second.

This view finds support in the system of time-limits in Article 35, which allows the Commission two months in which to define its position, and the interested party one month in which to institute proceedings before the Court.

Thus it is implicit in the system of Articles 33 and 35 that the exercise of the right to raise the matter with the Commission may not be delayed indefinitely.

If the interested parties are thus bound to observe a reasonable time-limit where the Commission remains silent, this is so *a fortiori* once it is clear that the Commission has decided to take no action.' [312]

§ 337. When the Institution has been called upon to act, it must act within two months. The action is not intended, however, to censure the Commission or the Council, but to obtain an act. If therefore the institution acts after the time limit, further proceedings may serve no purpose. In the *Hake Case*, where the Commission had answered after expiry of the two month period, the Court considered that its decision was no longer needed, but it did condemn the Commission to pay all the costs of the litigation. [313] On the other hand, in the *Steel Industries in Luxembourg Case*, when the High Authority had after the expiry of the time limit given a decision by letter, refusing to take the act requested and explaining why it had to be refused, the Court held that the letter justifying the refusal did not alter the fact that a refusal existed at the end of the time limit. On this account the action against failure to act could proceed. In reaching this conclusion the Court took into consideration the fact that the letter '*has not altered* [the] *situation any further*.'[314]

§ 338. When the two month period has passed without the institution acting, the same time limits apply as for the action for annulment, that is one month for the ECSC, two months for the EEC and Euratom, three months for civil servants.

d. CAPACITY TO BRING THE ACTION

(i) Actions by Member States and by other institutions

§ 339. Under the ECSC Treaty – where practically all acts are taken by the Commission – the action against failure to act is open to the (Member) States,

312. *Steel subsidies Case* (59/70), 6 July 1971, considerations 15-19, [1971] ECR 653, 654.

313. *Hake Case* (75/69), 8 July 1970, considerations 2, 11, [1970] ECR 541, 543; [1970] CMLR 432, 433.

314. *Steel Industries in Luxembourg Case* (7 and 9/54), 23 April 1956, [1954-56] ECR 194; 2 Jur. (1955-56) 94; 2 Rec. (1955-56) 89, 90.

the Council and 'as the case may be' to undertakings and associations. Under the EEC Treaty — where both the Commission and the Council are enabled to take acts — the action can be brought by the Member States, the other institutions and, in the case of decisions which should have been addressed to them, also by natural and legal persons.

Under the EEC Treaty the action by Member States and institutions can be brought in all cases where the Council or the Commission has failed to act, but in all other cases (all actions against failure to act under the ECSC Treaty and the actions by individuals under the EEC) the right to institute proceedings is restricted to the cases where a binding act should have been taken. The rules of admissibility differ, furthermore, in two respects from those concerning the action for annulment: (1) Unlike under EEC Article 173 the action against failure to act can be lodged in the EEC, not only by the Council and the Commission but also by 'the other institutions'. (2) The requirements for actions by private parties seem to differ.

§ 340. The 'other institutions', which may bring an action under Article 175 EEC while being unable to do so under Article 173, are the European Parliament and the Court of Justice. An action lodged by the Court seems extremely unlikely and has never even been seriously considered; an action by the European Parliament could be useful. The political power of the Parliament is limited, especially in relation to the Council. If the Council acts on the initiative of the Commission, the Parliament has some control over the latter institution; if the Council does not follow a proposal of the Commission, then it must be unanimous, so that each individual Council member can be held responsible to his own national parliament. But if the Council does not act at all (in practice this occurs when agreement cannot be reached), no one is politically responsible before any parliament. Therefore, it may be instrumental that the European Parliament is allowed to request the Court of Justice to establish the obligation to act. As yet the European Parliament has never lodged, nor initiated, an action against failure to act.

(ii) Actions by private parties

§ 341. Under ECSC Article 35 the action against failure to act may be brought by the (Member) States, the Council and undertakings or associations 'as the case may be'. The italicized words might suggest that undertakings and associations can institute proceedings on an equal footing with the States and the Council whenever the inaction pertains to them. However, the words refer back to Article 33 and therefore, in fact, mean: 'in as far as they are entitled to bring an action'. This refers to the capacity to bring an action for annulment should the act have been taken. Therefore, under the ECSC Treaty the Court of Justice requires the same conditions for the admissibility of actions for annulment as for actions against failure to act. [315] It considers the action

---

315. See e.g. *Steel Industries in Luxembourg Case* (7 and 9/54), 23 April 1956, [1954-56] ECR 189; 2 Jur. (1955-56) 87; 2 Rec. (1955-56) 83; *Second Limburg Coalmines Case* (30/59), 23 Feb. 1961, [1961] ECR 15; 7 Jur. (1961) 35; 7 Rec. (1961) 35.

of Article 35 as *'only a variation of the action for annulment of Article 33'*.[316] There is, therefore, no action for the failure to take a general decision nor for the failure to address to others individual decisions which would not concern the applicant.

§ 342. EEC Article 175 grants the right to institute proceedings against a failure to act to a natural and legal person when an institution of the Community 'has failed to *address to that person* any act other than a recommendation or an opinion'.[317] This wording is more restrictive than that of Article 173 which in addition grants the action for annulment to natural and legal persons when they are directly and individually concerned without being the addressees of the act. The Danish, French, Irish and German texts read the same as the English, but the Dutch and Italian texts permit a natural or legal person to appeal against inaction when an institution has failed to take any act other than a recommendation or opinion 'with respect to him' (*te zijnen aanzien; nei suoi confronti*).

§ 343. Advocate-General Roemer, referring to the French and German texts of Article 175, originally pleaded for a restrictive interpretation. The words *'de lui adresser un acte'* (to address an act to him) could only mean that the act must be addressed to the applicant.[318] Later he renounced this point of view, expressing that it was too formalistic and too narrow, as there are cases where a claimant has a direct and individual interest in acts which of necessity must be addressed to others. Taking into consideration the view repeatedly stated by the Court, that in case of doubt the right to institute proceedings should be widely interpreted, he considers it justified to permit the action against failure to act also in those cases when the act is not to be *addressed* to the applicant.[319]

§ 344. In the *First Mackprang Case* the Advocate-General Dutheillet de Lamothe strongly objected to an interpretation of Article 175 diverging from that of Article 173. He submitted:

'If the concept of a measure against which individuals could bring proceedings were different in scope with regard to the application of Article 173 from that with regard to the application of Article 175 the result would be that, in certain cases, the existence or absence of a judicial remedy would

316. *Schlieker Case* (12/63), 4 July 1963, [1963] ECR 89; 9 Jur. (1963) 193; 9 Rec. (1963) 185; [1963] CMLR 287.
317. Art. 148 Euratom reads the same. On that Article there is no case-law, but all remarks pertinent to Art. 175 EEC apply.
318. *Rhenania Case* (103/63), 2 July 1964, Opinion of the Advocate-General, [1964] ECR 433; 10 Jur. (1964) 896; 10 Rec. (1964) 858; [1965] CMLR 88. This opinion was supported by Advocate-General Gand in the *First Lütticke Case* (48/65), 1 March 1966, [1966] ECR 30; 12 Jur. (1966) 43; 12 Rec. (1966) 42; [1966] CMLR 381; CCH para 8044.
319. Karl Roemer, *Die Untätigkeitsklage im Recht der Europäischen Gemeinschaften*, SEW 1966, pp. 1-15 at 13, 14.

depend on the actions of the Community authorities to which the request was submitted.

If those authorities replied to the request either by accepting it or by rejecting it, the author of the request would be entitled to proceed under Article 173, even if he is not the addressee of the measure adopted or requested, provided that this measure is of direct and individual concern to him.

On the other hand, if the Community authorities did not reply to the person concerned he would, according to the Commission's argument, be deprived of any method of recourse if he is not the addressee of the measure requested, *even if the latter is of direct and individual concern to him.*' [320]

Furthermore, the Advocate-General referred to the *Chevalley Case* in which the Court of Justice had considered:

'The concept of a measure capable of giving rise to an action is identical in Articles 173 and 175, as both provisions merely prescribe one and the same method of recourse.' [321]

§ 345. In the light of the Court's opinion that the action against failure to act is a special form of the action for annulment one should interpret Article 175, with due consideration for the Dutch and Italian texts, in the sense that the action against failure to act may be brought by any natural or legal person who would have been directly and individually concerned by the act should it have been taken. As under the ECSC Treaty, individuals cannot institute proceedings against a failure to take general normative acts. [322]

e. BORDER-LINE BETWEEN THE ACTION FOR ANNULMENT AND THE ACTION AGAINST FAILURE TO ACT

§ 346. It was noted above (§ 344) that in the opinion of the Court the provisions of EEC Articles 173 and 175 (the action for annulment and the action against failure to act) '*both merely prescribe one and the same method of recourse*'. This does not solve the problem of when recourse should be made to one and not the other. In case of doubt, parties often institute both actions simultaneously. Although one of them will be held to be inadmissable, the other may succeed.

---

320. *First Mackprang Case* (15/71), 26 Oct. 1971, Opinion of the Advocate-General, [1971] ECR 807, 808; [1972] CMLR 55, 56; CCH para 8155.
321. *Chevalley Case* (15/70), 18 Nov. 1970, consideration 6, [1970] ECR 979; CCH para 8115.
322. See e.g. *First Holtz & Willemsen Case* (134/73), 15 Jan. 1974, consideration 5, [1974] ECR 11; CCH para 8255; *Third Granaria Case* (90/78), 28 March 1979, consideration 14.

(i) Admissibility of actions by States

§ 347. When the applicant is a Member State or a Community institution the EEC Treaty provides for the action for annulment against all acts of the Council and the Commission other than recommendations or opinions (Article 173(1)), and for the action against failure to act in all cases where the Council or the Commission takes no act (Article 175). This means that as soon as there is any form of action – be it only a letter in which it is stated that no act will be taken – then the applicant should not bring an action against failure to act but an action for annulment of the act (or letter) which has been issued. Also, when the Council or the Commission takes an act distinct from the one requested, the action should be for the annulment of the other act and not against a failure to act. [323]

§ 348. In the ECSC the relationship is different. Article 33 ECSC does not allow the action for annulment against any act but only against decisions and recommendations (i.e. directives). On the other hand Article 35 ECSC admits the action against failure to act when the Commission fails in its obligation to take a decision or to make a recommendation. This leaves more room for the action against failure to act. In contradistinction to the EEC Treaty recourse to this action remains possible when the Commission informs the applicant that it will not take the required decision. By giving such information the Commission may have acted, but it has not thereby taken a decision. In the *Steel Industries in Luxembourg Case* where the High Authority had, although belatedly, expressed its position, the Court of Justice reacted in the following way:

'Moreover, the subject-matter of the proceedings is not the silence of the High Authority but its refusal to take a decision within the meaning of Article 14 of the Treaty which, according to the applicant, it was under a duty to take.' [324]

§ 349. Also in the *Second Limburg Coalmines Case* the Court accepted the action under Article 35, although the High Authority had expressed its position within the required period of two months, for the reason that this position amounted to no more than a statement to the effect that no decision would be taken. [325]

If the Commission (the High Authority) responds by taking another decision than the one requested, then an action should be brought against that

---

323. See e.g. *Komponistenverband Case* (8/71), 13 July 1971, [1971] ECR 710, 711; 1973] CMLR 912; CCH para 8143; *Nordgetreide Case* (42/71), 8 March 1972, considera-tion 4, [1972] ECR 110; [1973] CMLR 187; CCH para 8174.
324. *Steel Industries in Luxembourg Case* (7 and 9/54), 23 April 1956, [1954-56] ECR 93; 2 Jur. (1955-56) 94; 2 Rec. (1955-56) 89.
325. *Second Limburg Coalmines Case* (30/59), 23 Feb. 1961, [1961] ECR 15; 7 Jur. 1961) 34, 35; 7 Rec. (1961) 34, 35; See also the opinion of Advocate-General Lagrange, 1961] ECR 37; 7 Jur. (1961) 70; 7 Rec. (1961) 68.

other decision and, as is the case with the EEC Treaty, the action against failure to act is no longer available. [326]

§ **350.** Though the demarcation between the action for annulment and the action against failure to act is different in the ECSC and the EEC Treaties, in both cases the two actions are complementary when brought by a Member State or another Community institution, for if the one procedure proves to be impossible, then the other may be utilised.

(ii)   Admissibility of actions by private parties

§ **351.** Under the EEC Treaty the system seems incomplete in as far as applications by private parties are concerned. [327] Article 173 para 2 does not allow them to institute proceedings against *any act* of the Community, but only against *decisions*. Assume that a Community institution fails to address a decision to a private party, the party calls upon the institution to act (Article 175(2)) and the institution replies that no decision will be taken. An action against failure to act is then rendered impossible as the institution has acted by dint of its negative communication; an action for annulment is equally impossible as no decision has been addressed to the individual. This seemed to be the situation in the *First Lütticke Case*, where Lütticke, invoking Article 175 EEC, had formally requested the Commission to initiate the procedure of Article 169 against Germany for violation of EEC Article 95. The Commission replied that there was no longer any question of a Treaty violation by the Federal Republic of Germany. Lütticke then brought an action for the annulment of this reply. Alternatively, he requested the Court to consider the action against failure to act. The Court did not admit the action for annulment, considering:

'No measure taken by the Commission during this stage (the preliminary phase of Article 169) has any binding force. Consequently, an application for the annulment of the measure by which the Commission arrived at a decision on the application is inadmissible.'

The Court did not admit the alternative claim under Article 175 either, considering:

'Under the terms of the second paragraph of Article 175, proceedings for failure to act may only be brought if at the end of a period of two months from being called upon to act the institution has not defined its position.
   It is established that the Commission has defined its position and has notified this position to the applicants within the prescribed period.
   The plea of inadmissibility is therefore well founded.' [328]

---

326. *San Michele Case* (5-11 and 13-15/62), 14 Dec. 1962, [1962] ECR 459, 460; 8 Jur. (1962) 921, 922; 8 Rec. (1962) 881, 882; [1963] CMLR 23, 24.
327. Toth (*op. cit.*, note 294) pp. 82, 83.
328. *First Lütticke Case* (48/65), 1 March 1966, [1966] ECR 27, 28; 12 Jur. (1966) 39; 12 Rec. (1966) 39; [1966] CMLR 387; CCH para 8044.

§ 352. At a closer look, the gap in legal protection proves to be much less substantial than one might fear. The Court could have replied that the letter in which the Commission communicated to Lütticke that it would not act was not a decision and that therefore the action for annulment was inadmissible, but it did not do so. The Court in fact replied that in the first phase of Article 169 the Commission can take no binding acts and that therefore no action for annulment is permitted against the reply of the Commission.

Lütticke did not lose his case due to a procedural gap between two forms of proceedings; he would have lost anyway because the Commission had not failed to fulfil one of its *obligations*.

§ 353. If an individual has a right to a decision by the Commission or the Council and that institution replies to a petition that it will not take the decision requested, the Court will either interpret the reply as a decision, since it changes the legal position of the applicant (see above § 245), or accept that the reply does not interrupt the procedure under Article 175. The former situation arose in the *Nordgetreide Case*, the Court considering that since the Commission had stated its position, '*the conditions for application of Article 175 were not satisfied and the admissibility of the action must, in consequence, be considered in the light of Article 173 alone.*' [329] Subsequently the case was declared inadmissible because it concerned a regulation against which individuals may never institute proceedings. The latter situation occurred in the *Borromeo Case* in which the department of the Commission concerned had sent a reply which the vice-president of the Commission subsequently acknowledged as the official position of the Community, but where the Court nonetheless permitted continuation of the procedure under Article 175. [330]

Finally, the Court may leave aside the question whether the case is to be decided under Article 173 or under Article 175. This occurred in the *Chevalley Case* quoted above (§ 344) where the Court considered that both articles merely prescribe one and the same method of recourse. [331]

(iii) Substitution of the action for annulment by the action against failure to act

§ 354. In 1961 Meroni objected to a provision of the High Authority for exemptions from the scrap levy, but could not appeal against it as the time limit (of one month) prescribed by ECSC Article 33(3) had passed. Meroni then requested withdrawal of the act and instituted an action against failure to act, because the High Authority had, in spite of Meroni's request, failed to withdraw the contested provision. Under the EEC Treaty Eridania took the same steps. It also wanted a number of decisions to be withdrawn and could no longer institute proceedings against them due to the elapse of the period allowed for the action for annulment. It requested withdrawal of the decisions

---

329. *Nordgetreide Case* (42/71), 8 March 1972, consideration 4, [1972] ECR 110; [1973] CMLR 187; CCH para 8174.
330. *Borromeo Case* (6/70), 15 July 1970, [1970] ECR 816, 819; [1970] CMLR 441; CCH para 8114.
331. *Chevalley Case* (15/70), 18 Nov. 1970, [1970] ECR 978, 980; CCH para 8115.

and lodged the action against failure to act when this request was not complied with. Both cases were declared inadmissible. In the *Fifth Meroni Case* the Court considered:

'The application must be dismissed because an applicant cannot be permitted, by using the procedural artifice of an action for failure to act, to ask for the annulment of decisions which might have been declared void if proceedings had been instituted within the time limit laid down in the third paragraph of Article 33.'[332]

And in the *Eridania Case*:

'Without stating under which provision of Community law the Commission was required to annul or to revoke the said decisions, the applicants have confined themselves to alleging that those decisions were adopted in infringement of the Treaty and that this fact alone would thus suffice to make the Commission's failure to act subject to the provisions of Article 175.

The Treaty provides, however, particularly in Article 173, other methods of recourse by which an allegedly illegal Community measure may be disputed and if necessary annulled on the application of a duly qualified party.

To admit, as the applicants wish to do, that the parties concerned could ask the institution from which the measure came to revoke it and, in the event of the Commission's failing to act, refer such failure to the Court as an illegal omission to deal with the matter would amount to providing them with a method of recourse parallel to that of Article 173, which would not be subject to the conditions laid down by the Treaty.

This application does not therefore satisfy the requirements of Article 175 of the Treaty and must thus be held to be inadmissible.'[333]

§ 355. The first paragraph quoted from the *Eridania Case* implies that Meroni and Eridania could have been successful if they could have demonstrated a legal obligation on the part of the Commission to withdraw the contested decisions. Such an obligation may exist in exceptional situations, for example when decisive facts have fundamentally changed. In such exceptional cases other legal systems, as is the case in French administrative law, permit recourse to the action against failure to act for obtaining withdrawal of existing rules.[334]

---

332. *Fifth Meroni Case* (21-26/61), 6 April 1962, [1962] ECR 78; 8 Jur. (1962) 157 8 Rec. (1962) 155, 156.
333. *Eridania Case* (10 and 18/68), 10 Dec. 1969, considerations 16-18, [1969] ECR 483 CCH para 8099 (pp. 8426, 8427).
334. J. Peters in SEW 1964, pp. 603-608.

3. The plea of illegality [335]

a. SCOPE OF THE PLEA OF ILLEGALITY

§ **356.** The right to bring an action against a regulation is very limited. Apart from the fact that the action must be instituted within a short period of time, varying from one to three months, it cannot normally be lodged by private parties.

Private parties may institute proceedings against decisions addressed to them or, if they directly and individually concern them, against decisions addressed to others. The vast majority of decisions is based on regulations rather than directly on the Treaties themselves. The plea, or exception, of illegality (EEC Article 184) provides that in proceedings against a decision the invalidity of an underlying regulation may be invoked. This prevents individuals from being obliged to respect illegal regulations. The plea is not often invoked. Up to 31 December 1973 the Commission reported 3 cases [336], since that date it has not found it worthwhile to report on its use.

The plea of illegality is actually an incidental ground of illegality in proceedings for the annulment of a decision. None of the normal grounds (see § 254-297) may be applicable if the decision itself has been correctly taken. The extra ground then is a means to establish that the underlying regulation is illegal. The annulment of the regulation itself is not at issue. If the Court considers it to be illegal, it will not be annulled, but declared inapplicable with respect to the specific case. This inapplicability means that the decision has no legal foundation and will be annulled, but the regulation stands and all other decisions which may have been based upon it remain in force. Of course, all future decisions based upon the regulation will run the same risk of being considered without proper legal foundation. The Commission or the Council will therefore in practice replace the regulation as soon as possible by a legal one.

b. IN WHAT PROCEEDINGS CAN THE PLEA BE INVOKED?

i) Actions for annulment

§ **357.** The ECSC Treaty provides for the plea of illegality only in the case of actions against pecuniary sanctions and periodic penalty payments. [337] In the

---

335. See also Ami Barav, *The exception of illegality in Community Law: a critical analysis*, 1974 CMLRev., pp. 366-386; Gerhard Bebr, *Judicial remedy of private parties against normative acts of the European Communities: the role of the exception of illegality*, 4 CMLRev. (1966-67), pp. 7-31; Lauwaars (*op. cit.*, note 143) p. 276-285; T.P.J.N. Van Rijn, *Exceptie van onwettigheid en prejudiciële procedure inzake geldigheid van gemeenschaps-handelingen*, Europese Monografieën No. 26, Kluwer 1978; Patrick Dubois, *L'exception, l'illegalité devant la Cour de justice des Communautés européennes*, 14 CDE (1978), p. 407-439.
336. *Community Law*, Extract from the Seventh General Report, Table 2.
337. ECSC Art. 36(3).

First Meroni Case the Court of Justice ruled that the plea of illegality is a general principle of law and should, therefore, also apply in cases for which it has not been expressly foreseen. It held in that case:

> 'That provision of Article 36 should not be regarded as a special rule, applicable only in the case of pecuniary sanctions and periodic penalty payments, but as the application of a general principle, applied by Article 36 to the particular case of an action in which the Court has unlimited jurisdiction.
>
> No argument can be based on the express statement in Article 36 to the effect that *a contrario* the application of the rule laid down is excluded in cases in which it has not been expressly stated. For the Court has decided, in its judgment in Case 8/55, that an argument in reverse is only admissible when no other interpretation appears appropriate and compatible with the provision and its context and with the purpose of the same. [338]
>
> Any other decision would render it difficult, if not impossible, for the undertakings and associations mentioned in Article 48 to exercise their right to bring actions, because it would oblige them to scrutinize every general decision upon publication thereof for provisions which might later adversely affect them or be considered as involving a misuse of powers affecting them.
>
> It would encourage them to let themselves be ordered to pay the pecuniary sanctions or periodic penalty payments for which the Treaty makes provision so as to be able, by virtue of Article 36, to plead the illegality of the general decisions and recommendations which they were alleged not to have observed.' [339]

A year later in the *First Snupat Case* the Court considered this wider applicability of the exception of illegality '*in accordance with the established case-law of the Court*' (see quotation below § 359). Twenty years later the Court again confirmed its position in the *Fourth Simmenthal Case*, this time with respect to the plea of illegality under the EEC Treaty (see below § 363a).

§ **358.** Only Member States and Institutions may institute actions for annulment against regulations (see above § 303, 312). These actions are rare, but if in such an action the validity of an underlying prior regulation is disputed, the plea of illegality can be used against that prior regulation. The Court confirmed this in the *Group Exemption Regulation Case*, in which Italy successfully invoked the plea of illegality against a prior regulation in a dispute concerning a subsequent regulation. [340]

---

338. *Fédéchar Case* (8/55), 29 Nov. 1956, [1954-56] ECR 300; 2 Jur. (1955-56) 324 2 Rec. (1955-56) 305.
339. *First Meroni Case (Meroni Milan)* (9/56), 13 June 1958, [1957-58] ECR 140; 4 Jur (1958) 27; 4 Rec. (1958) 26; and *First Meroni Case (Meroni Erba)* (10/56), 13 June 1958 [1957-58] ECR 162, 163; 4 Jur. (1958) 67, 68; 4 Rec. (1958) 66.
340. *Group Exemption Regulation Case* (32/65), 13 July 1966, [1966] ECR 409; 12 Jur (1966) 611; 12 Rec. (1966) 594; [1969] CMLR 65; CCH para 8048.

(ii) Actions against failure to act

§ 359. In the *First Snupat Case* the Court of Justice accepted that the plea of illegality can be invoked in an action against failure to act. Snupat had requested an exemption from the payment of a levy to the scrap equalization fund. When it did not receive any reply it instituted proceedings against failure to act under ECSC Article 35. The possibility of receiving an exemption was excluded by some generally-worded letters from the High Authority which in Snupat's submission were general decisions on scrap equalization. Snupat submitted that these general decisions were illegal. The Court held:

'According to the established case-law of the Court, an undertaking which contests an individual decision is entitled to raise the objection of illegality against the general decisions on which they are based.

The parties are in agreement about the fact that the letter from the CPFI of 12 May 1958 and the implied decision of refusal of 1 June 1958 are based on the principles set out in the abovementioned letters of the High Authority; and such indeed is manifestly the case. The question therefore arises whether those letters constitute decisions.' [341]

Though under the EEC Treaty a failure to act may not be considered as an 'implied decision of refusal' one may expect the same attitude from the Court on the ground that it considers the actions for annulment and against failure to act as *'merely prescribing one and the same method of recourse'* (see above § 344).

(iii) Actions against treaty violations by Member States

§ 360. Can a Member State on being accused of the violation of a rule of Community law, invoke the plea of illegality and plead that the allegedly violated rule is illegal? When discussing the judicial review of acts of Member States it will be seen that the Court of Justice rejects this plea. In the actions brought against Member States for failure to fulfil their obligations the plea of illegality cannot be invoked (see below § 386, 413-415).

(iv) Proceedings before national courts

§ 361. The provision on the plea of illegality in the EEC Treaty is not entirely clear, for EEC Article 184 provides that the inapplicability of a regulation may be invoked *'in proceedings in which [the] regulation ... is in issue'*. It does not expressly state before which court the proceedings must be conducted.

Wöhrmann invoked EEC Article 184 as a separate right of action before the Court of Justice when he had a case pending before his national court. The Court of Justice did not accept the action considering:

341. *First Snupat Case* (32 and 33/58), 17 July 1959, [1959] ECR 139; 5 Jur. (1958-59) 322, 323; 5 Rec. (1958-59) 300.

'More particularly, it is clear from the reference to the time limit laid down in Article 173 that Article 184 is applicable only in the context of proceedings brought before the Court of Justice and that it does not permit the said time limit to be avoided.

The sole object of Article 184 is thus to protect an interested party against the application of an illegal regulation, without thereby in any way calling in issue the regulation itself, which can no longer be challenged because of the expiry of the time limit laid down in Article 173.

It must be stressed that the Treaty clearly defines the respective jurisdictions of the Court of Justice and of national courts or tribunals. In fact, by virtue of both Article 177 and Article 20 of the Protocol on the Statute of the Court of Justice of the European Economic Community, the decision to suspend proceedings and to refer a case to this Court is one for the national court or tribunal.

If the parties to an action pending before a national court or tribunal were entitled to make a direct request to this Court for a preliminary ruling, they could compel the national court to suspend proceedings pending a decision of the Court of Justice. Neither the Treaty nor the Protocol, however, imposes such a limitation on the powers of the national court.'[342]

§ 362. In the *Hessische Knappschaft Case* one of the parties in proceedings before a national court again disputed the validity of a regulation. This time however, the national court had requested a preliminary ruling on the interpretation of that regulation so that the matter came before the Court of Justice. Once the matter had been brought before the Court of Justice could a party invoke a plea of illegality against the regulation whose interpretation was asked? The Court would then have to refuse to interpret the provision on the ground that the regulation was invalid and should therefore not be applied by the national court. Again the Court of Justice refused to entertain the plea of illegality, mainly on the ground that in proceedings under EEC Article 177 only the national courts may ask for rulings. Any additional request by one of the parties would therefore be inadmissible. The Court considered:

'Under Article 177 of the Treaty it is for the court or tribunal of a Member State, and not the parties to the main action, to bring a matter before the Court of Justice.

Since the right to determine the questions to be brought before the Court thus devolves upon the court or tribunal of the Member State alone the parties may not change their tenor or have them declared to be without purpose. Consequently the Court of Justice cannot be compelled at the request of a party to entertain a question when the initiative for referring it to the Court pertains not to the parties but to the court or tribunal of the Member State itself, or to entertain within the particular framework of Article 177 a claim based primarily on Article 184.

342. *Wöhrmann Case* (31 and 33/62), 14 Dec. 1962, [1962] ECR 507; 8 Jur. (1962) 1019, 1020; 8 Rec. (1962) 979, 980; [1963] CMLR 158; CCH para 8007.

Besides, the contrary view fails to recognize that the authors of Article 177 intended to establish direct cooperation between the Court of Justice and the courts and tribunals of the Member States by way of a non-contentious procedure excluding any initiative of the parties, who are merely invited to be heard in the course of that procedure.' [343]

c. AGAINST WHAT KIND OF ACTS CAN THE PLEA BE USED?

§ 363. The plea of illegality must be directed against regulations. In the *Third Dalmas Case* an individual decision had been addressed to the applicant against which he had not instituted proceedings. When, by a later decision, Dalmas was ordered to pay a penalty for not having complied with the previous decision, he brought an action against the penalty decision and pleaded that the previous decision was void. The Court of Justice did not accept this submission, considering:

'The third paragraph of Article 36 of the Treaty cannot enable an applicant to plead the illegality not only of general decisions and recommendations but also of decisions and recommendations addressed to him. Such an interpretation would conflict with the fundamental principle established by Article 33. In fact the strict time-limit for instituting proceedings laid down by this provision is in keeping with the necessity to prevent the legality of administrative decisions being called in question indefinitely.' [344]

§ 363a. The rule that the plea of illegality is to be used against regulations should not be interpreted in a narrow sense. In the *Fourth Simmenthal Case* the Court held that EEC Article 184 in the expression of a general rule of law which permits a party to challenge the validity of any prior act which forms the basis of a decision disputed before the Court, provided that the party has not been able to challenge that prior act in a direct action under EEC Article 173. [345]

§ 364. The reasoning that the plea of illegality may not be used against decisions which could have been challenged, might suggest that Member States may never invoke the plea, since they can bring an action for the annulment of all Community acts. The Court of Justice does not draw this conclusion, however. In the *Group Exemption Regulation Case* it permitted the Italian government to invoke the plea of illegality against regulations underlying the disputed acts. It held that under Article 184 '*any party may, in proceedings in which a regulation is in issue, plead the grounds specified in the first para-*

343. *Hessische Knappschaft Case* (44/65), 9 Dec. 1965, [1965] ECR 970, 971; 11 Jur. (1965) 1155; 11 Rec. (1965) 1198, 1199; [1966] CMLR 94; CCH para 8042.
344. *Third Dalmas Case* (21/64), 31 March 1965, [1965] ECR 187; 11 Jur. (1965) 248; 11 Rec. (1965) 244; [1966] CMLR 60.
345. *Fourth Simmenthal Case* (92/78), 6 March 1979, considerations 39-43. At the time of writing, no English text of the case was available.

*graph of Article 173, in order to invoke the inapplicability of that regula-
tion'.* [346]

§ 365. In the same case the Court held that the plea can be used only against
the regulations which form the basis of the act in dispute. Invoking the plea of
illegality, the Italian government also disputed the legality of a number of
other regulations. Rejecting this, the Court held with respect to Article 184
*'The intention of the said article is not to allow a party to contest at will the
applicability of any regulation in support of an application. The regulation of
which the legality is called in question must be applicable, directly or indirectly, to the issue with which the application is concerned'.* [347]

4. Preliminary rulings on the validity of acts [348]

a. COMPETENCE OF NATIONAL COURTS

§ 366. Community law is integrated into the national legal order and is
applied as part of that legal order with respect to its citizens by the national
courts (see above § 145-148). May the validity of Community acts be disputed at this stage of their application? The German Government contested
this in some early preliminary rulings on the validity of acts (see below
§ 371). Fortunately for the sake of the protection of individual rights against
invalid Community acts, Community law answers this question in the affirma-
tive. National courts are obliged to apply Community law, but are not obliged
to apply invalid acts. However, the decision that a Community act is invalid is
to be taken by the Court of Justice.

§ 366a. ECSC Article 41 expressly attributes to the Court of Justice 'sole
jurisdiction to give preliminary rulings on the validity of acts of the High
Authority and of the Council where such validity is in issue in proceedings
brought before a national court or tribunal'. For acts of the Council this is the
most appropriate way to decide on their legality as these acts may not be
challenged in an action for annulment. [349]

§ 367. EEC Article 177 provides a means for obtaining a decision on the
validity of a Community act by conferring jurisdiction on the Court of Justice

346. *Group Exemption Regulation Case* (32/65), 13 July 1966, [1966] ECR 409; 12 Jur.
(1966) 611; 12 Rec. (1966) 594; [1969] CMLR 65; CCH para 8048.
347. *Idem.*
348. On this subject see Gerhard Bebr, *Examen en validité au titre de l'article 177 du
traité CEE et cohésion juridique de la Communauté,* 11 CDE (1975) pp. 379-424; Henry
G. Schermers in LIEI 1974/1 pp. 105-106; Van Rijn, (*op. cit.,* note 335), pp. 229-272;
Jean François Couzinet, *Le renvoi en appréciation de validité devant la cour de justice des
communautés européennes,* 12 RTDE (1976), pp. 648-690. On the differences between
preliminary rulings on interpretation and on validity, see also Ami Barav, *Some Aspects of
the Preliminary Rulings Procedure in EEC Law,* 2 ELRev. (1977), pp. 7-14.
349. *CFDT Case* (66/76), 17 Feb. 1977, consideration 12, [1977] ECR 310; [1977] 2
CMLR 595.

to give preliminary rulings on the validity of acts taken by the institutions. The article, furthermore, provides that any court or tribunal of a Member State, before which such a question is raised, *may* ask a ruling of the Court of Justice thereon, if it considers this necessary to enable it to give judgement. Only courts in last instance are expressly *obliged* to ask for such rulings. The distinction drawn between lower courts which may, and highest courts which must request preliminary rulings has without doubt been made by the drafters of the Treaty with the intention of securing the prime goal of Article 177, that of providing for the uniform *interpretation* of Community law by the Court of Justice (see below § 557, 558). The notion of uniform interpretation has dominated both academic discussion and actual rulings relating to the Article. ECSC Article 41 which provides for preliminary rulings only on the validity of acts grants *sole* jurisdiction to the Court of Justice, thereby making clear that even lower national courts have no choice but to refer.

§ 367a.   If a preliminary ruling is asked on the interpretation of a Community act, then the Court of Justice may rule *ex officio* on the validity of that act, but it will not generally do so. [350] In the *First Milac Case* some doubt was raised whether EEC Regulation 725/74, on monetary compensatory amounts, was compatible with EEC Article 40(3). [351] The Court, however, did not rule upon this question, because the national court had not asked it. It did so only later when the national court, in a second reference, expressly asked this question. [352]

Similarly, in the *König Case* the Court refused to enter into the question of validity of its own motion, holding:

'For present purposes, the Court is not called upon to examine the compatibility with general principles of law of the provision in Article 2(1) of the Regulation, under which the Regulation, was to 'enter into force' on a date prior to its publication, this question not having been raised by the national court.' [353]

In the *Internatio Case* the Court of Justice did in fact examine a question of validity raised by one of the parties in the main action before the national court, but not asked by the national court. It then held:

'Since the failure to provide the necessary publicity can be considered by the Court of its own motion, this allegation should be examined.' [354]

---

350.   On this question see also B.H. ter Kuile, *Procedures over ongeldige gemeenschapsnormen*, 25 SEW (1977), pp. 621-623.
351.   *First Milac Case* (28/76), 23 Nov. 1976, [1976] ECR 1653; CCH para 8385.
352.   *Third Milac Case* (8/78), 13 July 1978, consideration 16, [1978] ECR 1731, 1732.
353.   *König Case* (185/73), 29 May 1974, consideration 7, [1974] ECR 617; CCH para 8275.
354.   *Internatio Case* (73, 74/63), 18 Feb. 1964, [1964] ECR 14; 10 Jur. (1964) 27; 10 Rec. (1964) 28; [1964] CMLR 221; CCH para 8021.

From the cases one might draw the conclusion that the Court will rule that an act is invalid, even when no question on its validity has been asked, in the case of a flagrant infringement of a superior rule of law, as it also does in an action for damages (see below § 478).

§ **368.** When the validity of a Community act is questioned before a lower national court the text of EEC Article 177 grants that court three alternative courses of action:

    a) to ask a preliminary ruling on the validity of the act,

    b) to consider the act valid without asking for a preliminary ruling,

    c) to consider the act invalid without asking for a preliminary ruling.

The selection of the last alternative creates grave problems, as it would actually result in the national court not applying Community law. Bebr presents six reasons why this alternative is unacceptable and should not be open to national courts:

    (1) The alternative would violate EEC Articles 173 and 174 which confer on the Court of Justice the exclusive competence to annul Community acts.

    (2) The alternative would be contrary to the fundamental principle of the uniform application of Community law.

    (3) It would violate the principle of the priority of Community law. The provision that regulations shall be binding in their entirety and directly applicable in all Member States would be frustrated.

    (4) The possibility of lower courts not applying Community acts would be incompatible with the importance of Community acts and to the ponderous enactment procedure.

    (5) In their national legal systems the lower courts of the Member States have no power to disregard national legal acts of a similar nature.

    (6) It would be paradoxical to grant lower courts powers which the highest courts would not have. [355]

Even if every single reason is not entirely convincing, taken together they strongly predicate that lower national courts must either apply Community acts or ask a preliminary ruling on their validity. These courts should *not* be considered competent to choose the third alternative. [356]

In its 'Suggestions on European Union' the Court of Justice proposed that a provision should be included to prohibit national courts from treating a Community act as invalid unless the European Court has so decided. [357]

§ **369.** In a relatively early case a lower German administrative court, the *Verwaltungsgericht* Frankfurt, ruled, without asking for a preliminary ruling, that an EEC regulation was invalid. It based its competence to do so on a textual comparison made with the provision in the German Constitution that

---

355. Bebr (*op. cit.*, note 348) pp. 381-383.

356. A.M. Donner, *Les rapports entre la compétence de la Cour de Justice des Communautés Européennes et les tribunaux internes*, 115 RdC (1965 II) p. 39; L.J. Brinkhorst in his Commentary to the Toepfer Case, AA 1964-65, p. 297.

357. *Suggestions of the Court of Justice on European Union*, Bulletin of the European Communities, Supplement 9/75, p. 21.

courts which consider a law unconstitutional *must* submit the question to the Constitutional Court. [358] The less stringent formulation of EEC Article 177 would then entitle the lower court to decide the question itself. [359] The decision of the *Verwaltungsgericht* has been severely criticized. [360] Naturally, the losing party appealed and in the higher court a preliminary ruling was asked. [361] . The Court of Justice decided that the EEC regulations concerned were valid [362] , so that finally the outcome was reached which could have been obtained at an earlier instance, had the *Verwaltungsgericht* properly applied EEC Article 177.

After having set aside EEC regulations on a number of occasions between 1966 and 1969 [363] , the *Verwaltungsgericht* Frankfurt changed its policy in 1970. Since then it has asked for preliminary rulings whenever it disputes the legality of Community regulations, rather than ruling itself. [364]

§ 370. In another German case it was suggested to a chamber (senat) of a German court that it might request a preliminary ruling on the question whether, in general, lower courts are obliged to ask for a preliminary ruling before they declare a Community act to be invalid. The 'Senat' held:

'The Senat did not follow the suggestion to refer to the European Court of Justice for a preliminary ruling the question whether national courts that are not of the last instance, are not only entitled, but also obliged to submit their question to the Court of Justice when they deem a legal act of a Community organ invalid.

The Senat was not presented with this question because (in accordance with the other courts of finance) it considers it advisable, as a general rule — especially when other questions on whose preliminary decision the decision concerned could depend are inconceivable — to submit for a preliminary ruling in the earliest possible stage of the judicial proceedings those questions which are of substantive relevance to the main decision. It is in the interest of the economy of the proceedings that in the earliest possible stage the European Court of Justice gets the opportunity to answer questions that concern the validity and direct applicability of decisions of the Commission'. [365]

---

358. German constitution Art. 100.
359. *German Exportbond Case*, 12 Dec. 1966, AWD 1967, p. 71; 5 CMLRev. (1967-68), p. 75.
360. R.H. Lauwaars, *Prejudiciële Beslissingen*, Europese Monografieën No. 19, p. 55; L. Constantinesco, AWD 1967, pp. 125-130.
361. By the *Hessische Verwaltungsgerichtshof*, decision of 21 April 1970.
362. *Köster Case* (25/70), 17 Dec. 1970, [1970] ECR 1161-1182; [1972] CMLR 255-259 and 288-295; CCH para 8127. See also *First Henck Case* (26/70), 17 Dec. 1970, [1970] ECR 1183-1195; [1972] CMLR 259-261 and 295, 296; CCH para 8128.
363. For an enumeration see [1972] CMLR 178, 179.
364. E.g. decisions of 25 Feb. 1970, 18 March 1970, 19 June 1972, see *Schroeder Case* (40/72), 7 Feb. 1973, CCH para 8206.
365. *German Rewe-Zentrale Case*, Finanzgericht Düsseldorf, 15 July 1970, AWD 1970, p. 377; L.J. Brinkhorst and H.G. Schermers, *Judicial Remedies in the European Communities*, 2nd ed. Kluwer 1977, pp. 280, 281.

For practical reasons this seems the correct approach for all lower courts. It makes no sense to postpone the ruling of the Court of Justice on the legality of an act, because such a ruling must inevitably be given at some stage of the proceedings whenever a lower court refuses to apply the act by reason of its presumed illegality.

b. GROUNDS FOR ILLEGALITY

(i) Validity versus legality

§ 371. In the *Internatio Case* the German government contended that a discussion of the legality of Community acts at the stage of their application would be contrary to the system and spirit of the EEC Treaty which intended to make Community acts final after the elapse of the time limits set for an action for annulment. Otherwise too great an uncertainty would hamper the development of the Community legal order. Basing its argument on the difference in wording of EEC Articles 173 and 177 the German government submitted that a review of the *validity* of an act under Article 177 was more restrictive than a review of the *legality* of an act under Article 173. [366] Under Article 173 the Court would therefore be competent to consider all grounds of possible illegality, while under Article 177 it would only be competent to verify the 'formal validity', bearing on the question of the existence of the act (see above § 213-219). Only when the act had not been taken by a Community institution, or when it had been withdrawn or (within the time limits prescribed for annulment) annulled, could the Court rule on its invalidity. [367]

§ 372. The Court of Justice did not follow the German government's submission. In reviewing the validity of acts under EEC Article 177 the Court looks at the same grounds of illegality as when it examines other applications, directed against the legality of acts (see above § 254-297), and interprets these grounds in the same way. [368] In the *Third International Fruit Company Case* the Court of Justice held:

> 'According to the first paragraph of Article 177 of the EEC Treaty 'The Court of justice shall have jurisdiction to give preliminary rulings concerning ... the validity ... of acts of the institutions of the Community'.
>
> Under that formulation, the jurisdiction of the Court cannot be limited by the grounds on which the validity of those measures may be contested.' [369]

---

366. A similar difference in wording exists in all other Community languages.
367. Observations made by the German Government in the *Internatio Case* (73 and 74/63), 18 Feb. 1964, [1964] ECR 19-20; 10 Jur. (1964) 37-39; 10 Rec. (1964) 39-41; [1964] CMLR 205-207; CCH para 8021.
368. See also Bebr (*op. cit.*, note 348), p. 402.
369. *Third International Fruit Company Case* (21-24/72), 12 Dec. 1972, considerations 4, 5, 1972 ECR 1226; [1975] 2 CMLR 20; CCH para 8194.

From this case it may be concluded that no distinction should be made between *legality* in Article 173 and *validity* in Article 177. Whenever asked, under the latter article, to rule upon the validity of an act the Court has examined all the grounds which could possibly affect its legality. In the *Second De Bloos Case* a national court expressly asked whether national courts can obtain preliminary rulings on the validity of decisions which are disputed by a party who is out of time to bring an action for annulment under EEC Article 173. [370] The Court of Justice did not reply to this question as the case could be decided on other grounds, but the case provides no reasons why the Court should refuse to give such a preliminary ruling when asked by the national court.

Only in two cases where a ruling on the validity of an act was asked due to a possible conflict with international law does the situation appear to be different. In the *Third International Fruit Company Case* and in the *Second Schlüter Case* the Court of Justice was requested to give a preliminary ruling on the validity of a Community act which allegedly violated international law. The Court held that the validity of Community acts can indeed be impaired by the fact that they are in conflict with a rule of international law, but that under EEC Article 177 such a conflict can be brought before the Court only if the rule of international law is of such a nature that individuals can invoke it before their national courts. [371] This, of course, is only rarely the case as most rules of international law are addressed to States. The review of legality under EEC Article 173 cannot be subject to a similar condition, so that a difference has been created between the review of the legality of an act which encompasses all rules of international law and the review of its validity which encompasses only those rules of international law which have direct effect.

(ii) Grounds applied

§ 373. So far there have been about a dozen cases in which the Court of Justice has declared Community acts (partly) void. [372] There is no indication that the Court will judge differently on the validity or legality of an act

---

370. *Second De Bloos Case* (59/77), 14 Dec. 1977, consideration 4, [1977] ECR 2368; [1978] 1 CMLR 528; CCH para 8444. On this question see Richard Clutterbuck, *Article 177 EEC: two important questions left unanswered*, 3 ELRev. (1978), pp. 292-295.
371. *Third International Fruit Company Case* (21-24/72), 12 Dec. 1972, consideration 8, [1972] ECR 1226; CCH 8194; *Second Schlüter Case* (9/73), 24 Oct. 1973, consideration 27, [1973] ECR 1157; CCH para 8233.
372. *Second Getreidehandel Case* (55/72), 10 Jan. 1973, [1973] ECR 25, 26; [1973] CMLR 480; CCH para 8203; *Niemann Case* (191/73, 28 May 1974, [1974] ECR 581; *First Roquette Case* (34/74), 12 Nov. 1974; [1974] ECR 1217; *Petroni Case* (24/75), 21 Oct. 1975, [1975] ECR 1149; *Rey Soda Case* (23/75), 30 Oct. 1975, [1975] ECR 1279; [1976] CMLR 158; CCH para 8321 and *EFFEM Case* (95/75), 9 March 1976, [1976] ECR 369; [1976] 2 CMLR 95; CCH para 8349; *First Dried Milk Case (Bela Mühle)* (114/76), 5 July 1977, [1977] ECR 1211; CCH para 8448; *Second Dried Milk Case (Granaria)* (116/76), 5 July 1977, [1977] ECR 1247; CCH para 8449; *Third Dried Milk Case* (Ölmuhle) (119, 120/76), 5 July 1977, [1977] ECR 1269; CCH para 8450; *Wine Levy Case (Commissionnaires Réunis)* (80, 81/77), 20 April 1978, [1978] ECR 948; *Second Milac Case* (131/77), 3 May 1978, [1978] ECR 1052; *Zipper Case* (34/78), 31 Jan. 1979; *Buitoni Case* (122/78), 20 Feb. 1979.

depending on the way it has been brought before it. Bebr considers that the Court should proceed more strictly in a case under EEC Article 177 than in one under EEC Article 173 for the reason that when a request is brought for a preliminary ruling the act may have been in force for a long time and as a result legal certainty would be seriously affected if non-validity were to be too easily established after the elapse of the time limits for the action for annulment. If no distinction were to be drawn the ruling on validity would come close to an 'eternal action for annulment'. [372a]

§ 374. Under German law courts questioning the validity of laws by way of reference to the Constitutional Court must reason *why* they think the law could be invalid. No such requirement exists in Community law. Being accustomed to the national situation, German courts questioning the validity of Community acts have always stated their reasons for questioning the validity of an act. [373] But what would happen if a national court asked whether a particular act was valid or not, without giving any reasoning? It is inconceivable that the Court of Justice would rule in the abstract that a Community act is valid, as there might always be a ground for invalidity which nobody had thought of and which might only be brought forward at a later juncture (see below § 530-537). The Court of Justice has never ruled that an act is valid; so far it has only stated that none of the grounds raised warranted a ruling of invalidity. [374]

Although the intervening governments and institutions and the parties to the dispute may not raise new questions before the Court of Justice (see below § 620-625) they may plead on the questions asked by the national court, and in their pleadings they may submit any reasons why the acts on whose validity a preliminary ruling is asked should be considered invalid.

Only when neither the national court nor any of the parties, governments or institutions have raised any ground for the invalidity of the act, should the Court declare the request inadmissible. [375]

c. IMPORTANCE OF THE REVIEW OF VALIDITY

§ 375. For the judicial review of Community acts it is of great importance that there are no limitations placed on the reasons for which the validity of acts may be contested under EEC Article 177. It opens up a means of challenging Community acts after the elapse of the time limits set out in EEC Article 173, and offers the chance of satisfaction to applicants who otherwise may not have any right to challenge such acts.

The action for annulment and the action against failure to act are restrictive. By means of the plea of illegality some guarantee has been given that

---

372a. Bebr (*op. cit.*, note 348), p. 403.
373. Other courts often do the same, see e.g. the Italian court in the *Tasca Case* (65/75), 26 Feb. 1976, [1976] ECR 294.
374. See e.g. *Triches Case* (19/76), 13 July 1976, consideration 19, [1976] ECR 1252.
375. See also Bebr (*op. cit.*, note 348) pp. 386-389.

invalid Community regulations will not be applied by the Court of Justice to individuals who have never had the opportunity of challenging these regulations. Article 177 as interpreted by the Court offers a similar guarantee that invalid Community law will not be applied to individuals by national courts.

In many national legal systems the legality of laws cannot be challenged at all. To some degree this can be remedied by the possibility of controlling such acts through the political mechanism of Parliament. In the Communities where political control is almost non-existent the additional judicial control presented by the system of preliminary rulings is therefore of even greater significance.

§ **376.** Attacking Community acts by way of preliminary rulings on their validity is relatively difficult as the challenge can be successful only if both the national and Community courts co-operate. [376] They must each play their part.

(a) National courts must apply Community law (see above § 145-149). Community law is directly applicable within all the national legal orders (see below § 158-174). Article 177 does not require that preliminary rulings be asked in all cases where Community law is to be applied. Only when the national court is faced with a question of interpretation or validity will it solicit the opinion of the Court of Justice. If the validity of a Community act is not in doubt, a preliminary ruling on its validity will not be requested, and normally the Court of Justice will not rule on its validity when it has not been expressly asked to do so.

The theory of the *acte clair* will be discussed in the context of preliminary rulings on interpretation (see below § 591-594). Several objections to this theory will be met, with the conclusion that national courts must not accept it too readily. In the case of a preliminary ruling on validity the situation may be different. There is no reason to require that every application of a Community act should be preceded by a preliminary ruling checking its validity. National courts may assume that Community acts are valid. Only in case of reasonable doubt should they ask for a preliminary ruling.

In the interest of legal certainty the validity of Community acts should not be disputed too readily. It is therefore thought that the additional prerequisite that the national court has to doubt the validity is reasonable.

(b) Once the national court has asked for a preliminary ruling the Court of Justice can decide on the question of validity. It does so according to the special procedure of Article 177 (see below § 680, 698) which permits the individual only a limited right to argue why the act should be considered illegal. He may present his argument in one written document, backed up subsequently by one oral plea. In this document he is unable to contest the arguments in favour of validity advanced in the documents submitted at the same time by the Member States, the Community institutions, or the opposing party in the national proceedings. This must be carried out in the oral procedure with all its attendant disadvantages of language difficulties (see below § 696).

376. For cases which were successful, see note 372 above.

d. PRELIMINARY RULINGS ON THE VALIDITY OF A FAILURE TO ACT

§ 377. Preliminary rulings may be asked on the validity of any act of the Communities. In consequence, is it possible to ask a preliminary ruling on the validity of a failure to act? In the opinion of the Court of Justice the concept of a measure capable of giving rise to an action is identical in the actions for annulment and against failure to act (*Chevalley Case*, see above § 344). Systematically, a failure to act could be classified as a specific form of a (non-existent) act (see above § 250). It is therefore submitted that a national court may request a preliminary ruling on the validity of a failure to act if it considers such a ruling necessary to pass judgment. It should take into consideration, however, that the parties to the national dispute may be entitled to bring an action against failure to act directly before the Court of Justice. If they have not done so this may lead to a presumption of legality, in the same way as an unchallenged individual decision may be assumed to be legal with respect to its addressee.

5. The action for damages

§ 378. Individuals who are not entitled to bring an action for annulment sometimes try to obtain a decision on the validity of a Community act in an action for damages (see below § 468-482). Prior to 1971 it was generally believed that a suit for damages could not be used for establishing the illegality of Community acts due to the Court of Justice ruling in the *Plaumann Case* that *'an administrative measure which has not been annulled cannot of itself constitute a wrongful act on the part of the administration inflicting damage upon those whom it affects'*. [377] It appeared that suits for damages, incurred by Community acts, would only succeed *after* the acts had been annulled and therefore that this action could not be used *in order to* obtain an annulment of the act or a declaration by the Court of its illegality.

Then, in 1971, the Court of Justice considered in the *Third Lütticke* and *Schöppenstedt Cases* that a claim for damages is *'an 'independent form of action with a particular purpose to fulfil within the system of actions'* [378] and admitted actions for damages caused by acts which had not already been annulled. In deciding on these actions for damages the Court ruled on the legality of the acts concerned.

For further details see the section below on 'suits for damages', § 446-508.

---

377. *Plaumann Case* (25/62), 15 July 1963, [1963] ECR 108; 9 Jur. (1963) 233; 9 Rec. (1963) 225, [1964] CMLR 48; CCH para 8013 (p. 7275).
378, *Third Lütticke Case* (4/69), 28 April 1971, consideration 6, [1971] ECR 336; CCH para 8136; *Schöppenstedt Case* (5/71), 2 Dec. 1971, consideration 3, [1971] ECR 983; CCH para 8153.

D. EFFECT OF JUDICIAL REVIEW

§ 379. An unsuccessful action against the legality or validity of a Community act will have no further effect. A rejection by the Court of Justice of the grounds on which illegality or invalidity was claimed does not protect the act against future challenges on other grounds. Its legal position is the same as that of any other act.

§ 379a. In the event of a successful direct action against the legality of a Community act, that is in an action for annulment, the Court shall declare the act to be void. [379] This means that the act has never lawfully existed. All payments made under it must be reimbursed, all further action based on it will be void as well. In the case of a regulation, however, the Court of Justice may state that some of its effects shall be considered as definitive. [380]

The following two examples may illustrate the need for such a provision. (a) In the *First Remunerations Adjustment Case* the Court came to the conclusion that some articles of a Council regulation on remuneration of Community staff were illegal. Wanting to prevent discontinuity in the system of remuneration it therefore applied EEC Article 174(2). It annulled Articles 1-4 of Council Regulation No. 2647/72 with the express declaration 'that these articles shall continue to have effect until the Regulation to be made in consequence of the present judgement comes into operation'. [381] (b) In the *De Dapper Case* the Court held that the Staff Committee of the European Parliament had been irregularly elected. It ordered the Parliament to disband the Committee, but it also provided that for the sake of legal certainty the arrangements adopted by the illegal Staff Committee should remain in force. [382]

In spite of the restriction to regulations, expressed in EEC Article 174, the Court of Justice has applied the same rule to other Community acts. In the *Fourth Simmenthal Case* the Court annulled Decision No. 78-258, addressed by the Commissions to the Member States, only in as far as it affected Simmenthal. For the sake of legal certainty the effects of the Decision on others were to remain. [383]

§ 379b. A Community act is not annulled when the Court holds in a preliminary ruling or in a suit for damages that the act is invalid. It may remain effective as an invalid act. The Court's decision only means that the Court of Justice itself, in a suit for damages, or the national court, in the suit for which it requested the preliminary ruling, must treat the act as inoperative in the particular case. The Court of Justice stressed this difference when it held in the Schwarze Case:

379. EEC art. 174(1); Euratom art. 147(1).
380. EEC art. 174(2); Euratom art. 147(2).
381. *First Remunerations Adjustment Case* (81/72), 5 June 1973, [1973] ECR 587; |1973| CMLR 659.
382. *De Dapper Case* (54/75), final judgment, 9 March 1977, consideration 56, [1977] ECR 488.
383. *Fourth Simmenthal Case* (92/78), 6 March 1979, considerations 106, 107.

'Although the Court may have no jurisdiction under Article 177 to declare such a measure void, as the French Government maintains, this provision does expressly confer jurisdiction on the Court to decide on the validity of such a measure'. [384]

Once the Court has stated in a preliminary ruling or in a suit for damages that an act is invalid, it may be expected that in all further applications individuals who are affected by the act will invoke the same invalidity before their national courts, and national courts will no longer apply the act. As it can no longer be sanctioned, the community institutions are compelled to replace the act.

§ 379c. National courts can refuse to apply express provisions of Community law which the Court of Justice has declared to be invalid. The national court cannot change Community law. They cannot give rulings when a Community act contains mistakes or omissions. Such unlawfulness cannot be removed merely by the fact that the Court of Justice, in proceedings under EEC article 177, rules that the contested provision is in whole or in part invalid. It is then up to the competent institutions of the Community to adopt the measures necessary to correct the illegal situation. [385]

§ 379d. The adoption of an invalid act constitutes a wrongful act which may lead to a suit for damages (see below § 450-455). The Court will grant such damages only when in adopting the invalid act the Community has manifestly and gravely disregarded the limits on the exercise of its powers (see below § 476). When an order to pay a specific charge has been declared invalid, we should assume that a refusal to repay the charge would constitute a violation of a superior rule of law, sufficiently flagrant for an action for non-contractual liability to be successful. In the *Nippon Seiko Case* the applicant claimed compensation for an anti-dumping duty, which it considered illegal, in a claim brought under EEC Article 215. The Court of Justice held, that *'as regards the amounts already paid ... the annulment* (of the regulation concerned) *has removed the obligation to pay them'*.[386] After that statement it finds no need to give any further ruling on these payments. Apparently, it considers a statement that the payments had no basis in law to be sufficient for the applicant's claim.

In the *Second Granaria Case* the Court of Justice made abundantly clear that national authorities are obliged to apply rules of Community law as long as the Court of Justice has not expressly declared them invalid. [387] Thus, the

---

384. *Schwarze Case* (16/65), 1 Dec. 1965, [1965] ECR 886; 11 Jur. (1965) 1117; 11 Rec. (1965) 1094; [1966] CMLR 186; CCH para 8039 (p. 7555). See also Advocate-General Gand in his opinion on the same case, 11 Rec. (1965) 1109, 1110; [1966] CMLR 184, 185.
385. *Ruckdeschel Case* (117/76, 16/77), 19 Oct. 1977, consideration 13, [1977] ECR 1771, 1772; CCH para 8457; *Moulins Pont-à-Mousson Case* (124/76, 20/77), 19 Oct. 1977, considerations 27, 28, [1977] ECR 1813; CCH para 8458.
386. *Nippon Seiko Case* (119/77), 29 March 1979, considerations 31, 32.
387. *Second Granaria Case* (101/78), 13 Feb. 1979, considerations 4-8.

Court's decision on the illegality of an act, though it may be a basis for a suit for damages against the national authorities if they subsequently apply the unlawful act, cannot serve as a ground for claiming compensation from the national authorities for their action prior to the Court's judgement.

III. JUDICIAL REVIEW OF ACTS OF MEMBER STATES

A. INTRODUCTION[388]

§ 380. International organizations cannot force their Members to obey their rules. As the constituent States wield the actual power, international organizations have little opportunity of influencing their behaviour. But they have nevertheless always attempted to do so and have consequently developed various supervisory procedures by means of which they can bring some pressure to bear on their Members. Most of these procedures are based on collecting and discussing reports on the Members' performance of their duties. [389]

In the European Communities supervision of the Members' behaviour is largely a task entrusted to the Commission, but the official establishment of breaches of Member States' obligations is assigned to the Court of Justice.

The Communities enforce their rules more effectively than other international organizations, in particular as result of the greater homogeneity of their Members and their stronger institutional structure. Notwithstanding this, the majority of breaches is not contested (see below § 389). The Commission voluntarily restricts its actions against breaches of Treaty obligations to the most important cases.

Member States may also institute proceedings against fellow Member States acting in breach of their Treaty obligations; but in practice they rarely do so. For political reasons they prefer to leave the initiative to the Commission.

The Court has also accepted an additional means of control instigated by individuals, in particular to check on minor breaches which would not be pursued by the Commission. This control is of great importance (see below § 435, 439).

§ 381. The Court of Justice can review only those acts of the Member States which they perform in their capacity as elements of the Communities, that is the acts which stem from their obligations under Community law and which therefore form part of Community law to some degree. Again, 'act' should be construed in a broader sense to include a failure to act.

In the beginning of this chapter much attention was devoted to the question of what acts taken by Community institutions are susceptible to judicial review. It would be difficult to answer the same question as to what acts of

---

388. See also above § 194.
389. See Schermers, (op. cit., note 2) Vol. 2, Chapter 10, pp. 557-621.

the Member States are susceptible to Community review as Community law does not usually require the Member States to take a specific kind of act. It rather prescribes that they are either obliged to achieve particular results, remaining free as to the choice of form and methods existing in their own legal systems, or, that they are prohibited from interfering with those rules of Community law directly applicable to their citizens. All manner of behaviour may constitute a breach of these obligations (see below § 392).

§ 382.   It was noted above (§ 254) that the legality of Community acts can be challenged only on specific grounds. No such limitations exist for the judicial review of the acts of the Member States. The Court has unlimited jurisdiction which means that any ground of illegality may be invoked.

In the judicial review of Community acts (see above sub II) the proceedings before the Court of Justice differ somewhat depending on whether they are instituted by the Member States, by other institutions or by private parties, but these differences are not fundamental. The judicial review of the acts of the Member States, on the other hand, varies distinctly according to who has instituted the proceedings.

The procedure of a review activated by the Commission will be discussed in section B, that by other Member States in section C and finally that by individuals in section D.

B.   REVIEW PROCEDURE INITIATED BY THE COMMISSION[390]

1.   Scope of the review

a.   SURVEY OF TREATY PROVISIONS

(i)   Supervision by the Commission

§ 383.   The Commission of the European Communities is entrusted with the task of ensuring the application of the Treaties, and of the measures taken by

---

390.   J. Mertens de Wilmars and I.M. Verougstraete, *Proceedings against Member States for Failure to Fulfil their Obligations*, 7 CMLRev. (1970), pp. 385-406; Manfred Zuleeg in Jahrbuch des öffentlichen Rechts der Gegenwart, neue Folge, Band 20 (1971), pp. 52-63; Jean-Victor Louis, *Ordre public communautaire et interêts des Etats dans la procédure en constatation de manquements*, in Miscellanea W.J. Ganshof van der Meersch, Brussels 1972, pp. 225-239; Hans Peter Ipsen, *Europäisches Gemeinschaftsrecht*, Tübingen 1972, pp. 233-237; Pierre Pescatore, *Responsabilité des états membres en cas de manquement aux règles communautaires*, Il Foro Padano, No. 10, Oct. 1972, 24 pages; Christian Tomuschat, *La Contribution de la Cour de justice des Communautés européennes au règlement des conflits entre états membres*, RGDIP 1974, pp. 40-59; Philippe Cahier, *Les Articles 169 et 171 du traité instituant la CEE à travers la pratique de la Commission et la jurisprudence de la Cour*, 10 CDE (1974), pp. 3-38; H.A.H. Audretsch, *Supervision in European Community Law*, North Holland, 1978; Ami Barav, *Failure of Member States to fulfil their obligations under Community Law*, 12 CMLRev. (1975), pp. 369-383.

the Community institutions. [391] This task includes the continuous supervision of the actions undertaken by the Member States. The EEC and Euratom Treaties expressly empower the Commission, within limits laid down by the Council, to collect any information and carry out any checks required for the performance of its tasks. [392] The Commission thus performs an active role of supervision. If it considers that a Member State has failed to fulfil an obligation under one of the Treaties, it first of all consults with the State concerned. [393]

In many cases these informal consultations lead to a termination of the breach; if not, the Commission 'shall give the State concerned the opportunity to submit its observations'. [394] In practice this means the opening of formal discussions between the Commission and the Member State in order to find a way of ending the breach of the Treaty. Such formal discussions are opened by means of an official letter in which the Commission defines the substance of its case, specifying the action or omission of which the State is accused and the rule of Community law which is considered to be violated. [395] When the formal discussions do not culminate in the desired result, the Commission has to act. The courses of action available differ between the ECSC Treaty on the one hand and the EEC and Euratom Treaties on the other.

In all three Treaties the procedure is not necessarily a means of rectifying an improper behaviour by the States. It may equally well stem from differences of opinion on the interpretation of Community law. [396] It then serves the purpose of promoting uniform application of the law.

(ii) ECSC Article 88

§ 384. Under ECSC Article 88 the Commission can record the failure of the Member State in a reasoned decision. In that decision a time limit is set during which the State still has the opportunity of fulfilling its obligation. If it fails to do so, economic sanctions can be taken. The Member State has a right to institute proceedings against the reasoned decision before the Court of Justice. In practice Member States have always done so. The final decision whether a Treaty obligation has been violated or not therefore lies with the Court of Justice.

The decision of the Commission taken under ECSC Article 88 differs to a certain extent from other ECSC decisions. It may only record a breach; it cannot create new rules of law, nor can it further specify existing rules of law. In the *Second Publication of Transport Tariffs Case* the High Authority had ordered the Netherlands Government to comply with its obligations under

---

391. EEC Art. 155; see also ECSC Art. 8.
392. EEC Art. 213; see also Art. 47 ECSC and thereon Ipsen (*op. cit.*, note 390), p. 234.
393. This is the general rule; some articles provide for special procedures, see EEC Artt. 93, 180 and 225; Euratom Artt. 38, 82. For the proceedings under Art. 93 EEC see Mertens de Wilmars and Verougstraete (*op. cit.*, note 390) pp. 395-398. On the precontentious phase, see also Cahier (*op. cit.*, note 390) pp. 5-15.
394. EEC Art. 169(1); ECSC Art. 88(1).
395. Louis (*op. cit.*, note 390) pp. 226-239.
396. See Mertens de Wilmars and Verougstraete (*op. cit.*, note 390) p. 401.

ECSC Article 70 in one of four expressly indicated ways. The Netherlands government denied the right of the High Authority to specify the obligations of the Treaty in a procedure under ECSC Article 88. The Court of Justice supported this view and held:

'Neither the wording nor the general structure of Article 88 allow the High Authority to rely on its provisions to exercise a power to make regulations ... Article 88 gives the High Authority only a power to record that a State has failed to fulfil an obligation under the Treaty.' [397]

§ 385.   Furthermore, the proceedings before the Court of Justice against decisions under Article 88 differ from the action for the annulment of other decisions. The Article expressly provides that the Court has unlimited jurisdiction, which means that there is no presumption of the validity of the decision and that the applicant does not have to demonstrate one of the grounds of illegality, specifically mentioned. The Court may look at all arguments for and against the validity of the decision and in its ruling is not limited to either declaring the decision valid or invalid. It may replace the decision by another of its own making.

§ 386.   In the *Railway Tariffs Case* the German Government submitted that the Court, as a consequence of its full jurisdiction, was also entitled to examine the legality of the legal rules whose violation was alleged. The Court rejected this view, holding:

'It cannot be argued that the authors of the Treaty intended to give a suspensory effect to actions under Article 88, for such a derogation from the general principle of Article 39 cannot be presumed from the silence of the text.
     Moreover, the particular scope of Article 88 runs counter to the proposition that an action under the second paragraph of that article can have suspensory effect. Since the decision taken by the High Authority under the first paragraph of that article was declaratory in nature, to accept that Application 19/58 has such effect would mean suspending not the execution of the said decision, but the binding effect either of the relevant provisions of the Treaty or of previous decisions of the High Authority, execution of which is concerned in the present case.' [398]

(iii)   EEC and Euratom provisions

§ 387.   Under EEC Article 169 and Euratom Article 141 the Commission delivers a reasoned opinion to a Member State if it considers that it has failed

397. *Second Publication of Transport Tariffs Case* (25/59), 15 July 1960, [1960] ECR 374; 6 Jur. (1960) 784; 6 Rec. (1960) 760. This statement was confirmed in Case 11/69 (the ECSC part of the *Rediscount Rate Case*).
398. *Railway Tariffs Case* (3/59), 8 March 1960, [1960] ECR 58, 59; 6 Jur. (1960) 133; 6 Rec. (1960) 130, 131. See also below § 413.

to fulfil an obligation under the Treaty. In that opinion a time limit is set for the State to repair the situation. If it fails to comply with the opinion within the time limit, the Commission may bring the matter before the Court of Justice. If the Court finds that the Member State has failed to fulfil an obligation, the State is required to take the necessary measures to comply with the judgment of the Court. [399] The Treaties do not provide for further sanctions.

§ 388. Apart from the general procedure contained in EEC Article 169 and Euratom Article 141, the Treaties contain a few articles permitting the Commission to bring specific breaches of the Treaty before the Court of Justice, without first delivering a reasoned opinion. In these cases some other form of consultation between the Member State and the Commission has been provided for.[400] If the matters is of such a confidential or urgent nature that a reasoned opinion is not considered appropriate, then the matter is referred directly to the Court. [401]

b. NUMBER OF CASES

§ 389. Since the entry into force of the EEC Treaty until 1 January 1979, the Commission has initiated formal discussions on breaches of the Treaty in some 750 cases. [402] The number of cases which were terminated at the informal stage is even greater [403] , and the number of breaches not contested at all by the Commission is greater still. It is estimated that cases falling under the latter group are twice as numerous as all the others taken together. [404]

About six percent of the formally discussed cases finally led to a decision by the Court of Justice. [405] This percentage has increased slightly recently.

Under the ECSC Treaty actions against States for breaches of the Treaty are much less frequent. Prior to 31 December 1969 the Commission (High

---

399. EEC Art. 171. On the proceedings before the Court, see also Cahier (*op. cit.*, note 390) pp. 15-25; Diane de Bellescize, *L'article 169 du traité de Rome, et l'efficacité du contrôle communautaire sur les manquements des états membres*, 13 RTDE (1977), pp. 173-213; Gérard Nafilyan, *La position des états members et les recours en manquement des articles 169 CCE et 141 CEEA*, 13 RTDE (1977), pp. 214-243.
400. EEC Art. 93; Euratom Artt. 38, 82.
401. EEC Art. 225; Euratom Art. 38.
402. The Commission does not always report separately on the number of cases initiated, the number of reasoned opinions issued, the number of cases brought before the Court and the number of cases decided by the Court. The following numbers have been published: 214 cases initiated until 31 December 1969 (Fourth General Report para 553; Answer of the Commission to parliamentary question Nr. 501/69 by Mr. Vredeling, OJ Nr.C 73, p. 1 of 18 June 1970); almost 50 cases a year between 1 Jan. 1970 and 1 Jan. 1976 (see Fifth to Ninth General Report); 90 in 1976, 68 in 1977 and 100 in 1978 (see Tenth to Twelfth General Report.
403. Fourth General Report, para 553.
404. Audretsch (*op. cit.*, note 390), p. 161.
405. Until 31 Dec. 1978 37 cases had been decided by the Court, 15 were pending, see Twelfth General Report, p. 368 table 2.

Authority) initiated about 20 cases.[406]   In four of them it finally issued a decision which came before the Court of Justice.[407]   After 1 January 1970 the Commission initiated less than one case a year on the breach of ECSC obligations by Member States.[408]   None of these cases have as yet reached the Court.

Under the Euratom Treaty only one case concerning a breach by a State has come before the Court.[409]

c. TIME INVOLVED

§ 390. The time taken up by informal discussions between the Commission and the violating Member State varies considerably. In the cases which finally came before the Court of Justice the period of time between the date on which the breach occurred and the commencement of the formal discussions ranged from less than a month[410] to 4 or 5 years.[411]

The formal discussions themselves can be finished within a few months[412] or even within a week[413], but often take longer.[414]   In most cases which finally came before the Court the period of formal negotiations was from 4 to 12 months.

In the reasoned opinion the Commission usually grants a relatively short period of time during which the State may remedy the situation to prevent the Commission having to take proceedings in the Court. In an urgent case the period may be less than a week. Usually it is a periode of some months which may be extended after mutual consultation. With extensions included these time limits often amount to less than 6 months, and generally to less than a year.[415]   In two exceptional cases, where national legislation was pending, the time limit exceeded two years.[416]

---

406. Fourth General Report, para 553; Answer of the Commission to parliamentary question Nr. 310/69 by Mr. Vredeling, OJ Nr C 159, p. 6 of 12 Dec. 1969.
407. For a list of cases under Article 88 ECSC, see Annex II.
408. See General Reports. There were none in 1976, 1977 and 1978.
409. *Euratom Case*, (7/71) 14 Dec. 1971, [1971] ECR 1003; [1972] CMLR 453.
410. *Sea Fisheries Case* (61/77), 16 Feb. 1978, [1978] ECR 422.
411. Four years in the *Cocoa Beans Case* (28/69), 15 April 1970, [1970] ECR 187; [1971] CMLR 448; five years in the *Euratom Case* (7/71), 14 Dec. 1971, [1971] ECR 1015. In the latter case the legality of the action was disputed, due to the length of time which had passed, see below § 426.
412. See *Pork Case* (7/61), 19 Dec. 1961, [1961] ECR 317; 7 Jur. (1961) 671; 7 Rec. (1961) 639; [1962] CMLR 39; CCH para 8001; *Premiums for Grubbing Fruit Trees Case* (30/72), 8 Feb. 1973, [1973] ECR 161. In the *Potatoes Case* (68/76), 16 March 1977, [1977] ECR 515 the formal discussions took less than three months.
413. *Sea Fisheries Case* (see above note 410).
414. 21 Months in the *Wool Imports Case* (7/69), 10 March 1970, [1970] ECR 111; [1970] CMLR 97; CCH para 8086 and *Cocoa Beans Case* (28/69), 15 April 1970, [1970] ECR 187; [1971] CMLR 448; CCH para 8088; more than two and a half years in the *Vineyards Registers Case* (33/69), 4 March 1970, [1970] ECR 93; [1971] CMLR 466; CCH para 8087.
415. *The Wine Import Case* (117/75) was brought before the Court of Justice approximately one month after the date on which the Commission declared France in default, see Ninth General Report para 521, p. 284.
416. *First Art Treasures Case* (7/68), 10 Dec. 1968, [1968] ECR 423; 14 Jur. (1968) 589;

A Court ruling is given 5 to 13 months after the Commission has brought the case before the Court [417] , but in case of urgency interim measures may be taken. In the *Sea Fisheries Case* such interim measures took two months, but this was mainly because the parties, by mutual agreement, twice requested an extension of the time-limits fixed by the Court. The total procedure, from the first formal steps of the Commission until the decision of the Court of Justice, has thus taken an average of almost two and a half years. [418]

The length of time involved is usually not so much due to differences of opinion with regard to the breach, but rather to the cumbersome nature of the national legislative procedures which, even when a solution of principle has already been found, often extend over years. [419]

§ 391. These long periods of time demonstrate one of the shortcomings of the Article 169-procedure: short term breaches can hardly be remedied. The Commission may bring a breach before the Court of Justice only when the State does not comply with the reasoned opinion within the period laid down. In other words no further action by the Commission is possible if the State terminates the breach during the period of informal or formal discussions, or even thereafter, as long as the time limit granted in the reasoned opinion has not elapsed. In practice the Commission deals with this problem by requiring in its reasoned opinion not only a termination of the breach, but also a compensation for the harmful effects caused by it. If, for example, a State has illegally levied an import duty for a short period of time, the Commission may no longer be able to require the withdrawal of the illegal measures as they have already been terminated by the time of its reasoned opinion, but it may still require in its reasoned opinion repayment of all duties, illegally paid to the importers concerned [420], and may request a declaratory judgment of the Court of Justice on the period in the past, which may then be used as a basis for decisions on damages by national courts (see below § 431, 432).

2. Prerequisites for Court action

a. THE EXISTENCE OF A BREACH

(i) Act causing the breach [421]

§ 392. The breach may be brought about by any act on the part of the State, not only by those taken by the government of the State (see below

---

14 Rec. (1968) 617; [1969] CMLR p. 1; CCH para 8057, (over three and a half years) and *Cocoa Beans Case* (28/69), 15 April 1970, [1970] ECR 187; [1971] CMLR 448; CCH para 8088 (almost two and a half years).
417. In the *Agricultural Tractor Case* (69/77), 21 Sept. 1978, [1978] ECR 1749; [1979] 1 CMLR 206, the Court ruling came after 15 months.
418. As an average of 33 cases.
419. Sixth General Report para 581; Seventh General Report paras 589, 590; Eighth General Report paras 473, 474; Ninth General Report paras 521, 522.
420. *Kohlegesetz Case* (70/72), 12 July 1973, considerations 12 and 13, [1973] ECR 829; [1973] CMLR 764; CCH para 8217. See also below § 404.
421. Barav (*op. cit.*, note 390) pp. 372-378.

§ 420-424). A failure to act is as much a breach as a positive act. [422]

It will be seen below (cf. quotation from the *Kohlegesetz Case* § 404) that not only the breach itself but also its consequences, past and future, may be the subject of the action.

§ 393.   Often a breach is caused by the existence of a national law which is contrary to Community law. In such cases the action against the Member State closely resembles an action contesting the validity of that law. The outcome of the case may be that the Court of Justice declares the law to be illegal (it cannot actually annul acts pertaining to the national legal order). However, the proceedings are usually not directed against that law but against the breach resulting from it. The expediency of not acting against the law itself was demonstrated in the *Tax Refund in Italy Case*. [423]   In Italy there existed a law, Law No. 103, which provided for the refund of taxes on exported steel products. The Commission considered such a refund as violating the EEC Treaty and instituted proceedings against Italy. It issued a reasoned opinion explaining that Italy had failed in the obligations incumbent upon it under Article 96 of the EEC Treaty by refunding taxes on export. The Italian Government alleged it had complied with that opinion by submitting a bill to the Italian Parliament which was intended to replace Law 103. The Commission was of the opinion that the bill was not substantially different from Law 103 and would not lead to a termination of the breach. It therefore proceeded with its action under Article 169 and brought the case before the Court. The Italian Government pleaded that the case was inadmissible because its substance was different from the substance of the administrative proceedings. In its submission the Commission should have reopened the discussions and issued a new reasoned opinion. The Court considered that the Commission's allegations against Italy, both in the administrative and in the judicial proceedings, concerned the actual application of the system of refunding taxes on export rather than the legal provisions on which the system might be based. As the system of refunds had not been terminated within the time limit granted in the reasoned opinion the appeal was considered admissible and the Court found that Italy had failed to fulfil an obligation under the EEC Treaty.

§ 394.   Five years later in the *Wool Import Case* the situation was somewhat different. Again at issue was an Italian law contrary to Community law. This time it concerned a law imposing a tax on imported wool. Italy had replaced the law by a new and different one after the Commission had brought the matter before the Court. The Italian Government pleaded that the Commission should stop its action before the Court as it had lost its substance on the replacement of the old law. The Commission was uncertain whether the new law sufficiently remedied the situation. It demonstrated in its pleadings that it

---

422. *Exports Rebate Case* (31/69), 17 Feb. 1970, consideration 9, [1970] ECR 32; [1970] CMLR 188; CCH para 8097.
423. *Tax Refund in Italy Case* (45/64), 1 Dec. 1965, [1965] ECR 864; 11 Jur. (1965) 1088, 1089; 11 Rec. (1965) 1068; [1966] CMLR 97 ff; CCH para 8038 (p. 7541).

had no interest in the action other than to obtain a termination of the specific breach at stake. Both parties asked the Court to rule on the situation as it existed, that is to take account of the new law as well. The Court considered that this meant a change in the action as originally brought. Any consideration of the new law, on which no administrative discussions had been held, would infringe the rights enjoyed by Italy under Article 169. Therefore the case as pleaded by the Commission was held to be inadmissible. [424]

From the two cases it may be concluded that the Commission's action against the behaviour of a State is not normally affected by the amendment or repeal of a national law, unless such an amendment or repeal substantially alters the situation under discussion before the Court.

§ 395. In the situation described above the Court indicated that it is not the text of the law, but the actual misapplication of the Treaty which is conclusive. This leads one to the question whether a law contrary to the Treaty is tantamount to a breach, or is the decisive factor whether that law is actually applied or not? In the *Cocoa Beans Case* the Court of Justice held that the alleged Treaty infringement could only exist to the extent that the disputed national rules had been actually applied. [425]

From this case it might be concluded that the breach should not be merely potential. [426]

A domestic law contrary to a Community obligation may, however, constitute a breach, even if it is not applied, because it may influence the behaviour of people who rely on the law being applied. This was the case in the *Marine Labour Code Case* against France. The Commission acted under EEC Article 169, claiming that France had violated its obligations by not amending its Marine Labour Code which conflicted with EEC Article 48 and with EEC Regulation 1612/68. The Commission considered that both Article 48 and Regulation 1612/68 had direct, effect and should be applied by the French courts. This could mean that in an actual case the French courts would set aside the French Marine Labour Code, so that EEC law would be properly applied notwithstanding the conflicting French legislation, but there would be no guarantee of this. The French government submitted that it had issued administrative instructions to its naval authorities not to apply the disputed provisions to Community nationals. This made their actual application still less likely.

The question then was, whether France had failed to fulfil its EEC obligations by having a law which conflicted with the Treaty or whether an actual case should be awaited. As to this question the Court held:

'It follows that although the objective legal position is clear, namely, that Article 48 and Regulation No 1612/68 are directly applicable in the terri-

---

424. *Wool Imports Case* (7/69), 10 March 1970, [1970] ECR 116, 117; [1970] CMLR 108, 109; CCH para 8086. See on this case Louis (*op. cit.*, note 390) pp. 227-230.
425. *Cocoa Beans Case* (28/69), 15 April 1970, consideration 14, [1970] ECR 195; [1971] CMLR 458; CCH para 8088.
426. Barav (*op. cit.*, note 390) p. 374, quoting Kovar.

tory of the French Republic, nevertheless the maintenance in these circumstances of the wording of the Code du Travail Maritime gives rise to an ambiguous state of affairs by maintaining, as regards those subject to the law who are concerned, a state of uncertainity as to the possibilities available to them of relying on Community law.

...

The uncertainty created by the unamended maintenance of the wording of Article 3 of the Code du Travail Maritime constitutes such an obstacle'. [427]

The Court concluded that France had failed to fulfil its obligations under the Treaty.

(ii) Breach of obligations

§ 396. Article 169 can be initiated whenever the Commission considers that a Member State has failed to fulfil an *obligation under this Treaty*. This includes all obligations under Community law as the entire legal system falls under the Treaty. [428]

But does it also include obligations arising from *additional treaties* which may be subsequently concluded? It is to be expected that such additional treaties will assume increasing importance. As the original Treaties age they will become increasingly unequal to the exigencies of the changing economic situation. Formally amended provisions of the Treaties will of course be covered by the provisions of Article 169, but as amendment is in practice extremely difficult, it is to be expected that many alterations will be brought about by means of additional treaties or conventions, such as those provided for in EEC Article 220. For the sake of consistency in Community law it is important that such supplementary treaties fall under the jurisdiction of the Court of Justice in the same way as the original ones.

The Court has had no cases on this question, which, therefore, remains open. [429]

§ 397. To what extent does a breach of the *general principles of law*, such as a violation of human rights, constitute a breach of an obligation under Community law? In this case it is essential to distinguish in what capacity the Member State has committed the breach (see above § 194 and § 381). If it is its capacity as an individual and independent State then the Community institutions cannot be involved. The fact that the Communities accept certain principles of law as binding in the performance of Community functions, does not legally oblige the Member States to accept the same principles in the exercise of other functions. Nor does it entitle the Community institutions to interfere with other tasks of their Member States.

427. *Marine Labour Code Case* (167/73), 4 April 1974, considerations 41 and 47, [1974] ECR 372, 373; [1974] 2 CMLR 230; CCH para 8270.
428. Mertens de Wilmars and Verougstraete (*op. cit.*, note 390) p. 388.
429. Pescatore (*op. cit.*, note 58) pp. 144, 145.

Only if the breach of the general principles of law is committed by a Member State in its capacity as an element of the Community, or in other words, in its performance of Community functions, can it amount to a breach of an obligation under Community law. In my opinion the Court of Justice is entitled to censure a Member State under EEC Article 169 if that State, for example, disregards human rights by its manner of collecting duties under the common customs tariff.

(iii) When must the breach exist?

§ 398. The text of Article 169 clearly demonstrates that its intention is to terminate breaches rather than to condemn States. If the breach is ended by compliance with the reasoned opinion no condemnation can follow. This leads one to the question of what the position is when a State, after the period prescribed in the reasoned opinion, belatedly remedies the situation. Is the Commission still free to continue its action before the Court?

In the *Pork Case* the Court of Justice stated:

'If the Member State does not comply with the opinion within the pre-scribed period, there is no question that the Commission has the right to obtain the Court's judgment on that Member State's failure to fulfil the 'obligations flowing from the Treaty.

In the present case, although it recognizes that the Italian Government finally respected its obligations, albeit after the expiry of the period re-ferred to above, the Commission retains an interest in obtaining a decision on the issue whether the failure occurred.' [430]

Because the Commission 'still retained an interest', the Court rendered a decision, in which it found that Italy had failed to fulfil an obligation under the EEC Treaty.

In practice the Commission usually withdraws the case when the breach is terminated during the course of the Court proceedings. [431]

§ 399. In the *Premiums for slaughtering cows Case* Italy was reproved for not paying the slaughter premiums. Italy submitted that the omission to pay the premium for non-marketing had become irremediable, because it would no longer be possible in reality to comply retroactively with obligations which should have been performed in the past. The action of the Commission had therefore lost its purpose. The Court of Justice did not accept that a breach which could not be remedied any more would no longer be subject to the procedure of Article 169, holding:

---

430. *Pork Case* (7/61), 19 Dec. 1961, [1961] ECR 326; 7 Jur. (1961) 692; 7 Rec. (1961) 653; [1962] CMLR 53-55; CCH para 8001 (pp. 7110, 7111).
431. Audretsch (*op. cit.*, note 390) p. 42. See, e.g., *Unloading Charges Case* (172/73), 1 May 1974, [1974] ECR 475, 476.

'The defendant cannot in any case be allowed to rely upon a *fait accompli* of which it is itself the author so as to escape judicial proceedings'. [432]

b. FORMAL DISCUSSIONS

§ 400. If the Commission considers that a Member State has failed to fulfil an obligation it delivers a reasoned opinion under the EEC and Euratom Treaties or a decision under the ECSC Treaty. In both cases, however, the State concerned must first be accorded the opportunity to submit its observations. The Commission will invite it to do so and may even repeat this invitation a number of times. [433]

In practice this leads to discussions, which are often detailed, between the Commission and the Member State.

Frequently these discussions persuade the Member State to terminate its breach in which case no further action is taken. The Commission may also abandon the action, if it is persuaded that no breach has in fact been committed. It cannot, however, take a decision signifying approval of any acts of the Member States. [434]

c. THE REASONED OPINION

(i) Designation of the breach

§ 401. In contrast to the judicial review of Community acts, where a specific act must be challenged, the review of the acts of the Member States is of a more general nature. It has within its ambit the entire behaviour of the Member States and may concern either a specific law, a group of laws or an omission to formulate legal rules.

It would be too vague to invoke 'the behaviour' or 'the legislation' of a State before the Court of Justice. The object of the action is, on this account, defined in greater detail in the reasoned opinion of the Commission in the case of the EEC and in the decision of the Commission in the ECSC. The Commission has a margin of discretion in formulating its reasoned opinion (see below § 425-428) for it need not attack the entire breach, but may indicate that it will be satisfied with particular measures to be taken by the State concerned.

The reasoned opinion, or the decision under the ECSC Treaty, serves as the basis for the possible ensuing Court proceedings; but since the Court has unlimited jurisdiction it may consider every aspect of the breach, even those which are not specifically denoted in the reasoned opinion.

---

432. *Premiums for slaughtering cows Case* (39/72), 7 Feb. 1973, consideration 10, [1973] ECR 112; [1973] CMLR 454; CCH para 8201.
433. See, e.g., *Slaughter of animals Case* (147/77), 6 June 1978, consideration 5, [1978] ECR 1312; [1978] 3 CMLR 431.
434. *First Limburg Coalmines Case* (17/57) 4 Feb. 1959, [1959] ECR 7; 5 Jur. (1958-59) 26; 5 Rec. (1958-59) 25.

§ 402. In the *Pork Case* the question was raised as to what extent the Commission is obliged to furnish the reasons which render the disputed behaviour illegal. In that case Italy contested the validity of the reasoned opinion, because it did not include an examination of the arguments advanced by the Italian Government. The Court of Justice then answered that a reasoned opinion under Article 169 must be held to contain legally sufficient grounds when it presents *'a coherent statement of the reasons which led the Commission to believe that the State in question has failed to fulfil an obligation under the Treaty'.* [435]

Thus a refutation of the arguments advanced by the State concerned is not necessary.

(ii) Grant of an opportunity for rectification

§ 403. In his conclusions in the *Pork Case* Advocate-General Lagrange submitted:

'The reasoned opinion referred to in Article 169 in reality has a dual purpose. First, it must set out the reasons of fact and of law for which the Commission considers that the State concerned has failed to fulfil one of its obligations and, secondly, it must inform the government of the State of the measures which the Commission considers necessary to bring the failure to an end. This second purpose of the opinion follows from the terms of the second paragraph of Article 169:
"If the State concerned does not comply with the opinion ..."
Therefore it does not suffice for the Commission to establish the failure to fulfil an obligation; it must, in addition, indicate the means calculated to bring it to an end.' [436]

The Treaties do not specify a particular *time limit* within which the reasoned opinion must be complied with. The Commission exercises full discretion, but it must be assumed that a reasonable time limit should be granted. [437] The Court decided under the ECSC Treaty that the time limit may be shorter than the time limit normally granted for bringing an action against Community acts. [438]

§ 404. It was noted above (§ 384) that the Commission may not designate a particular *method* for terminating the breach in its decision under ECSC Article 88. *A fortiori* it cannot do so in its reasoned opinion under EEC Article 169. It may only indicate ways and possible solutions. But it may

435. *Pork Case* (7/61), 19 Dec. 1961, [1961] ECR 327; 7 Jur. (1961) 693; 7 Rec. (1961) 654; [1962] CMLR 54; CCH para 8001 (p. 7110).
436. *Pork Case* (7/61), 19 Dec. 1961, [1961] ECR 334; 7 Jur. (1961) 709; 7 Rec. (1961) 670; CCH para 8001 (p. 7116).
437. Audretsch (*op. cit.*, note 390) p. 29.
438. *Railway Tariffs Case* (3/59), 8 March 1960, [1960] ECR 61, 62; 6 Jur. (1960) 137, 138; 6 Rec. (1960) 134, 135.

require the termination of the breach. In practice, the request to take specific measures and the requirement to terminate a breach of the Treaty cannot be entirely separated. Sometimes the Commission may succeed in pleading that the failure to take specific measures constitutes a breach of the Treaty. In the *Kohlegesetz Case* Germany had granted aid which the Commission considered to be contrary to the Treaty. In a procedure under Article 93, which in this respect is similar to that of Article 169, the Commission held that Germany failed to fulfil its obligations by not requiring repayment of the aid wrongly received by the recipients. The German Government submitted that under Article 171 the *Member State* is required to take the necessary measures to comply with the judgment of the Court. The Commission, therefore, could not order that particular internal measures should be taken and could only request termination of any possible breach. Furthermore, a judgment obliging Germany to require the repayment of the aid would in fact be against the eighteen undertakings which had received aid, which had not participated in the case and which could not even have the chance of intervening. This would be procedurally unjust as a case between a Community institution and a Member State should affect only the two parties to the action.

The Court did not share these opinions. It considered that the Commission is competent to require the amendment or abolition of illegal aid and that such requirements could only be of practical effect if they were to include an obligation to require repayment of any aid granted in breach of the Treaty. The Court then continued:

'Moreover, an application from the Commission, within the scope of the procedure under Articles 169 to 171, for a declaration that in omitting to take specific measures, a Member State has failed to fulfil an obligation under the Treaty, is equally admissible. Since the aim of the Treaty is to achieve the practical elimination of infringements and the consequences thereof, past and future, it is a matter for the Community authorities whose task it is to ensure that the requirements of the Treaty are observed to determine the extent to which the obligation of the Member State concerned may be specified in the reasoned opinions or decisions delivered under Article 169 and 93(2) respectively and in applications addressed to the Court'. [439]

The reasoning of this case, which the Commission lost on other grounds, seems acceptable. The harm suffered by the individual firms may be less than was suggested by the German Government. In an earlier series of cases, when the Court had authorized the return of illegal subsidies paid by the High Authority, it also granted damages to the firms concerned. It considered that the granting and paying of subsidies contrary to the Treaty, followed by a demand for their return, constituted a wrongful act for which pecuniary reparation should be ordered under ECSC Article 40. [440]

439. *Kohlegesetz Case* (70/72), 12 July 1973, consideration 13, [1973] ECR 829; [1973] CMLR 764; CCH para 8217.

Depending on the degree of 'innocence' of the firms concerned, these damages may come close to the amounts claimed back.

(iii) Legal status of the reasoned opinion

§ 405. The reasoned opinion forms part of the proceedings which may eventually lead to an action before the Court of Justice. This means that a separate action against the legality of a reasoned opinion is normally impossible. In the *First Lütticke Case* the Court stated that no action against the preliminary phase of the procedure of Article 169 was possible, as the measures adopted by the Commission in this phase of the proceedings had no binding effect. [441]

In the *Rediscount Rate Case* the Court held that the dispute on the legal validity of the reasoned opinion coincides with that of the action itself which the Commission had instituted before the Court pursuant to Article 169. [442] Normally this will be the case. Only when the Commission does not bring the case before the Court may the State concerned have a legal interest in a separate suit against the reasoned opinion. News of this opinion may have reached the press. If it is incorrect the State concerned may want a Court ruling. The reasoned opinion may create a situation of legal uncertainty which the State may wish to have terminated at short notice, especially if the Commission does not proceed to bring the matter before the Court.

In the *First Cement Convention Case* the Court considered that an act altering the legal position of the parties, thereby affecting their interests, can be challenged (see above § 245). This could be a reason for permitting the State involved to bring an action against a reasoned opinion if the Commission does not take the matter before the Court or at least not soon enough.

3. Alleged Justifications for breaches

§ 406. In the *First Publication of Transport Tariffs Case* the Court of Justice considered that against a decision of the High Authority under ECSC Article 88 not only all defences concerning the legality of the decision could be raised, but also all possible justifications for the failure to fulfil the obligations under the Treaty. [443] There is no reason why such justifications should not be permitted under the other Treaties since the Court has unlimited jurisdiction in such cases. The Member States have offered several reasons before the Court of Justice as justifications for their breaches of the Treaty.

---

440. *First Fives Lille Cail Case* (19, 21/60, 2, 3/61), 15 Dec. 1961, [1961] ECR 296, 297; 7 Jur. (1961) 624-626; 7 Rec. (1961) 590-592; [1962] CMLR 281-282; *Second Fives Lille Cail Case* (Laminoirs Case) (29, 31, 36, 39-47, 50, 51/63), 9 Dec. 1965, [1965] ECR 936-941; 11 Jur. (1965) 1230-1235; 11 Rec. (1965) 1156-1161 and 7 June 1966; 12 Jur. 1966) 205-207; 12 Rec. (1966) 202-204. See below § 453.
441. *First Lütticke Case* (48/65), 1 March 1966, [1966] ECR 27; 12 Jur. (1966) 39, 40; 12 Rec. (1966) 38, 39; [1966] CMLR 387; CCH para 8044 (p. 7603).
442. *Rediscount Rate Case* (6 and 11/69), 10 Dec. 1969, consideration 36, [1969] ECR 42; [1970] CMLR 67; CCH para 8105.
443. *First Publication of Transport Tariffs Case* (20/59), 15 July 1960, [1960] ECR 339; 6 Jur. (1960) 711; 6 Rec. (1960) 692.

a. STATEMENT OF RESERVATION

§ **407.** When the Council approved decision 66/532/EEC in July 1966 on the abolition of customs duties and quantitative restrictions for a large number of products, Italy made it clear that its assent was based on the understanding that it could continue payment of aid to its lead and zinc producers. As the decision was taken under Article 235 unanimity was required. The Italian government submitted that it had accepted the agreement with a reservation and that therefore the Commission could not act against Italy for a breach of the decision in so far as lead and zinc were concerned.

The Court considered that the decision was a Community act. It was an act of the Council, and did not constitute a multilateral treaty. Reservations were therefore impossible; the observations made during the preparation of the text were irrelevant as only the contents of the decision could be taken into account. [444]

b. AUTONOMY OF THE STATE

§ **408.** In 1968 the French Government established a special low rediscount rate to be charged by the *Banque de France* on medium and long term credits for exports to other Member States. As the low rate made exports cheaper the Commission considered them to be in violation of EEC Article 92. The French Government submitted that discount rates formed part of the monetary policy of a State, a field in which the Member States had retained their sovereignty. Notwithstanding this submission the Court considered that in any case the Member States, in the exercise of their reserved powers, may not unilaterally take measures prohibited by the Treaty. [445]

c. ABSENCE OF INTEREST

§ **409.** In the *Euratom Case* the French Government submitted that its behaviour had caused no damage at all to the other Member States and that therefore an action for breach of the Treaty (in this case an action under Euratom Article 141) was not justified. The Court considered, however, that Article 141 does not imply the precondition that an injury must be suffered by other Member States before the procedure can be implemented to establish a breach. [446]

---

444. *Lead and Zinc Case* (38/69), 18 Feb. 1970, considerations 5-13, [1970] ECR 55-5; [1970] CMLR 88-90; CCH para 8100. See also above § 8. The decision was confirmed in the *Premiums for slaughtering cows Case* (39/72), 7 Feb. 1973, consideration 22, [1973] ECR 115; [1973] CMLR 457; CCH para 8201, see also above § 8.
445. *Rediscount Rate Case* (6 and 11/69), 10 Dec. 1969, consideration 17, [1969] ECR 540; [1970] CMLR 67; CCH para 8105.
446. *Euratom Case* (7/71), 14 Dec. 1971, consideration 50, [1971] ECR 1021; [1972] CMLR 477. The Court gave a similar ruling in the *Metrology Case* (95/77), 11 April 1978, consideration 13, [1978] ECR 871; CCH para 8479.

In the *Marine Labour Code Case* the Court stressed that the Commission is not obliged to demonstrate any interest when acting under EEC Articles 155 and 169.[447] This does not mean, however, that some form of interest in a decision is never needed. This interest may be indirect; it may be to forestall future breaches or to provide a clarification of the law; but if the Court found that no interest could be established in a decision, it would declare the case inadmissible.[448]

410. What is the interest of the Commission? In the *Pork Case* two grounds of concern were mentioned: (1) the interest in the time limit of the reasoned opinion being observed, for this time limit would lose all force if a subsequent compliance were to lead to an immediate termination of the case, and (2) the interest in preventing a repetition of the breach, for if a case were to be simply struck off when a State ceased, or interrupted, the breach, the Commission might never be able to secure a clear condemnation of the particular practice in question. In the *Premiums for slaughtering cows Case* the Court added:

'In the face of both a delay in the performance of an obligation and a definite refusal, a judgment by the Court under Articles 169 and 171 of the Treaty may be of substantive interest as establishing the basis of a responsibility that a Member State can incur as a result of its default, as regards other Member States, the Community or private parties'.[449]

In the *Olive Oil Case* the Court examined on its own initiative whether the Commission had sufficient interest in continuing the action after the breach had been ended. It found that this was undoubtedly the case.[450]

1. ABSENCE OF FAULT

411. In the *Olive Oil Case* France was accused of violating Regulation 136/66. The Court of Justice considered that the Commission and the Council should have made explicit provisions when drafting that regulation to take account of the preference granted to Tunisia under Protocol 1/7, especially as an association agreement with Tunisia was contemplated. It held, that '*bearing in mind the equivocal nature of the situation thus brought about, the French Republic cannot be accused of any failure to fulfil its obligations*'.[451] The

---

447. *Marine Labour Code Case* (167/73), 4 April 1974, consideration 15, [1974] ECR 368, 369; [1974] 2 CMLR 227; CCH para 8270.
448. See Audretsch (*op. cit.*, note 390) pp. 40-46.
449. *Premiums for slaughtering cows Case* (39/72) 7 Feb. 1973, consideration 11, [1973] ECR 112; [1973] CMLR 454, 455; CCH para 8201.
450. *Olive Oil Case* (26/69), 9 July 1970, consideration 13, [1970] ECR 576; [1973] CMLR 458; CCH para 8077.
451. *Olive Oil Case* (26/69), 9 July 1970, consideration 32, [1970] ECR 578; [1970] CMLR 461; CCH para 8103 (p. 7140). See also below § 418.

French Government concluded from this case that there could be no failure under Article 169 when the State concerned was not at fault and it raised this as a defence in the *Euratom Case*. Advocate-General Roemer then discussed the question whether the establishment of a fault committed by the State concerned is required under Article 169 or not. He concluded that Article 169 'is concerned not with guilt and morality but simply with the clarification of the law'. [452] The Court of Justice did not expressly discuss this point, but it seems beyond doubt that it will adopt the same position. If the Commission is not obliged to establish fault, then the absence of fault cannot justify the conduct of the State concerned. [453]

e. EXCEPTIONAL CIRCUMSTANCES

§ **412.** In some cases the defendent States submitted that their acts were justified by special circumstances, foreseen in the Treaty. Between 1958 and 1960 Belgium and Luxembourg increased their special tax on the import of gingerbread because of serious difficulties in this particular sector of the economic activity. When the Commission acted under Article 169 the two Governments requested an authorization for their special measures, at that time possible under EEC Article 226. The Commission was prepared to entertain such a request, but only on the condition that the special tax should be suspended until a decision on the authorization could be taken. As this condition was not accepted the case came before the Court. [454]

In 1960 Italy violated the EEC Treaty by prohibiting all imports of pork for two months. When the Commission had already issued a reasoned opinion under Article 169, the Italian Government requested an authorization under Article 226 due to serious economic difficulties. The Commission considered that this request could not have suspensive effect on its action under Article 169 and took the matter to the Court. [455] In both the above-mentioned cases the Governments submitted that the Court could not condemn them before a decision on their requests under Article 226 had been taken, as the purpose of the Article 169 procedure is not to establish a condemnation of States but to eliminate a breach of the Treaty. An authorization under Article 226 would eliminate the breach concerned. Italy even submitted that its request for an authorization presented a means of compliance with the reasoned opinion of the Commission as it would lead to a termination of the breach of the Treaty.

The Court of Justice did not accept these submissions. It considered that a request for authorization to derogate from the obligations of the Treaty can-

---

452. *Euratom Case* (7/71), 14 Dec. 1971, Opinion A-G, [1971] ECR 1034; [1972] CMLR 469.
453. See Audretsch (*op. cit.*, note 390) pp. 70, 71 and further literature quoted there.
454. *Gingerbread Case* (2, 3/62), 14 Dec. 1962, [1962] ECR 429, 430; 8 Jur. (1962) 862 863; 8 Rec. (1962) 824, 825; [1963] CMLR 214; CCH para 8004.
455. *Pork Case* (7/61), 19 Dec. 1961, [1961] ECR 326, 327; 7 Jur. (1961) 692-694; 7 Rec. (1961) 653-655; [1962] CMLR 53-55; CCH para 8001.

not justify illegal unilateral measures. Article 169 would be devoid of its meaning if its application could be frustrated by a request for legalization. [456]

f. INVALIDITY OF THE INFRINGED RULE

§ 413. Can a State, accused of the breach of a rule of Community law, dispute the validity of that law in a procedure under Article 169? Or, in other words, can the plea of illegality be invoked in such procedures? As was noted above the Court of Justice does not admit the plea of illegality in such cases (see above, § 360). Nonetheless, a number of arguments could be made both for and against the use of the plea. On the one hand, it would be incorrect to find fault with a State for the breach of a rule which may be invalid; on the other hand there are the clear provisions of Articles 173 and 185 which hold that Community acts are final when no appeal is lodged within two months and that even when an appeal is lodged this has no suspensory effect. It would obstruct the system of the Treaty if States could pass over their right to institute proceedings before the Court and then raise objections to Community acts at a much later stage, when being prosecuted by the Commission. In the Railway Tariffs Case, brought under ECSC Article 88, the German Government submitted that in an action against a breach of the Treaty the Court should take into account the question of the legality of the act concerned. As the action under Article 88 is subject to its unlimited jurisdiction, the Court should consider all arguments which may justify the behaviour of the State (see above § 386).

The Court did not accept this submission, clearly stating that even when an action is still possible the Members are bound to apply Community acts (see quotation § 386). In the *Rediscount Rate Case*, and even more clearly in the *Rail Transport Subsidies Case*, the Court confirmed this position. [457]

§ 414. There is no reason why the situation should be different for *decisions* taken under the EEC and Euratom Treaties, but EEC Article 184 offers some basis for a different reasoning in the case of *regulations*. The Article provides that the inapplicability of regulations may be invoked in *proceedings in which a regulation is in issue*. On the basis of the wording of that article a State could dispute the applicability of regulations in proceedings under Article 169 notwithstanding the expiry of the period laid down in the third paragraph of Article 173. The Court of Justice has not supported this view, however. In the *Rail Transport Subsidies Case* it held:

'In view of the fact that the periods within which application must be lodged are intended to safeguard legal certainty by preventing Community

---

456. *Gingerbread Case* (2 and 3/62), [1962] ECR 430; 8 Jur. (1962) 863; 8 Rec. (1962) 824, 825; [1963] CMLR 214; CCH para 8004.
457. *Rediscount Rate Case* (6 and 11/69), 10 Dec. 1969, considerations 51 and 24, [1969] ECR 543 and 540; [1970] CMLR 68 and 66; CCH para 8105; *Rail Transport Subsidies Case* (156/77), 12 Oct. 1978, considerations 18-23, [1978] ECR 1896, 1897.

measures which involve legal effects from being called in question indefinitely, it is impossible for a Member State which has allowed the strict time-limit laid down in the third paragraph of Article 173 to expire without contesting by the means available under that article the legality of the Commission decision addressed to it to be able to call in question that decision by means of Article 184 of the Treaty when an application is lodged by the Commission on the basis of the second subparagraph of Article 93 (2) of the Treaty.' [458]

In this respect there can be no difference between the procedures of EEC Articles 93 and 169.

§ 415. The situation may be different when the question is not one of the validity of a Community act but one concerning its existence (see above § 213-226). The possibility of the non-existence of the act was raised in the *Rediscount Rate Case*. Here, the Commission had censured France for not complying with a decision which, in the opinion of the French Government, was taken in a field reserved to the competence of the Member States. The decision was final since an action for annulment was not brought within the time limit of Article 173. Nonetheless, the Court investigated the French submission, considering that if it was justified the decision would lack all legal foundation in Community law, and that in proceedings brought by the Commission in the interest of the Community, for failure to meet an obligation, it is a fundamental requirement of the legal system that the Court should examine whether this is the case (see quotation above, § 216). Thus, it should be concluded that in extreme cases when the non-existence of a Community act can be asserted, States can raise such a claim in an Article 169 procedure even when they have neglected to institute proceedings against the act within the prescribed time limits.

g. AVAILABILITY OF LOCAL REMEDIES

§ 416. Under the rules of the common agricultural policy the Member States have been obliged to pay export subsidies as from 1 July 1967. In February 1968 the Italian Government had still not paid any such subsidy. The Commission brought an action under Article 169. The Italian Government submitted that directly applicable rules of Community law were involved. As such rules formed part of the national legal system, their application should be invoked by the private parties concerned before the national courts. Only if these national courts refused to apply them, would there be a breach by the Member State. This submission resembles the requirement of the exhaustion of local remedies which is a normal condition for the admissibility of a suit

---

458. *Rail Transport Subsidies Case* (156/77), 12 Oct. 1978, consideration 21, [1978] ECR 1896. See also considerations 22-25.

under international law.[459] The theory advanced would be that the negligence of the Italian *Government* does not impute negligence on the part of the Italian *State* as long as remedies exist within that State, or in the present case, as long as the Italian courts may still remedy the situation.

The Court of Justice did not adhere to this view. It considered that the existence or non-existence of remedies before national courts can have no influence on the exercise of the remedy provided for in Article 169, since the two remedies have different objects and different effects.[460] In this respect it confirmed its decision in the *Van Gend en Loos Case* where the Netherlands Government had made the contrary argument that the case could not be brought before its national judiciary, as long as the remedy of Article 169 was available. In that case as well the Court held that the two remedies existed independently of each other (see below § 435).

It may be that the lack of a requirement for the exhaustion of local remedies deviates somewhat from the normal rules of State responsibility in international law; but in the interest of the supervision of Community obligations this is certainly fortunate. The Commission thus need not wait for an action to be brought by individuals directly affected by the breach, but can always act itself on finding a breach of the Treaty by a Member Government.

h. ، FAULT COMMITTED BY OTHERS

§ 417. Can a breach be justified by the fact that the other party was the first to violate its obligations? In the *Dairy-products Case* Belgium and Luxembourg submitted that the Community had failed to comply with its obligation to set up a common organization of markets for dairy products and that therefore they were justified in keeping their own protective measures in force. They argued that international law recognizes that a party affected by the failure of another party to comply with its obligations has the right not to fulfil its own obligations. The Court of Justice replied:

'This relationship between the obligations of parties cannot be recognized under Community law.

In fact the Treaty is not limited to creating reciprocal obligations between the different natural and legal persons to whom it is applicable, but establishes a new legal order which governs the powers, rights and obligations of the said persons, as well as the necessary procedures for taking cognizance of and penalizing any breach of it. Therefore, except where otherwise expressly provided, the basic concept of the Treaty requires that the Member States shall not take the law into their own hands. Therefore

---

459. See AA Cançado Trindade, *L'épuisement des recours internes dans des affaires interétatiques*, 14 CDE (1978), p. 139 ff.
460. *Exports Rebate Case* (31/69), 17 Feb. 1970, consideration 9, [1970] ECR 32; [1970] CMLR 188; CCH para 8097.

the fact that the Council failed to carry out its obligations cannot relieve the defendants from carrying out theirs.'[461]

§ 418. In the *Olive Oil Case* negligence on the part of the Commission, which failed to propose special rules, justified France in not honouring its obligations, an action not to be construed as a kind of retaliatory measure, but rather stemming from the fact that the negligence had created such an unclear and uncertain situation that France could not be blamed for acting independently. In this case France was accused of a breach of the Treaty by not applying the prescribed levy on olive oil on imports from Tunisia. The French Government contended that Tunisia was exempted from these levies by the *'Protocol on goods originating in and coming from certain countries and enjoying special treatment when imported into a Member State'* which is annexed to the EEC Treaty (Protocol I.7). The Court considered that such an exemption was not possible under the common agricultural policy, but that in some way the Community institutions should have provided for a special regime for these imports, in particular because they should have known that the association agreement with Tunisia — which was being prepared and which entered into force when the case was pending before the Court — would contain specific provisions for olive oil. Given that no special allowance had been made for Tunisian olive oil during the interim period between the entry into force of the common agricultural policy on olive oil and the association with Tunisia, a situation of uncertainty had arisen for which the Commission was to blame. France could therefore not be condemned under Article 169.[462]

§ 419. In the *Vegetable Seed Case* Italy was accused of failure to implement EEC Directive 70/458 on vegetable seed. The Italian Government submitted that the period prescribed in the directive for implementing its provisions was too short and sought to demonstrate this submission by establishing that none of the other Member States had implemented its provisions in time.
    The Court of Justice held:

'Any delays there may have been on the part of other Member States in performing obligations imposed by a directive may not be invoked by a Member State in order to justify its own, even temporary, failure to perform its obligations. The Treaty did not merely create reciprocal obligations between the various subjects to whom it applies, but established a new legal order which governs the powers, rights and duties of the said subjects as well as the procedures necessary for the purposes of having any infringement declared and punished.'[463]

---

461. *Dairy-products Case* (90, 91/63), 13 Nov. 1964, [1964] ECR 631; 10 Jur. (1964) 1292, 1293; 10 Rec. (1964) 1231, 1232; [1965] CMLR 72; CCH para 8028.
462. *Olive Oil Case* (26/69), 9 July 1970, [1970] ECR 575, 576; [1970] CMLR 458; CCH para 8103.
463. *Vegetable Seed Case* (52/75), 26 Feb. 1976, consideration 11, [1976] ECR 283 [1976] 2 CMLR 330 (here it is consideration 7); CCH para 8345.

In the *Steinike Case* the Court also ruled that a breach of obligations by one Member State cannot justify a breach of its obligations by another Member State. In the field of competition the effects of more than one distortion of competition in the Common Market do not cancel each other out, but are cumulative. [464]

4. Identity of the defaulter

§ **420.** Against whom should the Commission act under Article 169? Should it proceed against the Member State or against its Government? In all cases but one the Commission has acted against the State concerned, and in the one case where it did act against the Government of a State [465] it did not give any reasons for doing so. It appears to have been a procedural error rather than an intention to limit the action to one specific organ of the State. The substance of the case does not make clear why that case should have been addressed to the Government of the State any more than any other case. In its decision the Court did not refer to the Government but to the State, as in all other similar cases.

§ **421.** Even though the Article 169 action is directed against the State, in practice it is the Government which is brought before the Court, and which must plead and finally act to remedy the situation if the State loses the case. This creates problems when the Government is not responsible for the breach. In June 1967 a member of the European Parliament, Mr. Westerterp, asked the Commission whether EEC Article 169 is only applicable to breaches by the Governments of the Member States or also to the situation when a national parliament adopts a law contrary to the EEC Treaty or when a national court renders a judgment in breach of Article 177. The Commission responded that it considered Article 169 applicable to these cases also. [466] When, in March 1968, the French *Conseil d'Etat* had violated Article 177 by not asking a preliminary ruling in the *French Semoules Case* [467], another member of the European Parliament, Mr. Deringer, drew the attention of the Commission to that case and asked whether the Commission considered it ill-advised and, if so, what the Commission would do about it. The Commission confirmed that the procedure of Article 169 could be implemented when a national court violated Article 177 and stated that it 'was considering what steps would be appropriate in the case concerned'. [468]

---

464. *Steinike Case* (78/76), 22 March 1977, consideration 24, [1977] ECR 612; [1977] 2 CMLR 723; CCH para 8402.
465. *Alcohol Tax Case* (16/69), 15 Oct. 1969, [1969] ECR 377-386; [1970] CMLR 161; CCH para 8080.
466. Reply of 20 Oct. 1967 to Written Question No. 100, OJ 1967 No. 270, pp. 2-4, para 7.
467. *French Semoules Case*, Conseil d'Etat, 1 March 1968, Recueil Dalloz 1968, Jurisprudence p. 285; Brinkhorst-Schermers (*op. cit.*, note 365), pp. 197, 198.
468. Reply of 5 July 1968 to Written Question No. 28/68, OJ 1968 No. C 71, pp. 1, 2.

When the Commission had been deliberating for over a year without taking any action, Mr. Westerterp posed a new question on 10 November 1969 and asked the Commission what it intended to do. The Commission confirmed that it considered an action under Article 169 possible, but also stated that it had not acted as it seemed inappropriate to do so. It referred to a report of the Legal Committee of the European Parliament which expressed the fear that an action under Article 169 for a breach of Article 177 would affect the independence of the judiciary. The Commission had therefore chosen to proceed by way of persuasion, by better informing the national judiciaries and by mutual consultation. [469]

§ 422. The position of the Commission seems correct. The Court of Justice has repeatedly emphasized that Community law must be built upon co-operation between the Court of Justice and the national courts. Both bodies play their part, as the Community legal system depends as much on the national judiciary as on the Court of Justice itself. An Article 169 action against a national court would bring a conflict between the two court systems into the open and would result in compelling a State to ensure that its courts act differently in the future. This could lead to a form of government pressure on national courts when acting on Community law. As many Community law cases before national courts are brought against the Government, any such pressure is undesirable. It seems wise, therefore, that the Commission should first try all forms of informal persuasion. Only if no other remedy is available should an action under Article 169 be considered. [470] Since the *Conseil d'Etat* has asked for some preliminary rulings during ten years following the *French Semoules Case* [471], the informal persuasion seems to have had some effect. [472] But in 1978 the *Conseil d'Etat* bluntly violated Community law by a ruling which was contrary to established Community case law whilst refusing to apply for a preliminary ruling. [473]

§ 423. A few months after the Commission adopted its above-mentioned position a similar question came before the Court of Justice in the *Wood Case*. Belgium had levied an illegal tax on imported wood. When approached by the Commission the Belgian Government had recognized the illegality of the tax and on 27 June 1967 had introduced a bill in Parliament intended to adapt the law to EEC requirements. Parliament had been slow and the bill had

---

469. Reply of 30 Jan. 1970 to Written Question No. 349/69, OJ 1970 No. C 20, p. 4. This was confirmed in the Commission's answer to Written Question 608/78, OJ 1979, No C 28, p. 9.
470. The Commission initiated proceedings under EEC Article 169 against Germany after the *German Handelsgesellschaft Case* (see below § 171-173), *Europe* 27 Dec. 1974, No. 1657, p. 9, but this was not pursued further.
471. *Syndicat national céréales Case* (34/70), 17 Dec. 1970, [1970] ECR 1233; CCH para 8122; *Derived intervention prices Case* (11/74), 11 July 1974, [1974] ECR 877; [1975] 1 CMLR 75; CCH para 8281; *Charmasson Case* (48/74), 10 Dec. 1974, [1974] ECR 1383; [1975] 2 CMLR 208; CCH para 8291.
472. See also Mertens de Wilmars and Verougstraete (*op. cit.*, note 390) pp. 389, 390.
473. *French Cohn Bendit Case*, 22 Dec. 1978, see above § 163a.

lapsed when a new parliament had to be elected on 2 March 1968. Notwith-standing reminders by the Government the new parliament was again slow and as nothing had happened the Commission instituted proceedings before the Court on 22 December 1969. The Belgian Government submitted that it had made every effort to obtain an amendment of the legislation. Consequently, it should not be held responsible for the negligence of the Belgian Parliament. The Court of Justice held:

'The obligations (...) of the Treaty devolve upon States as such and the liability of a Member State under Article 169 arises whatever the agency of the State whose action or inaction is the cause of the failure to fulfil its obligations, even in the case of a constitutionally independent institu-tion.' [474]

The case is all the more interesting because of its wide wording. The Court did not refer to the parliament as such but to 'independent institutions'. Because of the discussions on the *French Semoules Case* which preceded this case it seems that the Court wanted to stress that an action under Article 169 is also possible when national courts violate their obligations to request a preliminary ruling under Article 177. Six months later, the Court confirmed its opinion in the *Wood Case* in a similar case against Italy. [475]

§ 424.   The position that the State as such and not its individual organs bears responsibility in international relations is in conformity with the general rule of international law. In one respect, however, the Court of Justice is more strict. Under general international law a State is responsible only after the exhaustion of its local remedies. In the *Export Rebate Case* the Court of Justice considered that the right of the Commission to act under Article 169 is not affected by the possibility for injured individuals to apply to national courts (see above § 416).

5. Discretion of the Commission

§ 425.   Is the Commission free to decide whether it will act or not? Arti-cle 169 provides that the Commission *shall* deliver a reasoned opinion if it *considers* that a Member State has failed to fulfil an obligation. This seems to indicate a freedom of the Commission to consider whether there is a breach or not and then, if it considers that there is a breach, an obligation to deliver a reasoned opinion. It is more likely, however, that the provision is intended to provide that the Commission is obliged to deliver a reasoned opinion before it can take any further action under EEC Article 169. The reasoned opinion is a

474.   *Wood Case* (77/69), 5 May 1970, consideration 15, [1970] ECR 243; [1974] 1 CMLR 210; CCH para 8089.
475.   *Administrative Services Case* (8/70), 18 Nov. 1970, [1970] ECR 966; CCH para 8116.

procedural condition which must be satisfied before the Commission may refer a breach of Community law to the Court, rather than an obligation on the Commission. [476] In practice the Commission enjoys full powers of discretion. When in the above-mentioned *French Semoules Case* (see § 421) the Commission had practically accepted that France had violated its obligations under the Treaty, but still decided not to act under Article 169, the European Parliament did not complain. It seemed to accept that the Commission was free to decide whether to act or not, even when it had found that there was a breach.

Paragraph 2 of Article 169 makes it entirely clear that the Commission is entitled not to bring the case before the Court of Justice even when the State does not comply with the reasoned opinion.

In one case the Commission brought an action under EEC Article 169 at the request of the government of the State concerned. After the Court of Justice had ruled in the *Second Rewe Case* that certain charges for compulsory inspection on importation were illegal [477], Dutch business circles began to dispute a phytosanitary charge levied on exports for the issue of sanitary certificates. The Dutch government did not want to withdraw the charge but wanted to be sure of its legality. It therefore invited the Commission to start an action under EEC Article 169 as soon as possible. The Commission brought the matter before the Court, which held that the Dutch charge was not contrary to EEC law. [478]

§ 426.   As to the *time* for initiating the action under Article 169 the Commission exercises full discretion as well. In the *First Art Treasures Case* the Commission had instituted an action against Italy only four days before the dissolution of the Italian Parliament, at a time when draft legislation for the repeal of the disputed measure was already pending. Italy therefore disputed the admissibility of the action. The Court replied:

'It is for the Commission, under Article 169 of the Treaty, to judge at what time it shall bring an action before the Court; the considerations which determine its choice of time cannot affect the admissibility of the action.' [479]

In the *Euratom Case* the French Government alleged that the action was inadmissible as France had repeatedly stated since 1965 that it no longer considered itself bound by Chapter VI of the Euratom Treaty. For years the Commission had not acted. It would therefore not be free to refer the matter to the Court in 1971. To this argument the Court replied that the action

---

476. See Andrew Evans, *Discretion of the European Commission as regards resort to the procedure contained in Article 169 of the EEC Treaty*, not yet published.
477. *Second Rewe Case* (39/73),11 Oct. 1973, [1973] ECR 1044; CCH para 8223.
478. *Phytosanitary Export Certificate Case* (89/76), 12 July 1977, [1977] ECR 1364-1366; [1978] 3 CMLR 641-644; CCH para 8415.
479. *First Art Treasures Case* (7/68), 10 Dec. 1968, [1968] ECR 428; 14 Jur. (1968) 597; 14 Rec. (1968) 625; [1969] CMLR 8; CCH para 8057.

under Article 141, the Euratom Article equivalent to EEC Article 169, was not bound by any time limits and that the Commission was entitled to choose the most suitable means and time to terminate any possible breach. [480]

§ 427.   As to the *State* against whom the action is to be addressed the Commission also has wide discretion. If two States were to similarly violate the Treaty, an action by the Commission against one of them would not be inadmissible for the reason that a similar action had not been instituted against the other. The former State or any other State could always institute an action under Article 170 to bring the other violating State before the Court.

In 1965 the Commission had addressed two directives to Germany in which the Federal Republic was requested to abolish certain taxes. Germany brought an action for the annulment of these directives under EEC Article 173. One of the grounds advanced was misuse of powers for the reason that the Commission had addressed these directives solely to Germany whilst other Member States had similar taxes and had not been requested to terminate them. The Court of Justice then replied that every Member State could call upon the Commission to act whenever it might fail to do so in infringement of the Treaty. A failure of the Commission to act against other States cannot release a Member State from its obligations. [481]

§ 428.   As to the *substance* of the action, the Commission has practically full discretion in deciding what breaches it will attack, and which elements in particular. It may, in its reasoned opinion, oppose only those aspects of the breach which it considers most important and it may limit its suggestions to the correction of these aspects.

As to those subjects which the Commission invokes before the Court, the Court is strict. It has already been seen (above § 393, 394) that the Commission need not concentrate its action upon a specific law but must give the State concerned the opportunity to submit its observations and must deliver a reasoned opinion on a law if it wants it to be discussed before the Court (*Wool Imports Case*). Under no circumstances may the Commission add further breaches by the State to the action after the termination of the formal discussions.

In the *Export Rebates Case* Italy was censured for the non-payment of export rebates as required by the agricultural system. Both in its introductory letter of 12 July 1968 and in its reasoned opinion the Commission had forwarded a general complaint, finding fault with Italy not only for the omission to pay in accordance with the specific regulations of 1967 but also for the more general failure to pay under this category of regulations, including those of 1968. The Court of Justice did not accept this general complaint. It consid-

480. *Euratom Case* (7/71), 14 Dec. 1971, consideration 5, [1971] ECR, 1016; [1972] CMLR 473.
481. *Administrative Fees Case* (52, 55/65), 16 June 1966, [1966] ECR 172; 12 Jur. (1966) 326; 12 Rec. (1966) 245; [1967] CMLR 44; CCH para 8049 (p. 7739).

ered that a procedure introduced in July 1968 could not concern the omission to pay under regulations which did not yet exist, or had only just come into force, at that time. It stated expressly that, under Article 169, it could only take into account failures existing when the Commission invited the Italian Government to submit its observations pursuant to Article 169 para 1. The opportunity for submitting such observations is an essential guarantee provided by the Treaty. It must be respected even if the State does not intend to make any observations. [482]

6. The decision of the Court and its application

a. CONTENT

§ 429. When the breach is a positive act of the State, that act cannot be formally annulled by the Court of Justice. According to the general principles of the relationship between national law and Community law such an annulment can only be undertaken by national courts (see below § 438).

When the breach results from a failure to act, such a failure is declared contrary to the Treaty in which case the obligation of the State to take the necessary measures is equivalent to the obligation borne by an institution when its failure has been declared illegal in an action against failure to act.

It is generally accepted that the Court of Justice − like the Commission (see above § 404) − may not prescribe specific measures to be taken by the Member State in order to terminate the breach. The Court can only find that the Member State has failed to fulfil its obligations, with the result that the Member State must then take the necessary steps to comply with the judgment of the Court. At the most, the Court may *indicate* what sort of measures would be needed. Such indications would be permitted as the Court has unlimited jurisdiction; they could be useful in order to avoid further actions on the breach of Treaty obligations. [483]

b. EXECUTION

§ 430. The Commission carefully supervises the execution of decisions rendered under ECSC Article 88 and EEC Article 169. In March 1975 a member of the European Parliament asked the Commission to state how long it had taken each of the Member States involved in judgments for the failure to fulfil their Treaty obligations to regularize the situation. In its answer the Commission stated that out of 17 judgments, 5 were executed before the Court had given its decision, 3 were executed within two months of the Court's decision, 5 others within 8 months, one more within a year and the other three within

---

482. *Exports Rebates Case* (31/69), 17 Feb. 1970, considerations 12-14, [1970] ECR 32, 33; [1970] CMLR 188; CCH para 8097.
483. Audretsch (*op. cit.*, note 390), pp. 74-78.

24, 43 and 48 months respectively.[484] The period of 48 months was attributed to particular difficulties faced by the Italian government in determining the fiscal charge to be imposed on a multitude of products; the period of 43 months related to the *First Art Treasures Case* of 10 December 1968. Several questions have been asked in the European Parliament concerning the execution of the Court's decision in that case.[485] The Commission exerted considerable pressure on Italy to comply with the Court judgment and finally opened a new procedure under Article 169, this time for breach of Article 171, which requires the State to take the necessary measures to comply with the judgment rendered under Article 169. In its pleadings the Italian Government maintained that the breach could only terminated by a new Italian law and that it had done its best to promote the adoption of such a law. When the case was already pending before the Court, the Italian Government remedied the situation by issuing a decree which repealed the illegal tax with retroactive effect as of 1 January 1962. Only after the Court's decision had been rendered was this decree confirmed by a formal law.[486] It seems that from different sources great pressure had been exerted on Italy to prevent the need for a second condemnation of the same breach. The Court itself may bring such pressure to bear by threatening that the second condemnation may be formulated in such a way and may censure the Government in power so directly that it will place the Government in an unenviable position before its national parliament. In the *Second Art Treasures Case* the second condemnation was formulated in mild terms as Italy had in the meantime taken the required measures.[487]

c. EFFECT

§ 431.   Under the ECSC Treaty the decision of the Court against a Member State has no legal effect in itself. The Court simply refuses to annul a decision of the Commission censuring the State, which means that the Commission's decision stands. As yet the Member States have complied with the decisions taken by the Commission, formerly the High Authority, under ECSC Article 88, so that economic sanctions have never been needed.

Under the EEC and Euratom Treaties the decision of the Court confirms that the Treaty has been violated. Though the Court's decision formally establishes the breach, it is not of a constitutive nature as the breach — and all its legal consequences — existed as from the date it was committed. The Brussels Tribunal, a lower Belgian court, held a contrary opinion in the *Belgian Fromagerie 'Le Ski' Case* when it held:

---

484. Question 22/75 (Cousté) of 14 March 1975, OJ 1975 Nr. C 138, p. 20.
485. Question 454/70 (Vredeling) of 18 Jan. 1971, OJ 1971, Nr. C 22, p. 11; question 138/71 (Vredeling) of 26 May 1971, OJ 1971 Nr. C 74, p. 19; question 309/71 (Vredeling) of 16 Sept. 1971, OJ 1971 Nr. C 115, p. 15.
486. Law No. 487 of 8 August 1972, G.U.R.L. No. 223 of 28 August 1972.
487. *Second Art Treasures Case* (48/71), 13 July 1972, [1972] ECR 531-533; [1972] CMLR 707, 708; CCH para 8172.

'Only since the Court of Justice gave its judgment has Belgium failed in its obligations under EEC Article 12; persons with an interest could personally bring an action against the *subsequent* demand for the illegal duties'.

The decision was reversed in appeal. [488]

§ 432.   In the *Second Art Treasures Case* the Court of Justice held:

'In the present case the effect of Community law, declared as *res judicata* in respect of the Italian Republic, is a prohibition having the full force of law on the competent national authorities against applying a national rule recognized as incompatible with the Treaty and, if the circumstances so require, an obligation on them to take all appropriate measures to enable Community law to be fully applied.
    The attainment of the objectives of the Community requires that the rules of Community law established by the Treaty itself or arising from procedures which it has instituted are fully applicable at the same time and with identical effects over the whole territory of the Community without the Member States being able to place any obstacles in the way.
    The grant made by Member States to the Community of rights and powers in accordance with the provisions of the Treaty involves a definitive limitation on their sovereign rights and no provisions whatsoever of national law may be invoked to override this limitation.' [489]

The fact that the national authorities are prohibited from applying national provisions which have been held incompatible with the Treaty in an action under EEC Article 169 amounts in practice to almost the same thing as bringing about an annulment of these national provisions by such an action. Any further application of the national provisions is illegal and that illegality can be invoked before the national courts. [490] A formal decision of the Court of Justice against a State may furthermore serve as a legal basis for actions for damages brought by individuals who have suffered from the illegal acts. A good example of such a suit is the *Belgian Fromagerie 'Le Ski' Case* mentioned above (§ 165).

C.   REVIEW INITIATED BY OTHER MEMBER STATES[491]

§ 433.   According to EEC Article 170 any Member State which considers that another Member State has failed to fulfil an obligation under the Treaty

---

488.   See Brinkhorst-Schermers (*op. cit.*, note 365), pp. 30-33, *Belgian Fromagerie 'Le Ski' Case*, first and second instance, italics added.
489.   *Second Art Treasures Case* (48/71), 13 July 1972, considerations 7-9, [1972] ECR 532; [1972] CMLR 708; CCH para 8172.
490.   See Pescatore (*op. cit.*, note 390), p. 23.

may bring the matter before the Court of Justice. Before doing so, however, it must bring te matter before the Commission. Apparently the Treaty prefers measures against breaches to be initiated by the Commission rather than by other Members. In practice, States also prefer the Commission to act, for no Member State has ever brought an action against another Member State before the Court.

Only if the Commission has not issued a reasoned opinion within three months, may the plaintiff State itself bring the matter before the Court of Justice.

Should the Commission have issued a reasoned opinion, then the procedure to be followed will be similar to that of Article 169: the Commission will grant the defaulting state a reasonable time limit within which to comply with the opinion. Should this time limit be too long, or if the reasoned opinion requires too few measures of the defaulting State, then it is to be assumed that the plaintiff State may go to the Court itself. The Treaty, however, does not expressly provide for this. The plaintiff State would have to base its action on general principles of law. An action against a defectively reasoned opinion seems problematical as the Court has decided that the opinion is not subject to review (see above § 405). The reason for this decision was, however, based on the assumption that an opinion can be discussed by the Court when the case is brought by the Commission. The Court might come to a different conclusion in a case which cannot be otherwise brought before it. As an alternative the Member State might institute an action against failure to act, which offers broad scope to Member States (see above § 339). In both cases it could be submitted that the failure to take a defaulting Member State before the Court is an infringement of the Treaty. So far only four requests have been submitted to the Commission under EEC Article 170. Two were resolved at an early stage [492], the third one came before the Court after a reasoned opinion by the Commission but was not continued [493], the fourth one is still pending. [494]

The Treaties expressly forbid Member States to submit a dispute concerning their interpretation or application to any method of settlement other than those provided for [495], thus precluding Member States from using traditional measures under international law, such as retaliation, when they consider that another Member has violated its obligations.

---

491. See Philippe Cahier in 1967 CDE, pp. 130-132; Mertens de Wilmars and Verougstraete (*op. cit.*, note 390), pp. 392-394; Ipsen (*op. cit.*, note 390), pp. 237-239; Audretsch (*op. cit.*, note 390), pp. 110-119.
492. See Ninth General Report on the Activities of the European Communities para 522.
493. Case 58/77. See Twelfth General Report on the Activities of the European Communities, para 547.
494. Case 141/78, *Idem.*.
495. EEC Art. 219; ECSC Art. 87; Euratom Art. 193.

D. REVIEW INITIATED BY INDIVIDUALS

1. Direct actions

§ 434. The Commission can be sued by other States [496], and even by individual undertakings, if it fails to act under ECSC Article 88 against a State which has failed to fulfil its ECSC obligations.[497] The position is different in EEC and Euratom: individuals cannot initiate action under EEC Article 169. On one occasion some German firms, *Lütticke* and others, tried to force the Commission to bring an action against Germany for breach of Article 95. After having failed to persuade the Commission in an informal way, they officially invited the Commission to act. On receiving a reply in which the Commission stated that in its opinion Germany no longer violated Article 95, the firms brought an action against that reply under EEC Article 173 (action for annulment). They also instituted proceedings against failure to act under EEC Article 175. The Court rejected the action against failure to act because the Commission had defined its position (see above § 351). It rejected the action for annulment because the action under Article 173 is only possible against binding acts and the first phase of the Article 169 procedure is of a non-binding character so that no measure adopted by the Commission in that phase had binding effect. [498] The latter argument does not seem strong as the Article 169 procedure as a whole is of a binding nature. But even if the Court had not used that argument it would have rejected the appeal as the required action against Germany certainly could not be of direct and individual concern to the German firms, and direct and individual concern is a strict condition for the admissibility of actions by individuals (see above § 314-324). The Commission's letter to the firms in question cannot be viewed as part of any binding decision the Commission was obliged to take, or had actually taken, and was on this account not subject to the action for annulment provided for in Article 173.

2. Preliminary rulings

a. USE OF PRELIMINARY RULINGS AGAINST NATIONAL LEGISLATION

§ 435. The impossibility of initiating proceedings under EEC Article 169 does not mean that individuals have no opportunity to obtain a decision from

---

496. See for example *Steel Subsidies Case* (59/70), 6 July 1971, [1971] ECR 639.
497. See Zuleeg (*op. cit.*, note 390), p. 55. In the following cases an action under Article 88 ECSC was initiated by individual undertakings; *Steel Industries in Luxembourg Case* (7 and 9/54), 23 April 1956, [1954-56] ECR 189, 190; 2 Jur. (1956) 87; 2 Rec. (1956) 83; *Chambre Syndicale de l'Est de la France Case* (24 and 34/58), 15 July 1960, [1960] ECR 299; 6 Jur. (1960) 625; 6 Rec. (1960), 609; *Second Limburg Coalmines case* (30/59), 23 Feb. 1961, [1961] ECR 15; 7 Jur. (1961) 35; 7 Rec. (1961) 34.
498. *First Lütticke Case* (48/65), 1 March 1966, [1966] ECR 27; 12 Jur. (1966) 39, 40; 12 Rec. (1966) 39; [1966] CMLR 387; CCH para 8044 (p. 7603).

the Court of Justice on the legality of a Member State's behaviour. By raising the question of legality before a national court, a preliminary ruling can be obtained (see below § 608) in which the Court of Justice can indicate whether the behaviour by the Member State is permitted or not, even though it is limited to interpreting the relevant rules of Community law.

This was first established in the *Van Gend en Loos Case*. Van Gend en Loos used to import urea-formaldehyde from Germany. Even before the EEC was established it had disputes with the Netherlands customs authorities on the classification of that product. In May 1958 the highest Dutch court for customs cases, the *Tariefcommissie*, had decided that the product should be classified in group 279-a-2, which was charged with a duty of 3 per cent. As the situation was still not entirely clear the Benelux rearranged its classifications and brought urea-formaldehyde in group 39.01-a-1, on which a duty of 8 per cent was applied. When van Gend en Loos was charged with this higher duty it again went to the Dutch customs courts and invoked EEC Article 12, which prohibits any increase of customs duties between EEC Members after 1 January 1958.

The *Tariefcommissie* requested a preliminary ruling of the Court of Justice *inter alia* on the question whether the imposition of a duty of 8 per cent represented an illegal increase within the meaning of EEC Article 12. As one of its defences the Netherlands Government, supported by the Governments of Belgium and Germany, submitted that this question was not one of interpretation but of application. In their opinion the procedure used by van Gend en Loos sought to evade the procedure of Articles 169 and 170 which did not permit individuals to complain about the attitudes of the Member States. The Governments concluded that it would not be admissible to bring an alleged breach of the Treaty before the Court on the basis of Article 177. The Court of Justice did not support this view, however. It held:

'In addition the argument based on Articles 169 and 170 of the Treaty put forward by the three Governments which have submitted observations to the Court in their statements of case is misconceived. The fact that these Articles of the Treaty enable the Commission and the Member States to bring before the Court a State which has not fulfilled its obligations does not mean that individuals cannot plead these obligations, should the occasion arise, before a national court, any more than the fact that the Treaty places at the disposal of the Commission ways of ensuring that obligations imposed upon those subject to the Treaty are observed, precludes the possibility, in actions between individuals before a national court, of pleading infringements of these obligations.

A restriction of the guarantees against an infringement of Article 12 by Member States to the procedures under Article 169 and 170 would remove all direct legal protection of the individual rights of their nationals. There is the risk that recourse to the procedure under these Articles would be ineffective if it were to occur after the implementation of a national decision taken contrary to the provisions of the Treaty.

The vigilance of individuals concerned to protect their rights amounts to an effective supervision in addition to the supervision entrusted by Articles 169 and 170 to the diligence of the Commission and of the Member States'. [499]

§ **436.** The position of the Court of Justice was clarified in the *Albatros Case*, in which an Italian Court had requested a preliminary ruling on the question whether EEC Articles 30-35 invalidated some specific French laws. The Court held that under Article 177, unlike under Articles 169 and 170, it was incompetent to rule on the validity of a provision of domestic law. From the wording of the request submitted it could, however, sift out those questions that call for a preliminary ruling on the interpretation of the Treaty. Thereupon, it considered that none of the provisions of the EEC Treaty mentioned by the Italian Court called for the immediate repeal of the quantitative restrictions in existence. [500] The conclusion that the French laws remained valid was left to the Italian Court.

§ **437.** A further clarification of the role of the courts in applying those rules of Community law which have direct effect was given in the *Salgoil Case*. Again the procedure was initiated by an individual before a national court. Two questions were asked, first whether EEC Articles 30-33 had direct effect and, second, what would the judicial protection thus accorded to the individual actually comprise. When the Court had affirmed that Articles 31 and 32 (1) had direct effect and therefore created rights in favour of individuals which national courts were required to safeguard, it replied to the second question that national courts are obliged to safeguard the rights granted by these Articles irrespective of any situation or any rule existing in national law. [501] The case provides an illustration of the importance of the direct effect of Community rules in allowing individuals to obtain an (indirect) condemnation of their States (see above § 175, 176). [502]

§ **438.** In a preliminary ruling the Court of Justice will not express an opinion on the conduct of the Member States, it will only interpret the rules of Community law and the extent to which they permit further national action. A decision on the validity or applicability of national acts is left to the domestic courts.

The Court's present position in this question was clearly expressed in the *Fifth Rewe Case* where it held:

'Although, in the context of proceedings under Article 177 of the Treaty, it is not for the Court to rule on the compatibility of the provisions of a

499. *Van Gend en Loos Case* (26/62), 5 Feb. 1963, [1963] ECR 13; 9 Jur. (1963) 24, 25; 9 Rec. (1963) 24, 25; [1963] CMLR 130; CCH para 8008 (p. 7215).
500. *Albatros Case* (20/64), 4 Feb. 1965, [1965] ECR 34-36; 11 Jur. (1965) 3: 8-11; 11 Rec. (1965) 3: 8-11; [1965] CMLR 176, 177, 179; CCH para 8029 (pp. 7441, 7442).
501. *Salgoil Case* (13/68), 19 Dec. 1968, [1968] ECR 462, 463; 14 Jur. (1968) 645; 14 Rec. (1968) 675; [1969] CMLR 196, 197; CCH para 8072.
502. See Pierre Pescatore, *L'effet direct du droit Communautaire*, Pasicrie Luxembourgeoise 1972, No. 5 and 6, first part, pp. 11-15; M-F. Gayet et D. Simon, *Manquement et effet direct*, 9 CDE (1973), pp. 298-324.

national law with the Treaty, it does, on the other hand, have jurisdiction to provide the national court with all the criteria of interpretation relating to Community law which may enable it to judge such compatibility.'[503]

In providing the national court with criteria of interpretation the Court of Justice may be very specific. In the *Russo Case*, for example, it answered to a question of an Italian court:

'It must therefore be concluded that the action of a Member State in purchasing durum wheat on the world market and subsequently reselling it on the Community market at a price lower than the target price is incompatible with the common organization of the market in cereals.'[504]

Similarly, in the *Schonenberg Case*, the Court held in a preliminary ruling '*that Article 7 of the EEC Treaty* [and several other provisions] *preclude a Member State from adopting measures such as are set out in the* [Irish Sea Fisheries Orders of 1977]'. The Court furthermore decided that:

'... where criminal proceedings are brought by virtue of a national legislative measure which is held to be contrary to Community law, a conviction in those proceedings is also incompatible with that law'.[505]

In the *Pigs Marketing Case* the Court of Justice left no doubt that some Northern Irish legislation was incompatible with Community law.[506]

In the *Meijer Case* the English High Court requested a preliminary ruling on the question whether Community law permitted the retention of quantitative restrictions on imports of potatoes. When giving a negative reply to this question, the Court of Justice annexed to its preliminary ruling, by way of reasoning a judgment rendered on the same day in a case brought by the Commission under EEC Article 169 in which it was held that the United Kingdom had failed to fulfil its obligations under the Treaty by not repealing or amending such quantitative restrictions.[507] This reference from the one procedure to the other demonstrates the close relationship between the two actions.

Although the Court's ruling may leave little choice to the national courts, this does not change the consistent position of the Court of Justice that it is the national court which must decide the question of whether national law is in conformity with Community law or not. The national judiciaries may

503. *Fifth Rewe Case* (45/75), 17 Feb. 1976, consideration 11, [1976] ECR 194; [1976] 2 CMLR 22; CCH para 8343.
504. *Russo Case* (60/75), 22 Jan. 1976, consideration 5, [1976] ECR 55; CCH para 8338. For other examples see the *SADAM Case* (88-90/75), 26 Feb. 1976, considerations 6 and 17, [1976] ECR 336, 339; [1977] 2 CMLR 200, 201, 206; CCH para 8355; *Bouhelier Case* (53/76), 3 Feb. 1977, consideration 11, [1977] ECR 204; CCH para 8399; *Van den Hazel Case* (111/76), 18 May 1977, consideration 27, [1977] ECR 912; CCH para 8421.
505. *Schonenberg Case* (88/77), 16 Feb. 1978, considerations 15, 16, [1978] ECR 491; [1978] 2 CMLR 526; CCH para 8474.
506. *Pigs Marketing Case* (83/78), 29 Nov. 1978, consideration 65, [1979] 1 CMLR 203.
507. *Meijer Case* (118/78), 29 March 1979, consideration 7.

decide, without requesting a preliminary ruling, that a national provision is incompatible with Community law and therefore void. No preliminary ruling is needed if such incompatibility would exist under all conceivable interpretations of Community law.

b.　EFFECT OF VIGILANCE OF INDIVIDUALS

(i)　Attention to minor breaches

§ 439.　The vigilance of individuals mentioned in the *Van Gend en Loos Case* (at the end of the quotation in § 435 above) has opened up the possibility of bringing to the Court those breaches which the Commission considered to be of insufficient general importance to initiate proceedings under Article 169, and those situations where the obligations of the State are so unclear that the Commission may not even recognize the breach of an obligation. Lütticke, one of the most vigilant companies, upon failing to persuade the Commission to follow the procedure of Article 169 (see above § 434) finally succeeded in obtaining a preliminary ruling, in which the Court of Justice indicated that the German tax on imported milk-products violated Community law. [508] Many minor breaches by States have been established by way of preliminary rulings. When the German authorities had added the 'reliability' of the exporter as an extra condition for obtaining the exemptions granted in EEC Regulations 805/68, 888/68 and 1082/68, a vigilant German exporter questioned the legality of this extra condition in court. This finally resulted in a preliminary ruling making it clear that the regulations do not permit additional requirements and, therefore, implicitly, that Germany had violated its obligations by adding the condition of reliability. [509]　In another case when the German customs authorities had classified turkey tails as 'poultry parts' Bollmann, considering this to be erroneous, initiated proceedings which led to a preliminary ruling declaring that turkey tails are 'edible offal' on which the duties are lower than on 'poultry parts'. [510]　Implicitly this meant that the German authorities had again incorrectly applied the EEC rules. When the Italian Government had failed to pay the slaughter premium provided by Regulations 1975/69 and 2195/69, Mrs. Leonesio claimed her right before her national court. In the requested preliminary ruling the Court of Justice made it clear that Italy had violated its obligations by not granting the necessary credits for this premium and that notwithstanding the absence of such credits Mrs. Leo-

---

508.　*Second Lütticke Case* (57/65), 16 June 1966, [1966] ECR 210, 211; 12 Jur. (1966) 354, 355; 12 Rec. (1966) 302, 303; [1971] CMLR 684, 685; CCH para 8045 (pp. 7611, 7612).
509.　*Reliable Importers Case* (39/70), 11 Feb. 1971, [1971] ECR 49-67; [1971] CMLR 294; CCH para 8132.
510.　*First Turkey Tail Case* (40/69), 18 Feb. 1970, [1970] ECR 69-84; [1970] CMLR 152-156; CCH para 8098.

nesio could claim the money from the Italian State.[511] In several other similar cases brought on the initiative of vigilant individuals the Court of Justice has reviewed the powers of Member States to make further rules on Community matters.[512]

(ii) Possibility of enforcement

§ 440. The control set in motion by vigilant individuals leads to national court decisions which are backed up by the enforcement measures of the national judicial systems. This fills part of the gap brought about by the weakness of the Article 169 procedure in not having effective sanctions. In December 1968, the Court of Justice had held in the *First Art Treasures Case*, that Italy had violated its obligations by continuing to levy a special tax on the export of art treasures.[513] Until August 1972 the law on which this tax was based was not withdrawn, however, and the Italian authorities continued to levy it. When in March 1970 Eunomia had been obliged to pay the illegal tax, it claimed restitution before the President of the Court of Turin. At the request of the President, the Court of Justice rendered a preliminary ruling in which it held that EEC Article 16, which prohibits customs duties between Member States, *'produces direct effects in the relations between the Member States and their subjects and confers on the latter rights which the national courts should protect'.*[514] By this ruling the Court indicated that national courts should no longer apply the illegal Italian law and that they should render it ineffective by allowing the exporters to claim back the illegal levy. The Italian courts subsequently gave effect to this ruling.[515]

§ 441. In the *Administrative Services Case* the Court of Justice decided that Italy had violated its obligations by levying a charge of 0.50 per cent on the importation of goods from other Member States as a fee for administrative services.[516] While this case was pending a vigilant importer, SACE, required repayment of the charge paid. At the request of an Italian court in Brescia the Court of Justice held in a preliminary ruling that the obligation to abolish the charge for administrative services was directly effective on the relations between the Member State to which it was addressed and its nationals and that

---

511. *Leonesio case* (93/71), 17 May 1972, [1972] ECR 292-297; [1973] CMLR 365-384; CCH para 8175. Without asking for a preliminary ruling the Brescia Tribunal had come to the same conclusion in its judgment of 5 Jan. 1972, see 10 VMLRev. (1973), p. 340.
512. See e.g. *Bremer Handelsgesellschaft Case* (72/69), 18 June 1970, [1970] ECR 427; [1970] CMLR 466; CCH para 8093; *Krohn Case* (74/69), 18 June 1970, [1970] ECR 451; [1970] CMLR 486; CCH para 8094; *Bakels Case* (14/70), 8 Dec. 1970, [1970] ECR 1001; [1971] CMLR 163; CCH para 8118; *Witt Case* (28/70), 8 Dec. 1970, [1970] ECR 1021; [1971] CMLR 188; CCH para 8119.
513. *First Art Treasures Case* (7/68), 10 Dec. 1968, [1968] ECR 428; 14 Jur. (1968) 597; 14 Rec. (1968) 625; [1969] CMLR 11; CCH para 8057.
514. *Eunomia Case* (18/71), 26 Oct. 1971, [1971] ECR 816; [1972] CMLR 11; CCH para 8148.
515. See 10 CMLRev. (1973), p. 340.
516. *Administrative Services Case* (8/70), 18 Nov. 1970, [1970] ECR 968; CCH para 8110.

it conferred on those nationals rights to which the national courts must give effect. [517] Again, this meant that the national courts should no longer give effect to illegal national rules, and again the ruling was finally carried out by the domestic court. [518] In these cases the Court of Justice had previously condemned the State concerned under Article 169. But even without such condemnation the Court of Justice has ruled several times that provisions of EEC law may be directly effective, so that individuals can invoke them in their national court and these courts should give effect to them regardless of possible contradicting national legislation. [519] This possibility to invoke EEC law in national courts independent of the position of the national government and notwithstanding possible contradictory national legislation adds considerable strength to the law of the European Communities.

§ 441a. When in a preliminary ruling the Court of Justice indicates that particular national legislation is in conflict with Community law, the national judiciary will no longer apply such national legislation. It depends on the national legal system whether effects produced by the legislation in the past can be remedied. In many cases damages may be granted, but in other cases national laws may not permit any form of remedy. When in the *Van Haaster Case* the Court of Justice had ruled that a particular Dutch penal law was incompatible with Community law, a person sentenced under that law applied for revision of the judgement. The Dutch Supreme Court, however, ruled that the fact that a legislative measure is non-binding falls outside the scope of the grounds on which application for revision may be made under the Dutch code of criminal procedure. [520] There could be no legal review of the judgement.

c. NEED OF SUPPORT BY NATIONAL COURTS

§ 442. The control of obligations incumbent on the State by individuals is only possible with the full co-operation of the national courts. These courts must be willing to apply Community law with priority over possibly conflicting national rules or possibly conflicting standpoints of their government. In general the national courts are prepared to extend their co-operation.

The case in which this was demonstrated most clearly was the *Belgian Fromagerie 'Le Ski' Case*, decided by the Belgian Supreme Court on 27 May 1971. In this case the Belgian Court expressly refused to apply a national law which violated a rule of Community law even though the national law was of a more recent date. [521] In a decision of 6 October 1972 the Italian *Cour de*

---

517. *SACE Case* (33/70), 17 Dec. 1970, [1970] ECR 1224, 1225; [1971] CMLR 133, 134; CCH para 8117.
518. See 10 CMLRev. (1973), p. 342.
519. See, for example, the *Van Gend en Loos Case* quoted above (§ 160).
520. *Dutch Ruigrok Case*, Hoge Raad 13 January 1976, [1977] 1 CMLR 308.
521. *Belgian Fromagerie 'Le Ski' Case*, *Cour de Cassation* (first chamber), 27 May 1971, JT 1971, pp. 460-474; [1972] CMLR 330-374.

Cassation followed this decision of its Belgian counterpart.[522] The Italian Constitutional Court took a similar decision on 18 December 1973.[523]

§ 443. When there is a domestic act violating Community law, non-application of the act may be a sufficiently effective remedy. But breaches by States do not always consist of acts which national courts can refuse to apply; many acts are applied by the government itself, without any court being involved. It depends on the national legal order whether a citizen can sue his government for damages caused by the government's breach of Community law. The Court of Justice indicated that it favours such a construction when it held in the *Premiums for slaughtering cows Case* that '*a judgement by the Court under Articles 169 and 171 of the Treaty may be of substantive interest as establishing the basis of a responsibility that a Member State can incur as a result of its default, as regards other Member States, the Community or private parties*'.[524] Subsequently, in its suggestions for the Tindemans Report, the Court of Justice remarked that the safeguarding of individual rights presupposes that '*in the event of a failure by a state to fulfil an obligation, persons adversely affected thereby may obtain redress before their national Courts*'.[525]

522. See 10 CMLRev. (1973), p. 345.
523. *Italian Frontini Case*, see above, § 167, 170.
524. *Premiums for slaughtering cows Case* (39/72), 7 Feb. 1973, consideration 11, [1973] ECR 112; [1973] CMLR 454; CCH para 8201.
525. *Suggestions of the Court of Justice on European Union*, Bulletin of the European Communities, Supplement 9/75, p. 18.

CHAPTER THREE

Other tasks of the Court of Justice

I. FIELDS OF JURISDICTION, OTHER THAN JUDICIAL REVIEW

A. LIMITED VERSUS UNLIMITED JURISDICTION[1]

§ 444. In the field of judicial review (see Chapter Two) there is a general presumption that public authorities are in the right unless the contrary is proven. Community acts are considered to be valid, unless it can be demonstrated on certain specific grounds that they are void. Though in practice the Court of Justice interprets these grounds very widely, the right to institute proceedings is limited. If the applicant cannot demonstrate that a legal rule has been violated, there will be no annulment. The Court has no need to search for legal rules independently. The Court is also limited in its powers of decision. It must annul the act in dispute or it must keep it in force; it cannot normally replace the act by an opinion of its own.

Apart from its tasks of judicial review the Court of Justice administers the law in a number of fields traditionally attributed to the civil courts in Common Law Countries and in many Continental States as well, for example, suits for damages brought against the Communities, disputes between civil servants and the institution employing them, disputes brought under an arbitration clause in a contract to which the Community is a party. Furthermore, the Court of Justice has penal law jurisdiction in disputes about penalties imposed by the Communities. Finally, several miscellaneous competences have been attributed to the Court, some of which have never been exercised.

In all these cases the Court has unlimited jurisdiction. Parties are not limited to specific grounds of illegality; the Court must seek out the relevant law, even where no specific rules have been invoked by the parties; it may go beyond the question of legality and also consider the expediency of the acts undertaken by the institutions.[2] In its decision the Court has a wider choice of action than in the context of cases involving judicial review. It can grant

---

1. Liliane Plouvier, *Le contentieux de pleine jurisdiction devant la Cour de Justice des Communautés européennes*, RMC 1971, pp. 365-379. On administrative law in general, see Z.M. Nedjati and J.E. Trice, *English and Continental Systems of Administrative Law*, North Holland, 1978.
2. B. van der Esch, *Pouvoirs discrétionnaires de l'Executif européen et contrôle jurisdictionnel*, Europese Monografieën, no. 12, Kluwer 1968, p. 32.

part of the damages claimed, or lower fines. One therefore speaks of unlimited jurisdiction, or, in French, of *pleine juridiction*.

§ 445. Had the Court of Justice been strict in its interpretation of the grounds of illegality, there could have been a great difference between the Court's limited and unlimited jurisdiction. Now that the Court interprets the grounds of illegality so widely the difference is not of such practical importance, the less so because in two fields of unlimited jurisdiction, the action against fines and the cases brought by civil servants, the Commission sits in judgment in first instance, so that the case before the Court is actually an appeal for the annulment of a decision taken by the Commission.

B. SUITS FOR DAMAGES[3]

1. Expediency

§ 446. As a rule, public international organizations are immune from the jurisdiction of their Member States. In order to guarantee their independence they have been accorded the same status in national law as foreign States. Without their agreement they cannot be summoned before a national court.[4] The European Communities do not have full immunity; as regards their contractual liability they can be sued before the national courts of the Member States.[5] There was no reason to grant immunity for suits concerning such liability. The national legal systems of the Member States are so similar and their courts of such a standing that neither significant national divergences in law nor discrimination against the Communities was to be expected or feared. The national courts normally adjudicate contractual obligations, and without strong reason they should not be deprived of this jurisdiction.

---

3. On the same subject see: Maurice Lagrange, *The non-contractual liability of the Community in the ECSC and in the EEC*, 3 CMLRev. (1965-66), pp. 10-36; Frédéric Dumon, *La responsabilité extracontractuelle des Communautés Européennes et de leurs agents*, 5 CDE (1969) pp. 3-48; Léon Goffin in *Les Novelles, Droit des Communautés Européennes* sous la direction de W.J. Ganshof van der Meersch, Brussels 1969, pp. 141-158 and 333-340; L. Goffin and M. Mahieu, *Responsabilité extracontractuelle des Communautés*, 8 CDE (1972) pp. 678-691; Wolf-Henning Roth, *Amtshaftung neben Nichtigkeits- und Untätigkeitsklage im Recht der EWG*, 138 Zeitschrift für das gesamte Handelsrecht und Wirtschaftsrecht (1974), pp. 80-100. Henry G. Schermers, *The law as it stands on the appeal for damages*, LIEI 1975/1, pp. 113-145; L. Goffin, *De niet-contractuele aansprakelijkheid van de EEG*, in Europese Monografieën no. 19, Kluwer 1975, pp. 75-101; Lord MacKenzie Stuart, *The 'non-contractual' liability of the EEC*, 12 CMLRev. (1975), pp. 495-512; W. van Gerven, *De niet-contractuele aansprakelijkheid van de Gemeenschap wegens normatieve handelingen*, SEW 1976, pp. 2-28; Durdan, *Restitution or Damages: National Court or European Court?*, 1 ELRev (1976), pp. 431-443; Bruno du Ban, *Les principes généraux communs et la responsabilité non contractuelle de la Communauté*, 13 CDE (1977), pp. 397-434; Ernst-Werner Fuß, *Die allgemeinen Rechtsgrundsätze über die auszervertragliche Haftung der europäischen Gemeinschaften*, Festschrift Hermann Raschhofer, 1977, pp. 43-57.
4. Henry G. Schermers, *International Institutional Law*, Vol. II pp. 633-642.
5. EEC artt. 215(1), 183.

§ 447. As regards non-contractual liability the situation is different. Here, the courts are not faced with a specific document, the contract, but with a more general form of behaviour by the party alleged to be liable. The liability may depend on whether that person committed a wrong or not. The decision on the non-contractual liability of the Communities will often entail passing judgment on Community policy. This should not be done by national courts. EEC Article 215(2) and ESCS Article 40 therefore allocate jurisdiction on non-contractual liability to the Court of Justice.

This jurisdiction is of increasing importance. Up to 31 December 1973 33 cases were brought before the Court of Justice under EEC Article 215(2). By 31 December 1975 this number had more then doubled to 70, and by 31 December 1978 it had risen to 125.[6] These figures' do not include the cases in which civil servants claimed damages from the Communities, and they represent about 12 per cent of all cases excluding those brought by civil servants.

2. Wrongful Acts

§ 448. There is no definition of the concept of a 'wrongful act' in Community law. The Court must operate 'in accordance with the general principles common to the laws of the Member States' which, in general, offer a sufficiently clear guideline. On the basis of these principles the Court requires: (1) a fault committed by the Communities, (2) damages suffered by the applicant, and (3) a causal link between the two: only damages *caused* by the wrongful act instigated by the Communities can be claimed.[7] The notion of 'fault' is gradually being expanded by the Court's case-law. The following categories can be distinguished.

a. CIVIL WRONGS

§ 449. The Communities may commit all sorts of torts in the same way as any private company may do so: the company driver may damage somebody else's car; tiles dislodged from their buildings may break other people's windows, etc. In practice, the Communities will pay such damages without taking the case to the Court of Justice. Notwithstanding the fact that the liability caused by such acts is non-contractual, taking them to the Court of Justice would lead to severe problems for the private party concerned. It is not easy to sue for a broken window in a court which is located more than a hundred miles away. It is preferable that the Communities, after stipulating that no official act is involved, simply waive their immunity in such cases and allow the case to be brought before a local court.

6. *Community Law*, extracts from the Seventh, Ninth and Twelfth General Reports, Table 2.
7. *Third Lütticke Case* (4/69), 28 April 1971, consideration 10, [1971] ECR 337; CCH para 8136.

b. ABUSIVE APPLICATION OF POWERS

§ 450. Article 22(2) of Regulation No. 19/62 empowers the Commission to approve measures taken by Member States to safeguard their markets, provided that such safeguard measures are justified. In the *First Kampffmeyer Case*, The Commission had approved safeguard measures which were not justifiable. In disallowing these measures, the Court held:

'The Commission applied Article 22(2) of Regulation No 19 in circumstances which did not justify protective measures in order to restore the situation resulting from the fixing by it of a zero levy. As it was aware of the existence of applications for licences, it caused damage to the interests of importers who had acted in reliance on the information provided in accordance with Community rules. The Commission's conduct constituted a wrongful act or omission capable of giving rise to liability on the part of the Community.

In trying to justify itself by the assertion that in view of the economic data at its disposal on 3 October 1963 a threat of serious disturbance was not to be excluded and that consequently its mistaken evaluation of the said data is excusable, the defendant misjudges the nature of the wrongful act or omission attributed to it, which is not to be found in a mistaken evaluation of the facts but in its general conduct which is shown clearly by the improper use made of Article 22, certain provisions of which, of a crucial nature, were ignored.'[8]

c. NON-PERFORMANCE OF OBLIGATIONS

§ 451. The Treaties oblige the institutions of the Communities to perform a number of duties. In the *Vloeberghs Case*, the applicant maintained that negligence by the High Authority to exert the necessary control constituted a wrongful act. The Court held:

'Consequently if the High Authority, which is required to have Article 4 (a) respected by the Member States and Community undertakings, does not carry out that duty, those who are subject to it are entitled to consider themselves to have suffered damage to their legitimate expectations or to their rights and to ask for reparation of the damage which has thus been done to them.'[9]

---

8. *First Kampffmeyer Case* (5, 7, 13-24/66), 14 July 1967, [1967] ECR 262; 13 Jur. (1967) 327; 13 Rec. (1967) 339; CCH para 8055 (pp. 7842, 7843).
9. *Vloeberghs Case* (9 and 12/60), 14 July 1961, [1961] ECR 216; 7 Jur. (1961) 452; 7 Rec. (1961) 429.

d. INADEQUATE ORGANIZATION OF THE ADMINISTRATION

§ 452. In the *First Feram Case* [10], the Court examined whether a fault might have been committed by a failure to organize the administration properly. At first glance, the fact that a fraud had continued for several years seemed to point to poor and insufficient organization, but after further analysis, the Court considered that the Community could not be blamed. By applying the reasoning of the Court, it might be concluded that the inadequate organization of an administration would be a fault, provided that it could be blamed on the Community. Whether this presumption will be confirmed will be dependent on the subjective determination by the Court that the Community has acted in a manner not expected of a good governmental body.

e. INADEQUATE SUPERVISION

§ 453. In the 1950's, European scrap prices were lower than those prevailing on the world market. This conferred an advantage on the European steel industry, which was quite essential to enable the industry to recover from the losses from the war. Since the amount of European scrap available was insufficient, it was feared that European prices would be pushed upward by the world market price. In order to forestall this, the European scrap users set up a fund to which each of them would make contributions based on the amount of scrap each had used. Subsidies would be paid from the fund on imports, so that the net import price would be the same as the European price. The High Authority of the Coal and Steel Community had accepted the system and delegated the necessary powers for its administration to the Joint Office of Scrap Consumers. After this delegation of powers had been declared illegal in the *First Meroni Case*, (see above § 257) the High Authority took over direct responsibility for the system of price equalization as from 1 August 1958. [11]
Since price compensation was based on the price at the port of arrival in the Community, the users imported their foreign scrap at points as close to their factories as possible to save transport costs. In 1958, it was considered desirable to stimulate shipbreaking in European harbours, mainly for reasons of employment. Users of foreign scrap were therefore asked to use scrap from foreign ships broken up in European ports. *Fives Lille Cail* and several other users of foreign scrap were prepared to do so, but drew attention to the fact that there were no shipbreaking facilities in their nearest harbours and that import through an alternative harbour would give rise to additional transport costs. The Joint Office of Scrap Consumers undertook to pay the extra costs of transport. In 1960, after it had paid out more than $ 500,000 the High Authority decided that transport subsidies were contrary to the ECSC Treaty and consequently illegal. Further payment was then refused and the amounts paid were claimed back. *Fives Lille* and some other firms brought an action

10. See quotation below § 454.
11. H.A. Decision 13-58.

against the refusal to pay further subsidies and against the decisions claiming
back the subsidies paid. They were unsuccessful in these efforts. The Court of
Justice did not consider that any Treaty provision authorized the payment of
such subsidies. Concurrently, the firms claimed damages. The Court held that
the High Authority had committed a wrongful act by exercising insufficient
supervison of the Joint Office of Scrap Consumers. When authority is delegated to another office, the delegator is not relieved of the burden to ensure
adequate supervision. The Court considered that the lack of supervision was
inexcusable [12] and subsequently granted damages. [13]

§ 454. In the *First Feram Case*, the High Authority accepted certificates of
origin issued by the Dutch Ministry of Economic Affairs. When such certificates proved to have been falsified, the High Authority was accused of exercising insufficient supervision. The Court, however, did not agree and held
that: '*In leaving to the competent national authority the task of issuing the
necessary certificates, the defendant pursued the course which appeared the
most appropriate and the most likely to afford the best guarantee against
abuse*'. [14] Here again, the standard of supervision required seems to depend on
what one could expect of a normally prudent governmental body.

f. ERRONEOUS INFORMATION

§ 455. In the *First Richez-Parise Case*, it was decided that an erroneous
interpretation of a rule of Community law was not, in itself, necessarily a
wrongful act, even when a department in the Commission had expressly presented the interpretation to the interested parties. However, after discovery of
the error, the interpretation should be immediately amended and the error
rectified. In this case, the Commission discovered the mistakes in its original
interpretation on 16 April 1968, but it was not until the end of the year that
the interested individuals were notified. The Court stated:

'A correction made shortly before or after 16 April, that is to say, before
the time when those concerned had to make their decision, would have
certainly enabled the defendant to avoid all liability for the consequences
of the wrong information.
    The failure to make such a correction is, on the other hand, a matter of
such a nature as to render the Communities liable.' [15]

12. *First Fives Lille Cail Case* (19/60, 2 and 3/61), 15 Dec. 1961, [1961] ECR 297; 7 Jur.
(1961) 626; 7 Rec. (1961) 592; [1962] CMLR 282.
13. *Second Fives Lille Cail Case (Laminoirs Case)* (29, 31, 36, 39-47, 50, 51/63), 9 Dec.
1965, [1965] ECR 934-941; 11 Jur. (1965) 1228-1236; 11 Rec. (1965) 1154-1162.
14. *First Feram Case* (23/59), 17 Dec. 1959, [1959] ECR 251; 5 Jur. (1958-59) 558; 5
Rec. (1958-59) 517. See also *Third Hauts Fournaux de Chasse Case* (33/59), 14 Dec. 1962,
[1962] ECR 389; 8 Jur. (1962) 768; 8 Rec. (1962) 737; *Second Meroni Case* (46, 47/59),
14 Dec. 1962, [1962] ECR 422; 8 Jur. (1962) 842; 8 Rec. (1962) 805.
15. *First Richez-Parise Case* (19, 20, 25 and 30/69), 28 May 1970, considerations 41 and
42, [1970] ECR 339, see also *Fiehn Case* (23/69), 9 July 1970, consideration 22, [1970]
ECR 560; *Heinemann Case* (79/71), 13 July 1972, consideration 12, [1972] ECR 589.

g. UNLAWFUL TERMINATION OF STAFF CONTRACTS

§ 456. Decisions to terminate staff contracts have not always been lawful, and when unlawful, they may be annulled by the Court with the result that the staff member is reinstated.[16] This does not preclude the possibility of the employee having suffered damages for which indemnification may be claimed, but often re-entry to the service is the sole reason for legal action being taken. Sometimes, the individual concerned does not want reinstatement, sometimes such re-entry is impossible. In those cases, the Court will not annul the decision terminating the contract but will grant damages instead.[17]

In the *Kergall Case*, the Court held that a contract which was not renewed for the sole reason that the post had been abolished was a wrongful act.[18]

In the *Algera Case*, the Court held that a hasty dismissal, while new rules on the harmonization of conditions of service were being prepared, constituted a wrongful act, and that another wrongful act was committed by the unlawful withdrawal of a nomination of a party as a civil servant.[19]

In the *Leda de Bruyn Case*, the Court ruled that a decision terminating a contract should be reasoned. Dismissal without stating the reasons is unlawful, and is a ground for indemnification.[20]

Before taking a decision to terminate a contract, the Commission, or the competent organs acting on its behalf, should actively collect all possible information that may be of advantage to the staff member concerned. In the *Luhleich Case*, the Commission's failure to do so and the fact that the justification for the termination rested on incorrect or insufficiently demonstrated facts, amounted to a wrongful act resulting in the Community's liability.[21]

h. INSUFFICIENT PROTECTION OF RIGHTS OF STAFF MEMBERS

§ 457. The Court of Justice has held in a number of cases that 'redundant criticism' of staff members would be a wrongful act, since it harms the individual position of the staff members concerned, and therefore leads to liability on the part of the Community.[22] In the *First Willame Case*, the Commission had taken insufficient care in judging Willame's capabilities. This constituted a wrongful act for which indemnification was granted.

16. See e.g. *Schmitz Case* (18/63), 19 March 1964, [1964] ECR 101-102; 10 Jur. (1964) 207, 208; 10 Rec. (1964) 195.
17. *Luhleich Case* (68/63), 8 July 1965, [1965] ECR 604; 11 Jur. (1965) 781; 11 Rec. (1965) 751, 752; [1966] CMLR 258.
18. *Kergall Case* (1/55), 19 July 1955, [1954-56] ECR 158; 2 Jur. (1955-56) 26; 2 Rec. (1955-56) 28.
19. *Algera Case* (7/56 and 3-7/57), 12 July 1957, [1957-58] ECR 65; 3 Jur. (1957) 136; 3 Rec. (1957) 128.
20. *Leda de Bruyn Case* (25/60), 1 March 1962, [1962] ECR 31; 8 Jur. (1962) 62; 8 Rec. (1962) 60; [1962] CMLR 183.
21. See above note 17.
22. *Leroy Case* (35/62 and 16/63, 5 Dec. 1963, [1963] ECR 207; 9 Jur. (1963) 437; 9 Rec. (1963) 420; [1964] CMLR 574; *De Vos van Steenwijk Case* (84/63), 25 June 1964, [1964] ECR 334; 10 Jur. (1964) 689; 10 Rec. (1964) 660; *Georges Case* (87/63),

i. BREACH OF INTERNAL RULES

§ 458. The Communities have promulgated many internal rules concerning the organization of their own administration. If these rules are violated uncertainty and injury may be caused to persons who have relied on them. The Court of Justice has accepted the breach of internal rules as a ground for liability. In the *Di Pillo Case*, the Court granted damages where the Community had violated its internal rules by failing to make probation reports within five months of the beginning of the trial period. [23]

j. INFRINGEMENT OF A SUPERIOR RULE OF LAW

§ 459. As will be discussed below (§ 478-481), a sufficiently flagrant infringement of a superior rule of law protecting individuals is another wrongful act for which damages can be claimed.

It may be submitted that an infringement of a superior rule of law is committed when the Community refuses to repay levies paid under a Community provision which has subsequently been annulled (see above, § 379[d]).

3. The special problem of wrongful legislation

a. THE PRINCIPLE OF LIABILITY FOR LEGISLATIVE ACTS [24]

§ 460. Is the Community liable for injuries caused by its wrongful legislation? For the ECSC Treaty the situation seems clear. Article 34 provides for equitable redress for harm directly resulting from decisions or recommendations which have been declared void. Wherever necessary, appropriate damages will be paid. Since the article is not limited to individual decisions, it may be interpreted to cover the possibility of liability for legislative acts on the condition that they have been declared void. [25]

---

7 July 1964, [1964] ECR 484; 10 Jur. (1964) 994; 10 Rec. (1964) 950; *Minot van Nuffel Case* (93/63), 7 July 1964, [1964] ECR 511; 10 Jur. (1964) 1051; 10 Rec. (1964) 1002; *Prakash Case* (19 and 65/63), 8 July 1965, [1965] ECR 557; 11 Jur. (1965) 613; 11 Rec. (1965) 704; [1966] CMLR 275; *First Willame Case* (110/63), 8 July 1965, [1965] ECR 667; 11 Jur. (1965) 922; 11 Rec. (1965) 823; [1966] CMLR 242.
23. *Di Pillo Case* (10 and 47/72), 12 July 1973, [1973] ECR 764-773; see also below § 484.
24. See also Peter Gilsdorf, *Die Haftung der Gemeinschaft aus normativem Handeln*, 10 EuR (1975). pp. 73-112; Wolf-Henning (*op. cit.*, note 3); Jörg Manfred Müssner, *Haftung der Europäischen Gemeinschaft für legislatives Unrecht*; 22 AWD (1976) pp. 93-95; Advocate-General Trabucchi in the *Compagnie continentale Case* (169/73), 4 Feb. 1975, [1975] ECR 139, 140; Ernst-Werner Fuß, *Zur Zulässigkeit der Schadenersatzklage wegen Gemeinschaftshaftung für rechtswidrige Verordnungen*, Festschrift Ipsen, Tübbingen 1977, pp. 617-643; Ami Barav, *'Injustice normative' et fondement de la responsabilité extracontractuelle de la Communauté Economique Européenne*, 13 CDE (1977), pp. 439-457; Trevor Hartley, *Damages for invalid regulations*, 3 ELRev (1978), pp. 300-303.
25. See Advocate-General Roemer in the *Schöppenstedt Case* (5/71), 2 Dec. 1971, [1971]

The EEC and Euratom Treaties are less explicit, and refer only to the general principles common to the laws of the Member States. In the legal systems of the Member States a distinction must be made between two groups of legislative acts: on the one hand, the statutory laws enacted by parliament, and on the other, the regulations issued by the administration or by individual ministers. In most Member States, the courts generally do not grant damages for the harmful effects of statutory laws, but they may do so for the effects of regulations. To find the general principles common to the laws of the Member States, one should consider both groups, since the EEC regulations are not quite equivalent to either one. In their purpose and legal effect they are equivalent to statutory laws, but in their origin they are more similar to national regulations, because no parliament has played a decisive role in their establishment. This origin criterion may be an argument for a maximum of judicial control to compensate to some extent for the inadequacy of the control exercised by the European Parliament.[26] In his opinion in the *Schöppenstedt Case*, Advocate-General Roemer expressed the opinion that the principle of governmental liability for legislative acts should be accepted as part of Community law, even though it is not known in all of the Member States. His principal argument was that such liability is widely accepted within the Member States and in some cases, even in relation to statutes.

The Court of Justice has decided that the Communities cannot be sued for damages when injury has been caused by the Treaties themselves, or by other acts of equal standing[27], but in a number of cases it has stated that parties would have standing to sue the Communities for injuries caused by other legislative acts.[28]

b. SEVERABILITY OF THE WRONGFUL ACT

§ 461. In many cases concerning legislative acts, harm is not caused by the act itself but rather by the manner in which the act was promulgated, or by the system which encompassed the act. Cases on these points, in fact, relate to a separate Community act, such as the promulgation or the setting up of the system, and are therefore not really concerned with the wrongful legislative act itself (see also below § 484). Often the actions against the validity of these separate acts are brought under EEC Article 173. At the same time, and

ECR 989, 990; CCH para 8153. For the question whether the normal action for damages under ECSC Art. 40 can also be used see the *Vloeberghs Case* (9 and 12/60), 14 July 1961, [1961] ECR 212-214; 7 Jur. (1961) 446-449; 7 Rec. (1961) 424-426.
26. See Roemer, quoted above, pp. 990, 991. See also L. Goffin and M. Mahieu in their comment on the *Schöppenstedt Case* in 8 CDE (1972), pp. 682-688.
27. *Compagnie Continentale Case* (169/73), 4 Feb. 1975, consideration 16, [1975] ECR 134; [1975] 1 CMLR 605; CCH para 8295.
28. *Schöppenstedt Case* (5/71), 2 Dec. 1971, [1971] ECR 983, 984; CCH para 8153; *Compagnie d'approvisionnement Case* (9 and 11/71), 25 June 1972, [1972] ECR 402, 403; [1973] CMLR 551; CCH para 8177; *First Haegeman Case* (96/71), 25 Oct. 1972, [1972] ECR 1015; [1973] CMLR 383; CCH para 8181.

usually in the same suit, damages may be requested. The Court then rules separately on the validity of the act and on the damages. As for the latter part of its decision all the rules mentioned in § 448 above will apply.

§ 462. Some of these cases concern the manner in which legislative measures were promulgated. In the *Leroy Case*, the Court considered whether the act concerned contained redundant criticism and was therefore inimical to the reputation of the applicant (see above § 457). In the *Chuffart Case*, the Court studied whether the act had been taken too hastily and whether necessary care had been taken.[29] In the *Labeyrie Case*, the question whether the reputation of the applicant had been unnecessarily damaged was again at issue.[30] In the *Espérance-Longdoz Case* the Court examined the allegation that the decision was not in keeping with prior information given by the High Authority, and that the applicant had therefore been unable to adapt his affairs sufficiently to the High Authority's position.[31]

In other cases it was claimed that the contested act formed part of a system which constituted in itself a wrongful act. *Modena*[32], *Simet*[33] and *Feram*[34] all claimed that the contested act was part of the general mismanagement of the High Authority and the Court considered whether such mismanagement existed; *Prelle* maintained that the contested act demonstrated the inadequate organization of the civil service.[35]

None of these submissions was declared inadmissible. Apparently the Court considered that the submissions, if proven, could give rise to damages. In all cases, however, the submissions were eventually rejected on the merits.

§ 463. *Heinemann* was more successful. On the basis of false information provided by the Commission, he had resigned his post without safeguarding his pension rights. He brought an action against the official act of the Commission in which the pension rights due to him were denied, but was unsuccessful as a result of the expiry of the statute of limitations. On the question of damages, the Court held that it would not interfere with the Commission's decision but would indemnify Heinemann for the Commission's false information and its failure to rectify the error in a timely fashion. Thus the Court based its grant of damages on the supplementary information supplied by the Commission — the sum being equivalent to the lost pension rights — even though the act itself remained valid.[36]

---

29. *Chuffart Case* (60, 61, 62/69), 15 July 1970, [1970] ECR 652.
30. *Labeyrie Case* (16/67), 11 July 1968, [1968] ECR 300, 301, 304; 14 Jur. (1968) 423, 427, 428; 14 Rec. (1968) 443, 447.
31. *Espérance-Longdoz Case* (3/65), 15 Dec. 1965, [1965] ECR 1082-1084; 11 Jur. (1965) 1398, 1399; 11 Rec. (1965) 1343, 1344; [1966] CMLR 166, 167.
32. *Second Modena Case* (55-59 and 61-63/63), 9 June 1964, [1964] ECR 229; 10 Jur. (1964) 476; 10 Rec. (1964) 449; [1964] CMLR 414.
33. *Third Simet Case* (67/69), 16 March 1971, [1971] ECR 212-214.
34. *Fifthe Feram Case* (70/69), 16 March 1971, [1971] ECR 236-239.
35. *Prelle Case* (5/70), 16 Dec. 1970, [1970] ECR 1081.
36. *Heinemann Case* (79/71), 13 July 1972, [1972] ECR 588-591. The underlying facts of the case were the same as those in the *First Richez-Parise Case*, see above (§ 455).

c. ACTIONS FOR DAMAGES CAUSED BY ACTS WHICH COULD HAVE BEEN CHALLENGED

§ 464. The actual result of an action for damages may be similar to that of an action for annulment. In both cases the Court will in fact state whether the Community act is valid or not. However, there are three reasons why the applicant may prefer to bring an action for damages, provided that a choice is open to him. (1) The strict conditions governing a suit for annulment brought under EEC Article 173 result in a far greater risk of the action being declared inadmissable than when an action is brought for damages. (2) An action for annulment must be lodged within two months[37] (one month under the ECSC-Treaty[38] and three months in civil servant cases[39]), while an action for damages may be brought within five years.[40] (3) A successful action for damages leads to financial compensation while an action for annulment only eliminates the act and damages must be claimed at a later date.

§ 465. The Court of Justice will declare the action for damages *inadmissable* if the cause of action is founded on the alleged illegality of an act against which proceedings could have been instituted; in other words, when its purpose is to replace an action for annulment.[41] Thus, when *Schreckenberg's* action, which was designed to bring him promotion to a higher grade, had been declared inadmissible, it was also inadmissible to claim damages for the difference between his salary at that time and that of the higher grade. The Court of Justice held:

'Although a party may take action by means of a claim for compensation without being obliged by any provision of law to seek the annulment of the illegal measure which causes him damage, he may not by this means circumvent the inadmissibility of an application which concerns the same illegality and has the same financial end in view.'[42]

§ 466. Similarly Mrs. *Müller-Collignon's* claim for damages was held to be inadmissible when her action for the annulment of the nomination of another[43] person to a post she desired, was filed too late. In her case the Court held:

'It is clear from this that the damage is founded on the non-appointment of the applicant and more exactly on the appointment of Mrs. Graf. The

---

37. EEC Art. 173(3).
38. ECSC Art. 33(3).
39. Staff Regulations, Art. 91(3).
40. EEC statute, Art. 43.
41. *Van Gerven* (*op. cit.*, note 3), pp. 5, 6, does not dismiss the possibility that an appeal for damages might succeed even in these cases.
42. *Schreckenberg Case* (59/65), 15 Dec. 1966, [1966] ECR 550; 12 Jur. (1966) 791 792; 12 Rec. (1966) 797.
43. An action for the annulment of the nomination of other people is possible and sometimes successful, see e.g. *Costacurta Case* (78/71), 22 March 1972, [1972] ECR 169

applicant could have avoided this damage by contesting the measures in question in good time. It is apparent from the foregoing that she has failed to do so.

In these circumstances she cannot repair this omission and, so to speak, acquire the opportunity of bringing a new appeal by means of a claim for damages.

Accordingly the inadmissibility of the request for annulment must inevitably bring with it the inadmissibility of the claim for damages.'[44]

§ 467. The Court ruled in a similar manner on the question of limitation periods in the cases following the *Sabbatini Case*. In 1972 Mrs. Sabbatini had successfully appealed against the decision cancelling her expatriation allowance as from the date of her marriage. The Court had considered that the rule that women lose their expatriation allowance at marriage while men do not, was discriminatory and therefore invalid (see above § 215). Prior to Mrs. Sabbatini's case, approximately 80 other women had lost their expatriation allowance as a consequence of the same rule. They could no longer bring an action against the cancellation of their rights as the period for an action for annulment had expired long ago. The Court considered whether damages were recoverable, but held thereupon that:

'Even if the applicants intended to claim compensation for damage caused by the institutions in the exercise of their functions, such an action in the present case has its origin in the alleged illegality of the institutions' decisions and cannot therefore be distinguished from an action for annulment.'[45]

d. ACTIONS FOR DAMAGES CAUSED BY ACTS WHICH COULD NOT HAVE BEEN CHALLENGED

§ 468. Generally, an individual cannot institute proceedings against regulations and directives nor against decisions addressed to persons other than himself unless they are of direct and individual concern to him. May he bring an action for injuries caused by such acts? The question first arose in the *Plaumann Case* where the applicant brought an action for the annulment of an import duty in 1963. He also requested damages as reimbursement for the import duties he had to pay. The Court declared his action for annulment inadmissible since the contested decision was not of direct and individual concern to him.

The Court did not declare Plaumann's claim for damages inadmissible as in the above cases where the applicant could have sued for the annulment of the contested act. However, in rejecting his action on its merits, the Court held:

44. *Müller-Collignon Case* (4/67), 12 Dec. 1967, [1967] ECR 373, 374; 13 Jur. (1967) 466; 13 Rec. (1967) 480.
45. *Mrs. Schots-Kortner* and 79 others (cases 15-33/73 etc.), 21 Feb. 1974, consideration 10, [1974] ECR 189.

'The conclusions of the applicant ask for payment of compensation equivalent to the customs duties and turnover tax which the applicant had to pay in consequence of the Decision against which it has at the same time instituted proceedings for annulment. In these circumstances it must be declared that the damage allegedly suffered by the applicant issues from this Decision and that the action for compensation in fact seeks to set aside the legal effects on the applicant of the contested Decision.

In the present case the contested Decision has not been annulled. An administrative measure which has not been annulled cannot of itself constitute a wrongful act on the part of the administration inflicting damage upon those whom it affects. The latter cannot therefore claim damages by reason of that measure. The Court cannot by way of an action for compensation take steps which would nullify the legal effects of a decision which, as stated, has not been annulled.'[46]

§ 469.   The Court may have been influenced by the fact that Plaumann had sought the annulment in the same case. It might also have reached this conclusion because this was the first action in which damages were claimed for legislative acts, and the Court was still searching for the most appropriate system. In any event, the *Plaumann Case* resulted in the general understanding that an act should be annulled before a claim for damages for the injuries caused by that act could be successful. The Plaumann decision may be the reason that for many years, no actions were brought against injuries caused by legislative acts.

§ 470.   In 1971, the *Third Lütticke* and the *Schöppenstedt Cases* were decided. *Lütticke* blamed the Commission for not acting against Germany when that country levied illegal taxes; and *Schöppenstedt* upbraided the Council for not making special provisions in a regulation on sugar. Normally an action against failure to act under EEC Article 175, (see above § 329-353) would have been brought, but the claimants in *Lütticke* and *Schöppenstedt* were incompetent to do so. Both defendants pleaded that the action for damages would not be open to the claimants either, but the Court of Justice stated in both cases that the claim for damages 'was established by the Treaty as an independent form of action with a particular purpose to fulfil within the system of actions'.[47]

In the latter case, the Court expressly held that the claim for damages 'differs from an application for annulment in that its end is not the abolition of a particular measure, but compensation for damage caused by an institution in the performance of its duties'.[48] Both cases were held admissible, but as to the merits, the Court held in the *Schöppenstedt Case* 'that the non-con-

46. *Plaumann Case* (25/62), 15 July 1963. [1963] ECR 108; 9 Jur. (1963) 233, 234; 9 Rec. (1963) 224, 225; [1964] CMLR 47, 48; CCH para 8013 (p. 7275).
47. *Third Lütticke Case* (4/69), 28 April 1971, consideration 6, [1971] ECR 336; CCH para 8136, *Schöppenstedt Case* (5/71), 2 Dec. 1971, consideration 3, [1971] ECR 983 CCH para 8153.
48. *Schöppenstedt Case*, consideration 3.

tractual liability invoked presupposes at the very least the unlawful nature of the act alleged to be the cause of the damage'. [49]

As the underlying act was not considered illegal the action for damages was finally rejected.

§ 471. Thus the Court made it clear that the act causing the damage need not have been previously annulled, but it must be declared illegal.[50] In the *Third Lütticke* and in the *Schöppenstedt Cases*, the Court studied the question of the legality of the underlying Community acts in the actions for damages, but in the *First Haegeman Case*, the Court required that the illegality be established *before* an action for damages can be brought. In that case the Court of Justice refused to consider the question of the legality of the act in the same proceedings as the claim for damages. It held that liability of the Community was dependent upon the legality of the Community levy concerned, and that questions pertaining to that legality should be brought before the national court since the levy was collected by the national authorities. In the interim, the claim for damages must be rejected.[51] It took Haegeman two and a half years to obtain a preliminary ruling on the legality of the levy.[52] Had the Court decided that the levy was illegal, which it did not, Haegeman would then have been able to commence a damage suit. It was to Haegeman's advantage that the preliminary ruling was requested by the Belgian court at first instance, as a considerably longer period would have elapsed if he had been obliged to go to the Court of Appeals or even to the Supreme Court to obtain the preliminary ruling. Since suits for damages must be brought within five years[53], this suit might even have been precluded by the statute of limitations. In its Seventh General Report the Commission expressed the opinion that it 'should not be assumed that the principle of the subsidiary nature of actions under Article 215, as expressed in the (Haegeman) judgement, is of general application, having regard to the particular circumstances of the case'.[54]

§ 472. At the first opportunity after the *First Haegeman Case*, the Advocate-General strongly pleaded in favour of permitting the illegality of the act to be

49. *Idem*, consideration 11. See also *Werhahn Case* (63-69/72), 13 Nov. 1973, consideration 30, [1973] ECR 1253; CCH para 8236.
50. When both issues are raised at the same time, the Court will decide them in the right order: see e.g. *First Fives Lille Cail Case* (19, 21/60; 2, 3/61), 15 Dec. 1961, [1961] ECR 295; 7 Jur. (1961) 623; 7 Rec. (1961) 590; [1962] CMLR 280, 281 or *Plaumann Case* (25/62), 15 July 1963, [1963] ECR 108; 9 Jur. (1963) 233; 9 Rec. (1963) 224; [1964] CMLR 48; CCH para 8013. For a list of cases in which indemnification was asked subsidiary to annulment, see Goffin and Mahieu (*op. cit.*, note 3) p. 73, note 12. Claims for damages brought *during* the proceedings for annulment are out of time and therefore inadmissible, see *Fiddelaar Case* (44/59), 16 Dec. 1960, [1960] ECR 542; 6 Jur. (1960) 1134; 6 Rec. (1960) 1093.
51. *First Haegeman Case* (96/71), 25 Oct. 1972, [1972] ECR 1014, 1015; [1973] CMLR 382, 383; CCH para 8181.
52. *Second Haegeman Case* (181/73), 30 April 1974, [1974] ECR 449; [1975] 1 CMLR 515; CCH para 8273.
53. EEC Statute, Art. 43.
54. Seventh General Report on the Activities of the European Communities (1973) para 569.

established in the same procedure as damages.[55] In the *Merkur Case*, the Court followed his opinion. Merkur sued for damages where injury had been caused by two EEC regulations which had not previously been declared invalid. In the suit for damages, the Court investigated the legality of the regulations. In reply to the submission of the Commission that the legality of the regulations should first be established in proceedings before the national court by means of a preliminary ruling the Court held:

> 'The Commission then maintains that the applicant should be sent back to pursue its claim before the administrative and judicial authorities in the Federal Republic of Germany, on the grounds that the event giving rise to the present dispute was the refusal by the competent customs office in that Member State to grant the applicant compensatory amounts on the exports it had made to third countries.
>
> If such a procedure were followed, it would result in a reference to the Court under Article 177 of the Treaty from the German courts on the question of the validity of Regulations Nos. 1014/71 and 1687/71.
>
> But the Court already has the case before it and within its jurisdiction and is therefore bound to see whether or not these regulations are tainted with the alleged irregularities. It would not be in keeping with the proper administration of justice and the requirements of procedural efficiency to compel the applicant to have recourse to national remedies and thus to wait for a considerable length of time before a final decision on his claim is made.
>
> The action is therefore admissible'.[56]

As in the previous cases, the Court subsequently held that the regulations were valid and rejected the appeal for damages.

§ 473. In the *Holtz & Willemsen Cases* the applicants contested the Community's support system for the processing of colza. The system was set up after the establishment of a uniform price for colza. Colza mills operating at a great distance from the colza fields became less competitive than the mills near the fields as the transportation of colza oil is considerably cheaper than that of the colza itself. As all Italian colza mills import colza and found themselves therefore in this unfavourable position, the Council had adopted special regulations for supporting these Italian mills. Holtz & Willemsen operated a colza mill in Germany at great distance from the colza fields and claimed to be in the same position as the Italian mills. In the *First Holtz & Willemsen Case* they had sued the Council and the Commission for failure to act because they had failed to make a regulation granting support for all colza processors operating at a great distance from where the colza was grown. The action had

---

55. Opinion of Advocate-General Mayras in the *Merkur Case* (43/72), 24 Oct. 1973, [1973] ECR 1077-1084; CCH para 8243.
56. *Merkur Case* (43/72), 24 Oct. 1973, considerations 5-7, [1973] ECR 1069; CCH para 8243.

been declared inadmissible as its purpose was to obtain a general rule and not an act concerning the applicants directly and individually.[57]

After this decision, Holtz & Willemsen sued the Council and the Commission for the damage caused by the absence of such a general rule. The Court of Justice confirmed its previous holdings on the admissibility of suits for damages caused by acts which could not be challenged. Again it accepted the claim for damages as an independent action, rejecting the contention that it would be inadmissible because of the fact that it aimed at a similar result as an action under the EEC Article 175. In its decision on the merits, the Court clearly abandoned its reasoning in the *Plaumann Case*. It no longer stated that the contested act, in this case the contested inaction, had not been previously condemned. On the contrary, the Court carefully studied the legality of the course of conduct undertaken by the Council and the Commission and came close to a condemnation. It actually held that the support for the industry in only one particular Member State was in violation of the Treaty, but ended up by accepting this policy as a transitional measure. The transitional character of the measure was underlined by the fact that it had been terminated, possibly as result of pressure from the Court action, after the 1973/74 season. Although the claim was rejected, the Court held in its decision on the costs:

'In the present case the applicant has had sufficient reason to refer the matter in question to the Court. In these circumstances instead of ordering the applicant to pay all the costs, it is fitting to leave it to bear only the costs which it has itself incurred'.[58]

Implicit in the Court's logic was a clear warning to the Council and the Commission that this sort of legislation is generally not acceptable.

§ 474. Then came the *CNTA Case*, in which a legislative act of the Commission was considered to be (partly) illegal, as a result of which the Commission was condemned to compensate CNTA for the loss suffered. The regime in force in January 1972 for the marketing of colza contained rules for 'refunds' to be granted to exports to third countries in order to compensate for the lower prices prevailing on the world market. These 'refunds' were paid on actual sales but could be fixed in advance. Apart from these 'refunds' the Member States were also authorized to grant 'compensatory amounts' when fluctuations in exchange rates of national currencies led to disturbances in trade. For France this compensatory amount was established by the Commission at FF 3.95 per 100 kgs. from 3 January 1972, and increased to FF 4.75 per 100 kgs. as from 24 January 1972. The compensatory amounts were granted on the date of export; they could not be fixed in advance.

On 6 January 1972 *Comptoir National Technique Agricole (CNTA)* had the

---

57. *First Holtz & Willemsen Case* (134/73), 15 Jan. 1974, [1974] ECR 1-12; CCH para 8255.

58. *Second Holtz & Willemsen Case* (153/73), 2 July 1974, consideration 19, [1974] ECR 697; [1975] 1 CMLR 109; CCH para 8277.

refunds fixed for the export of a specific amount of colza. In setting its price it took into account the refunds and the FF 3.95 per 100 kgs. 'compensatory amount', then in force. But on 26 January the Commission adopted a regulation, published on 28 January, by which all 'compensatory amounts' applicable to oils and fats were rescinded with effect from 1 February 1972, because the Commission considered that 'the present situation on the market is such that the application of these compensatory amounts no longer proves to be essential for avoiding disturbance to trade.'

CNTA performed its export contracts after 1 February 1972 and therefore received no compensatory amounts. It considered that the abolition of the compensatory amounts disturbed the performance of current delivery contracts and claimed damages.

The Court of Justice found that the Commission was entitled to rescind the compensatory amounts; that these amounts could *'not be considered to be tantamount to a guarantee for traders against the risks of alteration of exchange rates'* but that *'the application of the compensatory amounts in practice avoids the exchange risk, so that a trader, even a prudent one, might be induced to omit to cover himself against such risk'* and then went on:

'The Community is therefore liable if, in the absence of an overriding matter of public interest, the Commission abolished with immediate effect and without warning the application of compensatory amounts in a specific sector without adopting transitional measures which would at least permit traders either to avoid the loss which would have been suffered in the performance of export contracts, the existence and irrevocability of which are established by the advance fixing of the refunds, or to be compensated for such a loss'. [59]

§ 475. Thus, it may safely be concluded that a claim for damages is admissible in all cases where the injuries result from allegedly illegal legislative acts, with the exception of cases where the applicant could have sued for the annulment of the legislative act concerned and provided that by its act the Community has caused damage to the applicant. The case-law also leads one to the conclusion that the Court does not easily accept the illegality of legislative acts.

§ 476. However, even when the Court holds that the legislative act concerned is invalid, this does not necessarily mean that such invalidity will constitute a wrongful act for which damages can be granted. In the *First Feram* and the *Third Hauts Fourneaux de Chasse* Cases, the Court of Justice accepted the theory that responsibility in public law does not necessarily lead to liability. These cases concerned the liability of the High Authority of the Coal and

---

59. *CNTA Case* (74/74), 14 May 1975, consideration 43, [1975] ECR 550; [1977] 1 CMLR 190; CCH para 8305. On this case see Jörg Manfred Mössner, *Haftung der Europäischen Gemeinschaft für legislatives Unrecht*, 22 Recht der Internationalen Wirtschaft (1976), pp. 93-95. The action of CNTA finally failed as no damage could be proven, see decision of the Court of 15 June 1976, [1976] ECR 806; CCH para 8361.

Steel Community for the price equalization system for scrap. In the decision establishing the system[60], the High Authority created organs 'under the responsibility of the High Authority'. In the eighth recital to the Decision, the High Authority stated that: 'Considering that the High Authority is responsible for the correct functioning of the financial arrangement and that it must, in consequence, be at any moment in a position to intervene effectively'. From this, *Feram* and *Hauts Fourneaux de Chasse* concluded that the High Authority would be liable for damages caused by the poor functioning of the system. However, the Court held:

'The establishment of the financial arrangements and the principle enunciated in the recital to the abovementioned general decision, of the liability assumed by the High Authority for the regular functioning of this scheme, belong to the political and administrative sphere and cannot thus constitute an obligation to the undertakings under its authority or a guarantee giving rise to objective, contractual or legal liability on the part of the High Authority, even when no wrongful act or omission can be imputed to it'.[61]

This position was again demonstrated in the *Fourth Dried Milk Case*. After the Court had held in the first three *Dried Milk Cases* that EEC Regulation 563/76 was invalid[62], it refused to grant compensation to *Vermehrungsbetriebe* and others for the damage they had suffered from the invalid regulation. In the *Fourth Dried Milk Case* it held:

'It follows from these considerations that individuals may be required, in the sectors coming within the economic policy of the Community, to accept within reasonable limits certain harmful effects on their economic interests as a result of a legislative measure without being able to obtain compensation from public funds even if that measure has been declared null and void. In a legislative field such as the one in question, in which one of the chief features is the exercise of a wide discretion essential for the implementation of the Common Agricultural Policy, the Community does not therefore incur liability unless the institution concerned has manifestly and gravely disregarded the limits on the exercise of its powers'.[63]

§ 477. The final conclusion must, therefore, be that it will be difficult to obtain indemnification for illegal legislation. Nonetheless, the possibility of claiming damages where injuries have been caused by acts which cannot be

60. Decision 14-55 of 26 March 1955, O.J. 30 March 1955, pp. 685-688.
61. *First Feram Case* (23/59), 17 Dec. 1959, [1959] ECR 250; 5 Jur. (1958-59) 556, 557; 5 Rec. (1958-59) 516; *Third Hauts Fourneaux de Chasse Case* (33/59), 14 Dec. 1962, [1962] ECR 390; 8 Jur. (1962) 767; 8 Rec. (1962) 736.
62. *First Dried Milk Case (Bela Mühle)* (114/76), 5 July 1977, [1977] ECR 1211; CCH para 8448; *Second Dried Milk Case (First Granaria)* (116/76), 5 July 1977, [1977] ECR 1247; CCH para 8449; *Third Dried Milk Case (Ölmühle)* (119, 120/76), 5 July 1977, [1977] ECR 1269; CCH para 8450.
63. *Fourth Dried Milk Case (Vermehrungsbetriebe)* (83, 94/76 and 4,15, 40/77), 25 May 1978, consideration 6, [1978] ECR 1224; [1978] 3 CMLR 592.

challenged is of great importance for the judicial protection of individuals. It provides a new and additional opportunity for bringing court proceedings to dispute the legality of Community regulations, besides those of EEC Articles 173, 184 and 177. The main purpose of the action may even be to obtain a court decision that an act is illegal and thus to stop its application or to ensure its replacement in the future, rather than to obtain financial compensation for the past. The *Dried Milk Cases* offer a good example of the parallel application of the preliminary ruling procedure of EEC Article 177 and the suit for damages under EEC Article 215 for the same purpose of obtaining a ruling on the legality of EEC Regulation No. 563/76 which prescribed the use of milkpowder for animal food-stuffs. Four producers of food-stuffs had brought cases before their national courts, while five others had brought suits for damages before the Court of Justice by 5 July 1977, the date on which the Court first ruled on the legality of the regulation.

e. THE GROUND FOR ILLEGALITY OF A LEGISLATIVE ACT

§ 478. After concluding that the invalidity of a legislative act can be established in an Article 215 action, the next consideration should be the grounds upon which such legislative act may be declared invalid. To date the Court of Justice has accepted only one ground on which *legislative measures involving choices as to economic policy* have been declared unlawful and as such create liability on the part of the Community: when there is a *sufficiently flagrant violation of a superior rule of law for the protection of individuals.* [64] Two conclusions, one concerning the ground of illegality, the other the acts involved, can be drawn from the position of the Court.

(i) The ground of illegality

§ 479. In cases under EEC Article 215 the Court does not review the legality of the act on all the grounds mentioned in Chapter Two, IIB (§ 254-287), but only considers whether a 'superior rule of law protecting individuals' has been violated. [65] The formula has not yet been fully clarified, but the Commission

---

64. *Schöppenstedt Case* (5/71), 2 Dec. 1971, consideration 11, [1971] ECR 984; CCH para 8153; *Compagnie d'approvisionnement Case* (9 and 11/71), 13 June 1972, consideration 13, [1972] ECR 403, 404; [1973] CMLR 552; CCH para 8177; *Third Wünsche Case* (59/72), 12 July 1973, considerations 2 and 4, [1973] ECR 803; [1974] 1 CMLR 73; CCH para 8216; *Merkur Case* (43/72), 24 Oct. 1973, consideration 8, [1973] ECR 1070; CCH para 8243; *Werhahn Case* (63-69/72), 13 Nov. 1973, consideration 10, [1973] ECR 1248; CCH para 8236; *Second Holz & Willemsen Case* (153/73), 2 July 1974, consideration 7, [1974] ECR 693; [1975] 1 CMLR 107; CCH para 8277; *CNTA Case* (74/74), 14 May 1975, consideration 16, [1975] ECR 546; [1977] 1 CMLR 188; CCH para 8305. The wording in the English texts is less consistent than in the other languages. The differences in meaning are slight, however. On this ground see in particular Van Gerven (*op. cit.*, note 3), pp. 11-24.
65. In the *Merkur* and *Werhahn* cases the English version reads '... superior rule of law for the protection of the individual'. We assume that 'the individual' means individuals in general, as in the authentic (German) text the plural is used (as well as in the French text which is used most by the Judges *in camera*).

expects that once the various aspects have been more precisely defined, it will provide a reliable guide both for individuals and for Community institutions.[66] It may be deduced from the formula that the Court is primarily concerned about the protection of vested rights, more than it is about the question of validity.

From the Court's consideration in the *Van Gend en Loos Case* that the Treaty not only imposes obligations but also confers rights upon individuals, it may be concluded that an infringement of the Treaty will usually be covered by the formula (see quotation above § 160).

§ 480. There is some authority for the proposition that the general principles of human rights would also be considered as superior rules of law protecting individuals. In the *Handelsgesellschaft Case*, the Court held that, *'respect for fundamental rights forms an integral part of the general principles of law protected by the Court of Justice'*.[67]

The general principle of legal certainty — *in casu* a legitimate expectation — has been accepted by the Court of Justice as a superior rule of law protecting individuals in the *CNTA Case* where the Court of Justice held that the Commission violated a superior rule of law by failing to include in a regulation *'transitional measures for the protection of the confidence which a trader might legitimately have had in the Community rules'*.[68]

§ 481. In the *First Kampffmeyer Case*, the Court underlined that 'rules of law protecting individuals' need not be rules meant to protect the specific interests of the individual concerned.[69] On the subject of interests protected by Regulation No. 19/62 on cereals, the Court emphasized that:

'The fact that these interests are of a general nature does not prevent their including the interests of individual undertakings such as the applicants which as cereal importers are parties engaged in intra-Community trade. Although the application of the rules of law in question is not in general capable of being of direct and individual concern to the said undertakings, that does not prevent the possibility that the protection of their interests may be — as in the present case it is in fact — intended by those rules of law'.[70]

(ii) The acts involved

§ 482. The formula used by the Court of Justice appears to encompass only those legislative measures which involve *'choices as to economic policy'*.

66. Commission, Seventh General Report (1973) para 596.
67. *Handelsgesellschaft Case* (11/70), 17 Dec. 1970, consideration 4, [1970] ECR 1134; [1972] CMLR 283; CCH para 8126.
68. *CNTA Case* (74/74), 14 May 1975, consideration 44, [1975] ECR 550; [1977] 1 CMLR 190; CCH para 8305.
69. Concerning the intention of the law see for England *Gorris v. Scott* (1974) L.R. 9 Ex 125.
70. *Kampffmeyer Case* (5, 7, 13-24/66), 14 July 1967, [1967] ECR 263; 13 Jur. (1967) 328; 13 Rec. (1967) 340; CCH para 8055 (p. 7843).

However, one can hardly imagine that the aim was to control only a limited group of legislative acts. There is no compelling reason why the Court should exclude legislative measures based on, for example, social policy or transport. Rather, the correct interpretation seems to be that the formula is a further clarification of the term 'legislative', and that the purpose of the formula used by the Court is to distinguish policy choices from other Community acts which are governed by the rules for annulment under EEC Article 173.[71]

The negligence to remedy an illegal situation may create a legislative act involving choices of economic policy and may, therefore, give rise to damages.[72]

4. Liability for valid acts

§ 483. The 'non-contractual liability' of EEC Article 215 and Euratom Article 188 covers more than just liability for illegal acts. Unlike ECSC Article 40, EEC Article 215 does not require the plaintiff to prove that the authorities were at fault.[73] As regards Euratom one could perhaps argue that the drafters of Article 188 intended to include the requirement of fault by Community organs on the ground that they would not otherwise have added the provision of Article 28 whereby the Commission may be held liable in a particular case even if it has not committed a fault.[74] However, since the Court of Justice has repeatedly declared itself against the use of such *a contrario* reasoning (see above § 19), the argument is not persuasive. Rather, the texts of the treaties lead one to the conclusion that the two more recent Communities may be held liable for damages caused by their valid acts, provided that the general principles common to the laws of the Member States offer sufficient basis for this.[75]

So far, the case-law of the Court of Justice has not recognized the possibility of liability for valid acts. The Court has repeatedly stated that the illegality of the behaviour of the Community[76] or in the case of a legislative act, the violation of a higher rule of law[77] is a precondition for the Commu-

---

71. The Court uses this test in, e.g. the *Third Merkur Case* (97/76), 8 June 1977, consideration 5, [1977] ECR 1077, 1078; CCH para 8431.
72. *Fifth Kampffmeyer Case* (56-60/74), 2 June 1976, consideration 15, [1976] ECR 744; CCH para 8392.
73. M. Lagrange in 10 Sec. W (1962) p. 99.
74. Fuß (*op. cit.*, note 3), p. 361. The cases he mentions on the same page are all on the ECSC.
75. For the laws of the Member States, see Goffin, *De Aansprakelijkheid*, (*op. cit.*, note 3), pp. 114-116; Dumon (*op. cit.*, note 3), pp. 6, 43-45; Fuß (*op. cit.*, note 3), pp. 362, 363 pleads against the introduction into Community law of the German '*Sonderopfertheorie*', according to which anybody can obtain indemnification when a public act causes specific losses for him. In this respect the law of the new Member States is similar to that of the old ones.
76. *Third Lütticke Case* (4/69), 20 April 1971, consideration 10, [1971] ECR 337; *Schöppenstedt Case* (5/71), 2 Dec. 1971, consideration 11, [1971] ECR 984; CCH para 8153; *First Haegeman Case* (96/71), 25 Oct. 1972, consideration 15, [1972] ECR 1016; [1973] CMLR 383; CCH para 8181.
77. *Schöppensted Case* (5/71), 2 Dec. 1971, consideration 11; *Merkur Case* (43/72), 24 Oct. 1973, consideration 8, [1973] ECR 1070; CCH para 8243.

nity's liability. The sentence quoted above (§ 470) from the *Schöppenstedt Case* that *'the non-contractual liability invoked presupposes at the very least the unlawful nature of the act alleged to be the cause of the damage'* is particularly emphatic on this point.

For a successful suit for damages the Court requires that the Commission should be at fault. It held in the *Second Toepfer Case*:

'It is clear from the foregoing that in this case everything which the Commission did was in accordance with the rules in question and that the rules must be regarded as valid. Consequently there is nothing in the Commission's actions which could give rise to any right to compensation'. [78]

§ 484. In many cases a solution may perhaps be found by finding a separate wrongful act (see above § 461-463). This is actually what the Court did in the *CNTA Case* (above § 474) where it did not consider the disputed regulation to be invalid. Although it was ruled that the Commission was entitled to abolish the application of compensatory amounts it was held liable because it had done so *'with immediate effect and without warning'*. The wrongful act was therefore the failure to adopt transitional measures for imminent transactions and it was for that failure that the Commission was condemned to pay damages, not for a valid act which caused unreasonable injury to traders who had transactions pending.

The attempt has sometimes been made to first establish the illegality of a Community act or inaction in a separate suit. Even if such a suit fails the suit for damages may succeed. An example of this is the *Heinemann Case*, mentioned above (§ 463). Another example can be found in the *Di Pillo Case*. Di Pillo was employed on a trial basis with the Commission on 1 March 1971. According to the Staff Regulations, a report was to be prepared on him before 1 August 1971. [79] When a report with a negative outcome was finally made on 4 November 1971, Di Pillo brought an action for the annulment of the report, and also for the annulment of the decision notifying him of his dismissal which followed the report. He lost both actions, which meant that the report and his dismissal were considered to be legal. However, he succeeded in obtaining an indemnification for the unlawful prolongation of the state of uncertainty in which he was placed after the expiry of the probationary period. [80]

5. The suit for liability

a. THE SUITOR

§ 485. Any person who has suffered injury has a right to bring an action. However, under the ECSC Treaty a problem could arise, as that treaty is

78. *Second Toepfer Case* (112/77), 3 May 1978, consideration 22, [1978] ECR 1033.
79. Staff Regulations, Art. 34.
80. *Di Pillo Case* (10 and 47/72), 12 July 1973, [1973] ECR 771, 772.

generally applicable only to coal and steel firms. In the *Vloeberghs Case*
however, the Court of Justice accepted that an action for damages may be
brought by others as well [81]; it is not therefore anticipated that there will be
any particular difficulties as to who may bring an action under the ECSC
Treaty.

Civil servants may sue the Communities for damages; but for their cases
special procedures have been provided. They must claim their damages from
the Communities under the provisions of the Staff Regulations; if their claims
are rejected they may appeal against the rejection to the Court of Justice in
normal staff proceedings (see above § 325-328). In the *Meyer-Burckhardt
Case* the Court of Justice held:

> 'A dispute between an official and the institution to which he is or was
> answerable concerning compensation for damage is pursued, where it origi-
> nates in the relationship of employment between the person concerned and
> the institution, under Article 179 of the Treaty and Articles 90 and 91 of
> the Staff Regulations and as regards in particular the question of its admis-
> sibility, lies outside the sphere of application of Articles 178 and 215 of
> the Treaty and of Article 43 of the Protocol on the Statute of the Court of
> Justice of the EEC.' [82]

This means that claims for damages brought by officials are decided by a
procedure different from actions brought by other claimants. This does not,
of course, preclude a great similarity between the substantive contents of both
procedures.

b. SUITS AGAINST THE COMMUNITIES

§ 486. Suits for damages brought against the Communities can normally be
served on the Commission. In principle, the institutions do not operate in
isolation and thus share responsibility for any injury caused. As the Community is represented by the Commission [83], it can be sued through the medium
of that institution. If, however, the act in dispute is taken by another institution, that institution may be sued as well (see below § 653).

c. SUITS AGAINST CIVIL SERVANTS

§ 487. Normally, the action for damages can be lodged against the Communities *per se*. There is no need to act against the civil servant who committed
the act, as for example in Belgian law, or even to identify him, as for example

---

81. *Vloeberghs Case* (9 and 12/60), 14 July 1961, [1961] ECR 212-214; 7 Jur. (1961)
446-449; 7 Rec. (1961) 424-426.
82. *Meyer-Burckhardt Case* (9/75), 22 Oct. 1975, consideration 7, [1975] ECR 1181. See
also *Sixth Reinarz Case* (48/76), 17 Feb. 1977, considerations 4-11, [1977] ECR 297, 298.
83. EEC Art. 211.

in German law. [84] If it is clear, however, that a particular civil servant committed the wrongful act, should the action then be brought against that civil servant or against the Community? The appellant may prefer either course. An action against the civil servant may be less costly and easier since it can be brought in a local court; an action against the Community may accord greater security if the amount claimed is high as the solvency of the civil servant may not cover the grant of damages to be expected. The original text of the ECSC Treaty was not entirely clear. Before the Merger Treaty of 8 April 1965, ECSC Article 40, para 2 provided that the Court could order pecuniary reparation from the civil servant who had committed a wrongful act in the performance of his functions. If the civil servant would not pay, the Court could order reparation from the Community. This text suggested that action against the Community would be precluded if a particular civil servant could be sued. Since the Merger Treaty, the ECSC follows the system of the EEC, that is that the action should always be brought against the Community. [85] EEC Article 215(2) clearly provides that the Community must make good any damage caused by its servants in the performance of their duties. Personal liability of civil servants is an internal matter of the Communities and, as such, is governed by internal staff regulations.

§ 488. Unfortunately, this provision does not solve all problems which may arise in this context; it merely changes the nature of borderline cases. In the EEC Treaty it is clear that all suits for damages where injury has been caused by *official* acts should be brought against the Communities. On the other hand, suits for the reparation of injuries caused by *personal* acts of civil servants committed outside their functions should of course be brought against those staff members in a local court. [86] The problem that remains is: what are the criteria for determining what acts are committed 'in the performance of their duties?' This question came before the Court of Justice in the *Sayag Cases*. Sayag, in his function as an engineer of Euratom, went to Mol, Belgium. He drove there in his own private car and on the way caused an accident. Did the accident occur in the performance of his duties? The question first arose in relation to the possible immunity of Sayag from Belgian penal legislation. The Belgian Court of Cassation requested a preliminary ruling, and the Court of Justice replied:

'Hence, driving a motor vehicle is not in the nature of an act performed in an official capacity save in the exceptional cases in which this activity cannot be carried out otherwise than under the authority of the Community and by its own servants.

Finally it is appropriate to emphasize that the designation of an act with regard to immunity from legal proceedings, and any decision taken by the

---

84. See the opinion of Advocate-General Lagrange in the *First Feram Case* (23/59), 17 Dec. 1959, [1959] ECR 253; 5 Jur. (1959) 563-565; 5 Rec. (1959) 523-525 and in 10 SEW (1962), p. 99.
85. For problems of transitional law see Dumon (*op. cit.*, note 3), p. 3 (No. IV).
86. On the ground of Art. 40(3) ECSC 183 EEC or 155 Euratom.

competent institution with regard to waiver of the immunity, do not pre-judge any liability on the part of the Community, this being governed by special rules designed for a purpose separate from that of the provisions of the Protocol on the Privileges and Immunities.'[87]

§ **489.** Subsequently, a suit for damages was brought against Sayag by the victims of the accident. A preliminary ruling was again requested on the meaning of the term 'in the performance of their duties' and on the liability of the Community. In this case the Court held that:

'By referring at one and the same time to damage caused by the institutions and to that caused by the servants of the Community, Article 188 (*of the Euratom treaty, which is the same as 215 EEC*) indicated that the Community is only liable for those acts of its servants which, by virtue of an internal and direct relationship, are the necessary extension of the tasks entrusted to the institutions.

Only in the case of *force majeure* or in exceptional circumstances of such overriding importance that without the servant's using private means of transport the Community would have been unable to carry out the tasks entrusted to it, could such use be considered to form part of the servant's performance of his duties, within the meaning of the second paragraph of Article 188 of the Treaty.'[88]

§ **490.** By referring to the treaty provisions in the context of the general rules on immunity and considering both *Sayag Cases* the following conclusion may be made. A civil servant who causes damages by an act which may be considered private should be sued privately in a local court. If he invokes immunity of jurisdiction, the administrative head of the institution for which he works should be officially asked to waive such immunity. When the immunity is waived, the national court has jurisdiction and the civil servant personally is responsible. If immunity is not waived, the Community would thereby indicate that the act is within the performance of its functions, because immunity may only be invoked for such acts. An action can then be brought against the Communities before the Court of Justice.

This system, although easy to operate, may be subject to abuse: the Community might waive immunity in cases where it would be liable in order to protect itself against court action. This would leave the full burden to be borne by the official who may not always be solvent. The second paragraph quoted above from the *First Sayag Case* copes with this sort of abuse. It clearly states that in such cases, the Community can nonetheless be sued for damages. However, care must be exercised in interpreting this paragraph. The decision cannot be interpreted to mean that there is no relationship at all

---

87. *First Sayag Case* (5/68), 11 July 1968, [1968] ECR 402; 14 Jur. (1968) 559; 14 Rec. (1968) 585, 586; [1969] CMLR 22, 23.
88. *Second Sayag Case* (9/69), 10 July 1969, considerations 7 and 11, [1969] ECR 335, 336.

between the waiving of immunity and liability. If immunity has been waived, only then can the civil servant be sued before a national court. Since the Community authorities have indicated by their waiver that they consider no official act to be involved, it is doubtful whether the national court will ask further clarification on liability in a preliminary ruling. If it does, the Court of Justice may indicate that it does not share the opinion of the waiving authorities, because it considers the act to be an official one and, consequently, the Community and not its official should be liable. More probably, the civil servant will be found liable. Therefore, any action brought against the Community would be secondary, and only for unrecovered damages.

Furthermore, it would be hard to accept that the invocation of immunity in doubtful cases would not affect the liability of the Community. The conclusion that the Community could invoke immunity without then becoming fully responsible for the act would lead to the unacceptable result that no action would be possible at all.

d. SUITS AGAINST MEMBER STATES

(i) Court where the suit must be brought

§ 491. A substantial amount of Community law is executed by Member States. As with civil servants, they may commit errors in its execution. Can the Communities be held liable for acts taken by the Member States in the execution of Community law, or should the Member States be held liable, or both? The problem may be approached in several ways; but even before the question of liability can be raised, the practical question as to which court the action should be brought in, must be answered. Theoretically, this latter question need not be decisive. Both the Community Court and the national courts will come to the same decision on liability, provided they apply the same rules of law. When the matter concerns Community law the national courts will apply it only after having obtained a preliminary ruling on its interpretation, whilst in a similar case the Court of Justice will apply it directly.

In practice, however, it is important to decide which court to bring the action in as the national courts do not have the power to compel the Communities to pay damages, nor can the Court of Justice decide against a Member State in a suit for damages.

The applicant may, for two reasons, favour a judgment by the Court of Justice. (1) The proceedings before the Court of Justice are generally faster. They will be decided at least within a year, whilst national proceedings at first instance will normally take about the same length of time. In addition, however, more time may be required for an appeal and if a preliminary ruling is sought this will add at least another six months before the national court can give its final judgment. (2) In an action before the Court of Justice the parties are given a full hearing on the questions of Community law (see § 677, 688, 696), whilst in the case of a preliminary ruling the applicant is dependent upon the national court making the request and also the formulation of the question. His pleadings are, furthermore, limited to one written and one oral statement.

§ 492.   These two advantages might result in individuals bringing actions before the Court of Justice against the Communities for damages caused by acts of their own States whenever some aspect of Community law is involved. This could create an unacceptably large volume of cases being brought to Luxembourg. For reasons of self-defence the Court of Justice had to somehow restrict these direct actions. This the Court has done by ruling that the Member State should be sued whenever it has committed or authorized the execution of the wrongful act. Then the Member State can be ordered to repay the sums it has collected or to pay compensation for the damages it has caused. [89] This does not always lead to the most acceptable solution. Roquette, for example, had to pay a levy which it considered to be in breach of Community law. It sued both the French Government and the Community for damages, before a French court and the Court of Justice respectively. The French Government admitted that the levy was incorrect but submitted that it was obliged to collect it under Community law. The French court requested a preliminary ruling. In the *First Roquette Case* the Court of Justice held that the levy was void and in pursuance of this ruling the French court ordered the French Government to repay the levies paid. Roquette then restricted its claim for damages against the Communities to the interest (and some other minor costs) on the money which was illegally withheld for a considerable period of time from the firm. Though the levies were collected by the Member States they were subsequently passed on to the Communities. It must therefore be assumed that the latter profited from the interest on the illegal levies as they could dispose of the money between its illegal payment and its return.

The case also demonstrated that no fault could be attributed to the French Government in collecting the levies. A condemnation of the French Government for payment of the interest, therefore, seemed unlikely. As the national courts cannot condemn the Communities to pay damages, the Court of Justice decided the question whether the Communities were liable in the negative when it held:

'It is clear ... that the national authorities must ensure on behalf of the Community and in accordance with the provisions of Community law that a certain number of dues, including the monetary compensatory amounts, are collected.

Under Article 6 of the decision of 21 April 1970, the terms of which were repeated by Article 1 of Regulation No. 2/71, these collections shall be made by Member States in accordance with national provisions laid down by law, regulation or administrative action.

Disputes in connexion with the reimbursement of amount collected for

89.   See also Christopher Harding, *The choice of court problem in cases of non-contractual liability under EEC law*, 16 CMLRev. (1979), pp. 389-406.

the Community are thus a matter for the national courts and must be settled by them under national law in so far as no provisions of Community law are relevant.

In the absence of provisions of Community law on this point, it is currently for the national authorities, in the case of reimbursement of dues improperly collected, to settle all ancillary questions relating to such reimbursement, such as any payment of interest.'[90]

§ 492a.   The conclusion from the case-law of the Court of Justice should be that claims for repayment as well as payment of sums which have been wrongfully withheld must be brought before the national courts. The choice of which court to bring the other actions for damages in depends on the responsible for the harm committed. Such suits should come before the Court of Justice when the Community is to be blaimed and before the national courts when the national authorities are at fault. Harding's suggestion that the national court should be seized of the action whenever it can do anything concrete for the applicant or whenever a specific sum is claimed[91] will lead to almost the same result.

The Court of Justice has stated that it has no jurisdiction in cases in which the application is in fact directed against measures adopted by the national authorities for the purpose of applying Community law, but that it will gave a ruling under EEC Article 215 if the Community rules applicable are such as to cause damage.[92]

(ii)   Basis for community liability

§ 493.   In practice there may often be no ground for reprimanding the Community. In many cases it has no alternative but to leave the execution of particular functions to the Member States and it has no authority, to compel the Member States to utilize a specific method for executing their Community functions. In the case of its civil servants the Communities can at least be assumed to have the power to give orders and to lay down the course of action required. As regards the Member States the Communities only have the opportunity to bring pressure to bear under EEC Article 169 and even then this is a slow-moving procedure, as was described in Chapter Two (above § 380-432). The Community exercises no real authority over its Member States, even when they perform Community functions.

It therefore seems reasonable to submit that the Communities should be responsible for the performance of Community law even if it is delegated to the Member States, but that they cannot be held liable if it can be demonstrated that they have taken sufficient care to assure proper execution of this law.

90. *Second Roquette Case* (26/74), 21 May 1976, considerations 9-12, [1976] ECR 686; CCH para 8371.
91. Harding (*op. cit.* note 89), p. 392.
92. *Dietz Case* (126/76), 15 Dec. 1977, consideration 5, [1977] ECR 2441; [1978] 2 CMLR 621; CCH para 8459.

§ 494. The Court of Justice has so far not held the Community liable for tasks which it has delegated to its Member States. In the *Grands Moulins Case* it expressly held that an alleged fault committed by a Member State under Community law did not involve the non-contractual liability of the Community. The case concerned carry-over payments which could be granted by the competent authority of the Member State in whose territory stocks were situated.

Grands Moulins claimed the payment from the Community when it could not obtain it from the French authorities, and after the former's refusal to pay, it sued the Community for damages. The Court of Justice held:

'The refusal by a Community institution to pay a debt which may be owed by a Member State under Community law is not a matter involving the non-contractual liability of the Community. For an action involving non-contractual liability to lie it is necessary that an injury arising from an act or omission of the Community be alleged'.[93]

§ 495. In the *IBC Case* the Court of Justice again stressed that injuries caused by acts of national authorities in executing Community law should be brought before the national courts. In that case the Court of Justice held:

'The action in fact concerns decisions of the Italian authorities adopted in implementation of Community rules which the applicant regards as unlawful. It thus concerns the legality of the imposition of the sums in dispute by the national authorities responsible for the implementation and enforcement of the provisions concerning monetary compensatory amounts and seeks the reimbursement, by the Community rather than by the national authorities, of the sums which are said to have been improperly charged.

The provisions of these rules lay down criteria for the calculation of sums payable by way of equalization between the import charge and the compensatory amounts and therefore leave no doubt that the actual assessment and imposition of the sums due are matters for the national authorities.

The question of the legality of such implementing measures adopted in pursuance of Community law is, therefore, a matter for the competent national courts of tribunals to decide, using the procedures laid down under national law and after application, where appropriate, of Article 177 of the Treaty, in particular on questions concerning the validity of the Community provisions applied'.[94]

(iii) Shared liability [95]

§ 496. In my view the Community *should* be liable whenever it can be held responsible. This means that it should be liable also in those cases where

93. *Grands Moulins Case* (99/74), 26 Nov. 1975, considerations 16, 17, [1975] ECR 1439; CCH para 8325. See T.C. Hartley in 1 ELRev. (1976) pp. 299-304 and pp. 396-399.
94. *IBC Case* (46/75), 27 Jan. 1976, considerations 3-5, [1976] ECR 79; CCH para 8339.
95. See Durdan, (*op. cit.*, note 3), p. 238; Trevor C. Hartley, *Concurrent liability: a wrong*

responsibility is shared. For those cases a right of redress against the Member State is then needed. EEC Article 215(3) deals with the relationship between the Community and its civil servants. But there is no similar article governing the situation where injury has been jointly caused by the Communities and the Member States. If the liability of the Community is caused by a Member State performing its duties as a Member badly, the right of redress must be derived from the general principles common to the laws of the Member States, but so far this has not been attempted.

At this actual stage of the development of Community law, full responsibility and liability on the part of the Communities for all acts performed under Community law, together with a possibility for redress from the responsible executive authorities, is not realizable. This is partly due to the very independent position of the Member States in the Community legal system and partly to the practical problems which would arise from a substantial increase in cases taken before the Court of Justice as a result.

§ 497 In practice the Member States, in executing Community rules, and the Communities themselves are each held liable for their own wrongful acts. The decisions as to liability, however, are made by different courts: for the Member States the national courts must decide; for the Communities, the Court of Justice (see above § 491, 492).

§ 498. When liability is shared the most important problem to be solved is to establish what is the degree of liability of each party. Should the Court of Justice postpone the assessment of the Community's share of liability until the Member State's liability has been ascertained or should it be the other way round?

In the *First Feram Case* (under the ECSC Treaty) the Court of Justice seemed to reason that when a matter of Community law is involved an attempt should first be made to establish responsibility for the injury on the part of the Communities. In this case the Coal and Steel Community had left the task of issuing certificates for scrap imports to the national authorities. In the Netherlands some certificates had been falsified and Feram claimed damages by reason of being a contributor to the scrap equalization fund. The Court of Justice did not refer the claimant to the national (Dutch) court for action against the Dutch government, which might have been liable for the fraud committed by a Dutch civil servant. On the contrary, the Court carefully considered whether the Community had committed a fault. By reaching a negative conclusion, however, the question of sharing the responsibility was precluded.[96]

---

turning by the Court? 1 ELRev. (1976), pp. 465-469; *Idem* in 1 ELRev. (1976), pp. 555, 556; *Idem, Concurrent Liability in EEC law: A Critical Review of the Cases*, 2 ELRev. (1977), pp. 249-265.
96. *First Feram Case* (23/59), 17 Dec. 1959, [1959] ECR 252; 5 Jur. (1958-59) 558, 559; 5 Rec. (1958-59) 517, 518.

§ 499. In the *First Kampffmeyer Case* (under the EEC Treaty) the Court adopted a different line. According to the agricultural system which led to the dispute in this case, the EEC left the actual collection and administration of the levies to the Member States. The amount of the levies depended on the relevant Community provisions. The system provided for safeguard measures which the Member States could take under certain circumstances, but which had to be notified immediately to the Commission. The Commission could then annul, change, or uphold them. The German government had taken safeguard measures which the Commission had upheld, but which the Court, in another case, had considered illegal. It had, therefore, annulled the Commission's decision upholding them.[97] Kampffmeyer sued the Commission for damages based on this illegal decision. The Court of Justice found that the Commission had infringed upon the interests of the importers and that its conduct constituted a wrongful act entailing liability on the part of the Community. It then investigated the alleged injuries from which the liability arose and subsequently held:

'Before determining the damage for which the Community should be held liable, it is necessary for the national court to have the opportunity to give judgment on any liability on the part of the Federal Republic of Germany. This being the case, final judgment cannot be given before the applicants have produced the decision of the national court on this matter'.[98]

This decision marked the start of a period in which Kampffmeyer and other firms in the same situation were sent from pillar to post. It took more than seven years before the highest German court finally decided the matter in favour of the importers[99]; and it took about nine years before the applicants were able to withdraw their cases from the register of the Court of Justice due to the fact that their actions had been settled before the German courts.[100]

§ 500. Why did the Court of Justice not hold the Community liable for the full damage done to Kampffmeyer and indicate that Germany would be obliged to refund the Community for part of the paid compensation? There may have been several reasons. First, Kampffmeyer has asked indemnification only for the injuries caused by the acts of the Commission, and had not sued the Community for the injuries caused by the German government when acting in execution of Community rules, nor had it sued for all injuries caused by '*the Community*'. Second, the Court might have found it difficult to define the grounds on which it could hold that Germany was under a legal

---

97. *First Toepfer Case* (106-107/63), 1 July 1965, [1965] ECR 405 ff; 11 Jur. (1965) 507 ff; 11 Rec. (1965) 525; [1966] CMLR 111 ff; CCH para 8031.
98. *First Kampffmeyer Case* (5, 7, 13-24/66), 14 July 1967, [1967] ECR 266; 13 Jur. (1967) 331; 13 Rec. (1967) 344; CCH para 8055 (p. 7845).
99. *German Getreidehandel Case, Bundesgerichtshof*, 12 Dec. 1974. See Theodor Elster, *Non-contractual liability under two legal orders*, 12 CMLRev. (1975), pp. 91-100 and 254-257.
100. *Bulletin of the European Communities*, 1976 No. 2, para 2436, p. 73.

obligation to refund to the Community part of the compensation already paid out by the Community, though it was obvious that Germany should pay at least the sum total of the illegal levies which it had collected. Third, in this exceptional situation suits before national courts seemed easier. Kampffmeyer could bring a suit to recover unauthorized payment before a German court in well-established proceedings; whereas in the Community Court, it would have to resort to the general principles of the laws of the Member States which are vague and which may not even cover the relationship between the Community and its Members.

Whatever the reason for the decision, the outcome of the case is poor and demonstrates that dividing up cases on liability between the Court of Justice and national courts leads to serious complications.

So far no court has ever clearly divided responsibility for harm due to an applicant between Community and national institutions.

When both are liable the applicants will have to bring two suits: one before the national court against the Member State for damages caused by that State and possibly for repayment of illegaly collected sums, or for payment of sums which were illegally withheld, and a second before the Court of Justice for compensation of damages caused by the Community.

When a national court has been approached first in a case of shared responsibility, it might consider to request a preliminary ruling on the question to what extent the Community is jointly liable. If the Court of Justice would give a preliminary ruling indicating what percentage of the damage the Community should be held liable for, then the national court could condemn the Member State for the rest of the damages, whilst the Commission would probably be willing to pay the Community's share on the basis of the preliminary ruling. For the applicant it would then be sufficient to bring one case before his national court. In the *Second Granaria Case*, however, the Court of Justice refused to accept this kind of joining of the two suits for damages.

Presumably on the ground that in a preliminary procedure the Commission's right of defence would be insufficient, it ruled that questions concerning the Community's non-contractual liability cannot be decided in proceedings under EEC Article 177.[101]

6. Damages

a. THE SUBMISSION OF THE CLAIM

§ 501. In the action for damages, the applicant must clearly allege the injuries he has actually suffered and on what grounds he submits the Community is under an obligation to indemnify him. If the grounds for damages are insufficient, the Court may either declare the request inadmissible[102], or re-

---

101. *Second Granaria Case* (101/78), 13 Feb. 1979, consideration 10.
102. *Luhleich Case* (68/63), 8 July 1965, [1965] ECR 604; 11 Jur. (1965) 782; 11 Rec. (1965) 752, 753; [1966] CMLR 258.

ject it on the merits.[103] Similarly, a request for an unspecified amount of compensation may be declared inadmissible[104], or may be rejected on the merits.[105] However, this rule is not without exception. In the *Third Granaria Case* the Court held that Granaria's submission that is suffered damages from an EEC provision and that it would later specify these damages, did not meet the requirement that the application must describe the subject matter of the dispute. But then the Court went on to state that in the circumstances of the case the incompleteness of the application did not necessarily lead to inadmissibility, because considerations of economy of proceedings may move the Court to decide at the first stage on the question whether the behaviour of the Community institutions could lead to their liability, leaving to a possible later stage the questions of causal link, the nature and the amount of the damages.[106]

An action for damages where injury will, allegedly, be suffered in the future was considered premature and therefore inadmissible in the *Third Feram Case*.[107] Also, in the *First Richez-Parise Case*[108] the Court held that the injury must actually exist at the time of litigation, (*causé aux requérants un préjudice né et actuel*). In the *Fifth Kampffmeyer Case*, however, the Court revoked this position when it held:

'Article 215 of the Treaty does not prevent the Court from being asked to declare the Community liable for imminent damage foreseeable with sufficient certainty even if the damage cannot yet be precisely assessed.

To prevent even greater damage it may prove necessary to bring the matter before the Court as soon as the cause of damage is certain.

This finding is confirmed by the rules in force in the legal systems of the Member States, the majority, if not all, of which recognize an action for declaration of liability based on future damage which is sufficiently certain'.[109]

The applicant must be able to prove the nature and extent of the injury; if he cannot, he will lose on the merits.[110] The exact amount of the harm cannot

---

103. *First van Eick Case* (35/67), 11 July 1968, [1968] ECR 345; 14 Jur. (1968) 484; 14 Rec. (1968) 505.
104. *Lasalle Case* (15/63), 4 March 1964, [1964] ECR 39; 10 Jur. (1964) 76; 10 Rec. (1964) 74; [1964] CMLR 283; *Schöppenstedt Case* (5/71), 2 Dec. 1971, consideration 9, [1971] ECR 984; CCH para 8153.
105. *Second van Eick Case* (13/69), 4 Feb. 1970, [1970] ECR 14.
106. *Third Granaria Case* (90/78), 28 March 1979, considerations 5, 6 (at the time of writing no English translation of the case was available).
107. *Third Feram Case* (9, 25/64), 2 June 1965, [1965] ECR 320; 11 Jur. (1965) 404; 11 Rec. (1965) 414; [1965] CMLR 309, 310.
108. *First Richez-Parise Case* (19, 20, 25, 30/69), 28 May 1970, consideration 31, [1970] ECR 338.
109. *Fifth Kampffmeyer Case* (56-60/74), 2 June 1976, consideration 6, [1976] ECR 741; CCH para 8392. See also *Second Diverted Butter Case (Eier-Kontor)* (44/76), 2 March 1977, consideration 8, [1977] ECR 407; CCH para 8416.
110. See e.g. *Mirossevich Case* (10/55), 12 Dec. 1956, [1954-56] ECR 344, 345; 2 Jur. (1955/56) 415; 2 Rec. (1955/56) 390; *Fourth Meroni Case* (14, 16, 17, 20, 24, 26, 27/60

always be proved; particularly in cases of immaterial damages the Court will decide in equity (*ex aequo et bono*)[111] and may change the amounts asked.

b. IMMATERIAL DAMAGES

§ 502. The Court has granted compensation not only for actual losses suffered, but also for immaterial damage. For example, when the appointment of Miss *Algera* was illegally withdrawn, the Court considered that this entailed upheaval and discomfort to her which caused immaterial damage estimated at $ 100.[112] In another case, where Miss De Bruyn was dismissed without sufficient reason, she obtained compensation fixed by the Court *ex aequo et bono* at BF 40,000 ($ 800).

In various cases where damages were not granted the Court held:

'A measure which has not been shown to be unlawful cannot constitute a wrongful act or omission and thus unlawfully prejudice the honour and reputation of the person to whom it refers, unless it contains superfluous criticisms of that person'.[113]

The last part of the sentence indicates that in extreme cases of damage to one's reputation compensation will be possible.

In the *First Willame Case* the judgment in the report concerning the plaintiff's assimilation into the civil service of the Community was negative. When the Court found an irregularity in the making of this report it granted him a sum of BF 20,000 ($ 400) as compensation for immaterial damage.[114]

In the *Di Pillo Case* Di Pillo obtained an indemnification of BF 200,000 ($ 4000) for the unlawful prolongation of the state of uncertainty in which he was placed after the expiry of his probationary period. This had prevented him from looking after his interests adequately, in particular his career and his position in general (see above § 484).[115] Miss Mollet, who was left in a state

---

and 1/61), 13 July 1961, [1961] ECR 167; 7 Jur. (1961) 349; 7 Rec. (1961) 335, or *Lasalle Case* (15/63), 4 March 1964, [1964] ECR 39; 10 Jur. (1964) 76; 10 Rec. (1964) 74; [1964] CMLR 283.
111. The Court granted damages *ex aequo et bono* e.g. in the *Leda de Bruyn Case* (25/60), 1 March 1962, [1962] ECR 31; 8 Jur. (1962) 62; 8 Rec. (1962) 60; [1962] CMLR 183.
112. *Algera Case* (7/56, 3-7/57), 12 July 1957, [1957-58] ECR 67; 3 Jur. (1957) 138; 3 Rec. (1957) 130.
113. *Leroy Case* (35/62 and 16/63), 5 Dec. 1963, [1963] ECR 207; 9 Jur. (1963) 437; 9 Rec. (1963) 420; [1964] CMLR 574; *De Vos van Steenwijk Case* (84/63), 25 June 1964, [1964] ECR 334; 10 Jur. (1964) 689; 10 Rec. (1964) 660; *Georges Case* (87/63), 7 July 1964, [1964] ECR 484; 10 Jur. (1964) 994, 10 Rec. (1964) 950; *Minot van Nuffel Case* (93/63), 7 July 1964, [1964] ECR 511; 10 Jur. (1964) 1051; 10 Rec. (1964) 1002; *Prakash Case* (19 and 65/63), 8 July 1965; [1965] ECR 557; 11 Jur. (1965) 613; 11 Rec. (1965) 704; [1966] CMLR 275.
114. *First Willame Case* (110/63), 8 July 1965, [1965] ECR 667; 11 Jur. (1965) 922; 11 Rec. (1965) 823; [1966] CMLR 242.
115. *Di Pillo Case* (10 and 47/72), 12 July 1973, [1973] ECR 772.

of uncertainty regarding her state of health for too long a period, received BF 50,000 (then about $ 1500) as compensation for immaterial damage. [116]

c. LOST PROFIT

§ 503. In the *First Kampffmeyer Case* a number of applicants had suffered damages as result of the fact that the EEC Commission had illegally authorized the German authorities to refuse to grant import licences at a zero levy. The Court considered that the applicants should be paid compensation not only for the levy which had been illegally paid, but also for lost profit in cases where importers had cancelled their contracts. In the latter situation the Court took into account the speculative nature of the applicant's purchases. It found no justification for their claim to all the profit they could have realized by completing the transactions already initiated. Instead, their indemnification was estimated at 10 percent of the amount they would have paid in levies if they had performed the sales contracts which had been concluded and were then cancelled. [117]

In the *CNTA Case* the Court took into consideration the fact that the applicant had no guarantee and that CNTA could not therefore legitimately expect, in all circumstances, to make the profits which would have been accrued to it had the disputed action of the Commission not occurred. Therefore the protection it could claim was merely that of not suffering loss. [118]

In the *Heinemann Case* the Commission had wrongly told the applicant that he would receive pension rights from his 55th birthday. On the basis of that submission Heinemann had terminated his contract. When it turned out that pension rights would be paid only from Heinemann's 60th birthday, the Court granted compensation equal to the pension rights which Heinemann would have received between his 55th and his 60th birthday. [119]

d. PROOF

§ 504. If injury cannot be shown there will be no compensation (see above § 501). There has been some development in the case-law of the Court of Justice as to the amount of proof needed for a case to be successful. The Court was rather exacting in the *First Fives Lille Cail Case*, where it accepted that the High Authority had committed a wrongful act by exercising insufficient control (see above § 453). This wrongful act of the High Authority had caused Fives Lille Cail to believe that, when using shipbreaking scrap, it would get the difference in transport costs refunded. As damages, Fives Lille Cail

---

116. *Mollet Case* (75/77), 13 April 1978, considerations 26-29, [1978] ECR 908, 909.
117. *First Kampffmeyer Case* (5, 7, 13-24/66), 14 July 1967, [1967] ECR 266; 13 Jur. (1967) 331; 13 Rec. (1967) 334; CCH para 8055 (p. 7845).
118. *CNTA Case* (74/74), 14 May 1975, considerations 45, 45, [1975] ECR 550; [1977] 1 CMLR 190, 191; CCH para 8305.
119. *Heinemann Case* (79/71), 13 July 1972, consideration 14, [1972] ECR 590.

claimed that difference in transport costs. The Court considered, however, that the wrongful act did not stem from the refusal to pay a transport subsidy, but from the inadequacy of the supervision, and that loss could be compensated only if it could be established that the purchase of shipbreaking scrap, without the relief provided for by the transport rebate, would have been more onerous for the applicants than a straightforward purchase of imported scrap. Apart from the issue of transport costs, there were also questions of quality and availability. As Fives Lille Cail had neither advanced nor offered any further proof of specific damages the Court rejected its application. [120] Fives Lille Cail then brought a new case in which the Court ordered the parties to produce the figures necessary for establishing the injury. [121] In a third decision, the Court finally decided on the damages according to the figures produced (the damages were fixed at a far lower amount than were originally claimed).[122] Six years had then elapsed since the wrongful act had been committed, and four and a half years since the first judgment.

§ 505. Possibly because of the undesirability of such long Court proceedings, or perhaps because it was a clearer situation, the Court was less exacting in the *Di Pillo Case*. In this case the applicant had also enumerated some clear and specific losses (up to a total of BF 2,683,400,–) which he claimed as damages because of the unlawful prolongation of the state of uncertainty after his probationary period as an official of the Commission (see above § 484). As in the *First Fives Lille Cail Case* the Court rejected the specific claim, because the losses were due to certain measures. Di Pillo had himself taken and for which the Commission held no responsibility. Nevertheless compensation was granted to him, not on the ground of the specific losses incurred, but because the unreasonable delay after the expiry of the probationary period had prevented Di Pillo from adequately looking after his interests.

Unlike the plaintiff in the *First Fives Lille Cail Case*, Di Pillo was not compelled to start new proceedings. In the same proceedings the Court granted him compensation which, according to the Court *'may fairly be determined at BF 200,000'* ($ 4000).[123]

The simpler procedure of the Di Pillo Case seems to be the better one. As the Court has unlimited jurisdiction in deciding cases on damages, it must have sufficient freedom to decide both on the exact amount and on the exact grounds for damages. Had the Court ordered the production of figures in the *First Fives Lille Cail Case*, instead of in the second, the parties would not have wasted four years.

---

120. *First Fives Lille Cail Case* (19, 21/60 and 2, 3/61), 15 Dec. 1961, [1961] ECR 298; 7 Jur. (1961) 627; 7 Rec. (1961) 593; [1962] CMLR 283.
121. *Second Fives Lille Cail Case (Laminoirs Case)* (29, 31, 36, 39-47, 50, 51/63), 9 Dec. 1965, [1965] ECR 934-941; 11 Jur. (1965) 1228-1236; 11 Rec. (1965) 1154-1162.
122. *Idem*, decision of 7 June 1966, [1966] ECR 141-144; 12 Jur. (1966) 204-208; 12 Rec. (1966) 203-206.
123. *Di Pillo Case* (10 and 47/72), 12 July 1973, considerations 19-25, [1973] ECR 771, 772.

§ 506. In the *CNTA Case* the Court of Justice arrived at another simple solution. It did not settle the amount for damage forthwith as there was insufficient proof, nor it did oblige the parties to furnish the necessary proof. But it did order them to come to an agreement within six months, and in the absence of such an agreement to provide the Court within the same period with conclusions backed up by detailed figures. [124] When after six months it was demonstrated that CNTA could not prove specific damages, it lost its case. [125]

From the recent case-law of the Court it appears safe to infer that in order to establish the liability of the Communities the actual *amount* of the damages need not be proven. The Court is prepared to leave the actual assessment of the damages to a later decision. In the *Cooperatives Agricoles Case* it demonstrated this willingness in holding that it could deal with the '*preliminary matter of possible liability on the part of the Community*' even at a stage of the proceedings where it was impossible for the Court to reach a decision on the amount of the damages. [126]

It must, however, be obvious that the injury was caused by an illegal act of the Communities. In the *Second Roquette Case*, the action for damages was rejected, as the applicant was unable to prove that the damages claimed had been suffered. In that case the Court held:

'Although the Court expressly requested the applicant to supplement the particulars of its claim in this respect, the latter merely produced overall figures the interpretation of which is doubtful and it failed to prove any actual damage which it has specifically suffered in the course of its business or a causal connexion between this damage and the measures adopted by the Commission.

The fact that the applicant has reduced its claim to nominal damages does not relieve it of providing conclusive proof of the damage suffered.

Consequently this head of the claim must be dismissed.' [127]

e. CAUSAL LINK [128]

§ 507. Compensation for damages will only be granted if the injuries have been *caused* by the acts of the Community. The causal link is required in both ECSC Article 40 (injury *caused* by a wrongful act or omission on the part of

---

124. *CNTA Case* (74/74), 14 May 1975, [1975] ECR 551; [1977] 1 CMLR 191; CCH para 8305.
125. *CNTA Case* (74/74), 15 June 1976, [1976] ECR 806.
126. *Cooperatives Agricoles Case* (95-98/74, 15 and 100/75), 10 Dec. 1975, consideration 5; [1975] ECR 1635. On the action for a declaration of liability see also Advocate General Reischl's opinion in the *Fifth Kampffmeyer Case* (56-60/74), 2 June 1976, [1976] ECR 748.
127. *Second Roquette Case* (26/74), 21 May 1976, considerations 22-25, [1976] ECR 688; CCH para 8371.
128. On causality, see also Advocate-General Trabucchi's opinion in the *Compagnie Continentale Case* (169/73), 4 Feb. 1975, [1975] ECR 148-154.

the Community) and EEC Article 215(2) (damage *caused* by its institutions or servants). It also forms part of the general principles common to the laws of the Member States. The Court has accepted the notion of a causal link on a number of occasions, without any further elaboration. [129] The Advocates-General paid particular attention to the question whether inaction by the Communities can cause damages in cases where the illegal act has been committed by a Member State and the Communities have failed to use their powers to have the act withdrawn. Both Advocate-General Roemer [130] and Advocate-General Gand [131] were of the opinion that a failure to exercise adequate control can be considered as a *direct cause* of the damage. In the *First Kampffmeyer Case* where the act had been committed by the German government and expressly approved by the Commission, the Court accepted the causal link between the act of approval and the damage suffered.

§ 508.   The causal link can be severed by contributory negligence on the part of the applicant claiming damages. [132] In the *Compagnie Continentale Case* the Court of Justice considered:

'It is right, however, to inquire whether there is a chain of causation between the behaviour of the Council and the alleged damage.

One must ask not only whether the conduct in fact caused the wrong impression on the applicant's part that the compensatory amounts would remain fixed in spite of Article 55(6), but also whether it could and should have caused such an error in the mind of a prudent person.

...

The applicant, as a prudent exporter, fully informed of the conditions of the market, was not unaware and in any event could not be unaware that such was the position at the time the contracts were concluded, and of the consequences which would result therefrom as regards the compensatory amounts.'

The Court then considered that the applicant's correspondence demonstrated that he was effectively in a position to appreciate the situation and that '*accordingly the damage alleged has not been caused by the conduct of the Council*'.

The application was dismissed but the Council was condemned to pay its

129. For Art. 40 ECSC *inter alia* in the *Worms Case* (18/60), 12 July 1962, [1962] ECR 206; 8 Jur. (1962) 417; 8 Rec. (1962) 401; [1963] CMLR 12 and in the *Aciéries du Temple Case* (36/62), 16 Dec. 1963, [1963] ECR 298; 9 Jur. (1963) 630; 9 Rec. (1963) 603; [1964] CMLR 57; for Art. 215 (2) EEC in the *Third Lütticke Case* (4/69), 28 April 1971, consideration 10, [1971] ECR 337; CCH para 8136; *Produits Bertrand Case* (40/75) 21 Jan. 1976, considerations 5, 9, 14, [1976] ECR 8, 9; [1976] 1 CMLR 232, 233; CCH para 8337. On the causal link see also *Fuß* (*op. cit.*, note 3), pp. 363-366.
130. Opinion in the *Vloeberghs Case* (9 and 12/60), 14 July 1961, [1961] ECR 240; 7 Jur. (1961) 503; 7 Rec. (1961) 475.
131. Opinion in the *First Kampffmeyer Case* (5, 7, 13-24/66), 14 July 1967, [1967] ECR 278; 13 Jur. (1967) 347; 13 Rec. (1967) 360; CCH para 8055.
132. *Van Gerven* (*op. cit.*, note 3), p. 25.

own costs of the proceedings since *'the Court has found that the conduct of the Council was such as to make the Community liable'*.[133]

The reasoning leaves little doubt that another applicant who is not in a position to be so well informed would succeed in obtaining damages for the injury caused by the conduct of the Council which made the Community liable.

C. SUITS BROUGHT BY CIVIL SERVANTS

§ 509. By virtue of EEC Article 179 the Court of Justice has jurisdiction in any dispute between the Community and its servants. Almost a third of the Court's cases involve Community staff[134], but as they are decided in a Chamber of the Court (see below § 649) the actual time the judges spend on staff cases is less than proportional to the number of such cases. Recently, the percentage of staff cases has diminished. Since 1975 it has been less than a sixth of the total number of cases.[135]

The vast majority of these cases could equally well be decided by an administrative tribunal similar to those existing at the UN and the ILO. In the event of the Court of Justice being overloaded with cases, such a system could be resorted to. The Council in fact decided on 26 November 1974 that a special court for civil servants' cases would be desirable. The Court of Justice could then act as a court of appeals.[136] This decision was worked on by the Commission, which officially proposed the creation of a staff tribunal in September 1978.[137]

§ 510. All sorts of disputes may arise between the Communities and members of their staff. In practice such disputes are not brought directly before a court. The Communities settle disputes with civil servants by means of an official act which the civil servants may challenge before the Court of Justice. Civil servants on their part must bring their complaints to the notice of the appointing authority through their immediate superiors. This authority is then obliged to take a decision, which can again be challenged before the Court. In both cases therefore, the actual case brought before the Court of Justice is an action for annulment which the Court can decide upon under its powers of judicial review (see above § 325-328). No unlimited jurisdiction is required.

Only in one case has unlimited jurisdiction been expressly attributed to the Court; that is in disputes of a financial character.[138] The Court may then

133. *Compagnie Continentale Case* (169/73), 4 Feb. 1975, considerations 22, 23, 28, 31, 32, 33, 36, 37, [1975] ECR 135, 136; [1975] 1 CMLR 605, 606; CCH para 8295.
134. 524 out of 1875 cases up to 31 Dec. 1978. See *Twelfth General Report on the Activities of the Communities in 1978*, table 1, p. 367.
135. In 1978, 22 out of 268 cases were brought by officials, *Idem*.
136. Peter-Ernst Goose, *Neuere Entwickelungen im Verfahrensrecht des Gerichtshofs*, 10 EuR (1975), pp. 237-240.
137. OJ 22 Sept. 1978, No. C 225/6.
138. Staff Regulations Art. 91(1).

change the amounts established in the decisions adopted by the appointing authority in response to the complaints brought by civil servants.

D. ACTIONS AGAINST PENALTIES[139]

§ 511. In a number of articles the ECSC Treaty empowers the Commission, formerly the High Authority, to impose penalties for violation of those articles.[140] The High Authority has made considerable use of this power: up to 1969 it imposed some 60 penalties amounting to a total sum of almost 350.000 Units of Account.[141] Under the EEC Treaty the Council may grant the same power to the Commission by its regulations.[142] So far, the Council has made use of this competence on three occasions: Regulation 17/62 on competition,[143] Regulation 11/60 on transport[144] and Regulation 1017/68 on competition in the transport sector[145], of which the first regulation is by far the most important. Under that Regulation, by January 1979 the Commission had fined 102 undertakings, in 16 different cases a total sum of over 11 million Units of Account.[146]

The Court of Justice may impose a penalty, not exceeding 250 Units of Account, upon a witness who has been duly summoned and has failed to appear before the Court.[147] So far, this provision has never been applied.

1. Procedure before the Commission [148]

§ 512. The role of public prosecutor is performed by the Commission. Under EEC Regulation 7/6 it may collect information from the competent authorities of the Member States, from undertakings and associations of undertakings.[149] Undertakings as well as their representatives are obliged to supply the information requested.[150] If they provide false information they can be

139. See Rolf Winkler, *Die Rechtsnatur der Geldbusse im Wettbewerbsrecht der Europäischen Wirtschaftsgemeinschaft*, Tübingen 1971, Juristische Studien No. 25.
140. ECSC Artt. 47(3), 54(6), 58(4), 59(7), 64, 65(5), 66(6), 68(6).
141. Winkler, (*op. cit.*, note 139), p. 19, note 85.
142. See A. Mulder, *Handhaving van Europees Economisch Recht*, Speculum Langemeijer, Tjeenk Willink, Zwolle 1973, p. 353 and *Idem* in SEW 1962 pp. 642-646.
143. EEC Regulation 17/62, OJ 21 Feb. 1962 No. 13, p. 204; 10 July 1962 No. 56, p. 1655; 7 Nov. 1963, p. 2696; 29 Dec. 1971, No. L 285, p. 49.
144. EEC Regulation 11/60, OJ 1960 p. 1121.
145. EEC Regulation 1017/68, OJ 1968 No. L 175/1.
146. *Europa van Morgen*, 29 Jan. 1975, p. 54. For the individual fines imposed, see Barounos, Hall and James, *EEC Anti-Trust Law, Principles and Practice*, Butterworth 1975, p. 298.
147. Rules of Procedure of the Court, Art. 48(2).
148. See B.H. ter Kuile in *Europees Kartelrecht Anno 1973*, Europese Monografieën 16, Kluwer 1973, pp. 151-160; Jean Guyénot, *Droit Antitrust Européen*, Presses de l'Université de Quebec 1973, pp. 218-252; Barounos, Hall and James, (*op. cit.*, note 146) pp. 271-301.
149. EEC Regulation 17 (6 Feb. 1962), Art. 11(1).
150. *Idem* Art. 11(4).

fined [151] ; if they do not supply the information requested or if they supply incomplete information, the Commission shall by decision require the information to be supplied. That decision shall fix a time-limit and indicate the penalties in case of non-fulfilment. [152] In order to obtain further information and to verify the information received, the Commission is entitled to undertake investigations into undertakings; its officials are empowered inter alia to examine books and records, to make copies thereof and to ask for oral explanations on the spot. [153] If undertakings do not voluntarily submit to investigations, the investigations shall be ordered by decision of the Commission. That decision shall specify the subject matter and the purpose of the investigation and shall indicate the penalties for refusal to submit to it. [154]

§ 513. After the Commission has collected the necessary data and before it can impose penalties it must give the undertakings concerned the opportunity of being heard. [155] The undertakings are informed in writing of the objections raised against them and they must reply in writing. Further decisions of the Commission may deal only with issues raised in the statement of objections. [156] This does not mean that the final decision of the Commission must be a repetition of that statement. When in the *ICI Case* the applicant complained that the Commission in the decision referred to facts not mentioned in the statement of objections, the Court of Justice held that it sufficed that the essential factual elements in the case against the applicant are indicated in the statement of objections. In its final decision the Commission may make corrections as regards the exact details of the facts, in consequence of evidence obtained during the administrative proceedings. [157]

§ 514. Apart from the opportunity to reply in writing to the objections raised by the Commission the undertakings also have the opportunity to put forward their arguments orally. [158] Apart from the Commission's staff, officials of the Member States usually take part in the discussions, which are not open to the public. The essential contents of the statements made by each person during the oral proceedings are recorded and must be approved by him. [159] Failure to fulfil this requirement will invalidate the final decision of the Commission only if the records are incorrect. [160]

Prior to the Commission taking a decision on the case the Advisory Committee on Restrictive Practices and Monopolies, composed of the competent

---

151. *Idem* Art. 15(1)(b).
152. *Idem* Art. 11(5).
153. *Idem* Art. 14(1).
154. *Idem* Art. 14(3).
155. *Idem* Art. 19(1).
156. EEC Regulation No. 99/63 of the Commission of 25 July 1963, Artt. 2, 3, 4.
157. *ICI Case* (48/69), 14 July 1972, considerations 21-25, [1972] ECR 650, 651; [1972] CMLR 619; CCH para 8161.
158. EEC Regulation 99/63, art. 7.
159. *Idem* Art. 9(4).
160. *ICI Case* (48/69), 14 July 1972, consideration 31, [1972] ECR 651; [1972] CMLR 620, CCH para 8161.

officials of the Member States, must be heard. The opinion of the Advisory Committee is not binding, nor is it published. [161]

§ 515. Finally the Commission takes its decision by which — apart from the order to terminate particular practices — fines may be imposed. The decision can be appealed before the Court of Justice. Though such appeals have no suspensory effect[162], payment of fines is normally not required before the Court of Justice has decided on the appeal. EEC Regulation 11/60, on transport, expressly provides that the Commission may not proceed with the enforcement of a penalty until the period allowed for appeal has expired. [163] Though the Regulation does not forbid enforcement while an appeal is pending, the provision supports the position that immediate execution is not necessary.

In the *Commercial Solvents Case* the Commission had originally ordered that the fine should be paid within three months irrespective of whether an appeal would be brought by the parties. When the President of the Court of Justice extended that period until the point when the Court could take an interim decision on the application for a suspension of its execution, the Commission agreed not to demand payment of the fine before the Court's final decision in the case. [164]

The custom not to enforce penalties until a decision of the Court has been taken makes long Court proceedings financially favourable to the companies concerned.

2. Procedure before the Court of Justice

§ 516. The Commission combines the roles of law-maker, public prosecutor and judge at first instance. The Commission itself adopted many of the regulations which are to be enforced, it is charged with the execution of others, it collects the information necessary for their enforcement, it discusses possible violations with all persons concerned and, finally, it makes out the case against the undertakings concerned. Furthermore, as a judge the Commission imposes the fines for violation of the competition rules and of its own decisions based on these rules. This mixed role of the Commission means that it cannot be considered as a fully independent court at first instance, and that therefore the Court of Justice should not function as a court of appeal. In the *First Modena Case* the Court made it clear that the proceedings before the Court are independent from those before the Commission. Modena had invoked arguments which had not been put forward in the procedure before the

---

161. EEC Regulation 17, Art. 10.
162. EEC Art. 185.
163. EEC Regulation 11, Art. 25(2).
164. *Commercial Solvents Case* (6 and 7/73), 14 March 1973, consideration 20, [1973] ECR 360; [1973] CMLR 363; CCH para 8209; and 6 March 1974, [1974] ECR 226-258; [1974] 1 CMLR 309 ff; Ter Kuile in *Rechtsbescherming in de Europese Gemeenschappen* Europese Monografieën No. 19 Kluwer 1975, p. 128.

High Authority. The High Authority therefore submitted that these arguments could not be brought before the Court, but the Court held: *'To exclude the argument on this basis, which is in any event incompatible with the purely preliminary nature of the procedure laid down by Article 36,* (that is the procedure before the Commission) *would unduly restrict the applicant's rights of defence.'* [165]

§ 517.   As the Court of Justice is not a court of appeal it should decide cases involving fines in a fully independent manner and should not proceed from the presumption that the fine imposed by the Commission is correct.

The action against penalties is an independent action, governed by a separate article of the EEC Treaty (EEC Article 172). It can be distinguished from an action for the annulment of the decision by which the fine was imposed. This means that the provisions of the action for annulment, such as time limits, are not applicable of their own accord, though they may be applied by analogy. [166]   In practice, however, the Court of Justice treats the action against a penalty as an action for annulment of a decision. Its point of departure is not the alleged infraction, but the Commissions's decision. Thus it held in the *Alma Case, 'that the amount of the fine was not excessive,'* and that therefore the decision imposing it should not be annulled or changed. [167] Similarly it decided in the *TEPEA Case* that one fine did *'not seem to be out of proportion'* to the gravity and duration of the offence and that another *'appears to be completely justified'.* [168]   In the *Miller Case* it dismissed the application against the decision of the Commission as unfounded. [169]   This indicates that the Commission's fine is considered correct unless it is .obviously wrong. Also in the *Commercial Solvents* and in the *Sugar Cartel Cases,* where the Court *'reduced'* the fine imposed by the Commission instead of autonomously imposing a lower fine, such a presumption seems to be implied. [170]   Ter Kuile suggests that the Court wants to prevent the Member States from exercising too much influence over the implementation of the competition rules, and that it therefore buttresses the position of the Commission as much as is possible. Though conscious of the inherent danger to the position of individuals before the Court, he favours this approach. [171]

---

165. *First Modena Case* (16/61), 12 July 1962, [1962] ECR 302; 8 Jur. (1962) 602; 8 Rec. (1962) 575; [1962] CMLR 245.
166. Peter Oliver, *Limitation of Actions before the European Court*, 3 ELRev. (1978), p. 6.
167. *Alma Case* (8/56), 10 Dec. 1957, [1957-58] ECR 100; 3 Jur. (1957) 203; 3 Rec. (1957) 191, 192.
168. *TEPEA Case* (28/77), 20 June 1978, considerations 68, 72, [1978] ECR 1419, 1420; [1978] 3 CMLR 417, 418; CCH para 8467.
169. *Miller Case* (19/77), 1 Feb. 1978, [1978] ECR 153; [1978] 2 CMLR 354; CCH para 8439.
170. *Commercial Solvents Case* (6 and 7/73), 6 March 1974, consideration 52, [1974] ECR 257; [1974] 1 CMLR 346; CCH para 8209; *Sugar Cartel Case* (40-48, 50, 54-56, 111 and 113, 114/73), 16 Dec. 1975, consideration 624, [1975] ECR 2023; [1976] 1 CMLR 487.
171. Ter Kuile (*op. cit.*, note 148), p. 160.

The Court used more acceptable wording in the *First Dalmas Case* and in several other cases where it held that '*the amount of the fine is appropriate in view of the gravity of the infringements*'. [172]

§ 518. Having unlimited jurisdiction the Court of Justice is entitled to change a fine imposed by the Commission, and it often does so. On the other hand, the Court seems reluctant to change measures other than pecuniary sanctions. When in the case of a staff member a disciplinary measure was disputed, the Court held:

'The facts alleged against the applicant having been established, the choice of appropriate disciplinary measure is a matter for the disciplinary authority.

The subject matter not being of a pecuniary kind, the Court cannot substitute its own assessment for that of the authority in question, except in a case of a clearly excessive measure or of an abuse of power.' [173]

3. Penalties

a. NATURE OF PENALTIES

§ 519. The Commission and subsequently the Court may impose fines, periodic penalty payments, or both. Periodic penalty payments are coercive measures. They can be imposed in order to compel undertakings to terminate infringements or to supply information. [174] When the undertakings have satisfied the obligation belatedly they have to pay the penalty for each day they are late, but the Commission may fix the total amount at a lower figure than that which would arise under its original decision. [175]

There are two categories of fines, one resulting from procedural misconduct, such as supplying incorrect or misleading information, the other resulting from an infringement of substantive provisions such as EEC Article 85. The fines do not have the character of coercive measures. In the *First Boehringer Case* fines were imposed for infringements which had already been terminated. Boehringer contended that this fact should have been taken into account at least for the purpose of fixing the amount of the fine, but the Court of Justice held that the fines:

'are not in the nature of periodic penalty payments. Their object is to suppress illegal activities and to prevent any recurrence. This object could

172. *First Dalmas Case* (1/59), 17 Dec. 1959, [1959] ECR 205; 5 Jur. (1959) 460; 5 Rec. (1959) 427, 428. See also e.g. the *Dyestuffs Cases*, 14 July 1972, [1972] ECR 619-959; CCH para 8161-8169; and the *Quinine Cartel Cases* 15 July 1970, [1970] ECR 660-813; CCH para 8083-8085.
173. *Second De Greef Case* (46/72), 30 May 1973, considerations 45, 46, [1973] ECR 556.
174. EEC Regulation 17, Art. 16(1).
175. *Idem* Art. 16(2).

not be adequately attained if the imposition of a penalty were to be restricted to current infringements alone. The Commission's power to impose penalties is in no way affected by the fact that the conduct constituting the infringement has ceased and that it can no longer have detrimental effects.'[176]

§ 520. Decisions imposing fines are not of a criminal law nature.[177] The fines are imposed upon the undertakings and not upon their executives. They cannot be taken into consideration as a ground for increasing the punishment meted out in subsequent cases under national or Community law. Nor should they affect the reliability or good name of the undertaking concerned. For this reason AFC Chemiefarma submitted that the Commission had violated the principles of EEC Regulation 17 by publishing the decision by which AFC Chemiefarma was fined, notwithstanding the fact that such publication was not provided for in the regulation. This publication influenced public opinion to the detriment of AFC Chemiefarma's reputation and its position on the stock market. The Court, however, held that publication, though not prescribed, was not forbidden, and that it *may even contribute to ensuring the observance of the rules of the Treaty on competition.*'[178]

§ 521. It should be stressed that declaring a sanction to be of a non-penal nature cannot adversely affect the rights of the prosecuted person or undertaking. The non-penal nature of the sanction cannot, therefore, impinge upon the basic human rights guaranteed to everyone within the Communities by the European Convention on Human Rights to which all Member States are parties and whose content has been accepted by the Court of Justice as general principles of law (see above § 54, 134). These include the right to a fair and public hearing, within a reasonable time, by an independent and impartial tribunal, the right to be presumed innocent until proved guilty, and the right to have adequate time for the preparation of the defence.[179] Furthermore, national provisions which protect individuals against, for example, self-incrimination should also be applicable in the case of EEC fines.[180]

b. SPECIAL PROVISIONS

§ 522. Coercive penalties of a special nature have been introduced in several regulations on the import and export of agricultural products. In order to permit the competent authorities to constantly follow trade movements, im-

---

176. *First Boehringer Case* (45/69), 15 July 1970, consideration 53, [1970] ECR 805, 806; CCH para 8085.
177. EEC Regulation 17, Art. 15(4); EEC Regulation 11, Art. 19; EEC Regulation 1017/68, Art. 22(4).
178. *Quinine Cartel Case (AFC Chemiefarma)* (41/69), 15 July 1970, considerations 99-105; [1970] ECR 692; CCH para 8083 (p. 8196).
179. European Convention on Human Rights, Art. 6.
180. *English Rio Tinto Case*, Court of Appeal, 26 May 1977, [1977] 2 CMLR 420 and 436; *English Westinghouse Case*, House of Lords, 1 Dec. 1977, [1978] 1 CMLR 100.

ports into the Community and exports therefrom are subject to the issue of a licence. The issue of such licences is conditional on the lodging of a deposit guaranteeing that importation or exportation will be effected during the period of validity of the licence. The deposit is forfeited in whole or in part if the transaction is not effected, or is only partially effected within that period.

The legality of such coercive measures has been challenged several times before the Court of Justice, which in each case has held them to be legal. [181] In the *Handelsgesellschaft Case* the Court considered that the system of deposits *'cannot be equated with a penal sanction, since it is merely the guarantee that an undertaking voluntarily assumed will be carried out.'* [182] Though perhaps not formally a penal sanction, the forfeiture of deposits comes very close to constituting one. Some experts on penal law see no real difference. [183]

§ 523. In the Euratom Treaty four additional sanctions have been provided for, which are, in order of severity: (1) a warning, (2) the withdrawal of special benefits, (3) the placing of the undertaking under the administration of specially appointed persons, and (4) the withdrawal of source materials. None of these sanctions has ever been applied.

c. AMOUNT OF THE PENALTIES

§ 524. Under Regulation 17/62 periodic penalty payments can be from fifty to one thousand units of account per day. [184] The same amount can be imposed under Regulation 1017/68. [185] Regulation 11/60, on the other hand, charges the national governments to take the necessary coercive measures and therefore does not provide for periodic penalty payments. Under EEC Regulation 17/62 and under EEC Regulation 1017/68 fines for substantive violations can be imposed from one thousand to one million units of account and even in excess thereof, but not exceeding ten per cent of the turnover of the undertaking concerned. [186] Under EEC Regulation 11/60 the fines may not exceed 10,000 units of account or twenty times the carriage charge. [187] For procedural violations the fines range from 100 to 5,000 units of account. [188] The ECSC fixes the amount of possible fines in the Treaty itself. It does not provide for specific sums of money but relates the fines to the sums involved

---

181. *Handelsgesellschaft Case* (11/70), 17 Dec. 1970, considerations 5-20, [1970] ECR 1134-1137; [1972] CMLR 283-286; CCH para 8126; *Fourth Kampffmeyer Case* (158/73), 30 Jan. 1974, considerations 3-6, [1974] ECR 108, 109; CCH para 8261.
182. *Handelsgesellschaft Case* (11/70), 17 Dec. 1970, consideration 18, [1970] ECR 1136; [1972] CMLR 285; CCH para 8126.
183. See Mulder (*op. cit.*, note 142), pp. 350, 351, 356.
184. EEC Regulation 17/62, Art. 16(1).
185. EEC Regulation 1017/68, Art. 23.
186. EEC Regulation 17/62, Art. 15(2); EEC Regulation 1017/68, Art. 22(2).
187. EEC Regulation 11/60, Art. 18.
188. EEC Regulation 17/62, Art. 15(1), EEC Regulation 1017/68, Art. 22(1).

in the illegal action. [189] The actual fines imposed under the ECSC Treaty vary from 800 to 7,000 units of account.

In fixing the amount of the fine, the Commission takes account of the gravity and of the duration of the infringement. The gravity is influenced by the extent to which the violation runs contrary to the object of the Common Market. [190]

Apart from the upper limit the Commission is free to set the fine at any amount it considers appropriate. In the *BP Case* it did not even impose a fine at all. The Commission's decision simply stated that BP and others had infringed EEC Article 86. [191] BP challenged that decision, successfully, on the ground that even without a fine the critism expressed in the decision could be a basis for the commencement of an action for damages against BP before national courts. [192]

In the *First Boehringer Case* the Court of Justice held that the gravity of the infringement and its effect on the market should be taken into account when the amount of the fine is being settled. The Court had no objection to the Commission first fixing the total amount of the fine and subsequently distributing it between the undertakings involved. [193]

§ 525. Under Dutch tax law, taxes are calculated on the basis of the net profit of undertakings. Fines will lead to a lowering of this net profit and therefore result in lower taxation. In fact a substantial amount of a fine is covered by the reduction in the tax burden. Under German tax law fines must be paid out of the net profit after taxation. This means that no part of a fine is indirectly covered by a reduction in taxes. Because of this difference in national tax legislation, *Buchler* claimed in one of the *Quinine Cartel Cases* that the Commission in imposing fines should consider their real economic effect, but the Court held that the Commission is not required to take differences between the tax laws of the Member States into account. [194]

d. LIMITATION PERIODS

§ 526. The power of the Commission to impose penalties under the EEC regulations is subject to a limitation period of three years for periodic penalty

---

189. See e.g. ECSC Articles 54, last sentence, 58(4), 59(7), 64, 65(5), 66(6). According to Advocate-General Roemer the surcharges of ECSC Article 50(3) should also be regarded as pecuniary sanctions within the meaning of ECSC Article 36. *See Second Dalmas Case* (1/63), 16 Dec. 1963, Opinion of the Advocate-General, [1963] ECR 320; 9 Jur. (1963) 680; 9 Rec. (1963) 651, 652; [1964] CMLR 229.
190. See, e.g., the decision of the Commission concerning the *French and Taiwanese Mushroom Packers*, (75/77/EEC), 8 Jan. 1975, considerations 19, 20, [1975] 1 CMLR D90.
191. *BP Case* (77/77), 29 June 1978, considerations 3, 7, [1978] ECR 1523, 1524; [1978] 3 CMLR 189, 190.
192. *Idem*, consideration 11.
193. *First Boehringer Case* (45/69), 15 July 1970, considerations 54, 55, [1970] ECR 805, 806; CCH para 8085. See also *Quinine Cartel Case (AFC Chemiefarma)* (41/69), 15 July 1970, consideration 176, [1970] ECR 701; CCH para 8083.
194. *Buchler Case* (44/69) 15 July 1970, considerations 50, 51, [1970] ECR 761; CCH para 8084 (p. 8220).

payments and for the fines resulting from procedural misconduct, and to a period of five years for fines resulting from the infringement of substantive provisions. [195]

The power of the Commission to enforce decisions imposing penalties is subject to a limitation period of five years running from the day on which the decision becomes final. [196]

The harm caused by infringements depends on their duration. The Commission should, therefore, intervene as quickly as possible. In the *Commercial Solvents Case* the infringement had lasted for two years or more. The Court reproached the Commission for not intervening more quickly; this was one reason for lowering the fine imposed. [197] This is suggestive of a sort of gradual limitation period. Though the power of the Commission to impose fines is withdrawn only at the end of the limitation period, the amount of the fine which can be imposed diminishes at an earlier stage.

e. EFFECT

§ 527. There are limits placed on the effectiveness of imposing sanctions on undertakings. Fines may have a positive effect as long as they reduce the profit of a bona fide undertaking and thus lead to pressure imposed by shareholders on the management. If, however, an undertaking makes no profit at all, or if the penalties exceed the profits made, the effect of the sanctions may be so detrimental to the workers in the employ of the undertaking and to the employment situation in general that they may be counterproductive.

Apart from *bona fide* undertakings, there are many undertakings set up for a short period of time or for a particular purpose, which have little concern for the law, which are easily liquidated in the event of trouble and which lack the necessary financial resources for paying fines. Against such undertakings these non-penal sanctions of the Communities may have little effect. [198]

E. ARBITRATION

1. Domestic

§ 528. The Court of Justice has jurisdiction to give judgment pursuant to any arbitration clause contained in a contract concluded by or on behalf of the Community, whether that contract be governed by public or private law. [199] The reference to contracts governed by public law concerns the French legal system where contracts made with governmental authorities are

---

195. EEC Regulation 2988/74 of the Council, OJ 1974 No. L 319, Art. 1.
196. *Idem*, Art. 4.
197. *Commercial Solvents Case* (6 and 7/73), 6 March 1974, consideration 51, [1974] ECR 257; [1974] 1 CMLR 346; CCH para 8281.
198. See Mulder (*op. cit.*, note 142), p. 358.
199. EEC Art. 181, ECSC Art. 42.

governed by public law and therefore come under the jurisdiction of the administrative courts, while other contracts normally come before civil courts.

Euratom has included several arbitration clauses in its research contracts under Euratom Article 10 in order to prevent such contracts from being regulated by different national legal systems.

As yet the Court of Justice has had only one case brought before it under an arbitration clause and in that case the contract expressly provided that it was governed by Italian law. [200] Should ever a case be brought under an arbitration clause without such express provision, then the Court must find the applicable law for making its decision. It may be assumed that the general principles common to the laws of the Member States will play a paramount role, but it could also be that the Court of Justice would apply international law or any one of the national laws of the Member States.

2. International

§ 529. Disputes between Member States may be brought before the Court of Justice by special agreement between the parties if they relate to the subject matter of the Common Market. [201] The phrase, 'relation to the subject matter' must be interpreted widely as the provision is of no additional use in cases which are already covered by the Community Treaties themselves and may, therefore, be brought before the Court under EEC Article 170. The arbitration provision may be particularly useful for subjects which only partly affect Community law.

So far, no disputes between Member States have been brought before the Court of Justice under this provision.

F. NON-JUDICIAL OPINIONS OF THE COURT OF JUSTICE

§ 530. Apart from its judicial tasks, the Court of Justice performs some functions pertaining to the legislature rather than to the judiciary. Under ECSC Article 95 the Commission and the Council may jointly propose amendments to the Treaty which may not, however, conflict with the provisions of ECSC Articles 2, 3, and 4 or interfere with the relationship between the powers of the institutions. The Court of Justice must consider these proposed amendments and in doing so it has full power to assess all points of fact and of law. Only if the Court finds the proposals compatible with the above-men-

---

200. *Pellegrini Case* (23/76), 7 Dec. 1976, [1976] ECR 1807.
201. EEC Art. 182. See Claudius Alder, *Problematik der Schiedsgerichtsklauseln in Assoziationsverträgen der Europäischen Wirtschaftsgemeinschaft*, Symposium Europa, 1950-1970, College of Europe, Bruges 1971, pp. 179-194.

tioned conditions shall they be forwarded to the European Parliament for approval.

When an agreement between the Community and one or more States or an international organization is proposed, the Council, the Commission or a Member State may obtain the opinion of the Court of Justice as to whether the envisaged agreement is compatible with the provisions of the EEC Treaty. [202]

§ 531. In these cases the Court of Justice does not decide on a specific dispute but decides in a general way on the validity of a proposed act. It thus performs an advisory function within the legislative branch rather than a judicial one. As a rule the assignment of such advisory tasks to courts should be treated with circumspection as they detract from the freedom of the Court to rule objectively on specific cases in the future. If the legality of an act is challenged at a later date, possibly on completely novel grounds, a court is hampered in upholding such a challenge if on a former occasion it has officially declared that the act is valid. The Court of Justice tries to avoid such general statements. In response to an action for the annulment of an act and in reply to a national court requesting a preliminary ruling on the validity of an act the Court never declares that the act is valid; at the most it states that the arguments brought do not demonstrate any illegality. Thus the possibility is kept open that in future other arguments may be advanced to prove the illegality of the act. The above-mentioned requirements of general statements from the Court are, therefore, basically in conflict with the judicial function of the Court.

§ 532 For these reasons, the United States Supreme Court has always refused to render advice to other branches of government. In *Muskrat v. U.S.* it considered:

'In 1793, by direction of the President, Secretary of State Jefferson addressed to the justices of the Supreme Court a communication soliciting their views upon the question whether their advice to the Executive would be available in the solution of important questions of the construction of treaties, laws of nations and laws of the land, which the Secretary said were often presented under circumstances which *"do not give a cognizance of them to the tribunals of the country"*.

...

Chief Justice Jay and his associates answered to President Washington that, in consideration of the lines of separation drawn by the Constitution between the three departments of government, and being judges of a court of last resort, afforded strong arguments against the propriety of extra-judicially deciding the questions alluded to, and expressing the view that the power given by the Constitution to the President, of calling on heads of

202.   EEC Art. 228. On this article see Pierre Pescatore in 103 RdC (1961 II) pp. 126-129.

departments for opinions, "seems to have been purposely, as well as expressly, united to the executive departments".'[203]

The same concern was expressed by Justice Frankfurter in his concurring
opinion in *Youngstone Sheet & Tube Co, v. Sawyer* when he considered:

> 'Due regard for the implications of the distribution of powers in our Consti-
> tution and for the nature of the judicial process as the ultimate authority in
> interpreting the Constitution, has not only confined the Court within the
> narrow domain of appropriate adjudication. It has also led to "a series of
> rules under which it has avoided passing upon a large part of all the consti-
> tutional questions pressed upon it for decision". '[204]

§ 533.   After its creation in 1951 the German Constitutional Court, the *Bundesverfassungsgericht* was empowered to render advisory opinions to the highest legislative and executive authorities of the German Federal Republic. [205]
A dispute arose on the question to what extent the Constitutional Court itself
would be bound by such advisory opinions when in subsequent cases they are
invoked before it. The Constitutional Court attached great value to the consistency of its position and decided in December 1952 that in certain constitutional questions the Chambers of the Court, which normally render the
Court's decisions, would be bound by these opinions. [206] This increased the
opposition against the Court's advisory capacity and by law of 21 July 1956 it
was abolished. [207]

Under the Second Protocol to the European Convention on Human Rights
the European Court of Human Rights has been attributed competence to give
advisory opinions at the request of the Committee of Ministers of the Council
of Europe. Such opinions may not deal with any question relating to the
content or scope of the human rights themselves. Again, the legislators wanted
to avoid the possibility that the judicial task of the Court — and of the
European Commission of Human Rights — would be prejudiced by an advisory function.

§ 534.   It may safely be assumed that the Court of Justice shares the view
that in general the judiciary should not advise on the legality of proposed
legislative acts. However, both as regards ECSC Article 95 and EEC Article 228 there are exceptional circumstances as to the nature of the proposed
act which may lend justification to the advisory function of the Court of

---

203. *Muskrat v. U.S.* 219 US 346, 354 (1910), with reference to the *Correspondence and
Public Papers of John Jay*, vol. 3, p. 486. See also, e.g., Justice Frankfurter's concurring
opinion in *U.S. v. CIO* 335 US 106, 124.
204. *Youngstown Sheet & Tube Co. v. Sawyer*, 343 US 579, 595 (1951). The quotation is
from Justice Brandeis in *Ashwander v. Tennessee Valley Authority* 297 US 288, 341, 346.
205. Gesetz über das Bundesverfassungsgericht. § 97.
206. Ernst Friesenhahn, *Die Verfassungsgerichtsbarkeit in der Bundesrepublik Deutsch-
land*, in *Verfassungsgerichtbarkeit in der Gegenwart* edited by Hans Mosler, Max-Planck-
Institut, Karl Heymanns Verlag 1962, pp. 129-132.
207. Law of 21 July 1956, Bundesgesetzblatt I p. 662.

Justice, or at least make it less objectionable. In the *Local Cost Standard Opinion* the Court of Justice held:

'It is the purpose of the second subparagraph of Article 228(1) to forestall complications which would result from legal disputes concerning the compatibility with the Treaty of international agreements binding upon the Community. In fact, a possible decision of the Court to the effect that such an agreement is, either by reason of its content or of the procedure adopted for its conclusion, incompatible with the provisions of the Treaty could not fail to provoke, not only in a Community context but also in that of international relations, serious difficulties and might give rise to adverse consequences for all interested parties, including third countries.

For the purpose of avoiding such complications the Treaty had recourse to the exceptional procedure of a prior reference to the Court of Justice for the purpose of elucidating, before the conclusion of the agreement, whether the latter is compatible with the Treaty.'[208]

In this opinion the Court stressed that the procedure is exceptional and it also indicated why it is acceptable in the case of EEC Article 228: the agreements concluded by the Community are binding on the Community itself as well as on its Members.[209] According to the rules of international law the binding force of an international agreement cannot normally be terminated by an annulment of its provisions by a court of one of the parties.[210]

There will, therefore, be no opportunity at a later stage for challenging the legality of international agreements before the Court of Justice on specific grounds. The Court does not place any checks on any future judicial function by giving general opinions under EEC Article 228.

§ 534a. In the *Laying-up Fund Opinion* the Court of Justice held:

'It is not for the Court within the context of a request for an opinion pursuant to the second paragraph of Article 228(1) to give a final judgement on the interpretation of texts which are the subject of a request for an opinion'.[211]

It may therefore be expected that the advisory function of the Court under EEC Article 228 does not prejudice its normal judicial role as sole authoritive interpreter of Community law.

§ 535. The situation under ECSC Article 95 is a similar one. The provision concerns amendments to the Treaty. The validity of Treaty provisions cannot

208. *Local Cost Standard Opinion* (1/75), 11 Nov. 1975, considerations 10, 11, [1975] ECR 1360, 1361; OJ 1975 C 268 p. 21; [1976] 1 CMLR 90.
209. EEC Art. 228(2).
210. Vienna Convention on the Law of Treaties, Art. 42, 46.
211. *Laying-up Fund Opinion* (1/76), 26 April 1977, consideration 20, [1977] ECR 761; [1977] 2 CMLR 301; CCH para 8405.

be challenged before the Court of Justice. Again, a general opinion on the validity of a new Treaty provision cannot therefore prejudice any future Court decision in specific cases.

§ 536. So far, the Court of Justice has given five opinions, three under ECSC Article 95 [212] and two under EEC Article 228. [213] The opinions are separately numbered. In one respect their preparation differs fundamentally from that of the Court's judicial decisions: all the Advocates-General deliver a reasoned opinion, but these opinions are pronounced in the Deliberation Room [214] and, therefore, are not published.

§ 537. EEC Article 228 entitles the Council, the Commission and the Member States to obtain the opinion of the Court *as to whether an agreement is compatible with the Treaty*. This suggests that the Court should only look into the content of the agreement and not into the question whether it has been adopted in accordance with the correct procedure, or whether the Community was at all competent to conclude the agreement. As this would lead to unacceptable consequences the Court of Justice provided in its Rules of Procedure, which were unanimously approved by the Council:

> 'The Opinion may deal not only with the question whether the envisaged agreement is compatible with the provisions of the EEC Treaty but also with the question whether the Community or any Community institution has the power to enter into that agreement.' [215]

In the *Local Cost Standard Opinion* the Court was even more explicit when it stated, immediately following the passage quoted above (§ 534):

> 'This procedure must therefore be open for all questions capable of submission for judicial consideration, either by the Court of Justice or possibly by national courts, in so far as such questions give rise to doubt either as to the substantive or formal validity of the agreement with regard to the Treaty.
>   The question whether the conclusion of a given agreement is within the power of the Community and whether, in a given case, such power has been exercised in conformity with the provisions of the Treaty is, in principle, a question which may be submitted to the Court of Justice, either directly, under Article 169 or Article 173 of the Treaty, or in accordance with the preliminary procedure, and it must therefore be admitted that the

---

212. *Opinion* of 17 Dec. 1959, [1959] ECR 259; 5 Jur. (1958-59) 591; 5 Rec. (1958-59) 551; *Opinion* (1/60), 4 March 1960, [1960] ECR 46; 6 Jur. (1960) 107; 6 Rec. (1960) 107; *Opinion* (1/61), 13 Dec. 1961, [1961] ECR 252; 7 Jur. (1961) 534; 7 Rec. (1961) 505.
213. *Local Cost Standard Opinion* (1/75), 11 Nov. 1975, [1975] ECR 1355; OJ 1975 C 268 p. 18; [1976] 1 CMLR 90; *Laying-up Fund Opinion* (1/76, 26 April 1977, [1977] ECR 741; [1977] 2 CMLR 295; CCH para 8405.
214. Rules of Procedure of the Court, Art. 108(2).
215. Idem, Art. 107(2).

matter may be referred to the Court in accordance with the preliminary procedure of Article 228.' [216]

§ 537a. In practice, the Commission occasionally obtains unofficial advice from the Court of Justice on texts of a legal nature. The Court has rendered advice not only on issues directly affecting its own work, such as the establishment of a special tribunal for civil servants' cases, but also on texts of conventions. Article 18 para 2 of the Protocol on the protection, under criminal law, of the financial interests of the Community[217] for example, literally follows the amendments suggested by the Court of Justice with regard to a prior draft. [218] The Court, however, does not take any formal responsibility for such texts.

G. MISCELLANEOUS TASKS OF THE COURT OF JUSTICE

1. Authorization to enforce a garnishee order

§ 538. The property and assets of the Communities are immune from any administrative or legal measure of constraint without the authorization of the Court of Justice. [219] The Court exercises this power of authorization in order to preclude untimely and inappropriate obstacles arising to upset the independent functioning of the Community for the benefit of private interests. According to the Court it has competence *whenever an authority other than one of the institutions of the Community enforces against the Community a decision which alters its legal position.* [220] Originally this was construed to mean that an attachment on salaries of staff members needed prior authorization by the Court. Whenever a decision of a local court ordered such attachment, an authorization was asked of the Court of Justice, whereupon the Court decided in a private session after obtaining the observations of the institution employing the staff member concerned. [221]

More recently, the interpretation of the Protocol on Privileges and Immunities has changed. Nowadays, salaries of staff members are no longer considered to be the property of the Communities, but to be the property of the staff members themselves. This means that the Commission decides on requests for attachment. Only in case of dispute will this be brought before the Court of Justice.

216. *Local Cost Standard Opinion* (1/75), 11 Nov. 1975, considerations 11, 12, [1975] ECR 1361; OJ 1975 C 268, p. 21; [1976] 1 CMLR 90, 91.
217. O J of 22 Sept., 1976, No. C 222/9.
218. Advice of the Court of Justice of 19 March 1975, not published.
219. Protocol on the Privileges and Immunities of the European Communities, Art. 1.
220. *Hübner Case* (4/62), 13 March 1962, [1962] ECR 43; 8 Jur. (1962) 89; 8 Rec. (1962) 87.
221. Roger Michel Chevallier in *Les Novelles, Droit des Communautés Européennes*, para 1133. For an example, see *Potvin Case* (64/63), 1 July 1963, [1963] ECR; 9 Jur. (1963) 101, 102; 9 Rec. (1963) 97, 98.

2. Other tasks

§ 539. The Treaties attribute a number of other tasks to the Court of Justice:

a) The Court may deprive a Judge, an Advocate-General or a member of the Commission of his office, in case they no longer fulfil the necessary requirements. [222]

b) A Member State may not conclude agreements with third States or international organizations on matters within the purview of the Euratom Treaty against the objections of the Commission, unless the Court of Justice has ruled on the compatibility of the agreement with the Euratom Treaty. [223] This provision has been invoked once by Belgium, in which case the Court held that the agreement was compatible with the European Treaty only when the Community adhered to it as well. [224]

c) Under the Euratom Treaty compulsory licences may be granted by an arbitration committee. [225] The members of the Arbitration Committee are appointed by the Council acting on a proposal from the Court of Justice, and the Court of Justice may judge on appeal the formal validity of the decision of the Arbitration Committee. [226]

d) Several additional agreements, such as the Association Agreements with Greece and Turkey and the Luxembourg Convention on the Community Patent of 15 December 1975, attribute tasks to the Court of Justice for the sake of settling disputes.

Apart from the one application of European Article 103, mentioned above, none of these tasks have ever been actually performed by the Court.

---

222. EEC Statute Art. 6, 8; Merger Treaty Art. 10. See also below § 635.
223. Euratom Art. 103(3).
224. *Nuclear Materials Ruling* (1/78), 14 Nov. 1978, [1979] 1 CMLR 131.
225. Euratom Art. 17.
226. Euratom Art. 18.

CHAPTER FOUR

Other Courts applying Community law

I. INTERNATIONAL COURTS

§ 540. As yet, international courts have never applied Community law. It is unlikely that the International Court of Justice will ever do so. The Community Treaties provide that the Member States shall not submit a dispute concerning the interpretation or application of the Community Treaties to any method of settlement other than those provided for in the Treaties themselves.[1] This prevents them from bringing Community law before international courts. The chances that other States would do so seem rather remote.

§ 541. The possibility that regional courts might apply Community law is somewhat greater. The European Court of Human Rights may be confronted with Community law in two ways: (1) if a Member State accused of violating the European Convention on Human Rights were to invoke a rule of Community law as a lawful exception to the Convention or (2) if an individual were to claim that a rule of Community law violates the Convention. Under the European Convention on Human Rights domestic remedies must be exhausted before the international procedure may be initiated. Thus these questions would first have been raised in national courts and an authentic interpretation of Community law would normally have been obtained by the national judiciary, in a preliminary ruling from the Court of Justice. If not, the Human Rights Commission and Court could perhaps obtain such rulings themselves (see below § 567). It seems correct to say that the final decision on a possible violation of the European Convention on Human Rights would be given by the specialised Commission and Court created by that Convention. There is no reason to object to those organs then deciding the question whether the relevant provisions of Community law are in conformity with the requirements of the European Convention on Human Rights.

§ 542. The Benelux Court of Justice is charged with the promotion of the uniform interpretation of rules of law common to the Benelux countries.[2] Since these common laws are in such fields as excise duties, movements of capital and public tenders, rules of Community law may easily be involved.

---

1. EEC Art. 219; Euratom Art. 193; ECSC Art. 87.
2. For the Treaty establishing this Court see Trb. 1965 No. 71, for a list of provisions interpreted by that court see Trb. 1969, No. 127.

The competence of the Benelux Court is entirely within the field of the Common Market and all Benelux Members participate in the Communities. There is no reason why this court should not apply the rules prescribed for national courts applying Community law (see below § 554-556).

II. FOREIGN COURTS

§ 543. Under the rules of private international law foreign courts may have to apply Community law. For these courts such application would not be different from the application of any other foreign legal order and, therefore, the rules of private international law applicable before the court will provide to what extent Community law can be applied. It would be useful if foreign courts could ask preliminary rulings of the Court of Justice on the interpretation and validity of Community law (see below, § 566).

III. NATIONAL COURTS OF MEMBER STATES

A. TASK OF NATIONAL COURTS

1. Application of Community law

§ 544. It was noted above (§ 145-174) that the relationship between the Community legal order and the national legal orders is generally modelled on the established rules and principles of international law and those of the federal law of many federations. It was also seen that the international legal order has in most cases no court system of its own and can therefore only be applied by the national courts, so that precedents demonstrating a relationship between national and international court systems are much scarcer than precedents establishing a relationship between legal orders. Some examples may be found in the relationships between federal courts and state courts in some federations, but none of these examples has been followed by the Communities. The Community court system is quite unique. The Court of Justice of the European Communities is not a supreme court for the entire Common Market. It is charged with a number of specific tasks under the Community treaties, such as the review of the legality of Community acts (see above § 196-379), the judgment whether Member States have violated the Treaty (see above § 380-443) and jurisdiction in disputes relating to the compensation for injuries caused by the Communities (see above § 446-508). The application of Community law, however, is generally the function of the national courts of the Members. This has proved to be a wise separation of functions. Community law, being directly applicable within the legal orders of the Members, is so interwoven with national laws, that it would be very difficult to bring Community law and national law before different courts. The experiences of some federal States clearly indicate the problems which would have arisen if the two court systems had been fully separated.

As regards the Communities such a cleavage between the court systems would be impossible. Not only must Community law itself be applied, but also national law made in execution of Community obligations. Such national laws would inevitably come before national courts, and equally inevitably would contain elements of Community law. Furthermore, the Communities have no executive agencies of their own. The national authorities are charged with the execution of Community decisions. Some Community acts compel the Member States to penalize violation of Community rules. All such provisions inevitably confront national courts with Community law.[3]

§ 545. By virtue of this task of applying Community law to the actual cases which come before them the national courts perform an important rôle in the judicial system of the Community.[4] First of all, it devolves upon the national court to decide whether Community law is applicable to the case or not. From the law of conflicts it is clear how important this initial decision can be. If the national court considers Community law to be irrelevant and decides the case solely on the basis of national law then there is no remedy. The parties cannot appeal to the European Court of Justice.

Normally a national court will refer the decision whether Community law is applicable or not to the Court of Justice as they realize that only the Court of Justice can decide on questions of conflict in a way uniformly applicable throughout the Member States. Only the French Conseil d'Etat considered itself entitled to decide by itself whether Community law was applicable or not and even to decide this question contrary to established case law of the Court of Justice, when it ruled that directives adopted under EEC Article 56 could not have direct effect in France (see above, § 163a).

When the national courts apply Community law, they do so according to their own procedure. If, for example, the invalidity of a rule must be involved within a specific period of time then the Community rules are equally subject to that provision.[5]

2. Community law and overlapping national law

§ 546. Somtimes rules of national law and of Community law can cover the same issues. As long as they do not conflict with one another no problems will usually arise, whilst in the event of a conflict Community law should be accorded priority (see above § 159-174). Nevertheless, national courts have met at least two fields where the two legal orders overlap and questions have arisen as to what rule should be applied. (a) With regard to certain issues the Treaties transfer exclusive competence to the Communities, for example, in

---

3. R.H. Lauwaars, *Prejudiciële beslissingen*, Europese Monografieën No. 19, Kluwer 1975, p. 37.
4. Marcus Lutter, *Europäische Gerichtsbarkeit und nationale Gerichtsbarkeit*, 86 Zeitschrift für Zivilprozeß (1973), pp. 107-154.
5. See e.g. *Comet Case* (45/76), 16 Dec. 1976, considerations 13, 15, 17, [1976] ECR 2053; [1977] 1 CMLR 533; CCH para 8383. See also above § 141.

the field of customs duties. Does this mean that national courts must disregard all national legal rules regulating these specific topics? (b) For other subjects the power of administration is only partially transferred to the Communities and the national authorities retain competence to regulate certain aspects. An example is to be found in the law of competition where EEC Article 85 lays down rules on agreements which may affect trade between Member States, leaving it to the national authorities to regulate agreements which have no such effect. Which rules must be applied if the case is covered by both provisions?

a. NATIONAL RULES ON ISSUES OF COMMUNITY LAW

§ 547. In the *Turkey Tail Case* the Court of Justice held that the Member States are prohibited from taking steps, for the purposes of applying a regulation, which are intended to alter its scope or to supplement its provisions. *'To the extent that the Member States have assigned legislative powers (...) to the Community (...) they no longer have the power to make legislative provisions'.*[6] This means that in an actual case Community law predominates and that the courts cannot take diverging provisions of national law into consideration. It does not mean, however, that national law can never be of relevance. As the execution of Community rules is delegated to the national authorities, national rules relating to their execution will normally be applicable.[7] This will influence the way in which Community law is applied and, in practice, gives rise to important differences between the Member States. But the Court of Justice has held that the application of national rules may not lead to unequal treatment, nor may these rules in any way change Community law.[8] In the *Reliable Importers Case*, for example, the Court of Justice refused to recognise a German rule that only *reliable* importers could profit from the provision of Community law exempting meat from the import levy if it was imported for the sole purpose of being re-exported after some form of processing.[9]

§ 548. Binding national decisions on individual cases are permitted as long as they are not contrary to Community rules. Under German law importers may obtain an official opinion from the customs administration setting out under what particular tariff heading a product should be classified. This opinion is binding on the customs administration and is of assistance to importers in that it obviates the risk of losses caused by imported products being finally classi-

---

6. *Turkey Tail Case* (40/69), 18 Feb. 1970, consideration 4, [1970] ECR 79; [1970] CMLR 153; CCH para 8098.
7. *Reliable Importers Case* (39/70), 11 Feb. 1971, consideration 4, [1971] ECR 58; [1971] CMLR 293; CCH para 8132; *First Schlüter Case* (94/71), 6 June 1972, consideration 10, [1972] ECR 318, 319; [1973] CMLR 129; CCH para 8186.
8. *Idem*, See also below § 713.
9. *Reliable Importers Case* (39/70), consideration 6, [1971] ECR 59; [1971] CMLR 293; CCH para 8132.

fied under a tariff heading with a higher duty than had been expected. In the *Gervais-Danone Case* the Court of Justice held that such binding tariff opinions did not violate Community law as they contained no normative elements and were part of the usual rules for the application of tariff provisions to individual cases. [10]

The distribution of functions was further clarified in the *Third Balkan Case* when the Court of Justice held that national tax authorities may apply national rules in connexion with the formalities applicable to the imposition of a charge introduced by Community law, but that such rules may not be applied in so far as their effect would be to modify the scope of the provisions of Community law. A national rule that exemptions from taxes may be granted on grounds of natural justice could not be applied to charges prescribed by Community law. [11]

b. INFRINGEMENTS COVERED BY BOTH LEGAL SYSTEMS

§ 549. In the *Walt Wilhelm Case* it was recognised that one and the same agreement between undertakings may be the subject of two sets of parallel proceedings, one before the Community authorities under EEC Article 85, the other before the national authorities in application of the domestic law. This need not be objectionable when two fines are imposed for different aspects of the agreement: one fine for the limitation of competition on the national market and the other for ill effects resulting on the other markets. Taken together the two fines should then reflect the gravity of the infringement. In practice, however, examination of two aspects of the same agreement by two different courts may be difficult. The Court of Justice held that if an agreement is covered by Community law the parallel application of the national system *'should only be allowed in so far as it does not prejudice the uniform application, throughout the Common Market, of the Community rules on restrictive business agreements and of the full effect of the acts adopted in application of those rules.'* The Court held furthermore that conflicts between the Community rule and the national rules on competition *'must be resolved by applying the principle that Community law takes precedence'.* [12] This partly solves the problem: if national proceedings are initiated after Community proceedings have been completed, or have at least been started, the national judiciary must take the Community proceedings into account and may cover only that ground which has not been covered by the Community proceedings. But national courts cannot, manifestly, take account of Community proceedings which have not initiated. When national proceedings precede those of the Community, the national court will independently determine the

---

10. *First Gervais-Danone Case* (77/71), 15 Dec. 1971, considerations 11-13, [1971] ECR 1138; [1973] CMLR 428; CCH para 8152.
11. *Third Balkan Case* (118/76), 28 June 1977, consideration 5, [1977] ECR 1189; CCH para 8426.
12. *Walt Wilhelm Case* (14/68), 13 Feb. 1969, considerations 4, 6, [1969] ECR 13, 14; [1969] CMLR 118, 119; CCH para 8056.

fine for the violation of the national rules. The Court of Justice will then take the national fine into consideration when it subsequently imposes a Community penalty. This follows from the Court's ruling in the *Walt Wilhelm Case*, quoted above in § 64.

§ 550.   The highest German Court finally expressed the same opinion in its decision in the *Walt Wilhelm Case* when it held:

'It would certainly be intolerable and incompatible with the principle of the rule of law if a German state organ were to impose a fine without at the same time taking into consideration that the person in question had already been fined for the same act by a Community organ. The notion of justice inherent in the principle of the rule of law requires rather that in such case (...) the earlier but parallel proceedings should, vis-à-vis their effect on the person in question be taken into account in the imposition of later fines even if there are other points of law to be taken into consideration. [13]

Normally, it should indeed prove possible to solve problems when competences partly coincide by proper cooperation between the national courts and the Court of Justice. Such cooperation is facilitated by the possibility of national courts obtaining an authentic interpretation of Community law by means of preliminary rulings and by the Member States being entitled to intervene in all cases decided by the Community Court. This Court is, in addition, composed of judges from each of the Member States.

§ 551.   The situation is different when provisions of the Community legal order overlap with provisions of the legal order of third countries, as was demonstrated by the quotation of the *Second Boehringer Case* above in § 65.

In practice, the problem of infringements being covered by Community law as well as by the law of a non-Member State is greatly reduced by the attitude adopted by the Court of Justice, by virtue of which Community sanctions are imposed not simply because of the existence of agreements made to limit competition but because of the impact of these agreements on the Common Market. No foreign court will be easily moved to impose a fine for the effects of agreements restricting trade within the Common Market.

3.   National experience with parallel judicial systems

§ 552.   The application of Community law by national courts entails the risk of divergent interpretations. National traditions differ and consequently the attitudes of national courts differ. German courts, for instance, were more willing than Dutch courts to accept the nullity of agreements restricting com-

---

13. *German Walt Wilhelm Case, Bundesgerichtshof*, 17 Dec. 1970, AWD 1971, p. 83, NJW 1971, pp. 521-525; Brinkhorst-Schermers, *Judicial Remedies in the European Communities*, Second ed., Kluwer 1977, pp. 235, 236.

petition. In order to avoid discrepancies arising in the application of Community law it was essential that the interpretation of that law was ascribed to the Court of Justice. This means that the national courts must apply rules which they cannot interpret themselves. To allow for this situation precedents were found in the legal systems of the original Member States.

§ 553. Several of the original Member States have special judicial systems for dealing with special legal rules. [14] In France, all administrative law is adjudicated by special courts. Germany and Italy have a special constitutional court for deciding whether laws violate the constitution. Germany has special court systems for several branches of law, for instance administrative law, labour law, fiscal law, social law. In order to regulate the relationship between these court systems rules for mutual reference were developed, one of which was the reference by means of preliminary rulings: if the court of one judicial system needs to apply rules belonging to the competence of another system then it may request an interpretation of those rules from a court in the adjacent system. Generally, the courts exercise discretion whether or not to refer questions to courts in other systems, they need not do so if they consider the rules to be sufficiently clear to be able to reach an answer for the questions by themselves. A decision holding that a law is unconstitutional can only be pronounced by the constitutional courts. However, the other courts have discretion whether or not to bring the question of constitutionality before the constitutional court. In Germany, they may only do so if they consider a law to be unconstitutional; in Italy it is sufficient if there is reasonable doubt about the constitutionality of the law.

Drawing upon the latter experience the founders of the Communities introduced the system of *preliminary rulings* into the Community judicial system. In Community law these are rulings which are obtained from the Court of Justice, before the national court which is handling the case takes its final decision.

B. PRELIMINARY RULINGS[15]

1. Treaty provisions

§ 554. ECSC Article 41 attributes to the Court of Justice 'sole jurisdiction to give preliminary rulings on the validity of acts of the High Authority and of the Council where such validity is in issue in proceedings brought before a

14. See Maurice Lagrange, *L'action préjudicielle dans le droit interne des Etats Membres et en droit communautaire*, 1974 RTDE, pp. 271-277.
15. On preliminary rulings, see Jean de Richemont, *L'integration du Droit Communautaire dans l'ordre juridique interne*, Librairie du Journal des notaires et des avocats, Paris 1975, 149 pages; J. Mertens de Wilmars, *Procedurele aspecten van het prejudiciëel beroep*, 23 SEW (1975) pp. 78-98; Lauwaars (*op. cit.*, note 3) pp. 37-73; H.G. Schermers, *The Law as it stands on preliminary rulings*, LIEI 1974/1, pp. 93-112; Elisabeth Freeman, *References to the Court of Justice under Article 177*, 28 Current Legal Problems (1975), pp. 176-198; Franz Zehetner, *Zum Vorlagerecht nationaler Gerichte an den Gerichtshof*

national court of tribunal.' This provision prevents any one national court from rejecting the validity of a Community act while another court makes a ruling to the contrary, but it provides no guarantee that divergent interpretations will not occur. In practice, the application of ECSC law by national courts is so infrequent that divergent interpretations have never caused any problems. If they should ever do so, the legislator (the Commission) would have to decide on a solution.

§ 555. In the EEC and Euratom Treaties the provisions are more detailed. EEC Article 177 reads:

> 'The Court of Justice shall have jurisdiction to give preliminary rulings concerning:
> (a) the interpretation of this Treaty;
> (b) the validity and interpretation of acts of the institutions of the Community;
> (c) the interpretation of the statutes of bodies established by an act of the Council, where those statutes so provide.
>
> Where such a question is raised before any court or tribunal of a Member State, that court or tribunal may, if it considers that a decision on the question is necessary to enable it to give judgment, request the Court of Justice to give a ruling thereon.
>
> Where any such question is raised in a case pending before a court or tribunal of a Member State, against whose decisions there is no judicial remedy under national law, that court or tribunal shall bring the matter before the Court of Justice.' [16]

Apart from para 1(c) which is of little importance, the Article is crucial for the relationship between the Community legal order and the national legal orders of the Members. The courts of the Member States have realized this importance. Up to 31 December 1978, 192 of them (of which 19 Supreme courts) had made use of the Article in one or more cases (in a total of 616 cases). [17] In 1978 almost 60 percent of the decisions of the Court of Justice were preliminary rulings.

§ 556. Apart from the Community Treaties, preliminary rulings have been introduced in a number of conventions concluded under the auspices of the

---

der Europäischen Gemeinschaften(Art. 177(2)), 10 EuR (1975), pp. 113-128; Gerhard Bebr, *Article 177 of the EEC Treaty in the Practice of National Courts*, 26 ICLQ (1977), pp. 241-282; Walther J. Habscheid, *Der deutsche Richter und der Europäische Gerichtshof, Bemerkungen zur Dogmatik und Praxis des Vorlageverfahrens gem. Art. 177 E.W.G. Vertrag*, Festschrift von der Heydte, Berlin 1977, pp. 205-222; L. Neville Brown, *Article 177 of the Treaty of Rome in the British context*, 74 The Law Society's Gazette (1977), pp. 314-316; John Van Gelder, *Applications to the Court of Justice, From reference to judgement*, 23 Journal of the Law Society of Scotland (1978), pp. 383-387.
16. Apart from a minor difference in para l(c) Euratom Art. 150 reads the same.
17. Twelfth General Report, p. 368, Table 2. The number of national courts involved was kindly provided by the Registry of the Court of Justice.

Communities. On 3 June 1971 the representatives of the Member States adopted two protocols by which the Court of Justice was empowered to give preliminary rulings on the interpretation of the Convention of 29 February 1968 on the Mutual Recognition of Companies and Legal Persons and the Convention of 27 September 1968 on Jurisdiction and the Enforcement of Civil and Commercial Judgments. [18] The first protocol gives the Court of Justice the same powers as those contained in EEC Article 177. The procedure, however, in the second protocol differs in several respects from that described in the EEC Treaty. The most important differences are the more restrictive enumeration of the courts entitled to request preliminary rulings (see below § 561 and 577) and the power granted to authorities, other than national courts, to apply for such rulings (see below § 585). The second of the two protocols (concerning the convention on civil and commercial judgments) entered into force as between the original Members of the Community on 1 September 1975.

On 9 October 1978 the Convention of Accession of Denmark, Ireland and the United Kingdom was signed. [19] When it enters into force these Member States will become parties to the 1968 Convention on Jurisdiction and the Enforcement of Civil and Commercial judgments as well as to the second of the two protocols mentioned above. On 31 December 1978, 14 preliminary rulings had been given with respect to the second protocol and 3 more were pending. [20]

The Convention of 15 December 1975 on the European Patent for the Common Market contains provisions similar to those of EEC Article 177 with regard to preliminary rulings concerning the interpretation of the Convention and the interpretation and validity of rules made under that Convention. [21]

2. Function of preliminary proceedings

§ 557. EEC Article 177 has been included to ensure the uniform interpretation of Community law by national courts. [22] In addition to this important

---

18. Both Conventions have been published in the Supplement to Bulletin 2-1969 of the European Communities. The protocols can be found in Supplement 4/71. On the Convention see Peter Schlosser, *Der EuGH und das Europäische Gerichtsstands- und Vollstreckungsübereinkommen*, 30 NJW (1977), pp. 457-463; Andrea Giardina, *The European Court and the Brussels Convention on jurisdiction and judgements*, 27 ICLQ (1978), pp. 263-276. On the Protocol, see also Hans Arnold, *Das Protokoll über die Auslegung des EWG-Gerichtsstands- und Vollstreckungsübereinkommens durch den Gerichtshof in Luxemburg*, 25 NJW (1972) pp. 977-981; Jean Laenens, *Protocol betreffende de uitlegging door het Hof van Justitie van het Verdrag van 27 september 1968*, 39 Rechtskundig Weekblad (1976), pp. 1323-1330.
19. O J 30 Oct. 1978, No. L 304.
20. Twelfth General Report, p. 367, Table 1.
21. Convention on the European Patent for the Common Market, Art. 73. On this convention, see Oliver C. Brändel, *Die künftige Rolle der Europäischen Gerichtshofs in Patentstreitigkeiten*, 79 GRUR (1977), pp. 294-297; A. McClellan, *La Convention sur le Brevet Communautaire*, 14 CDE (1978), pp. 202-218; Iain C. Baillie, *Where goes Europe? The European Patent*, 58 Journal of the Patent Office Society (1976), pp. 153-185.
22. Wohlfarth-Everling-Glaesner-Sprung, *Die Europäische Wirtschaftgemeinschaft*, Franz

function the article has also assumed a role of importance in the field of judicial review. It is used to open up an additional channel (though it is an indirect one as the case must go through the intermediary of a national court) through which individuals may challenge the legality of both Community acts (see above § 366-378) and acts taken by Member States (see above § 435-443) before the Court of Justice. By recourse to this article, national courts faced with the problems of exercising such judicial review can refer the problem to the Court of Justice. This Court is best equipped for the task, not only because it has been charged to perform this function by other articles of the Treaty (173 and 169 respectively) and therefore can best guarantee uniformity, but also because of its supranational character.

§ 558.   Apart from the role it plays in the field of judicial review, the preliminary ruling procedure has at least three functions in the field of interpretation.

(a)   The most important function is to ensure uniformity in the interpretation of Community law. Because of the different legal traditions of the Members, or due to differences between the Community languages, variations in interpretation could arise not only between different individual courts, but also in the interpretations given to Community law in different Member States. The Common Market would suffer if particular rules were to develop along different lines in each of the Member States.

(b)   The system of preliminary rulings facilitates the application of Community law by helping the national courts to overcome the difficulties they encounter when applying Community law. If national courts had to apply Community law completely by themselves they might be inclined to shy away from doing so in order to avoid the difficult problems of applying a legal order unfamiliar to them.

The Court of Justice mentioned functions (a) and (b) in the *First Rheinmühlen Case* when it held:

'Article 177 is essential for the preservation of the Community character of the law established by the Treaty and has the object of ensuring that in all circumstances this law is the same in all States of the Community.

Whilst it thus aims to avoid divergences in the interpretation of Community law which the national courts have to apply, it likewise tends to ensure this application by making available to the national judge a means of eliminating difficulties which may be occasioned by the requirement of giving Community law its full effect within the framework of the judicial systems of the Member States.' [23]

(c)   A special function of the preliminary ruling procedure is to decide the question whether or not a Community act has direct effect (see above

---

Vahlen Verlag 1960, pp. 498-500; Von der Groeben-Boeckh. *Kommentar zum EWG-Vertrag*, Verlag August Lutzeyer 1960, pp. 142-147.
23. *First Rheinmühlen Case* (166/73), 16 Jan. 1974, consideration 2, [1974] ECR 38; [1974] 1 CMLR 577; CCH para 8265.

§ 175-192). If it has, then it can be invoked by individuals in their national courts, and it will have to be applied with priority over any national legislation.

3. Relationship between national and Community courts

§ 559. The Court of Justice does not claim superiority in its relationship with national courts. It has repeatedly stressed that both national and Community courts play their own roles in the application of Community law. In particular, in order to give assistance to the national courts (see above § 558(b)) the Court of Justice has always viewed EEC Article 177 as an article of co-operation, not as one of hierarchy. [24] The national judiciaries share this view. [25]

The attitude of the Court of Justice means that it is extremely informal in its manner of applying the Article, as may be illustrated by the following two cases:

(1) In the *Schwarze Case* a German Court has asked a question on interpretation (Art. 177, para 1(a)) while it had meant to ask a question regarding validity (Art. 177, para 1(b)). The French Government submitted that the Court of Justice therefore could not rule on the validity of the act, but the Court of Justice replied:

'If it appears that the real purpose of the questions submitted by a national court is concerned rather with the validity of Community measures than with their interpretation, it is appropriate for the Court to inform the national court at once of its view without compelling the national court to comply with purely formal requirements which would uselessly prolong the procedure under Article 177 and would be contrary to its very nature. Although this type of strict adherence to formal requirements may be defended in the case of litigation between two parties whose mutual rights must be subject to strict rules, it would be inappropriate to the special field of judicial cooperation under Article 177 which requires the national court and the Court of Justice, both keeping within their respective jurisdiction, and with the aim of ensuring that Community law is applied in a unified manner, to make direct and complementary contributions to the working out of a decision.' [26]

(2) In the *Wagner Case* a municipal court in Luxembourg required a preliminary ruling. It did not, however, ask for such a ruling but it referred the

---

24. In its *Suggestions on European Union* the Court speaks of the prevalent 'confidence and cooperation'. Bulletin of the European Communities, Supplement 9/75, p. 20.
25. See e.g., Walther Ecker, *Einige Besorgnisse bei Anrufung des Europäischen Gerichtshofs*, speech for the Judges of the European Court of Justice and of the Bundessozialgericht, Juristenzeitung 1974, pp. 608, 609.
26. *Schwarze Case* (16/65), 1 Dec. 1965, [1965] ECR 886; 11 Jur. (1965) 1117; 11 Rec. (1965) 1094, 1095; [1966] CMLR 186; CCH para 8039 (p. 7556).

parties to the Court of Justice. The registrar of the municipal court sent that decision and the file of the case to the Court of Justice. The Court of Justice gave the required preliminary ruling stating that the direct transfer of the decision and the file by the registrar was sufficient to comply with the requirements of Article 177. [27]

§ 560.   According to one of the basic rules for preliminary rulings the Court of Justice only interprets Community law. All questions concerning the facts of the case are left to the national courts (see below 603a). The spirit of cooperation between the courts also means that the Court of Justice does not reply to questions of interpretation in an abstract and theoretical way, but that it tries to give rulings which are helpful in solving the case being dealt with, even if that leads to an interpretation which may come close to application (see below § 611).

In general the Court of Justice tries to render assistance to the national courts by giving useful preliminary rulings. In the rare cases where it cannot give the requested ruling because it does not concern a question of Community law, the Court will still not declare the request inadmissible, but it will give a ruling holding that the question *pertains to national law alone and thus does not come within the jurisdiction of the Court of Justice.* [28] The Court may then subsequently give a preliminary ruling on a question of Community law which may help the national court in reaching its decision. [29] The Court of Justice occasionally gives a ruling on a question which has not expressly been asked, when it is of the opinion that the national court needs a clarification of such a question. [30]

In the *Tedeschi Case* the Court of Justice summarizes its position holding:

'Article 177 is based on a distinct separation of functions between national courts and tribunals on the one hand and the Court of Justice on the other, and it does not give the Court jurisdiction to take cognizance of the facts of the case, or to criticize the reasons for the reference.

Therefore, when a national court or tribunal refers a provision of Community law for interpretation, it is to be supposed that the said court or tribunal considers this interpretation necessary to enable it to give judgement in the action.

Thus the Court cannot require the national or tribunal to state expressly that the provision which appears to that court or tribunal to call for an interpretation is applicable.

27. *Wagner Case* (101/63), 12 May 1964; [1964] ECR 199; 10 Jur. (1964) 418; 10 Rec. (1964) 393. 394: [1964] CMLR 256.
28. see e.g. *Adlerblum Case* (93/75), 17 Dec. 1975, consideration 4, [1975] ECR 2151; [1976] 1 CMLR 240.
29. See e.g. *Dechmann Case* (154/77), 29 June 1978, considerations 7, 8, 10, [1978] ECR 1582.
30. See e.g. *Third Simmenthal Case* (70/77), 28 June 1978, consideration 57, [1978] ECR 1476; [1978] 3 CMLR 688, in which the Court gave a ruling on directives 64/433 and 64/432, though no question on those directives had been asked.

The Court may however provide the national court with the factors of interpretation depending on Community law which might be useful to it in evaluating the effects of the provision, which is the subject-matter of the questions which have been referred to it.'[31]

This confirms prior decisions in which the Court held that it may not take cognizance of the facts nor of the considerations which moved the national court to request the ruling[32], nor of the question whether the national court is at all competent to decide the case.[33]

Individuals may not interfere with the division of powers between the Court of Justice and the national courts. In the *Mattheus Case* the Court of Justice held:

'The division of powers thus effected is mandatory; it cannot be altered, nor can the exercise of those powers be impeded, in particular by agreements between private persons tending to compel the courts of the Member States to request a preliminary ruling by depriving them of the independent exercise of the discretion which they are given by the second paragraph of Article 177'.[34]

The Court declared that it had no jurisdiction to answer the questions referred to it by a German court on the ground of a provisional contract by which the parties referred a question to a decision by the Court of Justice.[35]

§ 560a. Close cooperation between the Court of Justice and national courts is the most essential condition for the succes of the preliminary rulings procedure. To foster mutual understanding, members of the Court of Justice regularly visit national courts, and the Court of Justice once or twice a year invites judges of national courts for a visit to Luxembourg. Speeches and informal talks may then help to promote co-operation.[36]

4. Jurisdiction to refer for a preliminary ruling

a. JURISDICTION ATTRIBUTED BY THE TREATY

§ 561. EEC Article 177(2) attributes the right to request a preliminary ruling to any court or tribunal of a Member State. In the *First Rheinmühlen Case*

---

31. *Tedeschi Case* (5/77), 5 Oct. 1977, considerations 17-20, [1977] ECR 1574; CCH para 8436.
32. See e.g. *Salgoil Case* (13/68), 19 Dec. 1968, [1968] ECR 459; 14 Jur. (1968) 641; 14 Rec. (1968) 672; [1969] CMLR 193; CCH para 8072; *Portelange Case* (10/69), 9 July 1969, [1969] ECR 315; [1974] 1 CMLR 417; CCH para 8075. See also Mertens de Wilmars (*op. cit.*, note 15), p. 86.
33. *De Cicco Case* (19/68), 19 Dec. 1968, [1968] ECR 478; 14 Jur. (1968) 665; 14 Rec. (1968) 698; [1969] CMLR 75.
34. *Mattheus Case* (93/78), 22 Nov. 1978, consideration 5, [1979] 1 CMLR 557.
35. *Idem* consideration 8.
36. See also L. Neville Brown and Francis G. Jacobs, *The Court of Justice of the European Communities*, Sweet & Maxwell, 1977, p. 145.

the Court of Justice held that a rule of national law cannot deprive national courts of this right [37] and in the *BRT-Sabam Case* it held that this right cannot be fettered by a regulation of the Communities. [38]

The Protocol Concerning the Interpretation by the Court of Justice of the Convention of 27 September 1968 on Jurisdiction and the Enforcement of Civil and Commercial Judgments is more restrictive. Apart from a minor exception contained in Article 37 of the Convention, only the Supreme Courts and those courts and tribunals hearing appeals in the Member States, which are parties to the Convention, are permitted to request a preliminary ruling from the Court of Justice.

§ 562. Article 177 is not entirely clear on the question whether any other body is permitted to make a reference for a preliminary ruling. Paragraph 1 attributes a general competence to the Court of Justice to give preliminary rulings; paragraphs 2 and 3 provide that national courts of the Member States are competent (or, as the case may be, obliged) to request such rulings. This need not exclude the possibility of other bodies also asking for preliminary rulings. Whether this would be possible under Article 177, para 1, is a question of interpretation of that article and therefore for the Court of Justice to decide. [39] So far only national courts or tribunals have ever asked for a preliminary ruling, but one could at least imagine other institutions which might want to do so, such as courts of foreign States, legislative organs and semi-judicial institutions. These questions as well as the question of which organs can be accepted as courts under EEC Article 177(1) will be briefly discussed below.

b. QUALIFICATION AS A COURT

§ 563. What constitutes a court and who decides upon this? There is no doubt that apart from the normal courts of a Member State special courts also qualify under EEC Article 177, irrespective of the kind of jurisdiction conferred upon them, civil, penal or otherwise. In the Netherlands, for example, customs tariff cases are not decided by the normal courts but by a special 'tariff-commission', the *Tariefcommissie*, composed of lawyers, who are experts in the field. This tariff-commission obtained one of the most famous preliminary rulings from the Court of Justice in the *Van Gend en Loos Case*. On the other hand a superior official judging an appeal within the administration is not normally considered to be a court under national law. Could it

---

37. First *Rheinmühlen Case* (166/73), 16 Jan. 1974, consideration 4, [1974] ECR 38, 39; [1974] 1 CMLR 577; CCH para 8265. For a critical note see Peter Ernst Goose. *Einschränkung der Vorlagebefugnis nach Art. 177 Abs. 2 EWGV durch die Rechtsmittelgerichte?* 21 AWD (1975), 660-663 and thereon Reinhard Riegel in 22 Recht der Internationalen Wirtschaft (1976), pp. 110, 111.
38. *BRT-Sabam Case* (127/73), 30 Jan. 1974, consideration 23, [1974] ECR 63; [1974] 2 CMLR 271; CCH para 8268.
39. See M.R. Mok, *Should the 'first paragraph' of Article 177 of the EEC Treaty be read as a separate clause?* 5 CMLRev. (1967-68) pp. 458-464.

then be considered as a court for the purposes of Article 177? There may be good reasons for doing so in cases where the superior official in fact decides the case, either because there is no judicial appeal, or because judicial appeal is so difficult that it is only rarely used in practice. In the *Widow Vaassen Case* Advocate-General Gand submitted that the notion 'court of law', in the sense of Article 177 need not coincide with the corresponding notion under national law. [40] In the *Politi and Birra Dreher Cases* the national courts requested a preliminary ruling at a time when the cases were not (yet) in a contentious phase, and therefore were not pending according to national law. The Court of Justice rejected the submission of the Italian Government that the requests were inadmissible and gave the preliminary rulings. (See below § 573).

§ 564. In one case the Court of Justice accepted a request for a preliminary ruling from an organ which is formally not a court, though substantively it fully operates as one. In the Netherlands the highest authority for many administrative law cases is the Crown. It is advised by a special section of the Council of State. This section functions as a court and takes its decisions after a procedure of full hearings for the parties and *casu quo* for witnesses. [41] In the *First Nederlandse Spoorwegen Case* the Litigation Section of the Dutch Council of State had requested a preliminary ruling. Could an organ acting in an advisory capacity to the Government ask for such a ruling? The Advocate-General pleaded that the preliminary ruling should be given as the Litigation Section of the Dutch Council of State exercised a judicial function. The Court of Justice in fact gave the ruling. [42]

c. REFERENCE BY THE LEGISLATURE

§ 565. In principle, preliminary rulings in response to questions posed by legislative organs are to be objected against. The task of the judiciary is to settle specific questions in specific cases. General rules are to be formulated by the legislature. Both these tasks are equally essential for the smooth running of society, but they are fundamentally different. General rules are needed, but they are never totally adequate for application to all possible future situations. Courts can then, to a great extent, forestall unacceptable individual cases by interpreting the rules and by applying general principles of law. Involving the Court of Justice in the legislative process may be attractive in

---

40. *Widow Vaassen Case* (61/65), 30 June 1966, Opinion of the Advocate-General, [1966] ECR 280, 281; 12 Jur. (1966) 284; 12 Rec. (1966) 404; [1966] CMLR 511; CCH para 8050. See also below § 568.
41. On the structure and task of the Litigation Section of the Netherlands' Council of State, see Advocate-General Mayras in *First Nederlandse Spoorwegen Case* (36/73), 27 Nov. 1973, Opinion, [1973] ECR 1317-1319; [1974] 2 CMLR 152-155; CCH para 8228. By Law of 1 May 1975 (Stb. 284) another section of the Council of State was charged with an independent function as a court of law.
42. *Nederlandse Spoorwegen Case* (36/73), 27 Nov. 1973, [1973] ECR 1308-1314; [1974] 2 CMLR 166-170; CCH para 8228. See also T.P.J.N. van Rijn, *De Raad van State en Artikel 177 van het EEG-Verdrag*, NJB 1974, pp. 516-518.

some specific instances and does occasionally occur under the Community Treaties, but this is nevertheless to be disapproved of in principle (see above § 531). If the Court has approved of legislative acts in any way, it is no longer free in future situations to set aside such acts or to interpret them in an entirely different way.

d. REFERENCE BY FOREIGN AND INTERNATIONAL COURTS

§ 566. For foreign courts preliminary rulings may be helpful. Questions of Community law, such as the question whether a particular agreement is void under EEC Article 85, para 2, are often complicated and there may be no other authority available to give guidance. Of course, all courts encounter such problems when they have to apply foreign law. Article 177 could, however, be of value in a field where traditional inter-state relationships have not yet invented adequate procedures for mutual legal assistance.

The chances that the Court of Justice would accept preliminary rulings from foreign courts seem remote. In its reasoning in the *Widow Vaassen Case* (see below § 568) the Court of Justice accepted the condition that the preliminary ruling must be asked by 'a judicial organ in the sense of EEC Article 177' which according to the article is *'a court or tribunal of a Member State.'* As other courts would not be obliged to apply preliminary rulings, such rulings given to them would have a purely advisory character.

§ 567. When international courts meet questions of Community law preliminary rulings could also prove useful. This is particularly true of regional European courts such as the European Court for Human Rights in Strasbourg. As was mentioned above (§ 541) it is unlikely that the Commission or the Court of Human Rights will ever be confronted with questions of Community law which have not been subject to a preliminary ruling in the national court proceedings, preceding the Strasbourg procedure, but this does not exclude the possibility that the Strasbourg institutions may want a further preliminary ruling. In the *CFDT Case* a French labour union submitted that its right to form trade unions was violated by the fact that its representatives could not be candidates for the Consultative Committee of the Coal and Steel Community. When the Court of Justice had held its application inadmissible[43], CFDT addressed a petition to the European Commission of Human Rights claiming that there had been a violation of Article 11 of the European Convention on Human Rights. The European Commission on Human Rights held this application inadmissible. [44] One could conceive of the usefulness of a preliminary ruling by the Court of Justice to the European Court of Human Rights if a similar case is held admissible by the Human Rights institutions and they would need an authentic interpretation of the Community rules involved in

43. *CFDT Case* (66/76), 17 Feb. 1977, consideration 15, [1977] ECR 311; [1977] 1 CMLR 595.
44. Decision of 10 July 1978 in Case No. 8030/77. See also above § 134.

order to establish whether any provision of the European Convention might have been violated. As the Human Rights Commission and Court can be seen as part of the judiciary of the Member States, there seems to be no reason why these institutions should not be entitled to request preliminary rulings if they consider that a decision on Community law is necessary to enable them to give judgment.

e. REFERENCE BY ARBITRAL TRIBUNALS

§ 568. There is only one case in which an arbitral tribunal has made a reference for a preliminary ruling: the *Widow Vaassen Case* [45], where an arbitral tribunal had to decide whether the widow in question was entitled to a pension under EEC Regulation 3. It asked for a preliminary ruling on the interpretation of that regulation. The Court of Justice did not hold that it could give preliminary rulings under Article 177 (1) to other than national courts and tribunals; on the contrary, it carefully discussed why this particular tribunal was a 'court' within the meaning of Article 177. When it had established this, it ruled that the request for a preliminary ruling was *therefore* admissible. In this particular case it was not difficult to establish that the tribunal could be considered as a court of law, as it was a permanent body founded in Dutch law; its members were officially appointed by the Government and were obliged to apply the rules of law. Most arbitral tribunals will resemble courts of law less closely, so that their competence to ask for a preliminary ruling will still have to be established in each individual case.

§ 569. Most authors deny arbitral tribunals the competence to ask preliminary rulings be enumerating one or more of the following grounds. (1) One of the basic principles inherent in arbitration is that the public authorities and courts are not involved in the decision. It would run counter to this principle to have one specific court involved with one specific sort of questions. (2) Often arbitral tribunals are entitled to make their decision by recourse to the rules of equity; they do not necessarily apply the law. (3) The raison d'être of arbitration is to obtain a decision quickly; this benefit would be frustrated if preliminary rulings had to be asked of the Court of Justice. (4) There are so many arbitral tribunals that their questions would overburden the Court of Justice. (5) The decisions of arbitrators do not form part of the case-law of the country and therefore are less important as precedents; they are, furthermore, not final, as additional judicial acts are required for their execution. (6) Arbitrators are not judges; they usually have neither the training nor the experience of professional judges. In addition they do not have the same public authority. (7) If arbitrators were obliged to request preliminary rulings, the parties would seek arbitration outside the Common Market; the underlying purpose of arbitration would thus be frustrated. [46]

---

45. *Widow Vaassen Case* (61/65), 30 June 1966, [1966] ECR 272, 273; 12 Jur. (1966) 275; 21 Rec. (1966) 394, 395; [1966] CMLR 518, 519; CCH para 8050.
46. Frédéric Dumon, *Le renvoi préjudiciel*, in Droit communautaire et droit national

Personally I share the view that arbitral tribunals are not courts and that they can therefore never be obliged to ask preliminary rulings, even if their decision is final. On the other hand, I see no objection to preliminary rulings at the request of arbitral tribunals. If an arbitral tribunal wants a preliminary ruling, it should be left free to ask for one. It sould at least be able to ask whether EEC Article 177 permits its request for a preliminary ruling.

f. REFERENCE BY COURTS IN INTERIM CASES [47]

§ 570. The competence of national courts to ask for preliminary rulings is not restricted to cases in which they deliver final decisions. Preliminary rulings may be also asked in actions for interim injunctions. The same ruling will apply as in the *Rheinmühlen Case* where the Court of Justice held:

'It follows that national courts have the widest discretion in referring matters to the Court of Justice if they consider that a case pending before them raises questions involving interpretation, or consideration of the validity, of provisions of Community law, necessitating a decision on their part.' [48]

§ 571. The provisions in the national legal systems for deciding urgent cases differ considerably. Usually in an urgent case an injunction can be asked from the court. The injunction − if given − is temporary and ceases to have effect if no proper court case follows. A court deciding on an interim injunction will only rarely find time for obtaining a preliminary ruling. In Germany the *Oberlandesgericht* Stuttgart was of the opinion that in proceedings for an interim injunction maintenance of the unity of the law is not involved and this would be another reason for not requesting a preliminary ruling. [49] Nonetheless in a number of cases courts have found the interpretation of Community law to be of such importance that they have requested preliminary rulings even for cases concerning (interim) injunctions. [50]

In the *English Löwenbräu Case* the High Court held:

'If the matter is doubtful, then presumably reference should only be made to the EEC Court for guidance in the case where an injunction is in fact

---

Semaine de Bruges 1965, pp. 219-221; Lagrange, (*op. cit.*, note 14), p. 283; Lauwaars (*op. cit.*, note 3), pp. 48, 49; M.R. Mok and H. Johannes, *Schiedsgerichtbarkeit und EWG-Vertrag*, 1966 AWD, pp. 125-130.
47. Hartmut Lübbert, *Vorläufiger Rechtsschutz und einheitliche Auslegung des Gemeinschaftsrechts*, Festschrift für Ernst von Caemmerer, Tübingen 1978, pp. 933-953.
48. *First Rheinmühlen Case* (166/73), 16 Jan. 1974, consideration 4, [1974] ECR 38; [1974] 1 CMLR 577; CCH para 8265. See also Advocate-General Roemer's opinion in the *Stauder Case* (29/69), 12 Nov. 1969, Opinion, [1969] ECR 427, 428; [1970] CMLR 114; CCH para 8077.
49. *German Bathing Fashions Case*, 23 Jan. 1976, consideration 18, [1977] 1 CMLR 136.
50. See e.g. *Stauder Case* (29/69), 12 Nov. 1969, [1969] ECR 419 ff; [1970] CMLR 112; CCH para 8077; *Variola Case* (34/73), 10 Oct. 1973, [1973] ECR 981 ff; CCH para 8226.

granted concurrently with the reference. If no injunction is granted it would not be justifiable to put the parties to the expense of going to the EEC Court unless they wished to do so. [51]

§ 572.   In the Netherlands, pressing cases are brought before the president of the court by means of a procedure called 'summary proceedings', which is simpler and faster than the normal one. In this procedure the courts do not sit in plenary session, time limits are shorter and the decision is taken more rapidly. This procedure can be followed by summary proceedings before the court of appeal, and again by summary proceedings before the supreme court, the Hoge Raad. In all three instances the decisions taken in summary proceedings stand unless they are overruled either by a decision in summary proceedings before a higher court or by a ruling given in normal proceedings by the same court sitting as a full court. The parties do not expect the full courts to overturn the decisions taken in summary proceedings and therefore they usually do not take the question to normal proceedings. Accordingly in the Dutch practice, the vast majority of decisions made in summary proceedings are final.

It will be clear that under these circumstances preliminary rulings are much more important than is the case with interim injunctions, for example, in the U.K. [52]

The Court of Justice has recognized the differences which exist between national interim proceedings. When it gave a ruling concerning a German interim order it mentioned the German name also in the translations of the case in the other languages, thus indicating that the ruling concerned the German interim proceedings only. [53]

§ 573.   In the *Politi* and in the *Birra Dreher Cases* no contentious procedure was at stake. A '*Pretore*' in Turin and one in Rome respectively were each making an order at the request of one party without the other party being heard. Such orders lead to actual court cases only when the other party raises objections. The Italian Government expressed doubts as to the jurisdiction of the Court of Justice to give preliminary rulings on questions raised in the course of an application for this kind of order, but the Court of Justice held in the *Birra Dreher Case*:

'It is sufficient to determine that the Pretore, in hearing the application for the grant of an order, is exercising the functions of a court or tribunal

---

51.   *English Löwenbräu Case, High Court, Chancery Division*, 27 Nov. 1973, [1974] 1 CMLR 10, 11. On this case see Lawrence Collins, *Art. 177 of the EEC Treaty and English interlocutory proceedings*, 23 ICLQ (1974), pp. 840-851.
52.   The *First Centrafarm Cases* (15/74 and 16/74), 31 Oct. 1974, [1974] ECR 1149, 1150, 1185; [1974] 2 CMLR 484; CCH para 8246, 8247, were brought by the Hoge Raad in summary proceedings. Lower Dutch Courts have never asked for preliminary rulings in summary proceedings.
53.   *First Hoffmann – La Roche Case* (107/76), 24 May 1977, considerations 1, 6, [1977] ECR 971, 973; [1977] 2 CMLR 352, 354; CCH para 8414.

within the meaning of Article 177 — as has moreover previously been decided — and that an interpretation of Community law has been considered by that court as essential for it to arrive at a decision, without its being necessary for the Court of Justice to consider the stage of the proceedings at which the question was put. Article 177 does not make the reference to the Court subject to whether the proceedings at the conclusion of which the national court has drawn up the reference for a preliminary ruling were or were not defended.' [54]

After these cases there can be no doubt that national courts are entitled to request preliminary rulings in interim cases whenever they want to do so.

5. Obligation to refer for a preliminary ruling

a. THE OBLIGATION ON LOWER COURTS

§ 574. In the section on the review of the legality of Community acts it was pleaded that lower courts should be considered *obliged* to request a preliminary ruling before they may rule that a Community act is invalid (see above § 368). Toth pleads that lower courts should also be obliged to request a preliminary ruling when the question of the direct applicability of a particular rule of Community law is raised for the first time. [55] I am dubious whether this might not overly curtail the freedom of the lower court which is provided for in the Treaty. There is no doubt that an immediate preliminary ruling on every question of direct effect is highly desirable, even if not obligatory. In all other cases lower courts have the right to ask for a preliminary ruling, and often they are to be advised to use that right (see below § 586), but they are not obliged to do so.

b. THE OBLIGATION ON THE HIGHEST COURT

(i) Highest court in the case, or highest court in the country?

§ 575. Article 177 of the EEC Treaty requires the courts against whose decisions there is no judicial remedy under national law, to ask for a preliminary ruling. The plural form of the word *decisions* suggests that only those courts are meant which normally render final decisions, in other words, the highest courts of the national judiciary. Some States, such as Germany, have different highest courts for different fields of law — such as fiscal courts, administrative courts, social courts — others may have only one supreme

---

54. *Birra Dreher Case* (162/73), 21 Feb. 1974, consideration 3, [1974] ECR 211; CCH para 8264. See also *Politi Case* (43/71), 14 Dec. 1971, consideration 5, [1971] ECR 1048; [1973] CMLR 69; CCH para 8159.
55. A.G. Toth, *Legal Protection of Individuals in the European Communities*, North Holland 1978, vol. II, p. 214.

court. The decisions of these highest courts comprise the case law which is likely to be followed by the lower courts. For the sake of the uniformity of Community law the decisions of the highest courts are the important ones. For those reasons the adherents to the *'abstract theory'* submit that only the highest courts are obliged to request preliminary rulings. [56]

Not all cases can be brought before the highest courts, however. In many legal systems cases on minor matters are decided by lower courts in final instance. If those courts were not obliged to ask for a preliminary ruling when faced with questions of Community law, a particular group of Community law questions, (that is those on minor matters), might never reach the Community Court and the rights of a particular individual (the party interested in the proper application of Community law) might be prejudiced. For these reasons the adherents of the *'concrete theory'* submit that each court judging in final instance is a highest court in the sense of Article 177 and is therefore obliged to bring questions on Community law to the Community Court.

For some Member States (France, the Netherlands) the question has no practical importance as appeals to the highest courts — at least on points of law — are always possible; but for others (Italy, the UK) the concrete theory means that many inferior courts would be obliged to request preliminary rulings in cases of minor importance. Now that practice has shown that requests for preliminary rulings may be quite costly this may not be appropriate in all circumstances. I would therefore not plead for an absolute obligation to be imposed on lower courts deciding in last instance, but that such courts should have very strong arguments for any decision not to refer.

§ 576. The Court of Justice opted for the concrete theory in the *Costa-Enel Case*. This leading case on the relationship between Community law and national law was brought before the Court of Justice by the lowest Italian Court, a Justice of the Peace, deciding in final instance as the sum of money involved was extremely small (less than 2000 Italian lire, or less than £2). In its decision on the admissibility of the question the Court of Justice held:

'Under Article 177 national courts against whose decisions, *as in the present case*, there is no judicial remedy, must refer the matter to the Court of Justice so that a preliminary ruling may be given upon the 'interpretation of the Treaty' whenever a question of interpretation is raised before them.' [57]

It is by no means certain that this *obiter dictum* of the Court of Justice was meant to settle the question. It is interesting that both Judge Donner, at that time President of the Court of Justice, and M. Lagrange, Advocate-General in

---

56. In support of this theory see Dumon (*op. cit.*, note 46), pp. 222-225; Lagrange, SEW 1962, p. 102 and Lord Denning in the *English Champagne Case, Court of Appeal*, 22 May 1974, [1974] 2 CMLR 113, 114.
57. *Costa-Enel Case* (6/64), 15 July 1964, [1964] ECR 592, 593; 10 Jur. (1964) 1217; 10 Rec. (1964) 1158; [1964] CMLR 454; CCH para 8023; *emphasis added.*

the *Costa-Enel Case*, consider the question as unresolved in their private writings after the case. [58]

§ 577. It is worthwhile noting that the Protocol concerning the Interpretation of the Convention of 27 September 1968 on Jurisdiction and the Enforcement of Civil and Commercial Judgments opted for the abstract theory. Article 2(1) enumerates the courts which are bound to request a preliminary ruling whenever they consider that an interpretation of the Convention is necessary in order to enable them to render judgment. [59] The courts, the highest in civil and commercial matters, are as follows:

in Belgium: la Cour de Cassation − het Hof van Cassatie and le Conseil d'Etat − de Raad van State;

in Denmark: Højesteret;

in the Federal Republic of Germany: die obersten Gerichtshöfe des Bundes;

in France: la Cour de Cassation and le Conseil d'Etat;

in Ireland: the Supreme Court;

in Italy: la Corte Suprema di Cassazione;

in Luxembourg: la Cour supérieure de Justice, when sitting as Supreme Court of Appeal;

in the Netherlands: de Hoge Raad;

in the United Kingdom: the House of Lords and the other courts to which appeals may be brought under the Convention.

(ii) Highest courts whose decisions may sometimes be appealed

§ 578. In most countries decisions from the highest courts may be reviewed under specific circumstances, or the Head of State may set aside penal sentences by granting a pardon. Such special appeals do not affect the position of a court acting as a court of last instance. Germany and Italy have special constitutional courts. These courts may overrule all other courts and are in this sense superior to the highest normal courts. However, due to their limited jurisdiction these courts do not constitute a higher instance, in the normal sense. Even under the abstract theory the *Bundesgerichtshof*, the *Bundessozialgericht*, the *Bundesverwaltungsgericht*, the *Bundesfinanzhof* and the *Bundesarbeitsgericht* should be considered as the supreme courts of Germany and the *Corte di Cassazione* and the *Consiglio di Stato* as those of Italy.

§ 579. In England a party who wants to appeal to the House of Lords must obtain leave to proceed there. That leave can be refused. What then is the position of the Court of Appeal? [60] It may be the court of last instance and it

58. A.M. Donner, *Les rapports entre la compétence de la Cour de Justice des Communautés Européennes et les tribunaux internes*, RdC 1965 (II) pp. 43, 44, translated in L.J. Brinkhorst and H.G. Schermers *Judicial Remedies in the European Communities*, second ed. Kluwer 1977, pp. 282, 283; Lagrange (*op. cit.*, note 14), pp. 283, 284.
59. Protocol of 3 June 1971, Art. 2, as amended on 9 Oct. 1978, OJ 30 Oct. 1978, No. L 304/98.
60. See also Freeman (*op. cit.*, note 15), pp. 185, 186; Francis Jacobs, *Which courts and tribunals are bound to refer to the European Court?* 2ELRev. (1977), pp. 119-121.

may not. In the *English Champagne Case* Lord Denning (Master of the Rolls) held that only the House of Lords would be obliged to refer and that the Court of Appeal would have 'complete discretion'[61], but on this point he was not supported by the two other judges in the case[62] and he was criticized by the Commission[63] and in the European Parliament.[64]

The discretion of the Court of Appeal is, in fact, not complete. It should take account of the possibility that leave to appeal to the House of Lords might not be granted and should therefore, in principle, make the reference itself. However, as long as it grants leave to appeal to the House of Lords the Court of Appeal is legally not a court against whose decisions there is no judicial remedy and, therefore, there is no strict legal obligation to refer. If the House of Lords were to refuse to rule on a case concerning Community law for which no preliminary ruling has been asked, then the House of Lords would violate the obligation incumbent upon it under the last paragraph of EEC Article 177.

In January 1979 the House of Lords requested a preliminary ruling in a case in which the Court of Appeal had refused to do so (for the reason that the EEC provisions were clear) and in which the Court of Appeal had also refused leave to appeal.[65] This may be an indication that the House of Lords is less reluctant than the Court of Appeal to use the preliminary ruling procedure.

§ 580. In the *English Holiday in Italy Case* a National Insurance Commissioner held that he did not constitute a tribunal against whose decision there is no judicial remedy under English law as his decision *'may be set aside by an order of certiorari made by the High Court on the ground of an error in point of law'*, even though an application for an order of *certiorari* cannot be made without the leave of the High Court.[66] At this much lower level an omission to refer seems less objectionable than in the case of the Court of Appeal, but the argument is the same: either the preliminary ruling should be asked or leave to go before the High Court should be granted.

§ 581. The courts which are obliged to ask for a preliminary ruling are the courts 'against whose decision there is no judicial remedy under national law'. The Dutch text of the EEC Treaty speaks of courts against whose decisions *'there is no appeal'* (*hoger beroep*). This caused some confusion as under Dutch law the last appeal is to the courts of appeal. Beyond them lies the Supreme Court, the *Hoge Raad*, where only *'cassation'* can be requested. This is more limited in its nature than an appeal as it does not lead to a fresh judgment on the case but only to a review of the points of law. One could,

61. *English Champagne Case, Court of Appeal*, 22 May 1974, [1974] 2 CMLR 114.
62. Lord Justice Stamp, *idem* p. 121, Lord Justice Stephenson, *idem* p. 125.
63. Eight General Report para 472.
64. Written question of Mr. Bayerl, OJ 17 July 1975 No. C 161, pp. 12, 13.
65. *English Smugglers Case*, Jan. 1979, Financial Times 15 Jan. 1979.
66. *English Holiday in Italy Case, National Insurance Commissioner*, 4 July 1974, [1975] 1 CMLR 188.

therefore, defend the argument that the courts of appeal are the courts which are obliged to refer. This position has, however, in the meantime been generally rejected. [67] In the *Da Costa Case* the Court of Justice clarified the point by reviewing the Dutch text of the Treaty. In that case, which is authentic in Dutch, the Court reformulated the provision when it held: '*Although the third paragraph of Article 177 unreservedly requires courts or tribunals of a Member State against whose decisions there is no judicial remedy under national law ... to refer to the Court every question of interpretation raised before them, ...* '. [68]

It is therefore, beyond doubt that the Dutch courts of appeal are not numbered amongst the highest courts obliged to request preliminary rulings. In one respect this limits the possibility of invoking Community law: as the cassation proceedings are limited to the question whether the law has been correctly applied by the lower courts, the parties cannot normally invoke, before the Supreme Court, questions of Community law which they had not previously invoked before the Court of Appeal. When in the *Netherlands Reinvoorde Case* the applicant invoked a number of questions of Community law for the first time in cassation, the *Hoge Raad* held:

'It does not appear that this plea has been submitted earlier in this dispute. It cannot be submitted successfully for the first time in cassation proceedings since it concerns questions which should also be judged in the light of the factual circumstances.' [69]

(iii) Highest courts granting interim injunctions

§ 582. Are the highest courts obliged to ask for a preliminary ruling when the case they have before them is not final? Again one encounters the arguments of the 'abstract' and the 'concrete' theories (see above § 575). On the one hand, as the highest courts set precedents, their case law, even in interim judgments, should be in conformity with Community law; on the other hand, their decisions are not necessarily final in the case concerned, normal procedures being still available. The legal situation was unclear and some German courts ruled divergently on this question. The *Bundesfinanzhof* (the supreme court for fiscal matters) expressly decided that it was not obliged to request a preliminary ruling in an interim case [70]; whilst the *Oberlandesgericht Hamburg*, the highest court of the Free State of Hamburg, was of the opinion that 'the obligation under EEC Article 177(3) also exists in relation to summary proceedings for an interim injunction'. [71]

---

67. See Dumon (*op. cit.*, note 46), pp. 226-228.
68. *Da Costa Case* (28-30/62), 27 March 1963, [1963] ECR 38; 9 Jur. (1963) 77; 9 Rec. (1963) 75; [1963] CMLR 237; CCH para 8010.
69. *Netherlands Reinvoorde Case, Hoge Raad*, 7 April 1970, consideration 19, [1973] CMLR 168.
70. *German Tapioca Case, Bundesfinanzhof*, 6 Dec. 1967 and 9 Jan. 1968, AWD 1968, p. 284; Brinkhorst-Schermers (*op. cit.*, note 58), pp. 276, 277.
71. *German Records Case, Oberlandesgericht Hamburg*, 8 Oct. 1970, AWD 1971, p. 40; Brinkhorst-Schermers (*op. cit.*, note 58), p. 277.

§ 583. In 1976 the *Oberlandesgericht Karlsruhe* requested a preliminary ruling on the question whether a national court is obliged to ask for a preliminary ruling under EEC Article 177(3) when a question of Community law arises during interlocutory proceedings for an interim order and when no appeal lies against the court's decision, but when an ordinary action is open to the parties. The Court of Justice then ruled:

'The third paragraph of Article 177 of the EEC Treaty must be interpreted as meaning that a national court or tribunal is not required to refer to the Court a question of interpretation or of validity mentioned in that article when the question is raised in interlocutory proceedings for an interim order (einstweilige Verfügung), even where no judicial remedy is available against the decision to be taken in the context of those proceedings, provided that each of the parties is entitled to institute proceedings or to require proceedings to be instituted on the substance of the case and that during such proceedings the question provisionally decided in the summary proceedings may be re-examined and may be the subject of a reference to the Court under Article 177. [72]

c. SANCTIONS AGAINST BREACH OF THE OBLIGATION

§ 584. It has been seen above (§ 421-423) that the Commission may act, under EEC Article 169, against a State whose highest court has failed to request a preliminary ruling in a case where it was obliged to do so, but that the Commission will usually not do so.

Whether the parties to the case will have any remedy in such a situation depends on the national legal system. Usually they have none. Under Dutch law a judgment rendered by the Court of Justice under EEC Article 169, establishing that the highest Dutch court has defaulted in its obligation to request a preliminary ruling, would be insufficient grounds for a retrial of the case [73], but such a judgment might be a ground for a suit for damages. It could be submitted that the State committed a wrongful act by not providing proper court proceedings, in violation of EEC Article 177 and perhaps also of Article 6 of the European Convention on Human Rights. [74]

§ 585. Even if the parties to the case in which the highest national court failed to request a preliminary ruling are able to claim damages (which they usually cannot), and even if they succeed in proving the injuries ensuing therefrom (which must be difficult), this still leaves a lacuna in the system because the required interpretation of Community law is not obtained. The Protocol of 3 June 1971 conferring on the Court of Justice jurisdiction to

---

72. *First Hoffmann-La Roche Case* (107/76), 24 May 1977, ruling, [1977] ECR 974; [1977] 2 CMLR 355; CCH para 8414.
73. Wetboek van Burgerlijke Regtsvordering, Art. 382.
74. See Lauwaars (*op. cit.*, note 3), pp. 65, 66.

interpret the Convention of 27 September 1968 on Jurisdiction and the Enforcement of Civil and Commercial Judgments, copes with this problem by providing that the Attorney-Generals at the national supreme courts or other designated authorities can lay a request for interpretation [75] before the Court of Justice.

Another solution would be to allow the Advocates-General, the Commission or the Member States to take such questions to the Court of Justice, not in order to decide a case but in order to obtain a precedent for similar situations that could arise in the future. [76]

In keeping with the English and German system of taking cases to the highest courts, the House of Lords and the *Bundesverfassungsgericht* respectively, a system could also be developed according to which the parties themselves would be permitted to obtain leave of the Court of Justice to bring their cases directly before the Court. In cases of general interest the Court of Justice could then grant such leave.

The Court of Justice has suggested that individuals should be provided with an appropriate remedy for infringement of Article 177 either by means of a direct application to the Court of Justice by the parties to the main action, or by means of an obligatory action for default or, finally, by an action for damages against the State concerned at the suit of the party adversely affected. [77]

6. Discretion not to refer for a preliminary ruling

a. DISCRETION OF LOWER COURTS

§ 586. Normally lower courts have a right to ask for a preliminary ruling but are not obliged to do so. There may be cases where it would be very unwise not to ask for a preliminary ruling, in particular when the preliminary ruling is essential for the solution of the case. Failing to ask a preliminary ruling at first instance would then compel the parties to appeal until the highest court had to ask for the ruling. This would lead to unnecessary costs and loss of time for the parties.

A prompt reference is not only of importance to the parties in the case before the court. Often a case is the consequence of a specific factual situation, a specific national rule, or a specific court interpretation which also applies to parties other than those to the case in dispute. A preliminary ruling at an early stage in the proceedings may, therefore, also be important for a larger group of people. [78]

75. Protocol of 3 June 1971, Art. 4, Supplement 4/71, Annex to Bulletin 7-1971 of the European Communities.
76. P.J.G. Kapteyn and P. VerLoren van Themaat, *Introduction to the law of the European Communities*, Kluwer 1973, p. 181.
77. *Suggestions of the Court of Justice on European Union*, Bulletin of the European Communities, Supplement 9/75, p. 18.
78. For examples see the *Bosch Case* (13/61), 6 April 1962, [1962] ECR 45; 8 Jur. (1962) 91; 8 Rec. (1962) 89, [1962] CMLR 1; CCH para 8003, or the *Van Haaster Case* (190/73), 30 Oct. 1974, [1974] ECR 1123; [1974] 2 CMLR 521; CCH para 8286.

§ 587. As a rule the Court of Justice does not have any control over the discretion exercised by national courts. It will give the requested ruling without asking whether it was necessary for solving the case.

In the *Sacchi Case* the Court of Justice held:

'Article 177, which is based on a clear separation of functions between the national courts and this Court, does not allow this Court to judge the grounds for the request for interpretation.' [79]

b. NECESSITY OF INTERPRETATION

(i) Lower courts

§ 588. A lower court may ask for a preliminary ruling on a question of Community law 'if it considers that a decision on the question is necessary to enable it to give judgment'. When is such a decision necessary?

In the *English Champagne Case* Lord Denning held as regards this question:

'The English court has to consider whether 'a decision of the question is *necessary* to enable it to give *judgment*'. That means judgment in the very case which is before the court. The judge must have got to the stage when he says to himself: 'This clause of the Treaty is capable of two or more meanings. If it means *this*, I give judgment for the plaintiff. If it means *that*, I give judgment for the defendant'. In short, the point must be such that, whichever way the point is decided, it is conclusive of the case. Nothing more remains but to-give judgment.'

and:

'It is to be noticed, too, that the word is 'necessary'. This is much stronger than 'desirable' or 'convenient'. There are some cases where the point, if decided one way, would shorten the trial greatly. But, if decided the other way, it would mean that the trial would have to go its full length. In such a case it might be 'convenient' or 'desirable' to take it as a preliminary point because it might save much time and expense. But it would not be 'necessary' at that stage. When the facts were investigated, it might turn out to have been quite unnecessary. The case would be determined on another ground altogether. As a rule you cannot tell whether it is necessary to decide a point until all the facts are ascertained. So in general it is best to decide the facts first.' [80]

79. *Sacchi Case* (155/73), 30 April 1974, consideration 3, [1974] ECR 426; [1974] 2 CMLR 201; CCH para 8267. See also e.g. *Mazzalai Case* (111/75), 20 May 1976, consideration 9, [1976] ECR 665; CCH para 8363.
80. *English Champagne Case, Court of Appeal*, 22 May 1974, para 27, 30; [1974] 2 CMLR 115, 116.

§ 589. This interpretation of the word 'necessary' is too narrow and was rightly criticized. [81] It would reduce the scope of EEC Article 177 considerably. Normally a court considers all aspects of a case and then makes its decision. According to the suggestion made by Lord Denning the court would first have to decide separately on the results of each of the possible interpretations of Community law, and only ask a preliminary ruling if these interpretations would produce contradictory results. In his submission there would be no need to ask for a preliminary ruling if an interpretation would be required only to shorten proceedings. If other courts desire to follow Lord Denning's interpretation, it would be wise first to obtain a more authoritative interpretation of the word 'necessary' from the Court of Justice.

(ii) Highest courts

§ 590. The last paragraph of EEC Article 177 does not reiterate the qualification that a decision on the question must be 'necessary'. Does that mean that courts of last instance are always compelled to ask for a preliminary ruling even if they do not consider a ruling necessary? It would be hard to accept that the highest courts are obliged to ask for rulings whenever a party raises any questions of Community law even if this is totally irrelevant to the case. This interpretation, therefore, is inappropriate and is not followed by the highest courts of the Member States. The supreme court of the Netherlands, the *Hoge Raad*, expressed this view in the *Netherlands Reinvoorde Case* when it held, after considering that the rules of Community law could not be successfully invoked for the first time in cassation (see above § 581):

> 'For this reason alone point 6 of the appeal, as it has been elucidated, cannot lead to cassation, the request for a preliminary ruling by the Court of Justice in Luxembourg submitted at this point in the appeal cannot be granted.' [82]

c. ACTE CLAIR [83]

§ 591. Under French law administrative courts do not have to refer questions of civil law to civil courts and *vice versa* when they consider the matter

---

81. See Mitchell in 11 CMLRev. (1974), p. 356, the Commission in its Eighth General Report, para 472 and in its answer to Parliamentary Question 25/75, OJ 17 July 1975, No. C 161, p. 13; Freeman (*op. cit.*, note 13), pp. 197, 198; R. Graupner, *Reference to the European Court according to Art. 177 of the EEC Treaty*, The Law Society's Gazette, 4 Dec. 1974, p. 1241; Francis G. Jacobs, *When to refer to the European Court*, 90 The Law Quarterly Review (1974), pp. 486-493; Brown and Jacobs (*op. cit.*, note 36), p. 146.
82. *Netherlands Reinvoorde Case, Hoge Raad*, 7 April 1970, consideration 20, [1973] CMLR 175.
83. On the theory of *acte clair* see Manfred Zuleeg, *Das Recht der Europäischen Gemeinschaften in innerstaatlichem Bereich*, 1969, p. 365, Pierre Pescatore, *L'interprétation du droit communautaire et la doctrine de l'acte clair*, Bulletin de l'association des juristes européens, 1971, pp. 49-72, English version in Legal Problems of an Enlarged European Community, Stevens & Sons 1972, pp. 27-46; Maurice Lagrange, *The theory of acte clair: a bone of contention or a source of unity?* 8 CMLRev. (1971) pp. 313-324.

sufficiently clear to be solved by themselves. Is this French theory of *'acte clair'* also applicable to Community law? As regards the lower courts there is no problem: under EEC Article 177 they are free to decide questions of Community law on their own if they consider them to be sufficiently clear; but the highest courts *must ask for a preliminary ruling* when ' *a question*' is raised on the interpretation or validity of Community law. Does every issue presuppose that there is a question or may courts find an issue so clear that no question is required? Parties may raise any point of Community law in a case possibly even as a delaying tactic, for a preliminary ruling takes at least six months. Is the highest court then always obliged to refer? Or should preliminary rulings be limited to cases where there is reasonable doubt on the interpretation or on the validity of Community law?

§ 592. The problem in the Communities is different from that in French law. In France the other legal system which must be interpreted is part of the law of the same State. It is in the same language; judges have met the problem before in their legal education and in their legal literature; the matter is familiar to them. It is, therefore, quite acceptable that easy questions with regard to one legal order are tackled by judges of the other.

In Community law the deviations between the different legal systems are greater. There are at least three reasons why national courts should not too readily accept that a rule of Community law is clear:

(1) Many legal concepts are clear to a lawyer because they have a specific meaning in his own legal system. The meaning in other legal systems may be different, however. Broad legal notions, such as 'legal security', 'public policy' or *'force majeure'* play an important role in many legal orders, but in each they do so in a different way and to a different degree. (2) Other legal concepts may be clear in one language of the Communities but may have a different meaning in one or more of the other languages. The wording in the six languages sometimes differs even in the EEC Treaty itself. [84] (3) Interpretations may be influenced by a general philosophy held by the national judiciary. If, for example, the general philosophy is that imported goods should be taxed – because consumers ought to buy national products – a court will be inclined to classify, in case of doubt, any imported products as being subject to duty. If, on the other hand, tariffs are seen as a burden to free trade, only to be resorted to when necessary, courts may rule differently. Similarly, in social legislation the philosophy of the court may be of crucial importance. As long as the contacts between courts are limited by national boundaries – judges rarely read foreign legal periodicals and rarely meet foreign colleagues – judges are insufficiently acquainted with other possible approaches for determining unclear questions of Community law.

Supreme courts, therefore, should not easily accept a plea of *'acte clair'*.

---

84. For an example (Art. 70) see Parry and Hardy, EEC Law, London-New York 1973, p. 256. See also the Court of Justice in the *Stauder Case* (29/69) 12 Nov. 1969, [1969] ECR 419; 7 CMLRev., 1970, p. 342; CCH para 8077, quoted above § 17.

Many European lawyers[85] have even submitted that they should never do so, but this extreme view is losing support.

§ 593. Gradually the opposition to any application of the *acte clair* doctrine whatsoever is decreasing. Since the national courts perform an important role in the Community judicial system and considering that especially the highest courts are composed of competent judges one may be confident that the theory of *acte clair* will not be abused. Unnecessary requests for preliminary rulings will only cause delay and extra costs to the parties.

In fact, the highest courts of the Member States do not ask for preliminary rulings when they consider the question clear enough to answer it themselves. Throughout the Communities there have been examples of supreme courts not asking for preliminary rulings when they considered the situation sufficiently clear.[86] Tacitly or expressly they have accepted the French legal doctrine of the *acte clair*.

The Commission seemed to accept the doctrine of *acte clair* in its answer to a parliamentary question in 1978. Without making any exception for courts of last instance it stated: 'In the opinion of the Commission, national courts are not required, under Article 177 of the EEC Treaty, to stay proceedings and systematically refer to the Court of Justice all questions concerning the interpretation of Community law which are submitted to them. They can decline to make a reference and decide the matter themselves in cases where such questions are perfectly straightforward and the answer is obvious to any lawyer with a modicum of experience.'[87]

Some authors have deduced from the *Second De Haecht Case* that the Court of Justice accepts the theory of *acte clair*.[88] In that case the Court held that in cases involving EEC Article 85 it devolves upon the national court to judge whether the proceedings before it should be suspended in order to allow

---

85. See e.g. Chevallier in 3 CMLRev. (1965-66) pp. 104-107.
86. Jean Boulouis, *General Report on the 1st theme of the 6th session of the International Federation for European Law (FIDE)*, Luxembourg 1973, p. 13 (French version). For France see the *French Shell-Berre Case, Conseil d'Etat* 19 June 1964, [1964] CMLR 481; Brinkhorst-Schermers (*op. cit.*, note 58), pp. 287, 288. For the Netherlands, see SEW 1970, pp. 465-486 and SEW 1971, pp. 100-106. For Germany see the *German Durum Wheat Case, Bundesverwaltungsgericht*, 14 Feb. 1969; *German Widow's Pension Case, Bundessozialgericht*, 22 Jan. 1970, [1971] CMLR 534; and *German Foreign Workers Case Bundesfinanzhof*, 9 July 1976, [1977] 1 CMLR 664 (with further references). For Belgium see e.g. the *Belgium Zettler Case* of the Court of Cassation, Michel Waelbroeck, *Belgian Report on the 1st theme of the 6th session of the International Federation for European law (FIDE)*, Luxembourg 1973, p. 24. For Luxembourg see the cases mentioned by Jacques Neuen, in the Luxembourg Report to the same session (pp. 37-39). For Italy see the cases mentioned by Luigi Ferrari-Bravo in the Italian report, pp. 35-37 and [1973] ELD 248. For more examples see Waelbroeck RCJB 1971, p. 569; For the UK the House of Lords has so far had no opportunity to apply the theory of acte clair. It was defended by Lord Denning in the Court of Appeal in the *English Champagne Case, Court of Appeal*, 22 May 1974, [1974] 2 CMLR 116, but not by the two other judges, [1974] 2 CMLR 121, 125.
87. Answer to Written Question No. 608/78 by Mr Krieg, OJ 31 Jan. 1979, No. C 28, p. 9.
88. Lauwaars (*op. cit.*, note 3), p. 61; M.R. Mok in 1973 Tijdschrift voor Vennootschappen, Verenigingen en Stichtingen, p. 138, noot 19.

the parties to obtain the viewpoint of the Commission unless, inter alia, '*there is no doubt that the agreement is incompatible with Article 85*'. [89] Apparently in such a case the national court may decide by itself and there is no need for a preliminary ruling.

§ 594. Though, in principle, courts should not readily consider a matter to be clear and should ask for a preliminary ruling whenever possible, an exception should be made for the question whether a Community act is valid or not (see above § 376). The validity of an act is the normal state of affairs and should therefore be assumed. As long as there is no reasonable doubt about the validity of an act even the highest national courts do not need to have it confirmed in a preliminary ruling from the Court of Justice.

d. PREVIOUS PRELIMINARY RULINGS

§ 595. The interpretation of Community law may be claer from a previous preliminary ruling (*acte éclairé*). In such a case should a highest national court refer the same question again? In practice it may be difficult to establish whether a question regarding the interpretation of Community law is really the same as a previous one. If the situation is not clear-cut the same rule applies as in the case of the *acte clair*: the court should make a fresh reference. Sometimes the situation is so similar to a case in which a preliminary ruling has already been obtained or the question of Community law is so plain from the facts that there can be no doubt that the former preliminary ruling of the Court of Justice should also apply to the latter case.

§ 596. This situation occurred in the *Da Costa Case* in which the Dutch *Tariefcommissie* (a highest court) was confronted with exactly the same question on which it had already asked, but not yet obtained, a preliminary ruling in the *Van Gend en Loos Case*. When it posed the same question again the Court of Justice rejected the Commission's allegation that the second reference was without object and was therefore inadmissible. It held:

'This contention is not justified. A distinction should be made between the obligation imposed by the third paragraph of Article 177 upon national courts or tribunals of last instance and the power granted by the second paragraph of Article 177 to every national court or tribunal to refer to the Court of the Communities a question on the interpretation of the Treaty. Although the third paragraph of Article 177 unreservedly requires courts or tribunals of a Member State against whose decisions there is no judicial remedy under national law — like the Tariefcommissie — to refer to the Court every question of interpretation raised before them, the authority of an interpretation under Article 177 already given by the Court may deprive

89. *Second de Haecht Case* (48/72), 6 June 1973, consideration 12, [1973] ECR 87; [1973] CMLR 302; CCH para 8170.

341

the obligation of its purpose and thus empty it of its substance. Such is the case especially when the question raised is materially identical with a question which has already been the subject of a preliminary ruling in a similar case.

It is no less true that Article 177 always allows a national court, if it considers it desirable, to refer questions of interpretation to the Court again. This follows from Article 20 of the Statute of the Court of Justice, under which the procedure laid down for the settlement of preliminary questions is automatically set in motion as soon as such a question is referred by a national court.' [90]

§ 597.   After the *Da Costa Case* national courts have often invoked prior preliminary rulings of the Court of Justice, even if the new case is not entirely identical to the previous one. In the *Belgian Van Boven Case*, for example, the Belgian Council of State had to decide whether an unemployment benefit was an advantage indirectly paid for by the employer in the sense of EEC Article 119. The Council of State referred to the *First Defrenne Case* [91], in which the Court of Justice had held that a State retirement pension was not such an advantage. In its opinion the same reasoning would *a fortiori* apply to unemployment benefits so that a new preliminary ruling was not needed. [92] In the *German Terrapin Case* the *Bundesgerichtshof* (Federal Supreme Court) held that no preliminary ruling was needed on a question which was clarified by the considerations of a prior preliminary ruling even though that prior ruling was in reply to other questions. [93]

The Court of Justice may have interpreted Community law not only in previous preliminary rulings but also in prior cases under other headings. [94] The invalidity of an act may have been demonstrated, for instance, in a case under EEC Article 184 or an interpretation may have been given under EEC Article 169. There is no reason why a highest national court should not be entitled to refer to such other rulings of the Court of Justice.

§ 598.   Can a national court which has requested and obtained a preliminary ruling ask for yet another ruling in the same case? The German *Bundesfinanzhof*, the supreme court for finance, considered that this would be permissible only '*where questions that require interpretation arise* in turn *from the decision of the European Court itself*'. [95] This could imply that normally no

90. *Da Costa Case* (28-30/62), 27 March 1963, [1963] ECR 38; 9 Jur. (1963) 77, 78; 9 Rec. (1963) 75, 76; [1963] CMLR 237; CCH para 8010. See also *Internatio Case* (73 and 74/63), 18 Feb. 1964; [1964] ECR 11; 10 Jur. (1964) 24; 10 Rec. (1964) 25; [1964] CMLR 219; CCH para 8021.
91. *First Defrenne Case* (80/70), 25 May 1971, [1971] ECR 452; [1974] 1 CMLR 508; CCH para 8137.
92. *Belgian Van Boven Case*, 27 June 1972, [1973] IV Pasicrisie Belge p. 116.
93. *German Terrapin Case*, *Bundesgerichtshof* 3 June 1977, [1978] 3 CMLR 114.
94. Advocate-General Roemer in the *Internatio Case* (73 and 74/63), 18 Feb. 1964, [1964] ECR 19; 10 Jur. (1964) 37; 10 Rec. (1964) 39; [1964] CMLR 205; CCH para 8021 (he refers to a case decided under EEC Art. 169).
95. *German Rheinmühlen Case*, *Bundesfinanzhof*, 8 Nov, 1972, [1974] 1 CMLR 552.

additional questions should be permitted. It should be taken into account, however, that the applicant had requested the *Bundesfinanzhof* to ask additional questions which would have had the effect of setting aside the answer given to the prior preliminary ruling, while the court considered this ruling to be adequate.

The Court of Justice is not strict in this respect. When in the *Third International Fruit Company Case* a Dutch court, the *College van Beroep voor het Bedrijfsleven*, posed two new questions in the same national case in respect of which it had already obtained a preliminary ruling, in the Court of Justice's *Second International Fruit Company Case* [96], neither the Court of Justice nor the Advocate-General raised any objection. [97]

7. Competence of the Court of Justice

a. ISSUES SUSCEPTIBLE TO PRELIMINARY RULINGS

(i) Community law

§ 599. EEC Article 177 enumerates four fields in which preliminary rulings may be asked:
  (a) interpretation of the Treaty,
  (b) interpretation of acts of the institutions,
  (c) the validity of acts of the institutions and
  (d) the interpretation of the statutes of bodies established by an act of the Council, where those statutes so provide (in Euratom: 'unless they provide otherwise').

This specific catalogue means that preliminary rulings cannot be given on all questions relevant to a case under Community law. Rulings are not possible if the questions relate to (1) the validity of Treaty articles; (2) general principles of Community law and *a fortiori* on (3) rules of other legal orders.

§ 600. The Treaties are the constitutions of the Communities. It seems appropriate that their legality cannot be challenged before the court established by these constitutions. If there should ever be a dispute on the validity of any of the Treaties it should be settled under international law, possibly before the International Court of Justice in the Hague. As the legality of the constitution cannot be disputed in any of the Member States the lack of legal control over the Treaties themselves has not raised any objections.

§ 601. In principle it should be regretted that preliminary rulings have not been expressly made possible for questions pertaining to all rules of the Com-

---

96. *Second International Fruit Compagy Case* (51-54/71), 15 Dec. 1971, [1971] ECR 1107; CCH para 8158.
97. *Third International Fruit Company Case* (21-24/72), 12 Dec. 1972, [1972] ECR 1219; [1975] 2 CMLR 1; CCH para 8194. Also in the *Schaap Case*, before the *Centrale Raad van Beroep* two preliminary rulings were asked: the *First Schaap Case* (98/77), 14 March 1978, [1978] ECR 707 and the *Second Schaap Case* (176/78), 5 April 1979.

munity legal order. This legal order must be applied as one whole, and uniform application of all its rules is of equal importance. If a national court should ever wish to decide a case on a general principle of Community law, it should be able to obtain a preliminary ruling thereon. In practice, however, it is not likely that problems will arise. General principles are only additional sources of Community law. They are used in cases which also concern other rules of Community law. Even if a general principle were promoted to an independent source of Community law, would this have to be brought about by some form of Community act whereupon preliminary rulings could be asked on the interpretation or validity of that act. The Court is not precluded from delivering explanations on general principles in its rulings given on Treaty articles or acts of the institutions.

§ 602. Those acts which may be challenged (see above § 196-253) may also be interpreted; but interpretation is not limited to those acts. Article 177 covers all acts taken by all the institutions. This means that preliminary rulings can be asked on acts which the national court cannot *apply*, either because the act is of a non-binding nature, or because it needs further action to be completed. [98] In the *Haaga Case* the German supreme court, the *Bundesgerichtshof*, asked for a preliminary ruling on a directive of the Council which had no direct effect within the German legal order but which was considered relevant for the interpretation of the German law adopted for the implementation of that directive. The Court of Justice had no objection against giving the requested ruling. [99]

§ 603. Article 177 also means that preliminary rulings can be asked on acts of the European Parliament. In his opinion in the *Wagner Case* Advocate-General Lagrange submitted that the Court was entitled to give a preliminary ruling on the interpretation as well as on the validity of the Rules of Procedure of the European Parliament. [100] In a subsequent article he expressed doubt as to the appropriateness of ruling on the validity of acts of the Parliament, due to the more or less sovereign nature of a parliamentary organ, however small its powers may be. [101] The Court of Justice has, in fact, never given a preliminary ruling on an act of the Parliament. In the *Wagner Case* it was able to give the requested ruling without interpreting the Parliament's Rules of Procedure.

More difficult is the question whether preliminary rulings can be asked on acts of the Court itself. In the *Second German Trockenrasierer Case*, the *Bundesgerichtshof*, a German supreme court, seemed to envisage this possibil-

---

98. Lagrange (*op. cit.*, note 14), p. 281; Lauwaars (*op. cit.*, note 3), p. 44, who names some dissenting authors; De Richemont (*op. cit.*, note 15), p. 60 who mentions a number of authors for and against the possibility of asking preliminary rulings on recommendations.
99. *Haaga Case* (32/74), 12 Nov. 1974, [1974] ECR 1201-1209; [1975] 1 CMLR 32 ff; CCH para 8289.
100. *Wagner Case* (101/63), 12 May 1964, [1964] ECR 204, 205; 10 Jur. (1964) 430; 10 Rec. (1964) 403; [1964] CMLR 248, 249.
101. Lagrange (*op. cit.*, note 14), p. 281.

ity, though it did not make use of it. [102] On the other hand, some authors have argued against this. [103] In practice, the need will not often arise as it may be easier to ask for an additional ruling on an act rather than for an explanation of the prior ruling on that act. However, if preliminary rulings are gradually recognized as having effect *erga omnes* subsequent preliminary rulings on them should be considered possible.

§ 603a. Preliminary rulings are given on questions of law. Interpretation and application of facts are left to the national courts. The Court of Justice is not competent to verify the facts of the case (see below § 624a). This does not mean, however, that the Court of Justice never needs to evaluate facts when giving a preliminary ruling. Cases may arise which the Court cannot decide without evidence, for example when the validity of an act is challenged on the ground that the act was founded on an error of fact. [104] Sometimes questions may be asked on the interpretation of Community rules which have been made for the situation in one particular Member State. Their interpretation may be so closely related to the national situation that the Court of Justice must take this into consideration.[105]

(ii) International law

§ 604. In as far as it is binding upon the Communities, international law has been incorporated into the Community legal order (see above § 127-138). Whenever international law is incorporated into another legal order, traditionally it is applied and interpreted by the courts of that legal order. As those rules of international law which form part of the Community legal order should be uniformly applied throughout the Communities it would be appropriate if the Court of Justice could give preliminary rulings on them.

In the *Vandeweghe Case* the Court was asked to give a preliminary ruling on the interpretation of a bilateral agreement concluded in 1957 by Belgium and the Federal Republic. The Court then ruled:

'The Court has no jurisdiction under Article 177 of the EEC Treaty to give a ruling on the interpretation of provisions of international law which bind Member States outside the framework of Community law.' [106]

---

102. *Second German Trockenrasierer Case, Bundesgerichtshof*, 14 June 1963, WuW 1964, pp. 180, 181; Juristenzeitung 1964, p. 219 with annotation Steindorff; [1964] CMLR 77.
103. See Dumon (*op. cit.*, note 46), pp. 207, 208.
104. See Advocate General Warner in the *EMI Case* (51/75), 15 June 1976, Opinion, [1976] ECR 854, [1976] 2 CMLR 246; CCH para 8350, Court of Justice in *Second Milac Case* (131/77), 3 May 1978, consideration 6, [1978] ECR 1050, 1051 and John Usher, *Article 177 EEC: when the facts matter*, 3 ELRev. (1978), pp. 298-300.
105. See e.g., *Brack Case* (17/76), 29 Sept. 1976, considerations 14, 30, [1976] ECR 1449, 1450, 1452, 1453; [1976] 2 CMLR 615, 616, 617.
106. *Vandeweghe Case* (130/73), 27 Nov. 1973, consideration 2, [1973] ECR 1333; [1974] 1 CMLR 455. In this case the Court reiterated the position it adopted in the *Hoekstra Case* (75/63), 19 March 1964, [1964] ECR 186; 10 Jur. (1964) 388; 10 Rec. (1964) 365; [1964] CMLR 332; CCH para 8022 in which it classified a German-Dutch

Would the situation be different as regards a multilateral treaty to which all Member States are parties? Under the present rules of Community law it does not seem likely that this is the case. In any event the Member States did not take this approach when they wanted to confer jurisdiction on the Court of Justice to interpret conventions concluded under EEC Article 220. They did not assume that the Court could give preliminary rulings on such conventions; neither were they of the opinion that they could attribute such competence to the Court by a simple resolution or by an interpretation of the existing texts. In each case they signed a special protocol conferring jurisdiction on the Court of Justice. [107]

§ 605. The position is different when the Community is itself a party to the international treaty concerned. In the *Second Haegeman Case* the Court of Justice considered the Association Agreement with Greece as an act of the Council in as far as it concerned the Community and on that ground accepted jurisdiction to give preliminary rulings concerning its interpretation (see above § 135).

By using the words '*in as far as it concerns the Community*' the Court demonstrated that its only purpose was to ensure the uniform interpretation of the agreement throughout the Communities and that it did not intend to bind the other party to the agreement. This restriction of the interpretation of international agreements to those matters which concern the Community also means that the Court will not rule upon treaty provisions which extend beyond the Community's field of operation. The importance of this restriction was demonstrated by the *Third Defrenne Case*. In that case, as in the other Defrenne Cases, the claim alleged was a violation of the principle of equality between men and women. The Court re-iterated its respect for fundamental human rights as general principles of Community law, the observance of which it has a duty to ensure, but it held that the Community had not assumed any responsibility for supervising and guaranteeing the observance of the principle of equality in working conditions other than with regard to remuneration. [108] Therefore, though it may protect the basic rights enumerated in the European Convention on Human Rights for situations involving Community law, the Court will not protect these basic rights in situations outside the field in which the Community operates.

§ 606. The issue raised by the *Second Haegeman Case* has wider significance than merely for treaties to which the Community is a party. In all cases where provisions of international law are to be applied by national courts these courts will interpret those provisions. This could lead to different interpreta-

---

treaty as domestic law and its stance in the *Torrekens Case* (28/68), 7 May 1969, consideration 6, [1969] ECR 134; [1969] CMLR 387, 388, in which it held that a Franco-Belgian treaty fell outside its competence.
107. Protocols of 3 June 1971, Supplement 4/71, Annex to Bulletin 7-1971 of the European Communities; 8 CMLRev. (1971) pp. 491-494.
108. *Third Defrenne Case* (149/77), 15 June 1978, considerations 26-30, [1978] ECR 1378; [1978] 3 CMLR 329.

tions in different Member States of the European Communities. If the subject matter of the international obligation falls outside the scope of the European Communities no harm is done. But is it acceptable that there might be divergent interpretations of international rules concerning Community matters, such as the General Agreement on Tariffs and Trade (GATT) or commodity agreements on sugar, tin, coffee, wheat etc.? There is no provision requiring national courts to request preliminary rulings on such international rules.

In the *Third International Fruit Company Case* and in the *Second Schlüter Case* the Court of Justice applied the GATT treaty (see above § 133). In both cases it considered the EEC to be bound by the GATT, and in both cases it also gave the interpretation that some articles of GATT have no direct effect. [109] This interpretation is authoritative within the Community legal order. It cannot of course bind third parties, but does it bind the courts of the Member States when they apply GATT in their national legal orders?

§ 607. A more general answer to this question requires a careful examination of the international obligation involved. (a) If it is a question of treaties to which (one of) the Communities as well as the Member States are parties, such as the Association Agreements with Greece and Turkey and the Lomé Convention, then the need for uniform interpretation is such that individual interpretations by national courts are unacceptable. Preliminary rulings should be asked. In the *Second Haegeman Case* the Court of Justice confirmed that it is possible to request such preliminary rulings by establishing that these treaties are acts of a Community institution.

(b) If they are treaties in which the Communities cooperated either as regards their conclusion (commodity agreements) or as regards their execution (GATT) then the same should apply. The need for uniform interpretation remains, but there is no rule of law which would oblige any national court to request a preliminary ruling when applying the international treaty within a national context. The Court of Justice seemed to indicate that there was no longer any national relevance as regards GATT, when it held that the Community has replaced the Member States in that organization. [110]

After its interpretation of some articles of the GATT agreement the Court of Justice will probably prove willing to give a ruling on this group of international obligations.

(c) If it is a question of a treaty or of a decision of an international organization in which the Communities did not cooperate then there may be insufficient ground to request the Court of Justice to give a preliminary ruling on that treaty or decision. Nonetheless, uniform application by the Member States of the Community is important with respect to many international conventions to which all or most of the Member States are parties, such as the Geneva Convention of 1931 on Bills of Exchange. The Court of Justice there-

---

109. For more interpretation of GATT by the Court of Justice, see *Markus Case* (14/69), 15 Oct. 1969, considerations 3-6, [1969] ECR 355, [1970] CMLR 212; CCH para 8081.
110. See *Second Nederlandse Spoorwegen Case*, quoted above in § 133.

fore suggested that the procedure for preliminary rulings could be extended to cover the interpretation of such conventions. [111]

Even without express provision, a preliminary ruling on the *content* of these conventions may often be feasible. If the convention concerns a matter of Community law then a preliminary ruling can often be requested on the corresponding Community legal rule involved. At this juncture the Court of Justice may be willing, and in important cases it ought to be willing, to interpret the international convention as well. In practice, the question will usually be whether the international convention has direct effect or not, and that question will often be decisive for the question whether a conflicting rule of Community law is binding or not.

(iii) National law

§ 608. The Court of Justice is not competent to interpret rules of the national laws of the Member States [112], even when these rules are based on provisions of Community law. [113] Sometimes national courts need to know whether particular national rules are in conformity with Community law (see above § 435-438). On such questions of conflict they can request preliminary rulings, provided that they present them as questions of Community law. Usually the Court of Justice then replies:

'Although the Court, when giving a ruling under Article 177, has no jurisdiction to apply the Community rule to a specific case, or, consequently, to pronounce upon a provision of national law, it may however provide the national court with the factors of interpretation depending on Community law which might be useful to it in evaluating the effects of such provision.' [114]

In its reply the Court of Justice may then leave little or no doubt about the validity of the national rule as, for instance, in the *Galli Case* where it ruled *'a national system which (...) has the effect of modifying price formation (...) is incompatible with Regulation No. 120/67 (...)'.* [115]

---

111. *Suggestions of the Court of Justice on European Union*, Bulletin of the European Communities, Supplement 9/75, p. 20.
112. This was stated *inter alia* by the Court of Justice in the *Dingemans Case* (24/64), 2 Dec. 1964, [1964] ECR 652; 10 Jur. (1964) 1335; 10 Rec. (1964) 1273; [1965] CMLR 156; CCH para 8037; and by the Belgian Court of Cassation in the *Belgian Peeters Case*, [1973] CMLR 190; 1973 ELD 85. See also the Court of Justice in the *Manghera Case* (59/75), 3 Feb. 1976, consideration 18, [1976] ECR 102; [1976] 1 CMLR 568; CCH para 8342.
113. *Rey Soda Case* (23/75), 30 Oct. 1975, considerations 50, 51, [1975] ECR 1307; [1976] 1 CMLR 212; CCH para 8321.
114. *Hirardin Case* (112/75), 8 April 1976, consideration 8, [1976] ECR 560; [1976] 2 CMLR 382. Compare also *Kuyken Case* (66/77), 1 Dec. 1977, consideration 10, [1977] ECR 2817, 2818; [1978] 2 CMLR 313, 314.
115. *Galli Case* (31/74), 23 Jan. 1975, [1975] ECR 66; [1975] 1 CMLR 230; CCH para 8294. The Galli Case was confirmed by the *SADAM Case* (88-90/75), 26 Feb. 1976, considerations 6 and 17, [1976] ECR 336, 339; [1977] 2 CMLR 205, 206; CCH para 8355. For another example see Mazzalai Case (111/75), 20 May 1976, considerations 15-17, [1976] ECR 666; CCH para 8363.

b. INTERPRETATION OF THE REQUEST

§ **609**. As mentioned above (§ 559) the Court of Justice seeks to strengthen cooperation with the national courts and therefore is not at all strict or formalistic in accepting questions from national courts. Furthermore, the Court of Justice does not assess whether the answer is needed for solving the case and does not usually check whether the national court is competent to handle the case (see above § 587).

Occasionally, national courts ask questions which the Court of Justice is not entitled to answer, for example on the application of Community law within the national legal order. In such cases the Court of Justice *'must extract, from the wording of the order referring the matter, those questions alone which relate to the interpretation of Community law'.* [116]

Questions which are wrongly formulated are rephrased by the Court. In the *Hein-Muller Case* a local court in Luxembourg had posed such a vague question that the Commission, in its observations made under Article 20 of the Statute of the Court, suggested that the Court should not answer at all. The Court, however, held:

'Despite the imprecise nature of the question, the grounds of judgement of the national court clearly show the subject-matter of this reference'.

and gave the ruling it considered most useful to the national court. [117]

In the *Van Wesemael Case* the Court did the same, expressly referring to the judicial cooperation between the Court of Justice and the national courts under EEC Article 177. [118]

§ **610**. Some national judges, in particular German ones, who are used to doing so under their national legal system, not only ask for a preliminary ruling, but also offer their suggestions for the answer. [119] The Court of Justice seriously considers such suggestions, but certainly does not blindly follow them. In its considerations the Court does not refer to them at all.

c. APPLICATION OF COMMUNITY LAW [120]

§ **611**. It is the task of the Court of Justice to interpret Community law, whereas the application of Community law is within the field of competence of the national courts. In the *Costa-Enel Case* the Court of Justice held:

116. Quoted from the *Fourth Getreide-Import Case* (11/73), 12 July 1973, consideration 3, [1973] ECR 925; [1974] 1 CMLR 57; CCH para 8222.
117. *Hein-Muller Case* (10/71), 14 July 1971, consideration 4, [1971] ECR 729; CCH para 8140 (p. 7606).
118. *Van Wesemael Case* (110, 111/78), 18 Jan. 1979, consideration 21.
119. See e.g. *Lorenz Case* (120/73), 11 Dec. 1973, [1973] ECR 1474, 1475; CCH para 8249; *Markmann Case* (121/73), 11 Dec. 1973, [1973] ECR 1498, 1499; CCH para 8250; *Hannoversche Zucker Case* (159/73), 30 Jan. 1974, [1974] ECR 123, 124; CCH para 8263.
120. See André M. Donner, *Uitlegging en Toepassing*, Miscellanea Ganshof van der Meersch, Vol. II 1972, pp. 103-126; Lauwaars (*op. cit.*, note 3), pp. 40, 41.

'This provision (*i.e. EEC Article 177*) gives the Court no jurisdiction either to apply the Treaty to a specific case or to decide upon the validity of a provision of domestic law in relation to the Treaty, as it would be possible for it to do under Article 169'. [121]

In later cases it has repeatedly confirmed this position. [122] Purely abstract interpretation is difficult, however, and may not be of any assistance to the national court. The Court of Justice, therefore, needs to be presented with the facts of the case. In the *LTM Case* one of the parties submitted that the question posed was one of application since the national court had not asked an abstract question but had informed the Court of Justice of the facts of the case. The Court of Justice held:

'Although the Court has no jurisdiction to take cognizance of the application of the Treaty to a specific case, it may extract from the elements of the case those questions of interpretation or validity which alone fall within its jurisdiction. Moreover the need to reach a serviceable interpretation of the provisions at issue justifies the national court in setting out the legal context in which the requested interpretation is to be placed. The Court may, therefore, draw from the elements of law described by the Cour d'Appel, Paris, the data necessary for an understanding of the questions put and for the preparation of an appropriate answer'. [123]

The Court of Justice has often indicated that it appreciates information about the background of the case as this facilitates the rendering of appropriate preliminary rulings.

§ 612. As the Court of Justice wants to be of practical help to the court referring the question it often gives such detailed answers that its interpretation is tantamount to application. Thus, in the *Van Leeuwen Case*, where the question was whether a school levy which depended on parental income was a tax for which Community staff members enjoyed immunity, the Court of Justice held:

'For these reasons a charge or due representing the consideration for a given service rendered by the public authorities, *such as the school levy in question in the present case*, which, moreover, is only payable in respect of non-compulsory education, is not a tax within the meaning of the second

121. *Costa-Enel Case* (6/64), 15 July 1964, [1964] ECR 592, 593; 10 Jur. (1964) 1217; 10 Rec. (1964) 1158; [1964] CMLR 454; CCH para 8023.
122. See e.g. *Dingemans Case* (24/64), 2 Dec. 1964, [1964] ECR 652; 10 Jur. (1964) 1335; 10 Rec. (1964) 1273; [1965] CMLR 156; CCH para 8037.
123. *LTM Case* (56/65), 30 June 1966, [1966] ECR 248; 12 Jur. (1966) 412; 12 Rec. (1966) 357; [1966] CMLR 373, 374; CCH para 8047. See also *Second Henck Case* (12/71), 14 July 1971, consideration 3, [1971] ECR 750; CCH para 8145 (p. 7668); *Third Henck Case* (13/71), 14 July 1971, consideration 3, [1971] ECR 704; CCH para 8146 (p. 7682); *Fourth Henck Case* (14/71), 14 July 1971, consideration 3, [1971] ECR 786, CCH para 8147 (p. 7689).

paragraph of Article 12 of the Protocol on the Privileges and Immunities of the Community, even if that charge or due is calculated on the basis of the salary paid by the Community to the person liable'. [124]

§ 613. In the *First Turkey Tail Case* the question was whether a turkey-tail was to be regarded as part of the turkey or as edible offal. This would have led to a considerable difference in the amount of the import levy. Was the Court of Justice entitled to decide this question or should it have given a general interpretation allowing the national court to decide? The Advocate-General, Roemer, considered:

'However I would just like to say an excessive scrupulosity in this matter is misplaced. In my opinion there can be no objection if the Court resolves directly the subsumed question of classification (naturally stating its reasons) and therefore does not limit itself to giving a circumstantial and abstract definition of the concepts which have to be interpreted by means of which the national judge then proceeds to answer the larger question.' [125]

§ 614. According to Judge Donner, the case-law of the Court of Justice is developing in the direction of giving interpretations for the specific case at hand. If the questions are general and abstract, the Court of Justice does not hesitate to look at the facts and to answer the question in the specific context of the case. [126] This development can be illustrated by many preliminary rulings on the classification of products under the common customs tariff, such as the *Turkey Tail Case*, but also by other cases, such as the *Cristini Case* on the rights of migrant workers. This case concerned the interpretation of Council Regulation No. 1612/68, according to Article 7 of which a worker who is national of a Member State 'shall enjoy, in the territory of other Member States the same social (...) advantages as national workers'. The Court of Appeal in Paris asked for a preliminary ruling on the question whether the reduction card issued by the French Railways to large families constitutes a 'social advantage' for the workers of the Member States within the meaning of this article. It sought this ruling in a case in which the widow of an Italian worker who had worked in France claimed the reduction. The Court of Justice held:

'Although the Court, when giving a ruling under Article 177, has no jurisdiction to apply the Community rule to a specific case, or, consequently, to pronounce upon a provision of national law, it may however provide the

124. *Van Leeuwen Case*, (32/67), 8 Feb. 1968, [1968] ECR 48; 14 Jur. (1968) 72; 14 Rec. (1968) 72, *italics added.* Also in the *Sayag Cases* (5/68 and 9/69), where abstract questions were asked, the Court gave very concrete answers, see also Waelbroeck in RCJB 1971, p. 577.
125. *First Turkey Tail Case* (40/69), 18 Feb. 1970, Opinion of the Advocate-General, [1970] ECR 88; [1970] CMLR 150; CCH para 8098.
126. Donner (*op. cit.*, note 120), p. 114, Summary in French p. 125.

national court with the factors of interpretation depending on Community law which might be useful to it in evaluating the effects of such provision.
...

Accordingly the answer to the question should be that Article 7(2) of Regulation (EEC) No. 1612/68 of the Council must be interpreted as meaning that the social advantages referred to by that provision include fares reduction cards issued by a national railway authority to large families and that this applies, even if the said advantage is only sought after the worker's death, to the benefit of his family remaining in the same Member State.' [127]

Another clear example of interpretation which comes very close to application is the Court's interpretation of EEC tariff heading 15.13 in the *Second Gervais Danone Case*. The Court ruled that the tariff heading '*was to be interpreted as not applying to mixtures of fats consisting of 85% pure butyric fat, 10% refined suet and 5% sesame oil*'.[128]

§ 615. Nevertheless, a division of competence still remains. The Court of Justice may decide very specifically into which category a particular product is to be classified for the purpose of customs duties, and whether the widows of workers have particular rights, but it is still up to the national court to decide whether the imported product is indeed the particular product involved, and whether the woman before the court is the widow of a worker in the sense of the social security regulations. [129]

d. REQUESTS WHICH HAVE BEEN APPEALED

§ 616. A request for a preliminary ruling will delay a case for about six months. When the request is necessary, it should be made as soon as possible; but it may also be unnecessary, for example if the case can be decided on grounds other than Community law. Whether or not an appeal is possible against the court decision by which a preliminary ruling was asked is a question of national law. [130] In the Netherlands the Supreme Court, the Hoge Raad, admitted such an appeal in order to allow it to '*decide whether the legal requirements for such a suspension of the proceedings exist, in so far as the parties' interests can thus be served and the requirements of good procedure are not violated*'. [131] In Belgium, Germany, France, Luxembourg and the United Kingdom, as well as in the Netherlands, appeals against requests for

127. *Cristini Case* (32/75), 30 Sept. 1975, considerations 6 and 19, [1975] ECR 1094, 1095; [1976] 1 CMLR 582, 583; CCH para 8330.
128. *Second Gervais Danone Case* (86/76), 23 March 1977, consideration 9, [1977] ECR 653; CCH para 8411.
129. See also Jean Amphoux in 10 CDE (1974) pp. 665, 666.
130. According to Mertens de Wilmars the problem is basically one of Community law, (*op. cit.*, note 15), p. 92.
131. *Netherlands Bosch Case, Hoge Raad*, 18 May 1962, NJ 1965 No. 115, Brinkhorst-Schermers (*op. cit.*, note 58), p. 269.

preliminary rulings are permitted. [132] In the *Second Rheinmühlen Case* the Court of Justice held that Article 177 does not preclude a decision, by virtue of which a lower national court has requested a preliminary ruling, *'from remaining subject to the remedies normally available under national law'.* [133] As a rule, therefore it may be concluded that an appeal can be lodged against the decision to make a reference. Whether such an appeal has suspensory effect depends on the national legal order. Some lower courts forward their cases to Luxembourg only after the decision on appeal has been decided [134] , others do not wait for the appeal. [135]

§ 617. What is the position of the request before the Court of Justice pending the appeal on the decision to make a reference? In the *Bosch Case* the interim judgment by which the Court of Appeal in the Hague had asked for the first preliminary ruling was appealed to the Dutch Supreme Court when the Court of Justice discussed the question. The Court of Justice did not declare that such an appeal is contrary to any rule of Community law, but it did not await the outcome of the appeal. It ruled that Article 177 does not require the Community court to examine the question whether the decision of the domestic court is final under domestic law. Whenever a preliminary ruling is requested by a national court, the Court of Justice is competent to give such a ruling. [136]

Seven years later the Court of Justice stayed the proceedings when it learned that another Dutch request for a preliminary ruling had been appealed. In distinction from the previous case the court requesting the preliminary ruling had itself informed the Court of Justice of the appeal and of its suspensory effect under Dutch law. When the higher Dutch court subsequently annulled the interim decision requesting the preliminary ruling – the case was settled in another way – the Court of Justice set aside the request as being without object, and gave no ruling at all. [137] In the *Second Simmenthal Case* the Court ruled:

---

132. Mertens de Wilmars (*op. cit.*, note 15), p. 94, see the facts of the *BRT-Sabam Case* (127/73), 30 Jan. 1974, [1974] ECR 54; [1974] 2 CMLR 242, 243; CCH para 8268, 8269 (Belgium); the facts of the *Biason Case* (24/74), 9 Oct. 1974, [1974] ECR 1001; [1975] 1 CMLR 60 (France); the *First Rheinmühlen Case* (166/73), 16 Jan. 1974, [1974] ECR 33-40; [1974] 1 CMLR 523; CCH para 8265 (Germany); Rules of the Supreme Court, order 114, Francis G. Jacobs and Andrew Durand, *References to the European Court: Practice and Procedure*, Butterworths 1975 (revised reprint from Atkin's Court Forms, Vol. 17), p. 213 (UK).
133. *Second Rheinmühlen Case* (146/73), 12 Feb. 1974, consideration 3, [1974] ECR 147; [1974] 1 CMLR 579; CCH para 8266.
134. *See Biason Case*, mentioned above (note 132); *Mertens Case* (178, 179, 180/73), 4 April 1974, [1974] ECR 385; CCH para 8272; *Regina Case* (30/77), 27 Oct. 1977, [1977] ECR 2001, 2002; [1977] 2 CMLR 802, 803; CCH para 8441.
135. E.g., the Dutch courts and the *Hessisches Finanzgericht* in the *Second Rheinmühlen Case* (146/73), 12 Feb. 1974, [1974] ECR 139-150; [1974] 1 CMLR 523-580; CCH para 8266.
136. *Bosch Case* (13/61), 6 April 1962, [1962] ECR 50; 8 Jur. (1962) 103, 104; 8 Rec. (1962) 101, 102; [1962] CMLR 26; CCH para 8003.
137. *Chanel Case* (31/68), 3 June 1969 and 16 June 1970, [1970] ECR 404, 405; [1971] CMLR 403-419.

'... in accordance with its unvarying practice the Court of Justice considers a reference for a preliminary ruling, pursuant to Article 177 of the Treaty, as having been validly brought before it so long as the reference has not been withdrawn by the court from which it emanates or has not been quashed on appeal by a superior court'. [138]

This is in conformity with the Court's opinion that national courts cannot be deprived of their right to ask for preliminary rulings (see above § 561).

8. Effects of preliminary rulings

§ 618.   In the *First Milch-, Fett- und Eier-Case* the Court of Justice stated clearly that a preliminary ruling is binding on the national court hearing the case for which the decision is given. [139]

In many decisions national courts have accepted the binding force of preliminary rulings. [140]   The obligation to recognise this was nicely formulated by the Court of Appeal in Paris which held in the *French Raffaele Case*:

'The decisions of the Court of Justice of the European Communities rendered for interpretation are of a general nature because they are designed to unify the case-law of the courts of the Member States; they are therefore binding on those courts'. [141]

§ 619.   Are preliminary rulings also binding in other, similar cases? Here the Continental courts tend to disagree. Several national courts have expressly held that preliminary rulings do not, as a matter of Community law, have the status of binding precedents in subsequent cases. Binding force will only be attributed to them if the national courts see fit to do so. [142]   Other courts have accepted the further binding force of preliminary rulings. Thus, for example, the French *Cour de Cassation* held in the *French Garoche Case* that a previous preliminary ruling on the same question, given in another case, is

---

138. *Second Simmenthal Case* (106/77), 9 March 1978, consideration 10, [1978] ECR 642; [1978] 3 CMLR 282; CCH para 8476. See also *BRT-SABAM Case* (127/73), 30 Jan. 1974, consideration 9, [1974] ECR 62; [1974] 2 CMLR 270; CCH para 8268.
139. *First Milch-, Fett- und Eier-Case* (29/68), 24 June 1969, consideration 3, [1969] ECR 180; [1969] CMLR 400; CCH para 8096. See also *Benedetti Case* (52/76), 3 Feb. 1977, consideration 26, [1976] ECR 183; CCH para 8406.
140. See Brinkhorst-Schermers (*op. cit.*, note 58) pp. 289-292; Lauwaars, Lyklema, Kuiper in SEW 1973 pp. 21, 34; Lauwaars (*op. cit.*, note 3) p. 71; Heinrich Matthies, *Die Bindungswirkung von Urteilen des Gerichtshofes der Europäischen Gemeinschaften*, Festschrift für Walter Hallstein, Frankfurt 1966, pp. 304-321; Bail and Lichtenberg in 9 CMLRev. (1972), pp. 236.
141. *French Raffaele Case*, Court of Appeals Paris, 13 Nov. 1970, Gazette du Palais, 1971, J. p. 206; 9 CDE (1973) pp. 64, 65.
142. See e.g. *Italian SAFA Case*, Court of Appeals Milan, 12 May 1972, consideration 12, [1973] CMLR 155, 156. This view is shared by several authors, inter 'alia Dumon in *Les Novelles, Le Droit des Communautés européennes* § 1000, 1001.

binding on national courts of law. [143] Similarly the German Federal Administrative Court, the *Bundesverwaltungsgericht*, held that a preliminary ruling given in another case, took precedence over a contrary interpretation which the *Bundesverwaltungsgericht* had given itself. [144] When the Court of Justice held in the *Molkerei-Zentrale Case* that *'resort by the national courts to Article 177 makes it possible to ensure a uniform interpretation of the Treaty and is capable of bringing about its identical application'* [145], it at least suggested some form of general application of preliminary rulings. How could these rulings otherwise bring about an identical application of the Treaty? On the other hand, the Court leaves to the national courts the option of asking a new preliminary ruling instead of following a previous one. In the *Da Costa Case* it held that national courts, even the highest ones, are entitled to follow a preliminary ruling given in a prior case, but that they are not obliged to do so; they can always ask for a further preliminary ruling (see above § 596). This seems the most practical approach. As national courts are always free to decide that a new question is not similar to the one on which a prior preliminary ruling was given, an obligation to follow prior rulings in similar cases would be void of any meaning.

In practice preliminary rulings may have considerable effect on the future application of the law. After the *Van der Hulst Case* [146], for example, in which the Court of Justice ruled that a Dutch internal levy on bulbs was illegal, the Dutch authorities repaid about 7,500,000 Dutch Florins. [147]

§ 619a. Special attention should be paid to the effect of preliminary rulings on interested parties who are not litigants in the case before the national court. In the *Benedetti Case* the outcome of the dispute between the parties largely depended on the question whether the conduct of a public cooperative, the AIMA, constituted a breach of Community law. However, the AIMA was not a party to the case and, therefore, could not appear before the Court of Justice either. Under these circumstances the Court was very reluctant to give a ruling affecting the position of the AIMA. It held that *'in the absence of accurate information relating to the nature of the alleged activities of the AIMA ... the Court cannot itself assess or classify those activities'*, the more so as the questions asked of the Court of Justice *'concern the conduct of a natural or legal person who was not yet a party to the action and who was not given an opportunity to state his case'*. [148] Subsequently the Court of Justice

---

143. *French Garoche Case, Cour de Cassation*, 8 May 1973, consideration 3, [1974] 1 CMLR 476. See also the Belgian *Cour de Cassation* in the *Belgian Advance Transformer Co. Case*, 24 Dec. 1970, 1971 SEW, p. 719. Several authors share this view, inter alia, Advocate-General Trabucchi, *L'effet 'erga omnes' des décisions préjudicielles rendues par la Cour de justice des Communautés européennes*, 10 RTDE (1974) pp. 56-87.
144. *German Bonsignore Case, Bundesverwaltungsgericht*, 2 July 1975, [1977] 2 CMLR 257.
145. *Molkerei-Zentrale Case* (28/67), 3 April 1968, [1968] ECR 154; 14 Jur. (1968) 219, 220; 14 Rec. (1968) 228; [1968] CMLR 218, 219; CCH para 8064.
146. *Van der Hulst Case* (51/74), 23 Jan. 1975, [1975] ECR 79; [1975] 1 CMLR 255; CCH para 8292.
147. Information obtained from the *Produktschap voor Siergewassen*.
148. *Benedetti Case* (52/76), 3 Feb. 1977, considerations 10, 12, [1977] ECR 179, 180.

replied to three questions submitted by the national court by referring to a previous case to which the AIMA was a party. To the fourth and the fifth questions the Court did not reply as these questions could not effectively be answered, *'owing to a lack of precision'*. The sixth question lost its purpose and to the seventh the Court replied that preliminary rulings are binding on the national courts. [149]

The case illustrates a general problem caused by the fact that the effects of a preliminary ruling extend beyond the underlying dispute. In cases where the legality or national laws are at stake there may be a need for a stronger procedural position of the authorities concerned (see below, § 685).

9. Role of the litigants

§ 620. Under ECSC article 41 there are no rules prescribing how preliminary rulings must be requested, or by whom the request must be made. According to Lagrange even the parties themselves can request a preliminary ruling from the Court of Justice under that article. [150] Under the other Treaties only national courts can refer cases to the Court of Justice. When a national court has asked for a preliminary ruling, the litigants in the case concerned may submit written observations to the Court of Justice. [151] They are also allowed to plead before the Court of Justice as to how in their opinion the questions should be answered. Can they submit further questions to the Court of Justice? This question has been raised in several cases of which the following may illustrate the position of the Court. [152]

§ 621. In the *Hessische Knappschaft Case* [153] the defendant asked the Court of Justice to rule that a regulation, the interpretation of which was asked, was invalid. The Court of Justice replied that it was for the national court and not for the parties to ask for preliminary rulings, that the parties could not change the content of the questions submitted nor have them declared moot and that consequently the Court of Justice could not be compelled to concern itself with additional questions raised by the parties.

§ 622. In the *Neumann Case* the additional question posed by the plaintiff was not even discussed by the Court of Justice. In his opinion the Advocate-General, Roemer, concluded, however:

'In principle, I tend to interpret the powers of our Court in this respect widely. Especially when the validity of such far-reaching legal acts of the Community organs is examined, we should not feel bound to deal only

---

149. *Idem*, considerations 16, 19, 22, 23, 26.
150. Lagrange (*op. cit.*, note 14), p. 291.
151. EEC Statute, Art. 20.
152. For a further enumeration of cases see Bebr in CDE 1975, p. 387, note 22.
153. *Hessische Knappschaft Case* (44/65), 9 Dec. 1965, [1965] ECR 970, 971; 11 Jur. (1965) 1155; 11 Rec. (1965) 1198, 1199; [1966] CMLR 94; CCH para 8042.

with points of law formulated by the national judge, but have to regard as permissible, if not the examination *ex officio* of all questions arising here, in any case of those questions raised by the parties'. [154]

§ 623. In the *First Getreidehandel Case* [155] the plaintiff wanted to add a question to the request for a preliminary ruling on the validity of a decision taken by the Commission. Knowing that the Court of Justice would not respond to a question directly posed by him, he wrote a letter to the national court which had asked for the preliminary ruling, requesting the court to add his specific question to its original questions. The national court forwarded this letter to the Court of Justice, leaving it to the latter to decide whether such an additional question was admissible or not. The Court of Justice considered that the question had come from a national court and that it could be derived from the wording of the covering note that that national court expected an answer. Therefore the additional ruling was given.

§ 624. The latter case demonstrates that the Court of Justice is prepared to accept suggestions from the parties whenever possible. When the questions asked by the national court are formulated in a broad and vague manner the Court of Justice will pay attention to a more specific delineation of the questions by the parties, but not without observing certain limits. In the *Second Scholten-Honig Case* the national court had only asked a general question on the validity of an EEC regulation. One of the parties put forward three specific grounds of invalidity and the Court of Justice replied to those specific grounds. [156] In the *IGAV Case*, on the other hand, the national court had made reference to some basic principles of the Common Market, such as the free movement of goods and the elimination of any form of discrimination, and IGAV had based its rights to raise additional objections to the existing system of importation of paper products into Italy, on these references. The court held, however, that there were '*no questions before the Court of sufficiently precise a nature to enable it to consider the objections raised by the applicant in the main action*'. [157]

§ 624a. In their submissions to the Court of Justice the litigants may not challenge the facts submitted by the national court. When in the *Oehlschläger Case* the applicant submitted that the goods described by the national court were not the goods he imported, the Court of Justice held that it could give rulings only on the basis of the facts which the national court put before it

---

154. *Neumann Case* (17/67), 13 Dec. 1967 [1967] ECR 460; 13 Jur. (1967) 581; 13 Rec. (1967) 597, 598; CCH para 8059.
155. *First Getreidehandel Case* (17/72), 8 Nov. 1972, [1972] ECR 1077, 1078. [1974] 1 CMLR 195; CCH para 8192.
156. *Second Scholten-Honig Case* (103, 145/77), 25 Oct. 1978, considerations 16, 17, [1978] ECR 2071.
157. *IGAV Case* (94/74), 18 June 1975, consideration 31, [1975] ECR 712; [1976] 2 CMLR 55 (there it is consideration 15); CCH para 8311.

357

and that it was not within its competence to verify whether such facts were correct. [158]

§ 625. From these cases it may be concluded that litigants are not permitted to submit additional questions directly to the Court of Justice, but when their questions can be seen as further qualification to the questions asked or when there is any form of acquiescent cooperation by the national court, their questions may be answered. Furthermore, the Court of Justice may decide on additional questions *ex officio,* if it considers them to be of a sufficient general interest to do so. For this latter reason, it may be prudent for a litigant to raise possible additional questions whenever they are in his interest.

10. Role of the Commission

§ 625a. In all preliminary proceedings the Commission submits written observations to the Court. [159] These observations are of great value to the Court as they contain all the factual information needed, which is particularly important in the case of complicated technical rules of secondary Community law. As with individual litigants the Commission may not add new questions to those requested by the national court. Neither does the Court feel bound to make statements at the request of the Commission on particular aspects of the questions referred to it for a preliminary ruling. [160]

---

158. *Oehlschläger Case* (104/77), 16 March 1978, considerations 3, 4, [1978] ECR 797; CCH para 8481.
159. Under the authority of EEC statute Art. 20.
160. *Pierik Case* (117/77), 16 March 1978, considerations 4-7, [1978] ECR 834, 835; [1978] 3 CMLR 351, 352.

CHAPTER FIVE

Structure and Operation of the Court of Justice

I. COMPOSITION OF THE COURT

A. THE JUDGES

1. Number of Judges

§ 626. Originally the Court consisted of seven Judges. Since January 1973 this has been increased to nine.[1] The Court must sit with an uneven number of its members.[2] If one Judge is unable to attend, the Judge most junior in office must also abstain from taking part in the deliberations of the Court.[3] Several issues may be decided by a Chamber of the Court, (see below § 649, 650), but issues which may not be delegated to a Chamber cannot be validly decided by less than seven Judges.[4] This is a high quorum which might easily give rise to problems if one or more judges were to fall ill for a lengthy period of time. As the Member States what their legal systems to be represented in the Court as far as is possible, a reduction in the quorum required seems inadvisable. As yet the Court has always succeeded in achieving the required quorum.

2. Nationality

§ 627. Nowhere in the Treaties is it provided that there should be a Judge from each of the Member States. It was not wished to make a reference to the nationalities of the Judges as the Judges perform a supranational task and should in no way be connected with particular Member States. In the International Court of Justice[5] and the European Court of Human Rights[6] there are provisions for the appointment of a judge *ad hoc* if there is no national of the State concerned in the court. There is no such provision for the Court of

---

1. ECSC Art. 32, EEC Art. 165, Euratom Art. 137. On the organization and composition of the Court, see also L. Neville Brown and Francis G. Jacobs, *The Court of Justice of the European Communities*, Sweet & Maxwell 1977, pp. 11-71.
2. EEC Statute Art. 15.
3. Rules of Procedure of the Court, Art. 26.
4. EEC Statute Art. 15.
5. ICJ Statute Art. 31.
6. European Convention for the Protection of Human Rights, Art. 43.

Justice. A party — even if it is a State — may not complain about the absence from the Court — or from a chamber of the Court — of a Judge of its own nationality. Neither may a complaint be made about the nationality of the sitting Judges.[7]

§ 628. Theoretically Judges could be appointed from non-Member as well as from Member States.[8] In practice, however, this would result in one of the national legal systems of the Member States being unrepresented in the Court, which would be most undesirable. It has been seen above that the general principles common to the laws of the Member States are an important source of Community law (§ 33-118) and that occasionally the Court must apply the national law of a Member State (§ 139-144). For both of these functions it is, accordingly, of great importance that the Court as a body is familiar with each of the national legal systems. To ensure that it operates in an optimum manner the Court, therefore, needs a member from each of these national systems. Furthermore, the judgments of the Court of Justice must subsequently be applied by the national judiciaries within the national legal orders. For this purpose they must be comprehensible to national lawyers and should not seem too alien. A national Judge from each of the Member States sitting in the Court can render assistance in making the judgments more understandable and therefore more readily applicable within the national judicial systems.

§ 629. As regards the International Court of Justice, Il Ro Suh has demonstrated that judges are inclined to support their own States. They did so in 167 out of the 203 cases examined, while they opposed their own State in only 36 of those cases.

These figures may lead to false conclusions being drawn as most of the judges involved were judges *ad hoc* nominated by their governments after the case had been brought to the Court. Once the case is already known, the government may choose a judge whose previous writings indicate that he holds the same opinion on the case as his government. His support for the government position may be due to his selection rather than to a lack or impartiality. But even when the judges *ad hoc* are disregarded from the survey, national judges have supported their Governments in more than two-thirds of the cases (59 out of 84).[9]

There is no reason to suspect the judges of the International Court of partiality as their support for their national governments can easily be explained on other grounds. International law is not a homogeneous legal system; there are very few rules of universal law. Most international law is codified in treaties which bind only a limited number of States; each State is

---

7. EEC Statute Art. 16.
8. Valerio Grementieri, *Le statut de la Cour de justice des Communautés européennes*, 3 RTDE (1967), pp. 818-822.
9. Il Ro Suh, *Voting Behaviour of National Judges in International Courts*, 63 AJIL (1969), p. 228, which covers the International Court's case law until September 1967. After that date, up to January 1975, there were six contentious cases. In none of them did a judge vote against his government's position.

bound to different rules and each State interprets these rules in its own way. To some extent it can be said that each State develops its own international law. Both the judges and the government officials have been educated in that particular discipline of international law and this explains why judges often hold the same views as the governments of their respective States.

In the case of the Court of Justice the situation is different. In the Communities there is a firm body of law created and developed by Community institutions; there are no national interpretations of Community law. Furthermore, legal traditions in a relatively small regional organisation are far more homogeneous than on the universal plane; the legal education and the legal and moral convictions held by the Judges of the Court of Justice are very similar. In those cases where national legal systems are not involved the nationality of the Judges is, therefore, irrelevant. Views held by individual Judges on what direction Community law should develop in are of far greater practical importance.

§ 630. Partly for reasons of tradition, partly because it was assumed that some national interest was at stake, but largely also because the Court needs some expertise in handling each of the national legal systems, the Member States have always appointed a lawyer from every Member State to the Court. Until July 1958 there was one extra Dutch Judge and from the end of 1958 until 1973 one extra Italian Judge in order to arrive at an odd number of Judges (the two Advocates-General at that time were German and French). [10] The intention was to retain the extra Italian Judge when four States were contemplating membership of the Communities in 1972. The Court would then have had eleven Judges and three Advocates-General. When Norway finally decided against joining the Communities the second Italian Judge became the fourth Advocate-General.

3. Requirements

§ 631. *'The Judges shall be chosen from persons whose independence is beyond doubt and who possess the qualifications required for appointment to the highest judicial offices in their respective countries, or who are jurisconsults of recognized competence'.* [11] This provision was introduced into the Community judicial system in 1958 when the EEC and Euratom Treaties entered into force. [12] Prior to that date the ECSC Treaty did not prescribe that Judges had to be qualified for national judicial offices and two of the original Judges (Rueff and Serrarens) did not in fact have a law degree. The present rule is not a rigid one as it does not require that the Judges have

10. Between 26 June 1958 and 4 Feb. 1959 no cases were decided. For a survey of the distribution of functions between the nationals of Member States see Werner Feld, *The Court of the European Communities: New dimension in international adjudication*, Nijhoff, The Hague 1964, pp. 16-18.
11. ECSC Art. 32(b); EEC Art. 167.
12. Convention on Certain Institutions Common to the European Communities, Art. 4.

experience as judges in national courts. In practice, the Judges of the Court have a varied background: some have been judges before, others were university professors, cabinet ministers, politicians, civil servants or practising lawyers. [13] Their wide range of experience is of advantage to the Court. Apart from proficiency in his own legal system each Judge also supplies the benefits of his own practical experience.

The Judges may not hold any political or administrative office and, without exemption by the Council, they may not engage in any other occupation, whether gainful or not. [14]

4. Appointment

§ 632. In order to avoid any suggestion of a hierarchy between the Community institutions the Judges are not appointed by the Council. The Treaties provide that the Member States shall appoint the Judges by common accord. In practice, this usually means that each of the Member Governments selects a candidate of its own nationality. Before doing so, however, informal consultations will have taken place with the result that the other Member States occasionally persuade a Member to propose another candidate during the course of these consultations.

There is no requirement that the Governments must consult national parliaments or courts when making this selection, but in practice they sometimes do so. [15] As one of the most important tasks of the Court of Justice is the judicial review of the acts taken by the Governments of the Member States it may seem objectionable that the Governments perform such an important role in the appointment of the Court's Judges. In practice, however, the system works reasonably well; participation by the other governments in the procedure apparently provides sufficient protection against overtly political appointments being made. A rule requiring a system of preselection of candidates by the national parliaments would offer no guarantee against political appointments. Preselection by the national judiciaries could lead to the appointment of aged and less dynamic Judges. As the Court of Justice is one of the most senior and best remunerated judicial bodies in Europe the national judiciaries might well forward their most senior and best known members in order to bestow some special 'pre-retirement honour' upon them.

When the names of the national candidates have been communicated to each of the Member States the appointment follows by the 'Member States acting in common accord'. This means in practice that the Ministers of Foreign Affairs, when they are already together for a Council meeting, adjourn in their capacity as Council members and proceed to meet in their capacity as representatives of their States. In the latter capacity they are entitled to conclude any agreement (for the legal status of such decisions of the representatives of the Members, meeting within the Council, see above § 222-224)

13. On the background of the judges see Feld (*op. cit.*, note 10), pp. 29-33.
14. EEC Statute Art. 4.
15. On the selection procedure in Germany and France, see Feld (*op. cit.*, note 10) pp

§ 633. When the Court of Justice was established it was an innovation and the Member Governments wanted to keep the option open of making changes in the Court's composition. On this account they recoiled from the prospect of freezing the membership of the Court by appointing the Judges for life or until retirement age, as would have been most in keeping with the European legal tradition. The Judges are appointed for six years, a term of office which is sufficiently long to guarantee a large degree of independence. At the end of this period the Judges are often re-appointed.

The limited period of appointment is to be objected to in principle. [16] It may lead to changes in the composition of the Court for purely political reasons. When a Judge with particular political sympathies, or — in a State like Belgium — from a particular part of the country, has served for six years, the governments may be under pressure to appoint someone with other political leanings, or from another region. In the case of a small country like the Netherlands, which does not hold many high posts within the Communities, the appointment of a Commissioner from a small political party might be a reason for not reappointing a Judge of that same party. In practice such considerations have not been of noticeable influence.

In theory the more fundamental objection against the short term appointment of Judges is that it could affect their independence. In practice, this objection has given rise to less problems than might be expected. [17] The independence of the judiciary is so strongly established in Western Europe that if a government were to object to the reappointment of a Judge due to his opinions being unfavourable to that government, it would probably encounter strong protests from public opinion and from parliament at home. Furthermore, governments usually do not learn of unfavourable opinions formulated by Judges as the deliberations of the Court remain secret (see below § 700).

§ 634. In order to obviate the risk of an entirely new court being appointed, the Judges are not replaced all at once. Every three years there is a partial replacement (five and four Judges alternately). [18] This ongoing and balanced process of replacement would be upset if Judges retiring in mid-term were to be replaced by others sitting for a full term. For this reason, it has been provided that a Judge replacing a member of the Court whose term of office has not expired shall be appointed for the remainder of his predecessor's term. [19]

'A retiring Judge shall continue to hold office until his successor takes up his duties'. [20] This makes it possible for the Court to complete cases in which

---

18, 19. See also Grementieri (*op. cit.*, note 8), pp. 822-824.
16. See e.g. Farewell speech by Judge Hammes, published in a booklet in four languages on the ceremonious public sessions of the Court, Luxembourg 1968, pp. 57, 58.
17. See statements of Judges Riese and Rueff, quoted by Feld (*op. cit.*, note 10), p. 20.
18. ECSC Art. 32(b)(2); EEC Art. 167(2).
19. EEC Statute Art. 7. For the Human Rights Court and Commission the original absence of a similar provision created considerable problems.
20. EEC Statute Art. 5.

a retiring Judge has participated. As only those Judges who are present at the oral proceedings may take part in the deliberations,[21] replacements before a case is decided may lead to the quorum not being reached. As the Court knows of replacements sufficiently in advance, it has always succeeded in organizing its work in such a way that no problems have arisen.

5. Special provisions

§ 635. It is highly unlikely that a Judge of the Court will commit a crime or will otherwise infringe the requisite conditions for serving in the Court, but such things could conceivably occur and therefore special procedures have been foreseen. [22] According to these procedures a Judge may be deprived of his office or of his right to a pension or other benefits in its stead, if, in the unanimous opinion of the Judges and Advocates-General of the Court, he no longer fulfils the requisite conditions or meets the obligations arising from his office. No provision has been made as to who can bring such questions before the Court and this renders the procedures inoperable. Had someone, for example, the First Advocate-General [23], been provided with the right to bring any misconduct indulged in by Judges and by Advocates-General to the attention of the Court, this person could then also have been in a position to informally accost Judges and Advocates-General whose behaviour was not entirely in conformity with their obligations, so as to persuade them to make the necessary redress.

Provisions have also been made for the privileges and immunities of all Court personnel, including the Judges and Advocates-General. [24] As in the case of all international civil servants, these privileges and immunities are meant to guarantee full independence from the Member States and they can be waived — by the Court sitting in plenary session — when they are not needed.

B. THE ADVOCATES-GENERAL[25]

§ 636. The Court of Justice has four Advocates-General who are of equal standing with the Judges. [26] The requirements for their appointment, term of office and replacement are the same as those for the Judges (see above § 630-635). The limited period of appointment of only six years is more objectionable than in the case of the Judges as the Advocates-General render their

---

21. Rules of Procedure of the Court, Art. 27(2).
22. See EEC Statute Art. 6 and 3.
23. His counterpart in the Netherlands has such a right.
24. See EEC Statute Art. 3.
25. See Ami Barav, *Le Commissaire du Gouvernement près le Conseil d'Etat français et l'Avocat Général près la Cour de justice des Communautés européennes*, 26 RIDC (1974) pp. 809-826; Paolo Gori, *L'avocat-général à la Cour de Justice des Communautés européennes*, 12 CDE 1976, pp. 375-393.
26. Rules of Procedure of the Court, Art. 6, 27(7).

opinions individually so that a possible disagreement with the appointing government is made quite public. This could mean that Advocates-General wanting to be reappointed feel less free to take up a position in opposition to that of their governments.

In every case one of the Advocates-General — normally the one attached to the Chamber to which the Judge Rapporteur belongs — delivers an opinion at the end of the oral procedure. [27] This opinion is a fully reasoned statement of the legal aspects of the case. It suggests one or more possible solutions and terminates with a specific conclusion. The opinions of the Advocates-General are sometimes called *conclusions* or *submissions*. [28] They are given with complete impartiality and independence. [29]

§ 637. The opinions of the Advocates-General, to some extent, make up for the fact that the Court of Justice operates only at one instance. In each of these opinions is to be found a view on the case which is independent from that of the Court. The opinion of the Advocate-General helps the Court to solve the case in much the same way as the decision of a court ruling at first instance assists a court of appeal. It provides the starting point for the Court's opinion.

If the Court does not follow the opinion of the Advocate-General, then it plays the same role as the dissenting opinions of judges in some other courts: it presents the legal argument for the other point of view; this may be valuable for the further development of the Community legal order. [30]

§ 638. By means of rotation an Advocate-General performs the function of First Advocate-General for the period of one year. [31] The First Advocate-General presides over the meetings of the Advocates-General and represents them on a number of occasions.

C. STAFF

1. The Registry

§ 639. The Court is served by the Registrar, a position which has been held from the outset by the Belgian lawyer, Mr. A. van Houtte. His functions are twofold. On the one hand he is involved in the judicial function of the Court: under his supervision a register is kept in which all pleadings and supporting documents are consecutively entered in the order in which they are lodged [32];

27. *Idem*, Art. 59.
28. *Conclusions* in accordance with the French usage; the word *submission* is used in the Treaties and Statutes; the Court uses *opinion*.
29. EEC Art. 166.
30. Feld (*op. cit.*, note 10), p. 22.
31. Rules of Procedure of the Court, Art. 10.
32. *Idem*, Art. 16.

he is reponsible for the documents [33], he has custody of the seals. [34] On the other hand the Registrar also plays a role in the internal administration of the Court, rather similar to that of the head of the chancellery in an embassy: he is responsible, under the authority of the President of the Court, for the administration, financial management and the accounts of the Court. [35] The officials and other servants attached to the Court are responsible to him. [36] The Registrar is assisted by an Assistant Registrar, who replaces him in case of absence and performs part of his duties. [37] Important administrative decisions, such as those on the appointment and promotion of higher officials, are taken by the Judges, the Advocates-General and the Registrar together in their administrative sittings (see below § 646).

2. Legal Secretaries

§ 640. Until 1979 each Judge and Advocate-General was supported by one legal secretary, a qualified lawyer charged with helping 'his' Judge prepare the cases. During 1979 their number was gradually increased so that by 1 January 1980 all judges and Advocates-General will have two legal secretaries. The role of these legal secretaries at the Court of Justice is similar to that of the law clerks at the United States Supreme Court.

Some legal secretaries have been permanently appointed from the early days of the Court. Recently, short-term appointments of about three years have become more customary. As the post offers an excellent training for European lawyers the Member States profit from appointments of a short duration which bring back lawyers trained in European law to their national States.

3. Research department

§ 641. Within the staff of the Court there is a special department for documentation and research which provides the judges and Advocates-General with information on national and Community law. Often this research consists of comparative studies made of the national legal rules on specific topics.

The department is made up of eleven lawyers of whom two qualified in German law, two in French, two in Italian, one in each English, Irish, Danish, Dutch and Belgian law.

4. Library

§ 642. The Court has its own library and a library staff to maintain it and to keep the catalogues well up to date. All important books and periodicals on

33. *Idem*, Art. 17.
34. *Idem*, Art. 18.
35. *Idem*, Art. 23.
36. EEC Statute Art. 11.
37. Rules of Procedure of the Court, Art. 13.

the subject of Community law are available. On other topics the Court is always able to borrow from the nearby library of the European Parliament if necessary.

5. Language department

§ 643. The largest single department of the Court's staff is that for translation and interpreting. On 1 April 1979 the professional staff of the Court (A and LA grades) numbered 96 officials of whom 54 belonged to the language department (LA grades).

6. Further Staff

§ 644. As the Court of Justice is an independent institution of the Communities, it has its own budget and its own personnel department. It also has a building of its own and employs the staff necessary for its maintenance. On 1 April 1979 the total staff of the Court of Justice numbered 270 (excluding auxiliary personnel).

D. SEAT

§ 645. The European Parliament and the Court of Justice are established in Luxembourg, the original seat of the ECSC (the Parliament often meets in Strasbourg). For the European Parliament the great distance from Brussels — where most of the executive organs are located — is a serious handicap. The Parliament would function more efficiently if it could keep in close contact with the Commission and (the Secretariat of) the Council.

As regards the Court of Justice the situation is different. There is no need to monitor political developments; the geographical distance from civil servants wanting to press their views upon Judges may even be advantageous. The Court is housed in a well designed building and is provided with good library facilities. The Court may meet outside its seat (see below § 646).

The Judges, the Advocates-General and the Registrar are obliged to reside at the place where the Court has its seat. [38]

II. ORGANIZATION OF THE COURT

A. SESSIONS

§ 646. The Court of Justice is a permanent institution. Apart from the holidays of 3 weeks for Christmas, 3 weeks for Easter and two months in sum-

---

38. EEC Statute Art. 13.

mer [39] the Court is permanently in session. [40] Its sittings and deliberations are normally held on Tuesdays, Wednesdays and Thursdays in the Court's building in Luxembourg. The Court may hold one or more particular sittings elsewhere, which it has done a number of times in ECSC Cases. [41]

Apart from its normal sittings the Court meets in administrative sittings in which the Advocates-General take part with the capacity to vote and the Registrar takes part without the capacity to vote. [42] At these sittings decisions are taken on the administrative aspects of cases, on the nomination of the professional staff, on the budget of the Court and on all sorts of other administrative questions.

B. THE PRESIDENT

§ 647. The Judges elect the President of the Court from among their number for a term of three years, which can be renewed. [43] This means that after each series of partial elections to the Court (above § 633) the President is elected. [44] The President presides over all sessions of the Court [45] and conducts its business. [46] In addition he performs a number of executive functions in the Court, *inter alia*

— He establishes the cause list, on which the order of the cases is arranged. [47]
— He assigns the cases to the Chambers. [48]
— If a Chamber is incomplete he designates another Judge to it. [49]
— He designates the Advocate-General and the Judge to act as rapporteur in each case. [50]
— For special reasons he may notify a Judge or an Advocate-General that he should not sit or give opinions in a particular case. [51]
— By way of summary procedure the President may provisionally prescribe interim measures or suspend the execution of Community acts. [52]
— He may extend the time limit during which the defendant in a case must lodge his defence [53]; he fixes the time limits for the pleadings [54], interven-

---

39. Rules of Procedure of the Court, Art. 28.
40. EEC Statute, Art. 14.
41. See e.g. *Fonderies de Pont à Mousson Case* (14/59), 17 Dec. 1959, [1959] ECR 224; 5 Jur. (1958-59) 503; 5 Rec. (1958-1959) 466; *Second Snupat Case* (42 and 49/59), 22 March 1961, [1961] ECR 72; 7 Jur. (1961) 141; 7 Rec. (1961) 141.
42. Rules of Procedure of the Court, Art. 27(7).
43. EEC Art. 167.
44. Rules of Procedure of the Court, Art. 7(1).
45. *Idem*, Art. 8.
46. See e.g. *Idem*, Art. 47, 56.
47. EEC Statute Art. 31.
48. Rules of Procedure of the Court, Art. 9(2).
49. *Idem*, Art. 26(3).
50. *Idem*, Art. 9(2), 76(3), 105(3), 108(1).
51. EEC Statute Art. 16.
52. EEC Statute Art. 36; Rules of Procedure of the Court, Artt. 83-90.
53. Rules of Procedure of the Court, Artt. 40(2), 105(2).
54. *Idem*, Artt. 41(2), 42(2), 84, 91(4).

tions[55] and sometimes for observations[56]; and he sets the dates on which the Judge Rapporteur is to present his preliminary report[57] and on which the oral procedure will be opened.[58]
- In special circumstances he may order that a case be given priority over others.[59]
- On the joint application by the parties the President may defer a case.[60]
- He supervises the work of the Registrar[61] and as such he is the most senior officer on the staff.

§ 648. Before the merger of the executive organs of the Communities the President of the Court had, apart from the above-mentioned Court functions, also the presidency of the ECSC Committee of Presidents which co-ordinated the administration of the four institutions of that Community.[62] In this important committee he exerted considerable influence. The Committee of Presidents was abolished by the Merger Treaty of 8 April 1965.[63]

C. CHAMBERS

§ 649. The Court has set up two divisions, called Chambers, each composed of four Judges of whom three sit in each case.[64] According to the Treaties Chambers can also be formed of five Judges, but this has never occurred in practice. To each of the Chambers two Advocates-General are attached. The President of the Chambers are designated by the Court for one year.[65]

The Chambers are charged with making preparatory enquiries and they decide on requests for legal aid and in disputes concerning the execution of the Court's decision on the costs.[66] When rendering judgment the Court normally sits in plenary session. An exception is made for cases brought by civil servants against the institutions of the Communities. These cases, which make up almost a third of the Court's total are normally decided by the Chambers.[67] In Germany there were formerly princes who attributed cases to judges of greater or lesser severity according to the outcome they wished. As a reaction to this practice it became an elementary rule of German law that everyone must be able to know in advance who will be the judge in his case. To respect this rule the Court has divided the staff cases between the Cham-

55. *Idem*, Art. 93(5).
56. *Idem*, Art. 107(1).
57. *Idem*, Art. 44(1).
58. *Idem*, Artt. 44(2), 54.
59. *Idem*, Art. 55(1).
60. *Idem*, Art. 55(2).
61. EEC Statute, Art. 11; Rules of Procedure of the Court, Artt. 14, 6(1), 17(1), 23, 53, 62.
62. ECSC (original version), Art. 78.
63. Merger Treaty, Art. 21.
64. ECSC Art. 32, EEC Art. 165; a third Chamber has been provided for by an amendment of the Court's Rules of Procedure on 15 July 1979.
65. Rules of Procedure of the Court, Art. 10.
66. *Idem*, Artt. 44(2), 76(3) and 74 respectively.
67. *Idem*, Art. 95(2).

bers: all cases concerning civil servants of the Commission come before the one Chamber, all cases concerning civil servants of any of the other institutions before the other.

§ 650.   Preliminary rulings, which nowadays constitute the largest group of cases, could originally not be decided by a Chamber. Questions of interpretation and validity were considered so important that the Treaties expressly provided that the Court must give preliminary rulings in plenary sessions. [68] When the Court began to receive an increasing number of references in which it had to decide on technical questions regarding the customs classification of imported goods, this opinion changed. By amendment of the Rules of Procedure (expressly allowed by EEC Article 165, last paragraph) the Council made it possible for preliminary rulings to be given by a Chamber of the Court, in questions of an essentially technical nature, or on matters for which there was already an established body of case-law. [69] Unlike staff cases references for preliminary rulings are not referred to a specific Chamber. [70] The Chamber of the Judge Rapporteur will take the case when, at the end of the written proceedings, it is decided to refer the case to a Chamber. When a Member State has submitted observations (see below § 680), preliminary rulings may only be assigned to a Chamber with the concurrence of that Member State. A case may not be assigned to a Chamber if an institution expressly requests that the case be decided in plenary session. [71]

A Chamber may refer a case to the plenary court. [72] It will do so when important new legal decisions must be taken, or in order to determine the prior position of the Court and thus to preserve the unity of the case-law of the Court (see e.g. the *Fiddelaar Case*). [73] The full case need not be referred to the plenary Court. It may happen that the Court settles one or two matters of principle and then remits the case to the Chamber. [74]

D. JUDGE RAPPORTEUR

§ 651.   In each case one of the Judges is charged with the preliminary preparation of the case. He makes an initial study of the files and presents a preliminary report (*rapport préalable*) to the Court containing the facts and an opinion on the question whether or not preparatory inquiries need to be

68.   ECSC Art. 32; EEC Art. 165.
69.   Rules of Procedure of the Court, Art. 95. For its first application, see *Riemer Case* (120/75), 15 June 1976; [1976] ECR 1003; CCH para 8364. The possibility to refer to Chambers was further extended on 15 July 1979.
70.   For example, there were two preliminary questions referred to Chambers on 16 Dec. 1976. The *Luma Case* (38/76), [1976] ECR 2028 went to the Second Chamber and the *Inzirillo Case* (63/76), [1976] ECR 2058 went to the First.
71.   Rules of Procedure of the Court, Art. 95.
72.   *Idem*, para 3.
73.   *Fiddelaar Case* (44/59), 16 Dec. 1960, [1960] ECR 541; 6 Jur. (1960) 1131; 6 Rec. (1960) 1091. See also *De Dapper Case* (54/75), 9 March 1977, [1977] ECR 474; CCH para 8343.
74.   See e.g. *Mills Case* (110/75), 15 June 1976, consideration 31, [1976] ECR 971.

carried out. Often the Judge Rapporteur, though he may not consider preparatory inquiries to be necessary, or the Advocate-General, will suggest posing specific questions to the parties, to the Commission or to a Member State in writing. The Court usually follows such suggestions and thus obviates the need for convening a special sitting for preparatory inquiries. The preliminary report also sets out the most important problems arising in the Case so that the Court, or its President, can plan its work accordingly.

§ 652. Before the oral procedure the Judge Rapporteur drafts the 'report at the hearing' (*rapport d'audience*). This report contains a survey of the facts of the case and of the submissions of the parties; it is usually reproduced with no or little amendment under the heading of 'facts' in the final judgment. After the oral procedure the Judge Rapporteur drafts the part of the judgment on the law. This part serves as no more than a basis for the discussion by the Court. In the course of this discussion the Judge Rapporteur may have a somewhat stronger position because of his better knowledge of the details of the case, but this position is by no means a dominant one. It may well be that after the discussion in the Court the Judge Rapporteur may have to re-write his draft in a completely different way. It may, therefore, happen that the final decision of the Court is decided against the vote of the Judge Rapporteur. For this reason the Court does not like to stress the influence of the Judge Rapporteur on the case and ceased publishing his name when one of the European law journals started publishing the cases under the name of the Judge Rapporteur involved. In recent years the workload of the Court of Justice has considerably increased. It may be expected that this development strengthens the influence of the Judge Rapporteur. When the other Judges have less time to study the case they will more easily be tempted to follow the studied opinion of the Judge Rapporteur.

According to the Statute of the Court, Assistant Rapporteurs may be appointed. [75] This has never occurred, however.

III. PROCEDURE[76]

A. PRELIMINARY POINTS

1. Representation

a. THE COMMUNITIES

§ 653. EEC Article 211, on the legal capacity of the Community and on its right to acquire or dispose of property and to be a party to legal proceedings, provides that the Community shall be represented by the Commission. Proceedings on behalf of the Community or the defence to actions brought

75. EEC Statute, Art. 12.
76. See also Brown and Jacobs (*op. cit.*, note 1), pp. 159-178.

against it will therefore be conducted by the Commission. In practice, however, many proceedings directly concern the other institutions: acts of the Council may be challenged; staff members may be in the service of any of the institutions. In those cases actions will be brought against the institution concerned and that institution will appear in court.

When injury is caused by the Communities, it seems most appropriate to sue the Commission for damages. In the *Werhahn Case* the Commission argued that one of its functions was to represent the Community before the Court in cases on the liability of the Community, irrespective of which particular institution caused the damage. The Court of Justice did not agree with this view. It held that EEC Article 211 deals with the legal capacity and the representation of the Community in the legal systems of the Member States, and that under the Community legal system it was in the interest of a good administration of justice that the Community should be represented before the Court by the institution or institutions against which the matter giving rise to liability is alleged. As the matter involved had its origin both with the Commission and with the Council, the first for having made a proposal, the second for having issued the legislation, the Court held that the plaintiff, Werhahn, was justified in bringing the proceedings against the Community as represented by the two institutions. [77] However, extension of an action to Council is no longer possible during the proceedings. [78]

b. PARTIES BEFORE THE COURT OF JUSTICE

§ **654.** As a rule, parties cannot themselves appear before the Court of Justice. States and institutions of the Community must be represented by an agent appointed for each case; other parties must be represented by a lawyer entitled to practise before a court of a Member State. [79] In proceedings for preliminary rulings the parties are represented in the same way as before their national court. If national law permits them to plead their own case, then they may also do so on the request for a preliminary ruling.

For parties from most Member States the requirement to be represented by a lawyer causes no problems as all lawyers which parties are likely to select are entitled to appear before national courts, but in the United Kingdom the situation is less clear. Only barristers (advocates in Scotland) may appear in court, but they have no contact with the party they represent. Solicitors, on the other hand, traditionally represent the parties, though they do not appear in court. [80] As solicitors can be regarded as being 'entitled to practise before a

---

77. *Werhahn Case* (63-69/72), 13 Nov. 1973, consideration 6-8, [1973] ECR 1247; CCH para 8236. On the question whether actions can be brought against the Economic and Social Committee, see G. Vandersanden and A. Barav, *Contentieux Communautaire*, Bruylant Brussels 1977, pp. 337, 338.
78. *Stimming Case* (90/77), Order of 10 Nov. 1977, [1977] ECR 2113, 2114.
79. EEC Statute, Art. 17; Rules of Procedure of the Court, Art. 38(3).
80. On the position of barristers and solicitors in relation to the Court of Justice see Valerio Grementieri and Joseph Golden jr, *The United Kingdom and the European Court of Justice: an Encounter Between Common and Civil Law Traditions*, 21 AJCL (1973), in particular pp. 675-681.

court' both categories can be considered as admissible representatives before the Court of Justice [81], and it is likely that both categories will act as representatives before the Court. The two professions have agreed that both will have the same rights before the Court of Justice, but on preliminary rulings requested by the High Court, the Court of Appeal or the House of Lords only barristers will plead. [82] The barristers changed their rules in order to facilitate their work before the Court of Justice, *inter alia* by allowing professional partnerships with foreign lawyers for European cases (for domestic cases this is not permitted). [83] In practice only a few law firms represent clients before the Court of Justice. Many cases are pleaded by the same lawyers.

§ 655. The agents and their advisers, as well as the lawyers of private parties enjoy immunity in respect of words spoken or written by them concerning the case or the parties. Their papers and documents are exempt from search and seizure. [84] The agents of States or institutions cannot be censured for anything they say, but their advisers and the lawyers of private parties may be excluded from the proceedings by an order of the Court if their conduct towards the Court is incompatible with its dignity or if they abuse their rights. [85]

§ 656. It is a general rule common to the laws of the Member States that lawyers may not disclose information confidentially obtained from their clients. To some extent, therefore, the so-called 'legal professional privilege' exists in the Communities, which guarantees to every client that what he tells his legal advisers and what they tell him will not be disclosed in any subsequent legal proceedings. The extent of this privilege under Community law has not been defined, however. It may be that letters between lawyers and their clients could be inspected by the Commission when they are in the files of companies which are subject to an investigation by the Commission. [86]

§ 657. The agent or private party's lawyer must sign the original of every pleading [87]; he must also deliver the oral submission. During the oral procedure he may be assisted by experts.

81. *The Treaty of Rome and the English Legal Professions: Proposed Solutions*, 68 Law Society Gazette (1971) p. 194, but see also Valentine, *The Court of Justice of the European Communities*, Stevens, London 1965, Vol. I, p. 48, note 47, who suggests that solicitors could represent the British Government or the Commission, but not a private party.
82. L. Neville Brown, *Les Juristes d'Outre-Manche*, Etudes offertes au Professeur Jacques Lambert, Lyon 1974, p. 465. Francis G. Jacobs and Andrew Durand, *References to the European Court: Practice and Procedure*, Butterworths 1975 (revised reprint from Atkin's Court Forms, Vol. 17), p. 178 which includes the text of the agreement.
83. Decision of the Extraordinary General Meeting of the Bar, 10 April 1972 on the report of a Special Committee of the Bar Council (Appendix B), The Times, 11 April 1972, p. 6.
84. Rules of Procedure of the Court, Art. 32.
85. *Idem*, Art. 35.
86. Stephen Stewart and David Vaughan, *Does Legal Professional Privilege Exist in the EEC?*, The Law Society Gazette, 5 Nov. 1975, pp. 1111, 1112.
87. Rules of Procedure of the Court, Art. 37(1).

2. Legal aid [88]

§ 658. In direct actions a party who is wholly or in part unable to meet the costs of the proceedings may at any time apply for legal aid. This application need not be made through a lawyer. The decision is taken by the Chamber to which the Judge Rapporteur belongs. This decision is not reasoned and not subject to appeal. At any time the Chamber may withdraw the aid. [89]

After the Chamber has decided that a person is entitled to receive legal aid, it makes an order for a lawyer to be appointed to act for him. In principle a person may choose his own lawyer. If he has not done so, or if his lawyer is unacceptable to the Court, the national authorities of the State concerned will suggest a lawyer which the Court appoints. [90]

Apart from one ECSC Case, legal aid has only been granted in cases brought by civil servants. Up to 1 June 1976 30 applications for legal aid were made, of which 11 were granted and 19 rejected. The amount is usually somewhere between 15.000 and 30.000 Belgian francs. Often a sum is indicated in advance. [91]

The aid may be revindicated. For the costs of preliminary rulings it seems logical that legal aid granted in the national proceedings should be extended to the costs of preliminary rulings. [92] In special circumstances the Court of Justice may grant, as legal aid, assistance for the purpose of facilitating the representation and attendance of a party. [93]

Before applying to the Court of Justice civil servants must submit their complaints to their superiors (see above § 327). For this internal procedure no legal aid can be granted. If the civil servant seeks a lawyer, he does so at his own risk and expenditure. [94]

3. Language of the case [95]

§ 659. Before filing the application instituting proceedings against a Community institution an applicant must choose the language of the case. He may pick any one of seven languages: Danish, Dutch, English, French, German,

---

88. See Karl Wolf, *Kostenrecht und Kostenpraxis des Gerichtshofs der Europäischen Gemeinschaften*, 11 EuR (1976), pp. 26-28; John Temple Lang, *A Referral to Luxembourg: Legal Aid*, 75 The Law Society's Gazette (1978), p. 37.
89. Rules of Procedure of the Court, Art. 76.
90. Supplementary Rules of the Court, Art. 4.
91. Wolf (*op. cit.*, note 88), p. 27.
92. See, for example the English High Court (Queen's Bench Division) in the *English Regina Case*, 17 Jan. 1977, [1977] 1 CMLR 269, also quoted in the facts of the *Regina Case* (30/77), 27 Oct. 1977, [1977] ECR 2002; [1977] 2 CMLR 802, 803; CCH para 8441.
93. Rules of Procedure of the Court, Art. 104.
94. *Herpels Case* (54/77), 9 March 1978, considerations 47, 48, 50, [1978] ECR 600, 601.
95. Lisbeth Stevens, *The principle of linguistic equality in judicial proceedings and in the interpretation of plurilingual legal instruments: the régime linguistic in the Court of Justice of the European Communities*, 62 Northwestern University Law Review (1967) pp. 701-734.

Irish or Italian. [96] Six of these languages will not cause any practical problems, but Irish has a weaker position in the Communities. Regulations and Court cases are not usually published in Irish [97]; the translation department would have difficulty in translating all pleadings into the other languages, and could not do so without considerable delay. It may therefore be expected (and hoped) that Irish parties will choose English as the language of the case.

The choice of language is important, not only because it will influence the choice of counsel available to the applicant, but also as it will be decisive as to who will be the agent of the Commission.

The applicant is not free to choose the language of the case when the application is made against a Member State or against a natural or legal person, having the nationality of a Member State. In those cases the language of that State shall be the language of the case, or, where that State has more than one official language, the applicant must choose one of them. [98]

The rules on the language of the case are not compulsory rules of public policy. [99] The Court may authorize another of the seven languages as the language of the case for all or part of the proceedings. [100]

The language of the national court concerned is the language of the case when a national court refers a case to the Court of Justice for a preliminary ruling, but the Member States may submit their statements and written observations in their own language.

Originally, French was the language most used before the Court, because most staff cases are in French. Since 1970, the language most used has been German. If staff cases are excluded, half of the cases decided since 1968 have been in German. Of the other half about 40 per cent were in French and about 30 per cent each in Italian and in Dutch.

§ 660. All statements, oral addresses and supporting documents must be in the language of the case or accompanied by a translation into the language of the case. The institutions of the Communities must, in addition, provide translations of all pleadings into the other languages mentioned in § 659, with the exception of Irish. [101] In the case of long documents translations may be confined to extracts. [102] The translators of the Court shall translate into the language of the case all statements of witnesses, experts, Judges or Advocates-General made in other languages. [103] When translation work carried out at the request of a party is excessive in the opinion of the Registrar, that party shall be charged for the costs. [104]

---

96. Rules of Procedure of the Court, Art. 29.
97. Council Regulation No. 1.
98. Rules of Procedure of the Court, Art. 29(2).
99. *Second Feram Case* (1/60), 10 May 1960, [1960] ECR 170; 6 Jur (1960) 371; 6 Rec (1960) 363.
100. Rules of Procedure of the Court, Art. 29(2)*b* and *c*.
101. *Idem*, Art. 37(2).
102. *Idem*, Art. 29(3).
103. *Idem*, Art. 29(4), (5).
104. *Idem*, Art. 72*b*.

There is a presumption *juris et de jure* that the Court itself knows all Community languages. When a document has been filed in the wrong language and it can be proven that the other party knows its content, the filing is not illegal on the ground that the Court could not read the document in the language of the case. [105]

4. Time limits [106]

a. NATURE

§ 661. It was noticed above (§ 67, 71-76) that time limits stem from a compromise between the need for the review of the legality of acts and the contrary need to respect legal certainty. This compromise has been expressed by the Court of Justice as a fundamental principle of law in the following manner:

'The limitation period for bringing an action fulfils a generally recognized need, namely the need to prevent the legality of administrative decisions from being called in question indefinitely, and this means that there is a prohibition on reopening a question after the limitation period has expired'. [107]

The Court has repeatedly stated that in actions against Community acts time limits are a matter of public interest. They cannot, therefore, be invoked at the discretion of the parties. [108] The Court examines them *ex officio*. [109] The Court has not made a similar statement with regard to actions for non-contractual liability. For these actions Advocate-General Lagrange was of the opinion that time limits are not a matter of public interest and therefore must be invoked by the parties. He reached this view on the strength of a comparison with similar national law. [110] In one staff case the Court was not strict in applying time limits *'in view of the difficulty which the applicant experienced in identifying the authority competent to receive his complaint and the uncertainty with regard to the period of notice'*. [111]

---

105. *Second Feram Case* (1/60), 10 May 1960, [1960] ECR 170; 6 Jur. (1960) 371, 372; 6 Rec. (1960) 363.
106. See Peter Oliver, *Limitation of Actions before the European Court*, 3 ELRev. (1978) pp. 3-13.
107. *Railway Tariffs Case* (3/59), 8 March 1960, [1960] ECR 61; 6 Jur. (1960) 137; 6 Rec. (1960) 134.
108. *Muller-Collignon Case* (4/67), 12 Dec. 1967, [1967] ECR 372; 13 Jur. (1967) 465; 13 Rec. (1967) 479; *Gunella Case* (33/72), 8 May 1973, consideration 4, [1973] ECR 480, see also Advocate-General Mayras, [1973] ECR 484.
109. *Müllers Case* (79/70), 7 July 1971, consideration 6, [1971] ECR 696.
110. *Fourth Meroni Case* (14, 16, 17, 20, 24, 26, 27/60 and 1/61), 13 July 1961, [1961] 172-174; Opinion of the Advocate-General, 7 Jur. (1961) 361-363; 7 Rec. (1961) 345-347.
111. *Schertzer Case* (25/68), 18 Oct. 1977, considerations 19, 20, [1977] ECR 1741.

b. DURATION

§ 662. Cases must be brought before the Court of Justice within specific time limits provided for in the Treaties or in other rules of Community law. The most important time limits are:

One month for the action for annulment under the ECSC Treaty. [112]

Two months for the action for annulment under the EEC and Euratom Treaties. [113]

Three months for actions by civil servants against Community Institutions. [114]

Five years for the action for non-contractual liability of the Communities. [115]

Actions by civil servants actually take much more time as the civil servants must first submit their complaints to the appointing authority within three months. [116] This authority must then take a decision on the case within a period of four months; this decision may then be appealed by the civil servant within three months before the Court of Justice. Hence, up to ten months may have passed between the time the disputed decision was taken and the day on which the action was brought before the Court of Justice.

§ 663. The Court of Justice grants a short extension to the prescribed time limits because of the distance which all parties, not habitually residing in the Grand Duchy of Luxembourg, live away from the Court. The extension varies between two days for Belgium, six days for Germany, France and the Netherlands, ten days for Denmark, Ireland Italy and the United Kingdom, two weeks for other European countries and one month for countries, departments and territories outside Europe. [117]

c. COMMENCEMENT OF THE PERIOD

(i) Regulations

§ 664. Publication of regulations has constitutive effect. [118] Before their publication regulations do not, therefore, exist and cannot be challenged. The time limit for actions against regulations runs from the 15th day after their publication in the Official Journal. [119]

(ii) Decisions

§ 665. The time for an action against a decision which has not been published runs from the day following the receipt of its notification by the person

112. ECSC Artt. 33(3), 38(2).
113. EEC Art. 173(3); Euratom Art. 146(3).
114. Staff Regulations, Art. 91(3).
115. EEC Statute Art. 43.
116. Staff Regulations, Art. 90, See above § 327, 328.
117. Decision of the Court of Justice of 4 Dec. 1974, OJ 28 Dec. 1974, No. L 350, p. 28.
118. CoJ in the *König Case* (185/73), 29 May 1974, consideration 5, [1974] ECR p. 616.
119. Rules of Procedure of the Court, Art. 81.

concerned, unless a delay in notification is attributable to that person. [120] In the absence of a notification the time limit runs from the day following that on which the decision came to the knowledge of the plaintiff. [121] For a decision of the Court thereon see above § 289.

The burden of proof of the commencement of the time limit rests with the Communities.

In the *First Snupat Case* the Community had failed to send the letter containing a decision by registered post and did not receive an acknowledgement of its receipt. It could not produce any evidence concerning the day on which the letter was posted. The Court of Justice then held:

'It is unlikely that a letter posted in Brussels and dated 12 May did not arrive a Saint-Michel-de Maurienne (Savoy) before 26 May, but it is not absolutely impossible, as the date on which the letter was sent is not certain.

... Therefore the applicant must be accorded the benefit of the doubt'. [122]

§ 666. For the commencement of time limits only the official decision is taken into account. When a civil servant was informed of a decision which was to be taken with respect to him but which was formally notified to him only much later, he could still bring the action within three months after the formal notification. [123]

Often addressees of decisions ask for further clarification thereof. Correspondence on the meaning of a decision normally does not interrupt the running of the time limits nor cause them to begin at a later date [124], provided that the decision was really taken. If the content of the decision was gradually built up in the course of correspondence between its addressee and a Community authority, the time limits *'commence to run only from the moment the competent administrative authority adopts a definite attitude.'*[125]

Only in staff cases may discussions on a final decision influence the commencement of the time limits. As mentioned above (§ 327), civil servants may not bring an action directly to the Court. First they must submit their complaints to the appointing authority. When it is not fully clear whether the response of the appointing authority is a final decision or not, the civil servant may be faced with the choice of either considering the answer as a decision and challenging it before the Court, or of continuing the administrative procedure until a final decision is obtained. Thus in the *Müllers Case* the Court of Justice held:

120. *Jänsch Case* (5/76), 15 June 1976, consideration 9 [1976] ECR 1034. See also Oliver, (*op. cit.*, note 106), p. 8.
121. EEC Art. 173(3); ECSC Art. 33(3); Rules of Procedure of the Court, Art. 81.
122. *First Snupat Case* (32 and 33/58), 17 July 1959, [1959] ECR 136; 5 Jur. (1958-59) 318, 319; 5 Rec. (1958-59) 297.
123. *Macevicius Case* (31/76), 12 May 1977, considerations 11, 12, 13, [1977] ECR 890.
124. See e.g. *Assessment for Social Fund Case* (2/71), 6 July 1971, [1971] ECR 676, 677; [1972] CMLR 444; CCH para 8144.
125. *First Guillot Case* (53/72), 11 July 1974, consideration 26, [1974] ECR 805 [1975] 1 CMLR 178.

'The applicant then had the choice of either directly lodging an appeal within the period of three months laid down by the first paragraph of Article 91(2) of the Staff Regulations of Officials, or of preserving the right of appeal by submitting to the appointing authority within that period under Article 90 of the same Staff Regulations a complaint against the decision taken relating to him.' [126]

In several other cases the Court has confirmed that a letter to the Community authority concerned, which may be regarded as an administrative appeal under Article 90 of the Staff Regulations, suspends the time limits. [127]

A confirmation of a previous decision does not reopen a time limit for appeal against it, but a reconsideration of such a decision is a new decision and may, therefore, be separately appealed against even if it has not led to any change in the position of the applicant. [128]

(iii) Non contractual liability

§ 667. Time limits for non-contractual liability begin *upon the occurrence of the event giving rise to the liability.* [129] In the *Second Meroni Case* the alleged injury was caused by a fraud resulting from inadequate supervision by the High Authority, but the High Authority was still trying to recover the amount lost. The Court of Justice then held that the time limit had not yet begun. [130] From this case it has been concluded that the time limit does not commence when the act is committed, but when the payments involved have been finally assessed, and when, therefore, the injury is established. [131]

d. RUNNING OF TIME

§ 668. In the reckoning of any time limit the day on which the event takes place and from which the period is to run is excluded. [132] The time continues to run on Sundays, public holidays and vacations but if the end of the period falls on a Sunday or on an official holiday it is extended until the end of the first following working day. [133] A list of ten official holidays has been published in the Official Journal of the Communities. [134]

126. *Müllers Case* (79/70), 7 July 1971, consideration 14, [1971] ECR 697.
127. See e.g. *Lacroix Case* (30/68), 28 May 1970, consideration 5, [1970] ECR 309; *Mulders Case* (8/69), 10 Dec. 1969, consideration 6, [1969] ECR 566.
128. *Herpels Case* (54/77), 9 March 1978, consideration 14, [1978] ECR 596.
129. EEC Statute Art. 43.
130. *Second Meroni Case* (46 and 47/59), 14 Dec. 1962, [1962] ECR 420; 8 Jur. (1962) 840; 8 Rec. (1962) 803.
131. Opinion of Advocate-General Gand in the *Third Feram Case* (9 and 25/64), 2 June 1965, [1965] ECR 327, 328; 11 Jur. (1965) 414; 11 Rec. (1965) 423; [1965] CMLR 309; Waelbroeck in RCJB 1971, p. 556.
132. Rules of Procedure of the Court, Art. 80(1).
133. *Idem*, Art. 80(2).
134. OJ of 28 Dec. 1974 No. L 350, p. 27. The official holidays are: New Year's Day, Easter Monday, 1 May, Ascension Day, Whit Monday, 23 June or 24 June when 23 June falls on a Sunday, 15 August, 1 November, 25 December, 26 December.

During the vacations of the Court [135] documents can still be served on the Court. [136] The functions of the President continue to be exercised either by the President himself or by one of the Judges on his account. In a case of urgency the President may convene the Court during the vacations.

§ 669. The Statute of the Court of Justice provides that the period of limitation (of five years) for non-contractual liability: 'shall be interrupted if proceedings are instituted before the Court or if prior to such proceedings an application is made by the aggrieved party to the relevant institution of the Community. In the latter event the proceedings must be instituted within the period of two months provided for in Article 173; the provisions of the second paragraph of Article 175 shall apply where appropriate'. [137]

An interesting question has arisen on the application of the statute of limitations. Normally an aggrieved party will not immediately sue the Communities for damages for non-contractual liability, but will first request compensation from the Commission for injuries suffered, whereupon the Commission will either reply that indemnification will not be paid, in which case the aggrieved party will have to bring an action before the Court for the annulment of that negative decision (this action must be lodged within two months, EEC Article 173) or the Commission will not reply within two months, in which case the aggrieved party must bring an action before the Court against failure to act (for this action the time limit is also two months, EEC Article 175). If the aggrieved party has not brought his action against the decision or against the failure to act of the Commission within the proper time limits, may he then avail himself of the action for damages instead? This question arose in the *First Kampffmeyer Case* and the Court held that:

'The defendant itself admits, however, that the reference to Articles 173 and 175 can only apply to the possibility of interruption of the period of limitation of five years laid down in the first sentence of the said Article 43. It follows from the actual wording of the second and third sentences of that provision that it is not intended to shorten the period of limitation of five years, but that it is intended to protect those concerned by preventing certain periods from being taken into account in the calculation of the said period. Consequently the aim of the third sentence of Article 43 is merely to postpone the expiration of the period of five years when proceedings instituted or a prior application made within this period start time to run in respect of the periods provided for in Articles 173 or 175. As the event which gave rise to the present applications occurred on 1 October 1963, that is to say, less than five years from the lodging of the said applications, they are therefore admissible.' [138]

135. See above § 646.
136. Rules of Procedure of the Court, Art. 28.
137. EEC Statute, Art. 43.
138. *First Kampffmeyer Case* (5, 7, 13-24/66), 14 July 1967, [1967] ECR 200; 13 Jur. (1967) p. 325; 13 Rec. (1967) p. 337; CCH para 8055 (p. 7841).

The second paragraph of this holding was further clarified in the *Giordano Case* in which the Court held:

> 'It is provided on this point that the period of limitation shall be interrupted either by the application brought before the Court, or by a preliminary request addressed to the relevant institution, it being however understood that, in such latter case, interruption only occurs if the request is followed by an application within the time limits determined by reference to Articles 173 and 175, depending on the case in issue'. [139]

e. TERMINATION OF THE PERIOD

§ 670. Time limits end with the close of their last day, but they may be extended by whoever prescribed them. [140] Periods expressed in weeks, months or years end with the expiry of whichever day in their last week, month or year is the same day of the week or falls on the same date, as the day from which the period runs. If that day does not exist in the last month, the period ends with the expiry of that month. [141] One month from 31 January is, therefore, 28 (or 29) February.

§ 671. The only relevant date with regard to the termination of time limits in proceedings before the Court is that of the lodging of the document concerned at the Registry of the Court. [142]

Time limits are strict but no right will be prejudiced in consequence of the expiry of a time limit if the party concerned proves the existence of unforseeable circumstances or of *force majeure*. [143] In the *Simet-Feram Case*, Simet had a right to bring an action until 30 April 1965, Feram until 29 April 1965. They dispatched their applications for initiating proceedings from Italy on 21 April 1965 by registered mail, but these applications reached the Court only on 4 May. The Court noted, however, that the arrival of the application was registered in Luxembourg on 30 April and it accepted the extra delay in reaching the Court as *force majeure*. Therefore, the application was considered to have been lodged on 30 April which meant that Simet's action was admissible whilst that of Feram was overdue and could not be received by the Court. [144]

---

139. *Giordano Case* (11/72), 5 April 1973, consideration 6, [1973] ECR 425.
140. Rules of Procedure of the Court, Art. 82.
141. Regulation 1182/71 of the Council, OJ 1971 No. L 124, Art. 3 (2c). Though this regulation is applicable only to time limits in regulations of the Council and the Commission, the Court will probably apply it by analogy in the cases where no other provisions have been made.
142. Rules of Procedure of the Court, Art. 37(3).
143. EEC Statute Art. 42.
144. *Simet-Feram Case* (25 and 26/65), 2 March 1967, [1967] ECR 42, 43; 13 Jur. (1967) 52, 53; 13 Rec. (1967) 52, 53.

5. Interim measures [145]

§ 672. Actions brought before the Court of Justice have no suspensory effect. [146] A party may, however, apply to suspend the operation of any Community act, but only if that act is challenged before the Court of Justice and if the matter is urgent [147], and, in the wording of the Court, if otherwise *'irreversible damage'* would be caused. [148] These factors are mutually related. When suspension causes little damage, the Court requires less urgency than in a case where grave practical problems will arise as a result of the suspension. [149] It is also possible to request the suspension of one particular article of an act, even when the action is brought against the entire act. [150] The suspension of a Community act is not in all cases sufficient to preserve the *status quo*. In the *Miles Druce Case*, for example, it was feared that an action would be brought by third parties during the period in which the case was pending before the Court. The Court then ordered the Commission *'to take all necessary measures to ensure that no action is taken during this period'.* [151] Orders for positive action are rare, however, in comparison to the orders for the suspension of acts. Until 31 Dec. 1978 the Court had given 95 interim orders. [152]

§ 673. When the Commission has issued a decision declaring that an agreement between undertakings violates the competition rules in EEC Article 85 and the parties dispute the validity of that decision, it may be important not to dissolve the agreement before the Court has decided on the validity of the Commission's decision. On the other hand, prolonging the agreement could finally lead to an increase in the fine imposed on the parties. *Fruit- en Groentenimporthandel*, therefore, asked for a suspension of the operation of the Commission's decision, and therewith requested that the prohibited agreement should be regarded as provisionally valid until judgment should be given in the main action. The Court, however, held:

'It is outside the jurisdiction of the Court, within the context of an interim procedure, to substitute its own appraisal for that of the Commission and

145. See Christine Gray, *Interim Measures of Protection in the European Court*, 4 ELRev. (1979), pp. 80-102.
146. EEC Art. 185; ECSC Art. 39.
147. EEC Statute Art. 36; Rules of Procedure of the Court, Art. 83.
148. *Fruit en Groentenimporthandel Case* (71/74 R and RR), 15 Oct. 1974, consideration 6, [1974] ECR 1034; [1975] 1 CMLR 649 (No. 9); *Johnson & Firth Brown Case* (3/75 R), 16 Jan. 1975, consideration 26 [1975] ECR 6; [1975] 1 CMLR 644.
149. See e.g., *Exportation des Sucres Order* (88/76R), 19 Oct. 1976, [1976] ECR 1588 or *NTN Toyo Order* (113/77R), 14 Oct. 1977, considerations 5-8, [1977] ECR 1725; *Simmenthal Order* (92/78R), 22 May 1978, consideration 9, [1978] ECR 1136.
150. This happened e.g. in the *Kali-Chemie Orders* (20/74 R), 3 April 1974, [1974] ECR 340 and (20/74 RII), 8 July 1974, [1974] ECR 789; [1975] 2 CMLR 154 and in the *United Brands Order* (27/76 R), 5 April 1976, [1976] ECR 429; [1976] 2 CMLR 151.
151. *Miles Druce Case*, second order (160, 161, 170/73 RII) 16 March 1974, [1974] ECR 284; [1974] 2 CMLR D 24.
152. J.P. Warner, *The evolution of the work of the Court of Justice*, Report to the Judicial and Academic Conference, Luxemburg 28 Sept. 1976, p. 17.

render provisionally valid an agreement which has been annulled on the basis of Article 85 (1) with the consequences prescribed by Article 85 (2).

In compliance with Article 185 of the EEC Treaty, the Court can, at most, grant a suspension of the operation of the contested Decision insofar as that suspension is established to be absolutely necessary, having regard to the urgency of the situation and to the irreversible nature of the damage which might ensue from immediate operation of the Decision before the Court's judgment in the main action, with regard to which such suspension is in any case without prejudice.

The Commission, moreover, has declared that 'it is not its practice to force the parties concerned formally to annul their agreements or to make them conform to the Treaty when an interim application is pending against a decision declaring an agreement incompatible with Article 85'.

It is therefore sufficient to suspend the operation of the Commission's Decision until the date of the Court's judgment, subject however to the non-application, during that period, of the clauses under which penalties may be imposed on the parties to the agreement. [153]

§ 674. The right to apply for the suspension of the operation of a contested act is granted to an applicant so that he may protect his own interests. It cannot be invoked in order to protect third parties from suffering any harm. [154] Nor is it possible for individuals to apply for the suspension of EEC regulations to protect the status quo. [155] The Court will not take interim measures when the Commission is able and willing to take the necessary measures. [156]

§ 674a. Interim measures may be prescribed in any case before the Court. They can be prescribed against Member States as well as against Community institutions. In May 1977 the Court ordered the United Kingdom as an interim measure to cease to apply an aid measure brought before the Court under EEC Article 93 by the Commission, which considered it to be incompatible with the common market. [157] In July 1977 Ireland was ordered to suspend the application of national rules on fisheries which were challenged by the Commission under EEC Article 169. [158] Without any specific reasoning the Court accepted its own competence to forbid, though temporarily, the application of national laws. [159]

---

153. *Fruit- en Groentenimporthandel Case*, Order (71/74) Rand RR) 15 Oct. 1974, considerations 5-8, [1974] ECR 1034; [1975] 1 CMLR 648.
154. *Second Küster Case*, order (22/75 R) 25 Feb. 1975, consideration 8, [1975] ECR 278.
155. *Köneke Case* order (44/75 R), 28 May 1975, consideration 2, [1975] ECR 640.
156. *NCC Case*, order (109/75 R), 22 Oct. 1975, considerations 7, 8, [1975] ECR 1201, 1202; [1975] 2 CMLR 469.
157. *Pig Producers Order* (31, 53/77 R), 21 May 1977, [1977] ECR 925.
158. *Second Sea Fisheries Order* (61/77 R), 13 July 1977, [1977] ECR 1414, 1415. For its execution see [1978] ECR 442.
159. See C.W.A. Timmermans in 26 SEW (1978), p. 236.

§ 675.   The application for interim measures must be in the same form as the written application initiating normal proceedings, but it must be in a separate document. Interim measures requested in the action itself are declared inadmissible. [160]   The Court of Justice is not formalistic about the formulation of the request for interim measures. When in the *Miles Druce Case* the applicant had applied for 'ex parte preliminary proceedings' according to the British procedure, the Court regarded this as an application for interim measures in the sense of the ECSC Treaty and Statute. [161]

§ 676.   The decision on interim measures is usually taken by the President of the Court, but he may refer the application to the Court itself which, in that case, postpones all other work in order to come to a decision as quickly as possible. [162]   Only when the application is referred to the Court, will the Advocate-General submit an opinion. [163]   The decision, either by the President or by the Court, is reasoned and not subject to appeal. [164]   It can be varied or cancelled at any time. [165]   In its decision on interim measures the Court of Justice is not restricted to either suspending or not suspending the Community act concerned. It may also subject the operation of the act to particular conditions, for instance, it may prescribe that voting rights attached to the shares of a specific company may not be exercised [166]   or that no further action may be taken. [167]

Interim measures can be invoked quickly. The President may grant the application even before the observations of the opposite party have been submitted. [168]   Interveners may put in their pleadings by telex. [169]   Usually an order of the President is obtained within the space of one week. [170]   In practice the President of the Chamber usually decides on interim measures in staff cases.

---

160.   *Merlini Case* (108/63), 21 Jan. 1965, [1965] ECR 9; 11 Jur. (1965) 12; 11 Rec. (1965) 12; *Customs Duties on Silk Case* (32/64), 17 June 1965, [1965] ECR 372; 11 Jur. (1965) 652; 11 Rec. (1965) 483.
161.   *Miles Druce Case*, first order (160, 161/73 R) 11 Oct. 1973, consideration 2, [1973] ECR 1053; [1974] 1 CMLR 228.
162.   Rules of Procedure of the Court, Art. 85.
163.   Mario Berri, *The Special Procedures before the Court of Justice of the European Communities*, 8 CMLRev. (1971), p. 21.
164.   Rules of Procedure of the Court, Art. 85.
165.   *Idem*, Art. 87.
166.   *Johnson and Firth Brown Case*, order, (3/75 R), 16 Jan. 1975, (1975) ECR 7; [1975] 1 CMLR 645.
167.   See *Miles Druce Case* quoted above § 672.
168.   Rules of Procedure of the Court, Art. 84(2).
169.   John A. Usher in 1 ELRev. (1976), p. 110.
170.   See e.g. *Exchange Rate Intervention Case* (50/69 R), 5 Oct. 1969 (a Sunday), [1969] ECR 450, 451; *Commercial Solvents Case* (6, 7/73 R), 14 March 1973, considerations 4, 5, [1973] ECR 358; *Johnson & Firth Brown Case* (3/75 R), 16 Jan. 1975, [1975] ECR 1; *Küster Case* (22/75 R), 25 Feb. 1975, [1975] ECR 277.

B. WRITTEN PROCEEDINGS

1. Application

a. DIRECT ACTIONS

§ 677. The case is actually brought before the Court by means of a written application addressed to the Registrar who gives the case a serial number, by which it is subsequently officially referred to. [171] Apart from the name and address of the applicant, the name of the other party and the subject matter of the dispute, the application must contain the grounds on which it is based. [172] These grounds must be clearly indicated, but not necessarily extensively. In the *First Fives Lille Cail Case* the Court of Justice held:

> 'With regard to the wording of the applications, although it must be accepted that the statement of the grounds for instituting the proceedings need not conform with the phraseology or the list in the first paragraph of Article 33, it may be sufficient for the grounds for instituting the proceedings to be expressed in terms of their substance rather than of their legal classification provided, however, that it is sufficiently clear from the application which of the grounds referred to in the Treaty is being invoked. A mere abstract statement of the grounds in the application does not alone satisfy the requirements of the Protocol on the Statute of the Court of Justice or the Rules of Procedure. The words 'brief statement of the grounds' used in those instruments mean that the application must specify the nature of the grounds on which the application is based. The ground of complaint relied upon must therefore be established in relation to the facts which have been set out.'[173]

The grounds of illegality must be enumerated separately for each case. A general reference to what has been stated in another action is not sufficient. [174]

§ 678. In principle an application cannot be changed, once it has been brought before the Court. [175] It is conceivable that fresh grounds of illegality may present themselves to the lawyer of a party only at a later stage of the

---

171. Instructions to the Registrar; adopted by the Court of Justice, 4 Dec. 1974, Art. 12, OJ 1974 No. L 350, p. 36.
172. EEC Statute Art. 19; Rules of Procedure of the Court, Art. 38. See also Werner Günther, *Die Präklusion neuer Angriffs-, Verteidigungs- und Beweismittel im Verfahren vor dem Gerichtshof der Europäischen Gemeinschaften*, Kölner Schriften zum Europarecht No. 12, Carl Heymanns Verlag 1970.
173. *First Fives Lille Cail Case* (19, 21/60; 2, 3/61), 15 Dec. 1961, [1961] ECR 295; 7 Jur. (1961) 622; 7 Rec. (1961) 588, 589.
174. *Beeringen Case* (9/55), 29 Nov. 1956, [1954-56] ECR 325; 2 Jur. (1955-56) 376; 2 Rec. (1955-56) 352.
175. On the changing of the application, see Detlev Möller, *Die Klageänderung im Verfahren vor dem Gerichtshof der Europäischen Gemeinschaften*, Thesis Bonn, 1976, 229 pages.

proceedings. In practice, there may be two ways to raise such additional arguments: (1) often further grounds can be adduced from an evaluation of the grounds raised in the initial document, in particular, when the initial grounds have not been too strictly defined; (2) when deciding on the validity of a Community act, the Court of Justice may examine of its own motion grounds which have not been raised; though the arguments brought at too late a stage of the proceedings should not be considered as being officially raised, they may help the Court in finding a ground for annulment of its own motion.

§ 679. If the necessary documents and certificates are not produced with the application, the Registrar will prescribe a reasonable period for producing them.[176] Usually the missing documents are not sufficiently relevant to delay the case. Documents such as a certificate that a lawyer is entitled to practise, or the statutes of an undertaking, can be sent in even after the application is served on the defendant. When important documents are missing the case will be held in abeyance. The Registrar will serve the application on the defendant when the considers it to be in order. Usually this means that he will forward the application by registered mail to the President of the Commission.

In the *CNTA Case* the Commission contended that the application was insufficiently complete and should therefore be declared inadmissible. The Court of Justice refused to do so holding:

'The alleged defects have not been such as to prevent the Commission from effectively defending its interests or to hinder the Court in the exercise of its judicial review, and the applicant has moreover provided all relevant information during the proceedings'.[177]

b. PRELIMINARY RULINGS[178]

§ 680. Because of the special nature of requests for preliminary rulings the provisions for their procedure[179] differ in some respects from the other procedural rules. It was noted above (§ 559) that the Court of Justice is informal in the way it receives requests from national courts. They can be sent in any form to the Registrar of the Court of Justice. He then informs the parties to the case, the Member States, the Commission and, if its acts are involved, the Council. All the parties have two months for submitting their remarks irrespective of whether they can demonstrate any interest in the Case. When the UK was not yet a party to the Convention on Jurisdiction and the Enforcement of Civil and Commercial Judgments, it was none the less per-

---

176. EEC Statute Art. 19; Rules of Procedure of the Court, Art. 38.
177. *CNTA Case* (74/74), 14 May 1975, consideration 4, [1975] ECR 544; [1977] 1 CMLR 187; CCH para 8305.
178. See also Jacobs and Durand (*op. cit.*, note 82).
179. EEC Statute Art. 20; Rules of Procedure of the Court, Artt. 103, 104.

mitted to submit its remarks in a case under that Convention. [180] Sometimes the Court expressly requests Member States to comment on a specific issue.[181] The Member States are, however, under no obligation to do so and they often abstain from issuing statements. The Commission, as a matter of policy, always sends in its remarks; the parties usually do so. The parties, the Member States, the Commission and the Council, if it is involved, will also be invited to make oral remarks, even if they have not submitted written ones. Unlike in the case of direct actions the parties are not required to select an address for service in Luxembourg. [182]

In contrast to direct actions there is no opportunity for defence, reply or rejoinder (see below § 688). This means that all arguments must be brought at one time. Only in the oral procedure may there be an opportunity to reply to the arguments of the other party (see below § 698).

Because of the short period of time and the limited opportunity to amplify the original statement, the British Government has suggested that in an early stage of the proceedings the Court of Justice should identify the important issues which it intends to cover in preliminary rulings. [183] It made this same suggestion in the *Pigs Marketing Case*. The Court of Justice then considered it impossible to give prior indications at the request of one of the parties '*without incurring the risk of seeming to commit itself to a definite position in advance of a final judgement and, what is more, without compromising the other parties' opportunities to put their case*'. [184]

2. The joining of cases

§ 681. As soon as a case has been brought, or at any time thereafter, the Court may, after hearing the Advocate-General, order that a number of related cases shall be dealt with jointly. [185] For the joining of direct actions the parties are to be heard in advance; in the case of preliminary rulings there are no parties before the Court and the Court may therefore join cases without hearing anyone but the Advocate-General.

Joint cases must be of the same nature. It is impossible to join an action of the Commission against a Member State for breach of a Treaty obligation to a request for a preliminary ruling. None the less in practice the Court of Justice came close to doing so in the *Sea Fisheries Case* against Ireland and the *Schonenberg Case* which concerned the same Irish regulations. The Court considered that it could refer from the one case to the other, because the parties in the first case were also involved in the second. [186]

180. *Tessili Case* (12/76), 6 Oct. 1976, considerations 5-8, [1976] ECR 1483, 1484; [1977] 1 CMLR 50, 51; CCH para 8375.
181. See e.g., *First De Bloos Case* (14/76), 6 Oct. 1976, [1976] ECR 1501; [1977] 1 CMLR 64; CCH para 8376.
182. Berri (*op. cit.*, note 163), p. 19.
183. See Editorial Comments, 16 CMLRev. (1979), pp. 3-6.
184. *Pigs Marketing Case* (83/78), 29 Nov. 1978, consideration 31, [1979] 1 CMLR 199.
185. Rules of Procedure of the Court, Art. 43.
186. *Sea Fisheries Case* (861/77), 16 Feb. 1978, considerations 21, 22, 56, [1978] ECR

Joining cases facilitates the work of the Court and often that of the parties as well. A large amount of needless repetition can be saved; often the lawyers of the parties can divide up tasks. But the parties do not always like their cases being joined. In the *Sugar Cartel Case*, for example, *Suiker Unie* submitted that its position differed from that of the other applicants (usually there will be at least some differences between the applicants or defendants in joint cases) and that it was inimical to its interests that different undertakings, accused of different acts, should be tried together. This would lead to the cases influencing each other. The flavour of the one case would prejudice the other. After the oral pleadings, for example, which lasted from 9 a.m. to 7 p.m., it must have been very difficult for the Judges to remember who said what.[187] Joint cases bear the serial numbers of each of the original applications and are usually referred to by the name of the first applicant.

3. Intervention [188]

a. IN DIRECT ACTIONS

§ 682. As soon as a case has been brought, even at the stage of an application for interim measures,[189] third parties may intervene when they have an interest in the result of the case. This happens a number of times a year. Up to 31 December 1978, States have intervened on 37, the Commission on 3 and individuals on 74 occasions. Under the EEC and Euratom Treaties individuals may not intervene in cases between Member States, between institutions or between Member States and institutions [190] ; under the ECSC Treaty the right to intervene is unlimited [191], but private parties intervening in cases between Member States and/or institutions cannot submit arguments which they would not be entitled to raise as a party before the Court. The *First Publication of Transport Tariffs Case* concerned the question whether the Netherlands had violated its obligations under the ECSC Treaty. The Court of Justice admitted the intervention of five private parties, but held:

'Although undertakings having an interest can be allowed to intervene in a dispute arising under Article 88, such intervention can, however, be for the sole purpose of obtaining an interpretation of the Treaty, to the exclusion of any consideration of determination of the time-limit which the High

---

441, 442, 447; [1978] 2 CMLR 510, 514; CCH para 8473; *Schonenberg Case* (88/77), 16 Feb. 1978, consideration 13, [1978] ECR 491; [1978] 2 CMLR 525; CCH para 8474.
187.   Lecture by the lawyer who had represented *Suiker Unie*, Mr. F. Salomonson, to the Amsterdam Student Society 'Europhilè', 29 Jan. 1976.
188.   See Berri (*op. cit.*, note 163) pp. 5-15: George Vandersanden, *Le recours en intervention devant la Cour de Justice des Communautés Européenes*, 5 RTDE (1969) pp. 1-27.
189.   See e.g. NTN Toyo Order (113/77 R-Int.), 14 Oct. 1977, considerations 1, 2, [1977] ECR 1724.
190.   EEC Statute Art. 37, Euratom Statute Art. 38.
191.   ECSC Statute Art. 34.

Authority can set that State for the fulfilment of its obligations or the detailed rules for the application of any restrictive decision by the Authority against that State since, in these various cases, the very nature of these acts, which take place at the level of the relationship between States, public authorities and the High Authority as the Community agency, preludes the intervention of private persons; and argument on these issues must, therefore, be conducted exclusively between the main parties.' [192]

§ 683. It may be of interest to one of the parties to a case that a particular person should intervene. No-one can be compelled to do so, however, either by the parties or by the Court. [193]

In the *Lasalle Case* the Court held that an intervener must have legal personality *'or those elements which constitute its basis'*, elements including in particular *'autonomy and responsibility'*. [194] Associations of interested persons especially may want to intervene even though they lack legal personality. In the *Générale Sucrière Case* the Court of Justice admitted the intervention of such an association when it held with reference to Article 37 of the EEC Statute of the Court:

'Pursuant to this provision, bodies not having legal personality may be permitted to intervene if they display the characteristics which are at the foundation of such personality, in particular, the ability, however circumscribed, to undertake autonomous action and to assume liability.' [195]

The intervener must demonstrate an interest in the case itself. It is not sufficient that he is in a similar position to one of the parties in such a way that the outcome of the case will indirectly influence his position. [196]

§ 684. The application to intervene must be made before the opening of the oral procedure [197] and may be filed in any of the official languages. [198] It must contain, *inter alia* the reasons for the intervener's interest and the submissions supporting or opposing the submissions of a party to the original

---

192. *Second Publication of Transport Tariffs Case* (25/59), 15 July 1960, [1960] ECR 389; 6 Jur. (1960) 815, 816; 6 Rec. (1960) 791, 792.
193. *Wonnerth Case* (12/69), 10 Dec. 1969, [1969] ECR 577, Berri regrets this (*op. cit.*, note 163), p. 8. On compulsory intervention see also G. Vandersanden, *Le recours en tierce opposition devant la Cour de justice des Communautés européennes*, 5 CDE (1969), pp. 670, 671.
194. *Lasalle Case* (15/63), Staff Committee intervening, Court Order 14 Nov. 1963, 10 Nov. 1963, [1964] ECR 51, 52; 10 Jur. (1964) 106, 107; 10 Rec. (1964) 100, 101; [1964] CMLR 267, 268.
195. *Générale Sucrière Order* (41, 43-48, 50, 111, 113, 114/73), 11 Dec. 1973, consideration 3, [1973] ECR 1468; [1974] 1 CMLR 216 (no. 2).
196. *Second Lemmerzwerke Case* (111/63), Klöckner intervening, Court order 25 Nov. 1964, [1965] ECR 716-718; 11 Jur. (1965) 983, 984; 11 Rec. (1965) 883-884; L.J. Brinkhorst and H.G. Schermers, *Judical Remedies in the European Communities*, second edition Kluwer 1977, pp. 324-325.
197. Rules of Procedure of the Court, Art. 93(1).
198. *Second Limburg Coalmines Case* (30/59), Court Order 18 Feb. 1960, [1961] ECR 48; 7 Jur. (1960) 95; 7 Rec. (1960) 93.

case. [199] Before deciding on the intervention, the Court hears the parties and
the Advocate-General. [200] As interventions are usually made shortly before
the opening of the oral procedure, they cause considerable delay in the proceedings. If the Court allows the intervention, the intervener must accept the
case as he finds it at the time of his intervention. [201] From then on, he will
participate in the proceedings and he will have to use the language of the case.
He must support the position of one of the parties and may not submit fresh
grounds of fact or of law which would modify the subject matter of the
original action, but, when supporting the defendant, he may raise objections
against the admissibility of the case even if the defendant has not done so. [202]
The intervener may use any arguments, including those which the supported
party rejects. [203] An intervener supporting the defendant may even file his
intervention before the defendant has lodged his defence. [204] An intervention
may be withdrawn during the further proceedings. [205]

b. IN PRELIMINARY RULINGS

§ 685. Parties who intervened in the case before the national court have the
same rights before the Court of Justice as the original parties: both in the
written and oral procedures they are invited to state how in their opinion the
questions should be answered, and why. [206] Parties who have not intervened
before the national court cannot do so before the Court of Justice; they are
not entitled to submit any documents to the Court of Justice. [207] This may
be disadvantage when a ruling is requested on the validity of a Community
act. In such a case others may have particular interests which they cannot
express before the Court. [208] As in the case of direct actions, the Court
cannot oblige parties to take part in the proceedings. [209]

4. Preliminary objections

§ 686. Individuals may not bring an action against regulations and only rare-

199. Rules of Procedure of the Court, Art. 93(2).
200. *Idem*, Art. 90(3).
201. *Idem*, Art. 90(5).
202. *Second Snupat Case* (42, 49/59), 22 March 1961, [1961] ECR 75; 7 Jur. (1961)
145; 7 Rec. (1961) 145.
203. *Second Limburg Coal Mines Case* (30/59), 23 Feb. 1961, [1961] ECR 17; 7 Jur.
(1961) 38; 7 Rec. (1961) 37, 38.
204. Berri (*op. cit.*, note 163), p. 11.
205. See e.g. *Papiers Peints Case* (73/74), 26 Nov. 1975, [1975] ECR 1496; [1976]
1 CMLR 595.
206. The intervening party made oral remarks in the *Reyners Case* (2/74), 21 June 1974,
[1974] ECR 646; [1974] 2 CMLR 309; CCH para 8256.
207. *Costa-Enel Case* (6/64), Order of 3 June 1964, [1964] ECR 614, 615; 10 Jur. (1964)
1257, 1258; 10 Rec. (1964) 1197, 1198; CCH para 8023.
208. See B.H. Ter Kuile, *Procedures over ongeldige gemeenschapsnormen*, 25 SEW
(1977), p. 623. See also above § 619a.
209. *De Cicco Case* (19/68), 19 Dec. 1968, [1968] ECR 479; 14 Jur. (1968) 666; 14 Rec.
(1968) 698, 699; [1969] CMLR 76.

ly against decisions addressed to others (see above § 314-324). If they do so nonetheless, is the Commission then obliged to reply to all their arguments? The rules provide that within one month after being served with the application the defendant must lodge his defence in which the points of fact and of law, on which he relies, must be enumerated. He cannot normally add new points later. This would mean that the Commission would be compelled to reply to all arguments made in the application when there is only the slightest chance that the case will be admitted. In order to save such extra work, the Commission may, in such cases, raise a preliminary objection on the admissibility of the action. In a separate document the Commission presents the grounds on which it considers the application to be inadmissible. The applicant is presented with the opportunity of replying in writing. Usually, this is followed by oral proceedings, but the Court may decide fortwith whether or not to decide separately on the admissibility of the case. The Court may then decide on the objection or reserve its decision for the final judgement. Rejection of the objection is extremely rare; in practice the Court either accepts it or reserves its decision for its final judgement. If the objection is accepted the Commission need not argue the substance of the case itself; if the objection is not accepted, the President will set a new time limit for the subsequent proceedings [210] in which all aspects of the case will be discussed.

§ 687. Apart from the question of admissibility, there may be other preliminary objections. Any question which may impede the normal course of the proceedings without touching upon the main issue may be raised as a preliminary objection. [211]

Apart from the parties, the Court itself may raise preliminary objections of its own motion when they constitute an absolute bar to proceeding with a case. [212]

5. Defence, reply and rejoinder

§ 688. Within one month after service of the application the defendant must lodge his defence, unless the President grants him an extension of this time limit. This is often done. [213] If the defendant, after having been duly summoned, fails to file written submissions in defence, judgment shall be given against him by default. An objection against that judgment may be lodged within one month of its being notified to the defendant. [214]

In his defence the defendant must state, apart from his name and address, the points of fact and of law relied on, the form of any order sought by him and the nature of any evidence submitted by him.

---

210. Rules of Procedure of the Court, Art. 91.
211. Berri (*op. cit.*, note 163), p. 23.
212. Rules of Procedure of the Court, Art. 92.
213. Rules of Procedure of the Court, Art. 40.
214. EEC Statute Art. 38.

The application originating the proceedings and the defence may be supplemented by a reply from the applicant and by a rejoinder from the defendant. The President of the Court fixes the time limits for these pleadings. [215]

6. End of written proceedings

§ 689. After the rejoinder, or when no reply has been lodged within the time limits fixed, or when the right to lodge a reply or rejoinder has been waived, the President fixes a date on which the Judge Rapporteur is to present his preliminary report as to whether a preparatory inquiry is necessary. The Court then decides, after hearing the Advocate-General, whether to order a preparatory inquiry or to open the oral procedure without an inquiry.[216] Usually no preparatory inquiry is ordered.

C. PREPARATORY INQUIRIES

1. General

§ 690. In order to collect the necessary facts and proof the Court may undertake a preparatory inquiry, or may assign the inquiry to the Chamber concerned with the case. Both the Court and the Chamber may conduct the inquiry by themselves or assign it to the Judge Rapporteur. [217]

Measures of inquiry that may be adopted are: (a) the personal appearance of the parties, (b) experts' reports, and (c) an inspection of the place or thing in question. [218]

Requests for information and for production of documents are frequently made, though usually as part of the preparation of the oral procedure rather than as part of the preparatory inquiries. The other forms of inquiries are rarely resorted to by the full Court. In staff cases before the Chambers other forms of inquiries occur more often but even then not very frequently. In those cases the inquiries are often held on the same day as the oral submissions in order to save the lawyers a second trip to Luxembourg.

The Court may request further information in writing before the oral submissions, or may ask the parties to adjoin them to these submissions.

§ 691. Witnesses and experts may be summoned. If they fail to appear witnesses may be fined[219], but against unwilling experts no sanctions have been provided.

As with most continental courts the witnesses are the Court's witnesses. Though the representatives of the parties may question them, most questions

---

215. Rules of Procedure of the Court, Artt. 41, 42.
216. *Idem*, Art. 44.
217. *Idem*, Artt. 44(2), 45(3).
218. *Idem*, Art. 45(2).
219. *Idem*, Art. 48(2).

are asked by the Chamber which performs the preparatory inquiry, or by its president. In practice, witnesses are heard on the day set for the oral procedure or on the preceding day, so that the parties can assist without extra travelling. [220]

2. Proof [221]

§ 692. The purpose of an inquiry is to determine the facts of the case. In principle, the parties must provide the necessary proof for their submissions, but the Court may order an investigation also of its own accord. Even when a party does not appear in Court a preparatory inquiry may be ordered, in order to verify the other party's submissions. [222] In a direct action by a private party against the Commission the rule that each party must prove its own submissions may present a serious handicap for the private party who cannot draw on the same enormous administrative machinery as the Commission. To compensate for this inequality the Court of Justice has tended to shift the burden of proof a little towards the Commission. It did so in one of its early staff cases where it found that the exceptionally small number of translations required from an official during her probationary period constituted a strong presumption in support of the official's contention that the probationary period had not been properly carried out. The Court then continued: '*Under these circumstances, it is for the defendants* (i.e. the High Authority) *to rebut this presumption*'. [223]

§ 693. It was mentioned above (§ 444) that in administrative law there is a presumption of validity: Community acts are presumed to be valid. The plaintiff in an action for annulment must therefore plead one or more of the required grounds of illegality (see § 254-297). There is no assumption however, of the *legality* of Community acts. [224] This means that there is no presumption that the act has been lawfully made, to such an extent that the plaintiff would be obliged to *prove* the illegality. When the validity of an act is regularly challenged, the Court of Justice will normally oblige the Community authorities to prove that the act has been lawfully made. [225] Thus, the Community will have to prove that, for example, the European Parliament has been consulted in cases where such consultation is prescribed and doubt has been raised on the question whether it has taken place.

§ 694. When the Commission imposes a penalty it must be able to prove that a violation has been committed. In doing so it may use any means of proof

220. Usher (*op. cit.*, note 169), p. 112.
221. See Achim André, *Beweisführung und Beweislast im Verfahren vor dem Europäischen Gerichtshof*, 6 Kölner Schriften zum Europarecht, Karl Heymanns Verlag 1966.
222. Rules of Procedure of the Court, Art. 94(2).
223. *Mirossevich Case* (10/55), 12 Dec. 1956, [1954-56] ECR 343; 2 Jur. (1955-56) 413; 2 Rec. (1955-56) 389.
224. André (*op. cit.*, note 221), p. 185 ff.
225. André (*op. cit.*, note 221), p. 237.

including *'correspondence exchanged between third parties, provided that the content thereof is credible'*. [226] This proof must be persuasive, however. Whenever it is possible that objectionable conduct or situations may have been caused by other circumstances than by a violation of Community law, the decision of the Commission imposing a penalty for the creation of that situation will be annulled. [227]

D. ORAL PROCEDURE

1. Report of the Judge Rapporteur

§ 695. According to the Statutes of the Court the oral procedure commences with the reading of the report presented by the Judge Rapporteur. [228] The report gives a survey of the facts and of the submissions of the parties. As the final decision of the Court is largely based on this report, it is of importance to the parties that their submissions are correctly presented. If not, they may suggest the necessary amendments during the further oral procedure. The report of the Judge Rapporteur may be in a language other than that of the case. [229] This would make it even more difficult to make the necessary corrections after only having heard the report read.

In practice, the report is not read, but presented to the parties before the oral submissions. This can be of advantage to the parties, provided they have sufficient time to carefully read the report. Sometimes this is not the case. [230]

2. Oral submissions

§ 696. The most important characteristic of the oral procedure is its multilingual nature. Whereas the written pleadings can be carefully translated by the translation department of the Court, oral proceedings are simultaneously translated by the interpreters of the Court. It is obviously impossible to translate a carefully balanced and argued oral statement simultaneously into other languages without substantially altering the meaning of the statement and thereby reducing the legal force of the arguments. The oral proceedings before the Court of Justice must therefore play a much less significant role than in the monolingual hearings in national courts. Lawyers prefer to advance their arguments in the written part of the proceedings. Furthermore, listening to long translations is even more difficult than listening to long speeches. The oral pleadings should, therefore, be short. For internal use all pleadings are recorded on tape.

226. See *Sugar Cartel Case* (40-48, 50, 54-56, 111, 113 and 114/73), 16 Nov. 1975, consideration 164, [1975] ECR 1940; [1976] 1 CMLR 424.
227. *Idem* considerations 210, 304, 354, 363, 418, 556.
228. EEC Statute, Art. 18.
229. Rules of Procedure of the Court, Art. 29(5).
230. B.H. ter Kuile, *'Enige Opmerkingen over 'Europees Procesrecht'*, Europese Monografieën No. 19, p. 121.

§ 697.   During the hearing the Judges and the Advocate-General may put questions to the agents, advisers or lawyers of the parties. [231]   They sometimes do so, perhaps even more so than in some Continental courts, but to a lesser extent than in British and Irish courts. The Court sometimes asks the agents, advisers or lawyers in advance to pay particular attention to specific questions in the oral submissions.

At the end of the oral procedure, some time after the oral submissions, the Advocate-General delivers his opinion. [232]   The method in which he does so may vary. Some Advocates-General send their opinions to the members of the Court a week in advance, others distribute them shortly before the session in which they will be read. Sometimes, the opinions of the Advocate-General is delivered at the end of the oral submissions, whilst the lawyers of the parties are still present. [233]   The reading of the opinion of the Advocate-General closes the oral part of the proceedings. Thereupon, no changes or additions to the pleadings are permitted.

Oral proceedings may be reopened if new facts are discovered which were not known at the time of the oral procedure. [234]

3.   Observations for preliminary rulings

§ 698.   The parties to the case, the Member States, the Commission and, if it is involved, the Council, can make oral observations before the Court of Justice makes its decision on preliminary rulings, even if they have not used the opportunity for submitting observations in writing (see above § 680). Again, the oral remarks are less noteworthy than the written ones; they can provide, however, a useful opportunity to reply to the remarks of other parties, since there is no opportunity to do so in writing.

In the *Fifth Rewe Case* the applicant in the main action sought the re-opening of the oral procedure on the ground that the replies given by the Government of the Federal Republic of Germany and the Commission to a question raised in another case might influence the Court's decision. The Court of Justice did not flatly declare the request inadmissible on the ground that the parties in the main action lacked the power to request the re-opening of a procedure concerning a preliminary ruling. It held that the replies were not decisive for the *Fifth Rewe Case*. [235]

---

231.   Rules of Procedure of the Court, Art. 57.
232.   *Idem*, Art. 59.
233.   E.G. in the *Sukkerfabrikken Nykøbing Case* (151/78), 16 Jan. 1979.
234.   See *Fourth Balkan Case* (26/77), 8 Nov. 1977, consideration 19, [1977] ECR 2045; CCH para 8452.
235.   *Fifth Rewe-Case* (45/75), 17 Feb. 1976, considerations 28, 29, [1976] ECR 200; [1976] 2 CMLR 26, 27; CCH para 8343.

E. DECISION

1. Character

§ 699. The decisions of the Court of Justice take the form of either judgments or orders. The judgments constitute the final decisions of the cases
both in direct actions and in preliminary rulings. Orders either come before
the final judgement in the case such as orders for interim measures and orders
admitting interventions, or they follow the judgment such as orders concerning its execution. Orders require less reasoning than judgments.

The Rules of Procedure of the Court contain one article enumerating what
factors the judgment must contain: the date, the names of the parties, the
Judges, the Advocate-General and the Registrar, the names of the agents and
lawyers of each party, the submissions of the parties, a statement that the
Advocate-General has been heard, a summary of the facts, the grounds of the
decision, and a decision as to the costs. [236]

2. Deliberation and voting

§ 700. If there is no reason for additional inquiries to be conducted or for
reopening the oral procedure, the Court or the Chamber comes to a decision
in the *'Deliberation Room'*. Though the Court has a special room for this
purpose, this expression does not so much distinguish the room used but
designates that the Judges are meeting in council to decide the case. The
deliberations are secret; only the Judges who were present at the oral proceedings may participate. The Advocates-General do not take part in the deliberations on cases. Only when the deliberation concerns questions of the Court's
administration will they participate and be accorded the right to vote. [237]

If no consensus is reached, votes are cast in the reverse order to the order of
precedence of the Judges and the decision is taken by majority vote. [238]
Voting in the reverse order to the order of seniority is an old judicial custom
in European courts and is designed to prevent the votes of the older and more
experienced judges from influencing their younger colleagues.

3. Dissenting opinions [239]

§ 701. In the International Court of Justice in the Hague and in many national judicial systems the dissenting judges make their views known by means
of *dissenting opinions*, and judges who agree with the court decision as to its

236. Rules of Procedure of the Court, Art. 63.
237. *Idem*, Art. 27.
238. *Idem*, Art. 27(5).
239. Kurt H. Nadelmann, *Due Process of Law before the European Court of Human
Rights: the Secret of Deliberation*, 66 AJIL (1972) pp. 509-525; *De dissenting opinion in
de rechtspraak*, Reports to the Netherlands Lawyers Association, NJV, by H. Drion and
O. de Savornin Lohmann, 1973.

final conclusions but who come to that conclusion by way of different reasoning can publish their *concurring opinions*. There are several arguments which can be advanced for such publicity.

(1) More arguments are brought out into the open: in the first place the arguments pleading for a different decision are voiced together with arguments which are intended to refute these arguments. This may lead to a more detailed reasoning of the final decision itself. Publicity may encourage the Judges to greater efforts to formulate judgments of a high quality. If no dissenting opinions are published arguments on which agreement cannot be reached may simply be left out of the final judgement.

(2) The individual answerability of each Judge will be enhanced. On the one hand this means that it will be more difficult for a junior Judge to follow the opinion held by the stronger personalities in the Court without expressly formulating his own point of view, and on the other hand it will be clear to the outside world that a Judge does not bear responsibility for a decision to which he objects.

(3) Judges who are continuously outvoted may become frustrated if they have no opportunity of expressing their own thoughts.

(4) If there are no dissenting opinions it may be that one Judge is taken less seriously than the others; his arguments may not attract sufficient attention from the other Judges. Publication of his views may compel the other Judges to give more weight to his objections.

(5) Dissenting opinions may assist the future development of the law. In those fields where the law is developing a prior dissenting opinion may act as a stimulus to bring a new case before the Court.

(6) Freedom of opinion is a basic human right. Dissenting opinions should, therefore, be possible as a matter of principle. The burden of proof should be brought to bear on those who reject any dissenting opinions.

§ 702. In the Court of Justice, as in the vast majority of Continental courts, neither dissenting nor concurring opinions are possible. The opinion reached by the majority of the Judges determines the decision of the Court [240] and the deliberations must be conducted in secret and must remain secret. [241] For at least four reasons it is important that the Court of Justice is guarded by secrecy.

(1) More than any other court the decision of the Court of Justice must enjoy authority. As a result of the poor legislative machinery of the Communities the Court of Justice must fill important gaps in the legal order and thus help to create legal certainty for those subject to Community law. Such legal certainty is more readily secured by firm rulings than by decisions characterised by hesistancy where the possibility exists that the Court could reverse its position when one of the Judges is replaced. A new legal order in particular needs firm and unequivocal rulings as a basis for its future development.

(2) As the Judges are appointed for only six years, their independence

240. Rules of Procedure of the Court, Art. 27(5).
241. EEC Statute Art. 32.

might be set at risk if their personal views were known. These could be elicited from dissenting opinions or from any failure to dissent. The reasons for the failure to re-appoint the second president of Euratom, M. Etienne Hirsch, considering that he had been generally regarded as a first class president, may have lain in his refusal to accept the views of the French government. This provides a strong warning to those who argue in favour of dissenting opinions. Even if the independence of Judges is not directly affected — for it is to be expected that Judges will not yield to irresponsible threats from government officials — good Judges might, nevertheless, not be reappointed. Actual pressure on Judges who do not support the position of their own State is not so much to be expected from the quarter of national governments, who are sufficiently aware of the importance of the independence of the judiciary, but from national public opinion which may, in some States and on certain issues, consider that their 'own' Judge should support the national interest.

(3)   The lack of any possibility to openly dissent promotes compromises within the Court of Justice. This aids the amalgamation of rules from all the national legal orders and their assimilation into Community law. [242] As with any well-conducted meeting the Court of Justice is not readily inclined to make its decisions by way of a vote. The members of the Court will first try to win their colleagues over to a common view, and to find a solution acceptable to all. When the discussions reach a certain stage a majority view and a minority view may well develop. The provision for dissenting opinions would then easily induce the President to advise the minority to formulate their dissenting opinion and then merely to accept the majority view as the view of the Court. When the minority has no such escape route, it is a far more serious matter within a harmonious group of colleagues for the majority simply to outvote the minority. The pressure will be greater to continue the discussions until a position is reached which is more acceptable to the minority. This means that some of the arguments put up by the minority will be taken into account.

In a national court the outvoting of a judge and the formulation of his argument as a dissenting opinion only means that the opinion of that judge is not reflected in the opinion of the court. If the two opinions are basically different this may even provide a clearer and more homogeneous decision. In the Court of Justice a Judge's viewpoint may also be representative of a national legal order. If, for example, the British and the Irish Judges were to dissent from the rest of the Court, the formulation of their views as a separate opinion would mean that regard for the Common Law system had been insufficiently incorporated in the decision of the Court.

(4)   If each Judge, directly or indirectly, expresses his own opinion, he may feel morally obliged to stand by that opinion in future cases. In the *Van Gend en Loos Case*, for example, it was decided that individuals can invoke the unconditional prohibition addressed to Member States in EEC Article 12 which lays down that: 'Member States shall refrain from introducing ... new

---

242. See A.M. Donner, *Handelingen 1973 der Nederlandse Juristen-Vereniging*, deel 2, pp. 17-19.

customs duties ...', (see above § 182). If one assumes that three Judges voted against this decision, which is not unlikely, given the opinion of the Advocate-General, then these three dissenting opinions would have been published. If so would not the same Judges have felt some moral pressure to dissent again in similar cases in the future? It may be true that this sort of personal restriction should not play any role in a Judge's reasoning, but people like to be consistent. If dissenting opinions are not published it is easier for the individual Judges to accept prior case-law as a definite basis on which to found further decisions.

§ 703. The arguments against the publication of dissenting opinions seem substantial, especially as regards international courts, such as the Court of Justice. It is worth mentioning that in the conference of the Netherlands Lawyers Association (the NJV) on dissenting opinions in 1973, the two rapporteurs who pleaded for the possibility of introducing dissenting opinions both wished to make a certain exception, the one rapporteur for international courts whose judges are appointed by a number of different States[243], the other for courts whose judges are appointed for a limited number of years. [244]

Several of the objections to the publication of dissenting opinions are equally valid for 'intermediary' solutions such as publishing dissenting opinions anonymously or merely publishing the voting results of the Court. Conversely the advantages to be gained by such intermediary solutions, in comparison to the present system, seem to be only minimal.

4. Costs [245]

a. DIRECT ACTIONS

§ 704. At the end of each decision the Court gives its ruling on the costs of the case. The services of the Court itself are free except where a party has caused the Court to incur avoidable or excessive costs. [246] The most important recoverable costs are (1) the remuneration of agents, advisers and lawyers, (2) their travel and subsistence expenses and the amounts payable to witnesses and experts. [247] Naturally the amount varies according to the case. Some charges, such as those for authenticated copies and translations have been fixed in advance by the Court. [248]

Normally the unsuccessful party is ordered to pay the costs of the action if

---

243. H. Drion, in *Handelingen 1973 der Nederlandse Juristen-Vereniging*, deel I, *eerste stuk*, p. 48.
244. O. De Savornin Lohmann, *idem*, pp. 61, 62.
245. See Wolf (*op. cit.*, note 88), pp. 7-30.
246. Rules of Procedure of the Court, Art. 72.
247. *Idem*, Art. 73. For an example of a case where a party was ordered to pay the costs of witnesses see *Second Guillot Case* (43/74), 7 July 1977, consideration 110, [1977] ECR 1338.
248. See Instructions to the Registrar, Artt. 17-22, OJ 1974 No. L 350, p. 37.

this has been asked for in the successful party's pleadings.[249] The Chamber that made the inquiries into the case takes the necessary decision if the parties cannot come to an agreement on the amount of the costs. In a number of cases brought under this provision the Chambers have developed some general rules: [250]

(1) All parties to the case, including those who intervened, may bring the settlement of the costs before the Chamber.

(2) There is no time limit.

(3) Agreement between the parties must have been attempted and proved impossible to obtain.

(4) The subject-matter, the importance and the intricacy of the case are taken into account.

(5) In general, travel and subsistance allowances for only one lawyer for each party are considered to be necessary expenditure.

(6) The honoraria for the lawyers are not necessarily fully covered. The Court is not bound by agreements thereon between a party and his lawyer, nor by national provisions or national custom.

In some cases parties sometimes failed to plead for the costs in good time and thus lost the opportunity for recovering them.[251] In the *Sugar Cartel Case* the Court of Justice accepted that a party can '*by implication*' ask that its costs be recovered.[252]

§ 705. There are exceptions to the rule that the loser must pay: in cases brought by civil servants against the institution employing them the institution bears its own costs even if it wins the case. [253] In practice the Court is benevolent towards civil servants. When their action only partially succeeds the Court grants them most of their costs. [254] But there is one other rule applicable to all cases, even to those initiated by civil servants: the Court may order even a successful party to pay costs which the Court considers that party to have unreasonably or vexatiously caused the opposite party to incur. [255] On the basis of this rule the Court may also order a civil servant who loses his case to bear the costs of the institution as well. [256] The Court has, in some cases, made use of this rule to indicate that disputed Community acts, though not invalid, were so doubtful that the party who instituted the proceedings could not be blamed for regarding them as illegal. [257] By ordering the successful Community institution to pay (part of) the costs the Court

---

249. Rules of Procedure of the Court, Art. 69(2).
250. See Wolf (*op. cit.*, note 88), pp. 24-26.
251. See e.g. *ERTA Case* (22/70), 31 March 1971, considerations 102, 103, [1971] ECR 283.
252. *Sugar Cartel Case* (40-48, 50, 54-56, 111, 113 and 114/73), 16 Nov. 1975, consideration 627, [1975] ECR 2024; [1976] 1 CMLR 487.
253. Rules of Procedure of the Court, Art. 70.
254. Günther Hesse, *Der Gerichtshof der Europäischen Gemeinschaften als Arbeitsgericht*, Diss. Frankfurt am Main 1972, p. 99.
255. Rules of Procedure of the Court, Art. 69(3). For an example, see *Barge Case* (18/62), 16 Dec. 1963, [1963] ECR 282; 9 Jur. (1963) 593, 594; 9 Rec. (1963) 570.
256. See e.g. *Third van Eick Case* (57/70), 24 June 1971, [1971] ECR 619.
257. See e.g. *Forges de Clabecq Case*, above § 27; *Holtz & Willemsen Case*, above § 473.

then exerts pressure on the institution in order to obtain a change in the disputed rules of Community law. Similarly the Court may express some disapproval of a national measure challenged by the Commission under EEC Article 169 by condemning the Member State to pay (part of) the costs even though the Commission is unsuccessful in its action against it.[258] When neither party fully wins the case, the Court allocates the costs in proportion to the success archieved by each litigant. If a party withdraws the case, he normally has to bear the costs, unless the withdrawal has been caused by the other party, e.g. when a State, sued for violation of its obligations, terminates the violation during the Court's proceedings, then that State must bear the costs even if the Commission withdraws the case. [259]

b. PRELIMINARY RULINGS [260]

§ 706. All costs of preliminary rulings which are incurred by the Court itself and by the other Community organs (which may submit written and oral statements) are borne by the Communities. States submitting statements bear their own costs. There remains the question of the costs of the parties. It has been the consistent policy of the Court of Justice to refer a decision on these costs to the national court which asked for the preliminary ruling and which will finally decide the case. A German court once asked what criteria it should use when condemning a party to pay the costs of the other party. [261] Should the costs — and in particular the legal fees — be established according to German law or according to Community law?

The Court of Justice ruled that in the present state of Community law the recovery of costs of preliminary rulings is governed by the provisions of the national law of the referring court. [262]

Even though the recoverable costs for preliminary rulings are limited to those incurred by the parties in the underlying case, they may be relatively important in cases on minor issues. This may induce a lower national court to refrain from asking a preliminary ruling in cases where lesser interests are at stake. It has therefore been suggested that the Governments of the Member States should bear the costs of preliminary rulings. [263] As these rulings are of general interest the suggestion is worth considering.

---

258. *Phytosanitary Export Certificate Case* (89/76), 12 July 1977, consideration 23, [1977] ECR 1366; CCH para 8415.
259. See e.g. *Unloading Charges Case* (172/73), 1 May 1974, [1974] ECR 476.
260. See also Reinhard Riegel, *Zum Verhältnis zwischen gemeinschaftsrechtlicher und innerstaatlicher Gerichtsbarkeit*, 28 NJW (1975), pp. 1055, 1056.
261. *Bundesfinanzhof*, 8 Aug. 1972, AWD 1972, p. 531.
262. *Second Turkey Tail case (Bollmann)* (62/72), 1 March 1973, consideration 6, [1973] ECR 275; CCH para 8205.
263. R.H. Lauwaars *Prejudiciële Beslissingen*, Europese Monografieën No. 19, Kluwer 1975, p. 70.

c. INTERVENTIONS

§ 707. The Court has full freedom to charge the intervening party with such costs as it considers justified. If the party supported by the intervention wins, then the losing party will normally bear the costs of the intervention, even if he is a staff member in a staff case and would therefore not normally have to pay the costs of the successful party. [264] In case his side loses the Court may sometimes order the intervening party to bear the costs of the action along with the party which he supported [265], while in other cases the intervening party is ordered to pay all costs caused by the intervention [266], or to pay solely his own costs. [267]

5. Publication

§ 708. Judgments are delivered in open court. [268] The original of each judgment is kept at the Registry; the parties are served with certified copies. [269] Preliminary rulings are sent directly to the registrar of the court which made the request. The Registrar is responsible for publishing all judgments of the Court. The full judgments and the opinions of the Advocates-General are published in Danish, Dutch, English, French, German and Italian in the 'Reports of Cases before the Court' (ECR). [270] These reports are considered to be so important for the development of European law that the cases published before 1 January 1973 are translated and published in English. The most important of them are published in Danish as well. Apart from the ECR, the Registrar also publishes the operative part of the decisions as well as notices of applications originating proceedings and notices of the removal of cases in the Official Journal of the European Communities.[271] The latter publication is of relevance to third parties as it starts the period during which they are entitled to lodge a third party application against the judgment (see below § 715). [272]

---

264. *Prais Case* (130/75), 27 Oct. 1976, consideration 24, [1976] ECR 1600; [1976] 2 CMLR 724.
265. See e.g. *Barbara Erzbergbau Case* (3-18, 25 and 26/58), 10 May 1960, [1960] ECR 198; 6 Jur. (1960) 422; 6 Rec. (1960) 413; *Geitling Case* (13/60), 18 May 1962, [1962] ECR 118; 8 Jur. (1962) 230; 8 Rec. (1962) 221, 222.
266. See e.g. *Chambre Syndicale de L'Est de la France Case* (34/58), 15 July 1960, [1960] ECR 301; 6 Jur. (1960) 629; 6 Rec. (1960) 613; *Second Limburg Coalmines Case* (30/59), 23 Feb. 1961, [1961] ECR 33; 7 Jur. (1961) 60; 7 Rec. (1961) 58; *Second Snupat Case* (49/59), 22 March 1961, [1961] ECR 90; 7 Jur. (1961) 166; 7 Rec. (1961) 162, 163.
267. See e.g. *Grundig Case* (56 and 58/64), 13 July 1966, [1966] ECR 351; 12 Jur. (1966) 526; 12 Rec. (1966) 506; *Meinhardt Case* (24/71), 17 May 1972, [1972] ECR 279; *Second Metro Case* (26/76), 25 Oct. 1977, consideration 25, [1977] ECR 1918; [1978] CMLR 36; CCH para 8435.
268. Rules of Procedure of the Court, Art. 64(1).
269. *Idem*, Art. 64(2).
270. For the way references are made, see above § 4.
271. Rules of Procedure of the Court, Art. 68; Instructions to the Registrar, Artt. 23-25, OJ 1974, L 350 p. 38.
272. Rules of Procedure of the Court, Art. 97(1).

6. Correction

§ 709. The Court may, of its own motion or on application by a party, rectify clerical mistakes, errors in calculation and obvious slips in a judgment within two weeks after its delivery. In preliminary rulings the Court decides by itself; in direct action the parties, who are notified of the corrections may lodge written observations if they wish to do so. [273]

In the same chapter of the Rules of Procedure of the Court the possibility of omissions is provided for. Substantially the same procedure is to be followed as applies to corrections. It therefore seems correct to consider that an application to the Court to supplement its judgment is a special form of the application for correction. An application to the Court to supplement its judgment can be made, within one month, by any of the parties if the Court has omitted to give a decision on a particular point at issue or to rule on costs. [274]

7. Interpretation

§ 710. In a written application similar to that described above (§ 677) a party or any institution of the Communities may make an application for the interpretation of a judgment, which is to be delivered to all the parties to the case. Interpretation is limited to clarifying obscurities arising from the case itself, and is not designed to clarify the law for other cases. [275] The parties are given an opportunity to submit their observations and the Court makes its decision after hearing the Advocate-General. The interpreting judgment is annexed to the original. [276]

Though the rules of procedure do not expressly state this, it must be understood from the general principles of law that requests for interpretation have no suspensory effect.

§ 711. Although, in principle, apart from the institutions of the Communities, only the parties to the original case may ask for an interpretation of the judgment, the Court held in the *Second Assider Case*:

'Where several actions are brought against the same decision of the High Authority and where, as the result of one of those actions the decision is annulled, the applicants in the other actions may be regarded as 'parties' to the action within the meaning of Article 37 of the Protocol on the Statute of the Court, subject expressly to the condition that the applicant has cited in his previous application the same ground on which the judgment to be

---

273. *Idem*, Art. 66. For an example of a correction, see *United Brands Case* (27/76), orders of 11 May 1978 and 26 June 1978, [1978] ECR 345, 346; [1978] 3 CMLR 83-86.
274. *Idem*, Art. 67.
275. *Collotti Case* (70/63 bis), 7 April 1965, [1965] ECR 279, 280; 11 Jur. (1965) 352; 11 Rec. (1965) 359.
276. EEC Statute Art. 40, Rules of Procedure of the Court, Art. 102.

interpreted has annulled the decision (...). Each of these parties is thus entitled to ask for the interpretation of the judgment which annuls the decision or declares one of the other actions well founded.'

In the same case the Court gave a rather wide interpretation to the words: 'If the meaning or scope of a judgment is *in doubt*'. [277] A difference of opinion between the parties is sufficient.

Furthermore, the Court decided in the same case:

> 'It is necessary to define the parts of the text of a judgment which may be the subject of interpretation. Obviously they can only be those which express the decision of the Court on the matter submitted to it: the operative part and such of the grounds as determine it and are essential for that purpose; those are the parts of the judgment which constitute the actual decision. On the other hand, the Court is not called upon to interpret ancillary matter which supplements or explains those basic grounds.' [278]

Finally, the Court stressed that interpretation can only determine the meaning and scope of an earlier judgment, it cannot be used for solving problems which have not been settled by that judgment; in other words, parties cannot ask for a new decision.

§ 712.   The parties before the national court cannot ask for the interpretation of preliminary rulings given by the Court of Justice. [279]

8. Enforcement

§ 713.   The enforcement of Court decisions has never caused any serious problems. [280]   In suits for damages and in cases of judicial review the Communities themselves or the Member States execute the Court decisions. In cases of pecuniary sanctions against individuals, enforcement is governed by the rules of civil procedure in force in the State in the territory of which the judgment of the Court is to be carried out. [281]   Under EEC Article 192 [282] each Member State has designated an authority, which appends the order for enforcement to the judgment of the Court of Justice without any other formality than verification of the authentity of the judgment. All Member States have appointed an authority to whom requests for orders of enforcement must be addressed. [283]   The authorities which actually perform these

---

277.   EEC Statute, Art. 40; ECSC Statute, Art. 37.
278.   *Second Assider Case* (5/55), 28 June 1955, [1954-56] ECR 141, 142; 1 Jur. (1954-55) 298-301; 1 Rec. (1954-55) 277-280.
279.   *Second Becher Case* (13/67), Order of the Court of 16 May 1968, [1968] ECR 196, 197; 14 Jur. (1968) 279, 280; 14 Rec. (1968) 290; CCH para 8066 (p. 8015).
280.   Apart from the *First Art Treasures Case*, see above § 430.
281.   ECSC Artt. 44, 92; EEC Artt. 187, 192.
282.   ECSC Art. 92.
283.   In Belgium: the Registrar of the Court of Appeals in Brussels to whom the matter is

functions vary: usually it is the Ministry of Foreign Affairs or of Justice. The express provision in the same Article that only the Court of Justice may suspend enforcement further demonstrates that the enforcing authorities are not entitled to review the content of the judgment: it must be executed even if under national law the case would have been decided differently. Save in the case of suspension, the procedure for enforcement comes under the jurisdiction of the national authorities. [284]

§ 714. In the *German Handelsgesellschaft Case* the German Constitutional Court held that German authorities may not cooperate in executing decisions which violate fundamental human rights (see above § 171-173). The Italian Constitutional Court has also ruled that the organs of the Community do not have the power to violate the fundamental principles of the Italian Constitution or the inalienable rights of man and that in such a case the Italian Constitutional Court would safeguard such fundamental rights and principles (see above § 170). The position of the supreme courts in the other Member States may be assumed to be similar, but it should be stressed that this is an extremely unlikely and purely theoretical situation. No one should be in a position to exercise absolute power, not even the Court of Justice of the European Communities, and if this court in a fit of madness, were to rule in such a way as to give rise to violations of human rights, whereby without any further inquiry or discussion it was *manifest* to the national judiciary that such a violation was about to be committed, it might be just as well for national courts to be able to stop the execution of the judgment. This does not mean, however, that parties would be entitled to reopen their case before their national courts in any normal event when the judgment of the Court of Justice is to be executed.

9. Third party proceedings[285]

§ 715. When a judgment is prejudicial to the rights of a third party, that party may initiate third party proceedings to be brought against all the parties

---

passed by the Ministries of Foreign Affairs and of Justice; in Denmark and Germany: the Ministry of Justice; in France: a specially designated authority (Journal Officiel 19 March 1957, p. 2885); in Ireland: the Minister of Justice who leaves the appending of the order to the Master of the High Court; in Italy: the Ministry of Foreign Affairs; in Luxembourg: the Ministry of Foreign Affairs who leaves the appending of the order to the Ministry of Justice; in the Netherlands: the Minister of Justice, who leaves both the verification and the appending of the order to the Registrar of the *Hoge Raad*; in the United Kingdom: the Secretary of State for Foreign and Commonwealth Affairs, but the registration of the judgment must be asked of the High Court (in England and Northern Ireland) or the Court of Session (in Scotland). See also Colette Constandinides Megret, *La loi du 6 Août 1967 et l'execution forcée de certains arrets communautaires*, RBDI 1969, pp. 69-79.
284. See *Second Nold Case* (4/73), Order of 11 Jan. 1977, consideration 3, [1977] ECR 3; [1978] 2 CMLR 185.
285. Georges Vandersanden, *Le recours en tierce opposition devant la Cour de justice des Communautés européennes*, 5 CDE (1969), pp. 666-682. See also Liliane Plouvier, *Les Décisions de la Cour de Justice des Communautés Européennes et leurs Effets juridiques*, Bruylant, Brussels 1975, pp. 103-107.

to the original case. specifying the judgment contested, stating how that judgment is prejudicial to his rights and indicating the reasons why he was unable to take part in the original case. [286] The application must be lodged within two months after publication of the contested judgment in the Official Journal. The Court may stay the execution of the judgment during the third party proceedings.

The purpose of third party proceedings is not the interpretation of the judgment but its review. The procedural requirements are rather strict as interested third parties may normally be expected to intervene in the case itself. It is for the purpose of enabling third parties to intervene that all cases are reported in the Communities' Official Journal as soon as pleadings are received by the Court.

The requirement that the *judgment* must be prejudicial to the rights of the third party means that no third party proceedings are possible against the *reasoning* of the judgment or against *orders* of the Court. In practice third party-proceedings will also be impossible against Court decisions in which actions were declared inadmissible or were rejected. [287]

So far there have been two cases of third party proceedings before the Court of Justice. [288]

10. Revision [289]

§ 716. If a new fact comes to light after a judgment has been given which is of such a nature as to be a decisive factor to the case the judgment may be revised. [290]   An application for revision may be made only by the parties to the case. Apart from the original plaintiff and defendant this also includes those parties who intervened in the original case. [291]

The Statutes of the Court impose two conditions on action for revision:

(a)   A fact must have been discovered which is of such a nature as to be a decisive factor to the case. A case decided by the Court of Justice between other parties does not constitute such a fact. [292]   In the *Fourth Elz Case* the Court ruled that a subsequent national court decision may constitute such a new fact, though it did not do so in that case. [293]

(b)   That fact must have been unknown to the Court and to the party claiming the revision at the time the original case was decided. [294]   Unlike the

---

286.   EEC Statute, Art. 39; Rules of Procedure of the Court, Art. 97.
287.   Vandersanden (*op. cit.*, note 285), p. 674.
288.   *Breedband Case* (42 and 49/59), 12 July 1962, [1962] ECR 145; 8 Jur. (1962) 289; 8 Rec. (1962) 275, and *Vloeberghs Case* (9 and 12/60), 12 July 1962, [1962] ECR 171; 8 Jur. (1962) 345; 8 Rec. (1962) 331.
289.   See Liliane Plouvier, *Le Recours en revision devant la Cour de Justice des Communautés Europeennes*, 7 CDE (1971), pp. 428-444.
290.   EEC Statute, Art. 41; Rules of Procedure of the Court, Artt. 98-100.
291.   Plouvier (*op. cit.*, note 289), p. 435.
292.   *Schots Kortner Case* (15-33/73 etc.), 21 Feb. 1974, consideration 36, [1974] ECR 191.
293.   *Fourth Elz Case* (56/75) Rev. 13 Oct. 1977, consideration 7, [1977] ECR 1621.
294.   EEC Statute, Art. 41(1).

Statute of the International Court of Justice which seems to have been used as a model [295], the Statutes do not expressly exclude facts which are unknown to the party requesting revision because of his own fault or negligence. In the *Second Mandelli Case* the court of Justice held, however, that the discovery of a new document did not constitute a new fact as the applicant could have known of its existence, and could have taken steps to bring it before the Court. [296]

The application for revision must be made within three months after the discovery of the new facts. After the lapse of ten years from the date of the original judgment, however, no application for revision may be made. [297]

The proceedings for the revision of a judgment have two stages: first, the Court decides on the admissibility of the application, judging whether there is a new fact of sufficient importance to reopen the case. If so, the second stage is the rejudging of the case itself. [298] In both stages the normal procedures are followed, with the exception that there are no oral submissions in the first stage. [299]

So far, revision has been requested on nine occasions; one of the requests was withdrawn, the others were all rejected.

295. Statute of the International Court of Justice, Art. 61.
296. *Second Mandelli Case* (56/70), 21 Jan. 1971, consideration 12, [1971] ECR 4.
297. EEC Statute, Art. 41(3).
298. EEC Statute, Art. 41(2); Rules of Procedure of the Court, Art. 100.
299. Plouvier (*op. cit.* note 289), p. 442.

TABLES

I. Table of Cases – Alphabetical

OPINIONS

II. Table of Cases – By number

60-62/69	Chuffart, § 462
64/69	Compagnie Française, § 206, 313
67/69	Third Simet, § 462
69/69	Alcan, § 323, 324
70/69	Fifth Feram, § 462
72/69	Bremer Handelsgesellschaft, § 439
74/69	Krohn, § 439
75/69	Hake, § 333, 337
77/69	Wood, § 423
1/70	Rochas, § 120
2/70	Riva, § 74
5/70	Prelle, § 462
6/70	Borromeo, § 331, 353
8/70	Administrative Services, § 423, 441
9/70	Grad, § 191
11/70	Handelsgesellschaft, § 46, 53, 107, 293, 480, 522
14/70	Bakels, § 21, 123, 128, 439
15/70	Chevalley, § 231, 331, 344, 353, 370
19/70	Almini, § 59
22/70	ERTA, § 220, 221, 265, 274, 279a
25/70	Köster, § 40, 107, 259, 261, 369
28/70	Witt, § 439
33/70	SACE, § 187, 441
34/70	Syndicat national céréales, § 422
37/70	First Rewe, § 13, 81
39/70	Reliable Importers, § 36, 439, 547
40/70	Sirena, § 31a
41-44/70	First International Fruit Company, § 202, 323
56/70	Second Mandelli, § 716
57/70	Third Van Eick, § 705
59/70	Steelsubsidies, § 72, 336, 434
62/70	Chinese Mushroom (Bock), § 98, 237, 319, 323
79/70	Müllers, § 244, 661, 666
80/70	First Defrenne, § 597
2/71	Assesment for Social Fund, § 666
5/71	Schöppenstedt, § 49, 378, 460, 470, 471, 478, 483, 501
7/71	Euratom, § 389, 390, 409, 411, 426
8/71	Komponistenverband, § 333, 347
9, 11/71	Compagnie d'Approvisonnement, § 255, 478
10/71	Hein-Müller, § 187, 609
12/71, 13/71, 14/71	Henck, § 77, 611
15/71	First Mackprang, § 344
18/71	Eunomia, § 187, 440
20/71	Sabbatini, § 94, 215, 467
24/71	Meinhardt, § 141, 707
30/71	Siemers, § 21
32/71	Bauduin, § 215
37/71	Jamet, § 241
40/71	Second Richez-Parise, § 244
42/71	Nordgetreide, § 324, 347, 353
43/71	Politi, § 189, 563, 573
48/71	Second Art Treasures, § 187, 430, 432
49/71	Hagen, § 140

TABLES

136/77	First Racke, § 282
139/77	Denkavit, § 141
140/77	Verhaaf, § 95
147/77	Slaughter of animals, § 400
149/77	Third Defrenne, § 54a, 605
150/77	Bertrand, § 141
154/77	Dechmann, § 560
156/77	Rail Transport Subsidies, § 413, 414
1/78	Nuclear Materials Ruling, § 27b, 539
1/78	Kenny, § 182
4, 19, 28/78	Salerno, § 279, 327
8/78	Third Milac, § 89, 367a
10/78	Belbouab, § 77
21/78	Delkvist § 191
24/78	Martin, § 27a
31/78	Bussone, § 189
33/78	Somafer, § 27a
34/78	Zipper, § 373
35/78	Schouten, § 25
83/78	Pigs Marketing, § 159, 187, 438, 680
85/78	Hirsch, § 141
87/78	Welding, § 95, 279
88/78	Kendermann, § 90
90/78	Third Granaria, § 345, 501
91/78	Hansen, § 187
92/78	Fourth Simmenthal, § 292, 297, 323, 363a, 379a, 672
93/78	Mattheus, § 560
98/78	Second Racke, § 80, 233, 287
99/78	Decker, § 80, 287
101/78	Second Granaria, § 379d, 500
103-109/78	Usines de Beaufort, § 313
110, 111/78	Van Wesemael, § 187, 609
115/78	Knoors, § 91a
118/78	Meyer, § 438
122/78	Buitoni, § 99a, 373
133/78	Gourdain, § 41
134/78	Danhuber, § 279
136/78	Auer, § 91a
141/78	(not decided), § 433
148/78	Ratti, § 191
151/78	Sukkerfabrikken Nykøbing, § 697
158/78	Biegi, § 85
176/78	Second Schaap, § 598

III. Table of citations of Treaty Articles

TABLE OF CITATIONS OF TREATY ARTICLES

IV. Table of Authors

1. Only the first reference in each Chapter is mentioned.

V. Index

Numbers refer to paragraphs.